# Evidence

# Evidence

Inns of Court School of Law
Institute of Law, City University, London

OXFORD
UNIVERSITY PRESS

# OXFORD

UNIVERSITY PRESS

Great Clarendon Street, Oxford OX2 6DP

Oxford University Press is a department of the University of Oxford.
It furthers the University's objective of excellence in research, scholarship,
and education by publishing worldwide in

Oxford  New York

Auckland  Bangkok  Buenos Aires  Cape Town  Chennai
Dar es Salaam  Delhi  Hong Kong  Istanbul  Karachi  Kolkata
Kuala Lumpur  Madrid   Melbourne  Mexico City  Mumbai  Nairobi
Sao Paulo  Shanghai  Taipei  Tokyo  Toronto

Oxford is a registered trade mark of Oxford University Press
in the UK and certain other countries

Published in the United States
by Oxford University Press Inc., New York

A Blackstone Press Book

© Inns of Court School of Law, 2004

British Library Cataloguing in Publication Data

Data available

Library of Congress Cataloging in Publication Data

Data available

ISBN 0-19-927294-8

1 3 5 7 9 10 8 6 4 2

Typeset by Style Photosetting Limited, Mayfield, East Sussex
Printed in Great Britain
on acid-free paper by
Ashford Colour Press, Gosport, Hampshire

# FOREWORD

These Manuals are designed primarily to support training on the Bar Vocational Course, though they are also intended to provide a useful resource for legal practitioners and for anyone undertaking training in legal skills.

The Bar Vocational Course was designed by staff at the Inns of Court School of Law, where it was introduced in 1989. This course is intended to equip students with the practical skills and the procedural and evidential knowledge that they will need to start their legal professional careers. These Manuals are written by staff at the Inns of Court School of Law who have helped to develop the course, and by a range of legal practitioners and others involved in legal skills training. The authors of the Manuals are very well aware of the practical and professional approach that is central to the Bar Vocational Course.

The range and \coverage of the Manuals have grown steadily. This year, the major revisions of last year have been consolidated and updated to ensure currency and to reflect the changing demands of Bar students.

This updating and revision is a constant process and we very much value the comments of practitioners, staff and students. Legal vocational training is advancing rapidly, and it is important that all those concerned work together to achieve and maintain high standards. Please address any comments to the Bar Vocational Course Director at the Inns of Court School of Law.

With the validation of other providers for the Bar Vocational Course it is very much our intention that these Manuals will be of equal value to all students wherever they take the course, and we would very much value comments from tutors and students at other validated institutions.

The enthusiasm of the publishers and their efficiency in arranging production and publication of the Manuals is much appreciated.

*The Hon Mr Justice Elias*
*Former Chairman of the Advisory*
*Board of the Institute of Law*
*City University, London*
*August 2004*

# OUTLINE CONTENTS

| | | |
|---|---|---|
| *Foreword* | | v |
| *Preface* | | xi |
| *Table of cases* | | xiii |
| *Table of statutes* | | xxi |
| *Table of statutory instruments* | | xxvi |
| 1 | Fundamentals of evidence | 1 |
| 2 | Burdens and standards of proof; presumptions | 30 |
| 3 | Presumptions | 49 |
| 4 | Witnesses | 57 |
| 5 | Witness evidence | 78 |
| 6 | Character evidence | 107 |
| 7 | The doctrine of similar fact evidence | 119 |
| 8 | Hearsay evidence | 134 |
| 9 | Confessions and illegally or improperly obtained evidence | 177 |
| 10 | Lies and silence | 184 |
| 11 | Identification evidence | 202 |
| 12 | Opinion evidence | 220 |
| 13 | Judgments as evidence of the facts on which they are based | 228 |
| 14 | Privilege and public policy | 237 |
| APPENDIX 1: | Activities | 255 |
| APPENDIX 2: | Small group questions | 294 |
| APPENDIX 3: | Multiple choice questions | 327 |
| *Index* | | 338 |

# DETAILED CONTENTS

| | | |
|---|---|---|
| *Foreword* | | v |
| *Preface* | | xi |
| *Table of cases* | | xiii |
| *Table of statutes* | | xxi |
| *Table of statutory instruments* | | xxvi |

| **1** | **Fundamentals of evidence** | **1** |
|---|---|---|
| 1.1 | About this Manual | 1 |
| 1.2 | What is evidence? | 1 |
| 1.3 | Facts in issue | 5 |
| 1.4 | Proof concepts | 9 |
| 1.5 | Proof of facts without evidence | 19 |
| 1.6 | Admissibility | 22 |
| 1.7 | Exclusion | 23 |
| 1.8 | Adducing evidence | 25 |
| 1.9 | Tribunals of fact and law | 27 |

| **2** | **Burdens and standards of proof; presumptions** | **30** |
|---|---|---|
| 2.1 | Introduction | 30 |
| 2.2 | Standards of proof | 34 |
| 2.3 | Burdens of proof | 37 |
| 2.4 | Allocating burdens of proof in civil cases | 37 |
| 2.5 | Burdens of proof in criminal cases | 41 |
| 2.6 | Burden and standard of proof on preliminary matters | 47 |

| **3** | **Presumptions** | **49** |
|---|---|---|
| 3.1 | Introduction | 49 |
| 3.2 | Classes of presumption | 50 |
| 3.3 | Irrebuttable presumptions | 50 |
| 3.4 | Rebuttable presumptions | 51 |
| 3.5 | Presumptions of fact | 54 |
| 3.6 | *Res ipsa loquitur*: a difficult case | 55 |
| 3.7 | Conflicting presumptions | 56 |

| **4** | **Witnesses** | **57** |
|---|---|---|
| 4.1 | Introduction to competence and compellability | 57 |
| 4.2 | Persons of limited understanding | 58 |
| 4.3 | The accused as a witness in criminal cases | 61 |
| 4.4 | Spouses of accused persons in criminal cases | 62 |
| 4.5 | Other classes of witnesses | 63 |
| 4.6 | Oaths and affirmations | 65 |
| 4.7 | Practical issues concerning witnesses | 66 |
| 4.8 | Activity | 77 |

| **5** | **Witness evidence** | **78** |
|---|---|---|
| 5.1 | Introduction | 78 |
| 5.2 | Examination-in-chief | 80 |
| 5.3 | Cross-examination | 91 |
| 5.4 | Re-examination | 102 |
| 5.5 | Suspect witnesses | 103 |

| **6** | **Character evidence** | **107** |
|---|---|---|
| 6.1 | Civil cases | 107 |
| 6.2 | Criminal cases | 107 |
| 6.3 | Criminal Justice Act 2003 — defendant's bad character | 117 |
| 6.4 | Children and Young Persons Act 1963, s 16(2) | 118 |

| **7** | **The doctrine of similar fact evidence** | **119** |
|---|---|---|
| 7.1 | Introduction | 119 |
| 7.2 | Criminal law | 122 |
| 7.3 | Similar fact in civil law | 133 |

| **8** | **Hearsay evidence** | **134** |
|---|---|---|
| 8.1 | Out of court statements | 134 |
| 8.2 | Hearsay evidence | 136 |
| 8.3 | Identifying hearsay evidence | 138 |
| 8.4 | Problem areas | 144 |
| 8.5 | Hearsay exceptions in civil cases | 150 |
| 8.6 | Statutory exceptions in criminal cases | 154 |
| 8.7 | Common law exceptions | 165 |
| 8.8 | Criminal Justice Act 2003 | 172 |

| **9** | **Confessions and illegally or improperly obtained evidence** | **177** |
|---|---|---|
| 9.1 | Confessions | 177 |
| 9.2 | Illegally or improperly obtained evidence other than confessions | 182 |
| 9.3 | Criminal Justice Act 2003 | 183 |

**10    Lies and silence                     184**

10.1    Introduction                        184
10.2    Civil cases                         185
10.3    Lies in criminal cases              186
10.4    Silence in criminal cases           187
10.5    Activities                          201

**11    Identification evidence             202**

11.1    Introduction                        202
11.2    Identification evidence and miscarriages
        of justice                          202
11.3    The special need for caution — *Turnbull*
        warnings                            203
11.4    Form of a *Turnbull* warning        205
11.5    Poor quality identification evidence —
        submissions of no case              205
11.6    Support for poor quality identification
        evidence                            206
11.7    Situations where a *Turnbull* warning may be
        unnecessary                         207
11.8    Appeals and identification evidence 208
11.9    Establishing a link between the accused and
        the crime                           209
11.10   Recap activities                    219

**12    Opinion evidence                    220**

12.1    General rule                        220
12.2    Witnesses of fact who offer their opinion    221
12.3    Expert opinion evidence             221

**13    Judgments as evidence of the
       facts on which they are based        228**

13.1    Introduction                        228
13.2    General rule                        228
13.3    Use of a previous judgment as evidence of
        the facts in civil cases            229
13.4    Use of a previous judgment as evidence of
        the facts in criminal cases         232
13.5    Recap activities                    236

**14    Privilege and public policy         237**

14.1    Introduction                        237
14.2    Privilege                           237
14.3    Public policy exclusion             248

APPENDIX 1: Activities                      255
APPENDIX 2: Small group questions           294
APPENDIX 3: Multiple choice questions       327

*Index*                                     338

# PREFACE

The law of evidence regulates the means by which facts may be proved in courts of law. It is for this reason that mastery of its basic principles and rules is essential to the practitioner. All too often, both before a trial and during its conduct in court, the rules of evidence must be applied on the spur of the moment, without the opportunity to consult books or articles. Perhaps instructions have been belatedly received. Perhaps a problem arises at the trial itself: during examination in chief, cross-examination or re-examination; when the admissibility of an item of evidence is suddenly questioned; or when it becomes necessary to deal with a judicial intervention or to make submissions about the contents of a summing-up.

This Manual, by its combination of text, materials, examples and problems, aims to develop not only a knowledge of evidence law, but also understanding of the ways in which it is applied in practice.

The references in this Manual to the PACE Codes of Practice are to the new Codes which came into force in April 2003.

This Manual has been written on the assumption that the Criminal Justice Act 2003 will be brought into force as enacted. At various points in the Manual the effect of changes made by this Act will be identified. However, the law as it stands prior to the coming into force of the 2003 Act is the basis for most of the rules identified in this book.

# TABLE OF CASES

A Chief Constable v A County Council [2002] EWHC 2198 (Fam) ... 239

Adjodha v The State [1982] AC 204 PC ... 178

Ajami v Comptroller of Customs [1954] 1 WLR 1405 ... 223

Alfred Compton Amusement Machines Ltd v Customs & Excise Commissioners [1974] AC 405 ... 240

Armchair Passenger Transport Ltd v Helical Bar plc [2003] EWHC 367 ... 223

Ashburton v Pape [1913] 2 Ch D 469 ... 246

AT&T Istel v Tully [1993] AC 45, HL ... 238

Attorney-General v Bowman (1971) 2 Bos & P 532 ... 107

Attorney-General v Hitchcock (1847) 1 Exch 91 ... 99

Attorney-General's Reference (No 3 of 1979) (1979) 69 Cr App R 411 ... 82

Attorney-General's Reference (No 2 of 2002) [2002] EWCA Crim 2373, [2003] Crim LR 192 ... 214

Attorney General's Reference (No 4 of 2002) [2003] EWCA Crim 762, [2004] 1 All ER 1 ... 45

Attorney General's Reference (No 1 of 2003) [2003] 2 Cr App Rep 453 ... 167

Aveson v Lord Kinnaird (1805) 6 East 188 ... 168

Barclays Bank plc v Eustice [1995] 4 All ER 411, CA ... 244

Barnes v Chief Constable of Durham [1997] 2 Cr App R 505 ... 84, 211

Bayerische Rückversicherung AG v Clarkson Puckle Overseas Ltd *The Times*, 23 January 1989 ... 69

Beckford v R (1993) 97 Cr App R 409 ... 207

Belabel v Air India [1988] Ch 317 ... 241

Benedetto and Labrador v The Queen [2003] UKPC 27 ... 180

Bessela v Stern (1877) 2 CPD 265 ... 185

BHP Billiton Petroleum Ltd v Dalmine SpA [2003] EWCA Civ 170 ... 37, 39

Blunt v Park Lane Hotel Ltd [1942] 2 KB 253 ... 238

Bowman v DPP [1991] RTR 263 ... 22

Bramblevale Ltd, Re [1970] Ch 128, CA ... 34

Bratty v A-G for Northern Ireland [1963] AC 386 ... 36, 42

Brennan v UK (2002) 34 EHRR 507 ... 181

Brinks Ltd v Abu Saleh (No 1) [1995] 4 All ER 65 ... 230

British Coal Corporation v Dennis Rye Ltd (No 2) [1988] 3 All ER 816 ... 243

Brown v Foster (1857) 1 H & N 736 ... 244

Brown v Stott [2001] 2 WLR 817 ... 240

Brutus v Cozens [1973] AC 854, HL ... 28

Buckinghamshire County Council v Moran [1990] Ch 623 ... 247

Burmah Oil Company v Bank of England [1980] AC 1090 ... 248, 250

Butler v Board of Trade [1971] Ch 680 ... 244

Butler v Mountgarret (1859) 7 HL Cas 633 ... 170

Buttes Gas & Oil Company v Hammer (No 3) [1981] 1 QB 223 ... 250

Calderbank v Calderbank [1976] Fam 93 ... 247

Castle v Cross [1984] 1 WLR 1372, DC ... 150

Chambers v Bernasconi (1834) 1 Cr M & R 347 ... 169

Chandrasekera v The King [1937] AC 220, PC ... 139

Chard v Chard [1956] P 259 ... 52

Chipchase v Chipchase [1939] P 391, DC ... 52

Chocoladefabriken Lindt & Sprungli AG v Nestle Co Ltd [1978] RPC 287 ... 247

Cleveland County Council v F [1995] 2 All ER 236 ... 239

Clingham v Kensington & Chelsea London Borough Council [2002] 3 WLR 1313, HL ... 150

Coldman v Hill [1919] 1 KB 443, CA ... 40

Condron & Condron v UK [2000] Crim LR 677 ... 191

Conlon v Conlon's Ltd [1952] 2 All ER 462 ... 242, 246

Constantine Line v Imperial Smelting Corporation [1942] AC 154 ... 37

Conway v Rimmer [1968] AC 910 ... 248

Corke v Corke [1958] P 93, CA ... 83

Coulson v Disborough [1894] 2 QB 316 ... 91

Crescent Farm (Sidcup) Sport Ltd v Sterling Offices Ltd [1972] Ch 553 ... 244

D (minor), Re [1993] 2 All ER 693 ... 247

D v National Society for the Prevention of Cruelty to Children [1978] AC 171 ... 251

D v NSPCC [1978] AC 171 ... 24

Daley v R [1993] 4 All ER 86 ... 206

Dawson v Lunn [1986] RTR 234 ... 225

Dean v Dean [1987] 1 FLR 517, CA ... 34

Dennis v A J White and Co [1916] 2 KB 1 ... 21

Doe d Church & Phillips v Perkins (1790) 3 TR 749 ... 82

Dolan [2003] 1 Cr App R 281 ... 131

DPP v A and BC Chewing Gum Ltd [1968] 1 QB 159 ... 290

DPP v Boardman [1975] AC 421 ... 125

DPP v Kilbourne [1973] AC 729 ... 9, 12

DPP v Morgan [1976] AC 182, HL ... 41

Dubai Bank v Galadari [1989] 3 All ER 769 ... 244

Duncan v Cammell Laird & Co Ltd [1942] AC 624 ... 248, 250

Duncan, Re [1968] P 306 ... 240

Dunn v Aslett (1838) 2 Mood & R 122 ... 98

English Exporters (London) Ltd v Eldonwall Ltd [1973] Ch 415 ... 224

English v Emery Reimbold and Strick Ltd [2002] 3 All ER 385 ... 224

Evans v Chief Constable of Surrey [1988] QB 588 ... 250

Ewer v Ambrose (1825) 3 B & C 746 ... 89

Factortame Ltd v Secretary of State for the Environment, Transport and the Regions (No 8) [2002] 3 WLR 1104 ... 223

Fairchild v Glenhaven Funeral Services Ltd [2002] 3 All ER 305, HL ... 223

Flanagan v Fahy [1918] 2 IR 361 ... 87

Folkes v Chadd (1782) 3 Doug KB 157 ... 221

Fox v General Medical Council [1960] 1 WLR 1017, PC ... 88

Francisco v Diedrick *The Times*, 3 April 1998 ... 185

Fraser v Warren (1956) 40 Cr App R 160 ... 90

Freemantle v R [1994] 3 All ER 225 ... 208

Funderburk [1990] 1 WLR 587 ... 109

G (a minor), Re [1996] 2 All ER 65 ... 239

GE Capital v Sutton [2004] EWCA Civ 315 ... 243

General Accident Fire & Life Assurance Corporation Ltd v Tanter [1984] 1 WLR 100 ... 243

Glendarroch, The [1894] P 226 ... 38

Gnitrow Ltd v Cape plc [2000] 1 WLR 2327 ... 247

Goddard v Nationwide Building Society [1987] QB 670, CA ... 246

Great Atlantic Insurance Co v Home Insurance Co [1981] 1 WLR 529 ... 243

Green v Bannister [2003] EWCA Civ 1819 ... 21

Greenough v Eccles (1859) 5 CBNS 786 ... 90

Greenough v Gaskell (1833) 1 My & K 98 ... 240

H v Schering Chemicals Ltd [1983] 1 WLR 143 ... 224

H (minors) (Sexual Abuse: Standard of Proof), Re [1996] AC 563, HL ... 35

H and A (Children), Re [2002] 1 FLR 1145, CA ... 52

Hall v R [1971] 1 WLR 298 ... 194

Harmony Shipping Co SA v Saudi Europe Line Ltd [1979] 1 WLR 1380, CA ... 68, 225, 244

Harris v DPP [1952] AC 694 ... 122

Harris v Tippett (1811) 2 Camp 637 ... 18, 98

Hart v Lancashire and Yorkshire Railway Co (1869) 21 LT 261 ... 13

Heather v P-E Consulting Group Ltd [1973] Ch 189 ... 22

Hellenic Mutual War Risks Association (Bermuda) Ltd v Harrison (The Sagheera) [1997] 1 Lloyd's Rep 160 ... 241

Henry Cox, The (1878) 3 PD 156 ... 169

Hickman v Berens [1895] 2 Ch 638 ... 66

Hickman v Peacey [1945] AC 304 ... 53

Higham v Ridgeway (1808) 10 East 109 ... 170

Highgrade Traders Ltd, Re [1984] BCLC 151 ... 242

Hinds v Sparks [1964] Crim LR 717 ... 229

Hobbs v C T Tinling and Co Ltd [1929] 2 KB 1, CA ... 96, 107

Hollingham v Head (1858) 27 LJ CP 241 ... 13

Hollington v F Hewthorn and Co Ltd [1943] KB 587 ... 228, 229

Hornal v Neuberger Products Ltd [1957] 1 QB 247 ... 34

Howe v Malkin (1878) 40 LT 196 ... 168

Hui Chi-ming v R [1992] 1 AC 34 ... 236

Hunter v Chief Constable of the West Midlands Police [1982] AC 529 ... 230, 231

Hurst v Evans [1917] 1 KB 352 ... 38

Inquiry under the Companies Securities (Insider Dealing) Act 1985, Re an [1988] AC 660 ... 252

International Business Machines Corporation v Phoenix International (Computers) Ltd [1995] 1 All ER 413 ... 246

ISTIL Group v Zahoor [2003] 2 All ER 252 ... 246

J v Oyston [1999] 1 WLR 694 ... 230

Jameel v Wall Street Journal Europe [2003] EWCA Civ 1694 ... 28

James v South Glamorgan County Council (1994) 99 Cr App R 321 ... 71

Jayasena v R [1970] AC 618, PC ... 36

Jones v DPP [1962] AC 635 ... 113

Jones v DPP [1962] AC 635, HL ... 111

Jones v Metcalfe [1967] 1 WLR 1286, DC ... 148

Joseph Constantine Steamship Line Ltd v Imperial Smelting Corp Ltd [1942] AC 154 ... 40

Judd v Minister of Pensions and National Insurance [1966] 2 QB 580 ... 34

Kajala v Noble (1982) 75 Cr App R 149, DC ... 213

Khan v Khan [1982] 2 All ER 60 ... 238

Khan v UK [2000] Crim LR 684 ... 182

Kilby v The Queen (1973) 129 CLR 460 ... 85

King of Two Sicilies v Willcox (1851) 1 Sim NS 301 ... 238

Klass v Federal Republic of Germany (1978) 2 EHRR 214, 232 ... 249

L (A Minor) (Police Investigation: Privilege), Re [1997] AC 16; [1996] 2 WLR 395 ... 243, 245

Lal Chand Marwari v Mahant Ramrup Gir (1925) 42 TLR 159, PC ... 52

Levene v Roxhan [1970] 1 WLR 1322 ... 231

Liverpool Roman Catholic Archdiocesan Trustees Inc v Goldberg (No 3) [2001] 1 WLR 2337 ... 223

Lloyde v West Midlands Gas Board [1971] 2 All ER 1240, CA ... 55

Lobban v R [1995] 2 All ER 602 ... 178

Lonhro Ltd v Shell Petroleum Company Ltd [1980] 1 WLR 627 ... 251

Lonrho plc v Fayed (No 4) [1994] QB 775 ... 252

Lowery v R [1973] 3 ALL ER 662 ... 132

M (A Minor) (Disclosure of Material), Re [1990] 2 FLR 36 ... 251

Mahadervan v Mahadervan [1964] P 233 ... 51

Makin v Attorney-General for New South Wales [1894] AC 57, PC ... 120

Manchester Brewery v Coombs (1901) 82 LT 347 ... 146

Mancini v DPP [1942] AC 1, HL ... 42

Marcel v Commissioner of Police for the Metropolis [1992] Ch 225, CA ... 250

Marks v Beyfus (1890) 25 QBD 494 ... 251

Maturin v A-G [1938] 2 All ER 214 ... 52

Mawaz Khan v R [1967] 1 AC 454, PC ... 144

Maxwell v DPP [1935] AC 309 ... 112

McQuaker v Goddard [1940] 1 KB 687 ... 22

Mechanical & General Inventions Co Ltd v Austin [1935] AC 346 ... 107

Mercer v Denne [1905] 2 Ch 638 ... 170

Miller v Minister of Pensions [1947] 2 All ER 372 ... 34, 35

Mills v R [1995] 1 WLR 511 ... 205

Minet v Morgan (1873) 8 Ch App 361 ... 243

Mitsubishi Electric Australia Pty Ltd v Victorian Work Cover Authority [2002] VSCA 59 ... 242

Monckton v Tarr (1930) 23 BWCC 504 ... 56

Mood Music Publishing Co Ltd v De Wolfe Ltd [1976] Ch 119, CA ... 133

Moor v Moor [1954] 1 WLR 927 ... 80

Muller v Linsley & Mortimer *The Times*, 8 December 1994 ... 247

Murdoch v Taylor [1965] AC 574, HL ... 115

Murray v DPP [1994] 1 WLR 1, HL ... 198

Myers v DPP [1965] AC 1001 ... 23, 144

Narracott v Narracott (1864) 3 Sw & Tr 498 ... 107

Nederlandse Reassurantie Groep Holding v Bacon & Woodrow [1995] 1 All ER 976 ... 242

Neill v North Antrim Magistrates' Court [1992] 1 WLR 1221 ... 158, 163

Nevill v Fine Arts and General Insurance Co Ltd [1897] AC 68 ... 28

Ng Chun Pei v Lee Chuen Tat [1988] RTR 298, PC ... 55

Nicholas v Penny [1950] 2 KB 466 ... 54

Nimmo v Alexander Cowan and Sons Ltd [1968] AC 107 ... 46

Nominal Defendant v Clement (1961) 104 CLR 476 ... 88

Noor Mohammed v R [1949] AC182 PC ... 122

Nye v Niblett [1918] 1 KB 23 ... 21

O'Connell v Adams [1973] RTR 150 ... 91

Office of Fair Trading v X [2003] 2 All ER (Comm) 183 ... 240

Oxfordshire County Council v M [1994] 2 All ER 269 ... 245

Oxfordshire County Council v P [1995] 2 All ER 225 ... 239

Palmer v Crone [1927] 1 KB 804 ... 22

Paragon Finance plc v Freshfields [1999] 1 WLR 1183 ... 246

Parkes v R [1976] 1 WLR 1251 ... 194

Paul v DPP (1989) 90 Cr App R 173 ... 22

Peacock v Harris (1836) 5 Ad & El 449 ... 168

Peete, Re [1952] 2 All ER 599 ... 51

Perry v Gibson (1834) 1 Ad & El 148 ... 66

Phené's Trusts, Re (1870) LR 5 Ch App 139 ... 52

Piers v Piers (1849) 2 HL Cas 331 ... 51

Pontifex v Jolly (1839) 9 Car & P 202 ... 69

Poulett Peerage Case, The [1903] AC 395 ... 52

Practice Direction (Criminal: Consolidated) [2002] 3 All ER 904 ... 99, 198

Price v Humphries [1958] 2 QB 353, DC ... 70

Prince v Samo (1838) 7 A & E 627 ... 102

Prudential Assurance Co v Edmonds (1877) 2 App Cas 487, HL ... 52

Pugsley v Hunter [1973] 1 WLR 578 ... 290

R (on the application of D) v Camberwell Green Youth Court [2003] EWHC 227 (Admin) ... 75

R (on the application of Grundy & Co Excavations Ltd) v Halton Division Magistrates' Court [2003] EWHC 272 (Admin) ... 44, 46

R (on the application of Hoare) v South Durham Justices [2004] All ER (D) (Feb) ... 242

R (on the application of McCann) v Manchester Crown Court [2002] UKHL 39 ... 34

R (on the application of S) v Waltham Forest Youth Court [2004] EWHC 715 (Admin) ... 73

R (Sullivan) v Crown Court at Maidstone [2002] 1 WLR 2747, CA ... 197

R (Thompson) v Chief Constable of the Northumberland Constabulary [2001] 1 WLR 1342 ... 181

R v A [1997] Crim LR 883 ... 198

R v A [2001] 3 All ER 1 ... 93

R v A [2003] EWCA Crim 3214 ... 102

R v Abadom (1983) 76 Cr App R 48 ... 224

R v Acton Justices, ex p McMullen (1990) 92 Cr App R 98 ... 156, 157

R v Agar [1990] 2 All ER 442 ... 251

R v Akaidere [1990] Crim LR 808 ... 206

R v Ali [2001] All ER (D) 16 ... 190

R v Anderson (1929) 21 Cr App R 178 ... 101

R v Anderson [1972] 1 QB 304 ... 223, 290

R v Andrews [1987] AC 281 ... 166

R v Argent [1997] Crim LR 346 ... 191

R v Ashford Justices, ex p Hilden (1993) 96 Cr App R 92, DC ... 158

R v Aves (1950) 34 Cr App R 159 ... 54

R v Aziz [1995] 3 All ER 149, HL ... 87

R v Aziz [1996] 1 AC 41 ... 108

R v B (Attorney-General's Reference (No 3 of 1999)) [2001] 1 Cr App R 475 ... 217

R v B (M T) [2000] Crim LR 181 ... 106

R v B [1997] Crim LR 220 ... 84

R v B [2000] Crim LR 48 ... 106

R v B [2003] EWCA Crim 2169 ... 144

R v Bailey (1978) 66 Cr App R 31 ... 223, 290

R v Ball [1983] 1 WLR 801 ... 133

R v Barnes [1995] 2 Cr App R 491 ... 127

R v Barrington [1981] 1 WLR 419 ... 128

R v Barry (1992) 95 Cr App R 384 ... 179

R v Bass [1953] 1 QB 680, CA ... 82

R v Beattie (1989) 89 Cr App R 302 ... 87, 102

R v Becouarn [2004] All ER (D) 369 (Feb) ... 199

R v Bellamy (1985) 85 Cr App R 222, CA ... 61, 66

R v Bentum (1989) 153 JP 538 ... 213

R v Bernadotti (1869) 11 Cox CC 316 ... 169

R v Birchall [1999] Crim LR 311, CA ... 199

R v Birks [2002] EWCA Crim 3091 ... 85

R v Blake (1844) 6 QB 126 ... 171, 172

R v Blastland [1986] AC 41 ... 13, 144, 168

R v Blenkinsop [1995] 1 Cr App R 7 ... 213

R v Bottrill, ex p Kuechenmeister [1947] 1 KB 41 ... 22

R v Bowden [1993] Crim LR 379 ... 204

R v Bowden [1999] 2 Cr App R 176 ... 243

R v Bowden [1999] 4 All ER 43 ... 192

R v Boyes (1861) 1 B & S 311 ... 238

R v Boyson [1991] Crim LR 274 ... 108

R v Bradley (1980) 70 Cr App R 200, CA ... 133

R v Bradshaw (1986) Cr App R 79 ... 224

R v Bray (1988) 88 Cr App R 354 ... 156

R v Breslin (1985) 80 Cr App R 226 ... 206

R v Brizzalari [2004] EWCA Crim 310 ... 190

R v Brown [1997] 1 Cr App R 112 ... 67

R v Brown [1998] 2 Cr App R 364 ... 91

R v Browning (1991) 94 Cr App R 109 ... 208

R v Bruce [1975] 1 WLR 1252 ... 116

R v Buckley (1838) 13 Cox CC 293 ... 168

R v Buckley (1999) 163 JP 561 ... 215

R v Burge [1996] 1 Cr App R 163 ... 186

R v Butler (Diana) [1999] Crim LR 835 ... 109

R v Butterwasser [1948] 1 KB 4, 32 Cr App R 81 CCA ... 108, 110

R v C and B [2003] EWCA Crim 29 ... 93, 101

R v Caldwell (1994) 99 Cr App R 73 ... 213

R v Callender [1998] Crim LR 337 ... 168

R v Cannan [1998] Crim LR 284 ... 91

R v Cannings [2004] EWCA Crim 1 ... 224

R v Cape [1996] 1 Cr App R 191 ... 207

R v Carnall [1995] Crim LR 944 ... 167

R v Carr-Briant [1943] KB 607 ... 36

R v Carrington (1994) 99 Cr App R 376 ... 161

R v Carter, 161 JP 207, CA ... 114

R v Cartwright (1914) 10 Cr App R 219 ... 84

R v Castillo [1996] 1 Cr App R 438 ... 157

R v Chance [1988] QB 932 ... 289

R v Chandler [1976] 1 WLR 585 ... 194

R v Chapman (1838) 8 Car & P 558 ... 71

R v Chapman [1969] 2 QB 436, CA ... 143

R v Cheng (1976) 63 Cr App R 20 ... 82

R v Chenia [2002] EWCA Crim 2345 ... 193

R v Chief Constable of the West Midlands, ex p Wiley [1995] 1 AC 274 ... 250
R v Christie [1914] AC 545 ... 84, 211
R v Churchill [1993] Crim LR 285 ... 158
R v Clare [1995] 2 Cr App R 333 ... 214
R v Clarke [1995] 2 Cr App R 425 ... 214
R v Cokar [1960] 2 QB 207, CCA ... 113
R v Cole [1990] 2 All ER 108 ... 162
R v Collins [2004] EWCA Crim 33 ... 186
R v Colwill [2002] EWCA Crim 1320 ... 98
R v Compton [2002] EWCA Crim 2835, CA ... 195
R v Condron [1997] 1 Cr App R 185 ... 191
R v Conway [1990] Crim LR 402 ... 210
R v Cook [1959] 2 QB 340 ... 25, 114
R v Cooke (1987) 84 Cr App R 286 ... 236
R v Coote (1873) LR 4 PC 599 ... 239
R v Corcoran [2003] EWCA Crim 43 ... 90
R v Cottrill [1997] Crim LR 56, CA ... 245
R v Coughlan [1999] 5 Archbold News 2, CA ... 157
R v Courtnell [1990] Crim LR 115 ... 207
R v Couzens [1992] Crim LR 822, CA ... 200
R v Cowan [1996] 1 Cr App R 1, CA ... 198
R v Cowan [1996] Cr App R 1 ... 190
R v Cox and Railton (1884) 14 QBD 153 ... 244
R v Crawford [1998] 1 Cr App R 338 ... 116
R v Cresswell (1873) 1 QBD 446, CCR ... 53
R v Cummings [1948] 1 All ER 551, CA ... 85
R v D [2002] 2 Cr App R 36 ... 156
R v Da Silva [1990] 1 WLR 31 ... 80, 81
R v Dallagher [2002] EWCA Crim 1903, [2003] 1 Cr App R 12 ... 216
R v Daly [2002] 2 Cr App R ... 193
R v Darby [1989] Crim LR 817, CA ... 90
R v Day [1940] 1 All ER 402, CA ... 70
R v Deenik [1992] Crim LR 578 ... 213
R v Delaney (1989) 88 Cr App R 338, CA ... 180
R v Derby Magistrates' Court, ex p B [1995] 3 WLR 681 ... 101, 244
R v Derodra [2000] 1 Cr App R 41, CA ... 161
R v Dervish [2002] 2 Cr App R 105 ... 189
R v Devonport [1996] 1 Cr App R 221 ... 172
R v Dillon [1982] AC 484, PC ... 53
R v Dixon [2001] Crim LR 126 ... 235
R v Dodson and Williams [1984] 1 WLR 971 ... 213
R v Doheny [1997] 1 Cr App R 369 ... 218
R v Donat (1985) 82 Cr App R 173 ... 172
R v Donovan [1934] 2 KB 498 ... 41
R v Doolan [1988] Crim LR 747, CA ... 180
R v Doolin (1832) 1 Jebb CC 125 ... 91
R v Downey [1995] 1 Cr App R 547 ... 127
R v Dragic [1996] 2 Cr App R 232 ... 163
R v Drummond [2002] EWCA Crim 527, [2002] 2 Cr App R 352 ... 44
R v Duffas (1994) 158 JP 224 ... 133
R v Duffy [1999] 1 Cr App R 307, CA ... 162
R v Duncan (1981) 73 Cr App R 359 ... 87
R v Edwards [1975] QB 27 ... 46
R v Edwards [1991] 1 WLR 207 ... 96, 98
R v Edwards [1996] 2 Cr App R 345 ... 19, 97
R v Edwards [2001] EWCA Crim 2185 ... 290
R v Fairfax [1995] Crim LR 949 ... 163

R v Forbes [2001] AC 473 ... 210
R v Fowden [1982] Crim LR 588 ... 213
R v Foxley [1995] 2 Cr App R 523 ... 160
R v Francis [1991] 1 All ER 225 ... 70
R v French (1993) 97 Cr App R 421 ... 157, 163
R v Friend [1997] 1 WLR 1433 ... 198
R v Fulling [1987] QB 426 ... 179
R v Funderbark [1990] 2 All ER 482, [1990] 1 WLR 587 ... 98... 101
R v Galbraith [1981] 1 WLR 1039 ... 28, 47, 205
R v Gall (1990) 90 Cr App R 64 ... 210
R v Garbett (1847) 1 Den CC 236 ... 239
R v Garrod [1997] Crim LR 445 ... 87, 177
R v Gayle [1999] 2 Cr App R 130 ... 208
R v Gill (1963) 47 Cr App R 166, CCA ... 42
R v Gloster (1888) 16 Cox CC 471 ... 168
R v Glover [1991] Crim LR 48 ... 167
R v Gokal [1997] 2 Cr App R 266 ... 162
R v Goldenberg (1989) 88 Cr App R 285, CA ... 180
R v Governor of Brixton Prison, ex p Levin [1997] 3 WLR 117, HL ... 150
R v Governor of Pentonville Prison, ex p Osman [1990] 1 WLR 277 ... 172
R v Grannell (1990) 90 Cr App R 149 ... 210
R v Gray [1995] 2 Cr App R 100 ... 171
R v Gray [2003] EWCA Crim 1001 ... 214
R v Grimer [1982] Crim LR 674 ... 213
R v Gummerson [1999] Crim LR 680 ... 213
R v Guttridges (1840) 9 C & P 471 ... 85
R v H [1995] 2 AC 596 ... 131
R v H [2001] Crim LR 815 ... 158
R v H [2003] EWCA Crim 2367 ... 93
R v H; R v C [2003] UKHL 2847 ... 249, 253
R v Hacker [1994] 1 WLR 1659 ... 133
R v Hampshire [1996] 1 QB 1 ... 104
R v Hampshire County Council, ex p K [1990] 2 All ER 129 ... 252
R v Haringay Justices, ex p DPP [1996] 1 All ER 828, DC ... 71
R v Harris [1927] 2 KB 587 ... 71
R v Hay (1983) 77 Cr App R 70 ... 236
R v Hayes [1977] 1 WLR 238 ... 60
R v Heath, The Times, 10 February 1994 ... 108
R v Henry [2003] EWCA Crim 1296 ... 157
R v Hersey [1998] Crim LR 281 ... 213
R v Hill (1851) 2 Den 254 ... 61
R v Hobson [1998] 1 Cr App R 31, CA ... 8
R v Holmes [1953] 1 WLR 686 ... 290
R v Honeyghon and Sayles [1999] Crim LR 221 ... 90
R v Horne [1990] Crim LR 188, CA ... 194
R v Horseferry Road Magistrates' Court, ex p Bennet (No 2) [1994] 1 All ER 289 ... 250
R v Howick [1970] Crim LR 403 ... 211
R v Hulbert (1979) 69 Cr App R 243 ... 177
R v Hunjan (1979) 68 Cr App R 99 ... 208
R v Hunt [1987] AC 352 ... 46
R v Ilyas [1996] Crim LR 810 ... 172
R v Inch (1989) 91 Cr App R 51 ... 221
R v Inder (1978) 67 Cr App R 143 ... 124
R v Inhabitants of Mansfield (1841) 1 QB 444 ... 52
R v Jackson [1992] Crim LR 214 ... 27
R v Jackson [1996] 2 Cr App R 420 ... 224

R v Jarvis and Jarvis [1991] Crim LR 374, CA ... 84
R v Jefford [2003] EWCA Crim 1987 ... 187
R v Jenkins (1869) 11 Cox CC 250 ... 169
R v Jenkins (1945) 31 Cr App R 1 ... 114
R v Jenkins [2003] Crim LR 107 ... 172
R v Jiminez-Paez [1993] Crim LR 596, CA ... 156
R v John [1973] Crim LR 113, CA ... 211
R v John W [1998] 2 Cr App R 289, CA ... 126
R v Johnson (Kenneth) (1989) 88 Cr App R 131 ... 251
R v Johnson [1995] 2 Cr App R 41 ... 126
R v Johnson [2001] EWCA 2312 ... 70
R v Jones (W) (1923) 17 Cr App R 117 ... 113
R v Jones [1997] 2 Cr App R 119, CA ... 171
R v Kachikwu (1968) 52 Cr App R 538, CA ... 47
R v Keane (1977) 65 Cr App R 247 ... 206
R v Keane [1994] 1 WLR 746, CA ... 249
R v Kearley [1992] 2 AC 228 ... 13, 139, 145
R v Kelly The Times, 27 July 1985, CA ... 69
R v Kelsey (1982) 74 Cr App R 213, CA ... 81
R v Kemble [1990] 3 All ER 116, CA ... 65
R v Kennedy [1994] Crim LR 50 ... 163
R v Khan (1981) 73 Cr App R 190, CA ... 60
R v Khan (Sultan) [1997] AC 558 ... 182
R v Khan [1991] Crim LR 51, CA ... 114
R v Khan [1999] 2 Arch News 2 ... 193
R v King [1967] 2 QB 358 ... 128
R v King [1983] 1 WLR 411, CA ... 244
R v Kirkpatrick [1998] Crim LR 63, CA ... 116
R v KM The Times, 2 May 2003 ... 163
R v Kolton [2000] Crim LR 761 ... 20
R v Kritz [1950] 1 KB 82 ... 35
R v L [1999] Crim LR 489 ... 105
R v Lake Estates Watersports Ltd [2002] EWCA Crim 2067 ...
    161, 163
R v Lambert [2001] 3 All ER 547 ... 42
R v Lamont [1989] Crim LR 813, CA ... 180
R v Lanfear [1968] 2 QB 77 ... 223
R v Latif; R v Shahzad [1996] 2 Cr App R 92, HL ... 183
R v Lawless (1994) 98 Cr App R 342 ... 91
R v Lawrence [1995] Crim LR 815, CA ... 99
R v Leckie [1983] Crim LR 543 ... 210
R v Lee (1912) 7 Cr App R 31, CA ... 85
R v Lewis (1982) 76 Cr App R 33 ... 127
R v Lillyman [1896] 2 QB 167 ... 84
R v Lobban [1995] 2 All ER 602 ... 24
R v Lobell [1957] 1 QB 547, CCA ... 42
R v Loosely [2001] 4 All ER 897 ... 25
R v Loosely; Att Gen's Reference (No 3 of 2000) 2002 1 Cr App
    R 29 ... 182
R v Lovelock [1997] Crim LR 821 ... 91
R v Lovett [1973] 1 WLR 241 ... 115
R v Lowe [2003] EWCA Crim 3182 ... 86
R v Lucas [1981] QB 720 ... 186, 206
R v Luffe (1807) 8 East 193 ... 21
R v Lumley (1869) LR 1 CCR 196 ... 55
R v Lydon (1987) 85 Cr App R 221, CA ... 149
R v M (T) [2000] 1 WLR 421 ... 130
R v M [1996] 2 Cr App R 56 ... 74
R v M [2004] All ER (D) 103 ... 94
R v MacKenney (1980) 72 Cr App R 78 ... 100
R v MacKenney (1983) 76 Cr App R 271 ... 290

R v Mahmood [1997] 1 Cr App R 414 ... 234
R v Makanjuola [1995] 1 WLR 1348 ... 104, 105
R v Maloney [1994] Crim LR 525, CA ... 157
R v Manchester Crown Court, ex p R The Times, 15 February
    1999 ... 243
R v Marshall [1989] Crim LR 819, CA ... 122
R v Marsham, ex p Lawrence [1912] 2 KB 362 ... 65
R v Martin [1996] Crim LR 589, CA ... 157
R v Mason [1988] 1 WLR 139 ... 25
R v Mattey [1995] 2 Cr App R 409 ... 156
R v Maw [1994] Crim LR 841 ... 90
R v McCay [1990] 1 WLR 645 ... 169
R v McFaden (1975) 62 Cr App R 187 ... 97
R v McGarry [1999] 1 WLR 1500 ... 193
R v McGillivray (1993) 97 Cr App R 232 ... 155
R v McGovern (1991) 92 Cr App R 228, CA ... 180
R v McGranaghan [1995] 1 Cr App R 559 ... 126
R v McGuinness [1999] Crim LR 318 ... 187
R v McLean (1968) 52 Cr App R 80, CA ... 148
R v McLeod [1995] 1 Cr App R 591, CA ... 114
R v McManus [2001] EWCA Crim 2455 ... 199
R v McNamara [1996] Crim LR 750 ... 214
R v Mendy (1976) 64 Cr App R 4 ... 98
R v MH [2002] Crim LR 73, CA ... 93
R v Miah [1997] Crim LR 351, CA ... 108
R v Miller [1952] 2 All ER 667 ... 132
R v Miller [1997] 2 Cr App R 178 ... 114
R v Mills [1962] 1 WLR 1152 ... 82
R v Mills [2003] 1 WLR 2931 ... 138
R v Moghal (1977) 65 Cr App R 56 ... 168
R v Mountford [1999] Crim LR 575 ... 192
R v Muir (1984) 79 Cr App R 153, CA ... 147
R v Mukodi [2003] EWCA Crim 3765 ... 92
R v Mullen [2004] EWCA Crim 662 ... 74
R v Muncaster [1999] Crim LR 409 ... 106
R v Munnery [1992] Crim LR 215, CA ... 71
R v Mutch [1973] 1 All ER 178, CA ... 211
R v Nash [2004] All ER (D) 207 (Jan) ... 187
R v Nathaniel [1995] 2 Cr App R 565 ... 217
R v Naudeer [1984] 3 All ER 1036 ... 200
R v Nazeer [1998] Crim LR 750 ... 164
R v Nelson [2004] EWCA Crim 333 ... 137
R v Newell [1989] Crim LR 906 ... 47
R v Newport [1998] Crim LR 581 ... 167
R v Newsome (1980) 71 Cr App R 325 ... 86
R v Nickolson [1999] Crim LR 61 ... 190
R v NK [1999] Crim LR 980 ... 84
R v Nye (1977) 66 Cr App R 252 ... 167
R v O'Connor (1986) 85 Cr App R 298 ... 233
R v O'Connell [2003] EWCA Crim 502 ... 143
R v O'Doherty [2003] 1 Cr App R 5 ... 213
R v O'Neill [1969] Crim LR 260 ... 102
R v Oakley (1979) 70 Cr App R 7 ... 291
R v Oliver [1996] 2 Cr App R 514 ... 22
R v Olivia [1965] 1 WLR 1028 ... 71
R v Osborne [1905] 1 KB 551, CA ... 85
R v Osbourne [1973] QB 678 ... 211, 148
R v Owen [1952] 2 QB 362 ... 71
R v Oyesiku (1971) 56 Cr App R 240 ... 87, 102
R v P [1991] 3 All ER 337 ... 124

R v P [2002] 1 AC 146 ... 182
R v Palmer [2002] EWCA Crim 2645 ... 210
R v Paris (1992) 97 Cr App R 99, CA ... 179
R v Park (1995) 99 Cr App R 270 ... 177
R v Parker [1995] Crim LR 223, CA ... 179
R v Patel (1981) 73 Cr App R 117 ... 147
R v Patel (1993) 97 Cr App R 294, CA ... 163
R v Patel [1951] 2 All ER 29 ... 14
R v Patrick [1999] 6 Arch News 4 ... 187
R v Paul [1920] 2 KB 183 ... 62
R v Pearce (1979) 69 Cr App R 365 ... 86, 178
R v Penny [1992] Crim LR 184 ... 210
R v Perry [1909] 2 KB 697 ... 169
R v Peterborough Justice, ex p Hicks [1977] 1 WLR 1371 ... 244
R v Petkar [2003] EWCA Crim 2668 ... 192, 193
R v Pettman (2 May 1985 unreported) ... 130
R v Phillips (1988) 86 Cr App R 18, CA ... 179
R v Pike (1829) 3 C & P 598 ... 169
R v Pipe (1966) 51 Cr App R 17 ... 61
R v Pitt [1983] QB 25 ... 238
R v Powell [1985] 1 WLR 1364, CA ... 114
R v Prager (1972) 56 Cr App R 151 ... 179
R v Quinn [1990] Crim LR 581 ... 210
R v R [1994] 4 All ER 260, CA ... 244
R v Radak [1999] 1 Cr App R 187, CA ... 163
R v Randall [2003] UKHL 69 ... 10, 14, 117
R v Randall [2004] 1 All ER 467 ... 132
R v Rankine [1986] QB 861 ... 251
R v Reading [1966] 1 WLR 836, CCA ... 129
R v Reid [1989] Crim LR 719, CA ... 116
R v Rice [1963] 1 QB 857, CA ... 148
R v Richardson [1969] 1 QB 299 ... 100
R v Richardson [1971] 2 QB 484 ... 80
R v Richardson [2003] EWCA Crim 2754 ... 94
R v Robb (1991) 93 Cr App R 161 ... 213
R v Roberts (1874) 14 Cox CC 101, CCR ... 53
R v Roberts [1942] 1 All ER 187, CA ... 83
R v Roberts [1998] Crim LR 682 ... 214, 287
R v Roberts [2000] Crim LR 183 ... 213
R v Robertson (1987) 85 Cr App R 304 ... 234
R v Roble [1997] Crim LR 449 ... 192
R v Rogers [1993] Crim LR 386 ... 211
R v Rogers [1995] 1 Cr App R 374 ... 170
R v Rothwell (1994) 99 Cr App R 388, CA ... 137
R v Rowson [1986] QB 174 ... 115
R v Rowton (1865) L & C 520 ... 108
R v Russell-Jones [1995] 3 All ER 239, CA ... 67
R v Rutherford [1998] Crim LR 490, CA ... 158
R v Samuel [1988] QB 615 ... 25
R v Sanderson [1953] 1 WLR 392 ... 71
R v Sang [1980] AC 402 ... 24, 182
R v Sat-Bhambra (1988) 88 Cr App R 44 ... 177
R v Sat-Bhambra (1989) 88 Cr App R 55 ... 25
R v Scaife (1836) 1 Mood & R 551 ... 169
R v Scarrott [1978] QB 1016 ... 124
R v Scott (1984) 79 Cr App R 49, CA ... 70
R v Seelig (1991) 94 Cr App R 17, CA ... 179
R v Seigley (1911) 6 Cr App R 106 ... 117
R v Sekhon (1987) 85 Cr App R 19, CA ... 82
R v Setz-Dempsey [1994] Crim LR 123 ... 156

R v Sharp [1988] 1 All ER 65, HL ... 87
R v Sharp [1988] 1 WLR 7, HL ... 137
R v Shone (1983) 76 Cr App R 72, CA ... 147
R v Silcot [1987] Crim LR 765 ... 178
R v Silcott The Times, 9 December 1991 ... 291
R v Silverlock [1894] 2 QB 766 ... 223
R v Simmonds [1969] 1 QB 685 ... 81
R v Sims [1946] KB 531, CCA ... 6
R v Skirving [1985] QB 819 ... 290
R v Slater [1995] 1 Cr App R 584 ... 207
R v Smith (1985) 81 Cr App R 286 ... 196
R v Smith (1987) 85 Cr App R 197, CA ... 28
R v Smith [1979] 1 WLR 1445 ... 289, 290
R v Smith [1989] Crim LR 900 ... 112
R v Smith [2003] EWCA Crim 1240 ... 68
R v Smurthwaite; R v Gill (1994) 98 Cr App R 437, CA ... 182
R v Snaresbrook Crown Court, ex p DPP [1988] QB 532 ... 245
R v Soffe, The Times, 5 April 2000, CA ... 110
R v Somers [1999] Crim LR 744 ... 98
R v South Ribble Magistrates' Court, ex p Cochrane [1996] 2 Cr App R 544 ... 80
R v Spencer [1987] AC 128 ... 104
R v Stamford [1972] 2 QB 391 ... 290
R v Sterk [1972] Crim LR 391 ... 71
R v Steward [1963] Crim LR 697 ... 172
R v Stockwell (1993) 97 Cr App R 260 ... 214, 222, 291
R v Storey (1968) 52 Cr App R 334, CA ... 86
R v Straffen [1952] 2 QB 911 ... 123
R v Stretton (1986) 86 Cr App R 7 ... 91
R v Stubbs [2002] EWCA Crim 2254 ... 148
R v Sullivan, The Times, 18 March 2003 ... 132
R v Surgenor (1940) 27 Cr App R 175 ... 60
R v Sweet-Escott (1971) 55 Cr App R 316 ... 96
R v Tahed [2004] All ER (D) 346 (Feb) ... 94
R v Tandy [1989] 1 WLR 350 ... 290
R v Tanner (1977) 66 Cr App R 56, CA ... 114
R v Taylor (1924) 17 Cr App R 109 ... 129
R v Teasedale (1993) 99 Cr App R 80, CA ... 109
R v Thomas (1982) 77 Cr App R 63 ... 41
R v Thomas (1999) LTL 22/11/99 ... 214
R v Thomas [1998] Crim LR 887, CA ... 163
R v Thompson (1976) 64 Cr App R 96, CA ... 90
R v Thompson [1918] AC 221 ... 129
R v Thomson [1912] 3 KB 19 ... 168
R v Thornton [1995] 1 Cr App R 578 ... 207
R v Tilley [1961] 1 WLR 1309 ... 290
R v Tobin [2003] Crim LR 408 ... 109
R v Tompkins (1977) 67 Cr App R 181, CA ... 245
R v Toner (1991) 93 Cr App R 382 ... 291
R v Tooke (1989) 90 Cr App R 417 ... 86
R v Treacy [1944] 2 All ER 229, CA ... 92
R v Turnbull [1977] QB 224 ... 17, 203, 205, 206, 207
R v Turner (1832) 1 Mood CC 347 ... 232
R v Turner (1975) 61 Cr App R 67, CA ... 61
R v Turner [1975] QB 834, CA ... 222
R v Turner [2000] 1 All ER 1025 ... 193
R v Turner [2004] 1 All ER 1025 ... 190
R v Uniacke [2003] EWCA Crim 30 ... 25
R v Valentine [1996] 2 Cr App R 213, CA ... 85
R v Van Vreden (1973) 57 Cr App R 818, CA ... 149

R v Varley (1982) 75 Cr App R 241, CA ... 115, 116
R v Vickers [1972] Crim LR 101 ... 114
R v Vye; R v Wise; R v Stephenson, 97 Cr App R 134 ... 108
R v Walters (1979) 69 Cr App R 115 ... 172
R v Ward [1993] 1 WLR 619 ... 248
R v Ward [2001] Crim LR 316 ... 148
R v Watts (W) (1983) 77 Cr App R 12, CA ... 115
R v Webber [2004] 1 All ER 770 ... 188, 190, 193
R v Weeder (1980) 71 Cr App R 228 ... 206
R v Weller [1994] Crim LR 856 ... 199
R v Welstead [1996] 1 Cr App R 59, CA ... 73
R v Weston-Super-Mare JJ, ex p Townsend [1968] 3 All ER 225, DC ... 114
R v Westwall [1976] 2 All ER 812 ... 80
R v Wheeler (2000) 164 JP 565 ... 197
R v Wheeler [1967] 3 All ER 829 ... 6
R v White [2004] All ER (D) 103 (Mar) ... 94
R v White [2004] All ER D 103 (Mar) ... 95
R v Whitehead (1848) 3 Car & Kir 202 ... 13
R v Wilkins [1975] 2 All ER 734, CA ... 133
R v Williams [1998] Crim LR 494, CA ... 88
R v Williams [2002] EWCA Crim 2208 ... 172
R v Willoughby [1999] 2 Cr App R 82 ... 212
R v Willshire (1881) 6 QBD 366 ... 51, 56
R v Wilmot (1989) 89 Cr App R 341 ... 88
R v Windass (1989) 89 Cr App R 258 ... 92
R v Wisdom (CA, 10 December 1989) ... 188
R v Wood (1982) 76 Cr App R 23, CA ... 149
R v Wood [1987] 1 WLR 799, CA ... 133
R v Wood Green Crown Court, ex p Taylor [1995] Crim LR 879 ... 91
R v Wright (1987) 90 Cr App R 91 ... 85
R v Wright [2000] Crim LR 510 ... 108
R v Wyatt [1990] Crim LR 343 ... 91
R v Y [1995] Crim LR 155, CA ... 88
R v Z [2000] 2 AC 483 ... 110, 236
R v Z [2000] 2 AC 483, HL ... 129
Rank Film Distributors Ltd v Video Information Centre [1982] AC 380 ... 238
Raphael, Re [1973] 1 WLR 998 ... 231
Ratten v R [1972] AC 378, PC ... 143
Reid v R (1990) 90 Cr App R 121 ... 204, 208
Renworth Ltd v Stephansen [1996] 3 All ER 244 ... 239
Rio Tinto Zinc Corporation v Westinghouse Electric Company [1978] AC 547 ... 238
Rogers v Home Secretary [1973] AC 388 ... 249
Rowe and Davis v United Kingdom (2000) 30 EHRR 1 ... 249, 253
Rowe v United Kingdom [2000] Crim LR 584 ... 105
Rudd (1948) 32 Cr App R 138 ... 178
Rush & Tompkins Ltd v Greater London Council [1989] AC 1280, HL ... 247
Salabiaku v France (1988) 13 EHRR 379 ... 44
Samuel [1988] QB 615 ... 181
Sangster v R [2002] UKPC 58 ... 214
Sattin v National Union Bank (1978) 122 SJ 367, CA ... 133
Schneider v Leigh [1955] 2 QB 195 ... 243
Science Research Council v Nasse [1980] AC 1028 ... 251
Scott v London and St Katherine Docks Co (1865) 3 Hurl &C 596 ... 55
Scott v R [1989] AC 1242 ... 208
Scott v Sampson (1882) 8 QBD 491 ... 107

Sealey v The State [2002] UKPC 52 ... 84
Secretary of State for Defence v Guardian Newspapers [1985] 1 AC 339 ... 252
Selvey v DPP [1970] AC 304 ... 113
Sheldrake v DPP [2003] 2 All ER 497 ... 44
South Shropshire District Council v Amos [1986] 1 WLR 1271 ... 247
Soward v Leggatt (1856) 7 Car & P 613 ... 39
Sparks v R [1964] AC 964, PC ... 23, 147
Stirland v DPP [1944] AC 315 ... 112
Studdy v Sanders (1823) 2 Dow & Ry KB 347 ... 243
Stupple v Royal Insurance Co Ltd [1971] 1 QB 50 ... 230
Sturla v Feccia (1880) 5 App Cas 623 ... 171
Subramaniam v Public Prosecutor [1956] 1 WLR 965, PC ... 143
Sumners v Moseley (1834) 2 Cr & M 477 ... 91
Taylor v Chief Constable of Cheshire [1986] 1 WLR 1479 ... 150
Taylor v Chief Constable of Cheshire [1987] 1 All ER 225 ... 213
Taylor v Director of the Serious Fraud Office [1999] 2 AC 177 ... 250
Taylor v Taylor [1965] 1 All ER 872 ... 56
Taylor v Taylor [1967] P 25 ... 51
Taylor v Taylor [1970] 1 WLR 1148 ... 230
Teper v R [1952] AC 480, PC ... 167
Thomas v Commissioner of the Police for the Metropolis [1997] 1 All ER 747, CA ... 99
Thomas v Connell (1838) 4 M & W 267 ... 144, 168
Thompson v R [1918] AC 221 ... 126
Three Rivers District Council v Bank of England (No 5) [2003] EWCA Civ 474, [2003] QB 1556 ... 241
Three Rivers District Council v Bank of England (No 10) [2004] EWCA 373, Ch ... 241
Tingle Jacobs and Co v Kennedy [1964] 1 WLR 638 ... 54
Tobi v Nichols [1988] RTR 343 ... 167
Tomlin v Standard Telephones & Cables Ltd [1969] 1 WLR 1378 ... 247
Toohey v Metropolitan Police Commissioner [1965] AC 595, HL ... 100, 290
Topham v McGregor (1844) 1 Car & Kir 320 ... 82
Triplex Safety Glass Co Ltd v Lancegaye Safety Glass [1939] 2 KB 395 ... 238
Tuck v Vehicle Inspectorate, 24 March 2004 (unreported) ... 71
United States of America v Philip Morris Inc [2004] EWCA CIV 330 ... 241, 242
USP Strategies v London General Holdings [2004] EWHC 373, Ch ... 241, 246
Vehicle and Operator Agency v Jenkins Transport Ltd [2003] EWHC 2879 (Admin) ... 160
Ventouris v Mountain (No 2) [1992] 1 WLR 817 ... 152
Vernon v Boseley (No 2) [1995] 2 FCR 78 ... 91
Walker v Wilshire (1889) 23 QBD 335 ... 247
Watson v Chief Constable of Cleveland Police [2001] EWCA Civ 1547 ... 99
Wauchope v Mordechai [1970] 1 WLR 317 ... 230
Waugh v British Railways Board [1980] AC 521 ... 240, 242
Waugh v R [1950] AC 203, PC ... 169
Wetherhall v Harrison [1976] QB 773 ... 22
Wheeler v Le Marchant (1881) 17 Ch D 675 ... 240, 242
White v R [1999] AC 210 ... 85
Wiedmann v Walpole [1891] 2 QB 534 ... 185
Wood v Mackinson (1840) 2 Mood & R 273 ... 91
Woodhouse v Hall (1980) 72 Cr App R 39, DC ... 143
Woolmington v DPP [1935] AC 462 ... 32, 35, 41

Worley v Bentley [1976] 2 All ER 449 ... 80
Wright v Doe d. Tatham (1837) 7 Ad & El 313 ... 145
Wyat v Wingford (1729) 2 Ld Raym 1528 ... 72

X Ltd v Morgan-Grampian (Publishers) Ltd [1991] 1 AC 1 ... 252
Young v Rank [1950] 2 KB 510 ... 28

# TABLE OF STATUTES

Administration of Justice Act 1920
  s 15...1.9.2.5

Bankers' Books Evidence Act 1879...4.5.2
  s 3...8.5, 8.6.5
  s 4...8.6.5
  s 6...4.5.2

Children Act 1989...4.2.2.1, 14.2.2.6, 14.3.3.3
  s 1(1)...14.2.2.6
  s 42...14.3.3.3
  s 96...4.2.2.1, 4.2.2.2, 4.6.2.2
  s 96(1)...4.2.2.1
  s 96(2)...4.2.2.1
  s 96(2)(b)...4.2.2.1
  s 96(3)–(5)...4.2.2.1
  s 98...14.2.1.4
  s 98(2)...14.2.1.4
Children and Young Persons Act 1933
  s 50...3.3.2
Children and Young Persons Act 1963
  s 16(2)...6.5
  s 16(3)...6.5
Civil Evidence Act 1968...13.3.4
  s 11...13.3.1, 13.3.2, 13.3.3, App.1
  s 11(1)...13.3.1, App.1
  s 11(2)...13.3.1, 13.4.1.1, 13.4.1.2
  s 11(2)(a)...13.3.1, 13.3.2, App.1
  s 11(2)(b)...13.3.1
  s 11(3)...13.3.1
  s 11(4)...13.3.1, 13.3.2
  s 12...13.3.5
  s 13...3.1.1, 3.3.1, 13.2, 13.3.2, 13.3.3
  s 13(1)–(3)...13.3.3
  s 14...14.2.1
  s 14(1)(b)...14.2.1.2
Civil Evidence Act 1972
  s 2(3)...12.3.5.1
  s 3(1)...12.3.1
  s 3(2)...12.2, 12.3.6.1, 12.3.6.2
  s 3(3)...12.2, 12.3.1
Civil Evidence Act 1995...1.4.2.2, 8.5, 8.5.3, 8.7, 8.7.1, 8.7.2,
    8.7.4, 8.8
  s 1...5.2.2.3, 5.2.7, 5.3.4, 8.5
  s 1(1)–(4)...8.5
  s 2...8.5.1, 8.7.4
  s 2(4)...8.5.1
  s 2(4)(a)...8.5.1

s 3...8.5.4, 8.7.4
s 4...8.5.4, 8.5.5, 8.7.4
s 4(2)...8.5.4
s 4(2)(a)–(f)...8.5.4
s 5...8.5, 8.7.4, 12.3.6.1
s 5(2)(a)...8.5.4
s 6...5.2.2.3, 5.2.4.5, 5.2.7, 5.3.4, 8.5, 8.5.2, 8.7.4
s 6(2)...5.2.4.6, 8.5.2, 12.3.6.1
s 6(3)–(5)...8.5.2
s 7...8.5, 8.5.5, 8.7.3
s 8...8.5.3
s 9...8.5.3
s 9(4)...8.5.3
s 10...8.5.3
s 13...12.3.6.1
Companies Act 1985
  s 434...14.2.1.4
  s 447...14.2.1.4
Consumer Credit Act 1974
  s 171(7)...2.4.3
Contempt of Court Act 1981
  s 10...14.3.3.4
County Courts Act 1984
  s 55...4.7.4.2
  s 68...1.9.2.5
Crime and Disorder Act 1998
  s 1...8.5
Criminal Damage Act 1971
  s 9...14.2.1.4
Criminal Evidence Act 1898
  s 1...6.3.3, 6.3.3.9, 6.4
  s 1(1)...4.3.2
  s 1(2)...6.3.3, 6.3.3.1, 14.2.1.4
  s 1(3)...6.3.3, 6.3.3.1, 6.3.3.2, 6.3.3.3, 10.4.5, 10.4.5.4, App.2
  s 1(3)(i)...6.3.3.1, 6.3.3.3, App.2
  s 1(3)(ii)...6.3.3.1, 6.3.3.4, 6.3.3.5, 6.3.3.6, 6.3.3.7, 6.3.3.8,
    App.1, App.2
  s 1(3)(iii)...6.3.3.1, 6.3.3.9, App.2
Criminal Evidence (Amendment) Act 1997...11.9.6.2
Criminal Justice Act 1967
  s 9...1.8.1, 4.7.1, 8.3.3.2, 8.6.5
  s 10...1.5.1.1
  s 10(1)...1.5.1.1
  s 10(2)...1.5.1.1
  s 10(2)(a)–(d)...1.5.1.1
  s 10(4)...1.5.1.1
Criminal Justice Act 1987
  Part I...14.2.1.4

s 1(5)...4.7.6.1
s 2...14.2.1.4
s 4...4.7.6.1
Criminal Justice Act 1988...8.6.1, 8.6.5
    s 21(3)...App.1
    s 23...8.6.1, 8.6.2, 8.6.2.2, 8.6.2.3, 8.6.2.4, 8.6.3, 8.6.3.2,
        8.6.4, 8.6.4.1, 8.6.4.4, 8.7.2, 8.8.2.1, 8.8.2.2, App.1,
        App.3
    s 23(1)...8.6.2
    s 23(2)...8.6.2, 8.6.3
    s 23(2)(a)–(b)...8.6.2.3
    s 23(3)...8.6.2, 8.6.2.3, 8.6.3
    s 24...8.6.1, 8.6.3, 8.6.3.1, 8.6.3.3, 8.6.4, 8.6.4.1, 8.6.4.4,
        8.7.2, 8.7.3, 8.8.2.1, 8.8.2.2, App.1, App.3
    s 24(1)...8.6.3
    s 24(2)...8.6.3, 8.6.3.2
    s 24(4)...8.6.3.3, 8.6.4.1
    s 25...8.6.1, 8.6.4.1, 8.6.4.2, 8.7.2, App.1
    s 25(1)...8.6.4.1
    s 25(2)...8.6.4.1
    s 25(2)(a)–(d)...8.6.4.1
    s 26...8.6.1, 8.6.2.3, 8.6.4.1, 8.6.4.2, 8.7.2, App.1
    s 26(i)–(iii)...8.6.4.1
    s 27...8.6.4.3, App.1
    s 28...App.1
    s 29...App.1
    s 30...8.6.4.4, App.1
    s 30(1)–(4A)...12.3.6.2
    s 31...8.6.4.4
    s 32...4.7.6.1
    s 34...5.5.2, 5.5.4
    s 134...9.1.2.3
    s 139...App.1
    s 139(1)...2.5.3.2, App.1
    s 139(2)...App.1
    s 139(4)...2.5.3.2, App.1
    s 139(5)...App.1
    Sched 2...8.6.4.2
        para 1(a)–(b)...8.6.4.2
        paras 2–3...8.6.4.2
        para 5...8.6.2.1
    Sched 5
        para 2...8.6.1
Criminal Justice Act 1991...5.5.2
Criminal Justice Act 2003...5.2.6, 6.4, 7.2.6, 8.3.1, 13.4.1.1
    Part 11...6.5, 8.8
    s 98...5.3.3.4, 7.2.6
    s 99...5.3.3.4
    s 100...5.3.3.4
    s 100(1)–(2)...5.3.3.4
    s 101...6.4, 13.4.1.1
    s 102...7.2.10
    s 108...6.5
    s 114...12.3.6.2
    s 114(1)...8.8.1
    s 114(1)(a)–(b)...8.8.1
    s 114(1)(c)–(d)...8.8.1, 8.8.4.1
    s 114(2)...8.8.1
    s 115...12.3.6.2
    s 115(2)...8.8.1, 8.8.5
    s 115(3)...8.8.1

s 116...8.8.2.1, 8.8.2.2, 8.8.2.4
s 116(2)(e)...8.8.2.1
s 116(4)–(5)...8.8.2.1
s 117...8.8.2.2, 8.8.4.1
s 117(6)–(7)...8.8.2.2
s 118...8.8.2.4, 8.8.4.1
s 118(2)...8.8.2.4
s 119...8.8.2.3
s 120...5.2.6, 8.8.2.3
s 120(2)...8.8.2.3
s 120(3)...5.2.2.3, 8.8.2.3
s 120(4)...5.2.6, 8.8.2.3
s 120(4)(b)...5.2.6
s 120(5)–(7)...5.2.6, 8.8.2.3
s 120(8)...5.2.6
s 121(1)(b)...8.8.2.1
s 122(2)...8.8.2.3
s 123(3)...8.8.4.1
s 124(2)(a)–(c)...8.8.4.2
s 124(3)...8.8.4.2
s 125...8.8.3.1
s 125(1)(b)...8.8.3.1
s 126...8.8.3.2
s 126(1)(b)...8.8.3.2
s 129...8.8.5
s 139...5.2.2.2, App.1
s 139(1)(a)–(b)...5.2.2.2
s 139(2)...5.2.2.2
Criminal Justice (International Cooperation) Act 1990
    s 3...8.6.4.4
Criminal Justice and Public Order Act 1994...5.5.2, 11.9.6.2
    s 5...4.7.2.4
    s 32...5.5.3, 5.5.4
    s 32(1)...5.5.3
    s 34...5.2.4.5, 10.4.1.1, 10.4.1.2, 10.4.1.3, 10.4.1.4, 10.4.1.5,
        10.4.1.6, 10.4.1.9, 10.4.1.10, 10.4.1.12, 10.4.2, 10.4.2.1,
        10.4.7, 14.2.2.4, App.1, App.3
    s 34(1)...10.4.1.1, 10.4.1.7
    s 34(1)(b)...10.4.1.3
    s 34(2)...5.5.7, 10.4.1.1, 10.4.1.9
    s 34(2A)...10.4.1.8
    s 34(2)(c)...App.1
    s 34(3)...10.4.1.12
    s 34(4)...10.4.1.7
    s 35...4.3.2, 4.7.2.1, 10.4.1.5, 10.4.1.12, 10.4.5, 10.4.5.2,
        10.4.5.3, 10.4.5.4, 10.4.7, App.1, App.3
    s 35(1)–(2)...10.4.5
    s 35(3)...5.5.7, 10.4.5
    s 35(5)...10.4.5
    s 36...10.4.2.1, 10.4.2.2, 10.4.7, App.1
    s 36(1)...10.4.2.1
    s 36(1)(a)(i)–(ii)...App.1
    s 36(2)...5.5.7, 10.4.2.1
    s 36(2)(c)...App.1
    s 36(3)–(5)...10.4.2.1
    s 37...10.4.2.2, 10.4.7, App.1
    s 37(1)...10.4.2.2
    s 37(1)(a)...App.1
    s 37(2)...5.5.7, 10.4.2.2
    s 37(2)(c)...App.1
    s 38(2A)...10.4.1.8

s 38(3)...5.5.7
Criminal Justices Act 2000
s 137...4.7.1
s 138...4.7.1
s 139(2)...4.7.1
Criminal Law Act 1967...3.5.1
s 3(1)...2.5.2
Criminal Procedure Act 1865...5.3.4
s 3...8.5.2
ss 4–5...5.3.4, 8.5.2
s 6...5.3.3.4, App.1
Criminal Procedure (Attendance of Witnesses) Act
    1965...4.7.4.1, App.1
Criminal Procedure and Investigation Act 1996...5.2.4.5,
    12.3.5.2, 14.3.4.1
Part I...14.3.1
s 3...14.3.4.1
s 5...10.4.4, App.3
s 5(6)...10.4.4
s 7...14.3.4.1
s 11...10.4.4, 10.4.7
s 11(5)...10.4.4
Sched 1
    para 26...9.1.3.1

European Communities Act 1972
s 3(2)...1.5.2.1
Evidence Act 1845
s 2...1.5.2.1

Factories Act 1961
s 29(1)...2.5.3.3
Family Law Reform Act 1969
s 20...3.4.2
s 21(3)...3.4.2
s 26...3.4.2
Firearms Act 1968
s 21...6.2
Forestry Act 19672.5.3.2...2.5.3.3

Human Rights Act 1998...2.4.2.3, 2.5.3.2, 9.1.1.3, 9.1.3.2
s 3...2.5.3.2, 5.3.2.2
s 4...2.5.3.2
Human Rights Act 2000...6.3.3.6

Insolvency Act 1986...14.2.1.4
s 433(1)–(2)...14.2.1.4
Interpretation Act 1978
s 3...1.5.2.1
s 22(1)...1.5.2.1

Law of Property Act 1925
s 184...3.4.3.3, App.1

Magistrates' Courts Act 1980
s 5A-5F...8.6.5
s 97...4.7.4.1
s 97(1)...4.7.4.1
s 97(3)...4.7.4.1
s 101...2.5.3.3, App.1

Matrimonial Causes Act 1973
s 19(3)...3.4.3.2
Misuse of Drugs Act 1971...App.1
s 5...2.5.3.3
s 5(3)...2.5.3.2
s 7...2.5.3.3
s 28...2.5.3.2
s 28(2)...2.4.3, 2.5.3.2
s 28(3)...2.4.3, 2.5.3.2
s 28(3)(b)...2.4.3, 2.5.3.2

Oaths Act 1978
s 1(3)...4.6.1
s 4(2)...4.6.1
s 5...4.6.1
Offences Against the Person Act 1861
s 18...App.1
s 20...App.2, App.3
s 47...App.2

Perjury Act 1911
s 1(1)...1.9.2.5
s 11(6)...1.9.2.5
s 13...5.5.7
Police and Criminal Evidence Act 1984...8.7.4, 9.1, 9.1.1,
    13.4.2
s 4...App.1
s 10...14.2.2.6
s 58...9.1.3.3, 10.4.1.8, App.1
s 58(6)...App.1
s 58(6)(a)–(b)...App.1
s 58(8)(a)–(c)...App.1
s 61...11.9.6, 11.9.6.1, 11.9.6.2, App.3
s 61(1)–(7)...11.9.6.1
s 62...10.4.3, 10.4.7, 11.9.6, 11.9.6.2, App.3
s 62(1)–(1A)...11.9.6.2
s 62(2)–(10)...11.9.6.2
s 63...10.4.3, 11.9.6, 11.9.6.2, App.3
s 63(1)–(3)...11.9.6.2
s 63(3A)–(3C)...11.9.6.2
s 63(4)–(9A)...11.9.6.2
s 64...11.9.6, 11.9.6.2, App.3
s 64(3B)(a)–(b)...11.9.6.2
s 65...11.9.6, 11.9.6.1, App.3
s 66...11.9.2, App.2
s 67(11)...9.1.2
s 73(1)–(2)...13.4.1.3
s 74...13.4.1, 13.4.1.2
s 74(1)...13.4.1.2, App.1, App.2
s 74(2)...13.4.1.2, 13.4.1.4, App.1, App.2
s 74(3)...13.4.1.1, App.1
s 75(1)...13.4.1.4
s 76...8.6.4.4, 9.1.2, 9.1.2.2, 9.3, 10.4.1.12, App.1, App.2
s 76(1)...9.1.1.2, 9.1.2
s 76(2)...2.6, 9.1.2, 9.1.2.1, 9.1.2.3, App.2
s 76(2)(a)...1.9.2.2, 9.1.2.3, App.3
s 76(2)(b)...1.6.1, 9.1.2.3, App.3
s 76(3)...9.1.2.1
s 76(4)...9.1.2.3, 9.3, App.1
s 76(5)–(6)...9.1.4, App.1
s 76(8)...9.1.2.3, 9.3

s 76A...9.3
s 77...9.1.2.4
s 78...1.7.2.2, 1.9.3, 7.2.13, 8.6.4.1, 8.7.1.1, 8.8.3.2, 9.1.2,
    9.1.3.1, 9.1.3.2, 9.1.4, 9.2, 9.3, 10.4.1.3, 10.4.1.12, 11.9.2,
    11.9.3.2, 11.9.6.2, 13.4.1.2, 13.4.1.4, 14.2.2.7, 15.1,
    App.2, App.3
s 78(1)...1.7.2.2, 9.1.3
s 78(2)...9.1.3
s 79...4.7.2.3
s 80...4.4, 10.4.6
s 80(2)...4.4.2
s 80(2A)...4.4.3
s 80(2A)(b)...4.4.3
s 80(3)...4.4.3
s 80(3)(a)...4.4.3
s 80(4)...4.4.2
s 80(4A)...4.4.2
s 80(5)...4.4
s 80A...10.4.6
s 81...12.3.5.2
s 82(1)...9.1.1
s 82(3)...1.7.2.2, 9.1.2, 9.1.2.2, 9.1.3
s 116...App.1
Codes of Practice...9.1.2, App.3
    Code C...9.1.2.3, 9.1.2.4, 9.1.3.2, 9.1.3.3, App.3
        para 10.4...10.4.1.3
        para 10.5A...10.4.2.1
        para 10.5B...10.4.2.2
        para 16.1...10.4.1.3
        Annex E...9.1.2.4
    Code D...11.9.2, 11.9.3, 11.9.3.2, 11.9.4, App.1, App.2,
        App.3
        para 2...11.9.3.2
        para 2.2...11.9.1
        para 2.3-para 2.10...App.1
        para 2.12-para 13...11.9.3.2
        para 2.14...11.9.2, 11.9.3.2
        para 2.15-para 2.20...11.9.3.2
        para 2.26-para 27...App.1
        para 3...11.9.6
        para 5...11.9.6.2
        para 5.8...11.9.6.2
        para 5.8A...11.9.6.2
        Annex A...11.9.3, 11.9.3.2, 11.9.5
            para 16...11.9.3.2
        Annex B...11.9.3, 11.9.3.2
            para 18...11.9.4
        Annex C...11.9.3, 11.9.3.2
        Annex D...11.9.3, 11.9.3.2
        Annex E
            para 2.27...App.1
Prevention of Crime Act 1953
s 1...App.2
s 1(1)...App.2
s 1(4)...App.2
Public Order Act 1986
s 1...4.7.2.4
s 3...App.1
s 4...8.1
s 8...9.1.2.3

Regulation of Investigatory Powers Act 2000...9.2
Rehabilitation of Offenders Act 1974
s 4...5.3.3.4
s 7...5.3.3.4
Road Traffic Act 1988...2.5.3.2
s 5(1)(b)...2.5.3.2
s 5(2)...2.5.3.2
Road Traffic Regulation Act 1984
s 89...5.5.7, 12.2

Supreme Court Act 1981
s 69(5)...1.9.2.5

Terrorism Act 2000...2.5.3.2
s 11(1)-(2)...2.5.3.2
s 118...2.5.3.2
s 118(5)...2.5.3.2
Theft Act 1968...14.2.1.4
s 27(3)...7.2.13
s 27(4)...8.6.5
s 31(1)...14.2.1.4

Youth Justice and Criminal Evidence Act 1999...4.2.2.3, 4.7.5,
    5.3.1.3, 5.3.2.2
Part II...4.7.5
s 16...4.7.5.1, 4.7.5.2, 4.7.5.3, 4.7.5.4, App.1
s 17...4.7.5.1, 4.7.5.2, 4.7.5.3, 4.7.5.4, App.1
s 17(2)...4.7.5.1
s 19(1)-(3)...4.7.5.3
s 20(1)-(2)...4.7.5.3
s 21...4.7.5.4
s 21(3)...4.7.5.4
s 23...4.7.5.3
s 24...4.7.5.3, 4.7.5.4
ss 25-26...4.7.5.3
s 27...4.7.5.2, 4.7.5.3, 4.7.5.4, 5.3.1.3
s 28...4.7.5.3, 4.7.5.4
ss 29-30...4.7.5.3
s 32...4.7.5.2
s 34...5.3.1.3
s 35...5.3.1.3
s 35(3)(a)...4.7.5.4
ss 38-39...5.3.1.3
s 41...5.3.2.2
s 41(1)...5.3.2.2
s 41(1)(b)...5.3.2.2
s 41(2)(a)-(b)...5.3.2.2
s 41(3)...5.3.2.2
s 41(3)(a)-(b)...5.3.2.2
s 41(3)(c)...5.3.2.2
s 41(3)(c)(ii)...5.3.2.2
s 41(4)-(6)...5.3.2.2
s 42(1)(c)...5.3.2.2
s 53...4.1.1, 4.2.2.1, 4.4
s 53(1)...4.1.1, 4.2.1.1, 4.3.2, 4.4.1
s 53(3)...4.2.1.1, 4.2.2.1, App.1
s 53(4)...4.3.1, 4.4.1
s 54(2)...4.2.1.1
s 54(4)-(6)...4.2.1.1
s 55...4.6.2.1
s 55(2)...4.2.1.2

s 55(2)(a)...4.2.1.2, App.1
s 55(2)(b)...4.2.1.2
s 55(3)...4.2.1.2, 4.3.1
s 55(4)...2.6
s 55(5)...4.2.1.2
s 55(8)...4.2.1.2
s 56(2)...4.2.1.2
s 56(4)...4.2.1.2
s 56(5)...4.2.1.2, 4.6.2.1
s 62...5.3.1.3
Sched 3...14.2.1.4

## International legislation

European Convention on Human Rights
Art 3...9.1.2.3
Art 6...2.1.3.4, 2.4.2.3, 2.5.3.2, 4.7.5.4, 5.3.2.2, 8.6.4.1,
    9.1.1.3, 9.2, 10.4, 13.4.1.2, 14.2.1.4, 14.2.2, 14.3.1, App.1
Art 6(1)...9.2, 14.2.1, 14.2.1.4, 14.3.4.1
Art 6(2)...2.5.3.23
Art 6(3)...9.1.3.3
Art 6(3)(d)...8.6.4.1
Art 8...9.2, 11.9.6.2

# TABLE OF STATUTORY INSTRUMENTS

Children (Admissibility of Hearsay Evidence) Order 1993 (SI 1993/621)...8.5
Civil Procedure Rules 1998 (SI 1998/3132)...1.5.1.2, 1.7.1
  Part 1
    r 1.1...4.7.2.1
  Part 3
    r 3.4...13.3.3
    r 3.4(2)(b)...13.3.2
  Part 14
    r 14.1(1)–(2)...1.5.1.2
    r 14.1(5)...1.5.1.2
  Part 16
    r 16.5(1)–(2)...1.3.2.1
  Part 18
    r 18.1...1.5.1.2
  Part 26
    r 26.5(3)...1.5.1.2
  Part 27
    r 27.8(4)...4.6.2.2
  Part 31
    r 31.17...14.3.4.2
    r 31.19(1)...14.3.4.2
    r 31.20...14.2.2.7
  Part 32
    r 32.1...1.7.1, 4.7.2.1
    r 32.1(1)...1.7.1, 4.7.2.1, 4.7.3.1
    r 32.1(2)...1.7.1, 4.7.2.1, 4.7.2.3, App.3
    r 32.1(3)...1.7.1, 4.7.2.1, 5.3.1.3
    r 32.3...4.7.6.2
    r 32.4(1)...4.7.1
    r 32.5...8.3.3.2
    r 32.5(2)...1.8.1, 4.7.1, 5.2.2.2
    r 32.18...1.5.1.2
  PD
    para.20...4.7.1
  Part 33
    r 33.2(1)–(3)...8.5.1
    r 33.4...1.8.1
  Part 34...4.7.4.2
    r 34.5(2)...4.7.4.2
  Part 35
    r 35.3...12.3.2
    r 35.7(1)...12.3.5.1
    r 35.11...12.3.5.1
    r 35.13...12.3.5.1
  Part 36...14.2.4
Crown Court (Advance Notice of Expert Evidence) Rules 1987 (SI 1987/716)...12.3.5.2
Crown Court (Advance Notice of Expert Evidence) (Amendment) Rules 1997 (SI 1997/700)...12.3.5.2

Family Proceedings Rules 1991 (SI 1991/1247)
  r 2.69...14.2.4

Magistrates' Courts (Advance Notice of Expert Evidence) Rules 1997 (SI 1997/705)...12.3.5.2
Misuse of Drugs Regulations 1973 (SI 1973/797)...2.5.3.3

National Police Records (Recordable Offences) Regulations 1985 (SI 1985/1941)...11.9.6.1

# Fundamentals of evidence

## 1.1 About this Manual

This Manual differs from a standard textbook. You are expected not only to read it but to carry out activities while doing so. These activities are varied but will all involve you thinking about the subject of evidence and, more importantly, putting your thought into concrete form (for example, by writing something down). It is hoped that by doing so you take a more active involvement in what you read and that you can therefore gain a deeper and better understanding of the subject areas. The activities relevant to each chapter are set out in **Appendix 1**. References will be made to that appendix where relevant. You may choose to read each chapter in full and then to attempt the relevant activities. Alternatively you may wish to deal with each activity when it arises. Often doing so will help you understand what you are reading. While it is possible to ignore the activities altogether you are advised to attempt them at some point or another.

This Manual is primarily intended for use on a taught course. There are therefore also questions and case studies for discussion in **Appendix 2** that would, normally, be used during a small group class.

The questions (both those in **Appendix 1** and those in **Appendix 2**, are not intended simply to test your comprehension of what you have already read. Instead the questions seek either to test your ability to *apply* what you have already read or to encourage you to explore principles and issues underlying what you have read or are about to read.

## 1.2 What is evidence?

Before looking at the Rules of Evidence (ie, the law governing what evidence will or will not be allowed into court) it is useful to be clear about some of the matters of fundamental importance in understanding how evidence works and therefore how and why the Rules of Evidence work. The subject matter of this chapter is therefore of considerable importance. You will find that the key terms that are being referred to in this chapter are used again and again in this book. You may find it useful to reread this chapter from time to time.

Consider the following scenario. Michaela cohabited with Jake. Jake has beaten Michaela a number of times, sometimes badly enough for her to require medical treatment. Eventually, Michaela has had enough and leaves Jake, going to stay at a Bed and Breakfast. Jake works out where Michaela is and visits her. There they have an argument in the course of which, Jake threatens to report Michaela to the police for drug dealing if she does not go back to him. He then leaves. Michaela goes to a nearby bar and drinks heavily. She then goes to Jake's house. There another argument takes place. Michaela snatches up a gun that Jake has left lying around and shoots him with it. Jake dies. Michaela is charged with murder.

What defences would be available to Michaela? As a student studying a criminal law course, you might identify defences such as diminished responsibility, provocation, intoxication (negativing intent), absence of a causative link, self-defence or even accident.

How might an advocate look at a case like this? The job of an advocate is not just to apply the law to a problem but to prove or disprove facts. That is what the trial process is about. It is why there are juries and why there are extensive rules of evidence. The real world does not come with the certain facts that are useful in learning the law. If a solicitor or barrister met Michaela to hear what her defence might be to these allegations, she might raise some of the defences in the paragraph above. On the other hand she might also say any of the following:

- 'I wasn't there.'
- 'I was there but someone else shot him.'
- 'I went to the house but found Jake lying in a pool of blood: someone else must have shot him.'

What Michaela is doing is challenging the facts that are alleged against her. For her to be convicted the prosecution must prove, for example, that she was there. Even if some of the defences like provocation or intoxication were raised, there might be a factual dispute as to whether they apply. Someone must prove or disprove whether there was an act of provocation or whether or not Michaela did drink enough to be intoxicated.

On a substantive law course, such as Criminal Law or Contract Law, you are required to work with factual scenarios in which the facts are taken for granted. This makes studying the principles and determining the *ratio decidendi* of cases simpler than it would otherwise be. This is also the way in which most Court of Appeal and House of Lords cases work. However, in the vast majority of cases being heard in the courts, there is not this factual certainty. While the law has its place, it is usually the disputes over facts that win or lose cases.

### 1.2.1  Facts and law

In the standard court case, whether in the criminal courts or in any of the civil courts, the legal sanctions that the court can impose depend upon the proven facts of the case. Therefore, before a judge in the Crown Court can impose a sentence on a defendant, he or she must be proven to have committed an offence. Further, which sentence is imposed on the defendant depends on which offence or offences that defendant is proven to have committed. A defendant who has been proven to have committed one offence of dangerous driving should not be sentenced in the same way as a defendant who has committed four burglaries. Which offence is appropriate depends on which offences are proven: in effect, which factual allegations the court has accepted.

Likewise a civil court could not award damages to a claimant for three breaches of contract if the claimant had only proven that the defendant had only breached the contract once. Furthermore, the amount of any damages award would depend on how much loss the claimant could prove from that breach.

It will be seen therefore that the court's power to exercise legal sanctions and to apply legal rules depends on *proof* of particular facts. The function of the law is to establish which facts have to be proven in any given case.

### 1.2.2  Proof

The word 'proof' is used commonly in evidential discussion. Later in this and the next chapter you will be exposed to concepts such as 'burden of proof', 'standard or proof' and 'probative value'. Before going into detail on these definitions, it is worth attempting a working definition of the word 'proof'.

It is worth considering what is generally meant by proof. The legal meaning of proof is not so different from its ordinary meaning. In ordinary speech 'proof' means a number of different things but for present purposes the most pertinent meanings of proof are *either* the process of convincing a person of a particular conclusion by the use of facts and logic *or* successfully convincing a person of a particular conclusion in that way. Therefore if A says to B, 'Prove it', A means that B should produce facts and make arguments on the point in question and also that the facts and arguments produced should be such as will convince A. It is worth noting the following points:

(a) Proof is achieved by combining facts and arguments.

(b) There is an implicit standard below which the conclusion would be 'unproven'. Some things are more difficult to prove than others. The more improbable the desired conclusion the harder it will be to prove it. By 'harder' we mean that more or better facts and more or better arguments will be required to convince the person to reach the conclusion in question.

(c) Facts and arguments are not all equally valuable in proving conclusions. We expect anyone deciding whether something is proven to treat facts and arguments differently for a variety of reasons. Some have less relevance or bearing on the matter in question. Some facts relied upon may be less reliable than others whether because the source of the fact is suspect or because there is an impression that the fact does not give the whole picture it purports to present.

(d) There is always someone who has to decide whether something has been proven. Proof requires an audience to determine whether something is proven.

The approach of the courts to proof is essentially the same as that set out above. However, as one might expect from the formal nature of courts, proof is subject to a system of rules and practices. These rules and practices are at the heart of the Rules of Evidence and most of this Manual will examine how the formal process of proof is based on these rules and practices. It is therefore worth noting some of the ways in which the points noted above are applied in a formal, legal setting.

#### 1.2.2.1  Facts and arguments

The process of proof in court requires a combination of facts and arguments to prove cases. The rules of evidence and of court procedure draw a distinction between facts, which are proven by the evidence (usually the calling of witnesses) and arguments, which are advanced later on by the advocates in the case. For example, an advocate in a Crown Court trial should not comment on the evidence given by a witness while conducting cross-examination (see the *Advocacy Manual*). Rather he or she will make comments upon that evidence (ie, make arguments about it) during a closing speech after all of the facts have been put before the jury (see the *Civil Litigation* and *Criminal Litigation Manuals*). Equally the rules of evidence draw distinctions between facts and opinions. As shall be seen in **Chapter 12**, evidence of the opinions of witnesses is not generally allowed into court. Even where it is (for example, where an expert gives evidence) the opinions must be based on proven facts.

### 1.2.2.2    Standards of proof

Every allegation in a case must be established to a particular 'standard of proof'. The standard for any particular allegation is set by the law. It is in this context that phrases you may have heard before like 'beyond reasonable doubt' and 'on the balance of probabilities' are used. The law has also regulated who must prove facts. The 'prove it' demand is generally but not always imposed upon the party bringing the case (ie, the claimant in civil cases and the prosecution in criminal cases) but, given the complexity of the litigation process, this is not always so. The requirement that a party prove a particular conclusion is called the 'burden of proof'. We shall examine the burden and standard of proof more closely in **Chapter 2**.

### 1.2.2.3    Facts and arguments are variable

The rules of evidence recognise that facts have differing capacity to prove conclusions in a number of different ways. While the rules of evidence generally seek to admit all facts that might prove a conclusion ('relevant facts') there are numerous safeguards that aim to prevent the trial process being undermined.

The formalised trial process has rules for how facts are proven (see **1.8** below) and there are also rules preventing some facts from being proven if the source of the fact in question is in some way potentially unreliable (for example, 'hearsay' evidence in **Chapter 8** and the requirement that an expert is proven to be an expert witness before expert opinion evidence can be given: see **Chapter 12**).

We shall see that some of these rules aim to prevent parties from wasting the time and resources of the court with facts of little value in deciding the issues of the case (for example, rules that limit the extent to which parties can prove that witnesses are of bad character: see **Chapter 5**).

Other rules seek to prevent the court from being distracted from deciding the real issues of the case (for example, rules that restrict parties from proving the bad character of the other party in the case: see **Chapters 6** and **7**). There is therefore a process of filtering out some facts from cases. This is more frequently the case in criminal trials than in civil trials, as shall become apparent.

At the heart of this filtering process is the concept of 'weight' (see **1.4.2** below), which is simply the legal recognition that some facts, or combinations of facts, or combinations of facts and arguments, are less capable of proving conclusions than others. The weight to be attached to any fact (or facts) is significant in two ways. First it often determines whether the court will entertain that fact at all (for example, where the fact seeks to prove the bad character of a criminal defendant: see **Chapters 6** and **7**). Secondly it is used to decide whether the fact or facts are sufficient to reach a particular standard of proof (as noted above and see **Chapter 2**).

### 1.2.2.4    The audience

A general term for the person or persons who must decide whether the facts in question are proven is 'the tribunal of fact' or the 'fact-finder'. Quite who this is depends on which court a party is appearing in. The classic audience in a legal dispute is the jury in a Crown Court trial. In the Crown Court the jury is responsible for reaching factual decisions and the judge with deciding points of law. This raises an important distinction that we will return to later (**1.9**). The 'law-decider' is generally referred to as a 'tribunal of law'. The legal decisions include matters such as what sentence to pass on a person who has been found guilty of an offence or what the effect of the frustration of a contract might be. However, they can also include decisions such as whether particular facts (ie, evidence) should be put in front of a tribunal of fact at all. Therefore the tribunal of law may occasionally have to examine the facts (and particularly the weight to be attached to the facts) to decide legal issues.

The tribunal of fact and the tribunal of law are often the same person or group of people. Most civil cases are heard by a single judge who determines both the facts of the case and the legal issues. This is also so with criminal cases heard in the magistrates' court. Although the fact-finder and the tribunal of law are the same in many cases the distinction between tribunals of fact and law is important.

### 1.2.3  Evidence

Facts and arguments combine to prove conclusions and this is so in cases brought before the courts as much as anywhere else. However, not all things asserted as 'facts' are accepted as such by other people. The term 'fact' is slightly misleading. The meaning given to the word by the *Oxford English Dictionary* is, '*Something that has really occurred or is actually the case; . . . hence, a particular truth known by actual observation or authentic testimony, as opposed to what is merely inferred*'. Although there is no formal definition of the term in law the word is most correctly used to illustrate matters that are accepted to have occurred by the tribunal of fact, which will consider various matters put before it and decide whether the alleged thing is true or not (ie, whether the alleged thing is a 'fact'). The matters it receives are evidence of that fact. Looking again at the definition given above, a tribunal of fact will not be relying on 'actual observation' and so will have to rely on 'authentic testimony' to reach its conclusions. We shall see that testimony is given a particular meaning at law but for the time being we can take testimony to mean evidence and note that evidence establishes facts.

It is worth noting at this point that evidence will not only prove a fact but that a proven fact may combine with other evidence (or proven facts) to prove some other fact. In other words a fact may be evidence of another fact.

In essence evidence is that which proves facts and the 'proof' is the process of converting evidence into facts.

## 1.3  Facts in issue

It was noted above that all issues in a case must be proven. These are often termed the 'facts in issue'. Identifying the facts in issue is not as straightforward as might first appear. First what the facts in issue are in a particular case depends on the relevant law. Secondly because of the adversarial nature of litigation in England and Wales, the parties to a case will make allegation and counter-allegation. A defendant may either challenge the allegations of the prosecution (in criminal cases) or claimant (in civil cases) or may raise some entirely different legal defence. Clearly, these counter-allegations have to be resolved. Finally, quite what the facts in issue are at trial is affected by rules of procedure (ie, rules dictating how the trial process will run). This means there are differences between civil and criminal cases.

### 1.3.1    Criminal cases

#### 1.3.1.1    General principle

In criminal cases, whether in the Crown Court or magistrates' court, trial starts with a process of arraignment or plea. The defendant is accused formally of the commission of an offence and asked to plead to it. If the plea is 'not guilty', *all* of the elements of the offence are put in issue (ie, the defendant has required the prosecution to prove them). Furthermore the defendant may raise defences during trial which will also be put in issue.

Therefore every element of the offence for which a defendant is being tried must be established in criminal cases. In addition any defence alleged and for which some evidence is admitted (see 'evidential burden of proof' in **Chapter 3**) will become a fact in issue. In *R v Sims* [1946] KB 531, CCA, Lord Goddard CJ said (at p 539):

The prosecution has to prove the whole of their case including the identity of the accused, the nature of the act and the existence of any necessary knowledge or intent.

Therefore the facts in issue in a criminal case are:

- the identity of the defendant;
- the *actus reus* of the offence;
- the *mens rea* in relation to the offence; and
- any defences raised at trial.

#### 1.3.1.2    Applying the general principle

Go back to the case study at **1.2** in this chapter (the murder case involving Michaela and Jake):

(a) The issues that must be proved by the prosecution in a murder case are:

    (i)   the *actus reus* of the offence, ie (in essence):
- Jake died
- as a result of unlawful violence;

    (ii)   the identity of the defendant: ie, that the *actus reus* was carried out by Michaela rather than by some other person.

    (iii)  that Michaela possessed the *mens rea* of the offence of murder ('malice aforethought'), ie, the unlawful violence was carried out with *either*:
- an intention to cause death to Jake; or
- an intention to cause Jake grievous bodily harm;

(b) These issues must be proved by the prosecution.

(c) Consider the effect of the following 'defences':

    (i)   Michaela alleges she did not go to the house at all, but stayed at the bar with her friend Alex. In this case, while Michaela is raising an alibi and proposing to call a witness, Alex, to establish it, she has not raised a new issue in the case. Rather she is challenging an existing fact in issue, namely that of the identity of the defendant. No new fact in issue has been added and it is still the prosecution that must prove Michaela's involvement in the offence.

    (ii)   She says that the argument with Jake became so heated that she got frightened and grabbed a gun, only pulling the trigger when Jake snatched up a bottle and ran at her with it. In this case, Michaela is alleging an act of self-defence. This is not strictly a defence (*R v Wheeler* [1967] 3 All ER 829) but a challenge to the prosecution case that the killing was unlawful. However, as will be seen in

**Chapter 3**, Michaela will have to raise the issue at trial before the prosecution are under an obligation to disprove it. Otherwise the prosecution would be under an obligation to disprove self-defence in relation to every offence of which unlawful killing was a part whether or not the defendant was alleging an act of self-defence.

(iii)   Michaela says that Jake kept shouting at her and insulting her and that he boasted about sleeping with other women. Something inside her 'snapped' and she suddenly found herself picking up a gun and shooting at Jake. This could raise the defence of provocation. This defence does not challenge either the *actus reus* or *mens rea* of the offence of murder. Michaela is neither challenging that there was an unlawful killing nor that when the killing took place she intended grievous bodily harm. She is alleging that her possession of that intent was due to a provocative act. There will therefore be another fact in issue: the defence of provocation.

It can therefore be seen that the facts in issue are a product of substantive law. When a barrister faces a case concerning a legal issue with which he or she is unfamiliar, as a starting point he or she would resort to a practitioner work like *Blackstone's Criminal Practice* or *Archbold: Criminal Pleading and Practice*. Both of these works deal with all of the major criminal offences. Often they set out the statutory definition of the offence and provide some detail concerning some or all elements.

To practise applying this rule, see **Activity 1** in **Appendix 1**.

### 1.3.2   Civil cases

#### 1.3.2.1   General principle

In civil cases, the process of making allegations begins much earlier and is more sophisticated than in criminal cases. Cases are initiated by the 'statement of case' process (see ***Civil Litigation Manual***). The claimant will make detailed allegations of some particular civil wrong (such as a breach of contract) in his or her 'particulars of claim'. The defendant will respond by way of a defence (assuming the defendant does not fully admit liability at this point). The defence will respond to each particular allegation made by the claimant.

The Civil Procedure Rules 1998 (CPR), r 16.5(1), provides:

*In his defence, the defendant must state—*
   *(a)   which of the allegations ... he denies;*
   *(b)   which allegations he is unable to admit or deny, but which he requires the claimant to prove; and*
   *(c)   which allegations he admits.*

Denial of an allegation puts the party denying under an obligation to state reasons for denial (CPR, r 16.5(2)). The requirement to prove in paragraph (b) recognises that there may be allegations made by a claimant that a defendant is simply not able to form a judgement on (particularly matters such as loss and damage that may be within the personal knowledge of the claimant).

Insofar as a party admits an allegation made by another party it ceases to be a fact in issue. Otherwise (ie, if the response is either a denial of a fact or a requirement that the other party prove a fact) the allegation remains a fact in issue.

In addition to responding to the case alleged by a claimant a defendant may raise new issues that would constitute a defence. For example, even if a defendant admits to having entered into a contract with the claimant, she might allege the existence of a frustrating event (ie, raise the defence of frustration). This would be done in her defence and would raise a new fact in issue.

To practise applying this rule, see **Activity 1.2** in **Appendix 1**.

There is therefore much more flexibility as to what may or not be a fact in issue in a civil case. First of all, the parties have far more control over what might be a fact in issue before trial. Secondly there is a greater variety of subject matter being litigated in civil courts. While all criminal cases are composed of an *actus reus* and a *mens rea*, civil cases are not so strictly categorised. Each area of substantive civil law will have different potential facts in issue.

As in a criminal case, a practitioner will resort to practitioner works as a starting point in identifying potential facts in issue in civil cases. However, while there are practitioner texts on civil litigation and evidence, they cannot be of as much assistance in identifying what needs to be proved or what could constitute a defence in a particular action. Instead a barrister would have resort to subject-specific practitioner works like *Chitty on Contract*. For a list of the usual practitioner works see the **Case Preparation Manual**. Furthermore because facts in issue are dictated by the Statement of Case process, great assistance will be gained from understanding how the courts expect cases to be pleaded. For the detail of this process and examples of Particulars of Claim and Defences see the **Drafting Manual** and *Atkin's Court Forms*.

### 1.3.3  Significance of facts in issue

It might be wondered why a lawyer will bother to identify the facts in issue in a case. In fact many lawyers who have experience in particular areas probably identify the facts in issue by instinct. The phrase 'facts in issue' is in fact not used widely in the courts. However, it is useful in understanding how evidence proves cases. By identifying the facts in issue in a case, three things are achieved:

(a) A list of matters to be established has been identified so that it is possible to go on to determine *who* it is that must prove which issue. In other words identifying the facts in issue is the first step in determining who bears the various *burdens of proof* in a case. This is dealt with in more detail in **Chapter 2**.

(b) This list places limits on the evidence that should and can be admitted at trial. The courts will not entertain evidence that does not assist in resolving the matters in dispute (ie, the facts in issue). In other words the facts in issue determine the *relevance* of evidence. Relevance in turn is one of the factors that determines the *admissibility* of evidence: evidence that is not relevant to one or more fact in issue is inadmissible at trial.

(c) Having methodically identified the facts in issue will also allow a lawyer to analyse the case, to identify evidence to be admitted and to formulate arguments about evidence more precisely. This is really a more precise use of relevance: it is not simply that the evidence has some relevance to an issue in the case but that it is possible to say that it has a particular relevance in a particular way to the case. For example, evidence that Michaela had been beaten regularly by Jake might assist in proving that she was suffering from diminished responsibility (following the case law in cases such as *R v Hobson* [1998] 1 Cr App R 31, CA). It might (depending on how it is presented) be relevant to the issue of self-defence (ie, a challenge to the unlawfulness of the killing, which ie, you will remember, was a different fact in issue). On the other hand, it might be relevant to intention as a fact in issue. The prosecution might seek to establish that she had decided to get revenge for the assaults by killing Jake. It is possible that the evidence could be used in more than one of these ways at trial. It will also be noted later on in this Manual (for example, in relation to the complicated subject of hearsay) that this identification of the exact *purpose* of the evidence may affect how particular rules of exclusion apply to it.

## 1.4  Proof concepts

The rules of evidence are based around four very important concepts: relevance, weight, probative value and prejudicial effect. One or more of these concepts is used in applying and understanding every rule of evidence. In fact these concepts are not only of use in understanding the rules (ie, in memorising the law on this subject) but they are also vital to the effective use of evidence as a litigator. Understanding the relevance and weight of a piece of evidence is vital to providing decent advice about a case to a client, to deciding when to agree to settle a case without going to court and in deciding how to fight the case if it goes to trial.

### 1.4.1  Relevance

As noted in **1.3.3** above, the concept of relevance is fundamental to all evidence. It is a necessary precondition for the admissibility of all evidence in both civil and criminal cases. Furthermore, a clear understanding of the relevance of a particular piece of evidence is necessary in applying a number of other rules of admissibility such as the rule against hearsay.

#### 1.4.1.1  Definition

There have been a number of attempts to define the concept of relevance. In *DPP v Kilbourne* [1973] AC 729, Lord Simon said (at p 756):

> Evidence is relevant if it is logically probative or disprobative of some matter which requires proof. It is sufficient to say ... that relevant (ie logically probative or disprobative) evidence is evidence which makes the matter ... more or less probable.

Note the stress upon logic in the above citation. Relevance does not stem from one's intuitions or feelings about a particular piece of evidence but from how one might rationalise and explain it. It is worth bearing in mind that an advocate will often be using the relevance of particular pieces of evidence in his or her closing speech. What he or she is persuading the jury to conclude from a particular piece of evidence is its relevance.

A slightly more complicated definition was given by Stephen in his *Digest of the Law of Evidence*, where it was said that relevance means:

> Any two facts to which it was applied are so related to each other that according to the common course of events one either taken by itself or in connection with other facts proves or renders probable the ... existence or non-existence of the other.

Both of these quotations show that evidence does not have to *prove* a matter to be relevant. Rather, it has to assist in proving a matter. As Stephen makes clear, one fact (the item of evidence) has a relationship with another fact (the conclusion from the item of evidence) because the evidence could prove the conclusion. However, it does not have to do so to be relevant. This is best understood by remembering the difference between a tribunal of law (eg a judge) and a tribunal of fact (eg a jury). The former filters the evidence to the latter. All evidence that might assist them in reaching a conclusion should be left to the tribunal of fact. It is for them to decide whether and how they will use it. As the concept of relevance is part of that filtering process, it is important that the test of relevance allows in evidence that could assist the fact finder to reach the right conclusions.

Therefore the test for the relevance of evidence is 'What *might* it prove?' and not 'What *does* it prove?'

In *R v Randall* [2003] UKHL 69, Lord Steyn noted (at [20]) that a judge in determining the issue of relevance 'has to decide whether the evidence is capable of increasing or decreasing the existence of a fact in issue'.

Lord Steyn also adopted the observation in Keane, *The Modern Law of Evidence*, 5th edn (2000) that the question of relevance 'is typically a matter of degree to be determined, for the most part by common sense and experience'. Relevance is therefore not a rule of law. There are no cases that set precedents for what will or will not be relevant in any particular situation. There are numerous cases in which the relevance of evidence was discussed and from which it is possible to discern principles about relevance. Each case will turn on its own facts. What is more important than the identification of precedents or examples is an ability to make a logical argument as to how evidence A might prove conclusion B. It is therefore useful to consider the concepts of direct and circumstantial evidence.

### 1.4.1.2   Direct and circumstantial evidence

Direct and circumstantial evidence show how relevance works.

*Direct evidence* is evidence that could prove a particular conclusion (a fact in issue) on its own. The evidence renders the conclusion more or less likely without any need for explanation or supporting evidence. For example, in the murder case referred to at the start of this chapter consider this witness:

*Witness 1*: 'I am Jake's housekeeper. I was standing at the door at the time. I saw Michaela pick up a gun during an argument and point it at Jake. She pulled the trigger and shot him in the chest.'

This witness has given direct evidence on a number of facts in issue. Her evidence that she saw Michaela shoot Jake could prove that Michaela was present at the shooting and that she carried out the shooting. It could do this without any need to find other evidence to show how this account is relevant. It is not direct evidence of Michaela's intention as we would at the best infer intention from the act of shooting.

*Circumstantial evidence* is evidence that cannot prove any particular conclusion on its own but could do so in combination with other evidence and by the drawing of inferences from the combined evidence.

Consider the following three witnesses in the murder example:

*Witness 2*: 'I was leaving Jake's house at 10.25 and met Michaela on the doorstep.'

*Witness 3*: 'At 10.30 I heard a gunshot from Jake's house. As I approached at about 10.40, I saw Michaela hurrying away from the house.'

*Witness 4 (a police officer)*: 'On searching Jake's house, I found Michaela's handbag lying on a table in the room in which Jake was shot.'

These three witnesses could not prove any issue in the case on their own. Their evidence has to be combined to achieve this. The facts that would combine as circumstantial evidence are:

- Michaela arrived at Jake's house at 10.25.

- At about 10.30 there was a gunshot.

- Michaela was seen rushing from the house at 10.40.

- Michaela's handbag was in the room where the shooting took place.

These facts will only have any relevance to the case in combination and even then only if further facts are established or presumed (eg that Michaela is a woman, that Jake was shot at his home, etc).

A learned theorist on evidence, Wigmore, constructed a complicated system of presenting this use of circumstantial evidence to prove conclusions. In a much simplified form it would look something like **figure 1.1**.

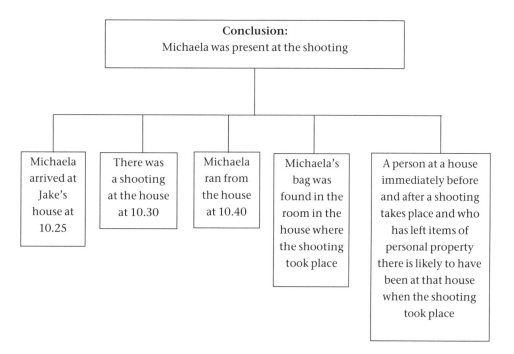

**Figure 1.1** Wigmorean analysis

In **figure 1.1**, the box at the top is the conclusion that we would want the jury to reach on this evidence. Note: that conclusion might itself just be one fact that will combine with a collection of other facts, as circumstantial evidence of an even more fundamental fact in the case. Ultimately all these strands of facts combine to prove the *facts in issue* and, once the facts in issue have been proved, the offence is established. This works equally well in civil cases, the only difference being how the facts in issue are determined in the first place.

Looking at the five adjacent boxes in **figure 1.1**, the four on the left set out part of the evidence of the witnesses. The prosecution would hope that the jury would first of all accept what the witnesses said as true and then combine these items of evidence to reach the conclusion in the conclusion box.

It is not obvious that a jury would accept that conclusion from simply hearing the evidence represented in these four boxes. Not one of those items of evidence would be particularly likely to convince a jury that Michaela was present when the shooting took place. It is only when they are combined *and* an explanation is given about the evidence, that they might convince a jury. The explanation is the statement set out in the box on the extreme right. This need for additional evidence or argument or generalisation makes the evidence circumstantial.

The use of argument or generalisation is an important feature of circumstantial evidence. It will often feature during closing speech or argument in a case, but this is not always the case. Sometimes an advocate might feel that the circumstantial evidence, taken in combination, speaks sufficiently for itself for it to be left to the jury (it would not be good tactics, after all, to be seen to be telling the jury the blindingly obvious). However, it is suggested an advocate should only decide that the generalisation is not needed after having worked out what it is. At the very least an advocate should never make a habit of omitting a careful formulation of the generalisation. He or she should always be live to the possibility that success may depend on the accuracy of the argument about the circumstantial evidence. At **1.4.2.2** you will come back to circumstantial evidence and will see that the generalisations and arguments are as much open to attack at trial as the evidence itself.

Turning back to witness 1, remember that what witness 1 saw was direct evidence of Michaela's presence and of the act of shooting. It would also be circumstantial evidence of any intention to kill or cause GBH (circumstantial because the jury would have to *infer* this from what the witness says she saw and an argument that people intend to do those things that directly and obviously flow from their conduct).

What exactly does this have to do with relevance? Have a look again at the example of circumstantial evidence above. If you left out the evidence that the shooting took place at 10.30 (and there was no other evidence of the shooting taking place at 10.30), how useful would the rest of the evidence in that example be? Without evidence that the shooting took place at 10.30, the rest of the evidence does not appear to prove much, if anything, of relevance to the case. All it would prove is that Michaela came to the house and left quickly but not that this had anything to do with the shooting. It is only when the small details of the circumstantial evidence combine to show something of significance to the current case that we would accept any particular piece of it or combination of it as relevant. Therefore the relevance of a particular piece of evidence is not wholly straightforward. There are two issues:

- Is there a *degree* of relevance or is evidence simply relevant or irrelevant?

- Can evidence be potentially relevant?

For more detail on Wigmorean analysis see the ***Case Preparation Manual***. While it is not essential to an understanding the subject of evidence, you may find it useful in analysing and understanding particular evidential topics as you work your way through this Manual.

### 1.4.1.3   Sufficiency of relevance

As we have just seen, it is sometimes tempting to say that something is 'not very relevant' or 'of marginal relevance' or to say that one fact is 'more' relevant than another. On the other hand, if relevance is determined by a strictly logical test of whether something makes a 'matter ... more or less probable' (per Lord Simon in *DPP v Kilbourne* [1973] AC 729), then it is something a piece of evidence either does or does not do. What Lord Simon did not say in *Kilbourne* is that evidence is relevant if it makes a matter more or less probable *to a sufficient extent*.

Consider an example in a civil case:

Arthur is being sued for negligence and breach of contract in respect of building works he has carried out for Amy. Amy wishes to show that he has been successfully sued in respect of a road accident in which he was alleged to have driven carelessly. Would this previous driving case be relevant?

If we were to adopt a literal approach to Lord Simon's test we might say that the driving case is relevant to the building works case. Our argument would be that at that previous case it was shown that Arthur had been less than careful. We would therefore say that he has set himself apart from all the people who have not been proved to drive carelessly. We would say that Arthur is therefore a relatively careless person and that this would show, to some small extent, that he may have been careless on this (building) occasion. By a very small degree it renders the conclusion that Arthur was negligent on this occasion more probable.

In fact a court would probably be unwilling to accept this evidence and this would be on the grounds that it is not relevant. It would therefore appear that the courts have qualified the strictness of the test for relevance. There is a concept of 'sufficiency of relevance' that appears to have gained some recognition in the courts.

Consider the following cases as examples:

- In *R v Whitehead* (1848) 3 Car & Kir 202, a doctor was tried for manslaughter of one patient, evidence that the doctor had treated other patients skilfully was held to be irrelevant. Only evidence of the skill used in treating the patient who died was held to be relevant.

- In *Hart v Lancashire and Yorkshire Railway Co* (1869) 21 LT 261, evidence that the defendant company had altered its practice in changing railway points after an accident was held to be irrelevant in an action concerning that accident which was alleged to have been caused by negligence in respect of railway points.

- *Hollingham v Head* (1858) 27 LJ CP 241 was a breach of contract case in which the defendant sought to prove certain terms of the contract that would excuse him from liability. The defendant sought to adduce evidence that the plaintiff had entered into contracts with other persons on those same terms to show that it was likely that he had included those terms in the contract with the defendant. The Court of Common Pleas held that evidence of contracting behaviour with other parties was irrelevant.

- *R v Blastland* [1986] AC 41 concerned the murder and buggery of a boy. The defendant wished to adduce evidence that showed that another person, M, had spoken about the murder of a boy before the boy's body had been found. The House of Lords held that evidence that showed that M knew of the murder was irrelevant to the issue in the case, namely whether the defendant was the murderer.

- In *R v Kearley* [1992] 2 AC 228, the House of Lords considered the relevance of statements made by third parties. In that case the police had raided a flat and, while they were searching, they received repeated calls to the flat by people asking for the defendant and requesting drugs. In so far as the callers made statements that the defendant sold drugs, these would be inadmissible as hearsay evidence. However, the fact that the callers *believed* drugs were sold at the premises would make it an exception to the hearsay rule. The House of Lords recognised this, but as in *R v Blastland* said that the state of mind of the maker of the statement was not relevant.

Do you agree with these judgments? Do you think that the evidence was excluded because it did not render the conclusion more or less likely or because it was not sufficiently effective in doing so?

In these cases, the courts often justified the conclusion that there was no relevance to the evidence by identifying or describing a test that is slightly different to that identified in *Kilbourne*. In *Hollingham v Head* the court said that the previous contracting behaviour was not relevant because it supported no *reasonable* inference as to how the parties had contracted. Clearly there was some requirement in addition to a simple change in probability of the sort described in *Kilbourne*. Rather the chance of such a term having been entered into had to have become a reasonable one. The justification (in *Whitehead*) for reaching different conclusions on the admissibility of evidence of general skilful treatment of patients generally and the skilful treatment of a particular patient must be that one is more (and sufficiently) relevant whereas the other is less (and insufficiently) relevant. In cases such as *Blastland* and *Kearley* it is not difficult to formulate arguments on the relevance of the evidence as follows:

*Blastland*:

- M said that the boy had been murdered before this was known.
- Therefore M had some peculiar knowledge of the death of the boy.
- Therefore M may have murdered the boy.
- Therefore the defendant may not have murdered the boy.

*Kearley*:

- Callers requested drugs at the defendant's flat.
- Therefore callers expected to receive drugs at the defendant's flat.
- Therefore the callers may have received drugs at the defendant's flat in the past.
- Therefore the defendant may have been selling drugs from his flat in the past.
- Therefore the defendant may still have been selling drugs from his flat.

Neither of these logical arguments is without its flaws and weaknesses but both of them are sustainable. Nonetheless the House of Lords on both occasions concluded that despite this sort of logical argument, the evidence represented by the first bullet point was not relevant to the conclusion in the final bullet point. This must be because the logic in each case is *insufficiently* strong or, in evidential terms, the evidence is *insufficiently* relevant.

The rationale for the restriction of evidence of marginal relevance is that it would increase the issues that have to be litigated with the resulting increase in cost and complexity of the trial process (see *R v Patel* [1951] 2 All ER 29).

It would therefore appear to be the case that the test for relevance is not simply whether the evidence might influence the chance of something being true or untrue in a very marginal way. Evidence has to influence that chance to a sufficient degree. There is no clear statement of *how* relevant evidence has to be. In part this is because relevance is, as Lord Steyn affirmed in *R v Randall* [2003] UKHL 69, not an issue of law but a matter of logic, common sense or experience. This means that the relevance or otherwise is a matter for the judge, not bound by precedent and case law but to be exercised in light of the facts of the particular case as a whole. In other words it is a matter for argument by the advocate in the case.

### 1.4.1.4  Conditional relevance

We have seen that some evidence does not have relevance on its own. Rather its relevance depends on other evidence in the case. Think about the three witnesses who gave circumstantial evidence in **1.4.1.2**. What the first witness says will not be relevant unless the second and third witnesses give their testimony. Of course, when witness 1 gives evidence the court will not know for certain that the other witnesses will say what they are supposed to. The court may nonetheless admit the evidence conditionally (or '*de bene esse*') upon the proof of such facts as render that evidence relevant. If the other evidence is not adduced, the judge will have to direct the jury to ignore the evidence that was conditionally admitted (or a civil judge or magistrate would have to disregard it). In extreme cases (where it will not be possible for the tribunal of fact to ignore it) the trial may have to be discontinued.

### 1.4.1.5    Importance of argument

To recap, the relevance of evidence is a matter of logic or of common sense. Relevance is a filter upon evidence; no evidence that is deemed irrelevant will be admitted. The test is whether it will increase or decrease the probability of a fact in issue being proved (or possibly whether it is sufficiently likely to do so or likely to do so to a sufficient extent). This will be a matter of argument or explanation. In many cases the relevance of particular pieces of direct evidence or particular collections of circumstantial evidence will be so clear that the argument does not need to be stated. Generally, however, some argument will have to be made at some point or another. It may be that this will be during the closing speech or submissions to explain what the evidence might prove. Alternatively it may be that the argument will also be used to justify the admissibility of the evidence in the first place. Given that relevance is not a matter of law but a matter of logic, it is not possible to lay down any rules about such arguments. However, the following points should be borne in mind:

(a) Evidence is not simply 'relevant'. Rather it is relevant to something. Identifying to which facts in issue evidence is relevant is necessary to constructing convincing arguments.

(b) Evidence might not simply be relevant to a fact in issue. Instead the evidence may be relevant to a fact which in turn is relevant to a fact in issue. In the example of circumstantial evidence in **1.4.1.2**, the evidence was all relevant to prove that Michaela was at the scene of the shooting of Jake. That in turn was relevant to prove Michaela may have shot Jake, which in turn is just part of what is necessary to prove that Michaela murdered him.

(c) It is not only necessary to identify *what* evidence is relevant to, it is necessary to identify *how* or *why* that evidence is relevant to that issue. This requires the drawing on logic or common sense to construct generalisations about human behaviour. Thinking again about the example in **1.4.1.2**, it was necessary to say something about the ordinary course of events that leads the audience to use the evidence presented to reach the conclusion that favours your case.

(d) Finally and most importantly, evidence is relevant if it *might* lead to a particular conclusion not if it *will* lead to that conclusion. When arguing that evidence ought or ought not to be admitted, keep this at the forefront of the mind. What you believe is not the point, nor is what the tribunal of fact will believe: it is what the tribunal of fact *could* believe that matters. When you are using the relevance of the evidence to make arguments to the tribunal of fact this still remains true. You are still using what the jury (for instance) could believe in making your argument. However, on this occasion you are asking the jury to accept your conclusions. Whether they will do so depends on how much *weight* they attach to the evidence and the argument you have presented to them.

## 1.4.2    Weight

We have seen in the preceding section that the *relevance* of evidence concerns what conclusions the evidence *might* prove or disprove. The *weight* of the evidence concerns *whether* the evidence does prove or disprove the conclusion. While it is still possible for people to disagree about what something might prove, this is not likely in most cases and even where it is, the disagreement is usually based on logical analysis. Weight is far more subjective. Among 12 jurors some may be inclined to reach a particular conclusion from a particular piece of evidence and others may not. There might be difficulty articulating why they do or do not do so. In so far as they can, they might draw on concepts like 'belief' or 'feelings' or 'instinct'. However, they may also draw on 'logic' and 'common sense' in deciding what they do or do not believe.

Weight is also known as credibility or credit. These terms are often used in the law of evidence. Often a rule will state that a certain type of evidence will only 'go to credit' or 'be relevant to credibility'. This means that that class of evidence is used to undermine the weight of another piece of evidence rather than to establish what did or did not happen in the particular case.

### 1.4.2.1   Importance of weight at trial

Weight is generally a matter for the tribunal of fact. Relevance matters when the tribunal of law (eg, Crown Court judge) decides whether or not to let the jury hear particular evidence. It is then a matter for the jury to decide how much weight to attach to it.

However, this does not mean that a lawyer can ignore the weight of the evidence. There are a number of ways in which weight will influence what a lawyer does:

(a) A lawyer may seek to *influence* the weight to be attached to evidence by the tribunal of fact. An advocate cross-examining a witness is generally seeking to reduce the weight to be attached to the evidence of that witness. An advocate must therefore be aware of how particular evidence or lines of questioning might affect the weight that might be attached to other evidence or the case as a whole.

(b) Lawyers do not always and only fight cases at trial. Many cases are settled before trial. Criminals plead guilty in the face of strong evidence or civil litigants compromise their claims in the face of strong opposition. Therefore lawyers must be able to *assess* the weight of evidence for both parties so that they can give clear advice about the prospects of success.

(c) Also lawyers will often have to *argue* about the weight to be attached to evidence. This arises in a number of different ways:

(i) In both civil and criminal cases advocates will make submissions or speeches to the tribunal of fact. This is done not simply to tell the tribunal what they have heard, but should also seek to persuade the tribunal to reach the desired conclusions. This is only possible if the advocate understands the strengths and weaknesses of the evidence as presented.

(ii) As will be seen in later chapters of this Manual (such as **Chapter 7** on similar fact evidence and later in this chapter), some evidence is excluded in part due to its lack of weight. To conduct arguments about the probative force of evidence, the weight of that evidence must be understood and explained.

(iii) It is possible that the failure to call sufficient evidence (ie, evidence of sufficient weight) on a particular issue or as a whole will have procedural consequences. The most dramatic is the submission of no case to answer (see the *Criminal Litigation and Sentencing Manual*). This procedure leads to the ending of a case at a very early stage due to the insufficiency of evidence (ie, the case for the relevant party lacks a minimum degree of weight). Furthermore as will be seen in **Chapter 2**, a party is only placed under a requirement to disprove an issue once his or her opponent has called evidence of sufficient weight to put the matter in issue.

### 1.4.2.2    Challenges to the weight of evidence

Look again at the testimony of witness 1 and that of witnesses 2 to 4 and the chart in **1.4.1.2**. How might the prosecution case on this matter be open to challenge? What flaws might there be with a prosecution case of this type?

The possibilities are too numerous to list in full here. However, we might categorise challenges as follows:

(a) Challenges to the truthfulness of particular witnesses (eg, witness 4 might have had a motive to lie due to his or her own involvement).

(b) Challenges to the ability of the particular witnesses to give an accurate account (eg, it might have been too dark for any witness to have a clear view of the person they say they saw so they could be mistaken).

(c) Challenges to the strength or validity of the arguments or generalisations made about the evidence (eg, a person could leave personal property at a house at any time)

(d) Alternative explanations about the evidence (eg, Was it possible that Michaela left the house before the shooting, came back after or as a result of hearing it and then left again in a hurry because Jake had been shot?).

(e) Gaps in the evidence or arguments (eg, Michaela might have been in the house but could have been in a completely different room).

Only some of these challenges would apply to direct evidence. We could question witness 1 in our example about her honesty or even her ability to see or comprehend what she saw (challenges (a) and (b) above).

Challenges (c) to (e) are more likely to be of application in relation to circumstantial evidence because, as we have seen, circumstantial evidence relies on the combination of evidence and on the strength of the generalisations about the combined evidence. Therefore it would be possible in principle to attack circumstantial evidence in one of three ways:

- asking the tribunal of fact not to believe any individual fact alleged by a witness that forms part of the circumstantial evidence (challenges under (a) or (b) above);

- inviting the tribunal of fact to conclude that the combined evidence does not suggest the generalisation proposed by the other side (challenges under (c) or (e) above); or

- proposing an alternative generalisation that assists your case rather than that of your opponent (challenge under (d) above).

Guidance on the weight to be attached to evidence is occasionally given in case law (eg, *R v Turnbull* [1977] QB 224 on identification, see **Chapter 11**) or by statute law (eg, Civil Evidence Act 1995, **Chapter 8**) on what might influence the weight to be attached to the evidence.

### 1.4.2.3    Collateral evidence

There is therefore a distinction between evidence that is relevant to the actual issues in the case (eg, whether the defendant committed the offence or breached the contract) and evidence that influences the likelihood that the tribunal of fact will reach that conclusion.

For example:

(a) Think back to the murder example and the questions posed in **1.4.2.2**. Witness 3 gave evidence that he saw Michaela hurrying from the house after hearing a gunshot.

(b) Imagine that during cross-examination these facts were suggested to witness 3:

    (i)    that witness 3 was short-sighted and could not have seen Michaela at the distance he says there was between them, or

    (ii)   that witness 3 has a grudge against Michaela and therefore lied that he saw her near the house, or

    (iii)  that witness 3 committed the offence and therefore is lying to hide his own involvement.

The first two suggestions do not *resolve* the issue: Did Michaela kill Jake? However, they will *influence* it because the acceptance of either suggestion by the jury will influence whether or not they accept as true the evidence that Michaela was present. Using a simplified version of Wigmore's analysis, we would represent these various alternative facts as follows:

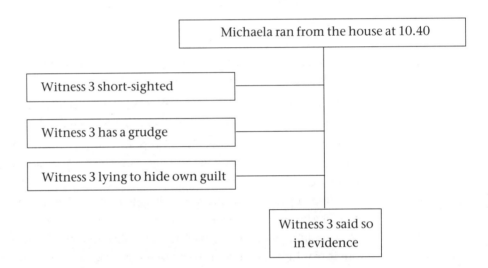

Wigmore attempted to illustrate their influence on the evidence by showing that they can influence whether we reach conclusion A (Michaela ran from Jake's house) from the fact of that having been said in evidence by witness 3. Each of those suggestions is not an alternative fact that contradicts the conclusion that Michaela was present. Rather each affects the inclination of the fact finder to reach the relevant factual conclusion. This is what is meant by labelling them 'collateral facts' or 'collateral evidence'.

Both civil and criminal courts seek to limit the extent to which collateral evidence will be admitted. While clearly of use to the tribunal of fact, to allow collateral facts to be admitted on all occasions could lead to a lot of evidence being admitted that does not directly bear on the issues in the case. This concern about keeping cases focused on the factual disputes has led to a general rule of limitation concerning collateral evidence, namely the rule of finality. This will be examined in detail in **Chapter 5** but it is worth bearing it in mind at this point. Essentially the rule states that evidence that only goes to credibility (collateral evidence) is not admissible. If a witness does not accept an allegation in cross-examination, the party cannot prove the allegation by independent evidence (*Harris v Tippett* (1811) 2 Camp 637). There are some exceptions to this general rule but its significance is that most evidence that would only assist in deciding whether to believe particular allegations by witnesses is not admissible.

Note that the third suggestion could be subject to proof by independent evidence because it goes beyond simply collateral matters. The allegation is that the witness rather than Michaela committed the offence. Evidence showing this would therefore not go only to collateral matters. While accepting that that witness committed the offence would render a jury less likely to believe that witness's testimony it also (and rather more significantly) would prove that Michaela probably didn't commit the offence. Therefore the evidence is not just collateral it is also relevant to a fact in issue. It would therefore not be kept out of court under the rule of finality (see *R v Edwards* [1996] 2 Cr App R 345 and **5.3.3** generally).

### 1.4.3  Probative value and prejudicial effect

Probative value and prejudicial effect are often balanced one against the other. As will be seen below (**1.6.2**) in a criminal case where the probative value of evidence is outweighed by its prejudicial effect, that evidence may be excluded (ie, it will never go before the jury). So what do these two concepts mean?

*Probative value* is a combination of relevance (what something might prove) and weight (whether it does prove it). Probative value is essentially an evaluation of the extent to which an item of evidence proves a case in a rational way.

*Prejudicial effect* is an evaluation of the *risk* that the evidence in question will be used by the tribunal in an inappropriate way, for example, becoming distracted from deciding the case to the requisite standard of proof (such as beyond reasonable doubt) or taking into consideration irrelevant or immaterial matters. Prejudicial effect includes an overwillingness on the part of the tribunal of fact to convict (or make some other adverse finding) contrary either to the relevance or the weight that ought to be attached to the evidence before it.

In so far as these concepts are to be compared and balanced, no real guidance has been provided on when one outweighs the other. As will be seen at **1.6.2**, the balance is exercised as a judicial discretion and therefore rules about how the test ought to be applied have been avoided.

## 1.5  Proof of facts without evidence

One party or another must prove each and every fact in issue. This is usually done by adducing enough evidence at court. Most of this Manual concerns the restrictions on the admissibility of that evidence. However, before examining those matters, it should be recognised that there are rules of practice and procedure that allow the court to reach conclusions on some facts in issue (or even on some very small details of a case) without calling evidence. Two of these will be examined: formal admissions and judicial notice. This section will also deal with the question of the extent to which a tribunal of fact or law can rely upon its own personal knowledge to fill gaps in evidence called by the parties.

### 1.5.1  Formal admissions

There are rules of procedure in both the civil and criminal courts that allow the parties to reduce the number of facts in issue in a case that have to proved by evidence. These rules allow a party to formally admit a fact in issue or a fact that might assist in proving a fact in issue. Formal admission of this sort determines that particular matter. It is proved and no further evidence will be admitted to prove or disprove it.

Formal admissions are often made to allow cases to be disposed of more quickly and efficiently where there is no serious dispute. Occasionally, however, a party might see a tactical advantage in admitting a particular fact rather than running extra risks in requiring the other side to call damaging evidence to prove it.

Note the distinction between formal and informal admissions.

(a) A *formal* admission is the result of a rule of procedure. The effect of the formal admission is that the particular issue is finally resolved: the admission is conclusive of that fact. Evidence that proves or disproves that issue alone is not relevant and will not be admitted.

(b) In contrast a party may make an *informal* admission, for example, by admitting to another person (including a police officer in a police station) particular relevant facts. This latter type of admission, commonly known as a confession, is only evidence on that particular fact. It is still possible for the tribunal of fact to disregard it. For detailed analysis of the rules of evidence concerning informal admissions see **Chapter 10**.

### 1.5.1.1   Criminal cases

Formal admissions are governed by the Criminal Justice Act 1967. Section 10(1) provides:

*Subject to the provisions of this section, any fact of which oral evidence may be given ... may be admitted ..., and the admission by any party of any such fact under this section shall, as against that party, be conclusive evidence ... of the fact admitted.*

Note that it is only possible to admit facts that could be proved by admissible evidence. Section 10 cannot be used to circumvent the rules of evidence.

Section 10(2) sets out how such formal admissions are made. In essence the section provides that formal admissions:

- Can be made at trial or before trial (s 10(2)(a)).
- Can be made orally in court. If made on the behalf of the defendant they must be made by the defendant's solicitor or barrister (s 10(2)(b), (d)).
- Can be made by the defendant (or the prosecutor if a private person) him or herself (s 10(1)).
- Can be made in writing either in court or outside of court. The written formal admission must be signed either by the defendant (or prosecutor) in person or, if the party making the admission is a company, by an appropriate officer of that company (s 10(2)(c)).

A formal admission may be withdrawn with leave of the court (s 10(4)). *R v Kolton* [2000] Crim LR 761 suggests that this will only happen rarely. The court will expect evidence from both the party making the admission and their legal representatives that shows the admission to have been made by mistake or misunderstanding.

### 1.5.1.2   Civil cases

The statement of case process provides in effect for the formal admission of facts (see **1.3.2.1**). However the Civil Procedure Rules also provide for situations in which parties may wish to admit facts once the statement of case process has ended. CPR, r 14.1, states:

*(1)   A party may admit the truth of the whole or any part of another party's case.*

*(2)   He may do this by giving notice in writing (such as in a statement of case or by letter).*

*(3)   The court may allow a party to amend or withdraw an admission.*

Such admissions can be made voluntarily by a party, usually to save costs and time. Furthermore there are various provisions of the CPR that allow one party to request or demand of another party admissions on particular points or issues such as the 'notice to admit facts' (r 32.18) and the rules relating to written requests or court orders to provide additional information (rr 18.1 and 26.5(3) respectively).

### 1.5.2 Judicial notice

In some cases a judge may take judicial notice of a fact. The taking of notice dispenses with any requirement to prove the fact in question. The matter is accepted by the court without evidence being adduced.

#### 1.5.2.1 Judicial notice without enquiry

There are some matters that are so obvious or so far beyond dispute that it would be a waste of court resources for them to have to be proved every time a case is litigated. In such situations it is possible for a judge to 'take notice' of the fact and to dispense with any requirement that it be proved.

Where a fact is so commonly agreed by people in general so as to be beyond serious dispute, a judge may take notice of it without hearing any evidence. Famous examples include:

- *R v Luffe* (1807) 8 East 193 (two weeks is too short a period for human gestation).
- *Dennis v A J White and Co* [1916] 2 KB 1 (that the streets of London are full of traffic).
- *Nye v Niblett* [1918] 1 KB 23 (cats are ordinarily kept for domestic purposes).
- *Green v Bannister* [2003] EWCA Civ 1819 (the existence of a 'blind spot' that cannot be observed in a car's wing mirror).

Some matters are taken on judicial notice by virtue of legislation. For example:

- Acts of Parliament do not have to proved by evidence. It is not necessary to prove an Act's content or that it was passed by both Houses of Parliament (Interpretation Act 1978, ss 3, 22(1)).
- European Community Treaties, the Official Journal of the Communities and decisions of the European Court are taken on judicial notice (European Communities Act 1972, s 3(2)).
- A judicial or official document that appears to have been signed and stamped by a judge of the Supreme Court shall be taken on judicial notice to have been signed or stamped by him or her (Evidence Act 1845, s 2).

#### 1.5.2.2 Judicial notice after enquiry

Where a fact is not so notorious or widely known, it is still possible for judicial notice of that fact to be taken. However, in such cases, the judge confronted with the issue in question will conduct an investigation. This will happen when the matter is one that is easily resolved by reference to sources of great reliability (such as ministerial certificates, learned works, etc).

This enquiry is not a trial on the matter. The rules of evidence do not regulate what the judge may consult and it is not possible to call evidence to rebut the judge's findings. Furthermore, the conclusions of the judge in the particular case constitute a binding legal precedent on the point.

This form of judicial notice will take place in relation to the following types of information:

(a) Facts of a general nature that can be readily demonstrated by reference to authoritative extraneous sources such as diaries, atlases, encyclopaedia, etc. In *McQuaker v Goddard* [1940] 1 KB 687, a judge resolved that a camel was a domestic creature by consulting books and hearing expert evidence.

(b) Facts of a political nature. Judicial notice can be taken of these following enquiry of political sources. In *R v Bottrill, ex p Kuechenmeister* [1947] 1 KB 41, judicial notice was taken of the fact that the country was still at war with Germany after examining a certificate from the Foreign Secretary to that effect.

(c) Customs and professional practices following consultation of suitably qualified experts in that field or area. For example, in *Heather v P-E Consulting Group Ltd* [1973] Ch 189 judicial notice was taken of accountancy practices.

### 1.5.3 Personal knowledge

To what extent can a judge take judicial notice of something within his or her own personal knowledge? May a juror or a magistrate do so? The general rule is that neither the judge or juror may apply their personal knowledge of facts (*Palmer v Crone* [1927] 1 KB 804) and jurors should be warned not to take steps to acquire such knowledge during trial (for example by visiting the scene of an alleged crime) (*R v Oliver* [1996] 2 Cr App R 514). In *Bowman v DPP* [1991] RTR 263 the use of personal knowledge was distinguished from judicial notice. It was also stated that any personal knowledge ought to be identified so as to allow comment by parties to the case.

However, the courts have allowed judges to use their general knowledge and magistrates may use their local knowledge (eg, *Paul v DPP* (1989) 90 Cr App R 173) in reaching decisions. In *Wetherhall v Harrison* [1976] QB 773, the Divisional Court drew a distinction between judges on the one hand and jurors and magistrates on the other. They said that the former ought not to use their personal knowledge but the latter could. The rationale for the use of juries and lay benches of magistrates was in part to facilitate the sharing of their personal experiences and local knowledge.

There are no clear rules on the extent to which personal knowledge of matters not established by evidence can be used to determine matters. In part this is due to the difficulty of separating the personal knowledge of a judge from judicial notice in many cases. So far as personal knowledge of jurors and lay magistrates are concerned, as their deliberations take place away from the public gaze it will rarely be apparent that they have not resorted to personal knowledge or experience.

## 1.6 Admissibility

So far, we have considered how evidence proves cases. However, we shall see in the rest of this Manual that much of the Rules of Evidence is concerned with whether evidence that clearly could prove a relevant fact will be allowed into court ('admitted') to do so. The starting point is that any item of evidence if sufficiently relevant is admissible unless there is a specific rule that it is not admissible. In other words, the vast majority of the Rules of

Evidence are about the *inadmissibility* of evidence: the Rules of Evidence are a series of filters keeping evidence out of court rather than a series of principles letting it in.

For example, an item of evidence might be relevant in a particular criminal case but it is hearsay evidence according to the law on that subject. This would mean that the evidence is *inadmissible*.

### 1.6.1 Preliminary facts

Some rules of evidence simply state that evidence of a particular class is admissible or inadmissible as a matter of law or logic. An example of this is hearsay evidence. It is not necessary to determine whether or not the evidence was obtained in any particular way. The court can determine the admissibility of this evidence without having to hear any evidence as to how it was obtained, for example.

However, some rules of evidence state that evidence will not be admissible if it was obtained in particular circumstances (such as the exclusion of evidence obtained by oppression under s 76(2)(b) of the Police and Criminal Evidence Act 1984) or that evidence will only be admitted if certain matters are proved (for example, an expert cannot give evidence unless he or she is proved to be an expert). Therefore admissibility depends on proof of particular facts. The facts that lead to the admission or exclusion of such evidence are not ordinary facts in the case. They do not go to prove the issues themselves. They are a necessary step for the admission of other evidence. These facts that make other evidence admissible or inadmissible are called '*preliminary facts*' because they have to be proved before the evidence to which they relate can be admitted. The process of determining these factual disputes is called a 'trial within a trial' or a '*voir dire*'.

## 1.7 Exclusion

There is no general judicial discretion to *include* evidence that is rendered inadmissible by a rule of evidence (see *Sparks v R* [1964] AC 964, PC and *Myers v DPP* [1965] AC 1001, HL).

*However*, there is a power to exclude otherwise admissible evidence in both civil and criminal cases.

### 1.7.1 Civil cases

The general exclusionary discretion to exclude evidence is contained in CPR, r 32.1, which provides:

> (1) *The court may control the evidence by giving directions as to—*
>   (a)  *the issues on which it requires evidence;*
>   (b)  *the nature of the evidence which it requires to decide those issues; and*
>   (c)  *the way in which the evidence is to be placed before the court*
> (2) *The court may use its power under this rule to exclude evidence that would otherwise be admissible.*
> (3) *The court may limit cross examination.*

This power should be exercised to give effect to the 'overriding objective' (see *Civil Litigation Manual*).

In so far as a civil case may not be covered by the Civil Procedure Rules, the position at common law would appear to be that there is no discretion to restrict what evidence can be admitted: *D v NSPCC* [1978] AC 171.

## 1.7.2   Criminal cases

There are important discretions to exclude evidence in criminal cases. There are two types of discretion that must be considered:

- discretion to exclude prejudicial evidence;
- discretion to exclude evidence obtained unfairly.

### 1.7.2.1   Discretion to exclude prejudicial evidence

In *R v Sang* [1980] AC 402, it was held that a trial judge had a discretion to exclude evidence tendered by the prosecution if its prejudicial effect outweighed its probative value. This discretion was an aspect of the judge's duty to regulate the trial process. It is important to be clear about the two important concepts.

*Probative value.* This has already been referred to above (**1.2.2** and **1.4**). Probative value is the likely effect of the evidence on the minds of a tribunal of fact that is acting rationally.

*Prejudicial effect.* This is the use of evidence in an irrational way. For example, we shall see (in **Chapters 6** and **7**) that evidence of an accused's bad character is not admissible to prove that the accused is the sort of person who would commit crimes. In so far as a jury might be inclined to use evidence of a person's bad character for this purpose, this would be prejudicial thinking.

This exclusionary discretion is aimed at situations in which evidence might have multiple uses by a tribunal of fact. On the one hand it will have probative value. On the other hand it will have one or more prejudicial effects. As stated above, previous criminal convictions are generally only admissible to prove the credibility of the accused. However, there is a risk that the jury will not use the knowledge of the accused's previous convictions to decide whether he or she is worthy of belief on oath (the probative value) but whether he or she is the type of person who is likely to have committed the offence in question (the prejudicial effect).

Note that this principle does not oblige the judge to admit or exclude such evidence, it is a matter of judicial discretion (see **1.7.2.3** below). The judge would have to weigh up the value of the evidence (this is why the word 'value' is used) and to compare that to the *risk* of prejudicial thinking on the part of the jury. As we shall see in **Chapter 7** this is not a simple exercise.

The exclusionary discretion only applies to evidence tendered by the prosecution not evidence tendered by a co-accused (*R v Lobban* [1995] 2 All ER 602). The discretion exists to protect the accused from wrongful conviction. Where co-accused A seeks to adduce evidence of previous wrongdoing on the part of co-accused B to show that B and not A committed the current offence, the judge would not be able to act without potentially *increasing* the risk of wrongful conviction on the part of one or the other. Therefore the judge has no discretion to intervene in such a situation.

The application of this rule is not restricted to evidence of previous convictions but applies to any situation in which the jury may follow an impermissible line of reasoning when they hear of a particular item of evidence. *R v Lobban*, for example, concerned prejudice deriving from the admissibility of statements made in confessions.

### 1.7.2.2   Discretion to exclude unfairly obtained evidence

There is a statutory discretion under s 78 of the Police and Criminal Evidence Act 1984 to exclude evidence as follows:

> *(1)   In any proceedings the court may refuse to allow evidence on which the prosecution proposes to rely to be given if it appears to the court that, having regard to all the circumstances, including the circumstances in which the evidence was obtained, the admission of the evidence would have such an adverse effect on the fairness of the proceedings that the court ought not to admit it.*

The detail of this discretion will be considered in **Chapter 9**. However, some preliminary points are worth noting.

(a) There is some overlap between this and the common law power noted above. The main difference is that the common law discretion focuses on the probative value of the evidence which is then compared to the irrational ways in which a jury will evaluate that same evidence. In exercising its discretion under s 78, both the probative value and the way in which the evidence might be misused are relevant matters, but s 78 goes much further. The court is required to consider the effect on the fairness of the proceedings and to examine how the evidence was obtained. This means that potentially probative evidence that would not lead to prejudicial thinking on the part of the jury could be excluded if it would have an adverse effect on the fairness of proceedings for other reasons. Examples of such exclusion include tricks played on the accused and/or his legal advisers with a view to obtaining confessions (*R v Mason* [1988] 1 WLR 139); denial of the accused's right to legal advice (*R v Samuel* [1988] QB 615) and the improper use of undercover surveillance (*R v Loosely* [2001] 4 All ER 897).

(b) This discretion only applies before evidence is admitted. Once it has been admitted, the defence will have to rely on the common law discretion to exclude the evidence that is preserved by s 82(3) (see *R v Sat-Bhambra* (1989) 88 Cr App R 55).

### 1.7.2.3   Appealing a refusal to exercise a discretion to exclude

As the exclusion of the evidence in both of these situations is discretionary, it will be very difficult to overturn a judge's decision on such a matter on appeal. In such situations the court will not intervene unless the discretion was exercised perversely by either refusing to exercise a discretion or erring in principle: see *R v Cook* [1959] 2 QB 340 and *R v Uniacke* [2003] EWCA Crim 30. However, the failure by a judge to apply (or show the application of) the concepts of relevance and weight may lead to his or her exercise of discretion being overturned.

## 1.8   Adducing evidence

An advocate cannot simply advance arguments based on evidence that has not been presented to court by legitimate means. The three bases of admitting (or 'adducing') evidence are:

- testimony;
- documentary evidence;
- real evidence.

### 1.8.1    Testimony

This is evidence that is given by a witness. Usually the witness will attend court, be sworn and stand in the witness box and relate, verbally, the information that will form the evidence in the case. What the witness says is testimony.

There are in fact rules of procedure that allow parties to rely on written witness statements in place of calling the witness. In criminal cases this is, for example, by virtue of s 9 of the Criminal Justice Act 1967 and this will be done if the witness would not say anything so controversial that there would be a need to cross-examine the witness to challenge it.

In civil cases the use of witness statements goes further. By virtue of CPR, r 32.5(2), where a witness is called to give evidence, his or her witness statement shall stand as his or her evidence in chief unless the court orders otherwise. This means that instead of hearing the witness give the evidence orally, the court may simply read the statement. The witness may then be cross-examined by the opposing party in the usual way (r 33.4). This approach allows cases to proceed more quickly.

In both cases, what is written down is still, technically, the testimony of the witness. Although contained in a document it is not documentary evidence.

### 1.8.2    Documentary evidence

Documentary evidence is evidence that is contained in a document. In contrast to the exceptional practices set out in **1.7.1** above, the contents of the documents are not treated as the testimony of the maker. They are 'out-of-court statements' (a concept that is very important when determining whether or not evidence is hearsay: see **Chapter 8**).

Documentary evidence must be 'proved' by a witness. This means that the origin and relevance of the document must be established. It does not mean that the author of the document must in all cases be established. An anonymous note found lying at the scene of a crime might be admissible to prove certain facts without actually establishing who wrote it (although such proof may often be necessary to establish the relevance of the document to the proceedings in question). What is required is that it is established that the document has some bearing on the case in question.

### 1.8.3    Real evidence

This is evidence that derives from the physical nature of an object. The item is produced in court (as an exhibit) or the court will visit the item, for example, when the court goes to the place where an incident took place (often referred to as the *locus in quo*) to view it. The significance of real evidence is that the tribunal of fact can reach conclusions based on the physical characteristics of the item or place rather than any words narrated. Therefore a book could be both documentary evidence (by reading and interpreting it) and real evidence (by examining its physical characteristics). Furthermore a witness in court would be giving testimonial evidence but would also be real evidence him or herself in so far as the tribunal of fact evaluates him or her as a person while giving evidence to determine, for example, whether they appear to be telling the truth or whether (where relevant to an issue in the case) they have particular physical characteristics.

It will be seen in **Chapter 8** that it has been resolved that some mechanically produced information or impressions (such as photographs) are real evidence as opposed to documentary evidence.

## 1.9  Tribunals of fact and law

### 1.9.1  General rule: distinction between tribunal of law and tribunal of fact

The general rule is that the tribunal of fact in any given case will decide the facts and that the tribunal of law will decide the law. In the Crown Court, this distinction is clear to see. The judge, as tribunal of law, deals with legal issues and will often do so in the absence of the jury. The jury deal with factual issues and the judge is under a duty to remind them that it is their function to decide factual issues not his (*R v Jackson* [1992] Crim LR 214). The direction is a follows:

It is my job to tell you what the law is and how to apply it to the issues of fact that you have to decide and to remind you of the important evidence on these issues. As to the law, you must accept what I tell you. As to the facts, you alone are the judges. It is for you to decide what evidence you accept and what evidence you reject or of which you are unsure. If I appear to have a view of the evidence or of the facts with which you do not agree, reject my view. If I mention or emphasise evidence that you regard as unimportant, disregard that evidence. If I do not mention what you regard as important, follow your own view and take that evidence into account.

### 1.9.2  Exceptions to the general rule

The tribunal of law will decide factual matters in the following cases.

#### 1.9.2.1  Summing up to the jury

The judge is not completely barred from considering and commenting upon the evidence in a case. As noted in **1.9.1**, it was said in *R v Jackson* [1992] Crim LR 214 that the judge should direct the jury on their respective functions. However, you will see by referring back to the detail of the direction that the judge could (indeed should) remind the jury of the evidence and review it. Clearly, this will involve some evaluation and consideration of the evidence. It is probably true to say, however, that judge is not in fact *deciding* factual issues.

Where the judge strays too far in commenting or sifting the facts of a case, there may be a ground of appeal. See *Blackstone's Criminal Practice 2004* or *Archbold 2004*.

#### 1.9.2.2  Preliminary facts and the *voir dire*

As noted at **1.6.1** some questions of the admissibility of evidence must be resolved by the proof of particular facts ('preliminary facts'). As the admissibility issue is an issue of law, the tribunal of law must determine it and this is so even where facts must be proved or disproved to determine admissibility. For example, by virtue of s 76(2)(a) of the Police and Criminal Evidence Act 1984, a confession is only admissible if the prosecution prove that it was not obtained by oppression. As the consequence of proving this is the admissibility or inadmissibility of a confession it must be resolved by the judge and it is therefore the judge who will have to decide whether there was in fact oppressive conduct that led to the confession.

Generally this process should be something of which the jury is unaware as their awareness of the evidence could lead to prejudice if it was excluded. In such circumstances the determination of admissibility is achieved by a 'trial within a trial' or *voir dire*, which takes place in the absence of the jury. As its name suggests, this is a trial to resolve a preliminary factual issue during or at the start of the main trial to which it relates. Both parties can call witnesses on the matter in question and make closing speeches. The judge will then decide the admissibility issue and give reasons for the conclusion reached. In this respect the judge is clearly exercising the role of a fact finder. For further details of the *voir dire* process see the **Criminal Litigation Manual**, *Blackstones Criminal Practice* or *Archbold*.

Not all determinations of preliminary fact issues take place in the absence of the jury. Many matters (such as whether a witness is qualified to give expert evidence) are conducted in the presence of the jury. This is generally the case where the matter would not take long to resolve and where the jury would not be likely to reach prejudicial conclusions from knowing of the existence of the evidence.

### 1.9.2.3    Sufficiency of evidence

As will be seen in **Chapter 2** one party or another must call sufficient evidence to put a matter in dispute at trial ('discharging the evidential burden'). This is a question of law that must be resolved by analysis of the evidence.

In criminal cases the prosecution have to prove that there is a case for the defence to meet on all of the elements of the offence. The test is that set out in *R v Galbraith* [1981] 1 WLR 1039, CA:

> (1)  *If there is no evidence that the crime alleged has been committed by the defendant there is no difficulty — the judge will stop the case.*

> (2)  *The difficulty arises where there is some evidence but it is of a tenuous character, for example, because of inherent weakness or vagueness or because it is inconsistent with other evidence: ... where the judge concludes that the prosecution evidence, taken at its highest is such that a jury properly directed could not properly convict on it, it is his duty on a submission being made to stop the case.*

This is determined at the end of the prosecution case and in the absence of the jury. Furthermore, the jury should not be told that the submission took place (*R v Smith* (1987) 85 Cr App R 197, CA). For further details on submissions of no case to answer see the **Criminal Litigation and Sentencing Manual**.

In civil cases with a jury, the judge has a discretion to rule that a party has no case to answer without that party calling evidence (*Young v Rank* [1950] 2 KB 510). Again this discretion is exercised having evaluated the evidence that has been called by the other party.

### 1.9.2.4    The meaning of words

In *Brutus v Cozens* [1973] AC 854, HL, it was stated that generally the meaning of words is a question of fact for the jury to determine. However, Lord Reid envisaged that words might require judicial interpretation if it is shown that they are being used in an unusual way in the statute in question or if there is an issue as to whether the jury reached a perverse interpretation of the word in question.

### 1.9.2.5    Other special cases

There are particular situations in which the law has given the judge the responsibility of determining questions of fact. For example:

(a)  In libel cases it is for the judge to determine whether a document is *capable* of bearing a defamatory meaning. It is then a matter for the jury whether the document does bear the defamatory meaning (*Nevill v Fine Arts and General Insurance Co Ltd* [1897] AC 68 and *Jameel v Wall Street Journal Europe* [2003] EWCA Civ 1694).

(b)  Under the Perjury Act 1911, s 1(1), a person commits perjury if he or she makes a false statement that is 'material' to a proceeding. It is a question of law whether a statement was in fact material (s 11(6)).

(c) Questions of foreign law are questions of fact to be determined after consideration of evidence. However, in criminal cases under s 15 of the Administration of Justice Act 1920 and in civil cases under s 69(5) of the Supreme Court Act 1981 and s 68 of the County Courts Act 1984, it is for the judge rather than the jury to decide this issue.

### 1.9.3 When the same person or persons are tribunal of law and tribunal of fact

In the magistrates' courts and in civil courts where a jury is not used, the function of tribunal of law and tribunal of facts are exercised by the same person or group of persons. Therefore a county court judge or a bench of three magistrates will determine both legal and factual issues. This often makes the process much simpler and more efficient but it also poses two practical difficulties for a lawyer.

(a) It can be difficult to determine the basis upon which a decision has been reached. In jury trials, while the same difficulty can arise, the appellate courts will consider the way in which the jury were directed by the judge to determine how they might have reached their decisions and to decide whether there is a valid basis of appeal due to an error. Where the same person or group is both tribunal of law and tribunal of fact there is no practical requirement for the tribunal of law to tell the tribunal of fact how to apply legal concepts. Therefore there is nothing upon which to base an appeal. To solve this difficulty, the rules of procedure for various courts set rules requiring the court to give reasons for its answers. Quite how much reasoning is required varies by the type of court. See the **Criminal Litigation and Sentencing Manual** and the **Civil Litigation Manual** for detail on the giving of reasons.

(b) The same person or group of people will both determine that evidence is inadmissible and will, at some later point, decide the factual issues in the case. In jury trials, where evidence is to be excluded, the decision to exclude evidence will be made in the absence of the jury. If the application succeeds, the jury will not have heard the evidence and will not have to discount it. Where there is no jury this is not possible. A bench of magistrates, for example, may decide to exclude a confession under the Police and Criminal Evidence Act 1984, s 78, and will then have to proceed on the assumption that they never heard it. Clearly there is a risk that the bench will not be able to disregard that evidence completely. However, it does appear to be an implicit feature of these court processes that the bench of magistrates or the judge in a civil court will be able to ignore evidence in such circumstances.

# Burdens and standards of proof; presumptions

## 2.1 Introduction

As was noted in **Chapter 1**, the issues the court has to resolve are called 'facts in issue'. This chapter considers *who* has to prove or disprove those issues.

### 2.1.1 Burden of proof

A burden of proof is an obligation placed on a party to convince the court with sufficient evidence. There are two types of burdens of proof, used to convince the court of two different but related things.

#### 2.1.1.1 Evidential burden of proof

This burden requires a party to call sufficient evidence to raise a fact in issue before the court. Until this burden is discharged, the other side is at no risk of an adverse finding on that fact in issue. Deciding whether an evidential burden has been met is a legal issue (determined by the tribunal of law) as part of trial management. Quite simply, where a party has not discharged an evidential burden in relation to a fact in issue the court has no jurisdiction to deal with that issue.

For example, as we shall see later, the defence in a criminal trial bear the evidential burden of proving self-defence. This means that the defendant must establish sufficient evidence to raise self-defence as an issue. If this is done, the prosecution have to prove that the defendant did not act in self-defence. If, however, the defendant fails to adduce sufficient evidence to raise self-defence, the prosecution do not have to disprove it. They do not, for example, have to establish that the defendant was *not* acting in self-defence.

#### 2.1.1.2 Legal burden of proof

Once a party has discharged the evidential burden, the court has to determine the issue. One party is then put under an obligation to convince the court on that matter. That party bears the legal burden of proof.

As we shall see below, the prosecution bear a legal burden of proving all elements of the offence (ie, the *actus reus* and *mens rea*). This means a jury, for example, will be directed that they must be satisfied that each element of the offence is proven against the defendant. We will also see below that if the defendant discharges the evidential burden or a defence such as self-defence the *prosecution* bear a legal burden of disproving that defence. In other words the prosecution *would* have to prove the defendant did not act in self-defence if the defendant *did* discharge the evidential burden referred to at **2.1.1.1** above.

## 2.1.2  Standard of proof

The standard of proof dictates the amount and quality (in other words, the weight) of evidence that must be put before the court to prove a fact in issue.

Quite how much evidence is required to prove a fact in issue depends on what area of law it is and which party has to prove it (ie, who bears the legal burden of proof on that matter).

## 2.1.3  Burdens and standards of proof in practice

Therefore for each fact in issue, there is an evidential burden of proof, a legal burden of proof and a standard of proof. Remember that there are a number of facts in issue in nearly all cases.

Before considering the rules for determining who bears which burden and standard of proof in any given situation, it is worth seeing the effect of the various rules in a straightforward case. For example:

You are instructed to represent Anton at trial for theft of £56 worth of food from a supermarket and also for assault occasioning actual bodily harm on the store detective who attempted to stop him from doing so.

For the purpose of this part of the chapter, we shall concentrate on the theft charge.

### 2.1.3.1  The facts in Issue

Using our knowledge of substantive criminal law, we would identify the facts in issue on the theft charge to be:

- Anton (ie, 'identity' as a fact in issue)...
- ...appropriated...
- ...property (ie, the food)...
- ...belonging to another (ie, the supermarket)...
- ...dishonestly...
- ...with intention permanently to deprive the owner of it.

Identifying the facts in issue is a starting point for determining who exactly must prove what and with how much evidence.

### 2.1.3.2  The burden of proof

Using the list of facts in issue identified above, we would apply the rules (that will be set out in the rest of this chapter to determine the incidence of the burden of proof (ie, which party must prove that fact in issue) as follows:

| Fact in issue | Evidential burden | Legal burden |
|---|---|---|
| Identity of Anton | Prosecution | Prosecution |
| Appropriation of food | Prosecution | Prosecution |
| Food was property | Prosecution | Prosecution |
| Food belonged to another | Prosecution | Prosecution |
| Dishonesty | Prosecution | Prosecution |
| Intention permanently to deprive | Prosecution | Prosecution |

The case is quite simple so far and you will note that the prosecution is having to prove everything.

The significance of this is that if the prosecution did not call any evidence that the food Anton was found to have in his possession was or could have been the property of the supermarket, they cannot have discharged the evidential burden. The effect of this is that the prosecution have not actually put an essential element of their case in issue and Anton must be acquitted following a 'submission of no case to answer' (see the **Criminal Litigation Manual**).

If they do manage to call enough evidence to allow the possibility that a jury (or bench of magistrates) can conclude that the shop could have owned the food then the prosecution will have discharged the *evidential* burden. They must then (as the table above shows) discharge the *legal* burden by calling sufficient evidence to prove that the shop did own the food.

### 2.1.3.3 Standard of proof

Having noted that the prosecution have to prove that the shop did own the food, the obvious question is how much evidence will prove that fact. This is the significance of the standard of proof. Applying the rules on the standard of proof to the above analysis would result in the following conclusions:

| Fact in issue | Evidential burden | Legal burden | Standard of proof |
|---|---|---|---|
| Identity of Anton | Prosecution | Prosecution | Beyond reasonable doubt |
| Appropriation of food | Prosecution | Prosecution | Beyond reasonable doubt |
| Food was property | Prosecution | Prosecution | Beyond reasonable doubt |
| Food belonged to another | Prosecution | Prosecution | Beyond reasonable doubt |
| Dishonesty | Prosecution | Prosecution | Beyond reasonable doubt |
| Intention permanently to deprive | Prosecution | Prosecution | Beyond reasonable doubt |

The standard of proof is the test that the tribunal of fact will apply to all of the evidence heard by the end of the case to decide whether each fact in issue is proven. A jury determining this case would have to be satisfied beyond reasonable doubt, for example, that Anton had been acting dishonestly.

### 2.1.3.4 The defence case: scenario 1

So far we have simply examined the incidence of burden and standard of proof in a simple theft case. By requiring the prosecution to prove all elements beyond reasonable doubt, the rules of evidence are simply safeguarding the presumption of innocence that is well recognised in English common law (*Woolmington v DPP* [1935] AC 462, HL) and is contained in Article 6(2) of the European Convention for the Protection of Human Rights and Fundamental Freedoms. However, we noted in the last chapter (at **1.3.1**) that the fact that a defendant advances a particular reason for not being found guilty, may create new facts in issue and it is then necessary to determine who bears the evidential and legal burdens of proof and to what standard for each of those new facts in issue.

Consider the following two alternative scenarios:

*Scenario 1*:

Anton does not give any evidence at trial and does not call any witnesses. Acting on his instructions you have challenged all of the prosecution witnesses on their evidence by suggesting that they are mistaken in saying that it was Anton who committed the offences and they are mistaken when they say that food found in Anton's possession had been taken from the shop.

In this situation, no new facts in issue have been raised. While new arguments are being advanced, your cross-examination has only challenged existing facts in issue (identity, appropriation of food and that the food belonged to another). The prosecution will still have to prove those matters beyond reasonable doubt. What you have done is commonly referred to as 'putting the prosecution to proof'.

*Scenario 2*:

Anton gives evidence during which he accepts that he took the food. However, he alleges that he did so because he had been threatened by John. Both Anton and John are homeless and John regularly threatens Anton and takes his food and any money he has obtained. On this occasion, John threatened to beat Anton up if he did not steal food for him.

In this situation, Anton has raised a new defence (duress). As a result of rules that we shall explore a little later in this chapter, the incidence of the evidential and legal burdens and the standard of proof do not work in quite the same way as for elements of the prosecution case. The effect of the rules of evidence in this area would lead to the following:

| Fact in issue | Evidential burden | Legal burden | Standard of proof |
|---|---|---|---|
| Identity of Anton | Prosecution | Prosecution | Beyond reasonable doubt |
| Appropriation of food | Prosecution | Prosecution | Beyond reasonable doubt |
| Food was property | Prosecution | Prosecution | Beyond reasonable doubt |
| Food belonged to another | Prosecution | Prosecution | Beyond reasonable doubt |
| Dishonesty | Prosecution | Prosecution | Beyond reasonable doubt |
| Intention permanently to deprive | Prosecution | Prosecution | Beyond reasonable doubt |
| Anton acted under duress | Defence | Prosecution | Beyond reasonable doubt |

In other words defendants and the prosecution are treated differently. We shall also see that different defences raised in criminal cases are also treated differently.

In the course of the remainder of this chapter we shall also see that in the civil courts deciding who bears which burden to prove which issue is also rather different.

You will have noted that determining the burdens and standards of proof in any case depends on understanding how facts in issue work. It is therefore strongly recommended that you reread **1.3** of this Manual before proceeding on with this chapter.

## 2.2  Standards of proof

Clearly it is necessary for any party to litigation to know when it has won a case (or to evaluate when it is likely to win a case). A lawyer advising a client or deciding whether or not to compromise or even begin a case must be able to determine whether the available evidence is sufficient. A party to a case must be able to determine whether it is worth risking litigation. It is therefore important to all parties and their advisers that there are clear rules about who should prove matters and how much evidence constitutes proof.

It will be seen that the standards of proof are expressed as degrees of probability. They are effectively yardsticks by which the tribunal of fact can decide a case. It makes sense to determine the standards of proof before tackling who bears the burden of reaching those standards.

### 2.2.1  Civil cases

#### 2.2.1.1  General rule

In civil cases the standard or proof is generally proof 'on the balance of probabilities'. In *Miller v Minister of Pensions* [1947] 2 All ER 372, Denning J described this standard as follows:

> If the evidence is such that the tribunal can say: 'We think it more probable than not', the burden is discharged, but, if the probabilities are equal, it is not.

#### 2.2.1.2  Exceptions

In some cases, the general rule does not apply. In such cases, the standard of proof is proof beyond reasonable doubt as in criminal cases. There is no general rule as to when these exceptions arise. This is determined by the substantive law of the proceedings in question. Examples include:

- Contempt of court: *Re Bramblevale Ltd* [1970] Ch 128, CA, and *Dean v Dean* [1987] 1 FLR 517, CA.
- Anti-social behaviour order proceedings in civil courts: *R (on the application of McCann) v Manchester Crown Court* [2002] UKHL 39.
- Where proof beyond reasonable doubt is required by statute (*Judd v Minister of Pensions and National Insurance* [1966] 2 QB 580).

At interim stages of civil proceedings, the court must reach conclusions without hearing all the evidence or full argument. In such situations, the balance of probabilities test cannot be usefully applied. In such situations (often of the court being required to predict what might happen at trial) a variation or modification of the balance or probabilities test is applied such as 'good arguable case'. This does not alter the general rule that the case must be established on the balance of probabilities. It simply adapts that standard to fit the needs of a pre-trial hearing where the issue is what might happen when the matter comes to trial.

#### 2.2.1.3  Civil cases in which crimes are alleged

Where, in civil proceedings a crime is being alleged (and that *type* of civil action does not fit within one of the exceptions referred to above), the party bearing the legal burden on the relevant issue still only has to prove that issue on the balance of probabilities (*Hornal v*

*Neuberger Products Ltd* [1957] 1 QB 247). Therefore a claimant following a road traffic accident would only have to prove the negligence of the defendant on the balance of probabilities even if the negligence alleged would also amount to a criminal road traffic offence such as dangerous driving.

However, vague use of language in *Hornal v Neuberger Products Ltd* has led to some confusion. In that case Denning LJ suggested that the more serious the allegation the 'higher the degree of probability that is required.' Similar reasoning was applied in relation to the care of children in *Re H (minors) (Sexual Abuse: Standard of Proof)* [1996] AC 563, HL, where it was said 'the more serious the allegation of abuse, the stronger the evidence required to prove it'.

The statements in those two cases do not seek to suggest that there is a third standard of proof somewhere between the balance of probabilities and beyond reasonable doubt. Consider an example. Parvin brings a claim against Arthur for conversion alleging that he took her car and sold it on, keeping the proceeds of sale. This allegation would most probably constitute a theft as well as a civil wrong. However, to succeed in her case, Parvin need only convince the court that it is more likely than not that he converted the car. Even though she has alleged a theft, she does not have to prove the theft beyond reasonable doubt (as the Crown would in a potentially simultaneous prosecution of Arthur). However, the judge in the civil case may legitimately state that before she is willing to conclude that Arthur did take the car for his own purposes, she would like to see strong evidence. This does not mean that she is setting a standard of proof higher than the balance of probabilities. Rather she is saying that given the seriousness of the allegation, it is inherently unlikely to have happened and therefore more evidence is required before she concludes that this is 'more likely than not' to have happened. Contrast, for example, an allegation of something more mundane or commonplace such as Arthur having damaged the car in a road accident. In such a case less evidence would probably convince the judge that the civil wrong (accidental damage) is more likely than not to have happened. In other words the more serious the allegation the more evidence is required to prove the matter on the balance of probabilities. This is not a rule of evidence but an observation on how the tribunal of fact might go about using its logic, reasoning or common sense in applying the balance of probabilities standard.

(It is worth noting at this point that where a civil wrong is also a crime, it is possible for a party to the civil action to prove any relevant criminal conviction in support of his or her case (see **13.3**)).

### 2.2.2    Criminal cases

#### 2.2.2.1    General rule: prosecution

In criminal cases the *prosecution* must prove evidence beyond reasonable doubt (*Woolmington v DPP* [1935] AC 462, HL). 'Beyond reasonable doubt' was described by Denning J in *Miller v Minister of Pensions* [1947] 2 All ER 372 as short of a certainty or 'beyond the shadow of a doubt' but justifying conviction where the only doubt was fanciful or 'possible, but not in the least probable'.

It is acceptable to describe beyond reasonable doubt as 'sure' (*R v Kritz* [1950] 1 KB 82). Clearly it is important that the jury are properly directed about what standard they ought to adopt when dealing with the prosecution case and the appellate courts have frowned upon glosses or qualifications on the 'beyond reasonable doubt' standard. The current specimen direction (obtainable from the Judicial Studies Board website at www.jsboard.co.uk) is:

How does the prosecution succeed in proving the defendant's guilt? The answer is — by making you sure of it. Nothing less than that will do. If after considering all the evidence you are sure that the defendant is guilty, you must return a verdict of 'Guilty'. If you are not sure, your verdict must be 'Not Guilty'.

### 2.2.2.2    General rule: defence

In so far as the defendant ever bears a legal burden to prove any issue in a criminal case, this is only ever on the balance of probabilities (*R v Carr-Briant* [1943] KB 607, CCA). The jury should be directed that the defendant does not have to prove issues to the same standard as the prosecution.

### 2.2.3    Standard of proof of the evidential burden

Where a party has to call sufficient evidence to put a fact in issue, how much evidence is sufficient? In *Jayasena v R* [1970] AC 618, PC, Lord Devlin said the following (at p 624) on the evidential burden:

How much evidence has to be adduced depends upon the nature of the requirement. It may be such evidence as, if believed and left uncontradicted and unexplained, could be accepted by the jury as proof. It is doubtless permissible to describe the requirement as a burden, and it may be convenient to call it an evidential burden. But it is confusing to call it a burden of proof. Further, it is misleading to call it a burden of proof, whether described as legal or evidential or by any other adjective, when it can be discharged by the production of evidence that falls short of proof.

In other words, a party bearing an evidential burden does not have to prove anything. That party merely has to call sufficient evidence for the tribunal of law to conclude that it is possible for the tribunal of fact to decide that the matter is proven on that evidence. Remember that the tribunal of law will often have to make the decision before all the evidence has been called at trial. For example a Crown Court judge will decide whether the evidential burdens have been discharged on all facts in issue at the close of the prosecution case. If it is concluded that sufficient evidence has been called, it will still be open for the defendant to call evidence to disprove (or undermine) the prosecution evidence. Also remember that the tribunal of law is exercising a different function (and is often a different person) to the tribunal of fact. Therefore the decision for the tribunal of law is whether it is *possible* that the tribunal of fact might decide the case has been proven rather than whether the tribunal of law itself decides that the case *has* been proven.

The test for the defendant in criminal cases depends on whether the defendant also bears the legal burden. Where the party only bears the evidential burden (and therefore does not have to prove the truth of his or her assertions) the test is that there is:

Such evidence as would, if believed and left uncontradicted, induce a reasonable doubt in the minds of the jury as to whether his version might not be true (*Bratty v A-G for Northern Ireland* [1963] AC 386).

Where the defendant bears the legal burden (and therefore will have ultimately to convince the court on the issue in question) the test is whether there is enough evidence as might satisfy the jury on the matter in question (*R v Carr-Briant* [1943] KB 607).

There is a lack of clear authority on the standard of the evidential burden in civil cases but as will be clear from the criminal cases evidential burdens require enough evidence to require some answer from the other side and this is deemed to be so when there is enough evidence to allow the possibility (as opposed to certainty) of successfully convincing the court on the point if no evidence to the contrary is adduced. It is likely that civil judges adopt a similar approach.

## 2.3    Burdens of proof

We have now seen what sorts of standards of proof must be borne by parties. Now we shall start to examine the various rules concerning who it is that must do this proving (ie, who bears the burden).

We saw at the start of this chapter that in relation to each fact in issue there is an evidential burden and a legal burden.

As we noted at the start of this chapter, the legal burden of proof on an issue requires a party to prove that issue to the standard we have already identified. The standard of proof does not vary much between cases. However, the incidence of the evidential and legal burdens of proof is more complicated. While there are some simple, straightforward rules, they are subject to many exceptions and provisos which it is necessary to understand. As will be seen these exceptions are often influenced by practical or policy considerations.

## 2.4    Allocating burdens of proof in civil cases

### 2.4.1    Evidential burden

As a general rule, in civil cases the party bearing the legal burden on a particular point will bear the evidential burden. Therefore if a party has to convince the tribunal of fact on a point at the end of trial, the same party will generally have to adduce sufficient evidence to put that point in issue.

### 2.4.2    Legal burden

The general rule in civil cases is that the party asserting a fact should bear the legal burden of proving that fact: *Constantine Line v Imperial Smelting Corporation* [1942] AC 154. This principle and many of the exceptions to it relate to the statement of case process. That is the main opportunity for the claimant to assert his or her case. A defendant will probably contest a claimant's allegations and may also make counter-allegations to support their defence. It will then be for the defendant to prove these new allegations. Therefore the burden of proof will generally be determined by consideration of how the parties have pleaded the case: *BHP Billiton Petroleum v Dalmine SpA* [2003] EWCA Civ 170. For more detail on the statement of case process see the **Civil Litigation Manual** and for fuller consideration of the tactics of drafting such documents see the **Drafting Manual**.

Sometimes the rule that the party making an assertion must prove it is difficult to apply. The parties will often attempt to place on the other side the obligation to prove the matter in hand. It was recognised in *BHP Billiton Petroleum v Dalmine* (above) that the general rule could not always apply where the pleading of the case was overly detailed or insufficient.

Even with properly pleaded cases the rule can be difficult to apply as the situations below illustrate.

#### 2.4.2.1    Contractual cases

There are two issues in contractual cases.

**Contractual terms concerning the burden of proof** First of all, a contract itself can impose the burden of proving a fact upon a particular party. Any rule based on reference to the pleadings should be made subject to this.

**Disputes about the meaning and significance of the terms of contracts** Secondly there may be difficulties in construing the contract, which affect the way the case is stated. This may lead both parties to argue that the other is in reality making the material assertion and should therefore bear the burden of proof. Consider the following examples:

(a) *Hurst v Evans* [1917] 1 KB 352. Jewellery was taken during a robbery and damaged. The plaintiff sought payment under the insurance contract and, when the defendant refused, brought an action for damages. The material term was that the plaintiff was insured against damage to the jewellery 'arising from any cause whatsoever ... except breakage ... and save and except loss by theft or dishonesty committed by any servant ... in the exclusive employment of the assured'. The defendant alleged that the loss was caused by a servant in the plaintiff's employment. The issue therefore arose whether it was for the defendant to prove or the plaintiff to disprove that the damage was due to the servant. Lush J held that the plaintiff bore the burden in this case and that for the defendant to bear it would lead to absurd results.

(b) *The Glendarroch* [1894] P 226. Cargo on a ship was damaged and the plaintiffs sought damages. The defendant shippers argued that the damage occurred due to 'perils of the sea' while the plaintiffs argued that the damage was a consequence of negligent navigation on the part of the defendants. The Court of Appeal determined that there was an implied term in contracts for marine shipping of this type that for perils of the sea to be a defence, they must not have been caused by the negligence of the ship's crew. It was, however, necessary to establish whether the plaintiffs had to prove that the crew was negligent or the defendants had to prove that they were not. It was held that the negligence issue should be proved by the plaintiffs. The facts in issue to be resolved in this case were held to be:

| Fact in issue | Legal burden |
| --- | --- |
| Contract for shipping | Plaintiff |
| Damage to goods | Plaintiff |
| Damage due to 'perils of the sea' | Defendant |
| 'Perils of the sea' due to negligence | Plaintiff |

In both of these cases the courts had regard to established pleading practice with a view to evaluating how the rule that the party that asserts a fact must prove it would apply in such a case.

However the courts had to look beyond the way in which the case had been pleaded and to assess how such an allegation would usually be pleaded. Clearly understanding this subject therefore requires an understanding of the skill and tactics of drafting and specific pleading practice in particular types of cases.

### 2.4.2.2   Negative assertions

The standard rule that the party asserting must prove may prove particularly difficult where a party is seeking to assert the non-existence of a fact. That something does not exist or did not happen is harder to disprove than the proof that something did in fact exist. Consider the following example:

Chris is alleged to have carried out negligent building work that resulted in the collapse of an extension. Should he have to prove he carried out the work carefully and skilfully or should the owner of the house, Doreen, have to prove that he was negligent?

In such a situation the court will require Doreen to prove negligent work. Usually this is not a problem. Doreen would initiate a claim in which she would include draft Particulars of Claim alleging negligent work. Therefore she would have asserted negligence and should prove it. However, what if the civil action was for Doreen's non-payment for Chris's work? In that case all that Chris needs to do in *his* Particulars of Claim is establish that he had a contract with a fee to be paid. It is not a fact in issue in his claim that the work was carried out carefully so he should not make that allegation. Doing so would technically put him at risk of having to prove something he never had to mention. If Doreen wants to allege that she is not required to pay the money because of the fundamental breach of contract by Chris (ie, the negligent work), she would allege this in her Defence.

Matters are not always as straightforward as this. One party may seek to manoeuvre the other into making an assertion by clever drafting. The court may look beyond the strict language of the documents stating the case to determine who in fact *should have* pleaded a particular fact rather than who in fact did plead the fact. In *Soward v Leggatt* (1856) 7 Car & P 613 a landlord brought an action against his tenant regarding non-performance of the obligations under the lease:

- In the Particulars of Claim the landlord alleged that the tenant 'did not repair' the premises.

- In the Defence the tenant alleged that he 'did well and sufficiently repair' the premises.

Who had in fact asserted the fact in issue and who was merely challenging it? Abinger CB held that the landlord could (and should) have alleged that the tenant had 'allowed the house to become dilapidated'. This was the real issue in the case and was why the case was being initiated. As the landlord *should* have alleged it in this way, he was taken to have done so and it was therefore held that he bore the burden of proof on that issue.

Sometimes a negative assertion may be implicit in the substantive law to which the pleadings relate. In *BHP Billiton Petroleum Ltd v Dalmine SpA* [2003] EWCA Civ 170, the claimants brought a claim due to fraudulent misrepresentation by the defendants about the chemical composition of underwater gas pipes that the defendants provided to the claimants. The issue in the case was whether the defendants had caused the claimant's loss. The claimants alleged that the misrepresentation by the defendants caused the claimants to use the defendants' pipes, which cracked and leaked gas, and therefore caused their loss. The defendants alleged that the pipes would have cracked for other reasons than the chemical composition and therefore the defendants had not caused the loss. Clearly this dispute went to the heart of the 'but for' test used to determine causation issues.

The claimants argued that as the defendants had pleaded an alternative cause of the cracking and leaks, the defendants had incurred the burden of proving the alternative cause. The defendants argued that the claimants had alleged causation and therefore, due to the 'but for' test, had 'implicitly pleaded' that there was no other cause. In other words the defendants argued that the claimants had to prove the absence of any other possible cause of loss (ie, prove a negative).

The Court of Appeal concluded that the defendants bore the burden of proving they had not caused the loss. They reasoned that the claimants would have proven causation when they proved both that the non-compliant piping failed and also that they would have rejected such piping if the defendants had not deceived them. Insofar as the defendants had raised an alternative reason for failure of the piping in their defence, they bore the burden of proving this alternative reason. In other words the 'but for' test did not require a claimant to prove the absence of all possible alternative causes but allowed a defendant to assert and prove and alternative cause to avoid liability.

Therefore the courts will tend to determine whether a negative assertion has to be proven by having regard to the actual pleadings in the case and the pleading requirements created by substantive law. They will not be bound by which party has asserted a fact but it will be a matter of great influence in the ordinary course of events.

### 2.4.2.3    Policy considerations

As noted above the actual pleading of a case and good or usual pleading practice will be highly influential in nearly all cases. However, in the most difficult cases the courts may have to look beyond pleading practice and to take into consideration other policy considerations too. Where, for example, it is unclear which party should have pleaded the issue, the court will consider which party would find it easiest to prove or disprove the matter in dispute.

In *Joseph Constantine Steamship Line Ltd v Imperial Smelting Corp Ltd* [1942] AC 154 the issue was whether a contract had been frustrated or not when a ship blew up at sea. The claimants (who alleged there was no frustration due to negligence) argued the defendants would have to prove the explosion *was* not caused negligently. The defendants argued that the claimants should prove it *was* caused negligently. The House of Lords upheld the defendant's argument. In part this was due to the fact that it would be easier to prove any specific allegation of negligence than to disprove negligence in general.

In contrast, in bailment cases it has been held that it is for the bailee (the person in the equivalent position to the defendant in *Joseph Constantine*) to prove a lack of negligence (*Coldman v Hill* [1919] 1 KB 443, CA). The logic of this, seemingly contradictory approach is, in part, that the person in possession would find it much easier to disprove any negligent conduct than for the person not in possession to prove particular negligent acts.

To see if you have grasped this complicated area have a look at **activity 2.1**.

### 2.4.3    Exceptions under statute law

Occasionally Parliament will state who should bear a burden of proof irrespective of who alleges the fact in question. Under the Consumer Credit Act 1974, s 171(7), where a debtor alleges that a credit agreement is extortionate, it is for the *creditor* to prove that the agreement is not extortionate.

## 2.5    Burdens of proof in criminal cases

In civil cases we have seen that the evidential burden and the legal burden are imposed upon the same party. However, in criminal cases this is often not the case. In criminal cases there are the following possibilities in respect of a particular fact in issue:

- The prosecution bear an evidential burden and also a legal burden to the standard beyond reasonable doubt.
- The defence bear an evidential burden but the prosecution bear a legal burden beyond reasonable doubt.
- The defence bear an evidential burden and also a legal burden on the balance of probabilities.

The main point to note is that the defence never bear a burden beyond reasonable doubt.

This approach reflects, to some extent, the principle that the party asserting an allegation must prove it. The prosecution are, in effect, asserting the elements of the offence and the defendant's involvement by bringing the case to court. They must therefore prove those elements. The defendant is asserting the defence by calling evidence in support of it. The difference with civil proceedings is threefold:

(a) There is no statement of case process. The defence is not under an obligation to set out its case in the same formal way as in civil cases. As a result there is no process of admitting, contesting or making counter-allegations equivalent to the statement of case process. Simply by pleading not guilty the defendant is denying *all* elements of the offence.

(b) Defence issues are therefore raised not by formal documents but by the evidence adduced at trial.

(c) The core principles of the criminal justice system, particularly the presumption of innocence, mean that the courts will only rarely impose a legal burden on the defence.

### 2.5.1    The prosecution bear an evidential and legal burden

The prosecution must prove the guilt of the accused. This means that they must discharge both the evidential burden (sufficient evidence to raise an issue upon which a jury could convict) and the legal burden (sufficient evidence to convince the jury beyond reasonable doubt) on all elements of the offence (*actus reus* and *mens rea*) and the issue of identity (*Woolmington v DPP* [1935] AC 462).

The substantive criminal law sometimes is unclear about whether a matter is an element of an offence or a defence. In such cases the court has to determine whether it is for the prosecution or the defence to discharge an evidential burden. For example, matters such as the absence of consent (*R v Donovan* [1934] 2 KB 498) or belief in consent (*DPP v Morgan* [1976] AC 182, HL, and *R v Thomas* (1982) 77 Cr App R 63) are elements of the offence for these purposes and therefore require the prosecution to discharge both evidential and legal burdens.

### 2.5.2    The defence bear an evidential burden but the prosecution bear a legal burden

The rule stated at **2.5.1** applies only to those facts in issue that prove the guilt of the accused. As we saw in **Chapter 1**, some facts in issue establish defences. In such situations
there has been a divergence of practice. The defence is **always** required to discharge an evidential burden on a defence (ie, they have to call sufficient evidence to put the matter in
issue at trial). However, once the evidential burden has been discharged who must discharge the legal burden depends on the defence in question.

For all common law defences except insanity, once the defence have put the matter in
issue by discharging the evidential burden, the prosecution must disprove that matter.
Examples include:

- Self-defence (*R v Lobell* [1957] 1 QB 547, CCA).
- Duress or threats (*R v Gill* (1963) 47 Cr App R 166, CCA).
- Non-insane automatism (*Bratty v A-G for Northern Ireland* [1963] AC 386).
- Intoxication.
- Provocation (*Mancini v DPP* [1942] AC 1, HL).

Some statutory defences also have to be disproved by the prosecution (eg the use of reasonable force to prevent a crime under the Criminal Law Act 1967, s 3(1)). This is because
the statute expressly requires the proof of the fact by the prosecution and is in contrast to
the statutory situations set out below.

### 2.5.3    The defence bear an evidential burden and a legal burden

In other situations the defence have not only to put the matter in issue by calling some evidence but also have to call enough evidence to prove the matter at the end of the trial on
the balance of probabilities.

#### 2.5.3.1    Insanity

In defining the defence of insanity in *M'Naghten's Case* (1843) 10 Cl & F 200, HL, the judiciary stated that the onus of proving the defence lies on the defendant.

#### 2.5.3.2    Express statutory exceptions

There are a number of ways in which a statute can make clear that it is for the defendant to
prove a defence. For example the Criminal Justice Act 1988, s 139(1), creates the offence of
having a bladed article in a public place. Subsection (4) provides:

> (4)   *It shall be a defence for a person charged with an offence under this section to prove that he had good
> reason or lawful authority for having an article with him in a public place.*

The imposition of a burden on the defence in such a situation is commonly called a
'reverse burden' as it is contrary to the usual principles.

The placing of a burden to prove a defence has been recently argued to be contrary to the
presumption of innocence and therefore in violation of Article 6(2) of the European Convention for the Protection of Human Rights and Fundamental Freedoms. In *R v Lambert*
[2001] 3 All ER 547, the House of Lords considered the impact of Article 6(2) and the
Human Rights Act 1998 on a statute that appeared to impose a burden on a defendant to
prove a defence.

Lambert was charged with possession of a controlled drug with intent to supply it under s 5(3) of the Misuse of Drugs Act 1971. He had been arrested in possession of a bag that contained cocaine. Upon arrest and at trial Lambert said that he had thought it contained scrap gold. To prove the offence under s 5(3), it is necessary to prove knowledge of possession of a controlled drug. Section 28(2) and (3) of the 1971 Act provide defences related to lack of knowledge. They read as follows:

> (2)   *Subject to subsection (3) below, in any proceedings for an offence to which this section applies it shall be a defence for the accused to prove that he neither knew nor suspected nor had reason to suspect the existence of some fact alleged by the prosecution which it is necessary for the prosecution to prove if he is to be convicted of the offence charged.*

> (3)   *Where in any proceedings for an offence to which this section applies it is necessary, if the accused is to be convicted of the offence, for the prosecution to prove that some substance or product involved in the alleged offence was the controlled drug which the prosecution alleges it to have been, and it is proved that the substance or product in question was that controlled drug, the accused*

> (a)   ...
> (b)   *shall be acquitted ...*
>> (i)   *if he proves that he neither believed nor suspected nor had reason to suspect that the substance or product in question was a controlled drug; ...*

Section 28(2), (3) therefore imposed a reverse burden on the accused to disprove relevant knowledge. In Lambert's case this meant the he had to 'prove' that he did not know or have reason to suspect that the item in the bag was cocaine. The question for the House of Lords was whether the reverse burden placed on him was compatible with the right to a fair trial protected by Article 6 of the European Convention of Human Rights. That right includes a presumption of innocence, which could be threatened by requiring a defendant to prove any aspect of his or her defence.

The House concluded that the burden placed on a defendant by s 28 was not contrary to Article 6 because the word 'proved' could be reinterpreted, pursuant to s 3 of the Human Rights Act 1998 to mean 'discharge an evidential burden' as opposed to 'discharge a legal burden'. Had s 28 placed a legal burden on the accused to disprove knowledge, the effect would be to require the accused to convince a jury on part of the offence, with the consequence that the accused could be convicted even though the jury had a reasonable doubt as to his knowledge but had not been convinced on the balance of probabilities that he did not know that the contents were drugs. However, when s 28 was reinterpreted to place an evidential burden on the accused, the effect was to require him to call some evidence to put knowledge in issue but still to require the prosecution to prove the offence (including guilty knowledge) beyond reasonable doubt. Such a situation, it was concluded would not undermine the presumption of innocence.

*Lambert* therefore established that reverse burdens may be reinterpreted, where possible, to place only an evidential burden on the accused where the language of the statue in question permits such an interpretation. However, it will not always be possible for this to occur. There are a number of reasons why the imposition of a reverse burden will not lead to this change:

(a) The language of the statute may not allow a reinterpretation under s 3 of the Human Rights Act. For example, the statute might use language such as 'for the defendant to prove on the balance of probabilities'. In such cases the question will be limited to whether the statute in question is contrary to Article 6 or not. No reinterpretation will be possible.

(b) The imposition of a reverse burden may not, on the facts of the case, be inconsistent with Article 6 (*Salabiaku v France* (1988) 13 EHRR 379). There are different reasons why this might be the case:

(i)    The imposition of a reverse burden may not in fact undermine the presumption of innocence. It was of significance to the House in *Lambert* that the matter that the accused was being required to disprove was central to the offence. Their lordships noted that this would not always be the case. Lord Steyn took the view (at [35]) that Article 6 would only be violated if the defence was required to prove something 'so closely linked with the mens rea and moral blameworthiness that it would derogate from the presumption to transfer the legal burden to the accused'.

(ii)   The imposition of a reverse burden that does in fact undermine the presumption of innocence may be justified as pursuing a legitimate aim in a proportionate way in that it achieves a proper balance between the general interest of the community and the protection of fundamental rights of the individual (per Lord Hope at paragraph 88). Lord Clyde noted (at [154]) that strict liability offences that regulate public activities (such as control of pollution or health and safety) may properly impose a burden on a defendant to prove some element of a defence such as lack of fault or the possession of a licence on the balance of probabilities. In such cases the offences carry less social stigma and fulfil necessary regulatory functions. See for example: *R (on the application of Grundy & Co Excavations Ltd) v Halton Division Magistrates' Court* [2003] EWHC 272 (Admin) concerning the Forestry Act 1967 and *R v Drummond* [2002] EWCA Crim 527, [2002] 2 Cr App R 352 concerning the Road Traffic Act 1988.

The effect of *R v Lambert* is to show that any imposition of a reverse burden may, but not must, be contrary to Article 6 and if so, may, but again not must, be reinterpreted to ensure that the burden imposed on the defendant is only an evidential burden. Whether the reverse burden in question is likely to either reinterpreted in accordance with s 3 of the Human Rights Act 1998 or to be subject to a declaration of incompatibility under s 4 of that Act will depend on a complicated analysis of not only the facts of the case but also the wider social and moral issues. It is strongly recommended that you read the judgment of their lordships in *R v Lambert* in full as an illustration of the considerations and factors the courts will take into consideration when determining the impact of Article 6 on the numerous reverse burdens imposed by statute.

In *Sheldrake v DPP* [2003] 2 All ER 497, the statutory provision in question was s 5(2) of the Road Traffic Act 1988, which provides that a defence to the offence of drink driving under s 5(1)(b) as follows:

> *(2)   It is a defence for a person charged with an offence under subsection (1)(b) above to prove that at the time he is alleged to have committed the offence the circumstances were such that there was no likelihood of his driving the vehicle whilst the proportion of alcohol in his breath, blood, or urine remained likely to exceed the prescribed limit.*

Clarke LJ (at [25]) identified a four-stage test to be applied in determining reverse burden cases:

1. Whether the true interpretation of the provision made an inroad into or derogate from Article 6?

2  Whether the provision was justified in doing so?

3    Whether the statutory provision was proportionate if it imposed a legal burden on the accused; and

4    Whether the provision could and should be read down in s 3(1) of the 1998 Act as imposing only an evidential burden on the accused.

To determine whether s 5(2) was in conflict with the presumption of innocence, the court considered the 'gravamen' of the offence (ie, what essentially the offence was aimed at curtailing) and concluded that this was likelihood of the accused driving. Therefore to require the defendant to prove that there was no such likelihood required the defendant to disprove a central feature (ie, the 'gravamen') of the offence was in conflict with the presumption of innocence. The court then concluded that such a reverse burden violated Article 6 of the Convention if it imposed a legal burden but that it could be 'read down' to impose only an evidential burden.

In *Attorney General's Reference (No 4 of 2002)* [2003] EWCA Crim 762, [2004] 1 All ER 1, the Court of Appeal stated that the in determining whether a reverse burden was in conflict with the presumption of innocence, it was necessary to interpret the statutory provision in question using the usual rules of statutory construction and to determine the mischief to which the statutory provisions are directed. The statute in question in that case was the Terrorism Act 2000 and the defendant was charged with membership of a proscribed organisation. Section 11(2) of that Act stated:

(2)    It is a defence for a person charged with an offence under subsection (1) to prove—
   (a) that the organisation was not proscribed on the last (or only) occasion on which he became a member or began to profess to be a member, and
   (b) that he has not taken part in the activities of the organisation at any time while it was proscribed.

Section 118 of the Act provided that where in any section specified under s 118(5) the Act required the defendant to 'prove' a fact, proof would be achieved by discharging an evidential burden not a legal burden of proof. Section 11(2) was not one of the sections specified in s 118(5). Therefore on the construction of s 11(2), 'prove' meant discharge a legal burden. The Court of Appeal also had regard to the purpose and context of s 11(2), which was to criminalise membership of dangerous organisations and of which it might be difficult for the prosecution to prove active and ongoing membership. As a result 'prove' was interpreted as to discharge the legal burden of proof on the balance of probabilities. The court then considered the 'gravamen' of the offence to determine whether requiring the accused to prove non-membership was in conflict with the presumption of innocence. In this case, the court decided it was not. The 'gravamen' of the offence had been fully identified in s 11(1) (being of professing to be a member of a proscribed organisation). All that s 11(2) did was create a specific defence that applied to a limited number of potential defendants. Therefore requiring a defendant to prove that membership pre-dated any illegality did not require that defendant to disprove the offence (which would offend the presumption of innocence) but to establish a particular defence (which did not). The court went on to consider that if the Act did conflict with the presumption of innocence, violation of Article 6 was justified in the circumstances of the offence.

There is therefore no simple answer to whether or not a statutory provision imposing a legal burden on the defendant will (a) be contrary to the presumption of innocence, (b) violate Article 6 and (c) be capable of reinterpretation pursuant to the Human Rights Act. Whether any such conclusion is appropriate will depend on a number of varying factors including the interpretation of the statute, the analysis of the offence to which it relates and a consideration of the social and moral function of the provision. The above principles will have to be applied to each statutory provision on a case by case basis.

### 2.5.3.3  Implied statutory exceptions

So far we have considered situations in which the statute expressly states that the defendant bears a burden. However, sometimes an Act of Parliament will create a defence without stating whether the defence is something for the defendant to prove or the prosecution to disprove. In some cases it is not even clear whether the provision in question is a defence or an element of the prosecution case. Language such as 'without lawful excuse', 'provided that' or 'other than' are examples of such exceptions.

The Magistrates' Courts Act 1980, s 101, states:

*Where the defendant ... relies for his defence on any exception, exemption, proviso, excuse or qualification, whether or not it accompanies the description of the offence or matter of complaint in the enactment creating the offence or on which the complaint is founded, the burden of proving the exception, exemption, proviso, excuse or qualification shall be on him: and this notwithstanding that the information or complaint contains an allegation negativing the exception, exemption, proviso, excuse or qualification.*

The 1980 Act applies to the magistrates' court. In *R v Edwards* [1975] QB 27, the Court of Appeal held that the law relating to the Crown Court is the same (it being considered that the 1980 Act reflected the common law in any event).

It was recognised in *R v Edwards* that determining whether something is an exception or proviso is a matter of statutory interpretation. It is therefore not possible to set down clear rules in advance that will apply to all cases. However, as an example consider the following case:

In a Scottish case, *Nimmo v Alexander Cowan and Sons Ltd* [1968] AC 107 the provision to be interpreted was s 29(1) of the Factories Act 1961, which provided that a workplace '*shall, so far as is reasonably practicable be made and kept safe for any person working therein*'. It was therefore necessary to determine whether the phrase 'so far as is reasonably practicable' created an exception or was part of the definition of the offence. The House of Lords concluded that it was an exception and that the defendant therefore had to prove on the balance of probabilities that he had kept the workplace safe.

In *R v Hunt* [1987] AC 352, the defendant was prosecuted for possession of a controlled drug, morphine, under s 5 of the Misuse of Drugs Act 1971. Section 5 is subject to regulations made pursuant to s 7. One such regulation (the Misuse of Drugs Regulations 1973, SI 1973/797) provides that s 5 has no effect in relation to products containing not more than 0.2% morphine. Was this an exception within the meaning of s 101? In the House of Lords it was recognised that determining where the legal burden lay was usually a matter of statutory interpretation. However, it was also stated that practical considerations such as the ease or difficulty of discharging the burden should also be considered. Applying this approach to construction to *Hunt's* case, the House of Lords concluded that the 1971 Act created an offence of being in possession of a controlled drug and that the provisions of the 1973 Regulations stated, in effect, whether a substance containing morphine was or was not a controlled drug. Therefore proof that the substance did contain more than 0.2% morphine was an element of the offence and not a defence and therefore should be proved by the prosecution.

Where a provision of a statute is interpreted as having imposed a burden on the defendant by virtue of *R v Edwards* and s 101 of the Magistrates' Court Act 1980, the defendant must prove the matter in question on the balance of probabilities: *R (on the application of Grundy & Co Excavations Ltd) v Halton Division Magistrates' Court* [2003] EWHC 272 (Admin).

Again, the question of the compatibility of this rule with Article 6(2) of the European Convention may arise. In *R (on the application of Grundy & Co Excavations Ltd) v Halton Division Magistrates' Court* (above) it was noted that the requirement that the defendant prove the existence of a valid tree-felling licence did derogate from the presumption of innocence. The court stated that there was no reason in principle why such implied statutory exceptions should not, potentially, derogate from Article 6(2). The court concluded, having regard to the nature and purposes of the Forestry Act 1967, that the requirement that a defendant prove the existence of an applicable licence on the balance of probabilities was a justified and proportionate derogation from Article 6(2). Whether this is the case in other cases falling under s 101 of the Magistrates' Court Act 1980 or the rule in *R v Edwards* will depend on the statute in question.

### 2.5.4 Practical consequences of the evidential burden in criminal cases

#### 2.5.4.1 Submissions of no case to answer

If the prosecution fail to call sufficient evidence to discharge the evidential burden on one or more issues, a submission of no case to answer made at the close of the prosecution case must succeed (*R v Galbraith* [1981] 1 WLR 1039). The defendant is entitled to be acquitted without having to call any further evidence.

On matters in relation to which the defence bear an evidential burden (whether or not they also bear a legal burden), the prosecution do not have to adduce any evidence to disprove that issue to succeed on submission of no case to answer.

#### 2.5.4.2 The jury

A judge is not obliged to direct jurors on a potential defence unless the defence have adduced sufficient evidence on the matter to discharge the evidential burden.

Tactically a defendant will not always actively allege all defences available to him or her. For example, a party who alleges that he was not present at the scene of the crime cannot realistically also argue that he was acting in self defence. However, if there is evidence (for example, from the prosecution witnesses) that this may have been the case, the matter ought to be left to the jury (*R v Newell* [1989] Crim LR 906). This is so even if the defendant expressly disclaims the defence (*R v Kachikwu* (1968) 52 Cr App R 538, CA).

## 2.6 Burden and standard of proof on preliminary matters

As will be remembered from **Chapter 1**, a preliminary matter is one which must be established before an item of evidence is admissible. Who bears the burden of proof and to what standard generally depends on the particular rules of evidence relating to that item. However, the general rule is that the party seeking to admit the evidence must prove it. Some examples include:

(a) The Youth Justice and Criminal Evidence Act 1999, s 55(4): it is for the party seeking to establish that a witness is able to give sworn testimony to prove the necessary preliminary facts (ie, that the person is aged 14 or older and that he or she has sufficient appreciation of the solemnity of giving evidence on oath).

(b) The Police and Criminal Evidence Act 1984, s 76(2): where a defendant challenges the admissibility of a confession on the ground that it has been obtained by oppression, the prosecution must prove beyond reasonable doubt that it was not so obtained.

Where the admissibility of evidence is disputed and must be resolved by the proof of such preliminary facts a *voir dire* will be held and the judge will resolve the disputes of fact. This means that the judge will decide whether the issue has been proved to the relevant standard.

# Presumptions

## 3.1 Introduction

### 3.1.1 What are presumptions?

In **Chapter 2** we saw that parties must prove cases to a certain degree. We have also seen that some facts in issue must be proved by one party and some by another.

We also saw (in **Chapter 1**) that there are situations in which the court will assume facts by taking judicial notice of them. This amounts to a simpler (and more cost-effective) way of resolving matters that would otherwise require the calling of witnesses and the making of argument. Another way in which the courts have simplified the process of proof is by the use of presumptions.

A presumption is a rule of evidence by which the proof of one fact (the 'basic fact') leads to a particular conclusion (the 'presumed fact'). Whether it is possible for the other party to disprove a presumed fact depends on which 'class' of the presumption applies.

Therefore in analysing any presumption it is necessary to identify:

- Its basic fact(s).
- Its presumed fact(s).
- The class of the presumption.

For example, s 13 of the Civil Evidence Act 1968 provides that in an action for libel or slander the proof that a person has been convicted of a criminal offence shall be conclusive evidence that he committed that offence. Therefore the elements of the presumption under s 13 of the Civil Evidence Act 1968 are:

- Basic fact: proof that C has been convicted of a criminal offence.
- Presumed fact: that C did commit the offence.
- Class of presumption: conclusive (C cannot call evidence to prove that he did not commit the offence).

This would mean that if Denise published an article alleging that Frederick was a thief and Frederick brought an action for libel, Denise could adduce evidence to prove *Frederick had been convicted of theft* (the basic fact). Proof of this would require the court to conclude that *Frederick had in fact stolen* as alleged (the presumed fact). As the presumption is conclusive, Frederick would not be allowed to attempt to disprove that matter (class of presumption). It ceases to be a fact in issue.

### 3.1.2   Why are presumptions important?

The tactical value of presumptions should not be underestimated. In the rest of this chapter you will be presented with a number of different presumptions that the law has recognised. Bear in mind that some facts are easier to prove than others. You will see that generally the basic fact that triggers the presumption is much easier to prove than the fact presumed as a result of it. In other words presumptions generally allow a party to prove a difficult fact by proving a simpler fact. Occasionally the proof of the basic fact creates a presumption that has the effect of placing a burden to prove a key fact upon a party who would not otherwise bear a burden on an issue.

## 3.2   Classes of presumption

There are broadly three classes of presumptions. One of the three classes of presumptions can be divided into two different types, as shown below.

(a) Irrebuttable (conclusive) presumptions of law.

(b) Rebuttable presumptions of law.

   (i)    evidential presumptions;

   (ii)   persuasive presumptions.

(c) Presumptions of fact.

The remainder of this chapter will look at each of these types of presumption in turn, identifying some examples of them.

## 3.3   Irrebuttable presumptions

Irrebuttable presumptions are usually rules of substantive law. They apply in particular classes or types of action (as opposed to rules of evidence that are of generally application to all types of cases). In fact often these apparent presumptions are simply ways of defining the substantive law. Two examples are set out below.

### 3.3.1   Civil Evidence Act 1968, s 13

This is the presumption used in the example in **3.1.1**. It only applies in defamation proceedings. In such proceedings, proof of the fact of a conviction in a criminal court (the basic fact) will lead to a conclusive presumption that the crime in question was committed. This will usually be relevant to the truth or falsity of the allegedly libellous comments and as the presumption is conclusive, the party against whom the allegation is proved cannot call evidence to prove that he or she did not commit the crime. See further **14.3.3**.

### 3.3.2   Children and Young Persons Act 1933, s 50

This is an example of a 'presumption' that is in effect stating the law of criminal responsibility. Section 50 states:

*It shall be conclusively presumed that no child under the age of 10 years can be guilty of an offence.*

## 3.4   Rebuttable presumptions

In contrast to irrebuttable presumptions, a rebuttable presumption can be disproved by calling sufficient evidence. As a matter of law, where this sort of presumption operates the court *must* presume the fact in question *unless* sufficient evidence is adduced to the contrary.

As noted above what amounts to sufficient evidence depends on what sort of presumption it is:

(a) With 'evidential' presumptions there is only a requirement of **some** evidence. In other words the other party must discharge an evidential burden to disprove the thing presumed. If he or she does so, the presumption ceases to operate.

(b) With 'persuasive' presumptions the party against whom the presumption operates bears a legal burden to disprove the presumed fact.

### 3.4.1   Presumption of marriage

#### 3.4.1.1   Formal validity

*Basic fact*: Proof that the parties to the marriage went through a marriage ceremony with the intention to marry (see *Piers v Piers* (1849) 2 HL Cas 331; *Mahadervan v Mahadervan* [1964] P 233).

*Presumed fact*: The marriage is presumed to have complied with all the formalities required for a valid marriage. (If this is not established then the marriage is voidable.)

*Class of presumption*: This is a persuasive rebuttable presumption. In other words the other party must prove that the ceremony was in some way flawed in form or procedure to show that no valid marriage took place.

#### 3.4.1.2   Essential validity

*Basic fact:* The party seeking to rely on this presumption must prove that a formally valid marriage ceremony was conducted (see above).

*Presumed fact:* The marriage is then presumed to be 'essentially valid' (ie, the parties were capable of marrying and consented to do so).

*Class of presumption:* This would appear to be a persuasive presumption although authority is not entirely clear on the point. See *Re Peete* [1952] 2 All ER 599 and *Taylor v Taylor* [1967] P 25. *R v Willshire* (1881) 6 QBD 366 took the view that this was an evidential presumption only.

### 3.4.2   Presumption of legitimacy

*Basic fact:* Proof either that a child was:

- born whilst the mother was married (*The Poulett Peerage Case* [1903] AC 395); or

- conceived whilst the mother was married (*Maturin v A-G* [1938] 2 All ER 214).

*Presumed fact:* The child born is the legitimate child of the husband to the marriage.

*Class of presumption:* Persuasive. The Family Law Reform Act 1969, s 26, provides that any presumption of legitimacy or illegitimacy in any civil proceedings can be rebutted on the balance of probabilities. Evidence of adultery will not generally rebut this presumption unless combined with evidence that the husband and wife were not having sexual relations at the time of conception (*R v Inhabitants of Mansfield* (1841) 1 QB 444).

*Note:* By virtue of the Family Law Reform Act 1969, s 20, the court has a power in any civil proceedings to direct the use of DNA testing to determine paternity and under s 21(3) a power to require a child under 17 years of age to provide a bodily sample for this purpose. This power does not extend to requiring an adult to provide a sample to match with the DNA of the child in question. There is extensive case law determining when an order under s 21(3) ought to be made. In *Re H and A (Children)* [2002] 1 FLR 1145, CA, the value of the presumption of legitimacy as an alternative to DNA evidence was questioned and a s 20 order was made despite the existence of this presumption.

### 3.4.3    Presumption of death

#### 3.4.3.1    Common law

*Basic fact:* In *Chard v Chard* [1956] P 259 by Sachs J at p 272 it was said that the presumption operates on the proof of the following facts:

- there is no acceptable affirmative evidence that a particular person was alive during a seven-year period;

- there are people who would be expected to have heard from the person during that seven-year period;

- those people have not heard from that person; and

- all due inquiries that are appropriate have been made in respect of the person.

*Presumed fact:* That the person is dead. However there is no presumption that the person died at any particular time. In *Re Phené's Trusts* (1870) LR 5 Ch App 139 the issue for the court concerned succession to a property right of a testator. One descendant, who might have succeeded, N, had not been heard of since 1860. While the court was prepared to presume that N was dead by the date of the trial in 1868, they were not prepared to presume he had died by the date the testator died in 1861. It would appear that the courts will presume that the person died at the end of the seven-year period (ie, in 1867). In *Chipchase v Chipchase* [1939] P 391, DC, a woman's capacity to remarry in 1928 depended upon the death of her first husband who had not been heard of since 1916: the court was prepared to accept that death could be presumed in 1928 as opposed to the date of trial. However in *Lal Chand Marwari v Mahant Ramrup Gir* (1925) 42 TLR 159, PC, the view was taken that it could only be presumed that the person was dead at the date of trial and not at any earlier point.

*Class of presumption:* The presumption is probably only evidential (*Prudential Assurance Co v Edmonds* (1877) 2 App Cas 487, HL). This would also appear to be implicit from the first of the basic facts identified in *Chard v Chard*. Sachs J stated there that the presumption would only operate if there was no acceptable affirmative evidence that a person was alive. Therefore some evidence of prima facie credibility would stop the presumption from operating.

### 3.4.3.2    Matrimonial Causes Act 1973, s 19(3)

*... the fact that for a period of seven years or more the other party to the marriage has been continually absent from the petitioner and the petitioner has no reason to believe that the other party has been living within that time shall be evidence that the other party is dead until the contrary is proved.*

*Basic facts:* (a) The other party to the marriage has been absent for a seven-year period and (b) the petitioner has no reason to believe the other party to be alive.
*Presumed fact:* The other party is dead.
*Class of presumption:* On the language of the statute this would appear to be a persuasive presumption.

### 3.4.3.3    Law of Property Act 1925, s 184

This section provides a presumption to determine the order of death for the determination of rights of succession:

*In all cases where ... two or more persons have died in circumstances rendering it uncertain which of them survived the other or others, such deaths shall (subject to any order of the court) ... be presumed to have occurred in order of seniority, and accordingly the younger shall be deemed to have survived the elder.*

*Basic facts:* It must be established that all of the people have died and the circumstances of death must render it uncertain which died first. In *Hickman v Peacey* [1945] AC 304, where the residents of a house were all killed from a bomb explosion, this presumption applied. It is not clear whether this presumption would operate if the deaths themselves have been presumed as set out above.
*Presumed fact:* The people died in order of seniority. The eldest died first and the youngest died last (therefore in *Hickman v Peacey* the youngest person was taken to have survived the other and therefore inherited the property).
*Class of presumption:* This would appear to be a persuasive presumption.

## 3.4.4    Presumption of regularity

This is a common law presumption of general application and is of two types.

### 3.4.4.1    Official regularity

*Basic fact:* Proof that a person acted in a judicial, official or public capacity.
*Presumed fact:* The act carried out by that person complied with all necessary formalities and the person was properly appointed. For example:

- *R v Cresswell* (1873) 1 QBD 446, CCR: where it was proved that a building had been used for marriage ceremonies, it was presumed that it had been duly consecrated.
- *R v Roberts* (1874) 14 Cox CC 101, CCR: where it was proved that a person had acted as a deputy county court judge, it was presumed that he had been duly appointed.

*Class of presumption:* Persuasive presumption. The party against whom the evidence is presumed may attempt to prove the lack of formalities or proper appointment on the balance of probabilities.

In *R v Dillon* [1982] AC 484, PC, it was stated that this presumption will not operate so as to prove a fact in issue directly. In that case the charge was negligently permitting an escape. One of the facts in issue was that the person in question was in lawful custody. The Privy Council refused to allow the presumption to prove that the person was lawfully in custody.

### 3.4.4.2  Mechanical regularity

*Basic fact:* Proof that a mechanical device is usually in working order.

*Presumed fact:* The mechanical device was in working order on the particular instance in question. For example:

- *Tingle Jacobs and Co v Kennedy* [1964] 1 WLR 638: traffic lights
- *Nicholas v Penny* [1950] 2 KB 466: speedometers.

*Class of presumption:* As above.

## 3.5  Presumptions of fact

These presumptions (unlike the other two classes set out at **3.3** and **3.4**) do not have the same strict legal status that *requires* the court to reach particular conclusions. Rather they are situations in whether the court may reach a particular conclusion. They are really principles that the courts have adopted to deal with commonly occurring disputes.

### 3.5.1  Presumption of intention

The intention of a party in criminal proceedings is often a fact in issue. It is almost impossible to prove the intention of a party by direct evidence. Generally intention has to be proved by circumstantial evidence. In other words intention is inferred from the conduct of the party. The Criminal Law Act 1967, sets out the position:

*A court or jury, in deciding whether a person has committed an offence—*
  (a)  *shall not be bound in law to infer that he intended or foresaw a result of his actions by reason only of it being a natural and probable consequence of those actions; but*
  (b)  *shall decide whether he did intend or foresee that result by reference to all the evidence, drawing such inferences from the evidence as appear proper in the circumstances*

The effect of this provision is to make clear that the tribunal of fact is not obliged to conclude that a party presumed the obvious consequence of his or her actions. Rather the tribunal may decide that he or she has done so. In other words the presumption is not a presumption of law (rebuttable or irrebuttable) but a presumption of fact only. A jury could decide that they were not willing to infer that the accused had the requisite intention even if the accused did not call any evidence to dispute intention.

### 3.5.2  Presumption of guilty knowledge

This presumption only applies in criminal cases in which the accused is charged with either theft or handling of stolen property and operates to establish the guilty *mens rea* of each offence. The presumption, as set out in *R v Aves* (1950) 34 Cr App R 159 is as follows.
  The *basic facts* are proof (beyond reasonable doubt) that:

(a) the accused was found in possession of stolen property soon after it was stolen; and

(b) the accused either:
   (i)   offered no explanation as to how he came to be in honest possession of the goods, or

(ii)  offered an explanation as to how he came to be in honest possession that the jury conclude is untrue.

The *presumed fact* is that either the accused stole the goods (on a theft charge) or knew the goods to be stolen (on a handling charge).

*Class of presumption:* As this is a presumption of fact the jury are not obliged to convict the accused even if they conclude that the basic facts are established beyond reasonable doubt.

### 3.5.3  Presumption of continuance of life

The presumption is simply a reflection of common sense. Where a person is proved to be alive on a particular date (the *basic fact*), they may be presumed to be alive on a subsequent date (the *presumed fact*). The presumption is not required by law and whether or not it is to be made will depend on factors such as the age and health of the person and the circumstances in which he was last seen. Clearly the longer it is since the person was seen the less likely it is that a tribunal of fact will reach this conclusion. See *R v Lumley* (1869) LR 1 CCR 196. As a matter of logic, this presumption cannot operate to displace a presumption of death (see **3.4.3.1** above).

## 3.6  *Res ipsa loquitur*: a difficult case

In *Scott v London and St Katherine Docks Co* (1865) 3 Hurl &C 596, at p 601, Erle CJ said:

... where the thing is shown to be under the management of the defendant or his servants, and the accident is such as in the ordinary course of things does not happen if those who have management use proper care, it affords reasonable evidence, in the absence of explanation by the defendants, that the accident arose from want of care.

Therefore the *basic facts* are:

- Something (whether an object or a location) is under the control of the defendant.
- An accident arose from that thing.
- The accident would not have happened if the thing had been properly managed.

The *presumed fact* is simply that the accident arose due to negligence.

What *class of presumption* is this? It is not finally resolved whether this is an evidential or a persuasive rebuttable presumption of law or a presumption of fact. The extensive case law is best found by referring to such works as *Charlesworth and Percy on Negligence*. The current view is that it is a presumption of fact (see *Lloyde v West Midlands Gas Board* [1971] 2 All ER 1240, CA; *Ng Chun Pei v Lee Chuen Tat* [1988] RTR 298, PC), which means the court *may* presume negligence but is not obliged to do so.

For a useful analysis of the case law and a justification of different approaches to this presumption in different circumstances see Keane, *The Modern Law of Evidence*, 5th edn (London: Butterworths) at p 652.

## 3.7  Conflicting presumptions

It should be clear from the analysis above that it is possible for two presumptions to conflict. Where this happens it would be possible in principle to conclude any of the following:

- One presumption must prevail over another presumption, this being decided on a case-by-case basis.
- That presumptions of a particular class must prevail over less probative presumptions.
- That presumptions cancel one another out.

In *Monckton v Tarr* (1930) 23 BWCC 504, it was held that presumptions cancel each other out where they are the same presumption: in that case, two conflicting presumptions of essential validity of marriage (see **3.4.1.2**). However, in *Taylor v Taylor* [1965] 1 All ER 872, Cairns J declined to adopt that approach and preferred the more recent presumption of validity to the older. Considerations of policy may have affected this approach but it is also partly based on an evaluation of the strength of the presumption in each case, the latter marriage appearing more probative.

However, where presumptions are not of the same type, the effect of each presumption upon the other must be considered as a matter of logic. In *R v Willshire* (1881) 6 QBD 366, W was charged with bigamy, having married C when B was alive. The prosecution therefore had to prove that the preceding marriage to B was valid and W had to prove that it was void. W had been married to A before he had married B. The parties sought to use presumptions as follows:

- W sought to prove that the marriage to B was void because A was alive when the marriage to B took place (presumption of continuance of life: see **3.5.3**).
- The prosecution sought to prove that the marriage to B was a valid marriage using the presumption of essential validity (see **3.4.1.2**).

It was held that the prosecution's presumption of validity, being only an evidential presumption, had been discharged by the operation of the presumption of continuance of life (note how the court concluded that the presumption of fact could discharge an evidential burden). As the prosecution's presumption had been discharged, it was necessary to prove the validity of the marriage to B by the normal rules of evidence.

It is therefore reasonably clear that there is no automatic order of preference for presumptions. Whether one presumption will overcome another depends on the basic facts, the presumed facts and the class of presumption of each and will be a matter of argument in each case, drawing on the logic of the presumptions in question but also on policy considerations.

# Witnesses

This Manual has so far concentrated on some of the fundamental issues that will influence how a case will be decided. We have seen that the courts work under rules stating who should prove which matters and how much evidence is required to do so (**Chapter 2**) and we have also seen (**1.7.1**) that there are a number of ways in which evidence can be brought before the court and that of these, the most common is by testimony. In fact other classes of evidence (documentary and real evidence) require proof and this proof will generally be effected by testimony.

Testimony is evidence given by witnesses. Although there are rules of procedure in both civil and criminal courts for a witness not to attend court and for his or her evidence to be tendered in a written format, these procedures do not supplant the witness. They simply, for pragmatic reasons, dispense with the need to call the witness *in person*.

It is therefore necessary to understand who the courts will allow to be called as witnesses to give testimony ('competence') and who the courts will force to give testimony ('compellability'). This chapter also deals with related topics. Some time will be spent considering the issue of sworn testimony (ie, whether witnesses should be permitted or required to make any particular promise to tell the truth during their testimony). Finally the chapter will consider some procedural and evidential issues concerning the calling of witnesses.

## 4.1 Introduction to competence and compellability

Defining a witness as competent means that he or she is *able* to give evidence in court. Defining a witness as compellable means that he or she can be *forced* to give evidence.

When a witness is compellable, the rules of procedure in both civil and criminal courts can force attendance and apply sanctions for a failure to do so (see **4.7.4** below).

A party who cannot compel a witness to attend court may attempt to have statements the witness made at earlier stages admitted as documentary evidence. In such cases the party is relying on 'hearsay' evidence. These matters are dealt with in the chapter on hearsay (**Chapter 9**). It will be seen that sometimes these rules allow a party to get round difficulties in getting the person who made the statement to attend court as a witness.

### 4.1.1 General rule

The general rule at common law is that:

- all persons are competent; and
- all competent persons are compellable

This general rule has been put on a statutory footing for criminal cases in the Youth Justice and Criminal Evidence Act 1999, s 53(1), which states:

*At every stage in criminal proceedings all persons are (whatever their age) competent to give evidence.*

In civil cases the rules are determined by a combination of the common law and statute law.

### 4.1.2   Exceptions to the general rule of competence

The general rule of competence was subject to considerable exceptions historically. These exceptions were either removed or placed on a statutory footing in recent years.

There are now specific exceptions concerning the *competence* of the following types of witnesses:

- Persons of limited understanding (eg, children and persons suffering from mental illness).
- Co-accused parties in criminal cases.
- The Sovereign (possibly).

### 4.1.3   Exceptions to the general rule of compellability

The rationale of the exceptions concerning compellability is different to that for competence, as the issue is whether they should be forced to give evidence rather than allowed to do so. As will be seen below, there are policy reasons why the following groups have been held not to be compellable. There are now specific exceptions concerning the compellability of the following types of witnesses:

- Co-accused parties in criminal cases.
- The spouse of an accused party in a criminal case.
- The Sovereign, heads of state and diplomats.
- Bankers.
- Members of the judiciary.

## 4.2   Persons of limited understanding

The competence of witnesses is based on an assumption that the person is able to give meaningful testimony on important matters. If the court concludes that they could not do so due to an inability to understand what has happened or what is being asked of them at court, the general rule of competence is not followed.

The common law developed a collection of rules and principles governing such witnesses. The position is now largely governed by statute law, although common law principles continue to operate in civil cases.

It is worth bearing in mind that, so far as children and persons of defective intellect are concerned, the courts draw a distinction between sworn and unsworn testimony. Competence and the issue of sworn testimony are related and are resolved at the same time procedurally. For the significance of sworn testimony see **4.7** below.

### 4.2.1  Criminal cases

#### 4.2.1.1  Competence to give any evidence

The general rule of competence set out in s 53(1) of the Youth Justice and Criminal Evidence Act 1999 is subject to an exception set out in s 53(3) as follows:

*A person is not competent to give evidence in criminal proceedings if it appears to the court that he is not a person who is able to—*

*(a)   understand questions put to him as a witness, and*

*(b)   give answers to them which can be understood.*

When the issue of the competence of a witness is raised (whether by a party or the court) the following procedures will be adopted:

- Competence is determined by the court (s 53(3)).

- The party calling the witness must prove the witness' competence on the balance of probabilities (s 54(2)) even if it is the prosecution calling the witness.

- Determining competence should take place in the absence of the jury (s 54(4)) but in the presence of the accused (s 54(6)).

- Questioning is conducted by the court (ie the judge or magistrates) (s 54(6)).

- Expert evidence may be called (subject to the various rules on expert evidence set out in **Chapter 12**).

- As will be seen at **4.7.5**, the court has various powers to make the giving of evidence by vulnerable or incapacitated witnesses more effective ('special measures directions'). The court, in determining competence under s 53(3) is required to presume that any available special measures have been taken to assist the witness in question (s 54(5)).

#### 4.2.1.2  Competence to give sworn evidence

If a witness is competent, there may still be an issue as to whether the witness may give sworn evidence. This is determined under s 55(2), which creates two requirements for sworn testimony:

- the witness must be aged 14 years or older (s 55(2)(a)); and

- the witness must have 'sufficient appreciation of the solemnity of the occasion and of the particular responsibility to tell the truth which is involved in taking the oath' (s 55(2)(b)).

A person is presumed (see **Chapter 3**) to have sufficient appreciation under s 55(2)(b) if able to understand questions put to him or her and to give understandable answers (s 55(3), (8)). This is an evidential presumption so will be rebutted if any evidence to the contrary is adduced. As the basic facts for the presumption are identical to the test of competence under s 53(3), the practical effect of this is that if a witness over 14 years of age has been held to be competent under s 53(3), he or she will be *presumed* to be capable of giving sworn testimony unless evidence to the contrary is adduced.

Where capacity to give sworn testimony is disputed:

- The matter is determined in the absence of the jury (s 55(5)) but in the presence of the accused.

- Expert evidence can be called (subject to the rules of evidence on expert evidence set out in **Chapter 15**).

- If the court decides that the witness cannot give sworn testimony, he or she shall give unsworn testimony (s 56(2)). This does not mean that the court cannot receive the evidence or that the conviction is rendered unsafe as a result of being based on unsworn testimony (s 56(4), (5)).

For the significance of unsworn testimony see **4.6**.

### 4.2.2  Civil cases

#### 4.2.2.1  Competence of children to give unsworn evidence

The Children Act 1989 applies to any person under the age of 18. Section 96 provides that:

(1)  *Subsection (2) applies where a child ... in any civil proceedings does not ... understand the nature of the oath.*

(2)  *The child's evidence may be heard by the court if, in its opinion—*

    (a)  *he understands that it is his duty to speak the truth and;*

    (b)  *he has sufficient understanding to justify his evidence being heard.*

Therefore the child's competence to give sworn evidence is determined alongside the competence to give any evidence at all. If the child witness cannot give sworn evidence, he or she may still be able to give unsworn evidence if he or she shows an understanding of the duty to tell the truth and an ability to give useful evidence.

Compare s 96(2) of the Children Act 1989 with s 53(3) of the Youth Justice and Criminal Evidence Act 1999. Section 96(2)(b) concentrates on the practical value of calling the witness in question, namely whether he or she can give useful answers to questions posed. In this respect it is similar to s 53(3). However, s 53 does not have any requirement that the child witness shows an ability or willingness to tell the truth. It is likely that this is so that younger child witnesses can be called in criminal cases given the importance of relying on very young witnesses. Often cases involving young witnesses may relate to crimes committed on the children themselves, so s 53 is as much available for their own protection as for the prosecution of particular persons. In the other class of cases intended to protect young children, civil cases brought under the Children Act 1989 itself, a different approach has been adopted. While the child may not be competent under s 96 to give testimony him or herself, what they say out of court may be admitted as an admissible hearsay evidence (s 96(3) to (5)).

#### 4.2.2.2  Competence of children to give sworn evidence

You will have noticed that the rules of witness competence in civil proceedings are related to the rules concerning the giving of sworn testimony and that both issues are referred to in the Children Act 1989, s 96. However, that section does not state when a child will be capable of giving sworn testimony. This and the procedure to be adopted are dictated by the common law.

It is a matter for the judge whether there is any need to investigate the capacity to give sworn testimony at all. In *R v Khan* (1981) 73 Cr App R 190, CA, it was stated that as a general rule of thumb inquiry should be conducted for children under the age of 14. The judge will determine whether a witness is capable of giving sworn testimony by asking questions of the witness (*R v Surgenor* (1940) 27 Cr App R 175).

The test to determine whether a child is capable of giving sworn testimony was laid down in *R v Hayes* [1977] 1 WLR 238, where it was said that the court should determine 'whether the child has sufficient appreciation of the solemnity of the occasion and the added responsibility to tell the truth, which is involved in taking the oath over and above the duty to tell the truth which is an ordinary duty of normal social conduct'.

### 4.2.2.3 Competence of other persons of limited understanding

In civil cases the competence of a witness suffering from a mental illness remains to be decided by the common law (which is derived from both civil and criminal cases pre-dating the Youth Justice and Criminal Evidence 1999). It should be noted that allowing a witness to give unsworn evidence is a specific statutory concession. The general common law rule is that the competence of a witness depends on competence to give sworn testimony. If the witness does not understand the nature of the oath then the witness cannot testify at all (see *R v Hill* (1851) 2 Den 254). In determining whether the witness can understand the nature of the oath, the courts have adopted the *R v Hayes* test for determining whether a witness suffering from mental illness can give sworn testimony (*R v Bellamy* (1985) 85 Cr App R 222, CA). Therefore the position in civil cases is that if a non-child witness cannot give sworn evidence he or she is not competent as a witness.

## 4.3 The accused as a witness in criminal cases

### 4.3.1 For the prosecution

The privilege against self-incrimination has ensured that the accused in a criminal trial will not be compelled to give evidence. Section 53(4) of the Youth Justice and Criminal Evidence Act 1999 states that any person 'charged in criminal proceedings' is not competent to give evidence for the prosecution.

What if a person is alleged to have been involved in criminal activity but, for whatever reason, is not being tried with others who took part? Section 55(3) states that a person is not 'charged in criminal proceedings' if they are no longer liable to be convicted of any offence in the proceedings. This will be the case where:

- The person has been acquitted.
- A *nolle prosequi* has been entered on the direction of the Attorney-General.
- The person has pleaded guilty.
- The person will be tried separately (therefore although still charged, that person would not be liable to conviction in the proceedings in question).

Where an accomplice still faces prosecution in respect of the crime in question, it is a matter of judicial discretion whether to allow the co-accused witness to be called (*R v Turner* (1975) 61 Cr App R 67, CA). In *R v Pipe* (1966) 51 Cr App R 17, it was held that where an accomplice was awaiting trial on the same matter but who was not going to be tried in the current proceedings, that accomplice should not be called unless he had receive an undertaking not to proceed with the case against him.

### 4.3.2 For the accused or co-accused

An accused is competent to give evidence on his or her own behalf (Youth Justice and Criminal Evidence Act 1999, s 53(1)) but cannot compelled to do so (Criminal Evidence Act 1898, s 1(1)).

Where, however, a witness does elect to give evidence is open to cross-examination by both the prosecution and by any co-accused party and this cross-examination may stray beyond the details of his or her own guilt. In *R v Paul* [1920] 2 KB 183, the accused gave evidence in chief to the effect that he was guilty. The prosecution were entitled to cross-examine him as to the involvement of the co-accused.

Although the accused cannot be compelled to give evidence, his refusal to do so may, in certain circumstances, lead to an inference being drawn against him under s 35 of the Criminal Justice and Public Order Act 1994. See **10.4.5** for further detail on this.

If the co-accused seeks to call the accused, s 53(1) of the 1999 Act also applies. The party called is competent to give evidence. However s 1(1) of the 1898 Act states that the accused shall not be called 'except on his own application'. This means that an accused cannot be compelled by a co-accused. Of course, if an accused is acquitted or otherwise ceases to be an accused party, he or she is subject to the rules that apply to any witness. He or she is compellable if he or she is competent.

## 4.4  Spouses of accused persons in criminal cases

There are a number of social and policy reasons why a spouse of an accused person should not be forced to give evidence against the accused. On the other hand spouses are often in a particularly strong position to give useful evidence. Occasionally they may even be the victim of the crime in question. The law relating to a spouse as a witness is set out in s 80 of the Police and Criminal Evidence Act 1984 ('PACE') and is effected by s 53 of the Youth Justice and Criminal Evidence Act 1999.

The provisions of s 80 do not apply to ex-spouses. Once spouses divorce ex-spouses are competent and compellable as normal witnesses (s 80(5)). The effect of this is that they can be compelled to give evidence even in respect of matters that arose while they were married.

Section 80 can be quite complicated. There is therefore a flow chart printed on p 64 to assist you in analysing this subject.

### 4.4.1  Competence of a spouse

A spouse is competent for any party in criminal proceedings (Youth Justice and Criminal Evidence Act 1999, s 53(1)). However, if both spouses are charged in the proceedings, neither spouse is competent for the prosecution (s 53(4)).

### 4.4.2  Compellability for the accused

Section 80(2) of PACE states:

> (2)  *In any proceedings the wife or husband of a person charged in the proceedings shall ... be compellable to give evidence on behalf of that person.*

However, if the spouse is a co-accused in the proceedings, he or she is not compellable unless he or she is no longer liable to be convicted (s 80(4), (4A)).

### 4.4.3   Compellability for the prosecution or a co-accused

Section 80(2A) provides:

> *(2A) In any proceedings the wife or husband of a person charged in proceedings shall ... be compellable—*
>
>> *(a) to give evidence on behalf of any other person charged in the proceedings but only in respect of any specified offence with which that other person is charged; or*
>>
>> *(b) to give evidence for the prosecution but only in respect of any specified offence with which any person is charged in the proceedings.*

Therefore a spouse will only be compellable for the prosecution or a co-accused if the proceedings are for a 'specified offence'. This is defined in s 80(3) of the act, which provides:

> *(3)   In relation to the wife or husband of a person charged in any proceedings, an offence is a specified offence ... if—*
>
>> *(a)    it involves an assault on, or injury or threat of injury to, the wife or husband or a person who was at a material time under the age of 16;*
>>
>> *(b)    it is a sexual offence alleged to have been committed in respect of a person who was at a material time under that age, or*
>>
>> *(c)    it consists of attempting or conspiring to commit, or of aiding, abetting, counselling, procuring or inciting the commission of, an offence falling within paragraph (a) or (b) above.*

The word 'involves' in paragraph (a) is ambiguous. Does it mean that the legal definition of the offence necessarily involves an assault or injury or threat of injury (such as robbery)? If so the ambit of this paragraph is relatively narrow. It will only apply where the offence charged includes these elements as part of its *actus reus*. However, a broader interpretation is that 'involves' means 'involves in this particular case'. On this interpretation, paragraph (a) would extend to any situation in which it is alleged that some force was used or threatened.

Note the use of the phrase 'but only in respect of any specified offence' in subsection (2A)(b) above. This would appear to mean that where an accused is tried for an offence that would be specified under s 80(3) and one that is not, the spouse is only compellable for the specified offence. He or she would therefore not be under any obligation to answer questions on the non-specified offence. Equally a co-accused can only compel a spouse if he or she (the co-accused) is charged with a specified offence and only in relation to that offence. Therefore where parties other than the co-accused are charged with a specified offence but the co-accused is not, the spouse is not compellable for that co-accused.

Note also that the spouse is only compellable under s 80(3)(a) if he or she (or a child under the age of 16) is the victim of a crime. Therefore where A and B are charged with assaulting A's wife, C, C is compellable but B's wife, D (not being a victim of the specified offence) is not.

To test whether you have grasped this complicated set of rules you may wish to consider the examples set out in **activity 4.1** in **Appendix 1**.

## 4.5   Other classes of witnesses

### 4.5.1   Heads of State

Neither the Sovereign of this State nor the sovereign or head of State of any other State is compellable. Furthermore, diplomats and consular officials may have immunity from compulsion under a number of laws.

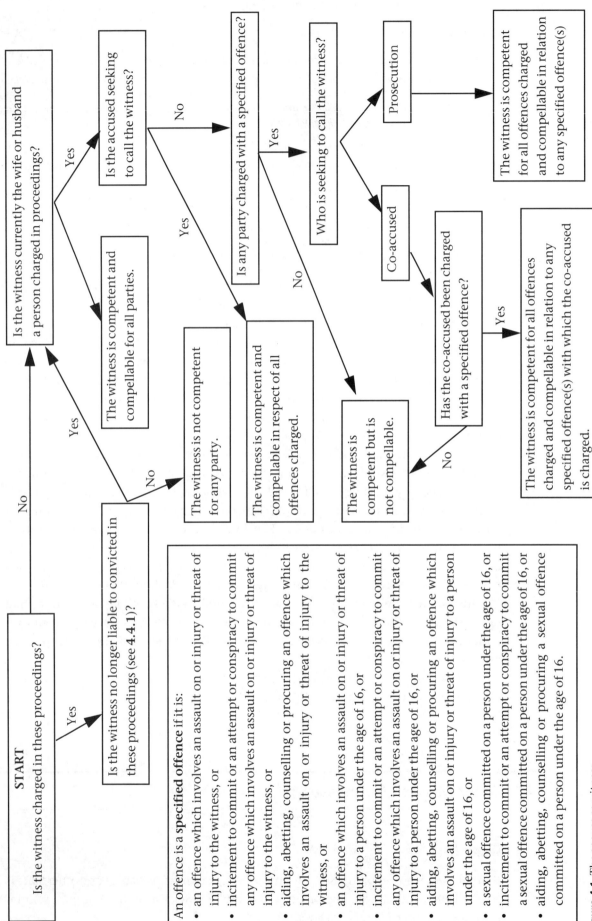

**Figure 4.1**  The spouse as witness

### 4.5.2 Bankers

The Bankers' Books Evidence Act 1879 provides for the admissibility of bankers' books in numerous proceedings. Section 6 of that Act states that a banker cannot be compelled to attend court to produce the book or answer questions concerning it unless the court orders otherwise.

### 4.5.3 Judges

Judges and masters are competent to give evidence about any matters arising in their court. However, they cannot be compelled to attend court to give evidence about their judicial function.

## 4.6 Oaths and affirmations

### 4.6.1 Sworn evidence

Generally a witness must be sworn to give evidence. Sworn evidence means that a witness has either taken an oath or has affirmed.

Under the Oaths Act 1978, an oath can be given in any lawful manner (s 1(3)). This means that:

- the oath appears to the court to be binding on the maker, and
- the maker states that he considers the oath to be binding on him or herself

Therefore in *R v Kemble* [1990] 3 All ER 116, CA, the evidence of a witness who was a Muslim was held to have been lawfully administered even though it had been administered on the New Testament whereas Islam requires that a binding oath is made on a copy of the Koran that is written in Arabic.

Section 4(2) states that an oath is binding even if the maker has no religious belief. However, usually such a person would choose instead to affirm under s 5 of the Act.

### 4.6.2 Unsworn evidence

#### 4.6.2.1 Criminal cases

In criminal cases unsworn evidence can be given by any witness who is competent but cannot give sworn evidence due to s 55 of the Youth Justice and Criminal Evidence Act 1999.

Section 56(5) states that the fact that a conviction is based on unsworn evidence does not of itself provide a ground for appeal.

#### 4.6.2.2 Civil cases

Generally, a witness who is not sworn cannot give evidence at all and a judgment based on such evidence will be set aside as a nullity (*R v Marsham, ex p Lawrence* [1912] 2 KB 362).

A person may give unsworn evidence if:

- The case is brought in the small claims track and the court does not require evidence on oath (CPR, r 27.8(4)).

- The witness is producing a document that can be identified by another witness on oath (*Perry v Gibson* (1834) 1 Ad & El 148).

- The evidence is of the terms of an agreement between parties and the witness is counsel for one of the parties (*Hickman v Berens* [1895] 2 Ch 638).

- The witness is a child and is not competent to give sworn testimony (Children Act 1989, s 96).

Unlike criminal cases, there is no general power on the part of the civil courts to accept the unsworn testimony of a person suffering from a mental illness or other mental disability (*R v Bellamy* (1985) 85 Cr App R 222, CA).

## 4.7 Practical issues concerning witnesses

### 4.7.1 Witness statements and video evidence

Generally the evidence of a witness is given orally.

In civil cases, CPR, r 32.5(2), states that where a witness statement has been served and a party intends to rely on that witness, the witness must be called to give oral evidence unless the court orders otherwise. However, by r 32.5(2), the statement shall stand as evidence in chief unless the court orders otherwise. Therefore a civil witness will generally give evidence in chief by way of the witness statement and be cross-examined orally.

For these purposes a witness statement contains only those matters that the person could give as oral evidence (r 32.4(1)). As the statement will stand as the evidence in chief of the witness, it must contain a signed statement of truth (PD 32, para 20). For details of the formal requirements of witness statements and procedural issues such as disclosure see the **Civil Litigation Manual** and *Blackstone's Civil Practice*, 2004, ch 48.

In criminal cases the witness statements will not stand as the evidence of the witness unless all parties agree. In that case a written statement can be admitted as their evidence under s 9 of the Criminal Justice Act 1967. This generally happens where the witness is not likely to give controversial evidence. If the statement is controversial, the defence should object to the use of the statement and the witness should be called. For detail on the use of 9 statements and the rules relating to disclosing them to other parties see *Blackstone's Criminal Practice*, 2004.

When ss 137 and 138 of the Criminal Justices Act 2003 are brought into force, statements made by witnesses and recorded on video may stand as the evidence of that witness if the court so directs. The video will only be treated as evidence if the witness asserts the truth of the statement in the video (s 139(2)).

### 4.7.2 Calling witnesses

#### 4.7.2.1 Who to call as a witness

To what extent can parties choose who they will call as a witness? Clearly a party cannot call a witness who is not competent to give evidence. However, even where a witness is competent there are two issues. First of all is any party under an obligation to call witnesses they would rather not call and secondly, can any party be prevented from calling competent witnesses for any reason. To some extent the answers to these questions depend on who exactly the party is.

### Civil cases

The parties in civil proceedings have considerable freedom to choose who they call. They are not under an obligation to call any particular witness. If a party chooses not to rely on the evidence of a witness, the witness does not have to be called (for an exception in relation to hearsay evidence see **Chapter 9**). However, there is one important restriction on the freedom of civil parties in this respect and that is CPR, r 32.1, which provides:

*(1) The court may control the evidence by giving directions as to—*
  *(a) the issues on which it requires evidence;*
  *(b) the nature of the evidence which it requires to decide those issues; and*
  *(c) the way in which the evidence is to be placed before the court.*
*(2) The court may use its power under this rule to exclude evidence that would otherwise be admissible.*
*(3) The court may limit cross-examination.*

This broad discretion allows the court to restrict which witnesses any party may call and should be exercised in accordance with the 'overriding objective' (r 1.1) to deal with cases justly.

### Criminal cases

As is usual in criminal cases, the prosecution is under different, and more extensive, burdens than the accused.

The accused is only restricted by the rules of competence and compellability set out above and the defendant is under no obligation to call any particular witness. As we saw earlier (**4.4.2**), even the accused cannot be compelled to give evidence (although the accused's failure might give rise to an adverse inference of guilt under s 35 of the Criminal Justice and Public Order Act 1994: see **11.4.5**).

Leaving aside the rules of competence and compellability of witnesses set out above, the prosecution is under important obligations to make witnesses available at trial as a result of its general duty to act fairly. These obligations were considered in *R v Russell-Jones* [1995] 3 All ER 239, CA and *R v Brown* [1997] 1 Cr App R 112 and the effect of these considerations is as follows:

(a) The prosecution has a discretion as to which witnesses will be relied upon as part of the prosecution case.

(b) The statements of witnesses that will be relied upon must be served upon the defence. The statements of witnesses that are not relied upon should generally be disclosed as unused material (see *Criminal Litigation and Sentencing Manual*).

(c) Where a witness's statement has been served upon the defence (ie, it is a statement that will be relied upon) the prosecution must have that witness at court unless the defence have agreed that there is no need to call him or her (in which case the statement can serve as evidence in their absence: see **4.8.1** above).

(d) The prosecution advocate has a discretion as to whether or not to call any witness that has been required by the prosecution to attend court. This discretion is, however, fettered:
  (i) The discretion ought to be exercised in the interests of justice and so as to promote a fair trial.

    (ii) The prosecution should call a witness who will give direct evidence on the primary facts unless, with good reason, they regard the witness's evidence as unworthy of belief:

- It is a matter for the prosecution to decide whether the witness's evidence is 'direct' or merely marginal.

- It is a matter for the prosecution whether or not a witness is unworthy of belief. However, this requires something more than inconsistency between the witness's evidence and the prosecution case: there must be such inconsistency or a lack of credibility that they cannot assist the jury in interpreting the case.

  (e) The prosecution advocate when exercising this discretion is not obliged to offer a witness merely to give the defence material with which to attack the prosecution case.

The effect of these principles is that the prosecution has the primary responsibility for making witnesses available and is under an obligation to inform the defence of witnesses that are not of use to the prosecution case. This allows the defence to choose whether or not to call the witness. As will be seen in **Chapter 5**, there is some significance in who calls the witness. Where a witness is called by one party the other party can then cross-examine that witness. The cross-examining party has a much freer hand in presenting the evidence to the witness and challenging the evidence of that witness. The *Russell-Jones* principles set out above have sought to balance the need for the prosecution to disclose their case to the defence on the one hand with the need to ensure that the prosecution are not forced to call witnesses who will undermine the prosecution case but cannot be challenged when they do so. In *R v Smith* [2003] EWCA Crim 1240, the Court of Appeal refused to quash a conviction where the prosecution refused to call a witness to material facts whom the prosecution would have to have treated as hostile (see **5.2.5** for the meaning of 'hostile witness'). The court noted that while the investigation of that case could have been conducted differently, there were no grounds for challenging the exercise of the prosecutor's discretion.

### 4.7.2.2    Can one party prevent another party from calling a witness?

Generally only one party or another will want to call a witness. However, there may be situations in which a witness is retained by one party or that party will want to prevent the witness from giving evidence for the other side. Such a situation occurred in *Harmony Shipping Co SA v Saudi Europe Line Ltd* [1979] 1 WLR 1380, CA. The plaintiffs had sought advice from an expert as to the validity of a document. The expert advised that it was not authentic (which was unfavourable to their case). The defendants then instructed the same expert who gave the same advice. They therefore sought to call the expert, who then realised he had already advised the plaintiff and refused to attend court on behalf of the defendants. The defendant sought a summons to compel him to attend on their behalf. The order was granted and approved by the Court of Appeal.

Note that discussions between the expert and the plaintiffs in that case would be *privileged* (see **Chapter 14**). The record of those discussions and any report he wrote for the plaintiffs would not have to be disclosed to the defendants. However in *Harmony Shipping* it was not the communications and the report that were in issue, rather it was whether the witness himself could be forced to attend court to give evidence. The principle is that there is no property in a particular witness. However, a witness who has given evidence for one party cannot then be called to give evidence for the other party (*R v Kelly* The Times, 27 July 1985, CA).

### 4.7.2.3   When to call a witness

There may be important tactical issues surrounding when witnesses should be called. Generally an advocate will seek to present the witnesses in an order that presents an understandable and compelling case. However, are there any rules of evidence that regulate when particular witnesses may be called?

**The accused in criminal cases**

There are no rules restricting the order in which prosecution witnesses may be called, but the defence case is controlled by s 79 of the Police and Criminal Evidence Act 1984, the effect of which is as follows:

(a) The section applies when:

   (i)    the defence intend to call two or more witnesses 'to the facts of the case';

   (ii)   one of those witnesses will be the accused.

(b) The effect of the rule is that the accused will be called first.

(c) The provision therefore does not apply where the witness is a witness to something other than the facts of the case (eg, an expert witness giving his opinion).

(d) This provision does not put the accused under an obligation to testify if he or she wishes to call other witnesses.

(e) The statute does allow the court to direct that this provision will not apply. This might happen if the witness to be called before the accused will give evidence that is merely uncontroversial or if the calling of the other witness will make the accused's evidence easier to understand (for example, the other witness will put the accused's evidence into a context by explaining preceding events).

**Expert witnesses in civil cases**

Many of the rules of evidence are treated differently if the witness is an expert witness giving admissible opinion evidence within his or her field of expertise (this concept is explained in **Chapter 13**). Given that often the function of the expert may be to provide an expert opinion on matters established during trial, the court may rule that the experts in the case give his opinion after all the evidence of the facts has been adduced. This was the position in *Bayerische Rückversicherung AG v Clarkson Puckle Overseas Ltd* The Times, 23 January 1989, in which it was stated that this principle applies where experts have been called to give opinion evidence on the professional competence of another person. It may be, however, that this principle could be applied in cases where the expert evidence is on another matter but it would be useful to hear all evidence before calling the expert for either side, particularly as CPR, r 32.1(2), now gives the judge the power to control the order in which witnesses give their evidence.

### 4.7.2.4   Calling witnesses after the close of the case

Generally a party must call all of its witnesses before the close of its case. Only once this is done will the other party bear any burden to disprove the case against it. It is clearly not appropriate to hold witnesses back until the other party has attempted to prove their case. The prosecution or claimant generally have to call evidence first as they bear the burden of proving at least one issue in support of their case. The only exception to this is in civil cases where the defendant bears the evidential burden on all issues in dispute (*Pontifex v Jolly* (1839) 9 Car & P 202). In such a case the defence will call all of their evidence first.

The requirement that one party calls all witnesses before another party calls any witnesses is a result of the burden of proof. The rationale is that a party must make out a case before the other party is under any obligation to call any evidence. By the end of the starting party's case the issue is whether enough evidence has been called for the other party (usually the accused or the defendant) to have to disprove the issues raised. If so the second party begins attempting to disprove those issues. This system allows clarity as to what exactly has to be disproved and prevents the parties from calling or recalling witnesses. Therefore in *R v Day* [1940] 1 All ER 402, CA, a conviction was quashed because the prosecution were allowed to call a handwriting expert after their case had closed even though it was foreseeable that the defence would challenge the handwriting in question.

After the party going last has called its last witness the case closes and the parties will make representations to the tribunal of fact (closing speeches or submissions). In a jury trial the judge will sum up the case. The general rule is that no further evidence can be adduced once speeches or submissions have begun.

There are occasions when this general rule is not appropriate or is unnecessary. The court will allow witnesses to call evidence after the close of their case in three situations:

(a) Where the evidence in question simply corrects an omission to call evidence that is merely formal (*Price v Humphries* [1958] 2 QB 353, DC). For example, the consent of the Director or Public Prosecutions is required before a party can be prosecuted for riot under s 1 of the Public Order Act 1986. If the prosecution were to overlook proof of this matter during their case, the judge could allow its proof should, for example, the defence seek to persuade the court that the accused should be acquitted due to this oversight during a submission of no case to answer.

(b) The trial judge has a discretion to allow the prosecution to call further evidence to rebut a matter the defence has sought to prove if the matter has arisen *ex improviso* (*R v Scott* (1984) 79 Cr App R 49, CA). That means the matter is one that could not reasonably have been foreseen or anticipated by the prosecution. *R v Day*, referred to above, is a case in which the court decided that the matter could have been foreseen.

(c) There is a further discretion held by the judge. In *R v Francis* [1991] 1 All ER 225, the Court of Appeal recognised that there is a further discretion beyond the two situations noted above. In *Francis*, the prosecution had called evidence showing that an identification procedure had been conducted by the police and that a witness had identified the person in position number 20. However, the prosecution did not prove that the person at position number 20 was the accused. Prosecution counsel was under the impression that this was not disputed. Note that in contrast to the *ex improviso* discretion this issue could have been anticipated but because of communications between the defence and the prosecution, the latter were under the impression that there was no dispute. The Criminal Justice and Public Order Act 1996, s 5, now requires that the accused in criminal cases dealt with in the Crown Court identify their case in a defence statement. This clearly should have an impact on what should be foreseen. In *R v Johnson* [2001] EWCA 2312, the accused made a submission of no case to answer on the grounds that the prosecution had not proved that the defendant was present at the scene of the assault he was alleged to have committed. His defence statement stated that his defence was that he was not present at the scene of the crime. The judge ruled that the prosecution should be entitled to call evidence to make good their failure to prove the identity of the accused. The effect of the defence statement was to suggest that the defence did not challenge the prosecution case that the accused was present at the relevant time. This is a judicial discretion and therefore may be difficult to appeal. This discretion should not be exercised where the defence have begun to call their evidence (*R v Munnery* [1992] Crim LR 215, CA). However this can, occasionally happen. In *James v South Glamorgan County Council* (1994) 99 Cr App R 321, an important prosecution witness had been told to attend the wrong court and arrived after the prosecution case had closed. The Divisional Court affirmed the conviction even though the magistrates had allowed that witness to give evidence after the defence case had started. The witness could not have been the only witness on a fact in issue as the absence of such a witness would have led to a successful submission of no case to answer. In *Tuck v Vehicle Inspectorate*, 24 March 2004 (unreported), the Divisional court adopted a more relaxed approach, refusing to overturn a decision of the Magistrates' Court to allow the prosecution to recall a witness after the close of its case, stating that the recalling of a witness in such a situation was a matter for the discretion of the magistrates to be exercised by balancing the interests of the defendant and the public interest.

The judge may allow a witness to be called while the judge is summing up the case (*R v Sanderson* [1953] 1 WLR 392) but once the jury have retired to consider their verdict, there is no power to call witnesses (*R v Owen* [1952] 2 QB 362).

### 4.7.3 Judge's powers to call and examine witnesses

#### 4.7.3.1 Civil cases

CPR, r 32.1(1), gives the court a power to control the evidence adduced. It is likely that this extends to a power to call or to require parties to call witnesses.

#### 4.7.3.2 Criminal cases

The judge in Crown Court proceedings may call witnesses without the consent of either party (*R v Chapman* (1838) 8 Car & P 558; *R v Harris* [1927] 2 KB 587). A similar power exists for magistrates (*R v Haringay Justices, ex p DPP* [1996] 1 All ER 828, DC. It would also appear from *R v Olivia* [1965] 1 WLR 1028 that the judge can invite the prosecution to call witnesses. In *R v Sterk* [1972] Crim LR 391, it was stated that the judge can *order* the prosecution to call witnesses.

### 4.7.4 Securing the attendance of witnesses

The rules and procedures for securing the attendance of witnesses are complicated. What follows is a summary of the relevant law.

#### 4.7.4.1 Criminal cases

Different procedures for securing the attendance of witnesses apply in the Crown Court and the magistrates' courts.

Where any party suspects that a witness will not attend the Crown Court voluntarily (ie, where they think that the witness will have to be compelled), a witness summons can be sought under the Criminal Procedure (Attendance of Witnesses) Act 1965. The party seeking the summons must show that the witness will give evidence of material facts and will not voluntarily attend court. Failure to comply with the summons can be summarily punished with up to three months' imprisonment unless there is a just excuse. For detail of this procedure see *Blackstone's Criminal Practice*, 2004 or *Archbold*, 2004.

In the magistrates' court the attendance of unwilling witnesses can be secured by using a witness summons or a warrant under the Magistrates' Courts Act 1980, s 97. The law relating to witness summonses under s 97(1) is essentially the same as in the Crown Court. However, where the magistrates are satisfied that a witness summons will not secure the attendance of the witness, they may also issue a warrant under s 97(3) so that the witness can be forced to attend. Failure to be sworn or to give evidence, whether having attended voluntarily or as a result of a summons or under execution of a warrant may lead to imprisonment for up to a month or a fine of up to £2,500. For detail on this procedure see *Blackstone's Criminal Practice*, 2004.

### 4.7.4.2    Civil cases

The attendance of a witness in a civil case is secured by the issuing of a witness summons under CPR, Part 34. A witness summons can require attendance at court to give testimony or to produce documents. The summons should generally be served at least seven days before the hearing to which it relates (CPR, r 34.5(2)).

Failure to comply with the witness summons leads to sanctions depending on the court that issued the summons. In the county court the sanction is a fine of up to £1,000 (County Courts Act 1984, s 55). In the High Court failure to appear is a contempt of court (*Wyat v Wingford* (1729) 2 Ld Raym 1528).

For detailed consideration of witness summonses see *Blackstone's Civil Practice*, 2004 and the *Civil Litigation Manual*.

### 4.7.5    Protection of vulnerable witnesses in criminal cases

Many witnesses may not wish to attend court (and have to be compelled) for reasons of fear of the court process or due to actual or perceived threats from the accused or those linked to the accused. Furthermore, as we have seen, the courts will only allow witnesses to give evidence if they are capable of doing so in a meaningful way. Clearly fear and an incapacity to communicate are two factors that could lead either to poor evidence being admitted or to no evidence being admitted at all. To tackle these difficulties, Part II, Chapter I, of the Youth Justice and Criminal Evidence Act 1999 introduced a statutory regime of 'special measures directions'. These measures are complicated and what follows is only a summary of the legal framework under that Act. For the text of the statutes and more explanation see *Blackstone's Criminal Practice*, 2004 or *Archbold*, 2004.

### 4.7.5.1    Who may be eligible for a special measures direction?

There are two classes of parties who are eligible in principle for a special measures direction. These classes are set out in ss 16 and 17 of the 1999 Act.

Section 16 seeks to tackle problems with the competence or vulnerability of classes of witnesses. A person may be eligible for protection under s 16 if he or she:

- is under 17;
- suffers from a mental disability to such an extent that it will diminish the quality of his or her evidence;
- has a 'significant impairment of intelligence and social functioning';
- has a physical disability or disorder

Section 17 applies to any witness where the court is satisfied that the evidence of the witness is likely to be of less quality due to fear or distress in connection with testifying. This is therefore a matter for the court to determine. Section 17(2) requires the court to consider factors such as the offence in question, the age of the witness and factors relating to their culture and ethnicity and any behaviour alleged towards the witness by the accused or his family or associates. While the availability of such a direction is generally a matter for the court to determine, a complainant in a sexual case is automatically eligible unless he or she informs the court otherwise.

Special measures directions are not available for the accused: *R (on the application of S) v Waltham Forest Youth Court* [2004] EWHC 715 (Admin).

### 4.7.5.2   What special measures direction may be made?

Special measures directions should be made to solve, cure or reduce any difficulties that the particular vulnerability of the witness in question causes. Most can be made whether a witness qualifies under s 16 or 17 but, as **Table 4.1** shows, that is not always the case. **Table 4.1** identifies the measures available. The column on the left identifies the section of the 1999 Act empowering the direction in question.

Table 4.1  **Special measures directions**

| Section authorising direction | Special measures direction available | Available | | Limits |
|---|---|---|---|---|
| | | s 16 | s 17 | |
| 23 | Witness prevented from seeing accused by screen or other means | Yes | Yes | |
| 24 | Evidence given by live link | Yes | Yes | |
| 25 | Exclusion of specified person from court | Yes | Yes | Only if:<br>• sexual offence; or<br>• reasonable grounds for believing that person other than accused has sought or will seek to intimidate the witness about testifying. |
| 26 | Wigs and gowns not worn | Yes | Yes | |
| 27 | Pre-recorded video interview with witness to stand as evidence in chief | Yes | Yes | |
| 28 | Cross-examination or re-examination to be pre-recorded | Yes | Yes | Only if s 27 direction has been made. |
| 29 | Examination of witness through interpreter or court-approved intermediary | Yes | No | |
| 30 | Use of devices to enable communication between witness and others during examination | Yes | No | |

Clearly there is a risk that the jury may interpret the use of screens, pre-recording or video links as grounds for believing the defendant is a dangerous criminal and therefore guilty. Therefore where a direction is made in a jury trial, the court should issue any warning necessary to ensure that the direction does not prejudice the accused (s 32).

Where pre-recorded videos are played to the jury, the judge may allow the jury to have transcripts of the recording if this would be of assistance in following the recording (and not as a matter of course) and the judge should warn the jury that the video not the transcript is the evidence of the witness both at the time they are provided and during summing up (*R v Welstead* [1996] 1 Cr App R 59, CA, applying pre-existing common law rules). Furthermore the replaying of the video evidence for the jury should only take place in exceptional circumstances: *R v M* [1996] 2 Cr App R 56. Such reasons may arise where the jury wish to review how the video evidence was given rather than simply to rehear what was said (*R v Mullen* [2004] EWCA Crim 662). Allowing the reviewing of video evidence is a matter of judicial discretion and can be exercised in relation to the video evidence of any witnesses. However when such a reviewing of video evidence takes place the judge should ensure that the jury are reminded that they should not attach any greater weight to such reviewed evidence than the testimony of any other witnesses (*R v Mullen*).

### 4.7.5.3  How are special measures directions obtained?

The court can make special measures directions on application by either party or of its own motion (s 19(1)). Where the issue has been raised the court must determine (under s 19(2)):

(a) whether the witness is eligible (under either s 16 or s 17);

(b) whether:
   (i) the making of any measures (under ss 23 to 30) would be 'likely to improve the quality of the evidence'; and
   (ii) if so which measures should be made.

The court is required to pay particular attention to the views expressed by the witness and the effect that any direction might have on the evidence tendered (s 19(3)).

The direction is binding while the proceedings to which they relate continue (s 20(1)) or until varied or discharged by order of the court under s 20(2).

### 4.7.5.4  Particular rules concerning children

The above procedure applies in relation to all witnesses who might be eligible under either s 16 or s 17 with the exception of child witnesses. Where a witness is a child witness (ie, is under the age of 17), the court must apply s 21(3), the effect of which is:

(a) The court must first determine whether the witness is a child witness (ie, less than 17 years old).

(b) If so, the court *must* then make a direction that:
   (i) any relevant pre-recording will be admitted as evidence in chief (a s 27 direction); and
   (ii) any evidence not given by pre-recorded video will be given by live link (a s 24 direction).

(c) These two compulsory directions are not required in the following situations:
   (i) Neither direction is required if the facilities are not available in the court in question.
   (ii) A s 27 direction (pre-recorded video) should not be made if the court thinks that it is not in the interests of justice (for example if the recording could lead to prejudicial evidence).
   (iii) Neither direction is required if the court is of the opinion that it would not maximise the quality of the witness's evidence as far as practicable. This may be either because the particular witness does not appear to be likely to benefit from the direction in question or because, in the case of a pre-recorded interview, the interview does not provide material assistance or because other special measures directions can cater more than adequately for any difficulties the witness might confront. However, this third limitation on the

requirement for a special measures direction does not apply if the child witness in question is in need of special protection (see below).

(d) Where the child witness is giving evidence in relation to a sexual offence specified in s 35(3)(a) of the 1999 Act or one that involves kidnapping, assault, false imprisonment or child abduction the witness is 'in need of special protection'. In such circumstances, the court must make the following special measures directions:

(i) Pre-recording of the evidence in chief under s 27 (unless it would not be in the interests of justice and only if facilities are available).

(ii) The provision of all evidence by live link under s 24 (if facilities are available).

(iii) The pre-recording of the cross-examination and re-examination by any person other than the accused under s 28 direction (if facilities are available and only if the witness has not informed the court that he or she does not want such a direction made).

In *R (on the application of D) v Camberwell Green Youth Court* [2003] EWHC 227 (Admin), the Divisional Court rejected arguments that the requirement to make directions in favour of children by virtue of s 21 violated a right of the defendant to confront accusers which was protected by Article 6 of the European Convention.

### 4.7.5.5  Chart

**Figure 4.2** is a chart that illustrates the considerations the court must take into account in determining which, if any, special measures directions are available to a witness.

## 4.7.6  Live television links

### 4.7.6.1  Criminal cases

Witnesses who are outside the jurisdiction can also give their evidence by live video link under s 32 of the Criminal Justice Act 1988. This is only permissible in criminal proceedings where the accused is being:

- tried in the Crown Court on indictment;
- appealing from a trial on indictment;
- tried in the youth court or appealing from the youth court to the Crown Court.

These provisions are currently only in force in relation to proceedings for murder or related offences or serious frauds under the Criminal Justice Act 1987, s 1(5) or s 4.

### 4.7.6.2  Civil cases

Witnesses in civil courts may give evidence by video link or by such other means as the courts allow by CPR, r 32.3. Note that this is not stated only to be possible if the witness is outside of the jurisdiction although it seems that there should be good reason for dispensing with the requirement that the witness attend court. As always, it would be necessary to ensure that the court has the facilities available to receive evidence by live link.

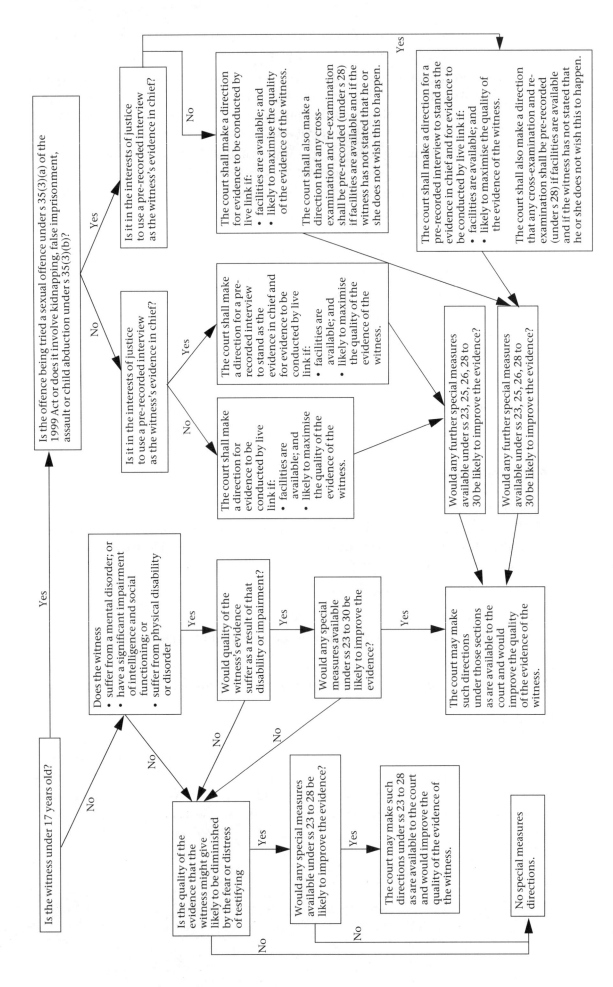

**Figure 4.2** Matters to be taken into account in making special measures directions

## 4.8  Activity

To test your understanding of many of the issues in this case, attempt **activity 4.2** in **Appendix 1**.

# 5 Witness evidence

## 5.1 Introduction

In the previous chapter we considered when a witness was able to attend court to give evidence and when they could be forced to do so. This chapter considers some of the rules of evidence that regulate how a witness may be questioned.

The examination of each witness goes through three stages:

- Examination-in-chief by the party calling him or her.
- Cross-examination by any other party.
- Re-examination by the party calling him or her.

In addition to examining the rules of evidence applicable at each of these stages, this chapter will examine the way in which the rules of evidence treat suspect witnesses.

It will be seen in this chapter that there are different rules restricting how each stage should be conducted. Before considering what these different rules are, it is worth attempting to understand *why* they should be different. What is the difference between examining your own witness and examining the witnesses of other parties?

1. The function of a witness at trial is to give truthful and accurate evidence on matters within his or her competence and knowledge with a view to assisting the tribunal of fact to reach conclusions on the facts in issue. We shall see later on in the Manual that there are various rules of evidence preventing witnesses from giving evidence that is not within their 'competence and knowledge' (the rule against hearsay in **Chapter 8** and the restrictions on opinion evidence in **Chapter 12**). We shall therefore concentrate in this chapter on the extent to which witnesses can give truthful and accurate testimony that will assist the tribunal in deciding the facts in issue.

2. There are a number of difficulties that might prevent a witness from giving truthful and accurate evidence. Even a willing witness giving evidence in court might forget important details or might fail to explain them sufficiently clearly. The details of an event might be forgotten in the time it takes the case to get to court. Also not all witnesses called by a party will attend willingly. As we saw in **Chapter 4**, some witnesses have to be compelled to give evidence on behalf of a party. While many compelled witnesses will give truthful and accurate testimony once they are at court, others will try not to help the party calling them (or even to harm their case).

3. It would be tempting to 'help' the witness by asking questions that suggest the answer to the question so that he or she is prompted to give the required answer. We shall see later in this chapter that a party cannot simply adopt this approach of asking 'leading' questions for his or her own witness. There are rules that prevent an advocate from telling the witness what to say so that the witness can repeat it. As we shall see, the rules for questioning your own witness in court are designed to ensure

that he or she gives his or her own evidence. However the court has approached this area practically. We shall see in the course of this chapter that some allowance is made to 'refresh' the memory of a witness. We shall also see that where a witness called by the party is considered to be 'hostile' to that party's case, the court will allow that party more freedom in the way that questions are posed.

4.  The primary purpose of cross-examination of witnesses for other parties is to 'put' your own case. Often this will involve challenging that witness on a fact-in-issue. In cross-examining a witness to an assault, for example, you would probably have to challenge the witness' evidence that your client struck the first blow. However cross-examination will go beyond simply arguing about the facts of the case. Often the questioning will seek to establish facts that will assist your client (not all witnesses called by other parties are completely hostile to every detail of your case). For example, the witness to the assault above might be prepared to agree that the victim of the assault was acting in an aggressive manner thereby assisting the defence of self-defence. Furthermore a lot of cross-examination challenges the credibility of the evidence of the witness. You might suggest that the witness to the assault was too far away to see clearly what was going on or was distracted by other events or that he or she is biased against your client and therefore not telling the truth. In all of these situations the issue in question is not what in fact happened at the time of the assault (ie the facts in issue) but the weight to be attached to the evidence of the witness when he or she gives evidence on those facts in issue (ie collateral facts). Note the importance of the concepts of relevance, weight, facts in issue and collateral facts. They are vital in understanding this chapter. Have a look at **1.3** and **1.4** to remind yourself of them.

5.  There are fewer restrictions on cross-examination than on examination-in-chief. However there are restrictions imposed for policy reasons. The cross-examination of complainants in sexual cases is restricted following concerns about the difficulties in getting such witnesses to give evidence due to the ordeal of doing so. More generally the courts have restricted the extent to which parties may attack the credibility of the witnesses for other parties (whether by cross-examination or by calling other evidence). This restriction seeks to keep trials focussed on the main issues so as to reduce the expense and inconvenience of trials both for the parties and for the state.

6.  The main purpose of re-examination is to cover matters that were *not* dealt with in examination-in-chief. As the cross-examination of a witness could raise matters for the first time, re-examination allows those and only those matters to be dealt with by the party calling the witness. It is not an opportunity to conduct the evidence-in-chief again.

7.  Leading questions are those questions that suggest the answer to the question posed such as, 'Did you see the tall man hit the shorter man?' Non-leading questions do not suggest the answer such as 'What did you see?' Technically the latter question suggests that the witness saw something but the courts have taken a pragmatic line on leading and non-leading questions. See the *Advocacy Manual* and *Blackstone's Criminal Practice*, 2004.

## 5.2   Examination-in-chief

### 5.2.1   The general rules of examination-in-chief

As has been noted above the general rule is that a witness cannot be asked 'leading' questions in examination-in-chief. That a question is leading does not affect its admissibility but can reduce the weight to attached to it (*Moor v Moor* [1954] 1 WLR 927).

The courts have however adopted a practical approach to leading questions. A witness may be led on introductory matters such has his or her name or occupation. Furthermore, a witness can also be led on matters that are not in dispute. Therefore if there is no challenge that a witness was present at an event, it would be permissible to ask a question such as 'Were you at the Freeholder Public House at 7 pm on the 7th of March?' rather than 'Where were you at 7 pm on the 7th of March'.

### 5.2.2   Refreshing the memory of witnesses

We noted above that even a willing witness might forget details of an event that he or she is called to give evidence about, especially given that litigation might take place months or even years after the initial investigation.

#### 5.2.2.1   Refreshing memory when not giving evidence

Before giving evidence, a witness may see a copy of any document made since the incident (note this does not have to be at or about the same time as the incident or events). The document will often be a statement prepared by the police or by a lawyer acting for the party calling the witness, but this is not a requirement; any private document can be used for this purpose. The use of such statements was approved in *R v Richardson* [1971] 2 QB 484, where it was recognised that requiring witnesses to give evidence without seeing such statements would cause more difficulty for honest than for dishonest witnesses and would make evidence-in-chief a test of memory rather than truthfulness. *Richardson* also ruled that where a number of witnesses are handed statements for the purpose of refreshing their memories in this way, they must not be allowed to compare the contents of each statement.

Where prosecution witnesses have refreshed their memory before giving evidence, it is desirable that the defence should be informed of this (*Worley v Bentley* [1976] 2 All ER 449). However a failure to do this will not, on its own, be a ground for acquittal (*R v Westwall* [1976] 2 All ER 812).

The judge may exercise his or her discretion to allow a witness who has started giving evidence to use a statement to refresh his or her memory (*R v Da Silva* [1990] 1 WLR 31). This will be possible if the witness:

- states that he or she cannot remember the details of the events
- made a document closer to the time
- did not read the document before giving evidence, and
- now wishes to read that document.

It would appear from *R v South Ribble Magistrates' Court, ex p Cochrane* [1996] 2 Cr App R 544, DC that the conditions are not strict requirements. In that case a witness who had read the document but had not remembered it properly was allowed to refresh his memory again.

Where a witness is allowed to refresh his or her memory outside of the court in this way, he or she must not be allowed to keep the memory-refreshing document when giving evidence.

### 5.2.2.2 Refreshing memory while giving evidence

There are also circumstances in which a witness can refresh his or her memory while giving evidence. The position in criminal proceedings is stated in the Criminal Justice Act 2003, s 139. Under that section, a witness may refresh his or her memory at any time in the course of giving evidence if the witness testifies that:

- the document from which memory is to be refreshed records his or her recollection at an earlier time (s 139(1)(a)); and

- his or her recollection was likely to be better when the statement was made (s 139(1)(b)).

Note that this test is similar to that for refreshing memory before giving evidence (**5.2.2.1** below) but that s 139 of the 2003 Act does not replace that test. The effect of s 139 is to harmonise the rules for use of memory refreshing documents before and during testimony in criminal proceedings.

Furthermore if a previous account was recorded and a transcript made of that recording, the witness will be able to use the transcript of the account in similar circumstances (s 139(2)).

In civil proceedings, the position is still governed by the common law. However, it is worth remembering that in most civil proceedings, the witness statement may be ordered to stand as the evidence-in-chief of a witness (pursuant to CPR, r 32.5(2)). For this reason, it is unlikely that a witness in civil proceedings will wish to rely on a memory refreshing document until the cross-examination or re-examination stages of testimony.

The circumstances in which a witness will be allowed to use a memory-refreshing document while giving his or her evidence at common law are:

(a) The document was made or verified at the time of the incident or events or so shortly thereafter that the facts were fresh in his or her memory.

(b) If the witness does not remember the events, the document must be the original if it is available.

(c) The document can be inspected by the court (see **5.2.2.3** below).

**Made or verified**

In *R v Kelsey* (1982) 74 Cr App R 213, CA it was held that where a note had been made by a police officer and read back to the eye-witness, who then confirmed it, that note had been 'verified' by the eye-witness.

**At the time of the events or shortly thereafter**

Whether a particular document was made sufficiently shortly after the event is a question of fact and degree (*R v Simmonds* [1969] 1 QB 685). In *R v Da Silva* [1990] 1 WLR 31, CA it was stated that whether a particular period was short enough will depend on the nature of the evidence. If the witness attempts to give detailed evidence about an event (for example, a conversation) the period between that event and the making of the memory-refreshing document would have to be shorter than if the witness simply attempted to give a general impression of the event. Note that this requirement is stricter than for documents used to refresh memory outside of court and for memory refreshing documents in criminal proceedings.

### Original documents

If the witness does not remember the details of the event at all and wishes to rely upon a memory-refreshing document ('past recollection recorded'), the original must be used if it is available (*Doe d Church & Phillips v Perkins* (1790) 3 TR 749). If it is not available, a copy may be used if it can be proved to be an accurate copy (*Topham v McGregor* (1844) 1 Car & Kir 320). If the witness wishes to use the document as a prompt so that he or she will then remember the events ('present recollection revived'), then it would appear that a copy of the document will suffice even if the original is available.

The court will sometimes treat documents written using other sources as the original document. In *R v Cheng* (1976) 63 Cr App R 20, an officer was allowed to use a committal statement prepared by referring to his notebook, which had since been lost. Although the statement was not a perfect copy it substantially reproduced the notes. In *Attorney-General's Reference (No 3 of 1979)* (1979) 69 Cr App R 411, a notebook record compiled from notes jotted down during two hours of interview could be used as a memory-refreshing document even though it was not claimed to be a complete record of the interview. In *R v Mills* [1962] 1 WLR 1152, a note made of a conversation between two accused that had been recorded could be used as a memory-refreshing document even though it had been compiled with the assistance of a tape recording of the conversation. That tape recording was not admitted in evidence.

### 5.2.2.3    Inspection and use of the memory-refreshing document

Generally a document that is used to refresh memory (whether before or during the giving of evidence) does not become evidence in the case. The evidence is the testimony of the witness that has been prompted by the document rather than the document itself.

However, any document used to refresh the memory of a witness should be available for inspection by the other parties. As it is not evidence it will not be seen by the tribunal of fact nor will it be exhibited.

However in *R v Sekhon* (1987) 85 Cr App R 19, CA it was stated that a memory-refreshing document may be shown to the tribunal of fact in the following situations:

(a) The document is used in cross-examination and goes beyond those parts for which it was used to refresh memory.

(b) The inspection of the memory-refreshing document by the tribunal of fact is necessary to determine a point in issue. In *R v Bass* [1953] 1 QB 680, CA the documents in question were two police notebooks which the defence alleged to have been concocted. The Court of Appeal stated that police officers could collaborate in writing up notes but that the jury should have had sight of the notebooks to determine the credibility of the police officers (who had denied any collaboration at all).

(c) The document becomes a previous inconsistent statement (see **5.3.4**).

(d) It would be necessary for the tribunal of fact to see the document so that they can follow the cross-examination of the witness (for example, if the cross-examination will refer to particular parts of the document in posing questions).

(e) It would be difficult for the tribunal of fact to follow the testimony of the witness who has refreshed his or her memory without having sight of the document (because the testimony is lengthy or complicated).

In situations (d) and (e) above, the document will not become evidence. Rather the document is shown as this will assist in the reception of other evidence (the testimony) and it was noted in *Sekhon* that care should be exercised before allowing a jury to see a document where the evidence was contested and where there was a risk that the jury would treat the document as evidence.

In the other situations the record may become evidence.

Situation (a) above requires further analysis. Consider the following example. You act for Alice, who is charged with assault on Bernice. A police officer gives evidence-in-chief, using his notebook, that he attended a street outside a nightclub where he saw an injured girl, Bernice, who was 'very upset' and that following a conversation he then arrested Alice. Alice's defence is she acted in self-defence. Upon inspection of the notebook you see that, in addition to the above matters, the notebook also records that Bernice was acting aggressively and appeared to be under the influence of drink or drugs. If you limit your cross-examination to matters that arise from the evidence-in-chief, ie that Bernice was not 'upset', the notebook does not become evidence. However, if you put to the police officer that Bernice was acting aggressively or appeared intoxicated, you have gone beyond the matters covered in evidence-in-chief and therefore the notebook will become evidence that can be inspected by the jury.

In civil cases, the statement in the memory-refreshing document will be evidence of the truth of the contents by virtue of ss 1 and 6 of the Civil Evidence Act 1995.

In criminal cases the current law is that the document is only evidence of the credibiiity of the maker. However when s 120(3) is brought into force, such statements will be evidence of the truth of the matters stated.

### 5.2.3  The rule against previous consistent statements

Consider the following two cases:

*Corke v Corke* [1958] P 93, CA: a husband alleged adultery against his wife, the wife wanted to give evidence that she had called her doctor requesting a medical examination to prove she had not had recent sexual intercourse.

*R v Roberts* [1942] 1 All ER 187, CA: the accused was charged with murder, having shot a girl. The accused gave evidence that the gun went off by accident and sought to call his father to give evidence that two days after the shooting the accused had said that it was an accident.

In each case the statement in question could have two potential purposes. In both cases they could have been evidence of the thing alleged. In *Corke* the wife's statement could have proved that she had not had sexual intercourse (on the logic that she would only have made the request for an inspection if she thought it would be favourable). In *Roberts* the statement could have shown that the shooting was an accident.

However the statements had another potential purpose. Each one would have supported the account given by the party in question when they came to give evidence on oath. In each case that was how the party was trying to use it. In other words, the statement would be admissible not to prove the thing alleged to be true but that when the party said that very thing in the witness box, they were more worthy of belief because they had said it previously.

In each case the statements were held not to be admissible. As a general rule the court will not allow statements that have been made by a person outside of court to be admitted to bolster their testimony.

If the statements were being admitted to prove the truth of the thing alleged by them, they would be governed by evidential rules of hearsay which are covered in **Chapter 8**.

The general rule is that a previous or self-serving statement made by a witness is not admissible to support their testimony. The rule applies whether or not the person seeking to prove the previous consistent statement is the witness himself or herself or another person.

### 5.2.4    Exceptions to the rule against previous consistent statements

#### 5.2.4.1    Hearsay

As noted above, statements made out of court could have the purpose of proving something in their own right rather than simply bolstering the credibility of a witness. These are hearsay statements. Generally out of court statements are not admissible for this purpose either, but there are numerous exceptions to the rule against hearsay evidence. See **Chapter 8**. When a statement is admissible as an exception to the rule against hearsay evidence or as 'original evidence' (see **Chapter 8**), it is admissible whether or not it happens to be consistent with the testimony of the witness.

#### 5.2.4.2    Memory-refreshing documents

As was noted above at **5.2.2.3**, a document used as a memory-refreshing document may become evidence at trial. In criminal cases the statement is relevant to the credibility of the witness. In civil cases the statement is evidence of the truth of what it alleges.

#### 5.2.4.3    Previous identifications

Identification of an accused person will generally take place before trial. The detailed rules on identification procedures is set out in **Chapter 13**.

Evidence of an out of court identification is admissible (*R v Christie* [1914] AC 545). In *Sealey v The State* [2002] UKPC 52, the Privy Council stated that a previous statement identifying the accused would be admissible if made by a person called as a witness, but not if made by a person not called as a witness. In the latter circumstance the statement would be an inadmissible hearsay statement. The out of court identification should generally be proved before the witness is asked to identify the accused in court. Also, where there has not been an out of court identification, a dock identification should be avoided (*R v Cartwright* (1914) 10 Cr App R 219). However, in the magistrates' court, it would appear that it is established practice (for practical reasons) to allow dock identifications in road traffic cases unless the accused has alleged he was not the driver or has requested an identification parade (*Barnes v Chief Constable of Durham* [1997] 2 Cr App R 505, DC).

#### 5.2.4.4    Complainants in sexual cases

If the complainant (ie the victim) of a sexual offence makes a voluntary complaint at the first reasonable opportunity then the person to whom the complaint was made may give evidence of what was said (*R v Lillyman* [1896] 2 QB 167).

The rule is limited to sexual cases (*R v Jarvis and Jarvis* [1991] Crim LR 374, CA).

Such evidence is relevant to two issues. First of all it shows the consistency of the complainant's allegations (ie to bolster the credibility of the his or her evidence) and to negative consent (if consent is in issue). The jury should be given the Judicial Studies Board standard direction, which is that the evidence 'may possibly help you to decide whether she has told you the truth. It cannot be independent confirmation of [the complainant's] evidence since it does not come from a source independent of her' (*R v NK* [1999] Crim LR 980).

The rule covers complaints whether they are made orally or in writing and will even apply to a private note not intended to be seen by anyone other than the complainant (*R v B* [1997] Crim LR 220).

As the complaint is evidence of consistency, if the complainant does not give evidence, there is nothing for the statement to be consistent with and it should therefore not be admissible (*R v Guttridges* (1840) 9 C & P 471). Equally a previous statement that is inconsistent serves no useful purpose and should not be admitted (*R v Wright* (1987) 90 Cr App R 91). If the statement could be consistent, it is for the jury to decide whether it is (*Lillyman*).

Insofar as the statement is to be used to show lack of consent, the best view appears to be that the statement is not admitted to prove lack of consent as such but to prove consistency with the denial of consent by the complainant in his or her evidence, and therefore such evidence should not be admitted if the complainant does not testify (*Kilby v The Queen* (1973) 129 CLR 460). The evidence of the previous consistent statement has to be given by someone other than the complainant as the purpose of the evidence is to bolster the credibility of the complaint. The complainant cannot give evidence of his or her own complaint (*White v R* [1999] AC 210).

The complaint has to be made at the first reasonable opportunity after the offence (*R v Osborne* [1905] 1 KB 551, CA), which is a question of fact to be determined by the judge in each case (*R v Cummings* [1948] 1 All ER 551, CA). Factors that the court will consider will include the character of the complainant and his or her relationship both with the person to whom the complaint was made and with other persons to whom the complaint might have been made. Furthermore the court recognised in *R v Valentine* [1996] 2 Cr App R 213, CA that victims of sexual offences may need time to be able to bring themselves to tell others that they have been attacked. To be an admissible previous consistent statement, the complaint does not have to be the first complaint made (*R v Lee* (1912) 7 Cr App R 31, CA). However in *R v Birks* [2002] EWCA Crim 3091, a complaint was made from six months or a year after the last in a sequence of sexual assaults that spanned a 12-month period. The Court of Appeal quashed the conviction resulting from the complaint having been adduced at trial. It was held that although the complaint had been made within a reasonable time, it was not 'recent'. The court noted that such statements as had been admitted in previous cases had all been made within a week of the act to which they related. It would therefore appear that to be admissible a statement must be made both at the first reasonable opportunity and also close enough in time to the alleged offence to be 'recent'.

The complaint must be voluntary in that it must not have been solicited by leading or suggestive questioning (*R v Osborne*) but the fact that the complaint is the response to questions does not automatically make it inadmissible. As Ridley J said in *Osborne*, questions such as 'What is the matter?' or 'Why are you crying?' would not render the complaint inadmissible but questions such as 'Did [the accused] assault you?' probably would do so.

### 5.2.4.5 Statements upon confrontation

The criminal courts will regularly allow evidence of what a person says when confronted by police officers or other investigators into a criminal act. The precise scope of this exception is not clear. This exception overlaps with the rules of evidence on confessions.

As a general rule there are three ways that a person might react to being confronted by a police officer about incriminating facts or upon being questioned:

(a) He or she might deny everything or give a complete excuse (such as being somewhere else entirely at the time). This is generally known as a exculpatory statement.

(b) He or she might admit everything. This is generally known as a confession or an inculpatory statement.

(c) He or she might admit some of the matters alleged but deny others. For example, he or she might admit to being at the scene of the crime and to having hit the victim but then state that he or she was acting in self-defence. This is a 'mixed' statement in that it could assist both the prosecution and defence at trial.

Wholly inculpatory statements (confessions) are admissible in principle as evidence of the truth of what is alleged as an exception to the rule against hearsay. Hearsay and confessions will be considered in **Chapters 8** to **9**. We need not bother with them for the minute, not least of all because they are unlikely to be a previous *consistent* statement when the accused goes on to plead not guilty. What, however, about statements that a person makes to the police that are complete denials of the accusations ('exculpatory') or partial denials ('mixed') statements?

### Exculpatory statements

Such statements are not admissible as truth of the matters alleged in them. In *R v Storey* (1968) 52 Cr App R 334, CA, the prosecution had been allowed to give evidence that the defendant, when confronted with drugs, had alleged that another person had brought them into her house against her will. The Court of Appeal held that, while admissible, the statement was not evidence of the truth of what was alleged. Instead it was held that the statement was admissible as evidence of the *reaction* of the accused upon being confronted with the incriminating facts or articles (in this case that she had come up with a denial and an explanation immediately upon being confronted).

In *R v Pearce* (1979) 69 Cr App R 365, CA, Lord Widgery CJ stated the following principles:

(a) Admissions are always evidence of the facts stated.

(b) A statement that is not an admission is admissible to show the attitude of the maker when it was made.

(c) This is not necessarily restricted to statements made immediately upon being confronted for the first time. However, the longer the period between the confrontation and the subsequent exculpatory statement, the less weight that might be attached to it.

(d) Not all exculpatory statements made in reaction to confrontation will be admitted. A written statement carefully prepared by the accused and handed to the police to form part of the prosecution case could be excluded by the trial judge (for an example of such an exclusion see *R v Newsome* (1980) 71 Cr App R 325).

This exception to the rule against previous consistent statements does not require the court to admit all previous consistent exculpatory statements. In *R v Tooke* (1989) 90 Cr App R 417, the accused sought to admit a written exculpatory statement after he had made an oral statement to the police. The Court of Appeal upheld the trial judge's decision to exclude the statement on the grounds that it added nothing to the previous oral statement. In *R v Lowe* [2003] EWCA Crim 3182, the Court of Appeal approved of a decision by the trial judge not to allow a defence statement prepared pursuant to s 5 of the Criminal Procedure and Investigations Act 1996. The Court of Appeal accepted that there was no basis for treating this as anything other than a previous consistent statement. Having been made over four months after the arrest of the accused the statement could not have been evidence of reaction to any accusation.

It is worth bearing in mind at this point that the *failure* of an accused person to mention exculpatory facts when questioned by police may be subject to an adverse inference of guilt by virtue of s 34 of the Criminal Justice and Public Order Act 1994.

As a result of s 34 and this common law exception to the rule against previous consistent statements, it is now standard practice for police interviews of the accused to be adduced as evidence as part of the prosecution case even if the interview consists wholly of denials or 'no comment' responses. Such denials or refusals to comment will constitute evidence of reaction to being confronted.

However it is important to remember that not all exculpatory statements are admissible. Exculpatory statements volunteered by an accused person are not admissible at all.

This exception to the rule against previous consistent statements appears to be confined to criminal cases. However in civil cases, a previous consistent statement is admissible, with permission of the court, as evidence of the truth of the matters alleged (ie, as admissible hearsay evidence) under s 6 of the Civil Evidence Act 1995 (see **Chapter 8**).

### Mixed statements

The result of the approach set out above is that in criminal cases inculpatory statements are admissible to prove what is said but that exculpatory statements are only admissible to prove the reaction of the accused to an accusation. What if the statement by the accused admits part of the offence but denies other parts or admits the offence but then raises a defence?

The approach adopted by the courts is that the whole of the statement is admissible to prove the truth of what is alleged (*R v Sharp* [1988] 1 All ER 65, HL). The logic of this approach is that to admit only inculpatory parts of the statement would be to put those admissions out of context. The jury should be directed to consider the statement as a whole (*R v Duncan* (1981) 73 Cr App R 359). Once the whole statement is put before the jury, it would be asking too much of them to use some parts of it as evidence of the truth of what is said and other parts as evidence of consistency or reaction. The whole of the statement is therefore evidence of the truth of what is said.

In fact nearly any statement could be said technically to be mixed, in that there will nearly always be something that could be said to be an admission, however small, of a relevant fact. However in *R v Garrod* [1997] Crim LR 445, the Court of Appeal held that before a statement could be treated by the court as 'mixed' it must include at least an admission of fact that was *significant* to an issue in the case in that it added some degree of weight to the proof of an issue that the prosecution had to prove.

In *R v Aziz* [1995] 3 All ER 149, HL it was stated that mixed statements are only admissible as truth of their contents if tendered by the prosecution. If the prosecution do not prove the statement, the defence cannot seek to tender it as evidence of the truth of its contents.

### 5.2.4.6   Statements in rebuttal of allegations of recent fabrication

This exception to the rule against previous consistent statements applies in both civil and criminal cases.

The mere fact that the cross-examination of a witness suggests that the witness is not worthy of belief does not allow the proof of previous statements by that witness that are consistent with the testimony he or she has just given. This is so even if the cross-examination shows that the witness previously said something inconsistent with what he or she is now saying (*R v Beattie* (1989) 89 Cr App R 302). To do so would make most cases much longer and more expensive where each parties call witnesses to testify as to what each witness did or did not say on numerous previous occasions.

However, where the cross-examination goes further than this and suggests that the witness has *fabricated* the evidence he or she gives, the party calling the witness may prove that the witness made consistent statements on previous occasions to rebut any suggestion that the witness's account was made up recently (*R v Oyesiku* (1971) 56 Cr App R 240; *Flanagan v Fahy* [1918] 2 IR 361). The allegation has to be that the account was made up at some time between the events in question and trial, not simply that the witness or the testimony is untruthful or unreliable (*Fox v General Medical Council* [1960] 1 WLR 1017, PC).

In *R v Oyesiku* the Court of Appeal approved the approach set out in the Australian case *Nominal Defendant v Clement* (1961) 104 CLR 476, which was in effect that the judge should not allow the evidence unless:

(a) The cross-examination has suggested that the witness's evidence has been recently invented or reworded.

(b) The previous statement is consistent with the testimony of the witness.

(c) The previous consistent statement, having regard to the time and circumstances in which it was made, tends to answer the suggestion of fabrication.

To illustrate this approach consider the case of *Flanagan v Fahy*:

(a) The cross-examination had suggested that the witness for the plaintiff had made up his testimony (that a will was a forgery) out of hostility to the defendant.

(b) The witness had made a previous statement to another person that the will was a forgery.

(c) That statement had predated the hostility between the defendant and the witness.

(d) The previous consistent statement was therefore admissible to rebut the suggestion that the testimony was fabricated.

As the evidence rebuts the suggestion of a subsequent fabrication, the justification for calling such evidence derives from the suggestion in cross-examination that the witness has recently fabricated the evidence (*R v Williams* [1998] Crim LR 494, CA), the statement has to disprove that the testimony has been recently fabricated. This is achieved by proving that the same thing was said before the motive or reason for fabrication arose.

The previous consistent statement can be proved either during the re-examination of the witness or by calling the other person to whom the statement was made (*R v Wilmot* (1989) 89 Cr App R 341).

What does the previous consistent statement prove? In criminal cases (where this rule is still a matter of common law), the statement is not evidence of the matters alleged but simply evidence that the testimony of the witness is worthy of belief. In other words, the statement is relevant to prove the credibility of the witness (*R v Y* [1995] Crim LR 155, CA).

In civil cases the common law rule has been abolished. The previous consistent statement is now admissible to prove the truth of what is alleged in it (s 6(2) of the Civil Evidence Act 1995).

### 5.2.5   Activity

To test your understanding of the rules relating to previous statements used during evidence in chief, attempt **activity 5.1** in **Appendix 1**.

### 5.2.6   Criminal Justice Act 2003

The admissibility of previous consistent statements has been altered by the Criminal Justice Act 2003. This Act is not yet in force. When it is brought into force, it will have the following effects.

The Act does not change the admissibility of previous consistent statements. However the Act does change the rule that such statements are relevant only to the credibility of the maker of the statement. Instead, pursuant to s 120, where the following statements are admitted under the existing common law rules, they will be admissible to prove the matters stated in them:

- A statement admitted to rebut a suggestion of fabrication (see **5.2.4.6**).
- A memory refreshing document that becomes evidence as a result of cross-examination (see **5.2.2.3** and **5.2.4.2**).

Additionally, s 120(4)–(7) provides that certain previous statements shall be admissible to prove the matters stated in them. This will only happen if the maker testifies that the statement was made by him or her and that it is true to the best of his or her knowledge and belief (s 120(4)(b)). In such circumstances a previous statement can be admissible to prove the matters stated in it if all three of the following conditions are made out:

- the statement is one of identification or description and the subject matter is a person, an object or a place (s 120(5));
- the statement was made 'when the matters stated were fresh in his memory' but the witness has forgotten those matters and 'cannot reasonably be expected to remember them well enough to give oral evidence of them' (s 120(6)); and
- the maker of the statement is the victim of at least one of the offences to which the proceedings relate and the statement is the complaint about the offence, freely made 'as soon as could reasonably be expected' after the incident (s 120(7)).

The effect of s 120(4)-(7) is to make a certain category of previous statement by a complainant admissible not to prove the credibility of the evidence given at trial (as is the case at common law: see **5.2.4.4**) but to substitute that testimony where the witness would not be able to recollect the matters complained of. Section 120 in this respect is broader than the common law in that it does not apply only to complainants in sexual offences (s 120(7)) and that the admissibility of such statements is not effected by having been elicited by the questioning of another (s 120(8)).

On the other hand s 120(4)–(7) is narrower in that the section does not apply where the witness is able to recall the detail of the complaint but a party wishes to prove it to support the testimony given by the complainant as a witness.

### 5.2.7  Unfavourable and hostile witnesses

As we have already seen, a party is not allowed to lead his or her witness to give any particular answer but must allow the witness to give the evidence in his or her own words. However, we also recognised that some witnesses will fail to say what it was hoped they would say or will have been compelled to attend and may not be willing to voluntarily support the case for the party calling him or her.

The simple failure of a witness to say what it was hoped they would say is commonly known as 'failing to come up to proof' (ie failing to say what was said in the proof of evidence). Such a witness is not a 'hostile witness' but an 'unfavourable witness'. Even a witness who flatly contradicts what was said in the proof of evidence or in a statement is not necessarily 'hostile'. An unfavourable witness of this sort cannot be contradicted by the party calling him or her. Previous inconsistencies cannot be put to him or her nor can suggestions be made in questioning or by calling other evidence that the witness is biased or dishonest in any way. All that a party can do is to call another witness to give the 'right' evidence on the matter in question (*Ewer v Ambrose* (1825) 3 B & C 746).

However, in more extreme situations the court may determine that a witness called by a party is 'hostile' to that party, in which case some of the restrictions that apply to examination-in-chief will be relaxed. Stephen in his *Digest on the Law of Evidence* defined a hostile witness as 'not desirous of telling the truth at the instance of the party calling him'. It is a matter of judicial discretion whether the witness is hostile or not (*Fraser v Warren* (1956) 40 Cr App R 160). The matter should be determined in the absence of the jury (*R v Darby* [1989] Crim LR 817, CA).

Relevant factors for determining whether a witness is hostile will include:

- The demeanour of the witness (including but not requiring animosity to the party calling him or her).

- The evidence he or she gives.

- The evidence he or she does not give including complete silence (*R v Thompson* (1976) 64 Cr App R 96, CA).

- The mere fact that the witness has made a previous statement that contradicts the witness's testimony in whole or in part does not automatically entitle the witness to be treated as hostile (*R v Maw* [1994] Crim LR 841). In such a situation the judge should consider allowing the witness to refresh his or her memory by looking at the document in question. In *R v Corcoran* [2003] EWCA Crim 43, it was noted that ordering an adjournment to allow a witness to reread a previous statement was not always appropriate and would often require careful explanation as to the sequence of events leading to a change of testimony where this process had been adopted.

- A witness who does not want to give evidence through fear is not necessarily hostile (*R v Honeyghon and Sayles* [1999] Crim LR 221).

Once a witness is treated as hostile, the witness may be asked leading questions (*R v Thompson*). Furthermore, the party calling the witness may ask the witness about previous inconsistent statements and, if they are denied, may prove them (Criminal Procedure Act 1865, s 3 and *Greenough v Eccles* (1859) 5 CBNS 786). For the rules relating to the proof of previous inconsistent statements, see **5.3.4** below. For now it is worth noting that in criminal cases the previous inconsistent statement is not evidence of the facts stated but only of the credibility of the witness (ie insofar as the testimony of the witness is different, it is less worthy of belief). In civil cases, as a result of ss 1 and 6 of the Civil Evidence Act 1995, the previous inconsistent statement is evidence of the facts it alleges.

There is no rule that the jury should attach less weight to the evidence of a hostile witness. However, where a previous inconsistent statement has been adduced, the judge should warn the jury about the dangers of relying on a witness who has contradicted himself or herself and the jury should first decide whether they can give any credence to the witness at all before deciding which part of the testimony they will give credence to (*R v Maw*). In *R v Corcoran* it was noted by the Court of Appeal that there would be a particular need to identify inconsistencies between the witness' evidence and previous statements where the party calling the witness had only solicited favourable evidence under cross-examination.

## 5.3   Cross-examination

### 5.3.1   General issues

#### 5.3.1.1   Liability to cross-examination

All witnesses are liable to be cross-examined except witnesses who produce documents without being sworn (*Sumners v Moseley* (1834) 2 Cr & M 477), those called by mistake (*Wood v Mackinson* (1840) 2 Mood & R 273) or a witness called by the judge unless the judge grants leave (*Coulson v Disborough* [1894] 2 QB 316). If a witness dies before being cross-examined (*R v Doolin* (1832) 1 Jebb CC 125) or the witness is determined by the judge to be incapable of answering further questions, the evidence adduced so far may be used if the judge can adequately direct the jury as to the prejudice faced by the accused in not having had the opportunity to cross-examine the witness (*R v Stretton* (1986) 86 Cr App R 7; *R v Wyatt* [1990] Crim LR 343; *R v Lawless* (1994) 98 Cr App R 342).

#### 5.3.1.2   The duty to cross-examine a witness

It was held in *R v Wood Green Crown Court, ex p Taylor* [1995] Crim LR 879 that a party who fails to cross-examine a witness on a fact is deemed to have accepted what the witness says on that fact and therefore cannot invite the tribunal of fact to disbelieve him or her on that matter. This is the obligation to 'put one's case' and is a fundamental requirement of cross-examination. Where the matter was not put to the witness by oversight, the witness may be recalled for cross-examination and the matter put to him or her (*R v Cannan* [1998] Crim LR 284).

The courts will approach this duty with some flexibility, looking to see the overall tenor of the cross-examination rather than whether any particular words were used (*R v Lovelock* [1997] Crim LR 821). In fact, the use of the phrase 'I put it to you ...' is generally frowned upon by members of the Bar and the judiciary alike. Furthermore, there is no need to put the same cross-examination to numerous witnesses that are giving essentially the same corroborative testimony. It would also appear that the failure to put a case clearly in the magistrates' courts does not prevent a party from inviting the magistrates to disbelieve the witness (*O'Connell v Adams* [1973] RTR 150), although putting the case would still be advisable in the interests of good advocacy.

#### 5.3.1.3   Restrictions on cross-examination in person

Generally the rules of evidence do not require a litigant in person to be treated differently from a litigant represented by a lawyer. However due to the inflammatory and occasionally sensitive nature of cross-examination, there are two restrictions upon an party who is not legally represented.

First of all, the judge has a power at common law to restrict both the length of the cross-examination and the issues to which it relates when conducted by a litigant in person (*R v Brown* [1998] 2 Cr App R 364, CPR, r 32.1(3) and *Vernon v Boseley (No 2)* [1995] 2 FCR 78).

Secondly, there are specific restrictions on the extent to which an accused may cross-examine a witness himself or herself. These restrictions are imposed by the Youth Justice and Criminal Evidence Act 1999. In summary the restrictions are:

(a) Under s 34 no cross-examination by the accused in person is permitted in relation to a sexual offence or any offence charged with a sexual offence. Sexual offences are defined under s 62 to include rape, burglary with intent to rape, indecent assault and other offences.

(b) Under s 35 no cross-examination by the accused in person is permitted in relation to a 'specified offence' in respect of a 'protected witness'.

(i) The specified offences include sexual offences, kidnapping, false imprisonment, offences of child neglect and offences involving assaults on, injury to or threats of injury to any person.

(ii) A protected witness is either the complainant to the specified offence or a witness to it *and* either a child or a person who has the benefit of a special measures direction that his or her evidence be video recorded under s 27 of the 1999 Act (see **4.7.5.2**).

(c) The court is given a residual power under s 36 to prevent cross-examination in person by the accused if of the opinion that the quality of the evidence will be diminished as a result.

Section 38 of the 1999 Act provides that where an order is made under any of the above sections, the court must offer the accused an opportunity to obtain his or her own legal representative and that if this does not happen should consider whether or not to appoint a legal representative for that purpose. Section 39 provides that the jury should be warned (if necessary) not to draw any inferences from the fact of cross-examination having been prevented or a legal representative having been appointed and that a court-appointed representative is not the accused's chosen representative.

### 5.3.2   Limits on cross-examination

#### 5.3.2.1   General limits

Cross-examination is subject to the rules of admissibility of evidence as much as is evidence-in-chief. Therefore questions seeking to elicit evidence that would not be admissible cannot be put to a witness in cross-examination (*R v Treacy* [1944] 2 All ER 229, CA). In *R v Windass* (1989) 89 Cr App R 258 the prosecution sought to cross-examine one co-accused about an admission made by another co-accused. Such an admission would only be admissible against the maker (the other co-accused: see **Chapter 9**). Therefore the Court of Appeal held that the prosecution cross-examination had been improper.

#### 5.3.2.2   Specific limits relating to complainants in sexual cases

The Youth Justice and Criminal Evidence Act 1999, s 41, places important restrictions on the extent to which a complainant to a sexual offence may be cross-examined about previous sexual experience. This restriction is in addition to the restriction upon cross-examination in person: it applies to cross-examination whether by the accused in person or by a legal representative.

The restriction only relates to questions or evidence about previous sexual behaviour; it does not restrict cross-examination about the sexual behaviour that is part of the incident or incidents for which the accused is being tried (s 42(1)(c)). In *R v Mukodi* [2003] EWCA Crim 3765, the Court of Appeal stated that it was not possible to define sexual behaviour. Rather what was meant by the term was a matter of 'impression and common sense' (at [14]). The behaviour in that case was the act of getting into the car driven by an unknown man who had pulled up alongside the complainant and the exchange of telephone numbers in the car. In allowing the appeal of the defendant, the Court of Appeal concluded that in the circumstances such behaviour was either sexual behaviour relevant to the complainant's consent at a later point (see below) or it was not sexual behaviour and therefore could have been the subject of cross-examination as s 41 did not apply.

If the defence is that the complainant is making false allegations against the accused and the accused seeks to support this by eliciting evidence of false allegations that have been made in the past, s 41 does not apply as the making of false allegations is not 'sexual behaviour' (*R v MH* [2002] Crim LR 73, CA). In *R v C and B* [2003] EWCA Crim 29 the Court of Appeal held that if the defence wished to question about previous false allegations of sexual offences, it would be necessary to determine whether there was a proper evidential basis for asserting that the allegation in question was (a) made and (b) false. If there were no such evidential basis the effect of questioning would be to prove the falsity of the previous allegation and would therefore be questioning about previous sexual behaviour. It is only if the falsity is shown by other evidence that the previous allegation would not be sexual behaviour. Therefore if the proof of falsity of the previous allegation would require cross-examination of evidence concerning the sexual behaviour on that previous occasion, the false allegation is sexual behaviour within the meaning of s 41 (*R v H* [2003] EWCA Crim 2367) but if it can be established by evidence of a non-sexual nature, the false allegation is not sexual behaviour.

The previous sexual behaviour does not have to be between the accused and the complainant. However, where the behaviour was with a third person there would have to be very special facts before cross-examination would be permitted.

Under s 41 such cross-examination will only be permitted if the court grants leave (s 41(1)). Leave can only be granted if:

- one of the four qualifying circumstances apply (s 41(2)(a)); *and*
- refusal to grant leave might render a conviction unsafe (s 41(2)(b)).

The four qualifying circumstances, one of which is required before cross-examination can be permitted, are:

(a) The cross-examination or evidence relates to an issue other than consent (s 41(3)(a)).

   (i)  Belief in consent is an issue 'other than consent' and therefore if the issue is belief in consent cross-examination may be permitted (subject to the other elements of the test) under this section (s 41(1)(b)).

   (ii) It would also include, for example, the defence that no sexual act took place. Where there is medical evidence of a sexual act having taken place, the accused would seek to be allowed to prove that the complainant had had sexual intercourse with another person at that time.

(b) The cross-examination or evidence relates to the issue of consent and the previous sexual behaviour took place 'on or about the same time' as the offence (s 41(3)(b)).

   (i)  In *R v A* [2001] 3 All ER 1, HL, it was observed that this meant a matter of hours rather than days.

   (ii) It would appear that this category of permissible questioning is aimed at defences using proof of the complainant's promiscuity to prove that at the time of the alleged offence he or she was likely to have consented to the sexual act in question.

(c) The cross-examination or evidence relates to the issue of consent and the previous sexual behaviour in question is very similar either to the alleged offence or other sexual behaviour at about the same time as the alleged offence (s 41(3)(c)).

    (i)    The exact phrase used by the Act is 'so similar ... that the similarity cannot reasonably be explained as a coincidence'.

    (ii)    This is potentially quite complicated but appears to be aimed at evidence of previous consensual sexual behaviour of a distinctive nature that bears such a strong similarity to what appears to have taken place during the offence that this similarity may raise a reasonable doubt as to the complainant's lack of consent.

    (iii)    For example, evidence that the complainant regularly had sexual intercourse in a particularly distinctive way with the accused on previous occasions might be admissible under this circumstance if there was evidence that the sexual act forming the charge had strongly similar characteristics.

    (iv)    It is submitted that if the sexual behaviour on the previous and current occasions were, due to their nature, incapable of suggesting consensual acts then such previous behaviour would not be admissible under s 41.

    (v)    Note that s 41(3)(c) relates not only to a similarity between a previous incident and the alleged offence where the nature of the two incidents could prove the existence of consent. Under s 41(3)(c)(ii), evidence of previous sexual behaviour which is similar to behaviour 'at or about the same time' as the alleged offence could be admitted. In *R v Tahed* [2004] All ER (D) 346 (Feb), where the alleged rape took place within a particular climbing frame at a public park, the conviction was set aside because the trial judge had not allowed cross-examination concerning a similar (consensual) sexual encounter within the same climbing frame three weeks earlier. The trial judge had wrongly considered that the similarity had to be between the acts comprising part of the sexual act and had neglected to consider acts that took place 'at or about the same time'.

    (vi)    In *R v Richardson* [2003] EWCA Crim 2754, the Court of Appeal concluded that evidence of a previous relationship and of a relationship after an alleged rape would not be permitted under s 41(3)(c) as the sexual behaviour in question (the relationship in general) would not bear sufficient similarity to the alleged offence.

  (d) The cross-examination or evidence is tendered to rebut evidence tendered by the prosecution about the previous sexual behaviour of the complainant and only goes as far as is necessary to rebut that evidence (s 41(5)).

    (i)    Note that this exception is not restricted to situations in which the defence is consent.

    (ii)    For example, if the prosecution tendered evidence that the complainant had no sexual experience before the act in question, the defence would be able to adduce evidence or ask questions that would establish that she had sexual experience in the past.

Note that no cross-examination will be permitted if its only purpose is to undermine the credibility of the complainant (s 41(4)).

In *R v M* [2004] All ER (D) 103, the Court of Appeal stated that where cross-examination would have the effect of undermining the credibility *and* of supporting the defendant's denial of the complainant's allegations then such evidence would not be excluded under s 41(4).

Even if the alleged sexual behaviour falls within the four categories of evidence set out in s 41(3)(5) identified above, such behaviour cannot be admitted unless it relates to specific incidents (s 41(6)). Therefore in *R v White* [2004] All ER (D) 103 (Mar), evidence of previous convictions of the complainant for prostitution were held to have rightly been excluded as such convictions would be too general.

The effect of s 41 is that the defence will have to convince the court to allow leave to question about *any* previous sexual behaviour of the complainant. The court cannot grant leave unless convinced both that there is some particular relevance to the evidence (ie, one of the qualifying circumstances set out above) and that the evidence is probative enough that a failure to allow it to be admitted would put the accused at risk of an unsafe conviction.

In *R v A*, the House of Lords considered the effect of this restriction in light of the right to a fair trial under Article 6 of the European Convention on Human Rights. They recognised that the right to a fair trial included the ability to put forward a full defence and that the restrictions imposed by s 41 of the 1999 Act created a risk that this would not be possible. They therefore invoked s 3 of the Human Rights Act 1998 to interpret s 41 to require that judges should consider the extent to which an accused would be deprived of a material defence and therefore a fair trial as a result of a refusal to grant leave. It would therefore appear that the restriction under s 41 is to exercised narrowly by the courts.

In *R v Richardson* (above), the Court of Appeal concluded that the strict interpretation of s 41(3)(c) that excluded cross-examination about ongoing sexual relationships between the complainant and the defendant was unfair within the meaning of *R v A* and therefore quashed a conviction where the trial judge, applying s 41(3)(c), had not permitted such cross-examination.

In *R v Mukadi* (above), the issue was whether the complainant had consented to sexual intercourse. The complainant's evidence was that she had gone to the defendant's flat with him not intending any sexual acts to take place but that she had allowed him to carry out various sexual acts short of intercourse in the hope that he would then not have full intercourse with her but that he had subsequently carried out sexual intercourse without her consent. The case for the defendant was that the complainant had willingly consented to all the sexual acts that took place. The Court of Appeal held the behaviour of getting into a car with an unknown person and exchanging telephone numbers a matter of hours before the events alleged would be sufficiently relevant and probative to prove that she may have intended, in going to the defendant's flat, to carry out sexual acts. It was noted that if her evidence had been that she had gone to the defendant's flat willing to engage in sexual activity short of full sexual intercourse, the previous event would not have been particularly probative and therefore probably not admissible. However, as she had stated in evidence that she had not intended to engage in any sexual acts, the previous event was probative in not only proving that she may have been willing to consent but also that her denial of consent was probably untrue. As such the previous event should have been admitted. *R v Mukadi* therefore illustrates that any analysis of the probative value and therefore of the fairness of refusing to allow questioning will depend on detailed analysis of the issues raised by the evidence of the parties and cannot be determined by simple categorisation of the evidence.

The previous sexual behavour does not have to have been between the accused and the complainant. However where the behaviour was with a third person more cogent evidence of potential consent would be required before cross examination will be permitted: *R v White* [2004] All ER D 103 (Mar).

### 5.3.3  Cross-examination as to credit and the rule of finality

#### 5.3.3.1  What questions may be asked concerning the credibility of a witness?

As noted earlier, a lot of cross-examination will go to matters such as the credibility either of the witness as a person or as to the particular testimony that he or she gives. There are many reasons why the testimony of a witness might be less worthy of belief. If you have not already done so, it is worth reminding yourself of what is meant by the 'weight' of evidence (see **1.4.2**), as this is what 'credit' and 'credibility' is about.

We have already noted the obligation to 'put' one's case to the witness. This involves identifying the relevant matters to which that witness testifies with which your instructions disagree. However, cross-examination is not simply a matter of disputing the facts of the case. It is also about providing the tribunal of fact with good reasons to favour your case over that of your opponents. In cross-examination this often involves showing how the evidence of the witness in question is less worthy of belief, ie by attacking the credit of the witness.

While a cross-examiner has more freedom as to what questions may be put to a witness, there are some restrictions. The courts have laid down rules as to the extent to which questions concerning the character of a witness may be asked. The simplest statement of the rule is that set out in *R v Sweet-Escott* (1971) 55 Cr App R 316 in which Lawton J said:

> Since the purpose of cross-examination as to credit is to show that the witness ought not to be believed on oath, the matters about which he is questioned must relate to his likely standing after cross-examination with the tribunal which is trying him or listening to his evidence.

In other words, if the cross-examination will not affect the way in which the tribunal will consider the witness's evidence but will show him or her to be a bad person in some other way it is not permissible. This principle reflects the approach identified in *Hobbs v C T Tinling and Co Ltd* [1929] 2 KB 1, CA where the court observed that cross-examination should not be allowed if the bad character in question occurred in the distant past or that it is out of proportion with the matters on which that witness will give evidence.

The court will therefore consider the potential probative value of the matters raised in cross-examination to determine whether they could assist the jury in deciding whether or not to believe the witness in question. This can cause difficulties if the evidence that the witness has acted dishonestly in the past is not clear. For example, *R v Edwards* [1991] 1 WLR 207 concerned allegations that a police officer had previously been disciplined for improper conduct. The court considered a number of options and concluded:

(a) An officer could be asked about previous convictions or disciplinary charges that had been found proved against him or her.

(b) An officer should not be asked about disciplinary charges that had not yet been proved against him or her.

(c) An officer should be asked about discreditable conduct of other officers in his or her squad.

(d) An officer could be asked about other cases in which he had been involved in certain limited circumstances:

    (i)    The mere fact that the officer had given evidence in previous cases and that the accused in those cases had been acquitted did not suggest anything about the credibility of the officer and therefore were not appropriate matters for cross-examination.

    (ii)   However, if it was alleged that (a) in the previous case the officer in question had given evidence that that accused person had made a confession, and (b) that accused person had been acquitted, and (c) the circumstances of that case suggest that the acquittal involved the jury disbelieving the evidence of the officer about the confession, and (d) the officer was alleging that the current defendant had confessed, then the officer could legitimately be asked about that previous acquittal.

*R v Edwards* provides a useful example of the approach that the court will adopt in determining what sort of matters should be considered. That it was stating general principles rather than laying down rigid rules is supported by the fact that in a different case, *R v Edwards* [1996] 2 Cr App R 345, the Court of Appeal concluded that there could be circumstances in which unproven allegations of perjury and other misconduct on the part of police officers *could* be legitimate matters for cross-examination. What appears to have made a difference in that case was that the numerous allegations had led prosecuting authorities to drop charges against other defendants in cases with which those police officers were involved. In other words the test is simply that laid down in *R v Sweet-Escott*: will the cross-examination affect the standing of the witness in the eyes of the tribunal? This is a matter of fact and argument in each case rather than rigid principle.

It must be remembered that in addition to the rules of evidence regulating the cross-examination of witnesses, a lawyer conducting cross-examination is regulated by his or her professional codes. For example, a barrister must comply with paras 701 and 708 of the Code of Conduct for England and Wales. These can be found in full in the **Professional Conduct Manual** but it should be noted that a barrister:

(a) Should act courteously and must avoid unnecessary expense or waste of the court's time (para 701(a)).

(b) Should not act outside of his or her client's instructions or devise facts to assist the client's case (para 708(e)).

(c) Should not ask questions that are scandalous or the only purpose of which is to 'vilify, insult or annoy' the witness or another person (para 708(g)) and must avoid naming third parties in open court who would be impugned as a result (para 708(h)).

(d) Should not criticise a witness he or she has had an opportunity to cross-examine unless the matters in question have been put to the witness in cross-examination (para 708(i)).

(e) Should not make allegations of fraud unless relevant to the case and supported by reasonable grounds (para 708(j)).

While the Code of Conduct is not binding on the court, it does have some persuasive force (see *R v McFaden* (1975) 62 Cr App R 187 concerning the Bar Council Rules which the Code of Conduct replaced).

### 5.3.3.2   The rule of finality

The preceding analysis concerned the questions that may be asked during cross-examination. However, it would be foolish to think that merely because a matter is put to a witness in cross-examination, he or she will agree to it. What can be done if a matter is put to a witness and that witness does not accept what has been suggested?

Strictly speaking what follows is not about cross-examination as such but about the consequences of cross-examination. The analysis concerns whether or not other witnesses can be called or evidence can be proved by other means; not what questions can be put to particular witnesses in cross-examination. However, it is worth considering this issue here as the rules and principles derive from the rules on cross-examination and the rules will also influence how cross-examination is conducted.

If the matter with which the witness will not agree concerns a fact in issue it is clearly necessary (and therefore possible) to call evidence to prove that what was put in cross-examination is true and that what the witness said is not. If the party conducting the cross-examination has not yet finished calling their evidence, then they can call (or recall) whichever witness can prove the matter in question. If the party has finished calling their evidence, they will generally have anticipated the matter and will have ensured that the relevant witness has given the necessary evidence. However, if the matter in question is unexpected, the court may exercise a discretion to allow them to call further witnesses. For details of when this will happen, see **4.7.2.4**.

However, if the matter upon which the witness is unwilling to concede goes only to the credibility of his or her testimony or that of another witness (ie it is a 'collateral fact'), the rule of finality applies.

The rule of finality is that where a witness answers a question on a collateral matter, the answer is conclusive and cannot be disproved or undermined by calling other witnesses to give evidence to the contrary (*Harris v Tippett* (1811) 2 Camp 637). Therefore a failure to disclose evidence relevant simply to a collateral matter such as the credibility of a witness will not render a criminal conviction unsafe as such evidence would not be admissible if the witness denied the allegation in cross-examination: *R v Colwill* [2002] EWCA Crim 1320.

As to whether the issue is collateral, the Court of Appeal in *R v Funderbark* [1990] 1 WLR 587 urged a flexible approach and discouraged an overly pedantic approach to such questions, even recognising that the test may be instinctive and depend upon the prosecutor's and the court's sense of fair play. Therefore the issue of whether or not a fact is collateral for the purposes of this rule is a matter for the judge and a question of fact rather than one of law and the Court of Appeal will only interfere with a ruling of a trial judge if it is wrong in principle or clearly wrong on the facts of the case (*R v Somers* [1999] Crim LR 744). *R v Funderbark* also recognised that where the issue in the case concerned sexual acts in private, it is almost impossible to distinguish between relevance to credibility and a fact in issue.

The rule against finality is subject to four exceptions. Also it might be argued that the rule permitting the proof of previous inconsistent statements could be an exception to the rule against finality. In *R v Edwards* [1991] 1 WLR 207 (discussed above at **5.3.3.1**) it was held that where such questions as had been permitted in that case had been asked of an officer, if the officer did not accept the truth of the allegations put to him they could not then be proved by independent evidence unless the allegations amounted to bias as set out below. The court concluded that there was not a further exception relating to the willingness of police officers to fabricate evidence.

### 5.3.3.3    Exception 1: bias or partiality

The prohibition on calling evidence to prove the lack of credibility of a witness does not apply where the witness has denied that he or she is biased against a party or has something to gain from giving the evidence in the way that he or she has. In such circumstances a party other than the one calling the witness can call evidence to prove that bias or partiality (*R v Mendy* (1976) 64 Cr App R 4; *Dunn v Aslett* (1838) 2 Mood & R 122).

Quite what could amount to bias or partiality will vary from case to case. However the courts will look closely at the alleged bias or partiality before allowing evidence to be called under this exception. For example, it is not the fact of having been *offered* but the fact of having *accepted* the bribe that is evidence of partiality (*Attorney-General v Hitchcock* (1847) 1 Exch 91).

### 5.3.3.4 Exception 2: previous convictions

Where it has been suggested in cross-examination to a witness that he or she has previous convictions and the witness denies the allegation, those convictions can be proved (Criminal Procedure Act 1865, s 6). In civil cases the trial judge has a discretion to limit such cross-examination both at common law (following *R v Sweet-Escott*) and under CPR r 32.1: *Watson v Chief Constable of Cleveland Police* [2001] EWCA Civ 1547.

The accused in a criminal trial is subject to further restrictions (see **Chapter 6**). What follows concerns all witnesses other than the accused.

For any witness there are two restrictions on the extent to which the previous convictions of any witness may be proved:

(a) A witness over the age of 21 cannot be questioned about any offence of which he or she was found guilty before he or she had reached the age of 14.

(b) No witness can be asked about any conviction that is spent under s 4 of the Rehabilitation of Offenders Act 1974 unless:

(i) In civil proceedings the leave of the trial judge is required (s 7 of the 1974 Act). Leave should only be granted if justice cannot be done without admitting the evidence. The court will consider what the previous conviction might prove and will only admit evidence of it if one of the parties could not have a fair trial without proving the previous conviction (*Thomas v Commissioner of the Police for the Metropolis* [1997] 1 All ER 747, CA).

(ii) In criminal proceedings section 4 does not apply. However, *Practice Direction (Criminal: Consolidated)* [2002] 3 All ER 904, para 6, provides that reference should not be made to spent convictions in open court without leave of the trial judge, such leave only to be granted in the interests of justice. In *R v Lawrence* [1995] Crim LR 815, CA it was stated that the *Practice Direction* created a judicial discretion and that although the Court of Appeal might disagree with the decision of a trial judge, that decision would only be overturned if it erred in principle.

Section 99 of the Criminal Justice Act 2003 (which is not yet in force) abolishes the common law rules on evidence of 'bad character' and s 100 of that Act (also not yet in force) allows the proof of 'bad character' evidence of non-defendants in limited circumstances (for the position of defendants in criminal proceedings, see **6.3.2.1**). Bad character is defined in s 98 as misconduct or a disposition towards misconduct other than that which has a relation with the events with which the accused is charged or the investigation into those events. Evidence of such bad character of someone other than the accused is only admissible if it is 'important explanatory evidence', if it has 'substantial' probative value on a fact in issue or if all parties agree (s 100(1)). 'Important explanatory evidence' is defined in s 100(2) as evidence without which the court or jury would find it impossible to understand other evidence in the case or is of substantial value for understanding the case as a whole.

Therefore s 100 places a limit on the admissibility of evidence of bad character where it is not directly relevant to the subject matter of the proceedings in question. However where the previous convictions do not amount to 'bad character' as defined in s 98, it is submitted the common law rules are not repealed and s 100 does not apply.

##### 5.3.3.5    Exception 3: reputation for untruthfulness

This is a common law exception to the rule of finality that is seldom used. In *R v Richardson* [1969] 1 QB 299, the following elements of the rule were identified:

(a) A witness may be called to give evidence of the general reputation for untruthfulness of another witness and whether *on the basis of that knowledge* he or she would believe the sworn testimony of the other witness.

(b) The witness may also give his or her personal opinion as to whether the person ought to believed on oath.

(c) Such a witness cannot identify in his or her evidence-in-chief particular details of the testimony he or she would not believe (but may do so in cross-examination).

In *R v Colwill* (above) the evidence of witnesses that a complainant was untruthful was held not to fall within this exception where the opinion of those witnesses was based on specific instances of untruthful behaviour.

##### 5.3.3.6    Exception 4: disability affecting reliability

Evidence may be called about any mental disability that would affect the capacity of the witness to give truthful or accurate testimony (*Toohey v Metropolitan Police Commissioner* [1965] AC 595, HL). Such evidence is not restricted to general reputation but may cover the basis of the assertion that the witness is unreliable due to a mental disability and to the extent to which his or her credibility is affected.

Proof of the mental illness may require the use of expert witnesses. As will be seen from **Chapter 13**, expert opinion evidence is only admissible in limited circumstances. It is for the tribunal of fact to assess the credibility of witnesses, so an expert will only be allowed if the expert testimony is that the witness is incapable of giving truthful or accurate testimony rather than unwilling to do so (*R v Toohey*; see also *R v MacKenney* (1980) 72 Cr App R 78).

#### 5.3.4    Previous inconsistent statements

We have already seen that previous *consistent* statements are generally not admissible at trial unless they fall within specific exceptions. What about statements made previously by a witness that are *inconsistent* with what the witness says in testimony?

As a preliminary matter it is worth bearing in mind that if one party has a document made by a witness for the other party and that document is inconsistent with the witness's testimony, there is nothing to prevent the document being used to *plan* the cross-examination of that witness. In other words, the advocate planning the cross-examination could use the information in the document to pose questions. The same is true if the statement was not made in a document but was something the witness had said to some other person. However to what extent can the document or the oral statement showing the inconsistency with the witness's testimony be proved in court if the witness denies ever having made that statement?

The general rule is that such statements may be admissible but will not necessarily be admissible automatically. The statement will only be admissible if the witness remains inconsistent, having been given an opportunity to consider the previous statement. The rules for both civil and criminal cases are set out in ss 4 and 5 of the Criminal Procedure Act 1865. This rule applies to both civil and criminal proceedings but the evidential effect of the statement differs (see below).

Section 4 sets out the basic rule for both oral and written previous inconsistent statements (*R v Derby Magistrates' Court, ex p B* [1995] 3 WLR 681). Section 4 provides that:

(a) A previous inconsistent statement may be proved if the witness 'does not distinctly admit that he has made it'.

(b) Before the statement is proved, however:

  (i)  the witness should first have the previous statement identified to him or her, and

  (ii)  should be asked whether he or she made it.

  For example, the witness might be asked 'Do you remember making a statement to the police on the 12th of November last year?' or 'Did you have a conversation about this matter with Thomas on the 12th of November last year?'

Section 5 makes additional provision for written statements:

(a) A party can cross-examine a witness about the subject matter of a previous inconsistent statement (ie he may put to the witness the facts that the witness said in the previous statement without proving that the statement was made).

(b) If a party seeks to prove that the previous inconsistent written statement was made, then those parts of the statement that are inconsistent should be shown to the witness.

(c) The judge may request sight of the written document at any time. Therefore the advocate seeking to cross-examine on the document must have it with him at all times even if he or she does not propose to prove it (*R v Anderson* (1929) 21 Cr App R 178).

There is an important limit on the application of the rule that must be remembered. These sections only apply to cross-examination about previous inconsistent statements on matters that relate to the facts in issue; they do not apply to statements on matters that relate to questions of the credibility of evidence (*R v Funderbark* [1990] 2 All ER 482, CA). If the statement in question only relates to the credibility of the witness, the Act does not apply. In *R v C & B* [2003] EWCA Crim 29, the Court of Appeal drew a distinction between cases where the previous statement related to matters that the prosecution had proven as part of its case and matters that it had not. In *R v C & B* the statements in question were allegations of sexual offences made against persons other than the defendant. In such circumstances the Court of Appeal concluded that such statements did not relate to facts in issue. The common law rules would apply. Assuming that the questioning about the previous statement would affect the standing of the witness after cross-examination, the fact of the statement could be put to the witness. However, if he or she denied it, the rule of finality (see **5.3.3.2** above) would apply, preventing the cross-examining party from proving that the statement was made.

How then do the sections work in practice? Remember that the function of the sections is to allow the proof of a previous statement having been made and that this is only possible if it is established that a person's statement is inconsistent with his or her subsequent testimony. The following sequence must therefore be adopted in examining the witness:

(a) Establish what the witness's testimony is on the matter in question (usually this is done by putting to the witness the version of events he or she gave in the previous statement and usually the witness will stick to his or her testimony).

(b) Establish that a previous statement was made (and if it is contained in a document, let the witness see the document).

(c) Put the matter in question to the witness again to establish whether or not he or she is consistent with the previous statement.

(d) If the witness changes the testimony (whether before or after the statement is put to him or her) and adopts what was said in the previous statement, there is no inconsistency so the previous statement will not be admissible evidence (you may have got the witness to give a more favourable account of the matter in question, however).

(e) If he or she sticks to his or her testimony, then the document or oral statement will be a previous inconsistent statement and will be admissible evidence with the following consequences:

   (i)   In civil proceedings it is admissible to prove the truth of what was said in it (Civil Evidence Act 1995, ss 1, 6).

   (ii)  In criminal proceedings it is only relevant to credibility (*R v O'Neill* [1969] Crim LR 260). In other words, it is admissible to prove that less weight should be attached to the witness's testimony but not to prove the truth of what was said. However when s 119 of the Criminal Justice Act 2003 comes into force in criminal proceedings previous circumstantial statements will be relevant to prove the truth of the matter stated in it.

   (iii) As it has become evidence, the jury are entitled to see it. However the judge has a discretion only to allow those parts of the statement on which the cross-examination was founded (*R v Beattie* (1989) 89 Cr App R 302, CA).

To check that you have understood this area, carry out **activity 5.2** in **Appendix 1**.

## 5.4  Re-examination

Once all parties have cross-examined the witness, the party calling him or her may conduct re-examination. The re-examination is restricted to matters that arose during cross-examination (*Prince v Samo* (1838) 7 A & E 627). Re-examination is subject to the same rules as evidence-in-chief.

In *R v Beattie* (1989) 89 Cr App R 302, the Court of Appeal confirmed that a party could not re-examine a witness on previous consistent statements merely because that witness has been cross-examined about previous inconsistent statements. In *R v Oyesiku* (1971) 56 Cr App R 240 at p 245, however, it was recognised that a trial judge had a residual discretion to allow re-examination where there was 'something either in the nature of the inconsistent statement, or in the use made of it by the cross-examiner, to enable such evidence to given'. In *R v A* [2003] EWCA Crim 3214, it was noted that this discretion was to be used to ensure that the jury were not 'positively misled as to the existence of some fact or as to the terms of an earlier statement' (at [33]) by the cross-examination. In other words re-examination would only be permitted on a previous statement if it fitted within one of the exceptions to the general rule of exclusion outlined at **5.2.4** or if the cross-examination went beyond undermining the testimony of the witness by creating a false impression of the facts of the case by using a previous statement out of context or incompletely.

## 5.5  Suspect witnesses

### 5.5.1  Introduction

Any witness may be unreliable. Historically, rules were developed for criminal trials which identified classes of witness who were particularly likely to give unreliable evidence. It was thought necessary to require evidence from independent sources to confirm their account, or for a warning to be given to the tribunal of fact about the danger of relying solely upon the evidence of such a witness. The typical tribunal of fact in a criminal trial is a juror or justice of the peace, neither of whom would usually be legally qualified or experienced in assessing the evidence of witnesses. In civil cases, by contrast, the judge decides factual disputes and should be aware of the potential pitfalls. For this reason, the situation is only addressed with regard to the position in criminal trials.

Although the courts do not think in terms of categories of suspect witnesses one might consider the following classes of witnesses as among those less likely to be reliable:

- those who have lied in this case (this may be a matter for the fact finders to determine, or the witness may simply have given contradictory accounts);
- those who have lied in a previous case (this may be plain from the judgment of the previous court);
- those who are of 'bad character' (typically, a prosecution witness with previous convictions);
- those who have a bias or prejudice against the accused (shown by evidence in this case);
- those who may benefit from testifying against the accused (again, shown by the evidence in the trial);
- those who are suffering from a mental handicap or mental disorder (dependent on expert opinion evidence).

However, historically, the courts have also treated the following types of witnesses with special care.

- any child witness;
- any complainant in a sexual offence trial.

### 5.5.2  Child witnesses

It used to be a rule of law that no defendant could be convicted on the unsworn evidence of a child whose account had not been corroborated (supported by independent evidence). There was also a rule of practice that required judges to warn juries of the danger of convicting a defendant on the uncorroborated evidence of a child (whether he or she had given sworn evidence or was unsworn). Those rules no longer exist. See the Criminal Justice Act 1988, s 34 (as amended by Criminal Justice Act 1991 and Criminal Justice and Public Order Act 1994 (CJPOA 1994)):

> *(12) Any requirement whereby at trial on indictment it is obligatory for the court to give the jury a warning about convicting the accused on the uncorroborated evidence of a child is abrogated.*

However, it is still suggested that trial judges should remind child witnesses of the importance of telling the truth, in the presence of both the defendant and the jury (see

Auld LJ in *R v Hampshire* [1996] 1 QB 1). The editors of the Specimen Directions in the Criminal Bench Book of the Judicial Studies Board suggest that it 'may be appropriate to warn the jury to take particular care with the evidence of a very young child'. See www.jsboard.co.uk/criminal for further guidance.

### 5.5.3   Complainants in sexual offence cases

There used to be a rule that a trial judge should direct the jury, in summing up the evidence, that it would be dangerous to convict a defendant on the evidence of the complainant in a sexual offence trial, if it was uncorroborated by other evidence.

Parliament no longer recognises any such propensity, either for females or complainants generally. See the Criminal Justice and Public Order Act 1994, s 32:

> *(1)   Any requirement whereby at a trial on indictment it is obligatory for the court to give the jury a warning about convicting the accused on the uncorroborated evidence of a person merely because that person is:*
>
> *(a)   an alleged accomplice of the accused, or*
> *(b)   where the offence charged is a sexual offence, the person in respect of whom it is alleged to have been committed,*
> *is hereby abrogated.*

### 5.5.4   Witnesses generally

The position now is simple: it is a matter for the discretion of the trial judge in every case whether or not to warn the jury to be cautious about the evidence of a witness. If the judge decides that no such warning is needed, the Court of Appeal is unlikely to interfere in the event of an appeal against conviction. Likewise, the terms of any such warning are largely a matter for the trial judge to determine.

There are a variety of motives for the defence to suggest that a witness's evidence is unreliable. How should that be dealt with by the judge in summing up the case? This was considered by Lord Hailsham of St Marylebone LC in *R v Spencer* [1987] AC 128, where it was said that a failure to 'warn the jury of the possible danger of convicting an innocent man if they convicted solely on the disputed but uncorroborated testimony' of a witness of bad character would make any subsequent conviction 'unsafe and unsatisfactory in the extreme.' Following the decision of the Court of Appeal in *R v Makanjuola* [1995] 1 WLR 1348, it will be a matter for the trial judge to decide exactly what to say to the jury about such a witness. It is beyond doubt, though, that they must be given some help on the appropriate use of such information.

The rules of evidence also have to make provision for allegations that a witness was an accomplice of the defendant. The allegation is made by the prosecution. The defence would usually say that the defendant was not a party to the crime at all, so it makes no sense for the defence to describe a witness as an accomplice. In the past, the evidence of alleged accomplices would have attracted a warning from the trial judge to the jury about the danger of relying simply on that evidence to ground a conviction. The CJPOA 1994, s 32, abolished any obligation to warn a jury where a prosecution witness was alleged to be an accomplice.

The judgment in *R v Makanjuola* requires there to be an 'evidential foundation' before any warning may be thought necessary. Even then, the following exchange would be insufficient.

Cross-examination of prosecution witness [W]:

| Defence Counsel [DC] | You have already admitted that you participated in the commission of this crime? |
|---|---|
| Witness [W] | Yes. I pleaded guilty at the start of this trial. |
| DC | And now you seek, quite falsely, to implicate my client? |
| W | She was involved. It was all her idea. |
| DC | I suggest that you are lying? |
| W | No. |
| DC | You have not been sentenced by the learned judge yet? |
| W | No. |
| DC | Again, I suggest that you are giving false evidence against my client, in the hope that your action may result in a lighter sentence for you? |
| W | No. I don't know what sentence I will get. |

Here, the prosecution witness [W] is a self-confessed participant in the crime for which the defendant now stands trial. The witness may say he was a principal party to the crime, or a secondary party (aider and abettor, counsellor or procurer). Whatever his own role, by pleading guilty and testifying for the prosecution, he is likely to receive a less severe sentence than would otherwise have been justified (because of his guilty plea and testimony for the prosecution). However, the Court of Appeal was quite clear in *R v Makanjuola* that there is no *obligation* on a trial judge to warn a jury about the potential unreliability of any witness, simply because the witness is alleged to be an accomplice of the defendant. This produces a grey area. Whenever an offender turns 'Queen's evidence' and testifies for the Crown against alleged former partners, there is a clear benefit for him regarding sentence. What more may be needed in order to lead the judge to warn the jury?

In *Rowe v United Kingdom* [2000] Crim LR 584, one alleged accomplice was in fact a police informer. He was paid £10,000 as a result of testifying against Rowe and the other defendants. That information (which was withheld from the defence at the trial on the ground of public interest immunity; see **Chapter 16**) could constitute the 'evidential foundation' that would lead to a *Makanjuola* warning.

Another example of an 'evidential foundation' may be found in *R v L* [1999] Crim LR 489. Here, a nine-year-old witness (J) testified that L had indecently assaulted her on several occasions. L and J's mother had separated, following a fight in a pub. Both had blamed the other. Subsequently, J had complained to her mother about L's behaviour towards her. It was said that J knew of the fight. Following CJA 1988, s 34, it was not necessary for the judge to warn the jury about the danger of relying upon the child's evidence. Further, following CJPOA 1994, s 32, it was not necessary to warn the jury about the evidence of J as a complainant in a sexual offence trial. However, given the history between J's mother and L, together with some significant differences between J's testimony at trial and earlier videotape evidence, a warning to assess J's evidence with special care was appropriate.

### 5.5.5  How judges deal with dishonest or 'unreliable' witnesses in criminal cases

Whether any witness is actually unreliable is a question of fact, to be determined by the jury (or magistrates). All that a judge can do is offer guidance to the jury (in a summary trial, the magistrates must guide themselves, with help from the defence closing speech and any assistance they can get from the clerk of the court). Next, the judge must determine whether a warning is necessary or not. As the Court of Appeal said in *R v Makanjuola* [1995] 1 WLR 1348:

It is a matter for the judge's discretion what, if any, warning he considers appropriate in respect of ... a witness. Whether he chooses to give a warning and in what terms will depend on the circumstances of the case, the issues raised and the content and quality of the witness's evidence.

For a judge to consider that any kind of warning is necessary, there must be an evidential basis for suggesting that the witness's evidence may be unreliable. In other words, there must be relevant and admissible evidence produced at the trial which suggests unreliability. It is not enough that counsel, when cross-examining the witness, asks questions that suggest unreliability. See the example given above (**12.3.4**).

If the judge feels that a warning *may* be necessary, it is good practice to hear the views of counsel on the matter before reaching a conclusion. The jury should be sent to their room while the matter is considered by judge and counsel. If the judge concludes that a warning is not needed, the jury is brought back into court and nothing more is said on the matter. If the judge decides that a warning is needed, it should be given during summing up to the jury, after all the evidence has been given and counsel have made their closing speeches. The strength of the warning and the words to be used are matters for each judge to decide.

A 'mild' warning might simply suggest that the jury be cautious before relying solely on the testimony of that witness. A stronger warning may invite the jury to consider if the witness has an 'axe to grind' against the accused (see for example, *R v B* [2000] Crim LR 48; compare *R v Muncaster* [1999] Crim LR 409). It could go on to suggest that the jury consider whether the testimony of that witness is supported by any other evidence. Where the judge makes that suggestion, it is good practice to explain what evidence in the case is capable of providing that support (see *R v B (M T)* [2000] Crim LR 181). Whether it does support the suspect evidence (or not) is a question of fact for the jury.

See further *Archbold*, 2004; *Blackstone's Criminal Practice*, 2004.

### 5.5.6    Cases where statute requires evidence from at least two sources

In several situations, statute requires evidence to come from at least two sources. These can be considered briefly.

(a) Perjury — a conviction for perjury (or attempted perjury) cannot be based 'solely upon the evidence of one witness as to the falsity of any statement alleged to be false' (Perjury Act 1911, s 13).

(b) Speeding — a conviction for speeding cannot be based solely upon the opinion of one witness that the accused was driving in excess of the speed limit: (Road Traffic Regulation Act 1984, s 89). However, evidence of a vehicle's speed may be determined by a radar gun or speedometer. That would not be opinion evidence and so s 89 would not apply.

(c) Inferences from silence — for any offence, magistrates or a jury may properly draw inferences from the silence of the accused in certain circumstances. See, for example, CJPOA 1994, ss 34(2), 35(3), 36(2) and 37(2). Such inferences may be relevant to the guilt of the accused but cannot by themselves justify a conviction (CJPOA 1994, s 38(3)). See further **Chapter 10**.

# 6

# Character evidence

May evidence be adduced to show the good or bad character of a witness during the course of a trial? What is the purpose of adducing such evidence?

This area of evidence will change once the Criminal Justice Act 2003 comes into force. The proposed date for the relevant sections to come into force, Part II, ss 98–111, is December 2005. In this chapter the current law will be the main focus; however, where the law is due to change a short explanatory note will be given.

## 6.1 Civil cases

Evidence of a party's good or bad character is admissible, in civil proceedings, if it is among the facts in issue in the case or of direct relevance to the facts in issue. A simple example is in a defamation case in which the defendant's defence is justification. Evidence of the claimant's character is also admissible, if he succeeds, on the question of quantum of damages: see generally *Scott v Sampson* (1882) 8 QBD 491.

Evidence of a party's good or bad character, if not among, or of direct relevance to, the facts in issue and if not relevant to credit (see below) is generally excluded even though it may have some relevance to the facts in issue. See *Narracott v Narracott* (1864) 3 Sw & Tr 498: in a divorce case a husband, in order to disprove a particular act of cruelty, cannot tender evidence of his general character for humanity. See also *Attorney-General v Bowman* (1971) 2 Bos & P 532.

Evidence of the character of a party to civil proceedings (or a witness called by him) may be adduced because of its relevance to his credibility. See generally **Chapter 5** and *Mechanical & General Inventions Co Ltd v Austin* [1935] AC 346 and *Hobbs v CT Tinling & Co Ltd* [1929] 2 KB 1, CA.

## 6.2 Criminal cases

In criminal cases evidence of a person's character is admissible when it is either a fact in issue in the case or of direct relevance to a fact in issue. One clear example of where evidence of bad character is a fact in issue is when it is an essential ingredient of the offence charged: see eg Firearms Act 1968, s 21 or driving whilst disqualified contrary to s 103, Road Traffic Act 1988. See generally **Chapter 2** and **Chapter 5**.

### 6.2.1  Witnesses other than the defendant

Evidence of the character of prosecution witnesses or any other witnesses other than the defendant is admissible where it is relevant to the facts in issue in the case and/or it is relevant to their credibility.

### 6.2.2  Good Character

#### 6.2.2.1  The defendant

The defendant may adduce evidence of good character either by calling witnesses him or herself, cross-examining the prosecution witnesses or giving evidence him or herself. The form of this evidence is confined to evidence of his or her general reputation that may be given by people known to him or her. Therefore a witness as to character is not allowed to speak to his or her own opinion of the defendant's disposition, but only as to the general reputation in which the defendant is held: *R v Rowton* (1865) L & C 520.

If evidence of good character is raised, the prosecution may in most cases rebut this by proving the defendant has previous convictions: *R v Butterwasser* [1948] 1 KB 4, 32 Cr App R 81 CCA. Where the prosecution seek to cross-examine a defendant on matters other than criminal convictions, but the weight to be attached to such evidence is in issue, a *voir dire* should be held: *R v Wright* [2000] Crim LR 510, CA.

In summing up character, the judge must follow the guidelines issued in *R v Vye: R v Wise; R v Stephenson,* 97 Cr App R 134. The guidelines state that the judge must indicate to the jury the two respects in which good character might be relevant:

(i)  credit;

(ii) likelihood of his or her having committed the offence charged.

Which limb applies depends on whether the defendant has given evidence, or has not given evidence but relies on exculpatory statements or answers given by him or her to the police or others.  In any such situation both limbs of the *Vye* direction are required.  The first principle in *Vye* suggests that the judge should clearly direct the jury that good character is relevant to credibility and not put good character 'in the scales': *R v Boyson* [1991] Crim LR 274; *R v Miah* [1997] Crim LR 351, CA.

In cases where the defendant has not given evidence (or made the sort of statement identified above) the judge may only direct on the second limb, ie, the likelihood of committing the offence charged. Good character cannot amount to a defence. However in cases where, for example, there is a long standing employee, relevance of good character to propensity to commit the crime should be emphasised by the judge in his or her summing up.

Where the case involves one defendant of good character and another of bad character the defendant of good character is entitled to a direction. This obviously has a detrimental impact on the co-defendant. What course and how the judge sums up must be decided in all the circumstances of the case and if character is one of the key aspects of the trial it may be that an argument for separate trials should be advanced.

A defendant may be treated as being of good character even though he or she has previous convictions: *R v Heath, The Times,* 10 February 1994. The *Vye* direction may be qualified by reference to previous convictions but stating that they are *not relevant* is wrong (*R v Aziz* [1996] 1 AC 41) because the defendant's previous conviction may have occurred a long time ago and/or relate to a different type of offence.

*R v Aziz* went further to assist on what to direct a jury where a defendant did not have previous convictions but has admitted to other criminal behaviour. Lord Steyn held that a judge has a residual discretion not to give a *Vye* direction where it would be an insult to common sense to give such a direction. However, it was held that this discretion is narrowly circumscribed and that directions *should* be given in order that a fair and balanced picture may be given by the judge to the jury by a qualified *Vye* direction.

In respect of a defendant with no previous convictions, where evidence is admitted of the background of an alleged offence and the detail of such evidence suggests the commission of earlier offences, *R v Butler (Diana)* [1999] Crim LR 835 hold that there should be no qualification to a standard good character direction. *Archbold* 2004, 4–408, suggests that this decision should be treated with caution as an unqualified good character direction may mislead or confuse a jury in their deliberations where evidence of other offences is clear, and it is open for the jury to accept this evidence.

Where a defendant pleads guilty to an offence, he or she is no longer a person of good character. However, if the count to which the defendant has pleaded is an alternative to that on which is he or she being tried and he or she is found guilty of the greater offence the guilty plea is vacated: *R v Teasedale* (1993) 99 Cr App R 80, CA. If this is the case a tailored good character direction may be given, as there is no conviction but some admission of guilt.

Where a defendant enters a plea for an offence other than to a lesser alternative, there may be cases where a form of good character direction may be given. For example, where a defendant has pleaded guilty, this may be relevant to his or her credibility on the issue of whether he or she is telling the truth in claiming innocence on the remaining counts on the indictment.

You may wish to carry out **activity 6.1** in **Appendix 1** at this stage.

### 6.2.2.2  Non-defendant's good character

As the defendant is the one who is on trial and will be sentenced if found guilty it is of paramount importance that the jury are directed on good character, as there may be an inference of guilt just because the person is standing in the dock. Prosecution witnesses are not on trial and are part of the case against the defendant, therefore the fact they are of good character is irrelevant. To allow the non-defendant's good character to put to the jury is seen as 'oath-helping'. However, there may be exceptional facts where this does become relevant, such as in cases of rebuttal when the defence have asserted bad character which is simply not true or where it is relevant to a fact in issue. *R v Tobin* [2003] Crim LR 408 was a case where the charge was indecent assault of a 16 year old girl in a motor car. The defence was that the complainant had initiated the sexual activity in 'circumstances that were bizarre'. The judge allowed evidence from the complainant's mother that included the statement '*I have never had any problems with [the complainant] throughout her childhood. She has always done really well at school. At home she gets on really well.*'. The Court's view was in sexual cases there was potential relevance of the complainant's characteristics and background, 'In the circumstances, our sense of fair play is not offended but rather affirmed by the admission of the very limited evidence of the complainant's characteristics and conduct'. In this decision the Court relied on *Funderburk* [1990] 1 WLR 587, '*where the disputed issue is a sexual one between two persons in private the difference between questions going to credit and questions going to the issue reduce to vanishing point*'. However, it must be stated that this is a *very exceptional* admission of evidence that is usually inadmissible.

### 6.2.3    The defendant: bad character — common law

The general rule is that the prosecution **may not adduce** evidence of the defendant's bad character nor cross-examine the defendant or any other witness with a view to eliciting such evidence. At *common law*, there are two exceptions:

(a) where the evidence is admissible under the similar fact doctrine (see **Chapter 6**); and

(b) where the defence adduces evidence of the defendant's good character and therefore it is rebuttal evidence.

If the defendant has asserted good character, this is only relevant to the likelihood of his or her having committed the offence and therefore evidence of bad character is only relevant to rebut this. The effect is to neutralise the evidence of good character.

Once the defendant puts character in issue his or her *whole character* can be cross-examined. Therefore evidence in rebuttal need not be confined to the character trait under consideration but may refer to any character trait of the defendant. The prosecution must first persuade the judge that the probative value of the evidence outweighs its prejudicial effect in order to admit it. The jury, however, if such evidence is admitted should be told that bad character may be relevant to an issue in the case, but the existence of previous convictions does not mean that the defendant is guilty of the offence charged. Moreover, bad character evidence should be treated with caution: *R v Soffe, The Times*, 5 April 2000, CA.

If the defendant does not give evidence and does not try to establish good character through cross-examination, evidence of his or her bad character is, at common law, inadmissible: *R v Butterwasser* [1948] 1 KB 4, CCA.

#### 6.2.3.1    Criminal Justice Act 2003

Section 99 abolishes the common law rules in relation to bad character. Section 98 defines character as evidence of misconduct, or of a disposition towards misconduct. This definition is intended to include previous convictions, as well as evidence on charges tried concurrently, and evidence relating to offences for which a person has been charged, but where the charge is not prosecuted, or for which the person was subsequently acquitted, In *R v Z* [2000] 2 AC 483, the defendant was charged with rape and had been acquitted of three previous allegations of rape, and the prosecution wished to adduce the testimony of the previous complainants to rebut the defence of consent. It was held that the evidence was relevant and may be admitted under similar fact doctrine and the principle of double jeopardy did not render it inadmissible.  It is likely that s 99 of the 2003 Act will apply to such situations.

Section 118 retains the common law rule that allows a person's bad character to be proved by his or her reputation and is preserved as a category of admissible hearsay. Many of the rules under s 118 were also preserved under the corresponding provisions in s 7, Civil Evidence Act 1995. However, on the issue of admissibility of bad character by reputation, this will be determined under s 101(1), Part II of the Act.

### 6.2.4    Defendant: bad character — Criminal Evidence Act 1898, s 1

Where the defendant gives evidence him or herself, further rules apply in regard to bad character. The common law position that the prosecution may not adduce evidence of bad character applies but there are important statutory exceptions.

These exceptions are set out in the Criminal Evidence Act 1898, s 1 (2)–(3).

(2) *A person charged in criminal proceedings who is called as a witness in the proceedings may be asked any questions in cross-examination notwithstanding that it would tend to incriminate him as to any offence with which he is charged in the proceedings.*

(3) *A person charged in criminal proceedings who is called as a witness in the proceedings shall not be asked. And if asked shall not be required to answer, any question tending to show that he has committed or be convicted or been charged with any offence other than the one with which he is then charged, or is of bad character, unless—*

    (i) *the proof that he has committed or been convicted of such other offence is admissible evidence to show he is guilty of an offence for which he is then charged; or*

    (ii) *he has personally or by his advocate asked questions of the witness for the prosecution with a view to establish his own good character, or has given evidence of his good character, or the nature and conduct of his defence is such as to involve imputations on the character of the prosecutor or the witness for the prosecution or the witness for the prosecution, or the deceased victim of the alleged crime; or*

    (iii) *he has given evidence against any other person charged in the same proceedings.*

### 6.2.4.1   The relationship between subsections (2) and (3)

The case on this point is *Jones v DPP* [1962] AC 635, HL. The CEA 1898 deals with three categories of question:

- those that would tend to incriminate the defendant as to the offence charged;
- those tending to show that he or she has committed or been convicted of, or charged with, some other offence; and
- those tending to show he or she is of bad character.

The first category of questions is permitted, the second and third are prohibited unless one of s 1(3)(i)–(iii) applies. It is assumed that all the classes of questions are exclusive of one another.

In *Jones v DPP,* Jones was charged with murder of a young girl. At trial he alleged that when the girl disappeared he had been with a prostitute in London. In his evidence-in-chief he explained that his wife had been concerned about articles in the Sunday papers concerning the disappearance of the murdered girl and that he had confessed to her where he had been. He gave details of the arguments that had ensued between them as a result of this confession.

However, when the police investigating the murder had questioned him, he had initially told them that he had been visiting his sister-in-law some distance away. She not only refused to confirm this but also was called as a prosecution witness. It was therefore necessary for Jones to explain during the course of the trial why he had originally lied. He said that he had previously been 'in trouble with the police' and that he had attempted to set up an alibi that he could substantiate with another witness (in contrast to the unknown prostitute). Jones' barrister had asked prosecution witnesses about this 'trouble' in the past and Jones had mentioned 'trouble' in his evidence-in-chief but that word had not been expanded upon before the jury. The defence gave no indication of the nature of the trouble.

When the prosecution came to cross-examine Jones, leave was obtained from the judge to ask particular questions of him. Jones was asked about the previous occasion when he had been in trouble. The questions related to the alibi that he had raised on that occasion and the conversation that had gone on between him and his wife. The conversation in relation to the previous occasion and that alleged in the murder alibi were almost identical in content. The prosecution sought to establish that, due to the similarity of the two conversations, the conversation in relation to the murder must have been fabricated and therefore the alibi was untrue.

Neither the defence nor the prosecution led any evidence in relation to the details of the previous conviction, which was the rape of a young girl. The only reference at the murder trial to the rape concerned the alibi that Jones had raised in relation to it and the conversation alleged to have taken place between him and his wife.

The defendant appealed, arguing that he had been improperly cross-examined on the details of the alibi and that this was not permissible under s 1(3) CEA 1898. The questions tended to show that 'he had committed or been convicted or been charged with' an offence other than that which he was charged. Such questions, it was argued, did not fall within any of the three categories of exception set out in (i)–(iii) of subsection (3).

The House of Lords by a majority rejected this argument on the grounds that the words 'tending to show' should be taken to mean tending to reveal for the first time. It follows that where the defendant's evidence-in-chief reveals that he has been trouble with the police, cross-examination by the prosecution will not contravene the prohibition. The reasoning being that it will not be questions 'tending to show' any of the prohibited matters. However, whether evidence has 'tended to show' a prohibited matter is a question of degree and if a defendant mentions one particular matter that will not give rise to the prosecution questioning him or her on any other convictions he or she may have.

The House of Lords further held that the questions 'tending to show', must be assessed by looking at the trial as a whole. In *Jones v DPP,* due to the evidence-in-chief of the defendant and the fact that the prosecution did detail the nature of this evidence, the prosecution had not revealed anything to the jury that the defendant had not revealed already.

In *Jones v DPP* the House of Lords also noted that:

(a) Subsection (2) permits questions which tend directly to incriminate the defendant (ie, questions relating to facts of the offence(s) which he or she is currently tried). The subsection confirms that the fact that it is the defendant, as opposed to another witness, giving evidence does not exempt him or her from cross-examination about the issue in the case (ie, his or her guilt or defence).

(b) Subsection (3) generally prohibits questions that would indirectly incriminate the defendant. These may be questions that reveal that the defendant has previous convictions or is of bad character or disposed to commit offences or that he or she ought not to be believed on oath. This evidence would only be permissible if it falls within one of the three categories set out by paragraphs (i)–(iii).

### 6.2.4.2   Section 1(3): the prohibition

As discussed above, 'any question tending to show' means 'tending to show for the first time'. This is known as the defendant's shield. The defendant may lose his or her shield if any of the subparagraphs apply and the questions are relevant: *Maxwell v DPP* [1935] AC 309. In *Jones,* Lord Denning stated that the question for the judge was what impact the cross-examination would have on the jury. If the question conveys two conflicting impressions (objectionable and not), it would 'tend to show' both, and should be excluded as the jury is likely to adopt the more prejudicial impression.

What is meant by 'charge' was held in *Stirland v DPP* [1944] AC 315 to mean 'accused is before the criminal court' and therefore does not cover the person who is 'suspected or accused without prosecution'. However, in *Maxwell v DPP* [1935] AC 309, the possibility of unrestrained cross-examination on past suspected behaviour (that did not fall under the prohibition) was considered and seen to be unfair. This conclusion was approved of in *Stirland* so that evidence of suspicion without prosecution must pass the common law test of relevance in order to be admitted. Questions in relation to pending charges are improper, as they undermine the accused's right to silence: *R v Smith* [1989] Crim LR 900.

### 6.2.4.3   Section 1(3)(i)

*the proof that he has committed or been convicted of such offence is admissible evidence to show that he is guilty of an offence with which he is then charged*

This section allows cross-examination about other offences that would be admissible to prove the guilt of the defendant but for this Act such as similar fact evidence or pursuant to another statute.  The direction to the jury will be that such evidence is relevant to the defendant's guilt.  In *Jones v DPP* [1962] AC 635, the House of Lords concluded that the prosecution would have to justify the admissibility of character evidence other than similar fact evidence before cross-examining about it, because such cross-examination if admitted would have the effect of 'tending to show for the first time' and therefore would undermine the prohibition under s 1(3).

Evidence of a defendant's previous acquittal should not be admitted in cross-examination under s 1(3)(i): *R v Cokar* [1960] 2 QB 207, CCA. This is due to a narrow approach to the section, which permits questions, relating to the 'commission' or 'conviction' of offences and not those relating to 'charges' or 'bad character'. However, where the defendant makes imputations and thereby loses his or her shield and is cross-examined on his or her convictions to discredit his or her testimony, it may be relevant to bring in previous acquittals as well.

### 6.2.4.4   Section 1(3)(ii)

*he has personally or by his advocate asked questions of the witnesses for the prosecution with a view to establish his own good character, or has given evidence of his good character, or the nature or conduct of the defence is such as to involve imputations on the character of the prosecutor or the witnesses for the prosecution; or the deceased victim of the alleged crime*

### 6.2.4.5   Attempts to establish good character (part 1 of s 1(3)(ii))

See **6.2.1** above where the defendant seeks to establish good character.  Where good character is alleged by the defendant, the prosecution may prove any previous convictions.

Now have a look at **activity 6.2** in **Appendix 1**.

### 6.2.4.6   Imputations (part 2 of s 1(3)(ii))

Section 1(3)(ii) gave rise to numerous interpretations in relation to the issue of 'imputation' until the House of Lords in *Selvey v DPP* [1970] AC 304 clarified the position. The following principles are now established:

(a) The words of the statute must be given their ordinary and natural meaning.

(b) The statute permits cross-examination of a defendant both when the imputation on the character of the prosecutor of Crown witness is cast to show that they are unreliable and also when casting the imputation as a necessary part of establishing his or her defence.

(c) In the cases of rape the defendant can allege consent without losing his shield.

(d) Where what is said amounts to an emphatic denial of the charge, is should not be regarded as an imputation. It is this area that can cause some confusion.

Police interviews are one example of what is seen to be a denial or an imputation. In *R v Jones (W)* (1923) 17 Cr App R 117, Lord Hewart CJ said (at p 120): 'It was one thing to deny that he had made the confession, but it is another thing to say that the whole thing was a deliberate and elaborate concoction on the part of the inspector; that seems to be an attack on the character of the witness'.  Whether a challenge to the prosecution evidence is a mere denial or an imputation would appear to be a question of fact and degree.  The determining factor will be the facts of the case, for example, where it is not a case of a single de-nial or a single answer, nor any suggestion of mistake it is likely that the conduct of the defence will involve imputation: *R v Tanner* (1977) 66 Cr App R 56, CA. There is a great deal of case law considering the issue of imputations as to whether or not an imputation has been asserted; the result tends to rest on the facts of each case. Therefore, there is no simple principle to apply and, in practice, the tendency is that counsel get a 'feel' for what de-fence will lose their shield and what will not. The term 'witness' is wide under this section, so that a statement that has been read by the prosecution is still deemed to be a witness who may be impugned, *R v Miller* [1997] 2 Cr App R 178. This is obviously in contradiction of the principle that s 1(3)(ii) does not apply to a person who is not a prosecution witness and who is not called as-a witness for the prosecution.  Note that s 1(3)(ii) also applies where the person against whom imputations are made is the deceased victim of the crime being tried.

Where counsel for the defence exposes the defendant to the risk of cross-examination as to character the judge should give a warning: *Selvey v DPP*. In a summary trial, where a de-fendant is unrepresented, the prosecutor and the clerk should give a warning in the ab-sence of the bench, at the request of the prosecutor: see *R v Weston-Super-Mare JJ, ex p Townsend* [1968] 3 All ER 225, DC.

The trial judge has a discretion to dis-allow cross-examination as to character. There-fore, leave should be sought before embarking on this course of questioning: *R v Carter,* 161 JP 207, CA. The discretion of the judge should be based on the circumstances in the case and an overriding duty to ensure that the trial is fair.

The general principle of fair trial and the requirement that the questioning must be rel-evant to a fact in issue has meant that the Human Rights Act 2000 has had little applica-tion in this area.

### 6.2.4.7   Purpose of cross-examination under s 1(3)(ii)

Evidence obtained under this subparagraph goes to credit only and therefore goes to show that the defendant should not be believed: see *R v Jenkins* (1945) 31 Cr App R 1 and *R v Cook* [1959] 2 QB 340. It is not to show that the defendant has a disposition to commit the type of offence with which he or she is charged: *R v Vickers* [1972] Crim LR 101, CA and *R v Khan* [1991] Crim LR 51, CA. Therefore, the judge, in summing up must tell the jury that the purpose of the questioning went only to credit and that they should not consider that it showed a propensity to commit the offence they were considering: *R v McLeod* [1995] 1 Cr App R 591, CA. A failure by the judge to give this direction will give rise to a ground of ap-peal.

The fact that the previous convictions are of a similar type to the offence with which the defendant is charged or that they have the incidental effect (whether because of the number of them or their type) of suggesting the defendant is disposed to commit the of-fence with which he or she is charged does not necessarily make cross-examination im-proper (*R v McLeod*).

In *R v Powell* [1985] 1 WLR 1364, CA, the appellant, P, was convicted of knowingly living on the earnings of prostitution. P alleged that the police had fabricated the evidence upon which the prosecution was based. He also put his character in issue, and thus came within both limbs of s 1(3)(ii). The trial judge then allowed cross-examination on his previous convictions, which were for allowing his premises to be used for the purposes of prostitu-tion. On appeal, it was argued that the judge should not have permitted the cross-exami-nation because the jury would have the greatest difficulty in relating the evidence strictly to the issue of credibility, but would have concluded that P had a propensity to commit offences relating to prostitution. The appeal was dismissed. Lord Lane CJ held that

Viscount Sankey's dictum in *Maxwell v DPP* could not be interpreted as meaning that convictions for the same or kindred offences can never be admitted. The defendant had lost his shield under both parts of s 1(3)(ii), but had either ground stood alone, the cross-examination should have been allowed.

*Limits on cross-examination*

In *R v McLeod* it was held to be undesirable that there should be prolonged or extensive cross-examination in relation to previous offences. This may divert the jury from the principal issue in the case, the guilt of the defendant on the *instant offence* and not the details of the earlier ones. Therefore, unless the evidence is admissible under similar fact doctrine, counsel should not seek to probe or emphasise the similarities between the previous offences and the instant one. Again, the purpose of cross-examination as to previous convictions must be to show that he or she is not worthy of belief, not to show disposition.

There may be a legitimate line of questioning where there were similarities in defences which had been rejected by a jury on previous occasions. In such cases the issue is whether or not the defendant was disbelieved having given evidence on oath. Further where there are underlying facts that showed particularly bad character over and above the facts of the case, these were not necessarily to be excluded. This is a difficult balancing exercise for the judge and one example of where questioning may be impermissible as it would be too prejudicial is where the previous offences are sexual offences (as for example in *R v Watts (W)* (1983) 77 Cr App R 12, CA, although this case has been questioned as can be seen in the commentary at F14.33, *Blackstones* 2004). The question of 'particularly' bad character should not have a bearing as the more extreme the assertion of bad character the more it is in fact being used to prove a disposition to offend rather than to establish the credibility of the defendant.

### 6.2.4.8   Cross-examination by co-defendant under s 1(3)(ii)

Section 1(3)(ii) applies to the defendant who loses his or her shield and therefore there is no restriction on a co-defendant who wishes to cross-examine in character. However, counsel for the co-defendant is also required to apply for leave before embarking on this line of questioning: *R v Lovett* [1973] 1 WLR 241, CA. *R v Rowson* [1986] QB 174 suggests that *Lovett* may have been decided differently today.

### 6.3.3.9   Section 1(3)(iii): evidence against a co-defendant in the same proceedings

The essential question that activates this subsection is whether the evidence damages in a *significant way* the co-defendant's defence. Therefore if the point is not in issue or supports the Crown but is not contentious, then the subparagraph does not apply: *Murdoch v Taylor* [1965] AC 574, HL and *R v Varley* (1982) 75 Cr App R 241, CA. The purpose of allowing cross-examination under s 1(3)(iii) is that the jury will be assisted, in deciding which defence case is to be believed, by the evidence going to the credibility of each defendant.

The leading case on s (1)(3)(iii) is *Murdoch v Taylor,* from which the following eight propositions derive:

(a) 'Evidence against' means evidence which supports the prosecution case in a material respect' or which undermines the defence of the co-accused.

(b) One test is to ask whether the evidence would be included in a summary of the evidence in the case which, if accepted, would lead to the conviction of the co-accused.

(c) Evidence which only contradicts something which a co-accused has said without further advancing the prosecution case in any significant degree is not 'evidence against'.

(d) 'Evidence against' may be given either in examination-in-chief or in cross-examination.

(e) Section 1(3)(iii) is not confined to cases where the 'evidence against' is given with hostile intent. The intention or state of mind of the person giving the 'evidence against' is irrelevant. What is material is the effect of the evidence on the minds of the jury. The test is objective not subjective.

(f) The purpose of cross-examination is to show the person giving 'evidence against' is not to be believed on oath.

(g) Subject to (h) below, where cross-examination is permissible, the judge has no discretion to prevent it: an accused, in seeking to defend him or herself, should not be fettered in any way. See *Corelli* [2001] Crim LR 913 allowing cross-examination of spent convictions.

(h) The prosecution may cross-examine under s (1)(3)(iii) but the court does have a discretion to prevent it as part of its function to exclude any prosecution evidence the prejudicial effect of which outweighs its probative value.

Note, in *Archbold* 2004, 8–207, 208 guidelines for determining whether defendant given evidence against a co-defendant are given from *R v Varley* (1982) 75 Cr App R 241, CA.

The evidence against the co-defendant must undermine his or her defence, ie, render it less likely that the jury will acquit him or her. In *R v Bruce* [1975] 1 WLR 1252 there were eight defendants. One of the defendants, M, admitted a plan to rob but denied being party to the actual robbery. Another, B, denied there was a plan to rob. At trial the judge ruled that B had given evidence against M and allowed M to cross-examine B about his previous convictions. The Court of Appeal held that B had not given evidence against M, as the evidence of denial was in effect a different and possibly better defence.

You may wish to explore the issue further by carrying out **activity 6.3** in **Appendix 1**.

Where the issue is one of joint venture the decision in *R v Varley* was reviewed in *R v Crawford* [1998] 1 Cr App R 338 and *R v Kirkpatrick* [1998] Crim LR 63, CA. In *R v Varley* two defendants were tried for robbery. The defence for D was that his involvement was because of duress exerted on him by A. A's defence was that he was not there at all. D was granted leave to cross-examine A under s 1(3)(iii) and A was convicted. On appeal, the Court of Appeal held that where one defendant asserts a view of the joint venture, which is directly contradicted by the other, such contradiction may be evidence against the co-defendant. A's defence had directly contradicted D's contention that he had been forced to participate in the robbery and thereby deprived him of his defence. Further the Court of Appeal noted that for s 1(3)(iii) to apply, a denial of participation in a joint venture 'must' lead to the conclusion that if one did not participate then it must have been the other who did.

*R v Crawford* held that *R v Varley* had gone too far in stating this proposition in mandatory terms and that the word 'may' would be more appropriate.

At trial, this subsection is often applied where defendants are running 'cut-throat' defences. However, this is not a pre-requisite as proposition (e) in *Murdoch v Taylor* confirms that there is no need for the evidence against the co-accused to be given with hostile intent.

In certain cases, the general principle that a defendant may be cross-examined about the fact but not the detail of his or her previous convictions may not apply. In *R v Reid* [1989] Crim LR 719, CA, R was one of four defendants charged with robbery. R was cross-examined on a previous conviction for robbery, following his defence, where he stated that he had got into the car last and only then discovered a robbery had taken place. At the previous trial for robbery his defence had been that he had got out of the car before the robbery took place. Therefore, counsel for the co-defendant argued that the detail of the previous conviction was relevant as he was running similar defences and further the dishonest defence involved the defendant seeking to falsely incriminate others.

Cross-examination under s 1(3)(iii) is in generally used by defence counsel; however, counsel for the prosecution are not excluded from applying under this subparagraph. In *R v Seigley* (1911) 6 Cr App R 106 the Crown applied to re-examine on the issue of the defendant's previous convictions. However, *Murdoch v Taylor* held that a discretion existed to prevent such questioning by the prosecution (as opposed to a co-defendant) must be given to the judge. The case of *R v Randall* [2003] UKHL 69 was a charge of murder against two defendants. Each lost the protection of s 1 CEA 1898 and therefore the previous convictions went before the jury as the defendants ran cut throat defences. The question of law was 'Where two accused are jointly charged with a crime, and each blames the other for its commission, may one accused rely on the criminal propensity of the other?' The House of Lords concluded that it was correctly stated by the Court of Appeal that in most cases the fundamental principle was that it was not normally relevant to enquire into an accused's previous character. However, in the particular circumstances of the case, where cut-throat defences were running, the antecedent history of the co-accused was not only relevant to his truthfulness but also to show who was more likely to have committed the offence. This was because of the imbalance of the antecedent history between the two co-accused, which tended to show that the version put forward by one accused was more probable than that put forward by the other. This is a very interesting case to read on the move towards bad character being directed as *to propensity* and also has a good summary of the case law in this area.

## 6.3  Criminal Justice Act 2003 — defendant's bad character

The Criminal Justice Act 2003, when it comes into force, will provide an inclusionary approach to a defendant's previous convictions and other misconduct or disposition, so that relevant evidence *is admissible* but can be excluded in circumstances if the court considers that the adverse affect on the fairness of the case so requires.

Section 101 states:

*In criminal proceedings evidence of the defendant's bad character is admissible if, but only if—*

*(a)   all parties to the proceedings agree to the evidence being admissible,*

*(b)   the evidence is adduced by the defendant himself or is given in answer to a question asked by him in cross-examination and intended to elicit it,*

*(c)   it is important explanatory evidence,*

*(d)   it is relevant to an important matter in issue between the defendant and the prosecution,*

*(e)   it has substantial probative value in relation to an important matter in issue between the defendant and co-defendant,*

*(f)   it is evidence to correct a false impression given by the defendant, or*

*(g)   the defendant has made an attack on another person's character.*

## 6.4 Children and Young Persons Act 1963, s 16(2)

A further restriction on the admissibility of evidence of previous convictions over and above the common law and statutory restrictions set out above is the CYPA 1963.

*In any proceedings for an offence committed or alleged to have been committed by a person of or over the age of 21, any offence for which he was found guilty while under the age of 14 shall be disregarded for the purposes of any evidence relating to his previous convictions; and he shall not be asked, and if asked shall not be required to answer, any question relating to such an offence, notwithstanding that the question would otherwise be admissible under section 1 of the Criminal Evidence Act 1898.*

The Criminal Justice Act 2003, s 108 will repeal s 16(2) and (3) of the Children and Young Persons Act 1963 when brought into force. The admissibility of this evidence will then fall under the general scheme set out in Part II of that Act, with two additional requirements:

(i) The offence for which the defendant is being tried and the offence for which he or she was convicted are triable only on indictment.

(ii) The court is satisfied that the interests of justice require the evidence to be admitted.

# The doctrine of similar fact evidence

## 7.1 Introduction

### 7.1.1 A cautionary tale

There was a barrister who, when quite junior, accepted a brief to prosecute a Crown Court trial. All appeared to go well throughout the prosecution case and the defendant chose to give evidence and was duly examined in chief. He was then cross-examined by prosecution counsel who, having put the allegation and received the expected vehement denial, asked the following question; 'You have done this sort of thing before haven't you?'

What do you think happened next?

(a) The defendant agreed and was convicted upon the basis that he had a propensity to commit the offence for which he was being tried.

(b) There was an immediate explosion from both defence counsel and the judge, the jury were immediately discharged and the judge demanded an explanation for prosecution counsel's behaviour and being dissatisfied with 'sorry, I got a bit carried away' ordered prosecution counsel to personally pay the wasted costs of the aborted trial.

Perhaps instinct would drive you to select the second proposition and you would be correct.

The first crucial question is to what extent can previous misconduct or discreditable behaviour of a party be adduced to prove an offence or a civil claim?

The second is this, if such evidence could be adduced, how would a jury be permitted to use it?

### 7.1.2 The general rule

As we saw in the previous chapter, the general rule is that evidence of a party's previous bad behaviour is not admissible to show that he or she is guilty of the crime or civil wrong of which he or she stands accused.

#### 7.1.2.1 Why?

This is because of the very grave risk that a tribunal of fact, and particularly a jury, would simply decide the case on the basis that 'he's done it before and so he must have done it this time', which in a criminal trial would inevitably result in a conviction.

Is it logical that if the prosecution can show that the defendant has a track record or propensity for committing a certain type of offence then a jury can be sure that he committed it on the occasion alleged?

Of course not. That would mean a conviction on a wholly incorrect basis.

### 7.1.2.2    Prejudice

It is occasionally said, 'all prosecution evidence is prejudicial'. That is not so. Prejudice arises when there is a serious risk that a tribunal of fact, usually a jury, will misuse a piece of evidence to the detriment of the defendant. The higher the risk, the greater the prejudicial effect.

Think about the following facts:

Peter is accused of indecently assaulting a small boy in a playground. In particular, it is said that he picked up the little boy in his arms and fondled his groin area. His explanation is that the little boy toppled off the slide and that he, Peter, was able to catch him. If he did put his hands between the boy's legs it was entirely accidental and completely innocent.

The judge allows the jury to know that Peter has two previous convictions for indecent assault on small boys.

(a) Does it follow that he must be lying about his intention on this occasion or could it be that this time he was behaving entirely innocently?

(b) Do you think there is a real likelihood that the jury will say that because he has a propensity to commit this sort of offence he must be lying about what happened on this occasion?

(c) Could there be situations where the fact of having done it before proves more than that the defendant has a disposition? For example, suppose on the other occasions he claimed the little boys had fallen off slides also.

### 7.1.3    Exceptions

Of course, there are exceptions to the general rule. This chapter deals with the principal common law exception, which has become known as the doctrine of similar fact evidence. Now perhaps wrongly named, it was once thought that to be admissible the previous bad behaviour had to bear a striking similarity to that of which the defendant is now accused. That is no longer the position. The recent approach is more complex and subtle. The question is not how similar is the previous misbehaviour but, taking all of the circumstances of the case, how powerful is the previous misbehaviour in proving something beyond a mere propensity on the part of the defendant to commit this type of offence.

Consider the facts of the leading case of *Makin v Attorney-General for New South Wales* [1894] AC 57, PC. The defendant and his wife were accused of the murder of an infant who they had taken from its mother on payment by her of a small sum of money. The couple were evasive when the mother tried to see the infant and moved away shortly after. A child's body was later found in the garden of their former home, dressed in the clothes of the infant. The Makins' defence was a denial of all knowledge of the infant. The trial judge admitted evidence that no fewer than 13 babies' corpses had been recovered from various premises occupied by the Makins in the past, as well as evidence that they entered into similar arrangements with other mothers to adopt their children on payment of small sums of money. Fairly inevitably they were convicted. The Privy Council dismissed the appeal and held that the evidence of the other corpses and arrangements was admissible because quite clearly this evidence went way beyond a mere propensity on the part of the Makins but went to undermine any explanation amounting to a defence.

It can be seen how powerful the evidence was that was admitted by the trial judge in the *Makin* case. This 'powerfulness' is now frequently referred to as its 'probative value'. The trial judge admitted the 'similar fact' notwithstanding its prejudicial effect in showing that they had behaved in an evil way in the past, because the probative value outweighed the prejudicial effect. Have another look at the analysis of probative value and prejudicial effect at **1.4.3** in **Chapter 1**.

### 7.1.4 The proper approach to case law

In this chapter there will be examples of similar fact evidence admitted to prove or disprove different things: to rebut a defence, to show something was designed rather then accidental, to show that the defendant was operating a system, to show that the perpetrator was the defendant, to give important background information to the jury without which they would get a distorted view of events.

Whether you are arguing for or against the admissibility of similar fact evidence it is essential to understand what the similar fact is supposed to prove, how it is supposed to prove it and to what extent it does so. The answers to these questions will depend on the whole matrix of facts and circumstances of the particular case. There will seldom be situations where one case can be said to be 'on all fours' with another. Care should be taken not to slavishly adopt old cases as authority. They are useful to illustrate principles and to demonstrate how the argument was made.

### 7.1.5 Situations where similar fact issues arise

You will notice from the *Makin* case that the defendants were only charged with one count of murder, although the jury heard evidence which strongly suggested that they murdered another 13 babies. The similar fact evidence relied upon could be described as 'off-indictment' in that the allegations of previous bad (in the Makins' case very bad) behaviour was not reflected in any count on the indictment (nor, you will notice, were they ever formally convicted of the other murders).

In some cases issues of similar fact arise 'on-indictment'. Here the 'similar fact evidence' is reflected in a count on the indictment. You will know that a defendant can, subject to the joinder rules, be tried for more then one offence in the same indictment (see the ***Criminal Litigation and Sentencing Manual***). Ordinarily, a trial judge must tell the jury to treat each count separately and not to use evidence in relation to one count in relation to another. Failure to 'firewall' each offence in this way will lead to a strong ground of appeal. There are cases where the judge will be invited by prosecution counsel to do the exact opposite, because the Crown's case is precisely that the evidence in relation to one count may be used as probative 'similar fact' in relation to another count by the jury. This was the situation in the two leading cases of *DPP v Boardman* and *R v P* (see below).

### 7.1.6 The principles

There is a marked difference of approach between similar fact in a criminal law context and that in civil law. In civil cases the tribunal of fact will almost always be a professional judge and as a consequence the risk of prejudice (the misuse of evidence) is reduced. Accordingly there is less emphasis on the prejudice versus probative focus and more on the simpler issue of relevance.

## 7.2    Criminal law

We have already given some thought to the *Makin* case. We find in that case not simply a good illustration of the probative value of evidence being so great as to outweigh its prejudicial effect but also the bedrock principles upon which the doctrine has been built. In his judgment Lord Herschell said:

In their Lordships' opinion the principles which must govern the decision of the case are clear, though the application of them is by no means free from difficulty. It is undoubtedly not competent for the prosecution to adduce evidence tending to show that the accused has been guilty of criminal acts other than those covered by the indictment for the purpose of leading to the conclusion that the accused is a person likely from his criminal conduct or character to have committed the offence for which he is being tried.

And then he said:

On the other hand, the mere fact that the evidence adduced tends to show the commission of other crimes does not render it inadmissible if it be relevant to an issue before the jury, and it may be so relevant if it bears upon the question whether the acts alleged to constitute the crime charged in the indictment were designed or accidental, or to rebut a defence which would otherwise be open to the accused.

### 7.2.1    Meaning and rationale for the rule

The first part of the pronouncement means that evidence which shows no more than that the defendant is disposed to commit offences or certain types of offences is not admissible.

In *Noor Mohammed v R* [1949] AC 182 PC, a goldsmith was accused of murdering his wife by cyanide poisoning. The trial judge admitted evidence that his first wife died of the same cause and that he had some motive to kill both of them as he believed that they had been unfaithful. As a goldsmith he had access to potassium cyanide. He appealed his conviction to the Privy Council. Lord Du Parc concluded that the 'similar fact' evidence should not have been admitted as it went no further than to suggest that the defendant might have a disposition to kill his wives but was otherwise of 'no real substance'.

Similarly in *Harris v DPP* [1952] AC 694, a police officer was accused of stealing from various shops in a market hall. Evidence was given that at various times when the thefts took place he was on duty patrolling the area and on the last occasion he was actually found outside the shop in question by detectives. Viscount Simon in the House of Lords stated, 'the fact someone perpetrated the earlier thefts when the accused may have been somewhere in the market does not provide material confirmation of his identity as the thief on the last occasion', and held that the evidence should not have been admitted on that basis.

In *R v Marshall* [1989] Crim LR 819, CA, the defendant was convicted of four burglaries. At his trial the jury was told that he had admitted committing some 87 other burglaries. The Court of Appeal held that this evidence should not have been admitted. There was no system disclosed by such evidence that could link the defendant to those burglaries for which he was being tried. The evidence simply showed a general propensity to commit burglary.

### 7.2.2    The exception to the rule

What about the second part of Lord Herschell's pronouncement?

We could do worse than to consider the judgment of Lord Cross at p 456.

Circumstances, however, may arise in which such evidence is so very relevant that to exclude it would be an affront to common sense.

*An affront to common sense?* Consider the 'similar fact' evidence in *Makin*. One dead baby in the back garden is one thing but another 13 found at the various premises where the defendants had lived is quite another. The similar fact evidence went beyond merely showing a disposition to kill babies but disclosed a system of what was described in the case as 'baby farming'. Surely it would have been an affront to common sense in that case if the jury had not been allowed to hear the 'similar fact' evidence.

Consider the case of *R v Straffen* [1952] 2 QB 911. The defendant was a patient at Broadmoor where he had be sent after murdering two young girls by strangulation. In relation to those offences there had been no attempt to conceal the bodies of the girls. They were not indecently assaulted nor did there appear to be any motive for the killings. He now stood accused of killing another young girl who was found strangled, again there was no attempt to hide the body, again no indecent assault or other motive and crucially, she was killed at a time when the defendant had absconded from Broadmoor. The evidence of the defendant's previous offences and his subsequent incarceration in Broadmoor were admitted by the judge at his trial and unsurprisingly, perhaps, he was convicted. The Court of Appeal held that the 'similar fact' evidence had been properly admitted.

It is important to understand that the 'similar fact' evidence was adduced not so the jury would say 'he's done it before so he must have done it this time', but because, given the particular circumstances, the 'similar fact' evidence represented highly probative evidence as to the defendant's guilt. It strongly suggested that all the killings were the work of the same person, they bore the 'hallmark' of the killer.

Do you think that it would have been an affront to common sense if the jury had not been allowed to hear about Straffen's previous convictions?

### 7.2.3   Striking similarity

As mentioned above, it used to be thought that the test for admissibility of 'similar fact' evidence was indeed similarity or as it was often put 'striking similarity'. Was the degree of similarity between the alleged offence and the evidence of other criminal or discreditable behaviour such as to provide power evidence of guilt?

The high water mark of this approach came in the House of Lords' judgments in *DPP v Boardman*. The defendant in that case was the headmaster of a boarding school. He was committed upon an indictment containing, inter alia, two counts. The first was buggery with boy A and the second was inciting boy B to commit buggery.

The judge directed the jury at trial that they could use both boys' evidence to prove each of the counts on the indictment as their accounts were so similar and the circumstances of the offences so unusual (on-indictment similar fact). Both boys had given evidence that they were woken around midnight by the headmaster in the dormitory and told to be quiet so as not to wake the other boys. Both alleged the use of similar words to persuade them to take part in sex and both said that the offences took place in the headmaster's sitting room. Furthermore, the House of Lords laid great store by the fact that the defendant, a middle aged man, requested that both boys take the active rather than the passive role in the act of anal sex. The House of Lords thought that this was very unusual!

The judgments emphasise that it was similarity that provided the key to the admissibility of similar fact evidence.

At p 453 Lord Hailsham said:

A mere succession of facts is not normally enough ... There must be something more than mere repetition. The test is whether there is such an underlying unity between the offences as to make coincidence an affront to common sense.

At p 462 Lord Salmon said:

It has ... never been doubted that if the crime charged is committed in a uniquely or strikingly similar manner to other crimes committed by the accused the manner in which the other crimes were committed may be evidence on which a jury could reasonably conclude that the accused was guilty of the crime charged. The similarity would have to be so unique and striking that common sense makes it inexplicable on the basis of coincidence.

The approach was followed in *R v Scarrott* [1978] QB 1016, where Lord Scarman referred to an 'underlying link' that had to be present between the alleged offence and the similar fact evidence. He also stressed that striking similarity could be found not only in the offence but in the circumstances surrounding it.

In *R v Inder* (1978) 67 Cr App R 143, the requirement of striking similarity was applied with some rigour. Here the method employed by the defendant to commit offences of indecency with young boys in the past was introduced into evidence as similar fact. The Court of Appeal held that the similarities went no further than to 'represent the stock in trade of the seducer of small boys and were not unique but appeared in the vast majority of cases that came before the courts'.

It must be arguable that the headmasters method in *DPP v Boardman* and his preference of role went no further than the stock in trade of a paedophile headmaster.

While it is possible to argue that *DPP v Boardman* might have misapplied the principle on its own facts, there is no doubt that it did lay down a clear principle that striking similarity was the test to be applied in 'similar fact' cases.

### 7.2.4   The decline of similarity

#### 7.2.4.1   *R v P* [1991] 3 All ER 337

P was accused of rape and incest in relation to his two daughters. There were similarities in what they said about their father's possessive and domineering behaviour, his use of force and threats, the acquiescence of their mother and the payment by P for abortions.

The allegations of both girls were reflected in different counts in one indictment. The defence sought separate trials in relation to both girls but this application was refused by the trial judge. P was convicted and appealed.

The Court of Appeal held that the evidence of the two girls should not have been left to the jury on the basis that what one girl said could be used to support the other and vice versa (ie on-indictment similar fact). The Court commented that the similarities did not go beyond 'the incestuous fathers stock-in-trade'. Upon the authorities the Court felt bound to say that more was required to justify the admissibility of the evidence.

The Court of Appeal allowed his appeal albeit reluctantly but granted leave to appeal to the House of Lords. The question of law certified by the Court of Appeal was as follows:

Where a father/step-father is charged with sexually abusing a young daughter of the family, is evidence that he has also similarly abused other young children of the family admissible (assuming there is no collusion) in support of such charge in the absence of any other 'striking similarities'?

Lord Mackay giving judgment in the House of Lords answered the question in the following terms:

... restricting the circumstances in which there is sufficient probative force to overcome prejudice of evidence relating to another crime to cases in which there is some striking similarity between them is to restrict the operation of the principle in a way which gives too much effect to a particular manner of stating it, and is not justified in principle.

He continued:

Once the principle is recognised, that what has to be assessed is the probative force of the evidence in question, the infinite variety of circumstances in which the question arises demonstrates that there is no single manner in which this can be achieved. Whether the evidence has sufficient probative value to outweigh its prejudicial effect must in each case be a question of degree.

And later in his judgment stated:

When a question of the kind raised in this case arises I consider that the judge must first decide whether there is material upon which the jury would be entitled to conclude that the evidence of one victim, about what occurred to that victim, is so related to the evidence given by another victim, about what happened to that other victim, that the evidence of the first victim provides strong enough support for the evidence of the second victim to make it just to admit it, notwithstanding the prejudicial effect of admitting the evidence. This relationship, from which support is derived, may take many forms and while these forms may include 'striking similarity' in the manner in which the crime is committed, consisting of unusual characteristics in its execution the necessary relationship is by no means confined to such circumstances. Relationships in time and circumstances other than these may well be important relationships in this connection. Where the identity of the perpetrator is in issue, and evidence of this kind is important in that connection, obviously something of the nature, of what has been called in the course of the argument a signature or other special feature will be necessary. To transpose this requirement to other situations where the question is whether a crime has been committed rather than who did commit it is to impose an unnecessary and improper restriction upon the application of the principle.

The appeal was allowed and P's conviction was restored.

Following *R v P* the test for admissibility for similar fact evidence can be summarised in the following two propositions:

- If the probative value of the similar fact material is sufficient it will be admitted notwithstanding its prejudicial effect.

- Probative value can be found in striking similarity or in some other 'relationship' between the allegation and the similar fact material.

To quote the learned editors of *Archbold* (2003 edn):

The great advantage of the decision in *P* is that it rid the law of the notion that had developed in the years since the decision of the House of Lords in *DPP v Boardman* [1975] AC 421, that the test of admissibility was that there should be a 'striking similarity' between the similar fact evidence and the evidence relating to the charge being tried. What is now clear is that the degree of similarity required will vary according to the issues in the case and the nature of the other evidence.

The disadvantage of the decision in *P* is that it gives little assistance as to what should be taken to invest the similar fact evidence with sufficient degree of probative value. This disadvantage is more apparent than real because the Lord Chancellor's conclusion was expressed to derive from the five speeches in *Boardman*, from which his Lordship quoted at length. Perusal of those speeches, it is submitted, gives a clear indication of what is to be regarded as investing the evidence with the requisite degree of probative force.

### 7.2.4.2  What about identity?

Interestingly, Lord Mackay appeared to require striking similarity in cases where identity was in issue and the prosecution sought to rely upon similar fact material.

This approach was followed in *R v Johnson* [1995] 2 Cr App R 41. In that case the defendant was accused of attempted rape. The victim awoke to find a man in her room lightly or gently touching her stomach. The trial judge admitted similar fact evidence of the defendant's previous convictions which involved the defendant waking a woman by gently stroking her thigh and waking a women by gently having intercourse with her. The Court of Appeal applying *R v P* held that the previous convictions should not have been admitted. The similarity did not go far enough.

In *R v John W* [1998] 2 Cr App R 289, CA a 13-year-old girl and a young woman were attacked in Aldershot and in Farnham respectively within two weeks of each other. The defendant was accused of both attacks. Some of the descriptions of the attacker fitted the defendant and his clothing but crucially the defendant had moved from Aldershot to Farnham between the two attacks. The trial judge directed the jury that the two counts on the indictment were mutually supportive of each other (on-indictment similar fact). The Court of Appeal found that the basis upon which the counts on the indictment were left to the jury was proper, finding between each allegation 'a relationship in time and circumstances' which was possessed of a high degree of probative value. Hooper J stressed that there was no special rule in identification cases and that Lord Mackay's observations in *R v P* should be interpreted to be applicable in cases where the only evidence against an accused was the similar fact evidence. In such cases the evidence would require such a high degree of probative value to achieve admissibility that there would usually have to be present something of the nature of a 'signature', but the principle was the same. What was required was still sufficient probative force.

Is the above what Lord Mackay really meant? A closer look at the relevant part of *R v P* is worth taking. Hooper J's interpretation has been described as 'strained and unconvincing'.

Was Hooper J making the law or merely restating the common law position prior to *Boardman*? In *Thompson v R* [1918] AC 221 the defendant was convicted of sexual offences of a homosexual nature when evidence was admitted that he was found in possession of powder puffs that were, at that time, thought to be indicative of homosexuality and therefore, on the facts of the case, as probative of the identity of the defendant. While social values have changed to the extent that it is certainly no longer the case that being found in possession of powder puffs would be thought to prove any criminal indication, *R v Thompson* was arguably decided with a requirement of something close to 'signature' being used as the test.

### 7.2.4.3  Identity — probative force proving what?

Consider the following facts:

The defendant is accused of three counts of rape and indecent assault on three separate women. All with similar features. All three victims identified the defendant but their identifications were weak and taken individually would not perhaps convince a jury. Can the judge direct the jury that each identification is capable of supporting the others on the issue of whether the defendant was the rapist (on-indictment similar fact)?

A similar situation occurred in the case of *R v McGranaghan* [1995] 1 Cr App R 559. McGranaghan had spent years in custody before it emerged from forensic evidence that he could not have been responsible for one of the rapes. The Court of Appeal allowed his appeal. It was said that the similar features were sufficient to permit the admissibility of one allegation in support of another on the basis that the rapes and indecent assaults were the work of the same man, but not that the man was the defendant. The jury should have been directed that they would have to be sure that the defendant committed at least one of the offences before they could use the identification evidence to prove that he committed all of the other offences.

In the words of Glidewell LJ:

> An identification about which the jury are not sure cannot support another identification of which they are also not sure however similar the facts of the two offences may be. The similar facts go to show that the same man committed both offences not that the defendant was that man.

A similar dilemma confronted the Court of Appeal in *R v Downey* [1995] 1 Cr App R 547. Here the robberies of two petrol stations took place within a few minutes of each other. The circumstances suggested strongly that it was the same man who committed both. In relation to one robbery there was CCTV footage evidence and in relation to the other a registration number of the robber's car. It was held that a direction that the jury could combine both pieces of identification evidence in determining whether the defendant had committed both robberies was proper because the offences were so 'welded together' that the jury were entitled to conclude that they were the work of the same man.

In *R v Barnes* [1995] 2 Cr App R 491, *Downey* was approved and *McGranaghan* was distinguished. The Court of Appeal held that where there was other (ie non-visual evidence) which proved that all the offences were the work of the same man, a jury could use separate identifications cumulatively on the issue of whether that man was the defendant.

The reconciliation of the two positions presents difficulties and seems only possible on the basis that the non-visual 'similar fact' was deemed to be less strong in *McGranaghan* than in *Downey* and *Barnes*. The court in *McGranaghan*, of course, had the benefit of hindsight in that evidence was produced before them that, notwithstanding the similar fact evidence, at least one of the offences could not have been committed by the same person as the other two. Indeed, it was the allegations arising from the strongest identification which were undermined by the forensic evidence.

### 7.2.5 Propensity by the back door?

#### 7.2.5.1 Circumstances in which probative force derives from the accused's propensity

It is sometimes suggested that Lord Hailsham's approach in *Boardman* regarding 'the forbidden chain of reasoning' goes too far, namely, any chain of reasoning leading from propensity to guilt. It is also suggested that his recommendation that in similar fact cases the jury should be directed to 'eschew the forbidden reasoning' is too cautious and has not been adopted in practice.

The basis of this suggestion appears to be that in some of the similar fact cases the appeal courts have upheld convictions notwithstanding the fact that a jury has heard evidence about a defendant's propensity.

What is forbidden, or at least should be, is evidence of 'mere' propensity, ie evidence which is merely about propensity and has no probative value beyond that.

In most of the cases where a jury has heard about a defendant's propensity there will be another reason for its admission. For example, in *R v Straffen* (**7.2.2** above) it wasn't the fact that the defendant had a propensity to strangle young girls that was the basis of the admission of the defendant's previous convictions but the peculiar circumstances of the murders, the opportunity and the proximity (his recent escape from Broadmoor) which added probative value to mere propensity.

It may be that there have been decisions that violate the principle stated by Lord Hailsham and should be regarded with circumspection as authorities.

In *R v Lewis* (1982) 76 Cr App R 33, the Court of Appeal were of the opinion that the nature of the particular case gave evidence of a paedophile tendency probative value sufficient to outweigh its prejudicial effect. Lewis' defence to allegations of indecency with his girlfriend's children was one of innocent association (ie, that the seemingly indecent acts were not motivated by indecency). Evidence of his sexual inclinations was considered to be of high probative value in evaluating that defence in the light of the prosecution evidence against him.

#### 7.2.5.2  Homosexuality

One might be forgiven for thinking that the doctrine of similar fact and homosexuality were in someway inextricably bound up, because of the volume of old cases wherein a defendant's homosexuality was an issue. Frequently sexuality was admitted into evidence to rebut innocent association and misidentification. It was at one point supposed that such cases represented a special category in the doctrine. Lord Hailsham in *Boardman* was at pains to point out that there is no such special category.

It might seem strange now that a jury should be allowed to hear evidence that the defendant was in possession of powder puffs to support an allegation of indecent assault on a boy as in *Thompson* (see above) or that the fact that a defendant was gay could be used by the jury to determine whether he had indecently assaulted a young man as in *R v King* [1967] 2 QB 358.

It is submitted that it is unlikely that today most people would find any 'striking similarity', 'hallmark' or 'high probative value' in the mere fact that a man might prefer having sex with men rather than women, even where the allegation was indecent assault on a boy. It hardly even amounts to evidence of mere propensity.

Contrast that position with Lord Sumners immortal words in *Thompson*:

Persons ... who commit the offences now under consideration seek the habitual gratification of a particular perverted lust, which not only takes them out of the class of ordinary men gone wrong, but stamps them with the hallmark of a specialised and extraordinary class as much as if they carried on their bodies some physical peculiarity.

It is submitted that in accordance with the modern perception of homosexuality it would not be surprising if it transpired that around say 10% of the population were gay. That quite clearly would not have been the perception of Lord Sumner and his contemporaries. Nobody was 'out' unless 'outed' by the criminal justice system. The settled world view of 'straight' men would perhaps have been that homosexuality was an absolute rarity and that such a 'class' was microscopically small. Certainly it would not have been in anybody's interest to fly in the face of such a settled view, particularly a judge. It is submitted that it was that perception coupled with extreme prejudice which sought to justify homosexuality as a 'hallmark' akin to some 'physical peculiarity'. At the time of *Thompson* homosexuality was perceived as possessing a high probative value that would not be attached to it in the early 21st century. It is worth considering that *what* is probative and therefore passes the test for similar fact evidence will change alongside changes in the nature of society.

### 7.2.6  Non-criminal behaviour as similar fact

What if the behaviour sought to be relied upon by the prosecution as similar fact evidence falls short of criminal behaviour? Could the fact of that behaviour be admitted to help to prove the allegation on the indictment? The answer to the latter question is yes so long as, in accordance with the principle set out in *R v P*, the fact has sufficient probative force to justify its inclusion. In *R v Barrington* [1981] 1 WLR 419 the charge was indecent assault on three young girls who had been lured to a house as babysitters. At the house they were shown pornographic material, induced by defendant to pose naked and thereafter indecently assaulted. In that case evidence that three other girls were lured to the house upon the same pretext and were subjected to the same treatment was properly admitted, even though what occurred in their case fell short of the offence of indecent assault because these girls left the house as a result of the approaches by the defendant.

The Criminal Justice Act 2003 defines bad character in much broader terms than having previous convictions. In s 98 (currently due to come into force in December 2005) the Act states:

> **Bad character**
>
> *References in this Chapter to evidence of a person's bad character are to evidence of, or of a disposition towards, misconduct on his part, other than evidence which—*
>
> *(a)   has to do with the alleged facts of the offence with which the defendant is charged, or*
>
> *(b)   is evidence of misconduct in connection with the investigation or prosecution of that offence.*

### 7.2.7   Previous acquittals

Does the law of similar fact go even further than that stated above and permit the jury to hear that a defendant has been acquitted of similar offences in the past? Such evidence is admissible so long as it is sufficiently probative. At first blush it is, perhaps, difficult to see how previous findings of not guilty could have relevance and therefore any probative value in relation to the offence on the indictment. Consider however the facts in *R v Z* [2000] 2 AC 483, HL. The defendant in that case had been acquitted of rape on three previous occasions. On each occasion his defence had been that of consent. He was tried on a fourth occasion for rape and again ran consent as his defence. The fact that he had been charged with rape three times before and on each occasion had explained himself by asserting that the woman had consented was so highly probative of the offence charged as to pass the *R v P* test. This was conceded by the defence. Indeed the argument on appeal was on the issue of double jeopardy rather than the admissibility of the previous acquittals.

### 7.2.8   Incriminating articles

The possession of an incriminating article or articles may go to prove that the defendant committed the alleged offence in that the article or articles in question may have been used or were intended for use in the commission of the offence. However, if the articles show no more than that the defendant has a propensity to commit this kind of offence, evidence of the possession would be inadmissible upon the principles set out in *Makin* and *Boardman*. This appears to have been the approach, but without much rigour, in *R v Thompson* [1918] AC 221 where it was assumed that the defendant had powder puffs about his person in furtherance of an intended homosexual assault on a young boy!

A clearer illustration may be found in the case of *R v Taylor* (1924) 17 Cr App R 109, where the defendant was seen running from the scene of a burglary. The prosecution were permitted to adduce evidence that a jemmy or crowbar was found in his house. There could not, in the circumstances, be any suggestion that the jemmy was used in the burglary with which the defendant was charged. It was held that evidence of the possession of the jemmy was wrongly admitted, its only purpose being to demonstrate that the defendant had a propensity to commit burglary. Contrast that situation with the one in the case of *R v Reading* [1966] 1 WLR 836, CCA. The defendants were charged with hijacking lorries and evidence of the possession of hijacking kit, ie a police uniform, walkie talkies and vehicle number plates, was held to have been properly admitted as the articles could well have been used in the alleged offences. This forms the justification for the admission of 'dealers kit', ie weighing scales, wraps, bags, cutting agent, etc in drug supplying cases.

### 7.2.9   'Background evidence'

As discussed above, the principles in *Makin* and *Boardman* represent a real protection for defendants from conviction upon the basis of prejudice rather than proof. It would seem to follow that in order to adduce other prejudicial evidence of a discreditable nature, ie 'off indictment' similar fact relating to the background of the offence charged, the prosecution would have to demonstrate, in accordance with *R v P*, that the evidence had such probative force that it would be right to admit it notwithstanding its prejudicial effect. That test of probative value would be achieved if the evidence was such that, without it, the jury would not be able to understand the real nature of the case against the defendant, for example, that the defendant threatened to kill the victim days before the victim was murdered.

Similarly, if the evidence is about something which is really part and parcel of the offence but prejudicial to the defendant, it would be proper for the jury to hear the evidence if it had strong probative force in relation to the offence charged. It would seem to follow that such evidence should be excluded if it does not possess powerful probative force in relation to the offence charged. For example, a defendant faces allegations of grievous bodily harm and affray. The charges relate to a fight outside a house in the same street as the defendant resides. During the fight the defendant was alleged to have kicked a young women while she lay on the ground. He was separated from her and appeared to calm down. There followed a certain amount of taunting from people in the house and he became enraged. After a few minutes he declared that he was going to get his 'f.....g sword'. He went to his own house and armed himself with a samurai sword and advanced upon a crowd who had gathered. They scattered in fear. He then demolished the garden fence of the house and went on to attack the front door but did not gain entry. He was duly arrested and charged. He pleaded guilty to the charge of affray, admitting his behaviour with the sword. He pleaded not guilty to the assault on the girl denying that he had touched her. On the trial for the assault, the prosecution were permitted to adduce evidence about the sword incident upon the basis that if formed part of the same transaction.

But how was it so probative of the assault? In what way could it assist the jury as to whether or not the defendant assaulted the girl? If it could assist at all, how could it be said to be so probative that it should be admitted notwithstanding the highly prejudicial nature of the evidence? In *R v Pettman* (2 May 1985 unreported) Purchas LJ stated:

> Where it is necessary to place before the jury evidence of part of a continual background of history relevant to the offence charged in the indictment and without the totality of which the account placed before the jury would be incomplete or incomprehensible, then the fact that the whole account involves including evidence establishing the commission of an offence with which the accused is not charged is not of itself a ground for excluding the evidence.

There is a recent tendency to distinguish background evidence from what is understood as similar fact evidence, and in doing so to establish as the sole gateway to admissibility the simple test of 'relevance' as opposed to powerful probative force. In *R v M (T)* [2000] 1 WLR 421 the Court of Appeal approved the distinction. In that case the defendant was charged with raping his sister on two occasions. The Court of Appeal upheld the trial judges decision to allow the jury to hear about other sexual offences committed against other siblings some years before, in which the defendant was forced to participate. The justification for admission of this evidence was that it was proper that the jury should hear about the culture of abuse wherein the offences took place in order to understand how the defendant felt able to abuse his sister with impunity. The basis of admission appears to have been that without the evidence the jury would be unable to fully understand an essential aspect of the case. It is submitted that the evidence would have been admitted under similar fact principles as set out in *R v P* as possessing powerful probative force.

It is further submitted that any distinction between similar fact and background evidence and the effect upon the test for admissibility may not give rise to a radical liberalisation of what the jury would be allowed to hear. Even if the trial judge decides that a particular piece of background evidence is admissible as simply relevant, the judge still has an inherent discretion to exclude evidence where the prejudicial effect outweighs its probative value. This position was confirmed in *M (T)*. The trial judge must exercise that discretion reasonably. In *Dolan* [2003] 1 Cr App R 281 the defendant was charged with the murder by shaking of his baby son. The evidence sought to be admitted against D, was that he had been violent towards inanimate objects such as the remote control for the television set. The Court of Appeal upheld the touchstones of the background evidence principle as being 'relevance and necessity'. This evidence was not relevant, nor could it be considered necessary for the jury to know about it. The judgment goes on to warn against the use of the background evidence principle as a device to illicit otherwise inadmissible similar fact evidence.

The Criminal Justice Act 2003, s 102 (currently proposed to come into force in December 2005) will put background evidence on a statutory footing. The section defines 'important explanatory evidence' as follows:

> ...... *evidence is important explanatory evidence if—*
>
> (a) *without it, the court or jury would find it impossible or difficult properly to understand other evidence in the case, and*
>
> (b) *its value for understanding the case as a whole is substantial.*

### 7.2.10 Collusion

What is the position where a defendant is accused of separate offences against two or more victims, and the prosecution argue that the allegations support each other (on-indictment similar fact) and the defence contend that any alleged similarity derives from collusion between the complainants or contamination of the account of one by knowledge of what another complainant has alleged?

The admissibility of one witness's evidence in support of another is dependent, since *R v P*, on its probative value. In a case of on-indictment similar fact, probative value is derived from the independent nature of the accounts given.

Where there exists a risk of collusion or contamination, the probative value of a given piece of evidence must be greatly reduced. If it is so reduced, how can it pass the admissibility test? One might argue that unless the risk of collusion can be dismissed, the evidence in relation to one allegation cannot be allowed to support another allegation.

The House of Lords were confronted with such an issue in the case of *R v H* [1995] 2 AC 596. Lord Mackay held that in such a situation the evidence would be admissible and should go before the jury. His reasoning, though perhaps surprising does, it is respectfully suggested, have the ring of common sense. If a judge has to decide whether any or all of the allegations made by the victims are true, he is doing the jury's job for them in that he is basically deciding guilt or innocence. He went on to say that the judge would have to direct the jury that if they were not satisfied of the absence of collusion they could not use the evidence of one allegation to help to prove another.

### 7.2.11  Discretion to exclude?

At common law the judge always has a discretion to exclude evidence as between the prosecution and the defendant where it is felt that the prejudicial effect upon the jury would outweigh its probative value. Of course, in relation to similar fact evidence, the test for admissibility under *R v P* is the same as the test for the exercise of common law judicial discretion. Consequently, if the judge decides the evidence is admissible, it would seem perverse for the judge to apply the same test again in relation to his or her discretion and come to a different conclusion.

### 7.2.12  Similar fact evidence as between co-accused

An accused can use similar fact against a co-accused (*R v Miller* [1952] 2 All ER 667) if the proof that the co-accused committed a crime is relevant to the defence of the accused (ie the fact that A committed offences previously must in some way suggest that B might not have done rather than simply making it more likely that A is guilty). In *Lowery v R* [1973] 3 All ER 662, It was stated that:

> If the crime was one which had apparently been committed without any motive, unless it was for the sensation experienced in the killing, then, unless both men had acted in concert, the deed was that of one of them and it would be unjust to prevent either of the accused from calling any evidence of probative value which could point to the probability that the perpetrator was one rather than the other.

In *R v Sullivan*, *The Times*, 18 March 2003 the defendant was charged with the torture and murder of a man who had starved to death locked in a cupboard in S's flat. His co-accused who lived in the same flat blamed him and explained their limited involvement with actions under duress exerted by S. It was held that:

(a) one co-accused is always entitled to adduce evidence that is relevant to this case, whatever the prejudicial effect on other co-accused;

(b) the test of relevance will be applied strictly;

(c) evidence of the propensity of a co-accused to commit crimes generally or the particular crime alleged cannot, generally speaking, be adduced by another co-accused as part of his or her case;

(d) However such evidence can be adduced by a co-accused (A) against a co-accused (B) if B has (i) put his or her own character or propensity in issue, or (ii) positively attacks A's case.

In *R v Randall* [2004] 1 All ER 467, R and G had been jointly charged with murder. Each defendant blamed the other for having inflicted the fatal blows. Both R and G had previous convictions, but G had a worse record than R, including offences for violence and robbery. These convictions were relied upon by R who was convicted whereas G was acquitted. The prosecution appealed the trial judge's ruling that the convictions were relevant. It was held that a co-accused's propensity might be relevant where a defendant sought to rely on such evidence in order to prove his innocence, applying *Lowery*.

In accordance with general principles, the judge does not possess the discretionary power to exclude (see **1.7.2.1**).

### 7.2.13  Statutory similar fact

The Theft Act 1968, s 27(3) provides that:

(3)  *Where a person is being proceeded against for handling stolen goods (but not for any offence other than handling stolen goods), then at any stage of the proceedings, if evidence has been given of his having or arranging to have in his possession the goods the subject of the charge, or of his undertaking or assisting in, or arranging to undertake or assist in, their retention, removal, disposal or realisation, the following evidence shall be admissible for the purpose of proving that he knew or believed the goods to be stolen goods—*

    (a)  *evidence that he has had in his possession, or has undertaken or assisted in the retention, removal, disposal or realisation of, stolen goods from any theft taking place not earlier than 12 months before the offence charged; and*

    (b)  *(provided that seven days' notice in writing has been given to him of the intention to prove the conviction) evidence that he has within the five years preceding the date of the offence charged been convicted of theft or of handling stolen goods.*

The above provision applies to all forms of handling (see *R v Ball* [1983] 1 WLR 801).

In *R v Wilkins* [1975] 2 All ER 734, CA and more recently in *R v Duffas* (1994) 158 JP 224 it was stated that the provision cannot assist the prosecution on any issue other than guilty knowledge or belief.

In *R v Bradley* (1980) 70 Cr App R 200, CA (applied in *R v Wood* [1987] 1 WLR 799, CA) the provision was given a restrictive construction in that it was held that, in relation to subsection (a) the only evidence which is admissible is that which is actually described, ie evidence of the defendant's possession etc but not how the stolen goods came to be in the defendant's possession.

In *R v Hacker* [1994] 1 WLR 1659 it was held by the House of Lords in relation to subsection (b) that the detail or description of the subject matter of the stolen goods was admissible.

The trial judge, as is usually the case, has a discretion at common law to exclude evidence otherwise admissible under the Theft Act 1968, s 27(3), where the prejudicial effect of the evidence would outweigh its probative value. Similarly, under s 78 of the Police and Criminal Evidence Act 1984, the judge has a discretion to exclude such evidence where it would have an adverse effect upon the fairness of the trial (see **Chapter 9**).

## 7.3  Similar fact in civil law

Similar fact arises in civil cases but tends to be less controversial. The test applied for admissibility is one of relevance rather than the principle arising from *R v P* (see above), ie strong probative force versus prejudicial effect. In *Sattin v National Union Bank* (1978) 122 SJ 367, CA, the defendant bank lost a diamond deposited by the plaintiff. The bank claimed that it had used all reasonable safeguards but the Court of Appeal held that the plaintiff was entitled to adduce evidence of another occasion when the bank had lost valuable jewellery. The evidence was relevant in that it tended to rebut the bank's assertion of taking all reasonable care. In *Mood Music Publishing Co Ltd v De Wolfe Ltd* [1976] Ch 119, CA, the plaintiff claimed infringement of their copyright in relation to the now immortalised piece of music 'Sogno Nostalgico'. It was alleged that the defendants had simply copied the piece and renamed it 'Girl in the Dark'. The defence case was that any similarity was merely coincidental. The plaintiffs were permitted to adduce evidence of three further pieces of music which the defendants appeared to have copied. The Court of Appeal upheld the judge's decision to admit such evidence as it was relevant as tending to undermine the defence of coincidence, on the basis that the evidence of previous copying was 'logically probative' that the music was copied on this occasion.

# Hearsay evidence

## 8.1 Out of court statements

This chapter will consider the concept of hearsay evidence. The rules relating to hearsay evidence restrict the extent to which statements made out of court will be admitted as evidence. Hearsay statements are not the only 'out of court' statements so it is worth exploring out of court statements generally before looking at hearsay statements in particular.

Take a minute to visualise a trial. It is likely that you will be thinking about a witness in the witness box giving evidence about some matter, perhaps an assault. It is likely that the witness you are thinking about will be an 'eye witness' in that he or she will be saying what he or she saw. The reason such a witness is called to give evidence is that he or she will be the best person available to give such evidence. What makes him or her the best person is the first-hand experience of the events in question. It makes more sense to call the witness to say what happened than to bring to court someone else the witness spoke to about the incident. Equally, it makes more sense to call the witness than to rely upon a document the witness wrote about the event.

In the course of this chapter we shall see that the courts prefer to hear evidence from such witnesses with first-hand experience. Why do you think that such witnesses are preferred? If witness A saw an event, what might be wrong with calling witness B to say what he or she had been told about the event by witness A.

Calling the witness of the event (witness A) to court as opposed to a person he or she told about the event (witness B) means that we have the best source of information for the court. There are a number of aspects to this:

1. The court receives the information with appropriate formality. Testimony is generally given on oath (see **4.6**). Even if the witness does not hold religious beliefs, the formality of the court environment and threat of a conviction for perjury form strong encouragement to the witness to give truthful testimony. A person making a similar statement out of court may not particularly feel a similar pressure to be honest.

2. There is less possibility of error. All witnesses can be mistaken in a number of ways. However, when witness B is used to prove what witness A saw by repeating what he has been told by A, we add to A's potential mistakes the chance that B has inaccurately repeated what witness A told him. B could have misheard, misinterpreted, forgotten or distorted what A had said or the account could simply be incomplete. The more people we add into the chain of communication between the actual witness to the event and the person testifying the greater the risk of such error.

3. If the testimony is given by the first-hand witness of the event, it will be possible to conduct the most critical examination of the account. A statement made out of

court clearly cannot be cross-examined. Further, any possible explanation advanced by the party against whom the evidence is admitted cannot be put to the actual witness if his or her account is conveyed by another.

4. Where evidence is given by way of a statement made out of court, the tribunal of fact is deprived of an opportunity to assess the demeanour of the person making the statement.

5. Added to this is the risk that inexperienced tribunals of fact, such as juries, may not be sufficiently aware of the weakness of out of court statements identified above.

The courts are therefore resistant to receiving out of court statements as evidence. There is a strong preference for receiving the evidence in court and from the person who had first-hand experience of the matters in question.

There are, however, various reasons for seeking to admit statements made out of court. Leaving aside the rules of evidence, a party may seek to prove that a statement was made out of court for the following purposes:

(a) To prove the thing said in the statement by relying on the truth or accuracy of what was said. The logic in such cases is, 'If A said X then X is true'. If this is the purpose of the statement, it is a *hearsay* statement.

(b) To prove that the statement was made. These statements are called *original* statements. There are a number of reasons why this might be useful in the case:

   (i) to bolster the credibility of a witness by being consistent with his or her testimony. This is a *previous consistent statement*, which was considered at **5.2.3**;

   (ii) to undermine the credibility of a witness by being inconsistent with his or her current testimony. This is a *previous inconsistent statement*, which was considered at **5.3.4**;

   (iii) to prove that the maker held a particular belief or knew a particular fact. The logic is that if a person speaks about a particular thing, he or she knows of that thing. Therefore a statement, 'Hello, Caroline, have you recovered from your illness?', could prove that the maker knew Caroline had been ill as much as it could prove that she had in fact been ill. Insofar as it is used to prove Caroline's illness, the tribunal of fact would have to rely on the truth of the statement (or what it implies). Insofar as the statement is used to prove that the maker of the statement knew that Caroline was ill, this does depend on the statement being true. However it does not prove the fact narrated in it (the illness): this would be proved by other evidence. Rather the evidential purpose is to prove a fact (the maker's knowledge) by proving (a) the fact of certain things having been said and (b) that the things said were true (this being achieved by independent evidence);

   (iv) to prove that someone other than the maker held a particular belief or knew a particular fact. For example, if the issue in the case was whether the accused acted under duress, evidence that a threat was made to that person would be relevant to prove that the accused *believed* that he or she had been threatened. It can do this whether or not the threat was genuine or true;

   (v) to prove that words were used because they have a particular legal significance. If I promise to sell you a painting for £100 and then refuse to do so, you could sue me for breach of contract. To prove that a contract existed and its terms you would have to prove that I had made you an offer, which you accepted. To prove the offer, you would have to prove the statement I made out of court: 'I will sell you this painting for £100'. To amount to an offer the promise to sell you a painting for £100 does not have to be true. In fact, if you think about it, most promises in breach of contract cases will have been untrue up to a point: that is why the breach of contract action is being brought. To use a criminal example, it is an offence under s 4 of the Public Order Act 1986 to use 'threatening, abusive or insulting words or behaviour'. If the prosecution allege that the offence was committed by use of threatening words they will have to prove that the words were used. If, for example, the words were 'You bastard, you're dead,' that statement will have to be proved at court. Clearly what is said does not have to be true. The relevance to the case is that the statement was made at all;

(vi)   to prove that the maker of the statement lied. Occasionally this sort of statement may overlap with the one above because proof that the maker of the statement lied may be a necessary feature of the case (for example in fraud, misrepresentation or deception cases). On other occasions the lie will be evidence that the maker was conscious of his or her own guilt and was trying to cover that guilt up (see **Chapter 10** for more detail on the probative value of lies). Obviously, the statement does not have to be true to be a lie!

## 8.2   Hearsay evidence

### 8.2.1   A cautionary note

This chapter will first consider what evidence is hearsay and then consider the exceptions to the hearsay rule. It is worth noting that many of the exceptions have evolved because the rule, strictly applied, would lead to the inadmissibility of a lot of evidence that (a) is highly probative and (b) could not be obtained by other sources available to the court. It is important to keep this in mind when reading this chapter because, unfortunately for anyone trying to understand hearsay, the courts have not always adopted a straightforward approach to getting such probative and necessary evidence into court. The law has not always developed exceptions to the rule that secure the admissibility of the best and most probative evidence. Instead the courts sometimes evade the hearsay rule by defining what one might think to be a hearsay statement as original evidence. As a result some of the hearsay cases are confusing and even, occasionally, wrong. This chapter will seek not to deal with all of the difficult cases but will concentrate on the identification of more common types of hearsay evidence. After the general rule has been identified, some of the more difficult areas and issues raised by the rule will be considered briefly. This chapter will then consider the main exceptions to the rule excluding hearsay (ie, situations in which hearsay evidence is admissible).

This area of law has also been altered by the Criminal Justice Act 2003. Although the Act is not yet in force some time will be spent considering these reforms.

### 8.2.2   Definition

Hearsay evidence is the use of words written or spoken out of court to prove something by getting the tribunal of fact to rely upon (ie put faith or belief in) the statement.

There is no single definition of hearsay evidence. However widely accepted ways of defining hearsay are:

(a) Any statement other than one made by a witness while giving testimony in the proceedings in question is inadmissible as evidence of the facts stated.

(b) An assertion other than one made by a person while testifying in the proceedings is not admissible as evidence of any fact asserted (*R v Sharp* [1988] 1 WLR 7, HL).

Any statement made out of court that is not a hearsay statement is termed 'original evidence'. Such statements are admitted not to prove a fact by relying on the truth of the words contained in it, but to prove something simply because the statement was made.

### 8.2.3  The rule against hearsay evidence

The general effect of the distinction between hearsay and original evidence is that hearsay evidence is generally inadmissible whereas original evidence is generally admissible (subject to particular rules relating to previous consistent and inconsistent statements by witnesses).

We shall see that there are a number of exceptions to the rule that hearsay evidence is not admissible. There is therefore an essential two-stage process for considering hearsay issues:

- Is the evidence hearsay evidence at all?
- If it is hearsay, is it admissible as falls into an exception to the rule against hearsay?

If the evidence is admissible for one purpose, it may still be inadmissible hearsay evidence for other purposes. In such situations the judge will have to direct the jury that they should not rely on the statement as evidence that what is alleged on that issue is true. In *R v Nelson* [2004] EWCA Crim 333, the hearsay statement in question was a record of a call made to the police by the defendant's father. The defendant was alleged to have stabbed another man and raised the defence of automatism. The father's call to the police, which was made soon after the incident, showed that the father was aware that a stabbing had taken place and that the defendant might be blamed. It was accepted by the Court of Appeal that such a statement could have been admitted as original evidence (see below) to show that the father may have been aware of the stabbing, which may have proved that the father had been told about it by the defendant, who therefore would not have been suffering from automatism. However the conviction was quashed because the jury were not directed that they should only use the evidence to decide whether they were sure that the father had been told of the event by the defendant who was not therefore suffering automatism. They were not directed that they should not use the statement to conclude that the defendant had in fact committed the offence (which would be a hearsay statement because the statement would then be used to prove a fact by virtue of being true).

The rule against hearsay does not just prevent a witness from relating what he or she had heard; it also prevents a witness from adopting as his or her knowledge something he or she has been told. Consider the example of the case of *R v Rothwell* (1994) 99 Cr App R 388, CA. The accused was charged with possession of heroin with intent to supply it. A police officer gave evidence that:

(a) He had seen the accused passing packages to other people and had seen him receive money in return.

(b) He knew that persons to whom the accused passed the money were drug dealers.

(c) He knew this because of his experience in the investigation of drugs offences and prosecutions in the Newcastle area where the events took place.

(d) (In cross-examination) he did not have first-hand experience of seeing the persons in question use drugs.

The Court of Appeal held that the police officer was not able to give such evidence. While it was not hearsay evidence in the obvious sense (his testimony was not 'PC Burnes told me that the persons were drug dealers') it was *based* on hearsay evidence (whatever he had in fact been told or heard in court at previous trials that led him to believe that the persons were drug dealers). It was just as inadmissible as if he had repeated every statement that he was relying on when he said that the people were drug dealers.

Nor will the courts allow hearsay to be side-stepped by proving that there was a conversation and then proving what a person immediately did as a result where that would, in effect, suggest to the tribunal of fact what the conversation was about. Using the case of *Rothwell* again, it would not be possible to prove that the police officer giving evidence said that:

(a) He had a conversation with PC Ings.

(b) As a result of that conversation he arrested Rothwell for possession of heroin with intent to supply it.

Quite simply only the stupidest jury would fail to interpret the conversation as being about supplying heroin in some way, which would almost certainly be hearsay if it had been repeated.

In *R v Mills* [2003] 1 WLR 2931, the Court of Criminal Appeal overturned a conviction on the grounds that inadmissible hearsay evidence had been admitted. The two appellants were charged with murder. During a police interview a police officer made incriminating allegations to one of the appellants about what had happened which were based on a statement made by one of the persons present at the incident, J, which the appellant denied. J was not called as a witness at trial but the interview, including those parts in which the police officer repeated what J had alleged, were admitted as evidence. The court ruled that the statements made by J and repeated by the police officer were hearsay statements and should not have been admitted at trial. It will be seen later that the interview itself (although an out of court statement and often tendered to prove the truth of some or all of it) is not inadmissible hearsay. It was what J had said to the police officer that was inadmissible hearsay.

---

## 8.3    Identifying hearsay evidence

Determining whether a statement is hearsay or original evidence is a skill that requires an understanding of proof and a logical approach to the evidence and, in particular, relevance.

As the definitions above suggest, identifying hearsay evidence requires the addressing of three questions:

• Is the evidence a statement or assertion at all?

• Was the statement made other than as testimony in the current case?

- Is the statement being used 'as evidence of any fact asserted': ie to prove a fact simply by the statement being accepted as true.

If 'yes' to all three questions, the statement is hearsay evidence. If the answer is not 'yes' to all three questions quite what the evidence is will depend on which of the above questions is answered in the negative.

### 8.3.1    Is the evidence a statement or assertion at all?

This is not generally a difficult stage of the analysis. However it is worth noting the scope of the statement for these purposes. A 'statement' includes:

(a) Both oral and written statements. Matters written in a document are statements for this purpose. This would also include electronic communications.

(b) Statements made by gestures or conduct. In *Chandrasekera v The King* [1937] AC 220, PC, for example, a victim of an attack had had her throat cut and could not speak. To illustrate that the accused, a local cow-herd, committed the offence, she made gestures and signs (including putting her hands to her head to impersonate a bull) and nodded when asked questions. These gestures were determined to be statements for the purposes of the hearsay rule.

(c) Matters that can be implied into another statement even if not expressly stated and even if the maker of that other statement did not intend to imply anything (*R v Kearley* [1992] 2 AC 228). Implied statements have proved to be an area of some difficulty and so will receive their own special treatment at **8.4**.

(d) Things stated whether or not there was an intention to communicate that information to another person (therefore a diary entry could be a statement for these purposes).

*Note*: the word 'statement' is commonly used in procedural rules to refer to a document written in preparation of proceedings. So far as the rule of hearsay is concerned, as can be seen from the analysis above, the word is being used in a much wider way.

If the out of court thing is not a statement it will either be part of a witness's account of what he or she saw happen (for example, the accused hitting the victim is probably not a statement) or real evidence (such as a document proved in court not for the content but to prove that a particular type of paper was used).

### 8.3.2    Was the statement 'other than as testimony in the current case'?

Put quite simply this part of the test is asking you to distinguish between a statement that is made for the first time as testimony and a statement in testimony that is a repetition of something said at another time. A common (if slightly misleading) short-hand term for such a statement is 'out of court'.

Note the following points:

(a) Statements made outside of any court (in the pub, at home, on the street, in a police station, onto a tape recorder) are clearly covered by this definition.

(b) Statements made in the witness box in *other* cases are also covered by this definition (*Berkeley Peerage Case* (1811) 4 Camp 401).

(c) Statements made in the courtroom but not in the witness box are also covered by this definition.

(d) Having been sworn does not prevent any of that witness's previous statements and utterances from potentially being hearsay evidence.

(e) However, a witness in a case will have made a statement to those preparing the case that outlines his or her testimony (a 'witness statement' or 'proof of evidence'). Insofar as the witness goes into the witness box and restates what is in that statement as his or her own testimony, the testimony is not the repetition of an out of court statement. All that document was doing was recording what the witness was intending to say as his or her evidence. However, if for some reason that statement must be produced before the court, it will be an 'out of court' statement for these purposes. Such statements may not be hearsay statements: this will depend on why they are admitted as evidence (see **8.3.3.3** below). See, for example, **5.2.2** (memory refreshing documents), **5.2.3** (previous consistent statements) and **5.3.4** (previous inconsistent statements).

(f) On the other hand, remember that there are certain rules of procedure that allow such earlier statements to stand as the evidence-in-chief of a party (CPR, r 32.5 and s 9 of the Criminal Justice Act 1967, for example: see **4.7.1**). The effect of these provisions is that these statements become the testimony of the witness in proceedings and cannot therefore be hearsay. This is because formalities and procedures have been complied with: otherwise such statements are just like any other 'out of court' statement.

It is important to look carefully at any statement or testimony to distinguish how much of it is (or will be) the testimony of the witness and how much will be the *repetition* of things said outside court. It is only the latter that will be potentially hearsay (ie to which you need to apply the third stage of the test, see **8.3.3.3**).

To test your understanding of hearsay evidence so far carry out **activity 8.1** in **Appendix 1**.

Merely because a statement is identified as an 'out of court' statement does not mean that it is automatically inadmissible or even that it is hearsay. It simply means that we need to apply the third stage of the test.

### 8.3.3 'Evidence of any fact asserted'

The really tricky but vital part of hearsay analysis is usually the third stage. It is this stage that distinguishes hearsay out of court statements from 'original' out of court statements.

The term 'hearsay' is only applied to 'out of court' statements or assertions with a particular purpose: those that are used to prove a fact by getting the tribunal to accept that the contents of the statement are true or accurate. If the statement has some other purpose, it will not be 'hearsay' but 'original' evidence. These are the various types of statements identified in **8.1**.

This stage can be broken down into two further stages:

• What is the relevant purpose of the statement (note that it may have more than one)?

• Will the tribunal of fact have to rely on the truth of the statement for that purpose to be achieved?

The key to this part of the test is, therefore, 'purpose': what you are trying to achieve with the evidence? This is a question of logic and proof rather than law.

Consider this example: A's out of court statement is 'B was on the High Street at 10 pm on Monday'. It has been put in evidence before a jury.

1.  Assuming there is no other evidence in the case, if the jury decides that the statement is true or accurate, what does it prove?

2.  What could the statement prove without being true or accurate?

If the statement is true, it proves what it says, namely that B was on the High Street at 10 pm on Monday. On these matters, the statement is evidence of those facts and they were asserted in the statement. Therefore for these purposes the statement is hearsay evidence.

In addition, by being true, the statement could also prove, for example, that A was on the High Street on Monday. This is done by:

(a)  Proving the statement above was made.

(b)  Proving that the statement was true (by use of evidence other than this statement).

(c)  Arguing that the fact that the statement was made and that it was accurate shows that A was in a position to know that fact and that he was therefore probably on the High Street.

In the second situation the statement is not 'evidence of any fact asserted' because it is not seeking to prove what it states. While it requires the statement to be true to prove something useful in the case, the statement achieves its evidential purpose by being proved to be true by independent evidence.

The statement is 'evidence of *knowledge of the facts asserted*'. It is the fact of the particular statement having been made plus proof by other means that the statement was accurate that allows the tribunal of fact to *infer* that the maker of the statement knew (or believed) a particular fact. If the maker's knowledge of belief is relevant, the statement could be relevant *original* evidence.

What could such a statement prove without being true?

The statement can be relevant to prove the following facts without being true (and would therefore be original evidence of these facts):

(a)  Facts it can prove by being false could include:

(i)     B lied about A's presence at 10 pm on Monday;

(ii)    B is prone to misidentify A;

(iii)   B cannot tell the time;

(iv)    etc.

(b)  Facts it can prove whether or not the statement is true:

(i)     A knows B (proved by the fact of having been talking about them);

(ii)    A knows there is a High Street (he mentioned it);

(iii)   A believed B was on the High Street at 10 pm on Monday (A could *believe* this whether or not it was true).

At risk of simplification, where the purpose of the evidence is to prove a conclusion by the fact of the statement having been made, the statement is original evidence. Where the purpose of the evidence is to prove a fact by the statement being *true*, the statement is hearsay. The over-simplification is that sometimes (knowledge cases) the conclusion is proved by the fact of the statement having been made and happening to be true. It is still, however, the fact of the statement having been made that determines its non-hearsay nature. The statement is not proving what it states.

While the word 'purpose' is of huge importance, do not overlook the word 'relevant'. Only relevant evidence is admissible. There is no point in determining that the statement could achieve some non-hearsay purpose if that purpose is not relevant in the proceedings. Have another look at **1.4.1.3** in this Manual and in particular the analysis of the cases of *R v Blastland* and *R v Kearley*. In both of those cases statements were determined to be hearsay if used to prove that what the maker said was true. In each case they could also have proved what the maker of the statement knew or believed and would be admissible if relevant. In both cases the House of Lords concluded that the state of mind of the maker was not relevant (or not sufficiently relevant) in the case in question. While it might be possible to disagree with the conclusions of the House of Lords in each case on the issue of relevance, the principle that relevance remains an absolute requirement for admissibility in unquestionably correct.

Leaving to one side issues of relevance for the time being, let us go back to the concept of purpose. By identifying the purpose of the evidence we can then work out whether it is 'evidence of the facts stated' or is 'tendered for the truth of its contents' (another way of explaining how hearsay statements can be distinguished from original evidence).

To test your understanding so far, carry out **activity 8.2** in **Appendix 1**.

The fact that statements are identified to be hearsay does not necessarily mean that they are not admissible. Some of them would fit into various exceptions to the rules against hearsay evidence. Other statements, although they would be inadmissible hearsay, could (and should) be proved from other sources. Remember that one of the purposes of the rule against hearsay evidence is to ensure that the evidence is given by the most authoritative source. Defining evidence as hearsay does not mean that the thing it proves can never be proven by any evidence. It simply means that it cannot be proven by the hearsay statement.

Now try **activity 8.3** in **Appendix 1**.

### 8.3.4  Recap

Identifying whether evidence is hearsay is a matter of applying the technique of proof to the facts of a particular case. Case law can illustrate principle but cannot set rules applicable in all cases that will determine whether a particular statement is hearsay or not.

The process for identifying hearsay evidence is:

(a) Determine whether it is a statement at all.

(b) Determine whether it has been made 'out of court' remembering quite how specific that is.

(c) Determine whether it is evidence of the facts stated by:

   (i)  Determining the relevant purpose or purposes of the evidence.

   (ii)  Determining whether the statement has to be true to achieve those purposes.

(d) If hearsay, determine whether any exceptions apply.

### 8.3.5  Examples of original evidence

The following cases illustrate the approach that the courts have taken in determining whether a statement was hearsay evidence or original evidence. As usual, the cases are illustrations of the application of the principle. In all of the cases, the statements were held not be hearsay but original evidence. While the cases have been put into categories below, that is for illustrative purposes rather than an attempt to define distinct categories. Each turns on its own facts and the purpose of the evidence identified in each case, applying the central principle that the statement must not be used to prove what it alleges. The categories reflect the ways in which statements will prove facts without being 'evidence of a fact asserted' as we identified in **8.1** and **8.3.2.3**.

### 8.3.5.1 Cases in which the truth of the statement is irrelevant

In the following cases the relevant purpose of the evidence is achieved irrespective of the truth or falsity of the statement. Quite simply it is the fact that the statement was made that achieves a relevant purpose in the case. That this is so is generally a matter of the substantive law in question.

*Subramaniam v Public Prosecutor* [1956] 1 WLR 965, PC: The accused was charged with a terrorism offence and pleaded the defence of duress. He alleged that he had been threatened by terrorists with death if he did not carry ammunition for them. The Privy Council concluded that such statements were not hearsay. The defence of duress applies if a person is threatened *not* if the person actually faces the harm that has been threatened. In other words it is the *fact* of the threat that is relevant rather than its genuineness or truth. Therefore the relevant purpose was to prove that the threat had been made not that it had been a genuine or 'true' threat that the terrorists would in fact carry out.

*R v Chapman* [1969] 2 QB 436, CA: The accused was charged with driving with excess alcohol. He would have had a defence to the charge if a doctor had objected to the provision of a breath specimen on health grounds. The prosecution were entitled to prove that the doctor did not so object. It was the fact of the lack of objection rather than the genuineness of that lack of objection that was relevant as a matter of substantive law. The purpose of the statement was to show that there was in fact no objection rather than that the doctor was genuinely not objecting. Again this was a matter of substantive law.

*Woodhouse v Hall* (1980) 72 Cr App R 39, DC: The accused was charged with 'acting in the management of a brothel'. The property, which appeared to be a massage parlour, would be a brothel if the prostitution was conducted there. The Divisional Court held that this, as a matter of substantive law, would derive not from the actuality of the patrons having sex with the occupants but from the occupants soliciting sex from the patrons. In other words the property was a brothel if sexual acts were offered rather than either intended or performed. Therefore undercover police officers were allowed to give evidence of statements made on the property offering the sexual acts. The purpose was to show that sexual acts were offered not that they were intended or performed.

*Ratten v R* [1972] AC 378, PC: The accused was charged with the murder of his wife by shooting her. His defence was that the gun went off accidentally. The prosecution were allowed to call evidence from a telephone operator that at the time of the killing a phone call was received from the accused's address in which a woman said in an hysterical and sobbing voice, 'Get me the police, please'. The accused had denied that any such call was made. The Privy Council held that the purpose of the statement was to prove the fact of a phone call and the fact of the hysterical nature of the call not that the lady wanted the police as such.

*R v O'Connell* [2003] EWCA Crim 502: After having been arrested on suspicion of drugs offences, the police intercepted two calls on the defendant's mobile telephone in which the callers impliedly requested drugs. On both occasions, the defendant, who was present at the time, called out that it was not him but the police on the 'phone and that the callers should end the call. The Court of Appeal stated that what was said by the callers was hearsay evidence (see *R v Kearley* below at **1.4.1.3**) but that what the defendant had said in reaction to those calls was admissible original evidence. The defendant's statement showed his reaction to requests on his telephone for drugs and therefore his awareness of his own guilt.

### 8.3.5.2 Cases in which the purpose was to prove the falsehood of the statement

*Mawaz Khan v R* [1967] 1 AC 454, PC: Two co-defendants were charged with murder. Each had made statements to the police that when the murder took place they were at a particular club. The prosecution were allowed to prove (a) that such statements were made and (b), by other witnesses, that the co-defendants were not at the club. The co-defendants appealed the admissibility of the statements as hearsay evidence. The Privy Council concluded that the statements were not hearsay evidence. The purpose of the statements was not to prove that the co-defendants *were* at the club but to prove the *fact* of having alleged that they were. This fact, combined with the fact that they were elsewhere would be relevant to prove that the co-defendants had lied about where they were (and therefore, potentially, that they were conscious of their guilty involvement in the crime). See also *R v B* [2003] EWCA Crim 2169. For further detail on the evidential value of lies, see **Chapter 10**.

### 8.3.5.3 Cases in which the purpose is the proof of knowledge of a fact that is either uncontested or proved by other means

To say that a statement is hearsay if it has to be true to achieve its relevant purpose simplifies matters a little too much. While that is generally true, there is a situation in which a statement does have to be true to achieve its purpose and that is where what is relevant in the case is that the person making the statement knew a particular fact. This is only achieved by proving it was correctly, accurately or truthfully stated. However the statement is not being used to prove that fact. Instead the fact is proved by other means and the statement is simply used to prove that the maker was aware of that fact. Have a look at the two cases that follow:

(a) *Thomas v Connell* (1838) 4 M & W 267: The issue was whether or not the defendant knew that he was insolvent. Proof of a statement in which he said that he was insolvent could prove *knowledge* of that fact. The fact that he was insolvent (another fact in issue in the case) was proved by other evidence.

(b) *R v Blastland* [1986] AC 41: In *Blastland* (referred to above and at **1.4.3.3**) it was accepted that the statements by M that showed he knew that there had been a murder would not be hearsay. While the statement had to be true to be achieve its purpose, the statement was *not proving the fact it alleged by being true*. Instead the fact that was alleged (there was a dead boy) was proved by other evidence. The purpose of the statement was to prove that M *knew* that fact. The statement was therefore not hearsay *insofar as it was used to prove that M knew of the death rather than to prove the death occurred*. However, the House of Lords concluded that M's knowledge was not (sufficiently) relevant to the trial issue (ie whether the accused killed him).

## 8.4 Problem areas

The analysis has thus far sought only to outline the central principle of hearsay evidence. However, this principle has presented the courts with various problems over the years, especially as society and technology has changed. The courts have occasionally resorted to the reinterpretation of the rule against hearsay to avoid its strictures rather than the creation of exceptions (especially since the creation of exceptions by the common law was stated no longer to be appropriate in *Myers v DPP* [1965] AC 1001). This occasional practice of evading the hearsay rule means that, in certain circumstances, the central principle becomes even more complicated in application.

### 8.4.1  Implied hearsay

#### 8.4.1.1  Implications from oral or written statements

A particular difficulty that the courts have faced is that often a statement is admitted at court not to prove what it literally states but what it implies. To what extent does the rule excluding hearsay apply to such implied statements?

The authorities were in conflict for a long time as to whether the rule against hearsay applied to matters to be implied from a statement or conduct. The case of *R v Rattan* (above) appeared to confirm that the courts would not concern themselves with what might be implied from the words uttered if the fact of the statement was relevant original evidence.

However, the matter was finally resolved in the case of *R v Kearley* [1992] 2 AC 228, where the House of Lords, by a majority, concluded that conclusions implied from statements were as much covered by the hearsay rule as those explicitly stated in them. The accused had been charged with possession of controlled drugs with intent to supply them. Drugs were found at his home and in his garden although not enough to be suggestive that he was a supplier. To prove this, the prosecution proved a number of calls to the flat while the police were searching it. The callers (both in person and on the telephone) had asked for the defendant and had requested drugs.

The requests made varied. However, the majority in the House of Lords concluded that insofar as the statements were requests of a 'usual' quantity of drugs, this implied that drugs had been sold at the property in the past. As this implication was made in an 'out of court' statement, it was subject to the rule against hearsay.

Insofar as those statements and others were used to prove *belief* that drugs were being sold at the house by the accused, the majority took the view that this was not a relevant purpose in the case (see **8.3.2.3** above).

In reaching these conclusions, the courts distinguished *R v Ratten* by saying that what the woman said on the telephone did contain hearsay by implication (that she wanted the police because she was about to be 'shot') but that such a statement was covered by the common law exception of *res gestae* (see **8.7.1**).

In *R v O'Connell* telephone calls to an alleged drug dealer were again intercepted by the police and again included implications of a request to buy drugs. The Court of Appeal held that it made no difference in deciding whether the requests by telephone were implied hearsay that the defendant was present when the police took the calls and overheard their content.

#### 8.4.1.2  Implications from conduct

Sensible as the House of Lords judgment may be insofar as it relates to assertive and deliberate communication carrying implications, unfortunately the House of Lords in *R v Kearley* did not state exactly how far the court can go in making implications. The House of Lords, in reaching its conclusions approved obiter dicta from the case of *Wright v Doe d. Tatham* (1837) 7 Ad & El 313, that suggested that the rule against hearsay applies to implications not only from oral or written assertions but also from conduct. An example that the House of Lords approved in *R v Kearley* was that of a ship's captain who boards a ship with his family and sets sail. It was held that such conduct would be a 'statement ... implied in or vouched for by actual conduct'.

The problem is that there is not really a clear distinction between implying a conclusion from the conduct of another person and inferring a conclusion from the conduct of another person. To what extent was the captain of the above ship trying to say anything?

Would you imply anything from the fact that the accused was seen running after the victim of a stabbing with a knife? Such evidence is exactly what juries would rely upon in such a case. In fact potentially anything anyone does could, technically, have implied hearsay statements that will not be admissible in them. This was clearly not what the House of Lords had in mind and not something that is likely to happen. However, there is the lack of a clear line distinguishing what is an implication from the conduct of a person and an inference from the conduct of a person.

Consider *Manchester Brewery v Coombs* (1901) 82 LT 347, in which it was said, obiter, by Farwell J, at 349, that the conduct of customers who ordered beer, tasted it and threw it away or left it could not be an implied hearsay assertion but admissible at common law as original evidence.

To the extent that *R v Kearley* has supported the proposition that it is possible for implications from conduct to be hearsay statements, such support was obiter. The statements carrying implications in *R v Kearley* were oral utterances. There is no direct authority to support the conclusion that conduct is capable of carrying implied hearsay in all cases. Some statements clearly are. Conduct that is 'assertive' like pointing is explicitly not implicitly communicating information. It almost seems meaningless to talk of implications from actions that are not intended to communicate anything. To what extent can such statements be 'evidence of the facts stated' when they are not stating anything? Quite simply, the matter has not yet been resolved by case law but it would seem likely that any development in the law in this area will have to be pragmatic and therefore will be unlikely to extend the ambit of implied hearsay by conduct at all far.

### 8.4.2  Negative hearsay

As we saw from the definition of hearsay in *R v Sharp* (see **8.3.2**), a hearsay statement is one that is evidence of any fact asserted. We have just seen that the allegation of fact A could also imply fact B and that could also, therefore, be covered by the rule against hearsay. But what if the things that a person states outside of the courtroom are notable not because of what the witness said but because of what the witness did not say. To what extent is this 'evidence of any fact asserted'?

Consider the following example. A theft takes place when some youths are on a hiking trip. The issue is whether the accused, Ed, was in a dormitory when an offence took place. Evidence is given that the person in charge of the trip, Peter, appointed 'Dormitory Monitors' for each dormitory and would call at each dorm asking the monitor who was there. At about the time the theft took place, the prosecution seek to prove that Ed was out of his dormitory.

To what extent should they be able to do so if the evidence they rely on is:

1. That Peter called out to the monitor, 'Is there anyone missing from your dormitory' to which Michael replied 'Yes, Ed'.

2. That Peter called out to the monitor, Michael, 'who is in there with you?' and that Michael replied, 'Me, Adrian, Jack, Steve and Asil'.

The courts have treated these two types of statements completely differently. In both cases the purpose of the statement is to prove that Ed was absent. The first statement does this by proving that what was said (or implied), namely that Ed is absent, was true. In the latter case, nothing has been asserted.

However the courts have taken the view that in the latter case it is not the truth of what was said that proves Ed was absent but the fact of not having said something and therefore the statement that is used to prove it is original evidence.

This concept of proof by the absence of a statement (sometimes confusingly called 'negative hearsay') was said recognised (obiter) in *R v Patel* (1981) 73 Cr App R 117, a case concerning illegal immigration, only to be arise if:

- It was proved by an officer responsible for compiling records that a particular method was used for making and storing entries as to the existence of a fact in that record.

- It was proved by the same officer that due to the process, the absence of a particular entry on the record meant the non-existence of the fact.

For examples of the application of the rule see:

(a) *R v Shone* (1983) 76 Cr App R 72, CA. There the accused was charged with theft, to prove which the prosecution had to establish that the goods alleged to be stolen had not been legitimately sold on. The prosecution were allowed to call two employees who testified to the system adopted and the absence of a record of onward sale.

(b) *R v Muir* (1984) 79 Cr App R 153, CA. The accused was alleged to have stolen a video recorder but stated in his defence that the recorder had been repossessed by the hire company. The prosecution were allowed to call the district manager of the hire company who gave evidence that if there had been a repossession he would have been informed. This was held to have been original (negative hearsay) evidence. However, the Court of Appeal held that the district manager should not have been allowed to give evidence that he had checked with his Head Office to determine whether they had any such record. The Court said that while an employee at the Head Office could have given admissible negative hearsay evidence as to their procedure and the absence of a record, the district manager would have to have relied on hearsay evidence as to what their system was and therefore his evidence was inadmissible.

### 8.4.3   Identification cases

As was noted in **Chapter 1**, it is always necessary in criminal cases to prove that the accused, as opposed to someone else, committed the crime in question. In *Sparks v R* [1964] AC 964, PC, Lord Morris of Borth-y-Gest said (at 981): 'There is no rule which permits the giving of hearsay evidence merely because it relates to identity'. Despite this we shall see that the rule has been evaded in response to two different problems in relation to identification.

#### 8.4.3.1   Identification of others outside of the witness box

As shall be seen in **Chapter 12**, there are complicated rules and procedures for the identification of persons between a crime and the trial of that crime. Part of the logic of encouraging such 'out of court' identifications is that it might be very difficult for a witness to remember the details of a face over a long period. Furthermore, as was noted at **5.2.4.3**, the practice of identifying the accused for the first time while he is in the dock has also been recognised to lack probative value (after all, who other than the accused sitting in the dock is likely to be identified by a witness in such circumstances).

Therefore out of court identifications have not only been recognised but are a central feature of the criminal trial process. However, it must be remembered that an identification at the police station is an out of court statement and is probably tendered for the truth of its content (eg 'He is the person who attacked me'). However, the courts have never formally stated that an exception to the rule against hearsay exists in relation to such evidence. In *R v Osborne and Virtue* [1973] QB 678, the Court of Appeal upheld a conviction based on the evidence of a police officer that another witness had identified the appellant (the witness could not remember having done so). The court did so without referring to the rule against hearsay or any exception.

On the other hand, the courts have clearly placed limits on the extent to which hearsay statements can be used to prove identification. In *Jones v Metcalfe* [1967] 1 WLR 1286, DC, out of court statements identifying the lorry the accused had driven were held not to be admissible to prove that the accused had driven carelessly. In *R v McLean* (1968) 52 Cr App R 80, CA the court applied this principle in ruling inadmissible an out of court of statement in which the number plate of a vehicle was recorded.

### 8.4.3.2   Self-identification

If the concept of hearsay is followed strictly, the identity of a person would be very difficult to prove. After all, we know who other people are because they tell us so in some way or another.

The courts have attempted to define statements of self-identification as original evidence. In *R v Ward* [2001] Crim LR 316, the Court of Appeal stated that the statement of personal details such as name, address and date of birth were not hearsay statements adduced to prove those facts. Rather the purpose of such statements was to show that the maker of such statements knew sufficient personal details of the person in question to be that person. Clearly to have this probative force, there must be sufficiently detailed statements. In many cases there is simply the statement of self-identification, 'I am X'.

The same principle was applied in *R v Stubbs* [2002] EWCA Crim 2254. In that case the defendant was charged with two robberies, both of which he denied having committed. While he was in custody on remand, a letter was intercepted at the institution at which he was located. The letter contained the name and prison number of the defendant and included the phrase 'Here are two of my CCTV pics from my robberies' and also included copies of two CCTV images showing the robbery. Also on the images were written comments such as 'This is me' and 'Me again'. They both also made reference to 'Jigga' which was a name shouted out during one of the robberies by one of the robbers. The Court of Appeal held that the intercepted letter had been properly admitted as evidence of self-identification. The only person in the remand institution where the letters were intercepted who could have known the details contained in the letter was the defendant.

A particular case in which the Court of Appeal attempted to tackle the evidential status of statements of self-identification was *R v Rice* [1963] 1 QB 857, CA. To prove that the accused had travelled to Manchester as part of the commission of a crime, the prosecution sought to tender in evidence a airline ticket stub with the name of 'Rice' upon it. The ticket had been found where used tickets would be located. The Court of Appeal held that the statement was not hearsay evidence because 'the balance of probability recognised by common sense and common knowledge that an air ticket which has been used on a flight and which had a name upon it has more likely than not been used by a man of that name'. However, the logic of this statement is flawed in that the probative value of that ticket in proving that Rice took the trip is dependent on one of two things, either:

> (a) The ticket itself is an out of court statement to the effect 'this ticket authorises Rice to travel', which implies that the owner or possessor of the ticket is Rice and there-

fore to achieve its relevant purpose, the statement implied into the ticket must be true.

(b) The ticket records information stated by someone when the ticket was booked, namely either 'my name is Rice' or 'the person travelling will be Mr Rice'. Therefore the ticket would be a record of a hearsay statement.

Either way, the ticket could only achieve its purpose via hearsay evidence. That *R v Rice* is wrong has been recognised by the House of Lords in *Myers v DPP* and in *R v Kearley*. Furthermore the principle that statements of self-identification are admissible due to their high probative value was questioned in *R v Van Vreden* (1973) 57 Cr App R 818, CA. In *Van Vreden* statements made to a credit card company by an applicant proved that the card in question had been issued to a woman. The accused charged with fraudulent use of the card was a man. However, the Court of Appeal held that the statement was hearsay. Its purpose was to prove that the legitimate holder of the card was a woman. This was proved by reliance on the statement for its truth. The Court of Appeal stated that there was nothing about statements of self-identification that prevented the hearsay rule from operating.

In *R v Lydon* (1987) 85 Cr App R 221, CA, the accused, Sean Lydon, was charged with robbery. To prove that he had committed the offence, various pieces of paper found with the gun that had been used in the robbery were admitted in evidence. These pieces of paper had 'Sean' and 'Sean Rules' written upon them. The Court of Appeal concluded that the statements were not hearsay as they were not used to prove what they stated (for example, that Sean ruled anything) rather it was the fact of the statement having been made that proved that the maker was Sean Lydon. However it might now be argued, following *R v Kearley*, that the statements proved the identity of the maker by implication and would therefore be hearsay.

The approach of the courts to the proof of identification by out of court statements is not, in fact, that different to the proof of any other issue. There are situations in which identification will be proved by the fact of particular statements having been made (for example, in *R v Ward* and, subject to *R v Kearley*, in *R v Lydon*). In other cases the statement of identification is being used as evidence of the fact stated, namely that the person is who he says he is (*R v Rice* and *R v Van Vreden*) and is hearsay.

### 8.4.4  Statements produced by mechanical devices

The rule against hearsay was not designed with modern technology in mind. Technological devices produce information that may appear to be statements but which the courts have held occasionally not to be hearsay but real evidence. Whether or not this is so will depend on the extent to which the process of the device is mechanical or is dependent on human input. Where a person types information onto a computer and saves it into a file, it will clearly be as much a statement as if it had been said or written. However, where the courts conclude that the machine or device in question is producing the record automatically, it has been held to be real not hearsay evidence. Again, using the definition in *R v Sharp*, we might say that a calculation or automated message is not an 'assertion' nor is the mechanical process asserting any fact.

Consider the following examples:

(a) In *R v Wood* (1982) 76 Cr App R 23, CA, the prosecution had to prove the chemical composition of metal alleged to have been stolen. The Court of Appeal held that the printouts from the computer were not hearsay but real evidence as the computer was performing a calculation that could have been done manually. Note, however, it is still necessary to prove by non-hearsay evidence the formula that had been programmed into the computer and the data that had been fed into it. Once this had been done the computer itself was not making any statement for hearsay purposes.

(b) In *Castle v Cross* [1984] 1 WLR 1372, DC, an intoxometer reading was similarly held not to be hearsay evidence. Again, the reading was a mechanical calculation rather than a statement produced by human agency or interpretation.

(c) In *R v Governor of Brixton Prison, ex p Levin* [1997] 3 WLR 117, HL, the mechanical record was of fund transfers made over the internet. The bank's computer system automatically recorded transactions made. The issue in the case was whether the defendant had used a computer to make such fund transfers. The House of Lords held that the computerised records of the transactions were no more hearsay to prove the fact of such transactions than a photocopy of a fraudulent cheque.

(d) In *Taylor v Chief Constable of Cheshire* [1986] 1 WLR 1479, the Divisional Court held that police officers could give evidence as to what they had seen on a CCTV video of an offence even thought the video had been lost. Rather than the video being an out of court statement it was said by Ralph Gibson LJ to be no different in principle from having witnessed the event when it took place.

## 8.5  Hearsay exceptions in civil cases

Most hearsay evidence is admissible in civil cases and the rules are therefore quite simple. The rules are stated in the Civil Evidence Act 1995. The 1995 Act has created a general rule of inclusion in civil cases, which is set out in s 1:

**1.**—*(1)    In civil proceedings evidence shall not be excluded on the ground that it is hearsay.*

*(2)    In this Act—*

*(a)    'hearsay' means a statement made otherwise than by a person while giving oral evidence in the proceedings which is tendered as evidence of the matters stated; and*

*(b)    references to hearsay include hearsay of whatever degree.*

*(3)    Nothing in this Act affects the admissibility of evidence admissible apart from this section.*

*(4)    The provisions of sections 2 to 6 (safeguards and supplementary provisions relating to hearsay evidence) do not apply in relation to hearsay evidence admissible apart from this section, notwithstanding that it may also be admissible by virtue of this section.*

In other words all hearsay evidence will be admissible in civil proceedings unless it is already admissible under another statute or is one of the common law exceptions preserved under s 7 of the Act. The 1995 Act applies to both documentary and oral statements and to 'multiple hearsay' (ie where the potentially hearsay statement itself contains or is based on hearsay).

It may not always be clear whether proceedings are civil or criminal. In *Clingham v Kensington & Chelsea London Borough Council* [2002] 3 WLR 1313, HL, proceedings in relation to an anti-social behaviour order under s 1 of the Crime and Disorder Act 1998 were determined to be civil because the order that would be imposed did not itself include a sanction (a sanction would have followed from non-compliance with the order).

These provisions do not allow the proof of out of court statements made by a person who would not be competent as a witness (s 5 of the 1995 Act: see **Chapter 4**).

The rule of admissibility under s 1 of the 1995 Act and the consequential provisions (set out below) do not apply if the statement is admissible under another statutory exception. Such exceptions include (but are not restricted to):

(a) Evidence in connection with the 'upbringing, maintenance or welfare of a child' will be admissible notwithstanding that it is hearsay evidence (Children (Admissibility of Hearsay Evidence) Order 1993).

(b) A copy of any entry in a bankers book is admissible to prove any transactions recorded in it: (Bankers' Books Evidence Act 1879, s 3). For more detail, see *Blackstone's Civil Practice*, 2004.

### 8.5.1 The requirement of notice

Where a party proposes to rely upon hearsay evidence, he or she must comply with the notice requirements set out in s 2 of the 1995 Act. The notice requirements are set out in detail in the *Civil Litigation Manual* or *Blackstone's Civil Practice*, 2004, chapter 51. However in short the main points are:

(a) Failure to give notice:
   (i)   does not render evidence inadmissible (s 2(4));
   (ii)  can lead the court to make procedural orders (for example the court could adjourn the hearing and/or order the party who has not complied with the notice requirements to pay costs) (s 2(4)(a));
   (iii) may lead the courts to attach less weight to the statement (s 2(4)).

(b) If the hearsay statement will be proved by the oral evidence of a witness (ie the witness will repeat what he or she has heard), service of the witness's statement is sufficient notice (CPR, r 33.2(1)).

(c) If the hearsay statement will be proved in a witness statement that stands as the evidence-in-chief, that witness statement constitutes compliance with the notice requirements (CPR, r 33.2(1)). Where the witness statement is going to be used instead of calling the witness, this fact must be identified to the other parties (CPR, r 33.2(2)).

(d) If the hearsay statement is not proved in the way set out above (for example the hearsay statement will be proved in a document) then a notice should be served on the other parties (CPR, r 33.2(3)). The reason for not calling the witness must be identified in the notice.

### 8.5.2 The requirement of leave

Generally leave is not required before such evidence will be admitted. The judge does not have to rule that the hearsay evidence is admissible.

There is one exception that evidence is admissible without leave which is set out in s 6(2) of the 1995 Act:

6.—*(2)   A party who has called or intends to call a person as a witness in civil proceedings may not in those proceedings adduce evidence of a previous statement made by that person, except—*
   *(a)   with the leave of the court, or*
   *(b)   for the purpose of rebutting a suggestion that his evidence has been fabricated.*

*This shall not be construed as preventing a witness statement (that is, a written statement of oral evidence which a party to the proceedings intends to lead) from being adopted by a witness in giving evidence or treated as his evidence.*

The effect of this is that leave will be required where a party seeks to both:

- call a person as a witness, *and*
- prove that the person has made a previous statement.

It is important to remember the rules relating to previous statements made by a witness. Re-read **5.2** of this Manual. Having done so you will remember that previous consistent statements are not generally admissible at common law. The effect of s 6 is that they now are generally admissible if the court grants leave. However, some of the types of previous statements have been mentioned specifically in s 6:

(a) *Previous inconsistent statements.* Generally a party calling a witness would not seek to prove they have made a previous *inconsistent* statement, however this might happen if the witness proves hostile (**5.2.5**). Section 6(3) provides that ss 3 to 5 of the Criminal Procedure Act 1865 still apply in such situations. The basic rule therefore has not changed the circumstances under which such statements can be proved.

(b) *Memory refreshing documents.* The common law rules concerning the admissibility of such documents as evidence (see **5.2.3.3**) has not been changed by this section (s 6(4)).

(c) *Statements admitted to rebut a suggestion of previous fabrication.* Such statements (formerly an exception to the common law rule against previous consistent statements: see **5.2.4.6**) are admissible *without leave*.

In contrast to the common law (and therefore criminal cases) any previous statements made by a witness to the proceedings, if admitted, will be evidence of the truth of what is alleged (s 6(5)). At common law such statements were only proof of the consistency of what the witness said (ie to bolster his or her credibility).

### 8.5.3  Proof of a hearsay statement

Although the 1995 Act renders hearsay statements admissible, they still must be proved. Where the statement is oral hearsay (ie the repetition of what someone *said* elsewhere), the statement is proved by the evidence of the person that heard it.

Where the hearsay statement is contained in a document, the document will be produced at court. The provenance of the document must be established (this is usually described as 'proving' the document). Section 8 provides that a document can be proved by producing it or a copy of it. This does not, however, mean that the document can simply be presented at court (*Ventouris v Mountain (No 2)* [1992] 1 WLR 817). A witness must establish that the document in question has something to do with the case. However this 'proof' of a document can be achieved by hearsay evidence. In *Ventouris v Mountain (No 2)*, the document in question was a tape recording of conversations between various people on matters relevant to an insurance fraud, which was being litigated. One of the participants to the conversation was G, who was not available to give evidence. A solicitor was allowed to 'prove' the tape recordings as relevant evidence of the conversations by repeating what G had told him about them.

Sections 9 and 10 of the 1995 Act make particular provisions for the admissibility of particular documents without having formally to 'prove' those documents.

(a) Section 9 concerns documents forming part of the records of a business or public authority. Instead of having to call a witness such a document will be proved if a certificate signed by 'an officer of the business or authority' is produced. 'Records' is defined, by s 9(4) as 'records in whatever form' and 'business' as 'any activity regularly carried on over a period of time, whether for profit or not, by any body ... or by an individual'. 'Public authority' includes any government department or public undertaking.

(b) Section 10 provides for the admissibility of actuarial tables in personal injuries cases.

### 8.5.4    Challenging the hearsay statement

Clearly a party against whom a hearsay statement is made has little power to prevent the statement from being admitted. There is only a requirement for leave if the statement was made by a witness. Even a failure to comply with the notice requirements will not prevent the statement from being admitted.

However, under the 1995 Act there are a number of ways in which another party can challenge the weight to be attached to the statement:

(a) Where the hearsay statement has been made by a person not called as a witness any party may call the maker of the statement to cross-examine him or her if the court grants leave (s 3).

(b) Section 4 lays down guidance upon what weight should be attached to the hearsay evidence. Section 4(2) states that the court may take into consideration the following:

  (i)    Whether it would have been reasonable and practical to secure the attendance of the witness rather than using the hearsay statement (s 4(2)(a)).

  (ii)   Whether the statement was made contemporaneously with the events to which they relate (s 4(2)(b)).

  (iii)  Whether the hearsay itself is based on the repetition of information from another source ('multiple hearsay') (s 4(2)(c)).

  (iv)   Any motive the maker has for concealing or misrepresenting matters (s 4(2)(d)).

  (v)    How complete the hearsay statement is as an account of the matters (s 4(2)(e)).

  (vi)   Whether the statement was made by numerous people in collaboration (s 4(2)(e)).

  (vii)  Why the statement was made (s 4(2)(e)).

  (viii) Whether the statement appears to have been produced in a way that would prevent other parties from fully testing or challenging it (s 4(2)(f)). In other words, failure to comply with notice requirements fully will probably lead the court to attach less weight to it.

(c) Where the witness does not attend for cross-examination, provision is made for attacking the credibility of the witness as if he or she had been called as follows:

  (i)    Evidence undermining the credibility of the witness may be called (s 5(2)(a)). This, however, would appear to be subject to the rule of finality (see **5.3.3**). Section 5(2)(a) states that the evidence is admissible for the purpose of attacking the credibility of the maker. It is therefore relevant only to the credibility of the maker of the statement not to prove the truth of the matters alleged.

(ii)  Evidence of previous statements inconsistent with the hearsay statements may be proved (see **5.3.4**).

### 8.5.5  Preservation of the common law rules

Section 7 of the 1995 Act preserves some of the common law exceptions. These exceptions concern various statements in documents of a public nature (see **8.7.3**) and include:

(a)  Statements contained in public documents (see **8.7.3** below).

(b)  Statements made by deceased persons to prove matters of pedigree (see **8.7.2.4**).

(c)  Statements made by deceased persons to prove the existence of a public or general right (see **8.7.2.5**).

(d)  Evidence of a person's general reputation (see **Chapter 5**).

Where these exceptions apply there is no need to comply with the notice requirements (**8.5.2**), the leave requirements (**8.5.3**) or the provisions in s 4 concerning the weight to be attached to such documents (**8.5.4**).

## 8.6  Statutory exceptions in criminal cases

The exceptions to the rule against hearsay in criminal cases are narrower than in civil cases. In particular, the statutory exceptions are far less extensive so it is necessary to rely upon the common law in many cases to get hearsay evidence admitted. It is far more likely in criminal proceedings that a hearsay statement will simply not be admissible than in civil proceedings.

### 8.6.1  Criminal Justice Act 1988: introduction

The Criminal Justice Act 1988 creates the most comprehensive of the statutory exceptions to the rule against hearsay. The statute applies only to documentary statements (ie the Act provides for situations in which documents that are adduced to prove the facts they allege will be admissible). Out of court oral hearsay statements repeated by a witness are not covered by the Act and will only be admissible if they fall within the common law exceptions set out at **9.4**.

Schedule 5, para 2 provides the following definitions:

- 'Statement' means any representation of fact, however made.
- 'Document' means anything in which information of any description is recorded.

Two sections of the Act create exceptions to the rule against hearsay. Section 23 creates an exception in relation to documents where the author of the document is unavailable to attend as a witness. Section 24 creates an exception in relation to documents created as part of a business or trade. These two exceptions are subject to an exclusionary discretion (s 25) and a requirement of leave in certain situations (s 26).

Both ss 23 and 24 require proof of certain facts before a document will be ruled admissible. Under either section, therefore, the party seeking to have the document admitted will have to convince the judge of these preliminary facts.

### 8.6.2    Section 23 of the Criminal Justice Act 1988

Section 23 allows parties to prove facts stated by a witness in a document as a substitute for calling that witness. As we shall see below, there has to be a good reason why the witness is not called to give the evidence himself or herself. Furthermore the rule does not allow the document to prove more than the witness would if he or she was called as a witness (ie the document is subject to all the restrictions of the rules of evidence).

The main provisions of s 23 are as follows:

> (1)  ... a statement made by a person in a document shall be admissible in criminal proceedings as evidence of any fact of which direct oral evidence by him would be admissible if—
>
> (i)    the requirements of one of the paragraphs of subsection (2) below are satisfied; or
>
> (ii)    the requirements of subsection (3) below are satisfied.
>
> (2)   The requirements mentioned in subsection (1)(i) above are—
>
> (a)    that the person who made the statement is dead or by reason of his bodily or mental condition unfit to attend as a witness;
>
> (b)    that—
>
>> (i)    the person who made the statement is outside the United Kingdom; and
>>
>> (ii)    it is not reasonably practicable to secure his attendance; or
>
> (c)    that all reasonable steps have been taken to find the person who made the statement, but that he cannot be found.
>
> (3)   The requirements mentioned in subsection (1)(ii) above are—
>
> (a)    that the statement was made to a police officer or some other person charged with the duty of investigating offences or charging offenders; and
>
> (b)    that the person who made it does not give oral evidence through fear or because he is kept out of the way.

It is therefore necessary to determine four things:

- whether the statement conveying the facts that must be proved was made in a document;

- who is the 'maker' of the statement;

- why the maker is not available to attend to testify as to those facts;

- whether the maker would have been able to testify as to those facts if he or she had been present.

#### 8.6.2.1    Whether the statement was made in a document

Generally it will not be difficult to determine whether a statement was made in a document, which is defined as 'anything in which information of any description is recorded' (Sch 2, para 5).

#### 8.6.2.2    Who is the 'maker' of the statement

Occasionally it will be a little more difficult to determine whether the person who provided the information is the 'maker' of the statement. Usually the person who wrote the document is the maker of the statement. Occasionally, however, it will not be clear whose statement it is. Where the statement has been written by one person on behalf of another, the document will be the statement of the latter person if he or she has acknowledged it by signing it. This is the case with a signed witness statement. Furthermore, where a witness provides information to another person (for example a police officer) and that other person writes that information down in his or her notebook, what is written will become the witness's statement if the witness checks and signs it. There is no strict requirement for a signature but for some form of authentication. In *R v McGillivray* (1993) 97 Cr App R 232, the victim of an attack was unable to sign the statement due to his injuries but the statement was treated as 'made' by the victim under s 23.

### 8.6.2.3    Why the maker is unavailable as a witness

Before such a document is admissible there has to be a reason why the witness could not give the evidence in question. The possible reasons are that the maker of the statement is:

- dead;

- physically unable to give evidence;

- mentally unable to give evidence;

- abroad and cannot be made to attend court;

- not traceable;

- kept away from court (whether by fear or by some other means) and the statement was made to a police officer or equivalent.

The party seeking to rely upon the document must prove one of the above reasons to the satisfaction of the judge. If it is the prosecution that is seeking to use the document, they must prove the reason beyond reasonable doubt (*R v Acton Justices, ex p McMullen* (1990) 92 Cr App R 98). The defence, when seeking to rely on one of the above reasons, need only prove it on the balance of probabilities (*R v Mattey* [1995] 2 Cr App R 409).

It is the state of the witness at the time of trial in all of the above situations which is important rather than the state of the witness when the statement was made. As for the particular reasons consider the following:

**The witness is dead or unfit to attend**

This reason is not restricted to being unable to attend court at all. In *R v Setz-Dempsey* [1994] Crim LR 123, the Court of Appeal held that it also applied where, although the witness had been able to attend, he or she could not give meaningful testimony due to his or her mental or physical condition. Furthermore, in *R v Millett*, 21 July 2000, unreported, it was stated that where the physical strain of giving testimony might lead to serious, permanent physical consequences (such as a stroke), the witness could be held to be physically unfit to attend under s 23(2)(a).

Where a witness is mentally unfit to attend, the issue of the competence of the witness to give any evidence might also arise. In *R v D* [2002] 2 Cr App R 36, an application was made under s 23(2)(a) to admit the statement of a witness with Alzheimer's disease. The defendant argued that the witness would not have been able to give 'evidence of any fact of which direct oral evidence by her would be admissible' as she would not have been a competent witness. The Court of Appeal held that the judge had not erred in admitting the statement. Competence was not a factor in determining whether a statement fell within s 23; rather it was one of the factors to which the judge had properly had regard when exercising his discretion to exclude evidence under s 26 (see below at **9.3.4**)

**The witness is outside the UK and it is not reasonably practicable to secure his or her attendance**

There are two aspects to this:

(a) *Outside the UK*. A diplomat resident in this country but who cannot be compelled to attend court is not 'outside the UK' (*R v Jiminez-Paez* [1993] Crim LR 596, CA). Note that the test is that 'it is not reasonably practicable' to secure his or her attendance.

(b) *Securing attendance*. Consider the following points:

    (i)    That it is not reasonably practicable to do so must be proved. In *R v Bray* (1988) 88 Cr App R 354 the maker of the statement had been suddenly sent to Korea. The prosecution were permitted to admit his statement as evidence of relevant facts. The accused successfully appealed on the grounds that the prosecution had not adduced evidence that it was not reasonably practicable to secure the attendance of the witness.

(ii)   Where a witness is not available at the date of trial, the judge should consider adjourning the case until he or she is available. However the judge should consider the practicability of securing attendance on the date of trial (or application to admit the statement under s 23) and should not have to look into the future to determine when a witness might be available (*R v French* (1993) 97 Cr App R 421, CA).

(iii)   Note that the language is 'reasonably practical'. This means that it is not necessary to prove that it is at all possible to get the witnesses to attend. In *R v Maloney* [1994] Crim LR 525, CA, the witnesses were Greek sea cadets and there was evidence that they were at sea, on leave or at college and that formal applications would have to be made to the Greek navy to secure their attendance. The Court of Appeal was satisfied that enough had been done in determining that they were not available for s 23(2)(b) to apply. Clearly lengthy procedures could have been adopted but these went beyond what was 'reasonably practicable'.

(iv)   Also as the phrase is 'reasonable practical to secure', a witness who could easily attend court *if he or she wished to do so* does not necessarily fall within s 23(2)(b). If there are no powers to secure the attendance of an unwilling witness because of the law of the country in which he or she is located, such a witness will fall within this category. In *R v French*, for example, the witness was Mexican and had already attended to give evidence at a trial that had been adjourned. There was no way of forcing the witness to attend again so the statement could properly have fallen within s 23(2)(b).

(v)   What is 'reasonably practicable' is a matter of fact to be determined in each case. However, in *R v Castillo* [1996] 1 Cr App R 438, the Court of Appeal stressed the following three factors:

- the importance of the evidence the witness could give;
- the expense and inconvenience in securing attendance; and
- the validity of the reasons put forward for not attending.

### All reasonable steps have been taken to find the witness

In determining whether all reasonable steps have been taken, it is permissible to take into account how important the witness's evidence will be in the case and the extent of available police resources for searching for the witness, but not the seriousness of the charge (*R v Coughlan* [1999] 5 *Archbold News* 2, CA; see also: *R v Henry* [2003] EWCA Crim 1296).

### The witness has been kept away from court through fear

Statements contained in documents will only be admissible on this basis if made to a police officer or other investigator. Note the following points:

(a)   The judge must conclude that the fear will prevent the maker from giving evidence: *R v Singh* [2003] EWCA Crim 2320.

(b)   There is no need to prove that the fear is reasonable or that it was caused by the incident that is being tried (*R v Acton Justices, ex p McMullen* (1990) 92 Cr App R 98). Further, it was resolved in *R v Martin* [1996] Crim LR 589, CA, that it is not necessary to prove that the fear was caused by a particular thing said or done by a particular person. In that case the fear had been triggered by a silent stranger outside the witness's house.

(c) In *R v H* [2001] Crim LR 815, the Court of Appeal stated that the court should consider whether the witness is in fear when the witness is due to give evidence rather than days or weeks beforehand. However it was recognised that there might be some practical necessity to resolve the matter at the beginning of the trial.

(d) The court should consider the extent to which steps have been taken to allay such fears such as resort to Special Measures Directions (see **4.7.5**) (*R v H*).

(e) Ideally the fear will be established by evidence from the witness in fear (*R v H*). It now appears settled that this can be proved by a written statement from the witness in question (*R v Rutherford* [1998] Crim LR 490, CA). Out of court statements by the maker of the statement to another person will also be admissible as evidence of the maker's fear if that witness testifies as to what was said. Such a testimony would be admissible as an exception to the rule against hearsay as it proves the state of mind or emotion of the maker (*Neill v North Antrim Magistrates' Court* [1992] 1 WLR 1221; see **8.7.1.3**).

(f) Section 23(3) can apply even where the witness has started giving evidence but stops doing so through fear (*R v Ashford Justices, ex p Hilden* (1993) 96 Cr App R 92, DC).

(g) A jury should not be told why the document has been proved instead of calling the witness as doing so might prejudice the accused (*R v Churchill* [1993] Crim LR 285).

### 8.6.2.4 Whether the maker would have been able to testify as to those facts if he or she had been present

Note the language of s 23: 'a statement ... shall be admissible ... as evidence of any fact of which direct oral evidence by [the maker] would be admissible'. The best way of understanding this is to imagine the document as the testimony of the person that wrote the document. Anything that would have been inadmissible evidence as testimony will be equally inadmissible as a fact narrated in a s 23 document.

### 8.6.3 Section 24 of the Criminal Justice Act 1988

Consider the following example:

Alf is charged with theft of computer parts from Stock Room D of the building where he works as a packer. The prosecution allege that the goods went missing on the evening of 3 March. The computer parts were found in Alf's house and the serial numbers for each part was identified. Consider the following items of evidence:

1. A timesheet written in hand recording that Alf was due to pack in Stock Room D on 3 March from 3 pm to 11 pm. The person who filled out the timesheet, Anil, can attend court but cannot remember any details. The system for filling out the sheet is that each stock room has a foreman who informs Anil who was in that room on each day, when they started and when they left.

2. A checklist which records the serial numbers of all parts consigned to each warehouse. On the list the serial numbers for the computer parts found at Alf's house appear in the column headed 'Stock Room D'. A witness can prove that the usual process for recording the information is either for the person compiling the list to look at the parts himself or for him to have a colleague call the numbers out to him.

Both documents relate to hearsay evidence. Furthermore, not one of the documents would be admissible under s 23:

1. The document is hearsay because its purpose is to prove that Alf had the opportunity to steal the computer parts when they must have gone missing. As Anil is available, the statement cannot be admitted under s 23. While it might serve as a memory-refreshing document, it might be difficult to convince the court that it was sufficiently contemporaneous. Furthermore, the information is based on hearsay evidence (what the foreman said to Anil) and therefore would not be admissible under s 23.

2. Again this is hearsay, being an out of court statement admitted to prove that the stolen parts were in Stock Room D. However it is not even possible to prove who created the document so as to comply with s 23(2) or (3). Furthermore it cannot be shown that the statement is or is not itself based on hearsay information given the ambiguity of how the list was compiled.

We shall see, however, that both documents could be admissible under s 24 of the Criminal Justice Act 1988 as they were both created in the course of business. Section 24 provides for the general admissibility of documents created in the course of business or professions. However the section also applies to documents created as part of a criminal investigation. However in cases of criminal investigations there are additional requirements before such documents are admissible (see **8.6.3.3** below).

Section 24 states:

> (1)  ... a statement in a document shall be admissible in criminal proceedings as evidence of any fact of which direct oral evidence would be admissible, if the following conditions are satisfied—
>
> > (i)  the document was created or received by a person in the course of a trade, business, profession or other occupation, or as the holder of a paid or unpaid office; and
> >
> > (ii)  the information contained in the document was supplied by a person (whether or not the maker of the statement) who had, or may reasonably be supposed to have had, personal knowledge of the matters dealt with.
>
> (2)  Subsection (1) above applies whether the information contained in the document was supplied directly or indirectly but, if it was supplied indirectly, only if each person through whom it was supplied received it—
>
> > (a)  in the course of a trade, business, profession or other occupation; or
> >
> > (b)  as the holder of a paid or unpaid office.

Section 24 is narrower than s 23 in that it relates to business documents only but is broader in that it allows the document to prove more hearsay statements and in that there is usually no need for the maker of the statement to be unavailable. At the heart of this difference is the logic that business documents are probably more reliable and also that it would be harder to expect a document created as part of someone's job or profession to contain the sort of information about which they would feel able to testify. It therefore makes more sense for the business document itself to prove the matters it alleges than to call the author of the document to attempt to remember the details of what he or she wrote at the time.

### 8.6.3.1  Types of documents to which section 24 relates

There are two features that must be proved before the document may be admitted under s 24.

- It must have been created by a person acting in the course of a trade, business, profession, etc.

- The information in the document must have been supplied by a person with (or likely to have had) personal knowledge. The fact of personal knowledge of the matter related in the document may be *inferred* from the document itself. There is no requirement to call any witness to prove that the maker had such personal knowledge: *R v Foxley* [1995] 2 Cr App R 523; *Vehicle and Operator Agency v Jenkins Transport Ltd* [2003] EWHC 2879 (Admin).

### 8.6.3.2    What the document may prove

The document cannot be used to prove anything that is inadmissible by other rules of evidence.

However, unlike s 23, the statement can be used to prove facts that would have been hearsay if they had been stated in testimony by the author. This is due to s 24(2). However such 'multiple hearsay' is only admissible if every person who received the *information* contained in the document *received* it in the course of a trade, business, etc. Note that the person who first *supplied* the information does not have to be acting in the course of a trade business or profession, etc. Consider the following examples:

(a) A guest tells a receptionist at a hotel that she saw a man outside room 203. The receptionist writes a note on piece of paper, which is then recorded in a daily log by an unknown employee. The hotel manager reads the daily log and makes an entry in a record book. Only the record book is now available. Can it be used to prove the man was outside room 203?

(b) Same as above but the guest says to the receptionist 'My husband says he saw a man outside room 203'.

In the first situation the record book could be admissible documentary evidence even though its author had no first-hand knowledge of the matters to which it relates. Each person received the information in the course of their business and it is reasonable to suppose that the guest had first-hand knowledge of the matters in question. However, in the second situation, the guest who passes on the information received it from her husband and therefore it has not been received in a trade or business capacity by 'every person through whom it was supplied'.

### 8.6.3.3    Documents prepared for the purposes of criminal investigations

Section 24(4) states:

(4)  A statement prepared ... for the purposes—

(a)    of pending or contemplated criminal proceedings; or
(b)    of a criminal investigation
shall not be admissible by virtue of subsection (1) above unless—

(i)    the requirements of one of the paragraphs of subsection (2) of section 23 above are satisfied; or
(ii)   the requirements of subsection (3) of that section are satisfied; or
(iii)  the person who made the statement cannot reasonably be expected (having regard to the time which has elapsed since he made the statement and to all the circumstances) to have any recollection of the matters dealt with in the statement.

Obviously a police officer or customs officer will be acting in the course of a profession and therefore any document created by them is potentially covered by s 24. Furthermore a police officer recording information given by a member of the public would be receiving such information in the course of his or her profession. To prevent s 24 from undermining the principle that witnesses attend to give evidence, the information contained a police notebook as a result of something a witness says (for example) is subject to same requirements as would be a document created by that witness. Before either can be used instead of the witness, there must be a good reason why the witness himself or herself cannot attend. However s 24 provides an additional justification for admitting the evidence. Therefore a s 24 statement created during a criminal investigation or for pending proceedings will be admissible if the maker of the statement is:

- dead;

- physically unable to give evidence;

- mentally unable to give evidence;

- abroad and cannot be made to attend court;

- not traceable;

- kept away from court (whether by fear or by some other means) and the statement was made to a police officer or equivalent; or

- likely (for justifiable reasons) not to be able remember the details contained in the statement.

However there has been some difficulty as to who is the 'maker of the statement' for these purposes. In various cases including *R v Carrington* (1994) 99 Cr App R 376, the courts have taken the view that it is the person who wrote the document who must be unavailable. Therefore in *Carrington*, A had reported a car registration number to B, who had made a note of it in the course of her duty. It was B's ability to testify not A's that was held to be relevant for the purposes of s 24(4). This approach, probably correct on a strict interpretation of the statute, was criticised in *R v Derodra* [2000] 1 Cr App R 41, CA. There the statement in question was the report of a burglary by B to a police officer, P. The Court of Appeal held that it was the statement made by B rather than the document written by P that was the focus of s 24. Therefore it was B rather than P who had to be unable to testify for s 24 to apply. This clearly makes more sense. The Court of Appeal in *Derodra* recognised that the police officer in such a case is simply an agent who passes on relevant information rather than the source of that relevant information (Buxton LJ described him as a 'conduit pipe'). Clearly it would be absurd if a witness tells a police officer about a road accident, the police officer dies and the police officer's notebook is admissible as proof of what happens even though the witness is perfectly willing and able to attend court to give evidence. *Derodra* was subsequently followed in *R v Lake Estates Watersports Ltd* [2002] EWCA Crim 2067 where the statements in question were responses to a questionnaire that had been sent to various local authorities concerning practice in ensuring that waterways were kept safe for watersports. In concluding that the maker could have been able to remember the details of the answers given, the court noted that the 'maker' was the person who provided the responses rather than the person who wrote them down.

### 8.6.4   Provisions consequential upon ss 23 and 24

#### 8.6.4.1   Exclusion of and leave to admit the document

That a document qualifies to be admitted under either s 23 or 24 of the 1988 Act does not mean that it must be admitted. Evidence that is admissible in principle under either section must pass one of two hurdles that are set out in ss 25 and 26 of the Act. It makes sense to consider the s 26 hurdle first.

**The leave requirement under s 26**

First of all, by virtue of s 26, where a statement has been prepared for the purposes of criminal proceedings or investigations, the document is not admissible unless the court grants leave. Therefore this requirement applies to any statement:

(a) to be admitted under s 24(4); and

(b) prepared during a criminal investigation or in preparation for proceedings that will be admitted under s 23 (such as the witness statement that was prepared for a witness who has since died).

Such leave ought only to be granted if it is in the interests of justice and the court is directed to consider:

(a) The contents of the document (s 26(i)).

(b) Any unfairness to any of the accused in the case arising from admitting the document, particularly but not exclusively due to the loss of any opportunity to cross-examine the person who supplied the information (s 26(ii)).

(c) Any other circumstances which appear relevant (s 26(iii)).

### The exclusionary discretion under s 25

Section 25(1) of the Act gives the court a discretion to exclude any s 23 or 24 statement 'in the interests of justice'. Section 25(2) requires the court, in exercising its discretion, to have regard to:

- The nature, source and likely authenticity of the document (s 25(2)(a)).

- How easy it would be to obtain the evidence from another source (s 25(2)(b)).

- The relevance of the information in the document to the issues in the case (s 25(2)(c)).

- Any unfairness to any of the accused in the case arising from *either* admitting or excluding the document, particularly but not exclusively due to the loss of any opportunity to cross-examine the person who supplied the information (s 25(2)(d)).

Note that this s 25 discretion does not prevent the operation of other discretions to exclude evidence such such as the common law discretion to exclude evidence (see **Chapter 1**) and under s 78 of the Police and Criminal Evidence Act 1984 (see **Chapter 10**).

In *R v Cole* [1990] 2 All ER 108, the Court of Appeal described the difference between ss 25 and 26 as follows:

> By s 25 ... the court must be made to hold the opinion that the statement ought not to be admitted. By contrast, under s 26 when a statement ... was prepared for the purposes of criminal proceedings, the ... court is not to admit the statement unless made to hold the opinion that it ought to admit it.

Note the following points:

(a) Where such a statement is admitted instead of calling the maker to give evidence, it will often not be possible to controvert it by cross-examination. Therefore the only way to challenge the statement will often be by the accused giving evidence. However the accused may wish not to do so. The fact that the accused would be put under pressure to give evidence as a result of the statement to be admitted will not dictate where the 'interests of justice' lie (*R v Cole*; *R v Gokal* [1997] 2 Cr App R 266). However, recently the courts appear to have been influenced by Article 6(3)(d) of the European Convention on Human Rights (the right of the accused to cross-examine witnesses against him).

(b) Whether under s 25 or 26, the 'interests of justice' test can cause difficulties where there is more than one accused. In such circumstances admitting the evidence may cause difficulties for one accused while not admitting the evidence may cause difficulties for another. For example, in *R v Duffy* [1999] 1 Cr App R 307, CA, two accused, D and H, were charged with murder and robbery. The statement by the son of the victim suggested D had attempted to dissuade H from killing the victim. The prosecution sought to prove the statement, which H opposed under s 26 on the ground that H would not be able to cross-examine the maker of the statement. The trial judge declined to grant leave to admit the statement. D, who had therefore been deprived of support for her defence, appealed. The Court of Appeal allowed her appeal. In doing so they contrasted the interests of justice of each accused. On the one hand, while H could not cross-examine the maker of the statement, he could still have controverted the statement by giving evidence himself. In contrast D had suffered by the decision not to admit the evidence as she was deprived of support for her evidence. Therefore the interests of justice should have favoured D over H and the statement should therefore have been admitted. In *R v Lake Estates Watersports Ltd* [2002] EWCA Crim 2067, the Court of Appeal considered that the trial judge should have had regard to the late stage in the proceedings at which the prosecution had sought to admit a statement under s 24. The court concluded that the statement should have been excluded under s 25 as the defendant had been deprived of a chance to call an expert witness to rebut the evidence contained in the statement.

(c) The quality of the evidence will be an important factor in determining whether or not to grant leave. Where the evidence is of marginal value, the court may decide not to admit it (see for example *R v Patel* (1993) 97 Cr App R 294, CA), whereas if the evidence is of high clarity and precision it is more likely to be admitted (*R v Fairfax* [1995] Crim LR 949).

(d) The significance of the evidence will also be an important factor. In *Neill v North Antrim Magistrates' Court* [1992] 1 WLR 1221, for example, the court concluded that if the statement contains evidence of identification, the court will generally be reluctant to admit it. Such evidence would be particularly difficult to challenge effectively given that the witness cannot be cross-examined. Where the evidence of the witness is central to the case, the approach of the courts has varied. In cases such as *R v French* (1993) 97 Cr App R 421, the courts have been reluctant to admit evidence where there is no other evidence on the issue. However, in cases such as *R v Dragic* [1996] 2 Cr App R 232, the courts have shown willingness to admit s 23 or 24 statements even when they are the only source of evidence on a crucial issue. The extent to which the statement provides the only evidence on a crucial issue would appear to be a strong factor. Furthermore the court will have regard to the extent to which the loss of the opportunity to cross-examine the maker of the statement conflicts with the right to a fair trial under Article 6 of the European Convention on Human Rights and in particular Article 6(3)(d) which provides for the accused's right to cross-examine witnesses: see *R v Thomas* [1998] Crim LR 887, CA in which regard to article 6(3)(d) did not lead to the exclusion of evidence and *R v Radak* [1999] 1 Cr App R 187, CA in which the court excluded a s 23 statement that it regarded as an essential link in the prosecution case. In *R v KM* The Times, 2 May 2003, the Court of Appeal overturned a conviction which was wholly based on a statement by a complainant witness who had been mentally unfit to attend. To base all of the prosecution case on evidence that the accused could not cross-examine was considered to be a breach of Article 6 of the European Convention.

Where the evidence is admitted under s 23 or 24, the jury should be reminded that the statement has not been tested in cross-examination (*R v Cole, R v Kennedy* [1994] Crim LR 50).

### 8.6.4.2    Attacking the credibility of the statement

Although the loss of the opportunity to cross-examine the maker of the statement is a factor that the courts will take into account in exercising its powers under s 25 or 26, Sch 2 to the 1988 Act does make provision for various ways in which the statement can be attacked in the absence of the maker. These provisions, which are based on the various rules concerning cross-examination of witness dealt with at **5.3**, are as follows:

(a) *The rule of finality* (see **5.3.3**). Clearly the logic of the rule of finality is that the attack on the credibility of the witness should generally be limited to the putting of questions in cross-examination and should not extend to calling evidence to prove the maker is not worthy of belief. As the maker will not be tendered for cross-examination, the rule and its exceptions are affected as follows:

   (i)    The common law exceptions are preserved. Any evidence that could have been called under the common law to attack the credibility of the maker of the statement is still admissible (Sch 2, para 1(a)).

   (ii)    However evidence that would normally not be admissible due the rule of finality, will be admissible to undermine the credit of the maker of the statement *if the court grants leave* (Sch 2, para 1(b)).

(b) *Previous inconsistent statements* (see **5.3.4**). Schedule 2, para 2 states that such statements are admissible. Clearly the procedure for putting the previous inconsistency to a witness to establish the statement as inconsistent cannot be adopted.

(c) The court is directed to have regard to 'all the circumstances from which any inference can reasonably be drawn as to [the statement's] accuracy' when determining how much weight to attach to the document (Sch 2, para 3).

### 8.6.4.3    Proof of the document

Section 27 of the 1988 Act states that either the original or a copy of the document (or even a copy of a copy, etc) will be admissible to prove the contents. If there are no available copies or the original, oral evidence as to the contents of the document may be admissible at common law (*R v Nazeer* [1998] Crim LR 750).

Just as in civil cases, where the hearsay that is being proved is a document, the document must be 'proved'. Section 27 provides that the document shall be 'authenticated in such manner as the court may approve'.

### 8.6.4.4    Scope of ss 23 and 24

Neither s 23 nor 24 applies in relation to:

(a) retrials ordered by the Court of Appeal (see the ***Criminal Litigation and Sentencing Manual***);

(b) documentary evidence used by expert witnesses under ss 30, 31 of the 1988 Act (see **Chapter 12**);

(c) documentary evidence adduced under the Criminal Justice (international Cooperation) Act 1990, s 3, which deals with letters of request for extradition from foreign countries.

Nor does either section restrict the operation of the rules restricting the admissibility of confessions under s 76 of the Police and Criminal Evidence Act 1984 (see **Chapter 10**).

### 8.6.5  Other statutory exceptions in criminal cases

With the exception of confessions (which are covered in **Chapter 9**) the statutory exceptions to the rule against hearsay in criminal cases all relate to documentary evidence. The Criminal Justice Act 1988 did not attempt to create a comprehensive category of exception relating to documentary evidence in criminal cases. Other statutes have also created exceptions to the rule against hearsay, including:

(a) The Bankers' Books Evidence Act 1879, ss 3 and 4, which provides for the use of bankers books to evidence banking transactions. See *Blackstone's Criminal Practice,* 2004, or *Archbold*, 2004 for further information.

(b) The Magistrates' Courts Act 1980, ss 5A–5F, which creates comprehensive rules for the admissibility of documentary evidence at committal proceedings in the magistrates' court. See *Blackstone's Criminal Practice*, 2004 for further information.

(c) The Criminal Justice Act 1967, s 9, which provides that the written statement of a witness shall be admissible 'as evidence to the like extent as oral evidence' of the maker. This will only happen, however, if no other party has objected to the use of the statement instead of calling the witness. For further details, see *Blackstone's Criminal Practice*, 2004, and *Archbold*, 2004.

(d) The Theft Act, s 27(4), which provides for the proof of facts by statutory declarations relating to goods in transmission. See *Blackstone's Criminal Practice*, 2004, and *Archbold*, 2004 for further information.

The above list is far from comprehensive. See *Archbold* 2004 for a more extensive list and *Blackstone's Criminal Practice*, 2004, for a more extensive consideration of documentary evidence in criminal cases. Furthermore, as we shall see there are some common law exceptions to the rule against hearsay that apply primarily to documentary evidence.

## 8.7  Common law exceptions

The exceptions that follow have evolved at common law over the previous centuries. At common law, these exceptions generally applied to both civil and criminal proceedings. However the Civil Evidence Act 1995 has replaced nearly all of these exceptions in civil cases. This part of the chapter will identify in which proceedings each common law exception applies.

### 8.7.1  *Res gestae*

Statements forming part of the *res gestae* fall into a number of different categories. The phrase '*res gestae*' is used by the law to identify the event in question. The various *res gestae* exceptions loosely conform to a principle that the statement must be made at or about the same time as the matter to which it relates. In other words, there is some requirement of contemporaneity. Quite what the statement relates to for each exception varies as shall be seen below. The logic of these exceptions is that statements made at the time of the event or matter are less likely to be made up or distorted than statements made at a later point.

In civil cases these exceptions have been replaced by the Civil Evidence Act 1995 (see above). Therefore the current position is that *res gestae* statements are of application only in criminal cases.

### 8.7.1.1    Statements contemporaneous to a startling event

This category of *res gestae* statement is one that is made by someone as an event is taking place and where the event is dominating or overwhelming the mind of the person making the statement.

The test for admissibility for this type of *res gestae* statement is set out in *R v Andrews* [1987] AC 281 where a man was attacked and mortally wounded by two men. The prosecution called police officers to give evidence that the victim told them that Andrews was one of the attackers. Clearly this was a hearsay statement adduced to prove that Andrews was the attacker. The House of Lords held that nonetheless the statement was admissible under the *res gestae* exception. In doing so Lord Ackner defined the test of admissibility (at p 300) as follows:

(a) The primary question which the judge must ask himself or herself is — can the possibility of concoction or distortion be disregarded?

(b) To answer that question the judge must first consider the circumstances in which the particular statement was made, in order to satisfy himself or herself that the event was so unusual or startling or dramatic as to dominate the thoughts of the maker so that his utterance was an instinctive reaction to that event, thus giving no real opportunity for reasoned reflection. In such a situation the judge would be entitled to conclude that the involvement or the pressure of the event would exclude the possibility of concoction or distortion, providing that the statement was made in conditions of approximate but not exact contemporaneity.

Therefore:

(a) The primary test is whether concoction or distortion can be disregarded.

(b) This test is passed if the judge concludes (ie it is proved to him or her that):
  (i)   There was an 'unusual or *startling* or dramatic' *event*.
  (ii)  That event therefore *dominated the thoughts* of the maker of the statement.
  (iii) As a result of that domination of the thoughts, the statement was an 'instinctive reaction' to the event. In other words, the statement was *spontaneous*.
  (iv)  The statement was *approximately contemporaneous*.

Lord Ackner made the following additional points:

(a) On the issue of spontaneity Lord Ackner said:
  (i)   The statement must be 'so closely associated with the event ... that it can fairly be said that the mind of the declarant was still dominated by the event'.
  (ii)  The judge must be satisfied that the 'event, which provided the trigger mechanism was still operative'.
  (iii) That the statement is a response to a question is only a factor to consider in deciding whether the statement was sufficiently spontaneous.

(b) The judge should consider any factors other than the passage of time that might, in the circumstances of each case, support any argument that the statement was concocted or distorted. In *R v Andrews*, for example, it was alleged that the victim had a malicious motive to fabricate evidence against Andrews. In such cases the judge must be satisfied that there was no possibility of any concoction or distortion having regard to the allegations of malice.

(c) Generally any risk that the person hearing and repeating the statement has made an error goes to the weight not the admissibility of the statement. However, a special feature is alleged to have caused the mistake such as drunkenness (as was the case in *R v Andrews*) or short sightedness, the judge must 'consider whether he can exclude the possibility of error'. If not, it would seem the judge may have to exclude the statement.

Note the importance of proof of these matters. Whether or not a particular statement fits within this exception will have to be established by evidence. In *Teper v R* [1952] AC 480, PC, the statement was made to a police officer by an unknown person. It was held that as it was not known who had made the statement, it was *unlikely* to be possible to rely on this exception. This is because it is unlikely that it will be possible to prove that the maker's mind was dominated by the event if it is not even known who the maker is. However, there may be circumstances in which there is evidence to suggest that the statement was made by an unknown person whose mind was dominated. This will be a matter of proof in each case.

The statement must be approximately contemporaneous. This will be a question of fact in each case. In *Tobi v Nichols* [1988] RTR 343 a statement made 20 minutes after a collision was determined not to be sufficiently contemporaneous. However it was also considered that the event was not sufficiently mind-dominating. It is submitted that there may be some correlation between the nature of the event and how long after it a statement may be roughly contemporaneous. The worse the event, the better the argument that it is still dominating the mind of the maker at a later point. In *R v Carnall* [1995] Crim LR 944, for example, a statement made an hour after a murderous assault was held to have been rightly admitted. As the statement must be a reaction to or part of the event, statements made before the event in question cannot be part of this category of *res gestae* exception (*R v Newport* [1998] Crim LR 581).

There are no particular requirements that the person who made the statement is dead or unavailable at the time of trial (*R v Nye* (1977) 66 Cr App R 252). Even statements made by the accused can be part of the *res gestae* and therefore admitted by either party. In *R v Glover* [1991] Crim LR 48, the accused said 'I am David Glover … we will not think twice about shooting you and your kids'. As the trial issue was identity, the prosecution were allowed to call this statement as part of the *res gestae*. However, in *R v Andrews*, Lord Ackner observed that it be wrong to use this *res gestae* exception to avoid calling the witness in question so as to deprive other parties of an opportunity to cross-examine the maker of the statement. However, in *Attorney General's Reference (No 1 of 2003)* [2003] 2 Cr App Rep 453, the Court of Appeal ruled that there was no requirement that a witness was unavailable before a statement made by that witness would be admissible under the doctrine of *res gestae*. However where the prosecution sought to rely on a *res gestae* statement made by a person who could be called as a witness but who the prosecution did not propose to call, the trial judge had a discretion under s 78 of the Police and Criminal Evidence Act 1984 to exclude the *res gestae* statements. In deciding whether to do so the court would have regard to the circumstances in which the statement was made and how easy it would have been to call the witness.

### 8.7.1.2 Contemporaneous statements relating to the maker's physical state

A statement made by a person in which he or she refers to his or her current physical state will be admissible to prove that physical state.

The statement can prove the physical state but not its cause (*R v Gloster* (1888) 16 Cox CC 471). Therefore in *R v Thomson* [1912] 3 KB 19 statements by a woman that she had recently operated upon herself were not admissible to prove the cause of a miscarriage.

The statements do not have to be made at the exact time that the feelings are being experienced: whether a statement is contemporary to the feeling is a question of degree. In *Aveson v Lord Kinnaird* (1805) 6 East 188, statements made by a woman as to symptoms she said she had been suffering for some time were admitted to prove that she not only was suffering those symptoms when she made the statement but also that she had suffered them some days earlier.

### 8.7.1.3    Contemporaneous statements relating to the maker's mind or emotion

You will remember from **Chapter 8** that statements revealing that a person was of a particular frame of mind could be original evidence (eg *Thomas v Connell* (1838) 4 M & W 267, as confirmed by the approach of the courts in *R v Blastland* [1986] AC 41, and *R v Kearley*). This is probably the best approach to cases from which a state of mind is inferred (ie, because A said a particular thing we can infer a particular state of mind or particular emotional state). Clearly, however, where a person expressly states that he or she is of a particular state of mind (such as 'I hate that man,' or 'I believe he is the one who stole my watch') there can be little doubt that the statement is hearsay evidence.

However such a statement will be admissible as an exception to the rule against hearsay evidence if it is sufficiently contemporaneous. Statements of one's state of mind at an earlier time are not admissible (*R v Moghal* (1977) 65 Cr App R 56).

A particular difficulty arises from this rule where a statement of a contemporaneous fact is used to prove what happened at a later date. The usual case is one in which the statement reveals the intention of the maker and the issue is whether the maker later acted on that intention. Consider the following cases:

(a) *R v Buckley* (1838) 13 Cox CC 293: a statement made by a police officer that he intended to keep a watch on the accused was admitted to prove that he had later been keeping a watch on the accused when he was murdered.

(b) *R v Moghal* (above): a statement made by S that she intended to kill R was held to be admissible to prove that she and not the accused had killed R even though the statement had been made six months before.

(c) *R v Callender* [1998] Crim LR 337: statements made by a person two weeks before he was arrested on explosives charges that he intended to carry false explosive devices for publicity purposes was held not to be admissible.

The case law in this area appears confused. It is submitted that the best view to take of cases about current intentions is that such statements of intention are admissible under this exception but only if relevant. If the statements are not sufficiently relevant, they should not be admitted. This was the view taken in *R v Blastland* in which the statement in *R v Moghal* was criticised as insufficiently relevant. For a further criticism of *R v Callender*, see *Blackstone's Criminal Practice*, 2004.

### 8.7.1.4    Contemporaneous statements relating to the maker's performance of an act

As with the exceptions above, such statements must be:

(a) Approximately contemporaneous to the act. In *Howe v Malkin* (1878) 40 LT 196, it was said that such a statement was admissible because it was mixed up with the event in question.

(b) Made by the person performing the act (*Peacock v Harris* (1836) 5 Ad & El 449).

(c) The act should itself be relevant to the issues in the case (in *R v McCay* [1990] 1 WLR 645, the statement 'It's number 8', was made at the same time as a person was identified in an identification parade).

### 8.7.2    Statements by persons now dead

The exceptions which follow all apply only where a person made a statement but has died by the time of trial. Clearly the courts are being pragmatic in allowing such evidence. However the rules also seek to ensure that only evidence that can, to some extent, avoid the risks of distortion or concoction will be admitted.

Owing to the effect of various statutes, this exception only really applies to oral statements in criminal cases. In civil cases, such statements would now be admissible under the Civil Evidence Act 1995 (see **8.5**). In criminal cases such statements made in documents would be admissible under ss 23 or 24 of the Criminal Justice Act 1988 (see **8.6**). It may be, however, that these exceptions will also apply where a documentary statement is not admitted in criminal proceedings due to the operation of either s 25 or s 26 of the 1988 Act.

#### 8.7.2.1    Dying declarations

This exception applies if all of the following conditions (laid down in *R v Perry* [1909] 2 KB 697) are met:

(a) The statement is to be admitted at a (criminal) trial for murder or manslaughter.

(b) The maker of the statement had a 'settled and hopeless expectation of death' when he or she made the statement. If the maker of the statement shows hope of recovery, such an expectation is not established (*R v Jenkins* (1869) 11 Cox CC 250). This does not mean that the maker of the statement has to die immediately (*R v Bernadotti* (1869) 11 Cox CC 316).

(c) The statement concerns matters of which the maker could have given direct oral evidence if he or she had lived (ie the dying declaration cannot contain what would have been hearsay evidence if it had been said as testimony) (*R v Pike* (1829) 3 C & P 598).

(d) The statement must be complete: *Waugh v R* [1950] AC 203, PC, where the last words of the victim were 'The man has an old grudge for me simply because ...'. The statement was not admitted because it was not possible to know what might have been said afterwards.

The statement can be admitted for the prosecution or for the defence (*R v Scaife* (1836) 1 Mood & R 551.

#### 8.7.2.2    Statements made in the course of a duty or business

A statement can be admitted to prove a particular act was carried out if:

(a) The person who made the statement was acting in the course of a business or duty to which the act related. That the person had a duty to perform the act must be proved before the evidence will be admissible (*Chambers v Bernasconi* (1834) 1 Cr M & R 347).

(b) The statement was contemporaneous with the act in question. In *The Henry Cox* (1878) 3 PD 156 a ship's log completed two days after the acts in question was not admissible under this exception.

(c) The person has since died.

### 8.7.2.3    Statements against the proprietary or pecuniary interest of the maker

Where a person makes a statement against his or her proprietary or pecuniary interest and then dies, the statement will be admissible to prove not only the adverse matter but also any incidental fact that is of relevance. In *Higham v Ridgeway* (1808) 10 East 109, for example, the deceased, a midwife, had recorded that he had been paid for assisting in the birth of a particular child. The statement was clearly adverse to the deceased in that it showed he was no longer owed the money for his services. However, the statement was held to be admissible to prove the date of birth of the child in question.

In *R v Rogers* [1995] 1 Cr App R 374, the Court of Appeal identified the following aspects of the test:

(a) The facts related in the statement that the deceased person has given must be something of which he or she had personal knowledge (ie had he or she been available to give evidence it would not have been hearsay).

(b) The statement must be adverse to a pecuniary or proprietary interest of the maker.

(c) It must have been adverse when the statement was made. It does not apply to possible future liabilities.

(d) The maker of the statement must have been aware that it was adverse when he or she made the statement.

In the *Sussex Peerage Case* (1844) 11 Ch & Fin 85, it was held that a person stating that he or she had committed a criminal offence was *not* necessarily adverse to a pecuniary or proprietary interest.

### 8.7.2.4    Statements as to pedigree

A statement made by a deceased person concerning a matter of pedigree (such as marriages, legitimacy, dates of birth, etc) will be admissible (*Butler v Mountgarret* (1859) 7 HL Cas 633) to prove the truth of the facts stated if:

- the maker of the statement and the person about whom it was made are blood relations or the one is married to a blood relation of the other.

- the pedigree matter is in issue as opposed to a collateral matter.

### 8.7.2.5    Statements as to public rights

Where the existence of a public right is relevant to an issue, any statement by a deceased person affirming the existence of a public right that was made before the dispute arose shall be admissible to prove the existence of that right (see, for example, *Mercer v Denne* [1905] 2 Ch 638). The statement must relate either to rights possessed by the general public or by particular classes of persons not to those possessed by an individual.

## 8.7.3    Statements in public documents

The common law exceptions set out below apply in both civil and criminal cases, having been expressly preserved by the Civil Evidence Act 1995, s 7 (see **8.5.5** above). It is likely that most such documents, would, however be admissible in criminal proceedings under s 24 of the 1988 Act rather than under this exception. The exception applies to:

(a) public works dealing with matters of a public nature and of public interest where the person recording the information is under a public duty to record and to ascertain the truth of the matters recorded (eg a dictionary or an atlas);

(b) public documents (eg public registers);

(c) public records (such as court records, treaties or town charters).

For detailed explanation of this exception, see *Blackstone's Criminal Practice*, 2004, and *Blackstone's Civil Practice*, 2004. However, in outline, the exceptions apply where the document in question is available to the public as of right. 'Public' was stated in *Sturla v Feccia* (1880) 5 App Cas 623 not to mean the whole world but all persons interested in the subject matter in question.

### 8.7.4 Confessions

An admission by a party that he or she has committed the offence with which he or she is tried or is liable in respect of the civil matter that is being litigated is clearly an out of court statement tendered to prove what is said in it and therefore hearsay. The common law and statute law have recognised that such statements are admissible. In civil cases these are now admissible under the Civil Evidence Act 1995 and therefore are subject to the provisions of ss 2 to 6 of it (see **8.5** above). In criminal cases such admissions are governed primarily by the Police and Criminal Evidence Act 1984. They are considered in more detail in **Chapter 9**.

### 8.7.5 Statements in furtherance of a common purpose

Where, in the course of committing a crime, A makes a statement which proves that B was also committing the same crime, the common law allows such matters to be admitted as proof of the fact that B committed the crime. This rule should be contrasted with the rule that generally a confession is only admissible against the person who makes it and not another person.

Before a statement will be admissible under this exception, however, it must be established that:

- there was a common criminal purpose; and
- The statement was made to pursue or further that purpose.

#### 8.7.5.1 Common purpose

A common purpose is wider than a conspiracy. In *R v Jones* [1997] 2 Cr App R 119, CA, for example, the doctrine was applied to the offence of evading the prohibition on the importation of drugs (drug smuggling) even though there was no charge of conspiracy on the indictment. However there does have to be some common element of commission of the offence. In *R v Gray* [1995] 2 Cr App R 100, there had been an allegation of a 'network' between various co-accused as to insider dealing but each accused was charged with separate offences. The Court of Appeal concluded that, in the absence of some allegation that the offences had been committed jointly, the rule did not apply. Usually such an allegation would arise from the way in which the accused persons were charged. Therefore even if there does not have to be conspiracy charged, the rule will generally only apply where the parties are jointly charged, whether as principals or as secondary parties. The court did leave open the possibility that future cases may involve a common purpose even if the various parties were charged with separate offences but did not define how that might be the case.

That there is a common purpose must be proved by evidence independent to the statement that will be admitted (*R v Blake* (1844) 6 QB 126). In other words, what is said in the statement cannot prove that there was a common purpose and the jury should be directed that they cannot rely on the statement itself to prove the existence of such a common purpose (*R v Williams* [2002] EWCA Crim 2208). However the court can conditionally admit the evidence of the statement subject to proof at some later stage that there was a common purpose (*R v Governor of Pentonville Prison, ex p Osman* [1990] 1 WLR 277). If it proves impossible to prove the existence of a common purpose by independent evidence, the statement will have to be excluded from the case against any co-accused (*R v Donat* (1985) 82 Cr App R 173) and, in jury trials, a direction will have to be given directing them to ignore the evidence or they may have to be discharged.

### 8.7.5.2    Furtherance of the common purpose

A statement that takes place after the criminal purpose has been achieved or simply explains what another member has done within the purpose without advancing it in any way, will not be 'in furtherance' of the common purpose and therefore not admissible (*R v Walters* (1979) 69 Cr App R 115; *R v Steward* [1963] Crim LR 697).

What is capable of being a statement in furtherance of a common purpose will depend on the facts of the case. In *R v Devonport* [1996] 1 Cr App R 221, the statement concerned the intended division of proceeds from a drug deal. This was treated as in furtherance of the common purpose. However, in *R v Blake* (1844) 6 QB 126, a cheque proving that B had received his share of the proceeds from a conspiracy was held not to be in furtherance of the common purpose. In the former case the statement assisted or encouraged the commission of the offence whereas in the latter case it was simply a consequence of it.

Where the evidence that is alleged to prove the common purpose is a document, it will be necessary to prove (a) it was either made in a particular (and relevant) way or to have been found in an incriminating way, and (b) that it suggests the involvement of the defendants in the common purpose (*R v Jenkins* [2003] Crim LR 107). Merely producing the document without proving it in this way will not render it admissible as evidence of the common purpose.

The courts have interpreted what furthers the purpose quite loosely. In *R v Ilyas* [1996] Crim LR 810, the diary of A was admitted to prove that B, C an D had received stolen cars, Latham J appearing to extend the definition to documents 'created in the *course of, or furtherance, of the conspiracy*'.

## 8.8    Criminal Justice Act 2003

As will be seen from the previous chapter, the law relating to hearsay has become complicated. We have also seen that the Civil Evidence Act 1995 largely removed any rules of exclusion relating to hearsay evidence in civil cases. The aim of the Criminal Justice Act 2003 is to do the same in respect of criminal cases.

The Act is not yet in force. What follows is a brief outline of the effect of the Act upon criminal evidence. The law relating to hearsay evidence is contained in Chapter 2 of Part 11 of the Act.

### 8.8.1    The basic rule

Hearsay evidence is defined as 'a statement not made in oral evidence in the proceedings' (s 114(1)) and a statement is 'any representation of fact or opinion made by a person by whatever means.' (s 115(2)).

Hearsay evidence is admissible as 'evidence of any matter stated' in one of five circumstances:

(a) a specific statutory rule other than the Criminal Justice Act 2003 (s 114(1)(a)) (see **8.6.5**);

(b) a rule of the Criminal Justice Act 2003 (s 114(1)(a)) (see **8.8.2**);

(c) specific common law exceptions that have been preserved (see s 114(1)(b) and **8.8.2.5**);

(d) agreement by the parties (s 114(1)(c); or

(e) under a discretion on the part of the court to admit such evidence 'in the interests of justice' (s 114(1)(d)).

The last two points are particularly noteworthy. There is no longer a requirement that evidence fits within a class to be admissible. Rather the evidence can be admitted if both of the parties or the court deems it appropriate. The court's decision in this respect should take into account the probative value of the statement, the availability of other evidence and the possibility of evidence on the matter in question being given from some other source, the importance of the evidence, the reliability of the maker and the making of the document and any difficulty of challenging the statement if admitted and any prejudice that the party against whom the hearsay statement is admitted may suffer as a result of it being admitted (s 114(2)).

As a possible change to the common law, the Act defines 'matter stated' as 'the purpose, or one of the purposes, of the person making the statement' if that purpose 'appears to have been (a) to cause another person to believe the matter or (b) to cause another person to act or a machine to operate on the basis that the matter is stated' (s 115(3)). This would appear therefore not to apply to some types of hearsay statement that the common law accepted as hearsay by implication. Before a statement would be implied hearsay under the Act one of the purposes identified in s 115(3) would have to be established.

### 8.8.2    Categories of admissibility under the Act

#### 8.8.2.1    The witness is unavailable (s 116)

Any hearsay evidence can be admitted if it would have been admitted as testimony and the person who made the statement can be identified 'to the court's satisfaction'. However before such evidence can be admitted one of five circumstances must be proven to exist:

(a) The maker of the statement is dead.

(b) The maker is unfit to attend court due to bodily or mental condition.

(c) The maker is outside the United Kingdom and it is not reasonably practicable to secure his or her attendance.

(d) The maker cannot be found despite all such steps as are reasonably practicable to find him or her having been taken.

(e) The maker is kept away from court through fear.

The effect of s 116 is to broaden the effect of s 23 of the Criminal Justice Act 1988 so that it applies to all types of hearsay evidence (documentary or oral). It is likely that the case law applicable to ss 23 and 24 of the 1988 Act will be applicable to determination of s 116 issues.

Generally where one of the factors identified above applies the evidence is admissible without leave. However, where the last ground for admissibility (fear under s 116(2)(e)) is relied upon, leave is required and should only be granted 'in the interests of justice' (s 116(4)). The court is to take into consideration the nature of the statement, any risks posed by allowing a hearsay statement rather than requiring the maker to give testimony and the possibility that any concerns of the maker could be solved by 'special measures directions' (see **4.7.5**).

Section 116(5) provides that a party cannot rely on hearsay evidence under s 116 if the circumstance set out above has been caused by his or her act (ie, if the defendant is alleged to have caused the death or disappearance, etc of the witness).

While s 116 does not preserve the requirement in s 23 of the 1988 Act that the statement must be something of which direct (ie, non-hearsay) testimony could be given, under s 121, a statement under s 116 cannot be proven by a hearsay statement unless all parties in proceedings agree (s 121(1)(b)) or the court admits the statement where the 'value of the evidence in question, taking into account how reliable the statements appear to be, is so high that the interests of justice require' such multiple hearsay to be admitted.

### 8.8.2.2   Business documents

Much as s 116 preserves (and expands) s 23 of the 1988 Act, s 117 preserves s 24 of the 1988 Act. Its provisions are essentially the same. Unlike s 116, s 117 applies only to statements contained in documents.

Like s 24, if the statement was prepared as part of a criminal investigation or in contemplation of criminal proceedings, there are added requirements and these added requirements correspond to those contained in s 24 of the 1988 Act (ie, the matters identified under s 116 or proof that the person who supplied the information cannot be expected to remember the matters contained in it). As a result of redrafting the difficulty identified in the case of *R v Derodra* (see **8.6.3.3**) has been solved: the person who cannot remember or be found, etc is the person who supplied the information. Note that the requirement of leave for witnesses in fear applies to s 117 as much as to s 116.

In contrast to s 24, s 117 has given the court a power to direct that any statement in a business document will not be admissible (s 117(6)). Such a direction can only be made if 'satisified that the statement's reliability as evidence for the purpose for which it is tendered is doubtful' (s 117(7)) having regard to the document, the sources of information, how the information was supplied and how the document was created or received.

### 8.8.2.3   Statements made by witnesses to proceedings

It has been already noted (in **Chapter 5**) that statements made by a party to proceedings may be admissible as relevant to the credibility of the witness but not to prove the matters alleged in the statement.

Insofar as the statement in question is a previous inconsistent statement (see **5.3.4**), s 119 of the 2003 Act now provides that such statements will be admissible to prove the matters alleged in it. In other words a previous inconsistent statement will be admissible to prove that what a witness said on a previous occasion is true. Section 119 has not, however altered the rules concerning *when* such statements will be admissible.

Where the previous statement is consistent with the testimony of the witness in question (ie, a 'previous consistent statement': see **5.2.3** and **5.2.4**), s 120 of the 2003 Act has altered some of the rules of admissibility of those statements *and* the effect of admitting them. For detail on when previous consistent statements will be admissible under the new Act see **5.2.5**. In brief the following previous consistent statements will be admissible, those that:

- are admitted to rebut a suggestion of fabrication (s 120(2)) (see **5.2.4.6** for the current law on statements in rebuttal of a suggestion of fabrication);
- are contained in memory refreshing documents made evidence as a result of cross-examination (s 120(3)) (see **5.2.2.3** for the current law on memory refreshing documents);
- are statements made by the victim of an offence identifying relevant matters and made when the matters were fresh in the memory of the maker (s 120(4)–(7)).

If a previous statement is proven under either ss 119 or 120, the document, if exhibited, can only be taken by the jury to the jury room when they retire if either the court orders so or all parties to the proceedings agree (s 122(2)).

### 8.8.2.4   Common law exceptions to the rule against hearsay

Section 118 of the 2003 Act preserves some of the common law exceptions to the rule against hearsay:

- statements in public documents (see **8.7.3**);
- statements concerning the general reputation of a person (see **6.3.2**);
- statements as to pedigree (see **8.7.2.4**);
- *res gestae* statements of all four types identified at **8.7.1**;
- confession (see **8.7.4**);
- admission by agents;
- statements in furtherance of a criminal purpose (see **8.7.5**);
- statements made by an expert in the course of giving expert opinion (see **Chapter 12**).

All other common law exceptions are abolished (s 118(2)). These will include, in particular statements by persons now dead. These will be covered by s 116 (see **8.8.2.1**).

## 8.8.3   Powers to exclude or restrict hearsay evidence

### 8.8.3.1   Power to stop the case

Section 125 gives the court a power in jury trials to withdraw the case from the jury where 'the case against the defendant is based wholly or partly' on a hearsay statement. The Act does not specify that the hearsay statement has to be one admitted under this Act and therefore it would appear that s 125 will also apply to hearsay statements admitted under preserved common law exceptions or under another statute.

The power to stop the case only arises if such a hearsay statement is 'so unconvincing that, considering its importance to the case against the defendant, his conviction of the offence would be unsafe' (s 125(1)(b)).

### 8.8.3.2   Power to exclude a statement

In addition to preserving the discretion to exclude evidence under s 78 of the Police and Criminal Evidence Act 1984 and at common law, s 126 of the 2003 Act gives the court a power to refuse to admit a hearsay statement. Again, the power to exclude such a statement is not restricted to a statement admitted under the 2003 Act. The court can only refuse to admit such a statement if 'the case for excluding the statement...outweighs the case for admitting it' (s 126(1)(b)). The section requires the court, when considering whether to exclude such evidence, to have particular regard to the danger that the evidence would waste court time when considering whether to exclude such evidence.

### 8.8.4    Other ancillary matters

#### 8.8.4.1    Competence of maker

Any statement admitted under the provisions set out above (but not including statements admitted by agreement of the parties under s 114(1)(c), by court order under s 114(1)(d) or under a preserved common law exception under s 118) can only be admitted if made by a person competent to do so. The test of competence set out in s 123(3) is the same as that contained in the Youth Justice and Criminal Evidence Act 1999, s 53 (see **4.2.1**). Where the statement is admitted under s 117 (ie, as a business document) the competence requirement applies to any person who received the document or information in question or who might be supposed to have done so.

#### 8.8.4.2    Credibility issues

Where a statement is admitted but the maker does not give testimony, evidence may be adduced before the court to undermine the credibility of the statement admitted (s 124(2)(a)) including evidence of previous inconsistent statements (s 124(2)(c)). However in addition to evidence that would be admissible if the maker had made the statement as testimony, s 124(2)(b) allows any party to admit evidence that would not normally be admissible under the rule of finality (see **5.3.3.2** to **5.3.3.6**) but only if the court grants leave.

Where evidence adduced under this section leads to the admission of evidence that undermines the credibility of the maker of a statement, the court may allow further evidence to be admitted 'for the purposes of denying or answering the allegation' (s 124(3)). In other words the court has a broader power to allow collateral evidence in respect of statements than it has in respect of witnesses giving testimony.

### 8.8.5    Mechanical devices

Section 115(2) defines a statement as a representation 'made by a person by whatever means'. Therefore statements made through a machine (such as dictation into a machine or typing or computer input) are clearly covered by the 2003 Act. However, where a representation is made 'otherwise than by a person, but depends for its accuracy on information supplied...by a person, s 129 states that such information is only admissible if the information provided is proved to be accurate. The Act therefore preserves the position at common law set out in *R v Wood* (see **8.4.4**).

# Confessions and illegally or improperly obtained evidence

- When can the prosecution use a confession to prove the defendant is guilty of the offence?
- When can the prosecution admit evidence that has been obtained illegally or improperly?

## 9.1 Confessions

The admissibility of a confession is governed by the Police and Criminal Evidence Act 1984 (PACE).

### 9.1.1 The definition of confession

Section 82(1) PACE provides that:

> 'confession' includes any statement wholly or partly adverse to the person who made it, whether made to a person in authority or not and whether made in words or otherwise.

As can be seen this is a very wide definition. However, the leading case, *R v Sat-Bhambra* (1988) 88 Cr App R 44, notes that there is a restriction on confessions in that the statement must have been adverse *when made*. Therefore, statements that were favourable when made, eg false alibis, but later proved to be adverse are not confessions: *R v Park* (1995) 99 Cr App R 270.

The whole statement is admissible, therefore a statement that is partly exculpatory and partly adverse 'mixed' cannot be divided and is taken as one confession *R v Garrod* [1997] Crim LR 445. See **5.2.4.5** for more detail on mixed statements.

### 9.1.1.2 Section 76(1) PACE

> In any proceedings a confession made by an accused person may be given in evidence against him in so far as it is relevant to any matter in issue in the proceedings and is not excluded by the court in pursuance of this section.

The confession must generally be based on facts that are known to the person who makes it. In *R v Hulbert* (1979) 69 Cr App R 243, the defendant was charged with handling stolen goods and confessed that the person from whom she bought the goods told her that they were stolen. This confession could not prove that the goods were stolen, but only went to Hulbert's knowledge of the goods.

### 9.1.1.3    The confession is only admissible against the defendant who made it

A confession made by one defendant is generally not evidence against a co-defendant. However, when the statement is made in the presence of the co-accused and he or she acknowledges the incriminating parts so as to make them, in effect, his or her own, the statement will be admissible against both parties. Note also that evidence that a co-accused gives on oath is evidence for all purposes, including being against the accused: *Rudd* (1948) 32 Cr App R 138.

Where X makes adverse statements about Y, X is entitled for the whole confession statement to be admitted even when parts incriminate Y: *R v Pearce* (1979) 69 Cr App R 365. Y is only protected by a direction by the judge to state that the confession is not evidence against Y.

The question of whether a statement should be edited was raised in *R v Silcot* [1987] Crim LR 765 and it was suggested that the trial judge had a discretion whether to do so. However, in *Lobban v R* [1995] 2 All ER 602, the Privy Council held that the discretion to exclude by balancing the probative value and prejudicial effect applies only to prosecution evidence and there is therefore no discretion in regard to defence evidence. This case was decided before the Human Rights Act was incorporated and it would be interesting to see whether Article 6, right to fair trial, would have led to a different result.

You may wish to carry out **activity 9.1** in **Appendix 1** at this point.

### 9.1.2    Statutory restrictions on admissibility of confessions (s 76(1) PACE)

*In any proceedings a confession made by an accused person may be given in evidence against him in so far as it is relevant to any matter in issue in the proceedings and is not excluded by the court in pursuance of this section.*

Section 76(1) is subject to subsection 76(2) which provides grounds on which such evidence will be excluded. Further, ss 78 and 82(3) provide discretionary grounds by which a confession may be excluded.

Further, the Codes of Practice provided for under PACE give weight to this issue. Section 67(11), PACE, provides that the court *shall* take account of the codes in determining any question (where relevant) arising in any proceedings.

### 9.1.2.1    The first barrier to admissibility, s 76(2) and (3), PACE

(2)  *If, in any proceedings where the prosecution proposes to give evidence of a confession made by an accused person, it is represented to the court that the confession was or may have been obtained—*

   (a)  *by oppression of the person who made it; or*

   (b)  *in consequence of anything said or done which was likely, in the circumstances existing at the time, to render unreliable any confession which might be made by him in consequence thereof,*

   *the court shall not allow the confession to be given in evidence against him except insofar as the prosecution proves to the court beyond reasonable doubt that the confession (notwithstanding that it may be true) was not obtained as aforesaid.*

(3)  *In any proceedings where the prosecution proposes to give in evidence a confession made by an accused person, the court may of its own motion require the prosecution as a condition of allowing it to do so, to prove that the confession was not obtained as mentioned in subsection (2).*

### 9.1.2.2    Making an objection under s 76

The leading case pre-PACE in relation to the admissibility of confessions was *Adjodha v The State* [1982] AC 204, PC. In this case Lord Bridge indicated that the confession should not be opened to the jury and the issue of admissibility would be resolved by a *voir dire*. A confession could be excluded where its 'voluntariness' was in doubt.

After PACE was enacted the procedure in *Adjodha* was followed. However, the case of *R v Sat-Bhambra* made no reference to *Adjodha* and did not see the defendant's position as one of choice. If there was to be an objection under s 76, the time to take the objection was before the confession was given in evidence: *Archbold* (2004) 151–284. The court went on to state that where a confession was admitted, following an objection or not, if during the course of the trial it emerged that the issue of admissibility was in doubt the judge was precluded from re-opening the s 76 issue. However, the judge could direct the jury in several ways:

- to disregard the statement;
- direct their attention to the matters which might affect the weight attached to the confession;
- or if the matter could not be solved by a suitable direction he or she could discharge the jury.

The judge's power to do the above derives from the preservation of the common law, under s 82(3), PACE, to take such steps that are necessary to prevent injustice.

### 9.1.2.3   Oppression and reliability in s 76(2)

Oppression is defined in s 76(8) of PACE as 'torture, inhuman or degrading treatment, and the use or threat of violence (whether or not amounting to torture)'.

In *R v Fulling* [1987] QB 426, Lord Lane held that 'oppression' was to be given its ordinary dictionary meaning:

The Oxford English Dictionary as its third definition of the word runs as follows: 'exercise of authority or power in a burdensome, harsh, or wrongful manner; unjust or cruel treatment of subjects, inferiors, etc., or the imposition of unreasonable or unjust burdens'

There is no reference to Article 3 of the European Convention on Human Rights nor are the words 'the use or threat of violence' further defined in PACE. 'Torture' is a criminal offence under s 134, Criminal Justice Act 1988 and 'violence' or 'force' is broadly defined in s 8, Public Order Act 1986 (where it includes violent conduct to property and person).

In *R v Paris* (1992) 97 Cr App R 99, CA, the fact that the defendant had a solicitor present did not deprive the interview of its oppressive character. The police had continued to shout at the suspect even though he had denied the charge over 300 times.

In *R v Parker* [1995] Crim LR 223, CA it was held that any breach of the PACE Codes of Practice would **not** automatically exclude the confession. It was important to look at the context in which the term oppression was used to judge whether or not the confession had been obtained by oppression. In determining whether oppression had been used, the court could have regard to the character and experience of the suspect: *R v Seelig* (1991) 94 Cr App R 17, CA.

When considering the issue of reliability of a confession, reference to pre-PACE law may be made to see whether the test has been passed. *R v Phillips* (1988) 86 Cr App R 18, CA relates to inducements: promises of bail and taking further offences into consideration, leading to unreliable confession. *R v Prager* (1972) 56 Cr App R 151 states 'questioning which by its nature or duration...excites hope (such as hope of release) or fears, or so affects the mind of the subject that his will crumbles and he speaks when otherwise he would have stayed silent'. Such could amount to oppression

Therefore, s 76 (2)(b), unlike s 76 (2)(a), may be inadmissible *without any impropriety*.

The case of *R v Barry* (1992) 95 Cr App R 384 sets out some useful guidelines when considering the reliability of a confession taken during police interview:

1. Identify the thing 'said or done' (the judge must take into account every thing 'said or done' by the police).

2. Ask whether or not the thing 'said or done' was likely in the circumstances to render unreliable the confession made in consequence.

3. Ask whether the prosecution have proved beyond reasonable doubt that the confession was not obtained in consequence of the thing 'said or done'.

1 and 2 are objective and the third step is a question of fact. See Code C, PACE 1984.

The words 'said or done' do not include anything said or done by the person making the confession: *R v Goldenberg* (1989) 88 Cr App R 285, CA. In this case a heroin addict was interviewed at a time when he may have been withdrawing from the effects of heroin. The police agreed that they would not have interviewed if they had known he was withdrawing. However, the fact that section states 'in consequence of' meant that a causal link had to be shown between what was said and done and therefore it followed that the words 'said or done' were limited to something external to the person making the confession.

Breaches of PACE Code C can amount to 'things done'. Examples include a failure to caution a suspect: *R v Doolan* [1988] Crim LR 747, CA, or improper denial of access to a solicitor: *R v McGovern* (1991) 92 Cr App R 228, CA. The test is whether the breach is significant: see *R v Delaney* (1989) 88 Cr App R 338, CA, where a confession made at the end of an interview which had not been recorded in accordance with Code C was ruled inadmissible.

The Privy Council in *Benedetto and Labrador v The Queen* [2003] UKPC 27 stated that in cases where the issue is the reliability of the witness who says the accused made a confession to him, counsel may suggest that the evidence is unreliable but the judge should also add weight to those submissions by explaining to the jury that they had to be cautious before accepting and acting upon that evidence. In that case a prisoner, who shared a cell with one of the appellants, alleged he had heard the appellants discussing the murder and that one had confessed to him.

### 9.1.2.4    Mentally handicapped persons

Section 77, PACE states '*the court shall warn the jury that there is a special need for caution before convicting the accused in reliance on the confession.*' If the judge fails to give this warning it is likely that the conviction will be quashed: *R v Lamont* [1989] Crim LR 813, CA.

The provisions for mentally handicapped and mentally disordered persons can be found in PACE Code C and are summarised in Annex E.

### 9.1.3    The discretion(s) to exclude

Section 78, PACE provides that:

(1) *In any proceedings the court may refuse to allow evidence on which the prosecution proposes to rely to be given if it appears to the court that, having regard to all the circumstances, including the circumstances in which the evidence was obtained, the admission of the evidence would have such an adverse effect on the fairness of the proceedings that the court ought not to admit it.*

(2) *Nothing in this section shall prejudice any rule of law requiring a court to exclude evidence.*

Section 82(3) PACE preserves the common law discretion to exclude evidence, pre-PACE and provides that:

*Nothing in part of this Act shall prejudice any power of a court to exclude evidence (whether by preventing questions being put or otherwise) at its discretion.*

### 9.1.3.1  Section 78 and the *voir dire*

A *voir dire* is necessary in the Crown Court to determine whether a confession should be excluded under s 78. However, s 78 has no application when magistrates are acting as examining justices, ie in committal proceedings (Criminal Procedure and Investigations Act 1996, Sch 1, para 26).

### 9.1.3.2  Deprivation of rights under the 1984 Act and Code C

The discretion to exclude a confession is likely to be exercised when deliberate impropriety or bad faith has obtained the confession and this has resulted in unfairness. Therefore, the fact that there has been a breach of the Code or a defendant's rights have been infringed by the actions of the police does not automatically lead to exclusion under s 78. Since the incorporation of the Human Rights Act 1998, the courts should be more 'rights oriented' in their application of s 78. One obvious example of this is where a confession has been obtained after an unjustified refusal of access to a solicitor.

### 9.1.3.3  Rights of access

A person who is arrested and held in custody at a police station has a right, at his request, to consult with a solicitor at any time, privately (s 58 Police and Criminal Evidence Act 1984). Article 6(3) ECHR requires that consultation must take place out of the hearing of a third party (in particular a police officer): *Brennan v UK* (2002) 34 EHRR 507. In the magistrates' court it is not a statutory right but it is a common law right to have access to a solicitor as soon as is reasonably practicable.

The right is a right to advice and not to be present during interview; however, Code C, para 6.8 states if the detainee has requested a solicitor and the solicitor is present before the interview starts, the detainee *must* be allowed to have the solicitor present during the interview.

The police may refuse access on the ground that allowing a particular individual access to the detainee may prejudice the investigation: *R (Thompson) v Chief Constable of the Northumberland Constabulary* [2001] 1 WLR 1342. In *Samuel* [1988] QB 615, the Court of Appeal stated that if the police seek to deny access to a solicitor they must show more than a substantial risk of their fears being realised. If delay is authorised the reasons must be given and noted in the custody record.

For a deeper understanding of this area, carry out **activity 9.2** in **Appendix 1**.

### 9.1.4  Effects of excluding a confession

Section 76(4), (5) and (6) provides that:

(4)  *The fact that a confession is wholly or partly excluded in pursuance of this section shall not affect the admissibility in evidence—*

   (a)  *of any facts discovered as a result of the confession; or*

   (b)  *where the confession is relevant as showing that the accused speaks, writes or expresses himself in a particular way, of so much of the confession as is necessary to show that he does so.*

(5)  *Evidence that a fact to which this subsection applies was discovered as a result of a statement made by an accused person shall not be admissible unless evidence of how it was discovered is given by him or on his behalf—*

(6)  *Subsection (5) applies—*

   (a)  *to any fact discovered as a result of a confession which is wholly excluded in pursuance of the section; and*

   (b)  *to any fact discovered as a result of a confession which is partly so excluded, if the fact is discovered as a result of the excluded part of the confession.*

These provisions have no effect in committal proceedings, as examining magistrates cannot rule on the admissibility of a confession.

The effect of s 76 (4)–(6) is that even where the confession is excluded, facts discovered as a result of the confession are admissible. However, the prosecution cannot prove that those facts were discovered due to the making of the excluded confession. If the confession is excluded under s 78 then s 76 (4)–(6) cannot be invoked. However, the common law principles of relevance will apply should the prosecution wish to admit facts arising from the confession. Furthermore any evidence obtained as a result of a confession excluded under s 78 may also be subject to a s 78 argument.

To test your understanding of this area, try **activity 9.3** in **Appendix 1**.

## 9.2  Illegally or improperly obtained evidence other than confessions

It is well established that a judge has, under his or her overriding duty to ensure a fair trial, a discretion to exclude evidence that may be admissible prosecution evidence where the prejudicial effect of the evidence outweighs its probative value. This is therefore a principle that is applied on a case by case basis and as was stated in *Sang,* should not be treated as a closed list of situations.

Where the police or State has obtained evidence unlawfully or improperly, a s 78 application may be made to exclude the evidence. In *R v Sang* [1980] AC 402 the House of Lords held that at *common law* the court did not have a discretion to exclude this type of evidence unless its probative value was outweighed by its prejudicial effect or that the evidence could be equated with a confession. An example of the latter is where a defendant was induced into providing a specimen, which was then used to show that he was unfit to drive: *R v Payne* [1963] 1 WLR 637.

Under both case law and recent statute law, the defendant is not *entitled* to have unlawfully obtained evidence excluded simply because it has been so obtained, *R v P* [2002] 1 AC 146 and the Regulation of Investigatory Powers Act 2000.

Therefore, any s 78 application to exclude unlawful or improperly obtained evidence must turn on its facts.

In *R v Khan (Sultan)* [1997] AC 558, the House of Lords upheld the Court of Appeal decision that evidence obtained by a bugging device, attached by the police to a private house without the knowledge of the owner, was admissible. Lord Nolan (at p 582) stated that the significance of any breach of any relevant law or convention will normally be determined by its effect on the fairness on the proceedings rather than its irregularity or unlawfulness. This case went to the European Court: *Khan v UK* [2000] Crim LR 684. The case was that there had been a breach of Article 8, respect for private life and therefore breach of Article 6(1), fair trial. The Court decided that there was no breach of Article 6, despite finding the UK had violated Article 8. Since this decision the Regulation of Investigatory Powers Act 2000 now governs the actions of the police for covert surveillance.

In *R v Smurthwaite; R v Gill* (1994) 98 Cr App R 437, CA, the court held that entrapment itself did not result in the exclusion of evidence but laid down a number of criteria that should be followed by the police. The first criterion being whether the officer enticed the defendant to commit an offence he would not otherwise have committed. *R v Loosely; Att Gen's Reference (No 3 of 2000)* 2002 1 Cr App R 29 reviewed the issue of entrapment and Lord Hoffman stated that the more appropriate remedy in cases of entrapment would be staying the prosecution as an abuse of process rather than excluding the evidence. For further comment on abuse of process see *R v Latif; R v Shahzad* [1996] 2 Cr App R 92, HL.

## 9.3  Criminal Justice Act 2003

Section 128 (which is not yet in force) inserts s 76A, PACE 1984, which in effect applies the same rule to co-defendant that applies to the prosecution when a confession has been made in breach of s 76 or s 78. Currently the prosecution may not use a confession if it has breached s 76 and s 78 but a defendant can use a confession to undermine the co-defendant's account or strengthen his or her case. Under the new Act, a co-defendant will no longer be able to use the confession where it has be obtained by oppression or rendered unreliable. The definition of these terms remains identical to s 76(8). However, the burden of proof is not the same as for the prosecution, so that the co-defendant needs to satisfy the court that the confession was not obtained by oppression or in circumstances likely to render it unreliable on the balance of probabilities. Subsection (4) maintains the rule that the exclusion of a confession does not affect the admissibility of facts discovered as a result of that confession.

# 10

# Lies and silence

## 10.1 Introduction

In the last chapter we considered how the courts will use confessions obtained (usually but not exclusively) by police officers investigating a criminal offence. Clearly not all persons questioned will confess. Others may seek to lie to deflect the police from investigating them further. So to what extent can the court use the fact either that someone remained silent or lied?

Consider the following scenario:

Ollie is alleged to have stolen a car. When arrested by the police he is in possession of a car radio (that, it later turns out, is the same as the car radio that has been taken from the stolen car). Ollie refuses to say anything about the radio when asked to do so by the police. Ollie is then taken to the police station he is interviewed and says that he does not know anything about the car in question and that when it went missing he was at work. The police then tell him (correctly) that they found his wallet in the back of the car. He then asks to see his solicitor and, having taken the solicitor's advice, he refuses to answer any other questions.

What if anything does Ollie's conduct prove? How might the following situations change the way in which a tribunal of fact might treat Ollie?

(a) At trial Ollie alleged that he lied about his whereabouts because he was visiting his girlfriend, of whom his parents do not approve and he didn't want them to know. He found the radio on the road.

(b) In addition to (a) above, his solicitor advised him not to answer any questions because the police officer interviewing him had a reputation for planting evidence.

(c) Instead of (a) and (b) above, Ollie alleges at trial that he didn't answer questions because his solicitor advised him that he had a right to remain silent and that it was for the police to get all the evidence to prove the case against him without his help.

(d) Instead of (a) to (c) above, Ollie gives no evidence at trial in his own defence but his barrister has cross-examined the police witnesses to suggest that the wallet was planted in the car by racist police officers (Ollie is black and has been in trouble with the police before).

The detail of the answers to these questions will be considered below. However, for the time being, it is worth considering the issues that the questions have raised:

(a) What is the evidential value of a lie? Does it show that the liar is guilty of the offence about which he has lied? Should it be admitted in evidence in a criminal trial?

(b) What is the evidential value of refusing to answer questions or allegations at the time of arrest and questioning?

(c) What is the effect of raising a defence for the first time at trial? Does it show that the accused was trying to hide his defence from the prosecution until he put it before the jury? If so does that mean that he is more likely to be guilty?

(d) What if the refusal to explain or answer questions is due to legal advice?

(e) What does the fact that an accused person does not testify in his own defence prove? Does this show that he or she is conscious of his or her own guilt?

(f) Does it make a difference if a person does not testify but gets his or her lawyer to advance the defence through cross-examination?

Before looking at these areas in more depth, it should be noted that what this chapter looks at is the evidential value of lies or silence on the part of a party. It is not about the evidential value of the thing that the party lied or was silent about. Consider the example above. Ollie was found with a car radio like the one from the car and his wallet was found in the car. These are items of circumstantial evidence unaffected by the law covered in this chapter. They are admissible insofar as they are relevant. What this chapter considers, amongst other things, is the evidential value of *failures to explain those other items of admissible evidence*. Do not mistake the two (it is very easy to do so).

As is common with the rules of evidence, we shall see that there is a very different approach between the civil and the criminal courts. We shall consider the civil rules (which are much simpler) first.

## 10.2  Civil cases

The common law governs the position in civil cases in respect of both lies and silence. The courts have treated the silence or lie like any other item of evidence: it is admissible if it is relevant to a fact in issue and the weight to be attached to it is a matter for the tribunal of fact and will depend on the facts and issues in each case. Examples include:

- *Bessela v Stern* (1877) 2 CPD 265 in which the plaintiff confronted the defendant over a promise to marry her. The defendant's silence was treated as admissible evidence to prove that there had been such a promise because he would have denied that fact if it had not been true.

- *Wiedmann v Walpole* [1891] 2 QB 534 in which the defendant did not reply to an accusatory letter written by the plaintiff. The court held that the letter was not admissible as evidence that the accusations were true. The failure to reply to the letter simply did not go far enough in proving that the accusation was true. There were a number of reasons why a person might not reply to such a letter.

- *Francisco v Diedrick* The Times, 3 April 1998 where a plaintiff had made out a prima facie case, the defendant's failure to testify was circumstantial evidence that supported the plaintiff's case.

## 10.3    Lies in criminal cases

The evidential value of lies, as opposed to silence in the face of accusation or questioning, is governed by the common law. Evidence of lies is generally admissible. The statements alleged to be lies will be admissible as original, as opposed to hearsay evidence (see **8.1**). The rules set out below apply to lies told both outside of court and in the witness box.

### 10.3.1    Directing the jury on lies

Where a lie is admitted, the judge will ensure that the jury is given careful guidance as to how they should deal with it as evidence. The leading case is *R v Lucas* [1981] QB 720, where Lord Lane CJ said (at p 724) that the jury must be directed that to be capable of being evidence against the accused the lie must be:

- Deliberate.
- Concerned with a material issue in the case.
- Motivated by a realisation of guilt and fear of the truth.
- Shown to be untrue.

All four matters must be identified to the jury in summing up and they must be told that before they use the alleged lie as evidence of the accused's guilt they must be satisfied beyond reasonable doubt that the statement is a lie (*R v Burge* [1996] 1 Cr App R 163).

On the issue of the motive for the lie, Lord Lane said:

The jury should in appropriate cases be reminded that people sometimes lie, for example, in an attempt to bolster up a just cause, or out of shame or out of a wish to conceal disgraceful behaviour from their family.

Clearly a statement made by the defendant that is alleged to be untrue will potentially be a lie within the meaning of *Lucas*. However, what if the statement is made by another person in the presence of the defendant? In *R v Collins* [2004] EWCA Crim 33, C and B were arrested together on suspicion of having recently kidnapped H. When B was asked where he had been he told the police officers (in C's presence) that both he and C had been at a particular public house. However, in interview and at trial C maintained that he had been with H but that he had not kidnapped him. At trial the judge gave a *Lucas* direction against C. The Court of Appeal quashed C's conviction. The court concluded that where a question was asked and an untrue answer was given in the presence of a defendant, the jury could conclude that his reaction to that question and answer could amount to his adoption of that answer, if the jury were satisfied that (a) the question called for some response from the defendant and (b) by his reaction, the defendant had adopted the answer made. In the circumstances of that case the jury had not been properly directed to adopt that approach and in any event there was not sufficient evidence adduced at trial for the jury to reach such a conclusion from the question and answer posed. Clearly whether this is the case or not will depend on the particular facts of each case.

### 10.3.2    When a *Lucas* direction is required

The direction set out above is not always necessary. In *R v Burge* the Court of Appeal identified four situations in which such a direction would be necessary:

(a) Where the accused raised an alibi;

(b) Where the judge has directed the jury to look for supporting evidence for particular witnesses and has made reference to potential lies as corroboration (on the need for the judge to issue such a direction, see **Chapter 11**);

(c) Where the prosecution have sought to rely on an alleged lie as evidence of the accused's guilt;

(d) Where the prosecution have not explicitly sought to rely on the alleged lie but there is a real danger that the jury will do so.

Situation (d) mentioned in *R v Burge* clearly places an obligation on the trial judge to consider the likely effect of any untrue statements made during or before trial. In *R v Nash* [2004] All ER (D) 207 (Jan), no *Lucas* direction was given. The defendant was charged with criminal damage, it being alleged that he had fired pellets from an air gun at car windows. The only evidence against the defendant was that (a) he was seen near the scene of the crime acting suspiciously, (b) he denied owning an air rifle and (c) an air rifle was found at his flat. The Court of Appeal concluded that, in such circumstances, a direction should have been given as there was a real danger that the jury might use the defendant's lie as evidence of guilt even though the prosecution did not so rely upon it.

The list identified in *R v Burge* is not exhaustive. In *R v Jefford* [2003] EWCA Crim 1987, the Court of Appeal noted that the categories identified in *Burge* did not reduce the general principle that a direction is required where there is a danger that the jury may regard the fact that the defendant has told lies as probative of his guilt. In any such situation a *Lucas* direction may be required. In *Jefford*, the need for the direction arose due to the significance that the judge attached to potential lies and inconsistencies even though the prosecution had placed no particular reliance upon those lies.

Although it should generally be clear whether such situations arise in each case, this may not always be so. The court in *R v Burge* stated that the judge and counsel should consider the need for a *Lucas* direction before the judge starts summing up. Further the Court of Appeal would generally be unwilling to overturn a conviction due to the lack of a *Lucas* direction if defence counsel did not identify the need for one at trial. This is because the lawyers and the trial judge are in a better position than the Court of Appeal to evaluate the issues and to determine whether a *Lucas* direction should have been given in any particular case. If the lawyers did not identify the need for a direction at trial, the Court of Appeal is unlikely to conclude that the absence of a direction renders a conviction unsafe (*R v McGuinness* [1999] Crim LR 318).

On some occasions where the jury rejects the accused's account (ie concludes he or she is lying) they will have no choice but to convict. In such circumstances, there is no need for the judge to direct the jury in respect of the lie (*R v Patrick* [1999] 6 Arch News 4). Clearly as the effect of rejecting the defence case is the conviction of the accused, there is little purpose to be served by also considering whether the lie is evidence that the accused was guilty of the offence.

## 10.4  Silence in criminal cases

Parliament has created a number of rules that allow the failure of the accused to answer allegations to be admitted as evidence of the accused's guilt.

It is not difficult to understand why a lie might prove that a person is guilty of an offence. A lie suggests that the person lying is trying to cover up for their guilty behaviour. But what about a refusal to answer questions or to explain matters? Clearly it is possible to infer from such silence that the suspect does not have an explanation that will stand up to scrutiny. However there are numerous reasons why a person would refuse to answer questions or explain incriminating evidence and being guilty is only one of them. Therefore, as we shall see, the courts have sought to ensure that juries are carefully directed only to use silence as evidence if any innocent explanations have been rejected.

Furthermore, using the silence of the accused as evidence of guilt offends some fundamental principles of the criminal justice process. Clearly such evidence runs contrary to the right to silence and the privilege against self-incrimination. These principles are enshrined in Article 6 of the European Convention on Human Rights. For this reason the statutory provisions set out below have been the subject of regular scrutiny to determine whether they comply with the right to a fair trial.

Instead of a single rule relating to inferences from silence, Parliament has provided different rules for inferences to be drawn in respect of silence at different stages in the criminal process. These stages are dealt with below.

### 10.4.1    Silence upon being questioned

Inferences may be drawn in certain circumstances if the accused has not explained his defence at an early opportunity. Before considering when this might happen, it is worth making sure that you understand the powers of the police to question suspects. Have a look at the *Criminal Litigation and Sentencing Manual*, **Chapter 2**.

#### 10.4.1.1    The Criminal Justice and Public Order Act 1994, s 34

Section 34 of the Criminal Justice and Public Order Act 1994 states:

> (1)  *Where, in any proceedings against a person for an offence, evidence is given that the accused—*
>> (a)  *at any time before he was charged with the offence, on being questioned under caution by a constable trying to discover whether or by whom the offence had been committed, failed to mention any fact relied on in his defence in those proceedings; or*
>> (b)  *on being charged with the offence or officially informed that he might be prosecuted for it, failed to mention any such fact,*
>>      *...*
> (2)  *Where this subsection applies—*
>>      *...*
>> (c)  *the court, in determining whether there is a case to answer; and*
>> (d)  *the court or jury, in determining whether the accused is guilty of the offence charged,*
>>      *may draw such inferences from the failure as appear proper.*

Section 34 places a suspect under an obligation to explain his or her potential defence under specified circumstances. These circumstances will be discussed in more detail below. The duty is not absolute. There is no automatic sanction for failing to explain a defence: the failure to mention a fact simply allows the tribunal of fact the option of treating that failure as something that can strengthen the prosecution case.

#### 10.4.1.2    No inference will be drawn if the fact relied on is true

In *R v Wisdom* (CA, 10 December 1989) it was stated that no inference should be drawn under s 34 if the fact in question has been shown to be true. This was approved in *R v Webber* [2004] 1 All ER 770.

### 10.4.1.3   The timing of the duty to explain

The court can draw inferences from the accused's failure to explain defences in two situations:

- Upon being questioned. But only if:
    - the accused has been cautioned;
    - the accused has not yet been charged with the offence.
- Upon being charged with the offence.

Therefore not all questions asked by a police officer are covered by s 34. There are situations in which questioning is possible both before caution and after charge (for detail, see Code C of the PACE Codes of Practice). However in such situations s 34 will not apply. To the extent that the prosecution seek to rely on a failure to provide answers to questions in those non-s 34 situations the common law rules apply (see below).

The text of the caution is:

> You do not have to say anything. But it may harm your defence if you do not mention when questioned something which you later rely on in court. Anything you do say may be given in evidence. (PACE Code C, para 10.4)

It is likely that the second situation (failure to mention facts in response to charge) would arise in the sort of situations where the police did not feel that there was a need to question the accused because they have sufficient evidence to charge the defendant. It would be rare for an inference to be drawn in this situation as under para 16.1 of Code C even if the police have sufficient evidence to charge they should only do so if 'the person has said all he wishes to say'. However, s 34(1)(b) will also apply if no inferences can be drawn from the interview because it has been excluded under s 78 (see **Chapter 10** above). In those circumstances inferences can be drawn from the failure to mention a defence on charge even though the accused was questioned fully prior to charge (*R v Dervish* [2002] 2 Cr App R 105).

Note that s 34 applies to situations in which the prosecution will be commenced other than by charging the accused (see the *Criminal Litigation and Sentencing Manual*, **Chapter 1**). In such circumstances the obligation to explain facts arises upon the accused being told he or she will be prosecuted.

### 10.4.1.4   The fact that is not mentioned must later be relied upon as part of a defence

This is a very important feature of s 34. Inferences cannot be drawn simply because the accused did not answer questions during interview (or upon caution). They may only be drawn if the accused:

- relies on a fact in his defence, and
- did not mention that fact when questioned under caution or charged.

In other words it is the last-minute use of a defence (or facts supporting a defence) that leads to the inference rather than simple exercise of the right to silence. But in what circumstances has a person relied upon a fact in his defence? Where the accused gives evidence this is relatively simple, but what if either the accused does not give evidence or the question as to s 34 inferences arises before the accused has had an opportunity to do so (for example during a submission of no case to answer)?

Think again about the case concerning Ollie at **10.1**. Have a look at situations (a) and (d) identified there. In which of the two situations does Ollie rely on a fact in his defence?

In situation (a) it is clear that Ollie has relied upon an alibi defence (he was visiting his girlfriend) and also that he found the radio on the road. In addition to any adverse inferences that might result from having lied, he could be subject to adverse inferences under s 34.

Situation (d) has presented more difficulty for the courts. To what extent does a defendant rely on a fact if he or she does not give evidence or call any witnesses? Does cross-examination of the police witnesses that the wallet was planted amount to reliance upon a fact? In *R v Webber* [2004] 1 All ER 770, the House of Lords considered the meaning of 'fact' within s 34 at some length. Lord Bingham said (at [33]) that the word 'fact' in s 34, 'should be given a broad and not a narrow or pedantic meaning. The word covers any alleged fact which is in issue and is put forward as part of the defence case: if the defendant advances at trial any pure fact or exculpatory explanation or account which, if it were true, he could reasonably have been expected to advance earlier, s 34 is potentially applicable'. For this reason, the House concluded that a party relies on a fact within the meaning of s 34 not only when the defendant gives evidence of that fact but also when the defendant's advocate 'puts a specific and positive case to prosecution witnesses, as opposed to asking questions intended to probe or test the prosecution case' and that was the case whether or not the witness in question accepted the allegation put to them by defence counsel.

It is therefore necessary to distinguish between cross-examination that tests the prosecution evidence (such as suggesting that an identification witness was mistaken) and cross-examination that suggests a positive defence (putting to the same witness that the accused was at another place at the time of the offence). The former will not amount to reliance on a fact under s 34 but the latter probably will.

The use of the phrase 'facts relied on in defence' may appear to give the prosecution and the court an opportunity to invoke s 34 whenever there is a small detail raised by the defendant at trial that he or she did not mention during a previous interview. However, in *R v Brizzalari* [2004] EWCA Crim 310, the Court of Appeal recognised that it was a matter for the trial judge to determine whether facts mentioned by the defendant were sufficiently important to fall within s 34.

### 10.4.1.5   The failure to mention the fact must be unreasonable

Section 34 states that a fact which is not mentioned must be 'a fact which in the circumstances existing at the time the accused could reasonably have been expected to mention'.

In many cases the defendant will have a reason for having failed to answer questions, which should be presented to the jury and which the jurors must consider. In *R v Cowan* [1996] Cr App R 1, a case concerning s 35 of the 1994 Act, which also allows adverse inferences to be drawn unless there are good reasons for the defendant's silence, it was noted that there would have to be evidence before the jury of the reasons for silence. It was not possible for counsel simply to give those reasons in the absence of an evidential foundation.

In *R v Nickolson* [1999] Crim LR 61, the Court of Appeal held that a suspect could not be expected to give an innocent explanation of potentially incriminating evidence that was not presented to him at interview.

In *R v Turner* [2004] 1 All ER 1025, the Court of Appeal stated that, where possible, the prosecution should challenge the defendant about any unmentioned fact in cross examination and give the defendant an opportunity to provide an explanation.

It would appear that s 34 will not apply if the accused mentioned the fact in a prepared statement even if he or she then refuses to answer questions (*R v Ali* [2001] All ER (D) 16).

Have another look at the scenarios concerning Ollie at **10.1**. Now consider situations (a), (b) and (c). In which of those situations should the jury be allowed to draw an adverse inference from Ollie's failure to explain his defence at the police station?

In relation to situation (a), the reason Ollie did not give the real explanation was fear of his parents. It will be a matter for the jury as to whether they believe this explanation. If not, they may decide that he did not give his defence because he was guilty. Note the similarity of approach adopted in relation to the lie he told: the jury will have to decide whether his reason for lying or not mentioning a fact was a consciousness of guilt. It should also be noted that no explanation appears to have been given for the failure to explain the radio. As he has not put forward any reason for failing to mention how he came by the incriminating radio, the jury would simply have to decide whether his failure to mention the finding of the radio was evidence that he might be guilty of the offence. In other words, where the defendant attempts to give an explanation for his failure to mention facts at trial, the jury will have to undertake a more complicated analysis before drawing adverse inferences against him or her.

In situations (b) and (c) Ollie's failure to put forward defences at the police station *are* explained at trial. However, the jury is not bound to accept the reasons he gives. Even legal advice does not determine whether or not inferences should be drawn. In *R v Condron* [1997] 1 Cr App R 185, two suspects being investigated for drug offences had been interviewed under caution but both remained silent. At trial the two accused put forward innocent explanations of all the prosecution evidence, which explanations could have been given at the police station. They also testified that their solicitor had advised them not to answer questions because he felt that they were suffering from heroin withdrawal. The police (acting on the advice of the police doctor) had decided the suspects were fit to be interviewed. The jury was directed that they could draw an inference from the failure of the accused to explain their defences at the police station. The Court of Appeal affirmed their convictions. Legal advice could not determine whether or not s 34 applied. Instead the jury should have regard to the reasons given by the accused (including legal advice) and consider whether it is the legal advice or the consciousness of guilt that is the reason for the failure to mention the fact. The matter was taken to the European Court of Human Rights (*Condron & Condron v UK* [2000] Crim LR 677) where it was decided that it was necessary that the jury be directed that they should only draw an adverse inference if they concluded (beyond reasonable doubt) that the *only* reason for failing to mention the fact was that the suspect had no answer to the questions (or none that would stand up to cross-examination).

In *R v Argent* [1997] Crim LR 346 the Court of Appeal stated that the jury should take into consideration the circumstances in which advice was given and the personality of the accused in deciding the real reason for remaining silent. It was also said that the reasons for the legal advice should not determine whether or not adverse inferences should be drawn. The jury should not be concerned with the correctness of the advice but its impact upon the accused's conduct at the police station. Therefore it is not the fact (or the accuracy) of the legal advice that determines whether or not it amounts to a good reason for remaining silent. Rather the jury will have to consider whether the advice was the cause of the silence or whether it was some other matter and should only infer guilt where they conclude that other reason was the guilty mind of the accused. There is no real difference between situations (b) and (c) except insofar as the jury is likely to accept one or the other as more or less likely to have influenced Ollie's decision. The fact that the advice in situation (c) is clearly wrong (in that it overlooks s 34) is simply a matter for the jury to take into account.

As legal advice can (but not must) be a good reason for failing to mention a fact it will occasionally be necessary to prove what legal advice was given. The accused could testify as to what his legal advisor told him (this would not be hearsay evidence because it is admitted to prove the fact not the truth of the advice: see **Chapter 8**). However, it may be necessary to call the legal advisor to testify as to what advice he gave to assist in deciding whether the decision to remain silent was really based on the legal advice given (*R v Roble* [1997] Crim LR 449). In *R v Bowden* [1999] 4 All ER 43, it was said that where the accused or his solicitor had given evidence as to not just the fact of advice having been given to keep silent but also the reasons for that advice, the accused 'voluntarily withdrew the veil of privilege and having done so could not resist questioning directed to the nature of that advice and the factual premises on which it was based' (per Lord Bingham CJ at p 47). While it is not generally permissible for one party to enquire into the legal advice that another has received (see legal professional privilege in **Chapter 15**), it is possible for this rule to be waived and following *R v Bowden* the giving of evidence as to the legal advice received constitutes such waiver. The witness (whether the solicitor or his or her client) could be cross-examined about that advice.

### 10.4.1.6    The nature of the questioning

Section 34 only applies if the questioning relates to whether or by whom the offence has been committed. A failure to explain other matters cannot be used to support an inference under s 34 (although it may do so at common law: see **10.4.1.10**).

### 10.4.1.7    Who must conduct the questioning

While s 34(1) refers to a constable, the section also applies to 'persons (other than constables) charged with the duty of investigating offences or charging offenders' (s 34(4)). Where questioning is conducted by someone who does not have a duty of investigating offences the rules at common law apply.

### 10.4.1.8    Access to legal advice

When questioning takes place in an 'authorised place of detention' (which includes but is not limited to a police station: see s 38(2A)) then no inferences can be drawn if the suspect was not allowed an opportunity to consult a solicitor (s 34(2A)). If the accused declines the right to consult a solicitor, it would appear that inferences could be drawn (as the opportunity has been allowed) although the matter has not been determined by case law. However if the police exercise the power to delay access to legal advice under s 58 of the Police and Criminal Evidence Act 1984 (see **Chapter 10**) then inferences could not be drawn from the failure to mention a fact.

### 10.4.1.9    The effect of the failure to mention the fact

Where the jury decide that there has been a failure to mention a fact in the circumstances set out above they may draw 'such inferences as appear proper' (s 34(2)). However in *R v Petkar* [2003] EWCA Crim 2668, the Court of Appeal accepted that the trial judge should give guidance as to what inferences might be drawn in each case.

### 10.4.1.10    Direction to the jury

There will always be a need to direct a jury when the judge concludes that the defendant has relied upon a fact and that the jury could conclude the failure to mention it was unreasonable. However in *R v Mountford* [1999] Crim LR 575, the Court of Appeal held that if the defence is raised for the first time at trial and the reasons for not mentioning it earlier were so related that the rejection of the defence would necessarily involve a rejection of the reasons, then a direction to the jury was unnecessary. Mountford's defence was that a prosecution witness (W) had committed the offence and that he had not mentioned this before trial out of fear of that witness. If the jury rejected the defence ('W did it') they must necessarily reject the reasons for not mentioning that defence ('W would kill me for saying so') and so a direction would serve no purpose. However in *R v Daly* [2002] 2 Cr App R 201, the Court of Appeal doubted that s 34 required any such restriction and thought that the direction should be given in all cases. Further in *R v Webber* [2004] 1 All ER 770, the House of Lords questioned the judgment in *R v Mountford*, noting that the jury could find assistance in deciding whether to believe W or Mountford from considering why Mountford had not offered the explanation he did at an earlier point.

Where the prosecution have not sought to rely on section 34 the judge should not invite the jury to draw an adverse inference from the alleged failure of the accused to mention a defence without first discussing the matter with counsel (*R v Khan* [1999] 2 Arch News 2).

The full specimen direction can be obtained from the Judicial Studies Board website (www.jsboard.co.uk). In essence the jury should be directed that:

(a) A suspect is not bound to answer police questions.

(b) An inference from silence cannot prove guilt on its own.

(c) The prosecution must have established a case to answer before any inference may be drawn.

(d) It is for them to decide whether the defendant could reasonably be expected to have mentioned the defence. If they think the defence should have been mentioned then the jury may, but not must, draw inferences against the accused.

(e) They can draw an inference *only* if satisfied that the defendant was silent because he had no answer or none that would stand up to investigation. See *R v Daly* [2002] 2 Cr App R.

The judge should identify the facts it is alleged the accused has relied upon that give rise to this inference (*R v Chenia* [2002] EWCA Crim 2345). Simple reference to a general failure to answer questions at interview creates the risk that the jury will convict on the silence at interview alone rather than on the failure to mention a fact later relied on in defence: *R v Turner* [2000] 1 All ER 1025.

The judge in summing up should not only identify any reasons given by the defendant for failing to mention a fact but should do so as part of the direction on s 34 rather than when summing up on the defence case: *R v Petkar* [2003] EWCA Crim 2668.

### 10.4.1.11   The position at common law

Section 34 will not apply if:

- The person questioning is not a police officer or authorised investigator.
- The questioning or accusation does not take place under caution.
- The questioning takes place after the accused has been charged.
- The accused does not rely on a fact in his defence.
- The questioning did not concern whether or by whom an offence had been committed.
- The failure to mention the fact now relied upon was not unreasonable.

As noted above if s 34 does not apply the common law rules on inferences from silence may apply (*R v McGarry* [1999] 1 WLR 1500). However, the common law rules will be of limited application because:

(a) A person could only be subject to adverse inferences arising from his or her failure to answer questions or accusations if :

   (i)    the accused had not been cautioned, and

   (ii)   the questioner/accuser and the accused were on equal terms: *Parkes v R* [1976] 1 WLR 1251.

(b) Where the person questioning or making accusations is a police officer or equivalent they will not be on equal terms (*Hall v R* [1971] 1 WLR 298) although an obiter dictum in *R v Chandler* [1976] 1 WLR 585 suggested that a person might be on equal terms with a police officer if he or she was accompanied by a solicitor. Furthermore in *R v Horne* [1990] Crim LR 188, CA an unprompted accusation was made by a victim of an attack in the presence of the defendant and police officers. The Court of Appeal ruled that the defendant's failure to respond to that accusation had been rightly admitted.

The main situation in which the common law rule will apply is where the person making the accusations or asking the questions is another member of the public (as was the case in *Parkes v R*).

### 10.4.1.12    'Counterweight' directions

If the accused does not advance a new defence or new facts in support of a defence at trial, s 34 will not apply. Because the accused was questioned under caution the common law rules concerning inferences do not apply either.

However, s 34(3) allows the prosecution to prove the silence under questioning (a 'no-comment' interview) before or after the accused relies on a fact. This is a pragmatic rule allowing to prove the accused's interview as an ordinary part of the prosecution case rather than requiring the prosecution to reopen their case when the accused later raises a new fact or defence and therefore triggers s 34. It is very rare in practice for an interview (other than those excluded under ss 76 or 78 of the Police and Criminal Evidence Act 1984) not to be proved during the prosecution case.

Where the prosecution have proved the interview but the accused does not then advance any new defence or facts, the tribunal of fact will have heard or read the interview and may draw an adverse inference of their own accord. In such situations not only should the judge not issue a s 34 direction, he or she should also issue a further direction (a 'counterweight direction') that they should not hold the accused's silence against him (*R v McGarry*). However the judge should have regard to whether on the particular facts there is any real risk that the jury would draw an adverse inference in the absence of any comment by the judge on the matter (*R v La Rose* [2003] EWCA Crim 1471). Where, for example, a direction will be made under s 35 (see **10.4.5** below) the jury would have been sufficiently warned about the right to remain silent so any further direction would simply be confusing.

### 10.4.2    Silence upon confrontation about particular types of incriminating evidence

There are two inferences of a similar nature. Both arise when a person is confronted about particular types of incriminating evidence. Unlike inferences under s 34, they do not arise because the accused later relies upon a defence which he or she has not mentioned at an earlier point but simply because he or she does not offer an explanation when invited to do so. In other words it is the simple exercise of the right to silence in incriminating circumstances that gives rise to the inferences.

### 10.4.2.1   Failure to account for objects, substances or marks

Section 36 of the Criminal Justice and Public Order Act 1994 provides:

*(1)   Where—*

    *(a)   a person is arrested by a constable, and there is—*

        *(i)   on his person; or*

        *(ii)   in or on his clothing or footwear; or*

        *(iii)   otherwise in his possession; or*

        *(iv)   in any place in which he is at the time of his arrest,*

    *any object, substance or mark, or there is any mark on any such object; and*

    *(b)   that or another constable ... reasonably believes that the presence of the object, substance or mark may be attributable to the participation of the person arrested in the commission of an offence specified by the constable; and*

    *(c)   the constable informs the person arrested that he so believes, and requests him to account for the presence of the object, substance or mark; and*

    *(d)   the person fails or refuses to do so,*

    *then if, in any proceedings against the person for the offence ... evidence of those matters is given, subsection (2) below applies.*

*(2)   Where this subsection applies—*

    *(a)   ...*

    *(b)   ...*

    *(c)   the court, in determining whether there is a case to answer; and*

    *(d)   the court or jury, in determining whether the accused is guilty of the offence charged,*

    *may draw such inferences from the failure or refusal as appear proper.*

*(3)   Subsections (1) and (2) above apply to the condition of clothing or footwear as they apply to a substance or mark thereon.*

In addition to the above points, it should be noted:

(a) Section 36 allows the court to draw adverse inferences from the failure to explain the object, substance or mark and only if the accused has been arrested and the effect of the failure to explain the incriminating object, etc, has been explained to the accused. Note, however, that the object, substance or mark itself is evidence in its own right and there are no particular rules or conditions for its admissibility (other than the usual rules of evidence).

(b) The inference can only be drawn if the suspect has been told of the reasons for suspicion and of the effect of failing to comply with this section (s 36(4)). The officer does not have to identify the precise offence. In *R v Compton* [2002] EWCA Crim 2835, CA, it was considered sufficient that the police officer had said that he was investigating 'drug trafficking'.

(c) Code C sets out the text of the special warnings that should be given to the accused under s 36 at para 10.5A.

(d) Section 36 applies to questions raised by customs and excise officers as well as police officers (s 36(5)). However, in contrast to s 34, other officers with a duty of investigating offences are not specifically mentioned. It would therefore appear that only confrontations or questions about objects, substances or marks by police or customs officers will lead to adverse inferences.

(e) Where the accused was in a place of authorised detention, inferences are only possible if the accused was offered access to a solicitor. This is likely to be a common feature of s 36 inferences as the section only arises upon arrest at which stage the police should generally take a suspect to a police station before questioning him.

### 10.4.2.2   Failure to account for presence at the scene of a crime

Section 37 of the 1994 Act provides:

(1)  Where—

    (a)  a person arrested by a constable was found by him at a place at or about the time the offence for which he was arrested is alleged to have been committed; and

    (b)  that or another constable investigating the offence reasonably believes that the presence of the person at the place at that time may be attributable to his participation in the commission of the offence; and

    (c)  the constable informs the person that he so believes, and requests him to account for that presence; and

    (d)  the person fails or refuses to do so,

    then if, in any proceedings against the person for the offence, evidence of those matters is given, subsection (2) below applies.

(2)  Where this subsection applies—

    (a)  ...

    (b)  ...

    (c)  the court, in determining whether there is a case to answer; and

    (d)  the court or jury, in determining whether the accused is guilty of the offence charged,

    may draw such inferences from the failure or refusal as appear proper.

The points noted in relation to s 36 above apply equally to s 37. However the text for the special warning is at Code C, para 10.5B.

### 10.4.3  Refusal to give body samples

Body samples are used to prove issues by scientific evidence, usually be DNA profiles. During the investigation of a crime samples or substances such as blood or semen might be taken, for example from the scene of the crime or from a victim. To prove that the accused committed the offence, the DNA profile of the sample and a profile from a sample taken from the accused must be matched.

The taking of bodily samples is governed by ss 62 and 63 of the Police and Criminal Evidence Act 1984. This is covered in more detail in **Chapter 12**. However at this point it is worth noting that bodily samples are defined in two classes:

(a) Non-intimate samples: such samples can be taken without the consent of the owner in certain circumstances (s 63). If the conditions for taking such a sample without consent do not apply and the owner declines to consent without good reason, the court may draw inferences of guilt from that refusal at common law (*R v Smith* (1985) 81 Cr App R 286).

(b) Intimate samples: such samples cannot be taken without the consent of the owner in any circumstances. However if the owner refuses to consent to the taking of such samples without good cause the court may draw such inferences from that refusal as appear proper. These inferences can be used in determining the issue of guilt and in determining whether there is a case to answer.

### 10.4.4  Failure to disclose the defence case

The inferences that we have already considered all relate to pre-trial investigation. Those that follow all relate to the trial process itself.

The Criminal Procedure and Investigations Act 1996, s 5 places the accused under an obligation to disclose his or her defence by way of a defence statement. See the *Criminal Litigation and Sentencing Manual*, *Blackstone's Criminal Practice*, 2004 or *Archbold*, 2004 for the detailed rules of procedure. In outline a defence statement should set out in general terms the nature of the accused's defence and matters with which he or she takes issue with the prosecution case and the basis of any such dispute (s 5(6)). The logic of this procedure is that the accused is then committed to the defence to be run at trial. Where the accused intends to rely on an alibi defence (ie that he was at some other specific place at the time of the offence) there are additional obligations. Section 11 of the 1996 Act makes provision for any failure on the part of the accused to comply with his obligations under s 5. The court may draw inferences when deciding the guilt of the accused *but not when deciding whether there is a case to answer* if the accused:

- does not give a defence statement;
- gives the defence statement late;
- runs a defence at trial which is inconsistent with that in his or her defence statement;
- seeks to establish an alibi without having complied with the additional notice requirements for alibi defences.

In summary proceedings the giving of a defence statement is voluntary (s 6) but must comply with the requirements in s 5 as to the form and content of the statement. However under s 11 inferences can be drawn if the accused:

- gives the defence statement late;
- runs a defence at trial which is inconsistent with that in his or her defence statement;
- seeks to establish an alibi without having complied with the additional notice requirements for alibi defences.

The accused cannot be convicted solely on the basis of an inference under s 11 (s 11(5)). The court should take care to ensure that the jury is properly directed as to the nature of any discrepancy and the reasons that the accused may give for it (*R v Wheeler* (2000) 164 JP 565). There may be particular difficulties where the accused states that the defence statement was not drafted under his or her instructions (in other words that a solicitor drafted it) and that therefore that its contents do not reflect his or her intended defence. It is not possible to force the accused to sign the statement (*R (Sullivan) v Crown Court at Maidstone* [2002] 1 WLR 2747, CA) so it is likely that the tribunal of fact will have first to decide whether the statement is that of the accused before applying s 11.

There is no specimen direction concerning inferences under s 11 but it would appear likely that such a direction should contain the features of an adverse inference direction: that the inconsistency is proven, deliberate, material and motivated by a consciousness of guilt.

### 10.4.5    Failure to testify

The traditional right of an accused not to testify has been modified by s 35 of the Criminal Justice and Public Order Act 1994, which provides:

> (1)  *At the trial of any person for an offence, subsection ... (3) below applies unless—*
>     (a)  *the accused's guilt is not in issue; or*
>     (b)  *it appears to the court that the physical or mental condition of the accused makes it undesirable for him to give evidence;*
>       ...
> (3)  *Where this subsection applies, the court or jury, in determining whether the accused is guilty of the offence charged, may draw such inferences as appear proper from the failure of the accused to give evidence or his refusal, without good cause, to answer any question.*

Such inferences can only be drawn if the accused has either been warned by the court of the effect of the failure to give evidence (s 35(2)) or has stated that he will give evidence and then fails to do so (s 35(1)). The text of any warnings to the accused is set out in the *Practice Direction (Criminal: Consolidated)* [2002] 3 All ER 904, para 44. The section applies to a person who refuses to answer questions in evidence unless the refusal is justified (under s 35(5)):

(a) on the grounds of legal privilege (see **Chapter 15**),

(b) because another statute excludes the evidence that would be contained in the answer (such as evidence of the bad character of the accused under s 1(3) of the Criminal Evidence Act 1898); or

(c) because the court rules that the question need not be answered.

Note that inferences can only be drawn when determining whether the accused is guilty. Inferences cannot be used to determine whether there is a case to answer not least of all because the accused has not had the opportunity to give evidence by that point in proceedings (*Murray v DPP* [1994] 1 WLR 1, HL).

Section 35 allows the judge to direct the jury (or requires the magistrates) to take into account the failure of the accused to testify if the conditions in s 35(1) are satisfied and the warnings have been issued under s 35(2). Further the prosecution are entitled to comment on the failure of the accused to testify.

### 10.4.5.1    The accused's guilt is not in issue

There are situations in which the accused could give evidence in his or her 'defence' even though his or her guilt is not in issue. The most obvious example is a 'Newton' hearing at which the issue is not whether the accused committed a particular crime but how serious his or her commission of the offence was so that an appropriate sentence can be passed: see the **Criminal Litigation and Sentencing Manual**, *Blackstone's Criminal Practice*, 2004, or *Archbold*, 2004.

### 10.4.5.2    'Physical or mental condition'

There must be evidence that the physical or mental condition of the accused is such that an inference should not be drawn (*R v A* [1997] Crim LR 883).

In *R v Friend* [1997] 1 WLR 1433, F was tried for murder. He did not give evidence and sought to avoid a s 35 inference on the grounds that he had a mental age of nine (he was 15 years old). The judge did invite the jury to draw an inference under s 35 on the grounds that, in light of the fact that he had been able to give a clear account of what he said had happened before trial, his mental age did not make it undesirable that he give evidence. The conviction was upheld by the Court of Appeal. Insofar as F would have had any special needs in giving evidence the court could have met these needs so the prejudice of having to give evidence could be accommodated.

### 10.4.5.3    The direction to the jury

In *R v Cowan* [1996] 1 Cr App R 1, CA, Lord Taylor CJ stated that a direction to the jury should contain the following elements:

(a) The accused has a right not to give evidence but he has been warned that a failure to do so may lead to the jury drawing inferences.

(b) A failure to give evidence cannot on its own prove guilt but it can assist in deciding whether the accused is guilty.

(c) If a reason for not testifying has been advanced the jury should consider it and:

    (i)    If they accept the reason advanced, they cannot draw any inference against the accused.

    (ii)   If they reject they reason advanced, they may draw an inference but are not obliged to do so.

(d) If the jury conclude that the only sensible explanation for his decision not to give evidence is that he has no answer to the case against him, or none that could have stood up to cross-examination, then it would be open to them to hold against him his failure to give evidence. It is for the jury to decide whether it is fair to do so.

In *R v Birchall* [1999] Crim LR 311, CA, a conviction was overturned where the trial judge had not required the jury to decide whether the prosecution had established a prima facie case before they could draw an inference, such consideration being an absolute requirement before an inference could be drawn under s 35.

Note that the jury can be invited to infer the fact of guilt from the failure to testify if a prima facie case has been made out. Lord Mustill described the matter in this way in *Murray v DPP* (a case concerning Northern Ireland legislation with provisions that were materially the same):

If ... the defendant does not go on oath ... the fact finder may suspect that the defendant does not tell his story because he has no story to tell or none which will stand up to scrutiny; and this suspicion may be sufficient to convert a possible prosecution case into one which is actually proved.

Lord Mustill also said that whether such inferences should be drawn depended upon whether the accused should be able to give his or her own account of the particular matter in question. Developing this point, the Court of Appeal concluded in *R v McManus* [2001] EWCA Crim 2455 that a direction under s 35 was inappropriate where there was no factual dispute in the case. The only issue in that case was whether a particular property could in law constitute a 'disorderly house', the facts that supported such a conclusion being agreed between the defence and prosecution. The accused's testimony could not have assisted on this matter so a s 35 inference was inappropriate.

### 10.4.5.4  The practical effect of s 35

While s 35 has not removed the right of the accused to remain silent, it has put a considerable practical burden on some defendants to give evidence.

In *R v Cowan*, Lord Taylor CJ observed that it would not be appropriate to permit an accused with numerous previous convictions to avoid a s 35 inference when he did not give evidence to avoid being cross-examined on them under s 1(3) of the Criminal Evidence Act 1898 (see **Chapter 6**). To do so would put an accused with no previous convictions in a worse position than an accused with a number of previous convictions. This was affirmed in *R v Becouarn* [2004] All ER (D) 369 (Feb), but the Court of Appeal certified a question of law of general public importance as to whether or not a s 35 direction was appropriate in such a situation.

### 10.4.6  Failure to call evidence

At common law it is permissible for the judge to comment on the failure of the accused to call a particular witness. The principle is that the judge should exercise care before doing so and the comments made to the jury should not generally invite the court to equate the failure to call the witness with the accused's account being untrue (*R v Weller* [1994] Crim LR 856). It is especially important that no comment should be made about the failure to call a witness if there may be a valid reason for not calling the witness (*R v Couzens* [1992] Crim LR 822, CA).

The Police and Criminal Evidence Act 1984, s 80A, provides that the failure to call a spouse should not be commented upon by the *prosecution* (the spouse of an accused person not being compellable on his or her behalf under s 80 of that Act: see **Chapter 4**). However, there is no prohibition on the *judge* commenting on the failure to call a spouse. However in *R v Naudeer* [1984] 3 All ER 1036, the Court of Appeal took the view that great care should be exercised by the judge before any such comment was made.

### 10.4.7   Conclusion on inferences from silence in criminal cases

There are two broad categories of inferences:

(a) Silence before a criminal prosecution is commenced:

    (i)    Silence under questioning (Criminal Justice and Public Order Act 1994, s 34).

    (ii)   Failure to explain objects substances or marks on the suspect's person (Criminal Justice and Public Order Act 1994, s 36).

    (iii)  Failure to explain presence at the scene of the crime (Criminal Justice and Public Order Act 1994, s 37).

    (iv)  Failure to provide bodily samples (Police and Criminal Evidence Act 1984, s 62).

(b) Silence after a criminal prosecution has been commenced:

    (i)    Failure to produce a defence statement (Criminal Procedure and Investigations Act 1996, s 11).

    (ii)   Failure of the accused to testify in his own defence (Criminal Justice and Public Order Act 1994, s 35).

    (iii)  Failure to call witnesses (common law).

There are many differences between the various sections but the essential difference between the two categories is that silence before commencement of a prosecution case can be used to raise a case for the accused to answer while silence after commencement cannot.

All of the inferences in criminal cases, however, have certain common features whether as a result of statute or common law. While expressed differently in different situations, the common features are that:

(a) Before an inference can be drawn it must be established that the motive for the failure must be a realisation of guilt rather than some other reason (and the jury should be told that they must rule out any other reason).

(b) The tribunal of fact are never obliged to draw an inference in any of the above cases: the facts simply establish that an inference may rather than must be drawn.

(c) The inference can never prove guilt on its own.

## 10.5  Activities

To test your understanding of the issues raised in this chapter, try **activities 10.1** and **10.2** in **Appendix 1**.

# Identification evidence

## 11.1 Introduction

We have already looked at situations where the fact-finders may need to be alerted to the possible danger of relying on a particular source of evidence — see **Chapter 5**. Usually, this happens on a case-by-case, witness-by-witness, basis. But there is one whole category of evidence where it is thought that the risk of unreliability is much greater than normal, or at least greater than the inexperienced fact-finder would expect. This is identification evidence. Courts have tried to minimise the danger by requiring a warning to be given by the judge to the jury where a case turns on such disputed evidence. We shall look first at the rationale behind the concerns (**11.2**) and next at the methods now used to deal with them (**11.3–11.8**). Finally, we will look at how evidence is produced to prove identification in court and the procedures that must be followed (**11.9**).

## 11.2 Identification evidence and miscarriages of justice

Intuitively, most people consider that identification evidence is very reliable and accurate. Indeed, identification witnesses themselves often think so and come into the witness box convinced that they have identified the criminal correctly. That there are dangers in over-reliance on such evidence has been plain since at least the early 20th century and the case of Adolf Beck. Beck was twice convicted wrongly (in 1896 and 1904) of offences of fraud. In the 1870s, when Beck claimed to have been in South America, a 'John Smith' was convicted in England of several frauds. Each offence alleged that Smith had become intimate with a woman, persuaded her to put valuable jewellery into his possession, and then disappeared. In 1895, several more women were called as witnesses at a new trial. The offences seemed identical. Each woman identified the accused, this time Adolf Beck. The prosecution even called two police officers to testify that Adolf Beck and John Smith were the same man. Beck was convicted and sentenced to seven years' imprisonment. After his release, the offences started again. In 1904, Beck was again convicted on the word of several women, each of whom claimed to have been intimate with him. Whilst Beck was held in custody, awaiting sentence, John Smith was caught committing another offence. Smith's appearance matched the descriptions given by the women, which included the fact that their seducer was circumcised. Prison records from the 1870s indicated that 'John Smith' was circumcised. Beck was not circumcised. Beck was released, pardoned and received a substantial sum in compensation. Following this case, the Court of Criminal Appeal was set up and the first set of general instructions on the conduct of identification parades was issued.

However, miscarriages of justice continued to occur in cases based upon identification evidence. As Lord Devlin has pointed out:

> In 1912 a man on a charge of murder was identified by no less than 17 witnesses, but fortunately was able to establish an irrefutable alibi. In 1928 Oscar Slater, after he had spent 19 years in prison ... had his conviction for murder quashed; he had been identified by 14 witnesses. Nevertheless, cases continued to be left to the jury as if they raised only a simple issue between the identifier and the accused as to which was telling the truth ... In 1974 two shattering cases of mistaken identity came to light within four weeks of each other. (Patrick Devlin, *The Judge*, 1981.)

## 11.3    The special need for caution — *Turnbull* warnings

In May 1974, Lord Devlin was invited to chair a committee to investigate the law and procedure on identification and his committee's report (*Report to the Secretary of State for the Home Department of the Departmental Committee on Evidence of Identification in Criminal Cases*) was published in April 1976. It made several recommendations for changes to the gathering of identification evidence and its treatment in the courtroom, all of which were intended to be effected by statute. However, as Lord Devlin has observed:

> The Court of Appeal decided to forestall legislation by giving in July 1976 ... a comprehensive judgment laying down a new approach ...

That judgment was given in *R* v *Turnbull* [1977] QB 224 by Lord Widgery CJ. The 'new approach' is as follows (see pp 228–30 of the report):

(a) First, whenever the case against an accused depends wholly or substantially on the correctness of one or more identifications of the accused which the defence alleges to be mistaken, the judge should warn the jury of the special need for caution before convicting the accused in reliance on the correctness of the identification or identifications. In addition he should instruct them as to the reason for the need for such a warning and should make some reference to the possibility that a mistaken witness can be a convincing one and that a number of such witnesses can all be mistaken. Provided this is done in clear terms the judge need not use any particular form of words.

(b) Secondly, the judge should direct the jury to examine closely the circumstances in which the identification by each witness came to be made. How long did the witness have the accused under observation? At what distance? In what light? Was the observation impeded in any way, as for example by passing traffic or a press of people? Had the witness ever seen the accused before? How often? If only occasionally, had he any special reason for remembering the accused? How long elapsed between the original observation and the subsequent identification to the police?

(c) Was there any material discrepancy between the description of the accused given to the police by the witness when first seen by them and his actual appearance?

(d) If in any case, whether it is being dealt with summarily or on indictment, the prosecution have reason to believe that there is such a material discrepancy they should supply the accused or his legal advisers with particulars of the description the police were first given. In all cases if the accused asks to be given particulars of such descriptions, the prosecution should supply them. Finally, he should remind the jury of any specific weakness which had appeared in the identification evidence.

(e) Recognition may be more reliable than identification of a stranger; but even when the witness is purporting to recognise someone whom he knows, the jury should be reminded that mistakes in recognition of close relatives and friends are sometimes made.

(f) When the quality (of the identifying evidence) is good, as for example when the identification is made after a long period of observation, or in satisfactory conditions by a relative, a neighbour, a close friend, a workmate and the like, the jury can safely be left to assess the value of the identifying evidence even though there is no other evidence to support it: provided always, however, that an adequate warning has been given about the special need for caution.

(g) When, in the judgment of the trial judge, the quality of the identifying evidence is poor, as for example when it depends solely on a fleeting glance or on a longer observation made in difficult conditions, the situation is very different. The judge should then withdraw the case from the jury and direct an acquittal unless there is other evidence which goes to support the correctness of the identification. This may be corroboration in the sense lawyers use that word; but it need not be so if its effect is to make the jury sure that there has been no mistaken identification.

(h) The trial judge should identify to the jury the evidence which he adjudges is capable of supporting the evidence of identification. If there is any evidence or circumstances which the jury might think was supporting when it did not have this quality, the judge should say so.

(i) Care should be taken by the judge when directing the jury about the support for an identification which may be derived from the fact that they have rejected an alibi. False alibis may be put forward for many reasons ... It is only when the jury is satisfied that the sole reason for the fabrication was to deceive them and there is no other explanation for its being put forward can fabrication provide any support for identification evidence. The jury should be reminded that proving the accused has told lies about where he was at the material time does not by itself prove that he was where the identifying witness says he was.

Note that identification evidence given by police officers has no special status. Typically, officers receive training in observation and they might be thought to possess greater ability to identify people than is possessed by ordinary members of the public. However, in *Reid v R* (1990) 90 Cr App R 121, the Privy Council stated that:

... experience has undoubtedly shown that police identification can be just as unreliable and is not therefore to be excepted from the now well established need for the appropriate warnings.

This remains the position, even where the police witness claims to have recognised the accused at the scene of crime, having known him previously (see *R v Bowden* [1993] Crim LR 379).

## 11.4  Form of a *Turnbull* warning

When a trial judge directs a jury about identification evidence, in the summing-up, there is no set form of words that is needed for the *Turnbull* warning. In *Mills v R* [1995] 1 WLR 511, the Privy Council stated that *Turnbull* was not a statute and did not require the incantation of a formula. A judge has:

a broad discretion to express himself in his own way when he directs a jury on identification. All that is required ... is that he should comply with the sense and spirit of the guidance in ... *Turnbull* ...

You may wish to attempt **activity 11.1** in **Appendix 1** at this point.

Notwithstanding the discretion that a judge clearly has, there is a specimen direction (number 30) formulated by the Judicial Studies Board:

This is a trial where the case against the defendant depends wholly or to a large extent on the correctness of one or more identifications of him which the defence alleges to be mistaken. I must therefore warn you of the special need for caution before convicting the defendant in reliance on the evidence of identification. That is because it is possible for an honest witness to make a mistaken identification. There have been wrongful convictions in the past as a result of such mistakes. An apparently convincing witness can be mistaken. So can a number of apparently convincing witnesses.

You should therefore examine carefully the circumstances in which the identification by each witness was made. How long did he have the person he says was the defendant under observation? At what distance? In what light? Did anything interfere with the observation? Had the witness ever seen the person he observed before? If so, how often? If only occasionally, had he any special reason for remembering him? How long was it between the original observation and the identification to the police? Is there any marked difference between the description given by the witness to the police when he was first seen by them and the appearance of the defendant?

See further the JSB website, www.jsboard.co.uk/criminal.

You may wish to attempt **activity 11.2** in **Appendix 1**.

## 11.5  Poor quality identification evidence — submissions of no case

You have seen, in **11.3** points (g) to (i), how the Court of Appeal in *R v Turnbull* [1977] QB 224 recognised that identification evidence may sometimes be of poor quality. The suggestion was that cases based on such weak evidence should be stopped on a submission of no case to answer unless there was some evidence which might support the accuracy of the identification.

At the conclusion of the prosecution evidence in a trial, the defence may make a submission of no case to answer (see **2.9.3.2**). Generally, such submissions are governed by the principles set out in *R v Galbraith* [1981] 1 WLR 1039 but in cases where evidence of identification is disputed, the submission will be based upon *R v Turnbull*:

(a) Where there is no identification evidence at all, the judge's decision is simple. The submission succeeds.

(b) Where there is identification evidence but it is of poor quality and is unsupported by other evidence, again the judge should withdraw the case from the jury. First, the judge should assume the identification evidence to be honest (that is, he or she does not need to form a view about the credibility of the prosecution witness). Then if the judge considers that the identification evidence has a base which is so slender that it is unreliable and thus not sufficient to found a conviction, he or she should uphold the submission and order the defendant's acquittal on the charge. See, for example, *Daley v R* [1993] 4 All ER 86.

(c) Where there is identification evidence of poor quality but which is potentially supported by other evidence, the judge will allow the case to go to the jury. The judge should tell the jury what other evidence is capable of supporting the accuracy of the identification. See **11.6**. According to *R v Akaidere* [1990] Crim LR 808, a judge should not tell a jury that the identification evidence is of poor quality and the case would have been withdrawn if there was no supporting evidence. The reason for this ban is that, whilst it is for the judge to decide if there is evidence *capable* of supporting the identification, it is a question of fact for the jury to decide whether it does support it. The jury might be inappropriately influenced in their decision if they knew of the judge's view.

We shall consider how identification evidence may be supported in **11.6**.

## 11.6  Support for poor quality identification evidence

One possible form of support was specifically considered in *R v Turnbull* [1977] QB 224 — the fact that the defendant had put forward a false alibi (see point (i), **11.3**). If a defendant's alibi is rejected as a lie, this fact can offer support but a careful direction is required (*R v Keane* (1977) 65 Cr App R 247). It does not follow that, because an alibi has been rejected by the jury as false, the defendant was wherever the identification witness says he was. The jury should consider if there is a reason why the defendant might have offered a false alibi, consistent with his innocence. An example might be where he was with a girlfriend and did not want his wife to find out about it, so offered a different, false, alibi. You will see the parallel with the general treatment of lies by the accused; *R v Lucas* [1981] QB 720, **10.3.1**.

In the absence of other sources of evidence to support a poor quality identification (for example, D's fingerprints on the murder weapon), the judge should consider whether several identification witnesses may support each other. If they have each been hampered in their observation (eg, passengers on a night bus passing an incident on the street), the judge may have to withdraw the case from the jury and direct an acquittal. If they have observed in satisfactory conditions (eg, several spectators at a sunny day-time football match observe an assault by a fellow spectator), then their evidence may be presented to the jury as capable of supporting each other's identification evidence. In that situation, the judge should also direct the jury that several honest witnesses can all be mistaken. See *R v Weeder* (1980) 71 Cr App R 228; also *R v Breslin* (1985) 80 Cr App R 226.

In some situations, several identification witnesses may offer mutual support even though they have each witnessed a different incident, where it is alleged that each incident involved the same offender. This is a form of similar fact evidence and is considered further in **7.2.4.2** above.

## 11.7 Situations where a *Turnbull* warning may be unnecessary

As you know by now, the concern that lay behind the decision in *R v Turnbull* [1977] QB 224 was that an identification witness may be mistaken but be persuasive because he appears to be sincere and convincing. In fact, he is sincere and has probably convinced himself that his identification is accurate. But he may still be wrong. The *Turnbull* warning is intended to alert the jury to the danger of being misled. But what if *mistaken* identification is not an issue at the trial? This may arise in three ways.

(a) There may be no possibility of mistake. If so, there is no need for a *Turnbull* warning. One example is when the only person who could be the offender is the defendant. In *R v Slater* [1995] 1 Cr App R 584, an offence took place in a nightclub and the accused accepted that he had been there. The accused was 2 metres tall and the Court of Appeal noted that there was no evidence to suggest that anyone remotely similar in height to the accused was present in the nightclub where the offence took place; no *Turnbull* warning was needed. Conversely, in *R v Thornton* [1995] 1 Cr App R 578, an offence occurred at a wedding reception. The accused accepted that he was at the reception. There were a number of people present who were dressed similarly to the accused (black leather jacket, black trousers) and several people were allegedly involved in the offence. The Court of Appeal thought that a mistaken identification was clearly possible; a *Turnbull* warning should have been given.

(b) Where the defence allege that the identification witness is lying. In this situation, mistake is simply not a live issue for the jury to consider. The issue now is simply the veracity of the witness. Does the jury believe the identification witness or not? In *R v Courtnell* [1990] Crim LR 115, the Court of Appeal accepted that point but noted that if there was evidence that might support the contention of mistaken identification, the judge should direct the jury accordingly, even though the defence had not raised that issue at the trial. In *R v Courtnell*, there was no such evidence and the judge had not erred in omitting a *Turnbull* direction. Similarly, in *R v Cape* [1996] 1 Cr App R 191, the defendants were alleged to have been involved in a fight in a pub. The pub landlord, who knew the men, testified that they were so involved. The defendants admitted being in the pub at the time but denied involvement; they suggested the landlord was lying and motivated by a grudge. The issue for the jury was simply whether they accepted the evidence of the landlord as truthful; that did not call for a *Turnbull* warning.

In *Beckford v R* (1993) 97 Cr App R 409, the Privy Council reiterated the need to consider carefully all of the issues before the jury. Beckford and two co-accused were tried for murder. The sole witness to the crime identified all three men as being present. At trial, the accused all ran alibi defences and alleged that the witness was lying because either (i) he was a compulsive and inveterate liar or (ii) he was susceptible to mental aberrations (having previously been a patient in a mental hospital). The Privy Council considered that there were two questions for the jury to consider:

(i) Is the witness honest? This was at the heart of the defence case. If the jury found he was not honest, they would disregard his evidence.

If the jury found him to be an honest witness, they would need to consider (and be directed on) a second question.

(ii)   Could the witness be mistaken? If this was a possibility, on the evidence, it would require a *Turnbull* direction from the judge. The direction should then be given even if the defence did not rely on the possibility of mistake.

(c)   Where the evidence does not identify a person. Where an eyewitness gives evidence only of *description* (for example, clothing or general characteristics), this is not identification evidence. In *R v Gayle* [1999] 2 Cr App R 130, the Court of Appeal noted that the danger of an honest witness being mistaken about distinctive clothing, or the general description of a person he or she has seen (eg, short or tall, black or white, direction of movement) is minimal. What the jury need to concentrate upon is the honesty of the witness.

Where the prosecution try to prove that a defendant was present at a particular place by calling witnesses who will say that they saw *a man* driving a car, and they can identify *the car*, then a full *Turnbull* warning is not needed. The prosecution will need to produce other evidence to prove that the defendant was driving the car at the material time. This was the view taken by the Court of Appeal in *R v Browning* (1991) 94 Cr App R 109. The explanation for the distinction between identification of a person and of a car was said to be that, whereas people may change their appearance frequently (eg, facial expression or bodily posture), cars do not change their shape, colour or size (unless of course they are altered deliberately). Nevertheless, a jury should still be directed about any difficulties regarding observation of the car (eg, if the witness was a driver who got a fleeting glance of the car whilst being overtaken).

## 11.8   Appeals and identification evidence

A failure to observe the *Turnbull* guidelines will often lead to a successful appeal: see *R v Hunjan* (1979) 68 Cr App R 99. Indeed, the Privy Council said, in *Reid v R* (1990) 90 Cr App R 121, that they had:

no hesitation in concluding that a significant failure to follow the identification guidelines as laid down in *Turnbull* ... will cause a conviction to be quashed because it will have resulted in a substantial miscarriage of justice ... If convictions are to be allowed upon uncorroborated [unsupported] identification evidence there must be strict insistence upon a judge giving a clear warning of the danger of a mistaken identification which the jury must consider before arriving at their verdict. It is only in the most exceptional circumstances that a conviction based on uncorroborated identification evidence will be sustained in the absence of such a warning.

An example of such 'exceptional circumstances' may be found in *Freemantle v R* [1994] 3 All ER 225. Here, the Privy Council said that if the identification evidence was of exceptionally good quality, this would be an exceptional circumstance. Amongst the factors which the Privy Council thought showed the exceptionally good quality of the identification evidence, was a dialogue between the accused, Freemantle, and one of the eyewitnesses, Campbell. Campbell shouted to the man he saw, 'Freemantle me see you'; the man's reply was regarded as an implied acknowledgement of the accuracy of that identification. See also *Scott v R* [1989] AC 1242.

## 11.9  Establishing a link between the accused and the crime

### 11.9.1  Ways to make a link

Suppose that a defendant (or suspect) denies being the offender, there are several ways to produce evidence which can show that he or she is the offender. For example:

- visual identification by an eyewitness;
- aural (voice) identification by an ear witness;
- prints left at the crime scene — these could be prints made by fingers, palm, foot or even ear;
- fibres left at the crime scene;
- DNA left at the crime scene;
- handwriting left at the crime scene;
- fingerprints, etc, or property from the crime scene which have been found to match ones found on the defendant or on his or her clothing, among his or her possessions or in his or her house.

We now need to consider what must be done in order to turn any of these pieces of information into admissible evidence that could be used in a trial. In all of these situations, there will be a witness as to the facts. This person must make a witness statement to say 'I heard something', 'I saw someone', 'I found this letter', 'I picked up this cigarette butt', and so on. A comparison must then be made between that information and the defendant (or suspect).

Comparison by an eye or ear witness is usually done by letting the witness see or hear the suspect in controlled conditions (for example, an identification parade). In order to insulate the witness from attack in cross-examination at trial, the witness should give a description of the person he or she saw or heard *before* comparing his or her recollection with the suspect's appearance or voice. See Code D, para 2.2.

Finders will need to send their discoveries elsewhere for testing. They should protect their discoveries by sealing them in plastic bags, to avoid possible contamination. Such bags must be labelled so that the expert making the comparison can show the connection between what he or she is testing and what was found. Defence counsel may object at trial either that a discovery has been contaminated by coming into contact with other material, or that there is no evidence to link the sample tested in a laboratory by an expert witness to what was found at the crime scene.

In the case of prints, fibres, DNA or handwriting, comparison must be made with a specimen obtained from the suspect. DNA and fingerprints may already be available to the police, following the suspect's conviction on an earlier occasion. Otherwise, a specimen must be obtained now. We will consider how that happens in **11.9.6**. Once we have the specimen, we need an expert to make the comparison. If there is a sufficient match, we will have our evidence of identity. The expert witness must provide an expert report, to be disclosed to the defence and used at trial. The probative value of that evidence will vary from case to case. A fingerprint or DNA match may be very probative but some fibres or types of glass, for example, may be in very common use and so have a low probative value. If they were rare, for example pieces of handblown mediaeval glass from a church window, the match would have a higher probative value. Even with a good match and uncommon material, we have only circumstantial evidence to link the suspect to the crime scene. This means that the match may be explained away at trial by the defence, or somehow shown to be less probative. For example, in the trial of several youths for the murder of Damilola Taylor at the Old Bailey in 2002, the prosecution alleged that the fatal injury to the victim was caused by a shard from a glass bottle. Fragments of the bottle were recovered at the crime scene. One of the accused youths possessed a pair of trainers on which was found a tiny piece of glass. Scientific tests showed it to match the type of glass which had been found at the crime scene. Thus, the police had evidence to make a link between the youth and the crime scene. At trial, the defence explained this apparently damaging match by showing that the youth had visited the crime scene a day or two after the death of Damilola Taylor. This was confirmed by police officers who were present at the time. The piece of glass could have got onto his trainer then, quite innocently. There are other ways to challenge expert evidence (on identification and other matters) which we will consider in **Chapter 12**.

### 11.9.2 Admissibility and exclusion of evidence

Quite apart from the risks which attach to identification evidence in general (to which the *Turnbull* direction relates), questions arise as to the ways in which identification evidence should be (a) gathered and (b) presented in court. Some forms of identification evidence, eg, dock identifications, are thought to carry such a risk of prejudice to the accused that the courts have frequently excluded such evidence. Exclusion is at the court's discretion either at common law or under the Police and Criminal Evidence Act 1984, s 78 (see **9.1.3**). In general the courts have sought to ensure that identification evidence is gathered in 'controlled circumstances' and to this end a code of practice (Code D) has been laid down by virtue of s 66 of the 1984 Act. Some aspects of the admissibility of identification evidence have already been dealt with in **Chapters 5** and **8** of this Manual.

Many Court of Appeal decisions illustrate that non-compliance with Code D may be an important factor in deciding whether to exclude the evidence pursuant to s 78 of the 1984 Act. See, for example, *R v Leckie* [1983] Crim LR 543; *R v Gall* (1990) 90 Cr App R 64 and *R v Conway* [1990] Crim LR 402.

However, breaches of Code D do not automatically lead to the exclusion of the identification evidence. See *R v Grannell* (1990) 90 Cr App R 149; *R v Quinn* [1990] Crim LR 581; *R v Penny* [1992] Crim LR 184; *R v Palmer* [2002] EWCA Crim 2645. For example, in *R v Forbes* [2001] AC 473, the House of Lords held that two street identifications by an eyewitness had been rightly allowed in as evidence at a trial, notwithstanding non-compliance with (what is now) Code D, para 2.14.

Whether there is a breach of Code D or not, s 78 of the 1984 Act would need to be considered. For example, evidence of a street identification, in the absence of an identification parade, *might* be excluded. In the final analysis, the fairness of allowing the other identification evidence to be called will depend on a variety of factors which are usually taken into consideration under s 78.

### 11.9.3 Cases where the link between the accused and the crime is based upon an eyewitness

This topic is dealt with generally in Code of Practice D, issued under PACE 1984. Code D can be found in *Blackstone's Criminal Practice* Appendix 2, or the *Archbold Supplement*. Code D and the Annexes A–D are particularly important. In considering the use to be made of an eyewitness, we must start by distinguishing between two situations:

(i) Where an eyewitness identifies the accused as the offender in court, while giving evidence at the trial (see **11.9.3.1**); or

(ii) Where an eyewitness identifies the accused as the offender before the trial begins (see **11.9.3.2**).

### 11.9.3.1   In-court eyewitness identification (usually called dock identification)

Dock identification should not generally be allowed (*R v Howick* [1970] Crim LR 403). The reason for this ban is the lack of probative value of a dock identification. It is easy for a witness to 'identify' the alleged criminal when he or she is standing rather obviously in the dock and the exercise adds little or nothing to a previous act of identification. In the absence of a previous identification by that witness, to allow a dock identification would flout the basic principles that govern the production of identification evidence (through an identification parade, for example).

A dock identification may be permissible when a defendant refuses to attend a parade (*R v John* [1973] Crim LR 113, CA) or renders a parade impracticable, eg, by changing his appearance (*R v Mutch* [1973] 1 All ER 178, CA).

There is no logic in making a distinction between a dock identification in a Crown Court and in a magistrates' court. However, in road traffic offences it is usually necessary to prove that the defendant was the driver of the car at the time of the offence. Generally, there is no dispute that the accused was the driver but a failure to call any evidence on that issue is likely to result in an acquittal. In summary trials for road traffic offences, the custom has evolved where a witness (usually a police officer) is asked, 'Do you see the driver in court?' Because of the sheer number of such offences which are tried by magistrates, if there had to be an identification parade in every case where the accused did not expressly admit that he or she was the driver, 'the whole process of justice in a magistrates' court would be severely impaired' (*Barnes v Chief Constable of Durham* [1997] 2 Cr App R 505). Thus, it seems that in this type of case the onus is on the accused to raise the issue of disputed identification before the trial starts, and seek an identification parade.

### 11.9.3.2   Out-of-court eyewitness identification

The obvious way to avoid the prejudice of a dock identification is to refer to an out of court identification made in less prejudicial circumstances. Code D lays down a regime for ensuring this (so far as is possible): see, in particular, Code D, para 2. All forms of out-of-court identification would seem to be admissible either as prior consistent statements (under the principle in *R v Christie* [1914] AC 545) or under the rules in *R v Osbourne* [1973] QB 678. See also *R v Rogers* [1993] Crim LR 386 confirming the admissibility of a street identification.

(a) When the *identity* of the *suspect is known* to the police *and* he or she is *available*, four forms of identification procedure may be used to confirm or refute identification. In a *video identification*, the witness is shown images of a suspect, together with images of at least eight other people who resemble the suspect. The images may be moving or still (see Code D, annex A). An *identification parade* puts the suspect into a line-up of at least eight other people who resemble the suspect as far as possible (see annex B). *Group identification* is less formal — the suspect is put into an informal group of people, perhaps walking through a shopping centre or in a queue at a bus station (see annex C). *Confrontation* involves a direct confrontation between witness and suspect. This will usually take place in a police station and the witness shall be asked, 'Is this the person?' (see annex D).

If the suspect does not dispute identification by a witness, no identification procedure is necessary unless the officer in charge of the investigation considers it would be useful (Code D, para 2.14). If identification is disputed, an identification procedure shall be held if practicable unless, in all the circumstances, it would serve no useful purpose in determining the suspect's involvement in the offence (paras 2.14 and 2.15). There will be no such useful purpose where it is not disputed that the suspect is already well-known to the eyewitness, or there is no reasonable possibility of the witness making an identification.

If an identification procedure is to be used, the officer in charge of the case will consult with the identification officer as to the suitability and practicability of holding either a video identification or an identification parade. (An identification officer is the officer responsible for the arrangement and conduct of identification procedures, usually an inspector: para 2.13). A video identification will normally be more suitable if it can be done sooner than a parade (para 2.16). The officer in charge of the case will then offer the chosen procedure to the suspect (para 2.16). A group identification may be offered to the suspect instead, if the officer in charge of the investigation considers it to be more satisfactory to do so (para 2.17). The suspect may refuse the offered procedure and may then make representations as to why a different procedure should be used. The identification officer shall then offer an alternative procedure if one is suitable and practicable. If the suspect refuses or fails to take part in any practicable identification procedure, arrangements may be made for covert video identification or covert group identification (para 2.19). As a last resort, if none of the other procedures are practicable, a confrontation may be arranged.

If an eyewitness makes an identification after an identification parade has ended, the suspect and his or her solicitor should be informed. The police should also consider whether to give the witness a second opportunity at a parade (Code D, annex A, para 16). Where two witnesses were put into the same room after taking part in a parade, and only one had identified the suspect, but later the second made a statement doing so, neither witness's evidence had to be excluded. See *R v Willoughby* [1999] 2 Cr App R 82, where the Court of Appeal held that merely 'firming-up' a tentative identification at a parade does not come within the ambit of annex A para 16. As to the witness who had not previously identified the suspect, the Court observed that even if para 16 is breached, so long as the breach is relatively minor and innocent (eg, no coaching has occurred), the trial judge may decide not to exclude that evidence under s 78 of the 1984 Act.

(b) When the *identity* of the *suspect is known* to the police but he or she is *not available*, the identification officer may arrange a video identification. The suspect will be 'unavailable' if not immediately available to participate in a procedure and will not become available within a reasonably short time. Failure or refusal to participate may be treated as not being available (see Code D, para 2.12).

(c) When the *identity* of the *suspect is not known* to the police, then clearly the steps outlined above cannot be taken. To discover the identity of the suspect an eyewitness may be taken to a particular neighbourhood (usually shortly after the alleged offence) to make a street identification (if possible) or given an opportunity to look through police photographs. See Code D, paras 2.17 and 2.18.

See also **activity 11.3**, to check your understanding.

### 11.9.4   Cases where the link between the accused and the crime is made by recognition of voice

An alleged recording of an accused's voice should be heard by the jury but expert evidence on it should also be presented (see *R v Bentum* (1989) 153 JP 538; *R v Robb* (1991) 93 Cr App R 161).

In *R v Deenik* [1992] Crim LR 578, a witness testified to recognising the accused's voice (as that of the person who had committed the offence) on overhearing the accused being interviewed. It was held that it was not necessary to exclude the evidence merely because the accused was unaware that the witness was listening to the interview. The Court of Appeal has said that where a witness identifies a suspect by hearing his or her voice, Code D has no application and there is no obligation to hold a voice identification parade. However, reference to Code D shows that a witness attending an identification parade may ask to hear any member speak (see Code D, annex B, para 18).

In any event, what the judge should do is to direct the jury using a suitably adapted form of *Turnbull* warning. Research suggests that identification by voice is less reliable than visual identification, so the warning should be in stronger terms. See further *R v Hersey* [1998] Crim LR 281; *R v Gummerson* [1999] Crim LR 680; *R v Roberts* [2000] Crim LR 183.

A tape of the perpetrator's voice may be played to the jury, if the accused has given evidence, so they may form their own judgement of the opinions of the experts. This was stated by the Court of Appeal in *R v Bentum* (1989) 153 JP 538 and approved by the Court of Appeal in Northern Ireland in *R v O'Doherty* [2003] 1 Cr App R 5. This is the position, notwithstanding that experts called for both prosecution and defence in *R v O'Doherty* had expressed the view that there are dangers in playing tapes to juries. The Northern Ireland Court of Appeal also said that where expert evidence is given of voice analysis, the evidence should normally deal with both auditory and acoustic analysis. Where a tape is played, the jury should be given a specific warning about the danger of relying upon their own untrained ears. The evidence of Dr Nolan, a Reader in Phonetics at the University of Cambridge, was effectively ignored in so far as he rejected the notion that there was any benefit in playing a tape to the jury. For example, 'jury members were already inevitably under psychological bias from the very fact that [the accused] was in the dock and had been confidently identified by a police officer of his acquaintance'. Dr Nolan made a comparison with identification parades, where the purpose of requiring at least eight other participants was to give a degree of protection to an innocent suspect. 'The jury were in effect given a line-up of one and asked "Is this the person or not[?]".' The Northern Ireland Court of Appeal rejected those concerns, and made a comparison with the case law on the playing of videotapes to a jury (see **11.9.5**). It might be that identical concerns could be raised about that, too.

### 11.9.5   Cases where the link between the accused and the crime is based upon security film/photographs etc

The jury can look at a CCTV film or a still photograph and form their own view as to whether the person shown is the accused sitting in the dock. See *Kajala v Noble* (1982) 75 Cr App R 149, DC, and *R v Dodson and Williams* [1984] 1 WLR 971. According to *R v Blenkinsop* [1995] 1 Cr App R 7 a full *Turnbull* warning would not be appropriate in such cases. However, it may be preferable to call a witness who knows the accused and recognises him on the film (in which case a *Turnbull* hearing would generally be appropriate).

*R v Fowden* [1982] Crim LR 588, *R v Grimer* [1982] Crim LR 674, *Taylor v Chief Constable of Cheshire* [1987] 1 All ER 225 and *R v Caldwell* (1994) 99 Cr App R 73 deal with the situation where witnesses (usually police officers) who know the accused are called upon to identify him as the person caught on film, etc. The propositions which emerge from these cases are:

(a) Where there are several witnesses, they should not be allowed to view the film etc together but should be asked to view the film individually and state whether they recognise the person on the film (see also Code D, annex A).

(b) At trial, attempts should be made not to reveal to the jury that the witness knows the accused through previous encounters in the course of investigations into other criminal offences.

(c) A *Turnbull* warning should be given to the jury.

All of these cases were considered and approved by the Court of Appeal in *Attorney-General's Reference (No 2 of 2002)* [2002] EWCA Crim 2373, [2003] Crim LR 192.

In *R v Stockwell* (1993) 97 Cr App R 260, the Court of Appeal accepted that the opinion evidence of a facial-mapping expert is admissible, particularly in cases where there is a possibility that the person caught on the film was disguised. However, one must take care that the opinion evidence of a facial-mapping expert stays within acceptable bounds. It is acceptable to call such an expert at trial to demonstrate to a jury particular characteristics or a combination thereof, with the aid of specialist enhancement techniques if appropriate. It is not acceptable for such an expert to offer an estimate of probabilities or to state the degree of support provided by particular facial characteristics. These are subjective opinions and will be inadmissible until such time as a 'national database or agreed formula or some other such objective measure is established'; see *R v Gray* [2003] EWCA Crim 1001.

In *R v Clarke* [1995] 2 Cr App R 425, the Court of Appeal held that evidence of facial mapping by way of video superimposition (of police photographs of the accused upon photographs of the offender taken by a security camera) was admissible as a species of real evidence to which no special rules applied.

In *R v Clare* [1995] 2 Cr App R 333, the Court of Appeal accepted that a police officer, who had viewed a security video of a crowd disturbance at a football match over 40 times (having the facility to stop the video and examine it in slow motion), had thereby become an expert on that video so as to justify calling him to give evidence interpreting the video and the role and identification of the person caught on the video. In *R v Thomas* (1999) LTL 22/11/99, the Court of Appeal held that there is no obligation on the prosecution to put the accused on an identification parade before people on whom neither the police nor the Crown ever intend to rely as identification witnesses. Before T was put on trial for four bank robberies, a police officer studied CCTV videos and single-frame shots of the robberies 'repeatedly'. The Court of Appeal said that the officer had 'acquired special knowledge that the [trial] court did not possess'; in effect, he had become an 'expert' and there was no purpose in seeing if he could pick out T on a parade.

In *R v McNamara* [1996] Crim LR 750 the Court of Appeal held that where a jury requested a view of the accused to compare with a man on a video, no inference could properly be drawn if the accused chose to absent himself from the dock.

Where a crime has been seen by an eyewitness as well as being recorded on a surveillance video, the witness may be allowed to view the video and to amend his/her witness statement in the light of what he or she sees on it (see *R v Roberts* [1998] Crim LR 682).

Where a security tape exists, and it shows an offence being committed, but does not show the accused who is now on trial, that tape is material evidence which must be disclosed to the defence. See *Sangster v R* [2002] UKPC 58.

### 11.9.6    Cases where the link between the accused and the crime is made by fingerprints or DNA profiles

The problem here is primarily how fingerprints or body samples can *properly* be obtained from the accused. The governing statutory provisions in this regard are to be found in the Police and Criminal Evidence Act 1984, ss 61 to 65 (as amended) and supplemented by Code D, para 3 (fingerprints) and para 5 (body samples).

#### 11.9.6.1    Taking fingerprints

Expert evidence on fingerprints is likely to be excluded if there are less than eight matching ridge characteristics. If there are no exceptional circumstances, the prosecution should not attempt to introduce such evidence. A judge would also consider whether there were any dissimilar characteristics between the print and that taken from the accused, and the size, quality and clarity of the print relied upon. See for example, *R v Buckley* (1999) 163 JP 561.

Police and Criminal Evidence Act 1984, s 61:

(1)  *Except as provided by this section no person's fingerprints may be taken without the appropriate consent.*

(2)  *Consent to the taking of a person's fingerprints must be in writing if it is given at a time when he is at a police station.*

(3)  *The fingerprints of a person detained at a police station may be taken without the appropriate consent—*

    (a)  *if an officer of at least the rank of superintendent authorises them to be taken; or*

    (b)  *if—*

        (i)  *he has been charged with a recordable offence or informed that he will be reported for such an offence; and*

        (ii)  *he has not had his fingerprints taken in the course of the investigation of the offence by the police.*

(4)  *An officer may only give an authorisation under subsection (3)(a) above if he has reasonable grounds—*

    (a)  *for suspecting the involvement of the person whose fingerprints are to be taken in a criminal offence; and*

    (b)  *for believing that his fingerprints will tend to confirm or disprove his involvement.*

(5)  *An officer may give an authorisation under subsection (3)(a) above orally or in writing but, if he gives it orally, he shall confirm it in writing as soon as is practicable.*

(6)  *Any person's fingerprints may be taken without the appropriate consent if he has been convicted of a recordable offence.*

(7)  *In a case where by virtue of subsection (3) or (6) above a person's fingerprints are taken without the appropriate consent—*

    (a)  *he shall be told the reason before his fingerprints are taken; and*

    (b)  *the reason shall be recorded as soon as is practicable after the fingerprints are taken.*

*[(7A) to (9) omitted]*

The definition of 'recordable offence' includes *all* offences punishable by imprisonment. See the National Police Records (Recordable Offences) Regulations 1985, SI 1985/1941.

Section 65 of the 1984 Act has the following definitions:

*'fingerprints' include palm prints;*
*'appropriate consent' mean—*

    (a)  *in relation to a person who has attained the age of 17 years, the consent of that person;*

    (b)  *in relation to a person who has not attained that age but has attained the age of 14 years, the consent of that person and his parent or guardian; and*

    (c)  *in relation to a person who has not attained the age of 14 years, the consent of his parent or guardian.*

Expert evidence may also be given of comparisons of ear prints: *R v Dallagher* [2002] EWCA Crim 1903, [2003] 1 Cr App R 11.

### 11.9.6.2   Body samples (DNA profiles)

The governing provisions are the Police and Criminal Evidence Act 1984, ss 62 and 63, as amended by the Criminal Justice and Public Order Act 1994. These are set out below. Section 62 deals with intimate samples and s 63 deals with non-intimate samples.

'*Intimate sample*' means (a) a sample of blood, semen or any other tissue fluid, urine or pubic hair; (b) a dental impression; (c) a swab taken from a person's body orifice other than the mouth; ('intimate search' means a search which consists of the physical examination of a person's body orifices other than the mouth).

'*Non-intimate sample*' means (a) a sample of hair other than pubic hair; (b) a sample taken from a nail or from under a nail; (c) a swab taken from any part of a person's body including the mouth but not any other body orifice; (d) saliva; (e) a footprint or a similar impression of any part of a person's body other than a part of his hand.

Section 62 of the 1984 Act provides:

(1)   *An intimate sample may be taken from a person in police detention only—*

   (a)   *if a police officer of at least the rank of superintendent authorises it to be taken; and*
   (b)   *if the appropriate consent is given.*

(1A) *An intimate sample may be taken from a person who is not in police detention but from whom, in the course of the investigation of an offence, two or more non-intimate samples suitable for the same means of analysis have been taken which have proved insufficient—*

   (a)   *if an officer of at least the rank of superintendent authorises it to be taken; and*
   (b)   *if the appropriate consent is given.*

(2)   *An officer may only give an authorisation under subsection (1) or (1A) above if he has reasonable grounds—*

   (a)   *for suspecting the involvement of the person from whom the sample is to be taken in a recordable offence; and*
   (b)   *for believing that the same will tend to confirm or disprove his involvement.*

*[(3) to (9) contain various procedural rules about the taking of intimate samples.]*

(10) *Where the appropriate consent to the taking of an intimate sample from a person was refused without good cause, in any proceedings against that person for an offence—*

   (a)   *the court, in determining whether ... there is a case to answer; and*
   (b)   *the court or jury, in determining whether that person is guilty of the offence charged,*
   *may draw such inferences from the refusal as appear proper.*

For the definition of 'recordable offence' see the note following s 61 in **11.9.6.1**.

Section 63 of the 1984 Act provides:

(1)   *Except as provided by this section, a non-intimate sample may not be taken from a person without the appropriate consent.*

(2)   *Consent to the taking of a non-intimate sample must be given in writing.*

(3)   *A non-intimate sample may be taken from a person without the appropriate consent if—*

   (a)   *he is in police detention or is being held in custody by the police on the authority of a court; and*
   (b)   *an officer of at least the rank of superintendent authorises it to be taken without the appropriate consent.*

(3A) *A non-intimate sample may be taken from a person (whether or not he falls within subsection 3(a) above) without the appropriate consent if—*

   (a)   *he has been charged with a recordable offence or informed that he will be reported for such an offence; and*
   (b)   *either he has not had a non-intimate sample taken from him in the course of the investigation of the offence by the police or he has had a non-intimate sample taken from him but either it was not suitable for the same means of analysis or, though so suitable, the sample proved insufficient.*

*(3B) A non-intimate sample may be taken from a person without the appropriate consent if he has been convicted of a recordable offence.*

*(3C) A non-intimate sample may also be taken from a person without the appropriate consent if he is a person to whom section 2 of the Criminal Evidence (Amendment) Act 1997 applies (persons detained following acquittal on grounds of insanity or finding of unfitness to plead).*

*(4)  An officer may only give an authorisation under subsection (3) above if he has reasonable grounds—*

*(a)  for suspecting the involvement of the person from whom the sample is to be taken in a recordable offence; and*

*(b)  for believing that the sample will tend to confirm or disprove his involvement.*

*[(5) to (9A) contain various procedural rules about the taking of non-intimate samples. See also Code D, para 5.]*

Section 63 (especially s 63(3A) and (3B)) brings the position with regard to obtaining *non-intimate* samples into line with the position relating to obtaining fingerprints (see above). Thus a *non-intimate* sample can be taken from a person for the first time without the appropriate consent in a variety of circumstances, for example, whenever the person has been convicted of a recordable offence (s 63(3B)). Even where a non-intimate sample cannot be taken without the appropriate consent, the refusal to consent may form the basis for an inference of guilt (at common law; see **10.4.3**). Section 63(3C) and s 63(9A) were inserted by the Criminal Evidence (Amendment) Act 1997.

Section 64 of the 1984 Act makes provision for the destruction of samples where suspects are eventually cleared of any offence — see Code D, paras 5.8 and 5.8A. Regarding the effect of breaches of these statutory rules, see *R v Nathaniel* [1995] 2 Cr App R 565, in which it was held that the trial judge should have applied PACE 1984, s 78, to exclude evidence obtained from a blood sample which should have been destroyed. Lord Taylor CJ said:

> To allow that blood sample to be used in evidence ... when the sample had been retained in breach of statutory duty and in breach of undertakings to the accused must ... have had an adverse effect on the fairness of the proceedings.

Subsequently, the House of Lords has drawn a distinction between, on the one hand, trying to use a DNA profile as evidence in a trial when it should have been destroyed (as was the position in *R v Nathaniel*) and using such a profile as part of a criminal investigation. The position is governed by different parts of s 64 — s 64(3B)(a) and (b), respectively. In *R v B (Attorney-General's Reference (No 3 of 1999))* [2001] 1 Cr App R 475, the House of Lords considered the use of a DNA profile from a man (B) acquitted of burglary. The profile had been placed on the national DNA database but, contrary to s 64(3B)(b), was not removed following his acquittal. Subsequently, the profile provided a match with DNA obtained from a rape victim. B was arrested and one of his hairs was removed, legally but without his consent. The hair provided another DNA match. At trial, the prosecution did not rely on the first DNA profile. B was convicted and appealed. The House of Lords held that the 1984 Act did not stipulate a consequence for a breach of s 64(3B)(b) and that the subsection did not legislate that evidence obtained as a result of the prohibited investigation was inadmissible. Section 64(3B)(b) had to be read in conjunction with s 78 of the 1984 Act. Section 64(3B)(b) prohibited the use of a sample liable to destruction for the purposes of any investigation of other offences. It would not prohibit the use of any evidence resulting from such investigation in any subsequent criminal proceedings. The House also considered article 8 of the European Convention on Human Rights and concluded that its interpretation of s 64(3B)(b) did not contravene the Convention.

### 11.9.6.3    Adducing evidence of DNA profiles

In *R v Doheny* [1997] 1 Cr App R 369, the Court of Appeal laid down the following guide-lines as regards the adducing (in court) of DNA evidence:

(a)    The scientist should adduce the evidence of the DNA comparisons between the crime stain and the defendant's sample together with his calculations of the random occurrence ratio.

(b)    Whenever DNA evidence is to be adduced the Crown should serve on the defence details of how the calculations have been carried out which are sufficient to enable the defence to scrutinise the basis of the calculations.

(c)    The Forensic Science Service should make available to a defence expert, if requested, the databases upon which the calculations have been based.

(d)    Any issue of expert evidence should be identified and, if possible, resolved before trial. This area should be explored by the court in the pre-trial review.

(e)    In giving evidence the expert will explain to the jury the nature of the matching DNA characteristics between the DNA in the crime stain and the DNA in the defendant's blood sample.

(f)    The expert will, on the basis of empirical statistical data, give the jury the random occurrence ratio — the frequency with which the matching DNA characteristics are likely to be found in the population at large.

(g)    Provided that the expert has the necessary data, it may then be appropriate for him to indicate how many people with the matching characteristics are likely to be found in the United Kingdom or a more limited relevant sub-group, for instance the Caucasian, sexually active males in the Manchester area.

(h)    It is then for the jury to decide, having regard to all the relevant evidence, whether they are sure that it was the defendant who left the crime stain, or whether it is possible that it was left by someone else with the same matching DNA characteristics.

(i)    The expert should not be asked his opinion on the likelihood that it was the defendant who left the crime stain, nor when giving evidence should he use terminology which may lead the jury to believe that he is expressing such an opinion.

(j)    It is not appropriate for an expert to expound a statistical approach to evaluating the likelihood that the defendant left the crime stain, since unnecessary theory and complexity deflect the jury from their proper task.

(k)    In the summing-up careful directions are required in respect of any issues of expert evidence, and guidance should be given to avoid confusion caused by areas of expert evidence where no real issue exists.

(l)    The judge should explain to the jury the relevance of the random occurrence ratio in arriving at their verdict and draw attention to the extraneous evidence which provides the context which gives that ratio its significance, and to that which conflicts with the conclusion that the defendant was responsible for the crime stain.

(m)    In relation to the random occurrence ratio, a direction along the following lines may be appropriate, tailored to the facts of the particular case: 'Members of the jury, if you accept the scientific evidence called by the Crown this indicates that there are probably only four or five white males in the United Kingdom from whom that semen stain could have come. The defendant is one of them. If that is the position, the decision you have to reach, on all the evidence, is whether you are sure that it was the defendant who left that stain or whether it is possible that it was one of that other small group of men who share the same DNA characteristics.'

## 11.10  Recap activities

If you want to test your understanding of some of the principles covered in this chapter, turn to **activities 11.4** and **11.5** in **Appendix 1** and work through the cases of Barry Borrower and *R v Gilbert*.

# 12

# Opinion evidence

## 12.1 General rule

You may recall an occasion when someone (a parent or teacher perhaps) said to you, 'When I want your opinion, I'll ask for it!' In the courtrooms of England and Wales, the approach is effectively the same. In civil and criminal cases, the opinions of witnesses are not generally admissible.

Opinions, and conclusions, are for the court to reach, based upon the information placed before it. If a conclusion on a point of law is required, the court will base its conclusion upon the legal arguments put before it by the advocates. Any factual conclusion will be based upon the evidence in the trial (or other form of hearing). Any witness should normally be confined to stating the facts.

When reaching conclusions of fact, the court should make its decisions for itself. So, a rule evolved that a witness should not be asked questions, or offer answers, which require the witness to venture an opinion on a fact in issue. To do so could appear to exert improper influence over the court. This is sometimes known as the 'ultimate issue' rule.

There is also a risk that the court might be unaware of the factual basis (or lack of it) on which the witness's opinion is founded. What the court really needs are the original facts, upon which the witness's opinion is based.

Finally, in situations where the court is quite capable of forming an opinion on the fact in issue, it would be a waste of time to allow a witness to state his or her opinion on that fact.

Before continuing, try **activities 12.1** to **12.3** in **Appendix 1**.

Any description of the rule against opinion evidence, even if it is supported with examples, fails to give a true impression of the impact of the rule upon the questioning of witnesses. An objection to a particular question is often made (and sustained) on the basis that the witness is being invited to state opinion. Sometimes the question itself is really nothing more than comment on the witness's evidence.

The general rule excluding opinion evidence is subject to two important exceptions. These arise in cases where the court lacks the witness's competence to form an opinion on a particular issue. That may arise through (a) lack of the necessary direct knowledge or (b) lack of the necessary expertise.

## 12.2   Witnesses of fact who offer their opinion

To test your understanding of the difference between statements of fact and opinion, turn to **Appendix 1** and work through **activity 12.4**.

Statements of opinion by an eyewitness (E) to the facts in issue are often really a convenient way of stating several facts. Thus an assertion by E that the defendant was drunk is a convenient way of stating the various facts which E saw (or heard or smelt) which led him to form that opinion. Such a statement will generally be admissible as long as a proper appraisal of the facts does not call for any special expertise.

In civil cases this exception has been put into statutory form: the Civil Evidence Act 1972, s 3(2):

> *It is hereby declared that where a person is called as a witness in any civil proceedings, a statement of opinion by him on any relevant matter on which he is not qualified to give expert evidence, if made as a way of conveying relevant facts personally perceived by him, is admissible evidence of what he perceived.*

If a degree of precision is required, then a witness's best guess or estimate by itself will probably not do. In a case concerning a road accident it will often be necessary to consider the speed at which the vehicles involved were travelling and E may be allowed to state his opinion on this issue. However, if the charge is driving over the speed limit or driving with an amount of alcohol in the blood which exceeds the maximum prescribed by law, precision is needed. See, for example, the Road Traffic Regulation Act 1984, s 89 (see **12.6**), which states that it is insufficient to use the opinion of just one witness to prove a speeding case.

In the 'blue car' example, the defendant may have been on trial for the offence of dangerous driving. The manner of her driving would be one of the most important facts in issue in the trial. Whether the driving was dangerous is for the court to decide but it should not be thought that Mrs Hill-Start would be prevented from offering her opinion. The court will simply pay little, if any, attention to it. In civil cases, factual witnesses are clearly entitled to offer their opinion on such ultimate issues. See Civil Evidence Act 1972, s 3(2), above and s 3(3):

> (3)   *In this section 'relevant matter' includes an issue in the proceedings in question.*

## 12.3   Expert opinion evidence

### 12.3.1   General principle

There are many situations in which an issue the court is required to determine is so far removed from the court's experience that it needs the opinions of experts to help it determine the issue in question. When such need arises the opinion of an expert *is* admissible. This was recognised as long ago as *Folkes v Chadd* (1782) 3 Doug KB 157. The converse is also true: if an issue calls for expert evidence, the evidence of a non-expert should not be admitted; see *R v Inch* (1989) 91 Cr App R 51.

It is not possible to list all the matters in respect of which expert evidence is required; some matters (eg, medical and scientific) obviously call for the opinions of experts. However, the line between matters which do call for expert evidence and matters which do not is often extremely fine (especially in relation to psychiatric evidence) and the courts consider the question most carefully. In *R v Turner* [1975] QB 834, CA at p 841 Lawton LJ put the point very effectively in this way:

> The fact that an expert witness has impressive scientific qualifications does not by that fact alone make his opinion on matters of human nature and behaviour *within the limits of normality* any more helpful than that of the jurors themselves; but there is a danger that they may think it does. (Emphasis added.)

As we saw above, expert evidence will usually be excluded if it merely offers an opinion on normal human behaviour. But this sometimes begs the question, 'What is normality?' In a development from the position in *R v Turner*, expert evidence may now be called not merely where the accused is alleged to be suffering from a recognised mental illness, but also if it could show that the accused is suffering from a personality disorder which would tend to affect the reliability of the confession or other evidence. See, for example, *R v Pinfold* [2003] EWCA Crim 3643.

There are particular difficulties in criminal cases when there *is* evidence of *abnormality* but the central issue in the case turns on the application of an objective test. By definition the 'reasonable man' cannot be assumed to be abnormal. In so far as an expert's evidence would *only* be relevant if such an assumption could be made then it would appear to be inadmissible. You should refer to practitioner works to review the (sometimes contradictory) case law on this subject. It has affected such issues as duress, recklessness and provocation.

To examine the sorts of issues which can require expert evidence, turn to **Appendix 1** and work through **activity 12.5**.

This list has been drawn exclusively from criminal cases but this does not mean that expert evidence is less common in civil cases. Indeed, it is probably encountered more frequently in civil cases (and there are many rules of civil procedure which relate to expert evidence — see the *Civil Litigation Manual*).

We saw earlier that witnesses of fact can express their opinion on an issue, even though it may be an 'ultimate issue' for the court to decide. The same is true for an expert witness. In civil cases, this is established by the Civil Evidence Act 1972, s 3(1) and (3):

> (1)   *Subject to any rules of court made in pursuance of this Act, where a person is called as a witness in any civil proceedings, his opinion on any relevant matter on which he is qualified to give expert evidence shall be admissible in evidence ...*
>
> (3)   *In this section 'relevant matter' includes an issue in the proceedings in question.*

Sometimes, an expert may seem to trespass into ultimate issues in criminal cases, for example, *R v Stockwell* (1993) 97 Cr App R 260 — an early use of facial mapping evidence. There is no statutory equivalent of the CEA 1972 to permit experts in criminal cases to offer their opinions on ultimate issues but it seems to be a matter of the form that questions take now, rather than their substance. See further *Blackstone's Criminal Practice*, 2004.

### 12.3.2   Who is an expert?

Where a matter calls for expert evidence, only a suitably qualified expert can give it. Indeed the starting point in examining in chief an expert witness is to establish his or her expertise. But this does not necessarily mean that there must be formal qualifications. See, for example, *R v Stockwell* (1993) 97 Cr App R 260, where the 'expert' in facial mapping had 'no scientific qualifications, no specific training, no profeessional body and no database'.

Other examples are *R v Silverlock* [1894] 2 QB 766 — a solicitor who had for many years studied handwriting as a hobby (handwriting expert); *Ajami v Comptroller of Customs* [1954] 1 WLR 1405 — a banker with 24 years' experience of Nigerian banking law (foreign law expert). (Matters of *foreign* law are generally treated as calling for expert evidence: obviously matters of English law are for the judge to determine.) However, it will not be easy to satisfy a judge that a witness is an expert in a field if he lacks formal qualifications.

It has sometimes been said that an expert witness would be disqualified from giving evidence in a trial if he or she had an interest in the proceedings (see, for example, *Liverpool Roman Catholic Archdiocesan Trustees Inc v Goldberg (No 3)* [2001] 1 WLR 2337). Such a situation might arise where the expert is an employee of one of the litigants, or is related to one. It ought to be clear that the expert owes an overriding duty to the court, not to himself or herself or to a litigant (see, for example, CPR, r 35.3). Currently, the position is that a litigant who wishes to call an expert as a witness should disclose to the other litigant(s) and the court any interest that the expert has, or may seem to have. That interest will not automatically disqualify the expert, although disqualification may be required on the facts of the particular case. It has been said that it is 'the nature and extent of the interest or connection which matters, not the mere fact of the interest or connection' (see Nelson J in *Armchair Passenger Transport Ltd v Helical Bar plc* [2003] EWHC 367). Apparent bias is not enough to disqualify an expert from being called as a witness. The key questions are:

- Does the person have relevant expertise.

- Is he or she aware of the overriding duty as an expert to the court, and is willing and able to fulfil it?

If allowed to testify, the interest or connection may still be relevant to the weight of the evidence given by the expert. In conclusion, 'it is always desirable that an expert should have no actual or apparent interest in the outcome of the proceedings in which he gives evidence', according to Lord Phillips MR in *Factortame Ltd v Secretary of State for the Environment, Transport and the Regions (No 8)* [2002] 3 WLR 1104.

### 12.3.3  Status of expert evidence

Expert evidence should be treated like the evidence of any other witness. It is a misdirection to tell a jury that they must accept it. See, for example, the speech of Lord Diplock in *R v Lanfear* [1968] 2 QB 77. However, in *R v Anderson* [1972] 1 QB 304 it was held that it would equally be a misdirection to tell a jury that it could disregard expert evidence which had been given by only one witness and which, if accepted, dictated one answer. See also, to the same effect, *R v Bailey* (1978) 66 Cr App R 31.

In civil cases, it has been said that:

even though it is always for the judge rather than for the expert witness to determine matters of fact, the judge must do so on the basis of the evidence, including the expert evidence. The mere application [by a judge] of 'common sense' cannot conjure up a proper basis for inferring that an injury must have been caused in one way rather than another when the only relevant evidence is undisputed scientific evidence which says that either way is equally possible.

See Lord Rodger of Earlsferry in *Fairchild v Glenhaven Funeral Services Ltd* [2002] 3 All ER 305, HL. Similarly, where two or more experts have been called as witnesses:

'a coherent reasoned opinion expressed by a suitably qualified expert should be the subject of a coherent reasoned rebuttal'. This does not mean that the judgment should contain a passage which suggests that the judge has applied the same, or even a superior, degree of expertise to that displayed by the witness. He should simply provide an explanation as to why he has accepted the evidence of one expert and rejected that of another. It may be that the evidence of one or the other accorded more satisfactorily with facts found by the judge. It may be that the explanation of one was more inherently credible than that of the other. It may simply be that one was better qualified, or manifestly more objective, than the other. Whatever the explanation may be, it should be apparent from the judgment.

See Lord Phillips of Worth Matravers MR in *English v Emery Reimbold and Strick Ltd* [2002] 3 All ER 385.

The dilemma for judges (and other fact-finders) in relying on expert evidence is well illustrated in the tragic case of Angela Cannings (*R v Cannings* [2004] EWCA Crim 1), a mother convicted of the murders of two of her children on the basis of expert evidence as to sudden infant deaths. Quashing her convictions, the Court of Appeal observed that:

> Not so long ago, experts were suggesting that new born babies should lie on their tummies. That was advice based on the best-informed analysis. Nowadays, the advice and exhortation is that babies should sleep on their backs...This advice is equally drawn from the best possible known sources. It is obvious that these two views cannot both simultaneously be right...[R]esearch in Australia [suggests] that the advice that babies should sleep on their backs had not achieved the improvement in the rate of cot deaths attributed to modern practice ...Our point is to highlight the fact that even now contrasting views on what might be thought to have been settled once and for all are current.

### 12.3.4    Upon what can an expert base an opinion?

An expert's opinion will be based upon much more than the facts of the particular case he is considering. It will be based on the expert's experience and any information that he has obtained from extraneous sources such as textbooks, articles and journals. Such information (often referred to as secondary facts) is not treated as hearsay but simply as part of the basis for the expert opinion. Obviously the facts of the particular case on which the opinion is given (the primary facts) should be proved by admissible evidence (whether or not by the expert).

For example, an expert valuer of antiques may be called to give opinion evidence of the value of certain Chinese vases. Her opinion may be based on her own knowledge of previous sale prices of similar vases; it may also be based on secondary facts — reports of sales at foreign auction rooms, or books published for the antiques trade specialist. However, if her valuation is based on the 'primary fact' that these vases date from the era of the Ming dynasty in China and are in excellent condition, these primary facts must themselves be proved by admissible evidence. This might be done either by this witness testifying about what she observed when looking at the vases (maker's marks, absence of cracks, chips, etc) or by calling other witnesses who have examined the vases. Thus, our expert may need dual expertise — first, on current sale room prices for excellent quality Ming vases; secondly, how to identify an 'excellent quality Ming vase'. See generally *English Exporters (London) Ltd v Eldonwall Ltd* [1973] Ch 415 and *H v Schering Chemicals Ltd* [1983] 1 WLR 143. Compare *R v Bradshaw* (1986) Cr App R 79, in which 'as a concession to the defence' a psychiatrist was allowed to base his opinion as to the accused's mental state upon statements made out of court by the accused (ie, hearsay).

In *R v Jackson* [1996] 2 Cr App R 420 the Court of Appeal held that although strictly speaking an expert witness should not give an opinion based on scientific tests which had been made by assistants (in the expert's absence), maximum use should be made of written statements and formal admissions in proving such tests where it is not disputed that the tests were properly carried out.

A good example of the difference between primary and secondary facts is *R v Abadom* (1983) 76 Cr App R 48. A was charged with robbery. An expert gave opinion evidence that glass found on A's shoes came from a window which had been broken during the robbery. Samples of glass taken from the shoes and the window had the same refractive index. The expert stated that, according to statistics produced by the Home Office Research Establishment, the chances of the glass being from two distinct sources were minimal. A was convicted and appealed on the grounds that the statistics were hearsay. The Court of Appeal held that the statistics were secondary facts supporting the expert's opinion. So long as the primary facts (ie, that the samples compared were (a) glass taken from A's shoes and (b) glass from the robbery scene and they shared the same refractive index) were proved by admissible evidence, the expert could (indeed should) state why he arrived at his opinion on those facts.

Secondary facts cannot be introduced as evidence in the absence of an expert's opinion. For example, on a drink-driving charge a defendant who is not a medical expert cannot refer to a medical journal to support his defence. See *Dawson v Lunn* [1986] RTR 234. Note that when the CJA 2003, s 127 comes into force, it will allow proof of the primary facts through hearsay evidence in criminal cases.

### 12.3.5   Advance notice of expert evidence

#### 12.3.5.1   Civil cases

The Civil Evidence Act 1972, s 2(3), made provision for rules of court to be made in relation to advance notice of expert evidence in civil cases. By CPR, r 35.13, a party who fails to disclose an expert's report may not use the report at the trial or call the expert to give evidence orally unless the court gives permission.

A party should be sure that he wishes to use the expert's report as evidence in his case *before* disclosing it to the other side. CPR, r 35.11, provides that *any* party to whom such a report is disclosed can put it in evidence. In general an expert's advice which is sought by a party for the purposes of pending or contemplated litigation would be protected from disclosure (at any stage of the proceedings) by legal professional privilege (see **Chapter 14** of this Manual) but r 35.11 makes it clear that the privilege is lost once the report has been disclosed under the advance notice procedure.

Even where a party relies on legal professional privilege in respect of an expert's opinion, it should be remembered that there is no property in a witness. A party who chooses not to use an expert's evidence can claim privilege in respect of the expert's opinion given to that party but he cannot muzzle the expert. Other parties to that litigation are entitled to instruct the expert and seek his opinion (subject to the procedural restrictions): see *Harmony Shipping Co SA v Saudi Europe Line Ltd* [1979] 1 WLR 1380, CA.

The amount of expert evidence which can be used in civil cases is affected by CPR, r 35.7(1), which provides:

*Where two or more parties wish to submit expert evidence on a particular issue, the court may direct that the evidence on that issue is to be given by one expert only.*

Unless the parties agree on the expert under this rule, the court may select an expert from a list submitted by the parties, or direct how the expert should be selected. Once selected, each instructing party may give instructions to the expert, sending a copy to the other instructing parties.

#### 12.3.5.2   Criminal cases

The prosecution are obliged to disclose their expert evidence to the defence (see the *Criminal Litigation and Sentencing Manual*). The defence are also obliged to disclose such evidence. In the Crown Court, rules require any party proposing to adduce expert evidence to furnish the other parties with a written statement of the expert's finding or opinion. Such party then, *on request* in writing by any other party, must provide a copy of, or opportunity to examine, the record of any observation, test or calculation on which the finding or opinion is based. For the Crown Court rules, see the Crown Court (Advance Notice of Expert Evidence) Rules 1987, SI 1987/716, made pursuant to the Police and Criminal Evidence Act 1984, s 81, and the Crown Court (Advance Notice of Expert Evidence) (Amendment) Rules 1997. By virtue of the Criminal Procedure and Investigations Act 1996, similar provisions now apply to expert evidence in the magistrates' court (see SI 1997/705).

A party may elect not to comply with the rules on disclosure if that party has reasonable grounds for believing that compliance might lead to intimidation or attempted intimidation of an expert witness or to interference with the course of justice. In those circumstances, the party must give notice of the grounds for non-compliance to the other parties. If the rules are not complied with in other circumstances, the expert evidence can only be used with the court's permission.

### 12.3.6    Opinion evidence and the hearsay rule

#### 12.3.6.1    In civil cases

In civil proceedings, hearsay statements are rendered admissible by the Civil Evidence Act 1995, subject to ss 5 and 6(2) of the Act. 'Statement' is defined in s 13 of the Act for the purpose of civil proceedings as 'any representation of fact *or opinion* however made' (emphasis added). Accordingly, the fact that opinion evidence is presented as hearsay will not generally affect its admissibility in civil cases. This will apply to both expert opinion evidence (typically in the form of an expert report) and also to statements of opinion by witnesses of fact (where covered by CEA 1972, s 3(2)).

#### 12.3.6.2    In criminal cases

By the Criminal Justice Act 1988, s 30:

*(1)   An expert report shall be admissible as evidence in criminal proceedings, whether or not the person making it attends to give oral evidence in those proceedings.*

*(2)   If it is proposed that the person making the report shall not give oral evidence, the report shall only be admissible with the leave of the court.*

*(3)   For the purpose of determining whether to give leave the court shall have regard—*

> *(a)   to the contents of the report;*
> *(b)   to the reasons why it is proposed that the person making the report shall not give oral evidence;*
> *(c)   to any risk, having regard in particular to whether it is likely to be possible to controvert statements in the report if the person making it does not attend to give oral evidence in the proceedings, that its admission or exclusion will result in unfairness to the accused or, if there is more than one, to any of them; and*
> *(d)   to any other circumstances that appear to the court to be relevant.*

*(4)   An expert report, when admitted, shall be evidence of any fact or opinion of which the person making it could have given oral evidence.*

> *In this section 'expert report' means a written report by a person dealing wholly or mainly with matters on which he is (or would if living be) qualified to give expert evidence.*

*(4A) Where the proceedings mentioned in subsection (1) above are proceedings before a magistrates' court inquiring into an offence as examining justices this section shall have effect with the omission of—*

> *(a)   in subsection (1) the words 'whether or not the person making it attends to give oral evidence in those proceedings', and*
> *(b)   subsections (2) to (4).*

This section applies to statements of fact *and* opinion in the expert report. The effect is clear. It creates a hearsay exception specifically directed at expert reports. When the expert attends as a witness the report is admissible without leave. However, where the expert is not available as a witness the court's leave to use the report is required.

There is no specific provision applicable to criminal cases to allow out-of-court statements which are essentially shorthand for facts perceived (cp. the CEA 1972, s 3(2)). However, when the CJA 2003, ss 114 and 115 come into force, they will allow out-of-court statements to be used in evidence, whether they are statements of fact or opinion (see **9.5**).

# Judgments as evidence of the facts on which they are based

## 13.1 Introduction

How might a case which has already been decided be relevant to a current case?

The judgment in the earlier case may have established a legal principle or precedent that is relevant to the legal issues in the current case.

Alternatively, the parties and the issues in the two cases may be the same. It may be necessary to refer to the judgment in the earlier case to prevent unnecessary repetition of litigation. In a civil case, we might refer to the concept of *res judicata*, and say that the earlier case establishes an issue estoppel (or a cause of action estoppel) between these litigants. Legal certainty requires an end to litigation. Likewise, in a criminal case, the accused can enter a special plea, either *autrefois acquit* or *autrefois convict*, to prevent successive proceedings for the same crime. This principle is often described in criminal cases as the rule against double jeopardy. For more information, you should consult the practitioner texts concerned with these topics.

A third possibility is that the facts that were proved in the earlier case may be relevant to the facts in issue in the current case. An example is the use of similar fact evidence (see **Chapter 6** above).

## 13.2 General rule

The general rule is that such judgments are inadmissible if offered in later trials as evidence of the facts upon which they were based. This rule is often regarded as having been established in a civil case: *Hollington v F Hewthorn and Co Ltd* [1943] KB 587 (hence, the rule is often referred to as the rule in *Hollington v Hewthorn*). Mr Hollington brought a civil claim for damages for the death of his son, caused in a road accident. His cause of action was the allegedly negligent driving of the defendant's employee. The court held that it was not possible to call evidence of the employee's conviction for driving without due care and attention on that specific occasion in order to prove the facts on which that conviction was based. To succeed on the issue of negligence, Mr Hollington had to call evidence, starting from scratch. The driver's conviction was not conclusive on the issue of negligence (it was not an irrebuttable presumption). It did not place the legal burden of proof on the party disputing the fact in issue to refute the conviction (it was not a rebuttable presumption). The conviction did not weigh in the scales at all — it was simply inadmissible and so unusable as evidence.

One consequence of this judgment was that proceedings in the civil courts were often extended unnecessarily because (unless the facts were admitted by the convicted party) the same issues had to be proved all over again. The inconvenience of this general rule is obvious. A further unfortunate consequence was that in some civil trials, matters which had already been established beyond reasonable doubt (in a criminal trial) were not found to be established to the lower standard of proof, on the balance of probabilities. That inconsistency was a matter for serious concern (although, in fairness, we should observe that the evidence in the two trials might have been different).

An example of the sort of problem thrown up by this rule is found in *Hinds v Sparks* [1964] Crim LR 717. Hinds had been tried for and convicted of a robbery and had appealed unsuccessfully to the Court of Criminal Appeal. Later, a journalist, Sparks, published a statement asserting that Hinds had committed a robbery some years previously. Hinds sued Sparks for defamation. The law of defamation requires the defendant to prove the truth of his assertion. Sparks was unable to produce any evidence to support his assertion, other than the robbery conviction. Unfortunately, the rule in *Hollington v Hewthorn* made that evidence inadmissible to show Hinds had committed a robbery. Hinds won his claim.

There are now a number of exceptions to the rule in civil and criminal proceedings. With one exception, these relate to the admissibility of previous convictions. In only one example is the conviction conclusive evidence of the facts upon which it was based (see Civil Evidence Act 1968, s 13, **13.3.3** below). We shall look at the exceptions in civil cases, then criminal cases.

## 13.3   Use of a previous judgment as evidence of the facts in civil cases

### 13.3.1   Use of a criminal conviction as evidence of the facts upon which it was based in a subsequent civil case

The Civil Evidence Act 1968, s 11, reverses the actual decision in *Hollington v F Hewthorn and Co Ltd* [1943] KB 587 (ie, the conviction for driving without due care would now be admissible evidence in the civil trial to help Mr Hollington prove negligence). It therefore creates a major exception to the general rule. Section 11 puts the legal burden of proof on to the party (let's call him X) who denies that the person convicted of the offence in question did commit it. Section 11 does not say that the conviction is conclusive of the facts; it simply creates a rebuttable presumption.

*Civil Evidence Act 1968, section 11*

(1)  *In any civil proceedings the fact that a person has been convicted of an offence by or before any court in the United Kingdom or by a court-martial there or elsewhere shall (subject to subsection (3) below) be admissible in evidence for the purpose of proving, where to do so is relevant to any issue in those proceedings, that he committed that offence, whether he was so convicted upon a plea of guilty or otherwise and whether or not he is a party to the civil proceedings; but no conviction other than a subsisting one shall be admissible in evidence by virtue of this section.*

(2)  *In any civil proceedings in which by virtue of this section a person is proved to have been convicted of an offence by or before any court in the United Kingdom or by a court-martial there or elsewhere—*

(a)  *he shall be taken to have committed that offence unless the contrary is proved; and*

(b)    *without prejudice to the reception of any other admissible evidence for the purpose of identifying the facts on which the conviction was based, the contents of any document which is admissible as evidence of the conviction, and the contents of the information, complaint, indictment or charge-sheet on which the person in question was convicted, shall be admissible in evidence for that purpose.*

(3)    *Nothing in this section shall prejudice the operation of section 13 of this Act or any other enactment whereby a conviction or a finding of fact in any criminal proceedings is for the purposes of any other proceedings made conclusive evidence of any fact.*

(4)    *Where in any civil proceedings the contents of any document are admissible in evidence by virtue of subsection (2) above, a copy of that document, or of the material part thereof, purporting to be certified or otherwise authenticated by or on behalf of the court or authority having custody of that document shall be admissible in evidence and shall be taken to be a true copy of that document or part unless the contrary is shown.*

To test your understanding of s 11, turn to **Appendix 1** and try **activity 13.1**.

### 13.3.2    Challenging a conviction

Remember, X is the party against whom the presumption in s 11 will operate. How should X go about rebutting this presumption? This question has been considered by the courts on several occasions. The prevailing view is that it will not avail X simply to challenge the technical correctness of the conviction. X must prove either:

- that he or she (or whoever else was convicted) did not commit the crime; or

- that the crime was not committed at all.

The practical consequence of s 11 is that it is extremely difficult for a party to challenge successfully the presumption that the person convicted did in fact commit the offence in question. One need simply note the different standards of proof involved in securing the criminal conviction (beyond reasonable doubt) and in the civil trial (balance of probabilities). See *Stupple v Royal Insurance Co Ltd* [1971] 1 QB 50, *Taylor v Taylor* [1970] 1 WLR 1148 and *Wauchope v Mordechai* [1970] 1 WLR 317.

It has been said (in *Brinks Ltd v Abu Saleh (No 1)* [1995] 4 All ER 65 by Jacob J) that a convicted defendant must adduce fresh evidence which 'entirely changes the aspect of the case' in order to be permitted to contest a civil action based on the same facts. Others have since argued that this requirement to adduce fresh evidence which 'entirely changes the aspect of the case' is a very difficult one to surmount and, if it were applied generally, the effect would be to prevent a convicted defendant from ever contesting a civil claim. The matter was considered in *J v Oyston* [1999] 1 WLR 694.

The defendant [O] was convicted by a jury of raping J, and indecently assaulting her. Subsequently, J sued the defendant for damages. O now wished to call evidence about J (the claimant/complainant), which had not been produced at his criminal trial, although it had been put before the Court of Appeal when he appealed unsuccessfully against his conviction. J asserted that to allow O to call evidence which was intended to show that no crime had been committed would constitute an abuse of process and should not be allowed. Smedley J rejected that assertion. Smedley J ruled that it was entirely legitimate for O to seek to disprove allegations of rape and indecent assault, notwithstanding his convictions for both offences. In effect, J wanted to stop O from doing precisely that which s 11(2)(a) permitted him to do. That would be quite contrary to the intention of Parliament as enshrined in s 11 and as interpreted by Lord Diplock in *Hunter v Chief Constable of the West Midlands Police* [1982] AC 529. It may be difficult for a party successfully to rebut a presumption under s 11, but it must be a matter for that party to decide whether or not he or she wants to attempt it.

Conversely, it seems that where a *claimant* seeks to re-litigate a matter which has already been determined against him or her by a criminal court (that is, a convicted defendant seeks to challenge the correctness of the conviction by initiating a civil claim against the prosecuting authority), the claim is likely to be struck out as an abuse of process under CPR, r 3.4(2)(b); see *Hunter v Chief Constable of the West Midlands Police* (and cf. Civil Evidence Act 1968, s 13, below).

Section 11 only applies to subsisting convictions. If a party in a civil claim wishes to use a conviction under s 11, the civil proceedings should be adjourned until any pending criminal appeal has been heard: see *Re Raphael* [1973] 1 WLR 998. A party seeking to rely on s 11 should state this clearly in the appropriate statement of case (see the **Drafting Manual** at **9.3**, for example). This should include details of the conviction and the issue to which it is relevant. Section 11(4) allows a certified copy of the conviction, indictment etc to be used to prove the facts on which the conviction was based.

### 13.3.3   Use of convictions in defamation cases

A convicted criminal might try to use libel proceedings to reopen a criminal case which resulted in his conviction (in similar vein to Mr Hinds, **13.2**). Section 11 would not prevent this because it only creates a rebuttable presumption. Now, in this situation a defendant could try to persuade the judge that the claim should be struck out as an abuse of process (under CPR, r 3.4; cf *Hunter v Chief Constable of the West Midlands Police* [1982] AC 529, **13.3.2**). That application might or might not succeed. This specific situation was addressed by s 13 of the Civil Evidence Act 1968, which creates an irrebuttable presumption that the person convicted of the crime did in fact commit it.

*Civil Evidence Act 1968, section 13*

(1)  *In an action for libel or slander in which the question whether a person did or did not commit a criminal offence is relevant to an issue arising in the action, proof that, at the time when that issue falls to be determined, that person stands convicted of that offence shall be conclusive evidence that he committed that offence; and his conviction thereof shall be admissible in evidence accordingly.*

(2)  *In any such action as aforesaid in which by virtue of this section a person is proved to have been convicted of an offence the contents of any document which is admissible as evidence of the conviction, and the contents of the information, complaint, indictment or charge-sheet on which that person was convicted, shall, without prejudice to the reception of any other admissible evidence for the purpose of identifying the facts on which the conviction was based, be admissible in evidence for the purpose of identifying those facts.*

(3)  *For the purposes of this section a person shall be taken to stand convicted of an offence if but only if there subsists against him a conviction of that offence by or before a court in the United Kingdom or by a court-martial there or elsewhere.*

The effect of s 13 is that an action in defamation will be struck out if it is based on the defendant's assertion that the claimant committed an offence for which the claimant has been convicted. In other words, in defamation cases a person convicted of an offence is *conclusively* presumed to have committed it. Some care still needs to be taken, though — s 13 does not give publishers carte blanche to make *general* attacks on the character of convicts (see *Levene v Roxhan* [1970] 1 WLR 1322).

### 13.3.4    Use of a criminal acquittal as evidence of the facts upon which it was based in a subsequent civil case

An acquittal is not covered by any exception in the Civil Evidence Act 1968, so it appears that the rule in *Hollington v Hewthorn* still applies: the acquittal is inadmissible evidence if it will be used to show that the criminal defendant did not commit the offence. This may be justified by reference once more to the different standards of proof which apply in the two trials. See further *Blackstone's Civil Practice*, 2004.

### 13.3.5    Use of a civil judgment as evidence of the facts upon which it was based in a subsequent civil case

There is no *general* provision allowing for previous civil judgments to be used as evidence of the facts on which they were based. However, s 12 of the Civil Evidence Act 1968, allows a very limited range of civil judgments to be used as evidence of the facts on which they are based. See *Blackstone's Civil Practice*, 2004.

## 13.4    Use of a previous judgment as evidence of the facts in criminal cases

### 13.4.1    Use of a criminal conviction as evidence of the facts upon which it was based in a subsequent criminal case

Remember that previous judgments are often used in criminal cases. When a witness is cross-examined, they may be asked about their convictions with a view to undermining their credibility (see **5.3.3.4**). Where similar fact evidence is admissible, the defendant's previous convictions may be produced as evidence (see **Chapter 7**). If the defendant attacks the character of a prosecution witness, or asserts his own good character, his previous convictions may be put in as evidence in the trial (see **Chapter 6**). In most of these situations, all that matters is the fact of the conviction — the offence, the date — not the facts upon which it was based.

Until relatively recently the common law rule excluding judgments as evidence of the facts on which they are based was of general application in criminal cases. For example, where A was charged with handling stolen goods, it was not permissible to prove that B was convicted of the theft of the goods in question to show that the goods were stolen. You may wonder why a rule established in a civil case (*Hollington v Hewthorn*) should hold sway in criminal cases, too. In fact, the rule in criminal cases pre-dates *Hollington v Hewthorn*. The example that you have just read is taken from *R v Turner* (1832) 1 Mood CC 347.

For convictions, the rule has been changed by the Police and Criminal Evidence Act 1984, s 74. A distinction needs to be drawn between (a) convictions of the accused and (b) convictions of persons other than the accused.

#### 13.4.1.1    Convictions of the accused

Police and Criminal Evidence Act 1984, s 74(3), as amended by the CJA 2003, provides:

> *In any proceedings where evidence is admissible of the fact that the accused has committed an offence, if the accused is proved to have been convicted of the offence—*
>
> (a)  *by or before any court in the United Kingdom; or*
>
> (b)  *by a Service court outside the United Kingdom,*
>
> *he shall be taken to have committed that offence unless the contrary is proved.*

The general rule is that evidence that the accused has previously offended is inadmissible at his trial (see **Chapters 6** and **7**). This is so, regardless of whether or not the accused was actually convicted of the earlier offence. In exceptional situations, the fact that the accused has previously offended *may* be relevant and admissible (see CJA 2003, s 101). Where one of these exceptional situations applies, the prosecution can take advantage of s 74(3). This provision works in the same way as CEA 1968, s 11(2). It sets up a rebuttable presumption that the convict did indeed commit the crime.

Section 74(3) does *not* deal with questions of admissibility. All it says is that, where it is relevant and admissible to prove that D committed an offence, the act of adducing evidence that he has been convicted of it results in a rebuttable presumption. It will then be for D to try to prove, on a balance of probabilities, that he did not commit the offence.

To test your understanding of this, try **activity 13.2** in **Appendix 1** now.

So, remember what we are looking for. These are situations where it is relevant and admissible to show that the accused has previously *committed* an offence. In such situations, if the prosecution prove his conviction for the earlier offence, they can rely on s 74(3) to reverse the burden of proof on that fact. This still begs the question, How does the prosecution prove the conviction? See **13.4.1.3**.

### 13.4.1.2  Convictions of persons other than the accused

In 1972, the 11th Report of the Criminal Law Revision Committee had recommended the abolition of the rule in *Hollington v Hewthorn* in criminal proceedings. The Committee apparently thought that it was recommending simply that a conviction would be admissible in evidence to deal with the situation 'where it was necessary as a preliminary matter for it to be proved that a person other than the accused had been convicted of an offence' (see *R v O'Connor* (1986) 85 Cr App R 298, per Taylor J). This would ease the burden on the prosecution in the following situations, for example:

- In a trial for handling stolen goods, in order to prove that the goods were stolen the prosecution could prove the conviction of the thief.

- In trials for harbouring offenders, the prosecution could prove the conviction of the offender.

The Police and Criminal Evidence Act 1984, s 74(1) and (2), provide:

> (1)  *In any proceedings the fact that a person other than the accused has been convicted of an offence by or before any court in the United Kingdom or by a Service court outside the United Kingdom shall be admissible in evidence for the purpose of proving, where to do so is relevant to any issue in those proceedings, that that person committed that offence, whether or not any other evidence of his having committed that offence is given.*
>
> (2)  *In any proceedings in which by virtue of this section a person other than the accused is proved to have been convicted of an offence by or before any court in the United Kingdom or by a Service court outside the United Kingdom, he shall be taken to have committed that offence unless the contrary is proved.*

That seems quite straightforward. The effect of s 74(2) is very similar to the effect of the Civil Evidence Act 1968, s 11(2), in civil cases. That is, it puts the legal burden of proof on the party who denies that the convicted person committed the offence in question (of course the *standard* of proof in a criminal case will vary according to whether that party is the prosecution or the defence). However, judicial interpretation of s 74(1) has caused considerable difficulties in practice.

Those difficulties began with the judgment of the Court of Appeal in *R v Robertson* (1987) 85 Cr App R 304. The court considered the proper interpretation of the phrase in s 74(1) 'where to do so is relevant to any issue in those proceedings'. Lord Lane CJ observed that this clearly encompassed an issue which is an essential ingredient of the offence charged. That was consistent with the thinking of the Criminal Law Revision Committee. However, Lord Lane continued, 'The word "issue" ... is apt to cover also less fundamental issues, for example evidential issues arising during the course of proceedings'.

*Robertson* itself involved the use in evidence of guilty pleas to several burglaries given by R's co-accused. All of the defendants were originally charged with conspiracy to commit burglary and R was tried on that allegation. The prosecution introduced the guilty pleas to prove that there was a conspiracy. The only live issue left then was whether R had been a party to it or not.

The Court of Appeal said in *Robertson* that s 74 was 'a provision that should be sparingly used'. Following the judgment, there have been several reported cases where the prosecution allege that the accused was very closely involved in an offence, of which another person has been convicted, and the prosecution wish to use that conviction in evidence. It seems that the conviction is admissible subject to the discretion to exclude it pursuant to s 78 of the 1984 Act. The most common reason for invoking s 78 is where the conviction clearly and of itself implies the guilt of the accused standing trial. See *Blackstone's Criminal Practice* 2004 or *Archbold* 2004 for more detailed reviews of the relevant cases.)

In *R v Mahmood* [1997] 1 Cr App R 414, the Court of Appeal held that in deciding whether evidence of a guilty plea should be admitted, a judge is required to apply a two-stage test:

(a) The judge must determine whether the guilty plea is clearly relevant to an issue in the accused's trial (application of s 74(1)). If it is, then

(b) the judge should consider any prejudice to the accused in respect of the fairness of the proceedings (application of s 78).

The judge must then exercise his or her discretion accordingly.

In *Mahmood* the two accused and a third man, L, were charged with raping the complainant (C) one after another. L pleaded guilty. There were several live issues at the trial:

- whether C consented;
- whether the accused believed C was consenting;
- whether C was incapable of consenting.

The trial judge allowed the prosecution to call evidence of L's guilty plea. The Court of Appeal held the judge had erred. The main difficulty was that the judge had not known the basis on which L had pleaded guilty. There were several bases on which he could have done so which were consistent with being guilty of rape. It was essential that the judge should have had that information in order to be able to identify the relevant issue for the jury in the appellant's trial.

To test your understanding, try **activity 13.3** in **Appendix 1**.

It should be noted that s 74(1) only provides a short cut for proving matters which otherwise may be proved by calling a witness. For example, in a case where one of several defendants has entered a guilty plea, the prosecution can then call the former co-defendant to testify for the Crown against the rest. In that event the remaining defendants can then cross-examine the former co-defendant, on both the facts and his credibility. The trial judge may also warn the jury to take care when assessing the evidence of the former co-defendant. By using s 74(1) instead, the opportunity of cross-examination and the need for a 'care' warning are both removed. It is arguable that this situation could deny the accused a fair trial, contrary to the European Convention on Human Rights, art 6. Perhaps this is why the Court of Appeal said (in *Robertson* and subsequent cases) that s 74(1) is to be used sparingly.

Section 74(1) will be amended by the Criminal Justice Act 2003, when Sch 36 of the CJA comes into force. The troublesome phrase from s 74(1) — *'where to do so is relevant to any issue in those proceedings, that that person committed that offence'* — will be deleted. The replacement looks like this — *'that that person committed that offence, where evidence of his having done so is admissible'*. This may be intended to make s 74(1) fit better with the new provisions on using evidence of non-defendants' bad character (in s 100 of the CJA 2003). It remains to be seen if this will be a significant change at all, let alone one for the better.

### 13.4.1.3 Proving a conviction

This is a two-limb process that can be done using PACE 1984, s 73(1) and (2).

One limb is that the prosecution must call a witness to produce the certificate of conviction. What qualifies as a certificate is explained in s 73(2). The other limb is that the prosecution must call a witness to say that the person named in the certificate is the accused in the dock. It could be the same witness for both limbs, usually a police officer.

> (1)  Where in any proceedings the fact that a person has in the United Kingdom been convicted or acquitted of an offence otherwise than by a Service court is admissible in evidence, it may be proved by producing a certificate of conviction or, as the case may be, of acquittal relating to that offence, and proving that the person named in the certificate as having been convicted or acquitted of the offence is the person whose conviction or acquittal of the offence is to be proved.
>
> (2)  For the purposes of this section a certificate of conviction or of acquittal—
>
>   (a)  shall, as regards a conviction or acquittal on indictment, consist of a certificate, signed by the [proper officer] of the court where the conviction or acquittal took place, giving the substance and effect (omitting the formal parts) of the indictment and of the conviction or acquittal; and
>
>   (b)  shall, as regards a conviction or acquittal on a summary trial, consist of a copy of the conviction or of the dismissal of the information, signed by the [proper officer] of the court where the conviction or acquittal took place or by the [proper officer] of the court, if any, to which a memorandum of the conviction or acquittal was sent;
>
>   and a document purporting to be a duly signed certificate of conviction or acquittal under this section shall be taken to be such a certificate unless the contrary is proved.

### 13.4.1.4 What does the conviction prove?

Where a conviction is introduced into evidence in a trial, the judge must be careful to direct the jury as to:

- what issue in the trial it relates to; and
- what the effect of the conviction is.

First, it is important for judge and counsel to be clear on the exact issue to which the conviction is said to be relevant. If it is liable to be misused by the jury, the judge should probably exclude evidence of the conviction, using PACE 1984, s 78. Secondly, the conviction is *not* conclusive evidence that an offence was committed by anyone. That is shown by s 74(2), which creates a rebuttable presumption. It was confirmed in *R v Dixon* [2001] Crim LR 126 that if the defendant testifies that no such offence was committed, it is for the jury to decide whose account to believe.

By PACE 1984, s 75(1):

*Where evidence that a person has been convicted of an offence is admissible by virtue of section 74 above, then without prejudice to the reception of any other admissible evidence for the purpose of identifying the facts on which the conviction was based—*

    *(a)   the contents of any document which is admissible as evidence of the conviction; and*

    *(b)   the contents of the ... indictment ... on which the person in question was convicted,*

    *shall be admissible in evidence for that purpose.*

### 13.4.2   Use of a criminal acquittal as evidence of the facts upon which it was based in a subsequent criminal case

This situation is unaffected by PACE 1984. If the acquittal is that of the defendant, D, then generally it will be inadmissible as evidence in the current trial. However, facts involved in the offence of which D was acquitted may be relevant now as similar fact evidence. The acquittal may then become admissible (see *R v Z* [2000] 2 AC 483; *R v Hay* (1983) 77 Cr App R 70).

If the acquittal is of someone other than the accused, generally it is inadmissible. Again, it may be relevant to an issue in the current case. An example may occur if the credibility of a witness is challenged (and the witness has previously testified for the prosecution in a trial where he allegedly fabricated a confession) (see *R v Cooke* (1987) 84 Cr App R 286). The general principle is illustrated by the decision of the Privy Council in *Hui Chi-ming v R* [1992] 1 AC 34. A man was killed. D1 and D2 were charged with his murder. D1, the alleged killer, was tried first. The jury acquitted him of murder but convicted him of manslaughter. At D2's trial, as an accomplice to murder, the defence wanted to use evidence of D1's acquittal for murder. The trial judge ruled that it was inadmissible. The ruling was upheld by the Privy Council on appeal, because the verdict of the first jury was irrelevant, being only evidence of their opinion. You may feel that this produces exactly the same result as *Hollington v Hewthorn*, nearly 50 years earlier, and could also be criticised. It may make more sense if you bear in mind that there are often seemingly inconsistent verdicts involving different parties to a single crime. Also, an acquittal simply records a failure by the prosecution to prove their case beyond a reasonable doubt. It does not do the opposite and prove that D is innocent. Of course, in a case like that of *Hui Chi-ming*, it would have been better for justice to have held a single trial of D1 and D2 before the same jury on the same evidence.

### 13.4.3   Use of a civil judgment as evidence of the facts upon which it was based in a subsequent criminal case

Due to the lower standard of proof in civil trials, any finding of fact would seem to be insufficiently probative to be admissible as evidence in a criminal trial.

## 13.5   Recap activities

To consolidate your understanding of this part, turn to **Appendix 1** and try **activity 13.4**.

# Privilege and public policy

## 14.1 Introduction

Most of the rules of evidence involve analysis of the value of the evidence to be admitted and lead to the exclusion of evidence that will not, for various reasons, be valuable evidence. However we did see that there are occasional wider social, political or moral considerations (for example the exclusion of 'unfair' evidence under s 78 or improperly obtained confessions even though they are prejudicial). However, generally the main concern of the rules of evidence in both civil and criminal cases is ensuring that the evidence that goes before the tribunal of fact will assist in proving the case. Even when policy reasons for excluding evidence arise, those policies (such as fairness or proportionality) are aspects of the interests of justice. However in this chapter we shall see situations in which the courts have excluded evidence irrespective of the demands of the interests of justice.

The rules of evidence considered in this chapter reflect this concern to ensure that the interests of justice do not lead to admitting evidence that will cause a greater damage to society. With 'privileged' evidence, the concern for broader interests of justice, have been taken to outweigh the interests of justice in any particular case. In the case of public policy exclusion the interests of justice are weighed against social and moral questions other than the interest of justice (for example national security).

Both privilege and public policy arguments are most likely to arise during the disclosure/discovery procedures. This is so in either civil cases (see the *Civil Litigation Manual* or *Blackstone's Civil Practice*, 2004, Chapter 48) or criminal cases (see the *Criminal Litigation and Sentencing Manual*, *Blackstone's Criminal Practice*, 2004 or *Archbold*, 2004).

## 14.2 Privilege

In broad terms the privileges which follow allow one (or in the case of 'without prejudice' correspondence either) party to prevent evidence from being put before the court on specific grounds. The types of privilege covered in this chapter are:

- The privilege against self-incrimination.
- Legal professional privilege
- 'Without prejudice' correspondence.

### 14.2.1    Privilege against self-incrimination

The privilege against self incrimination is a principle of English law that influenced the development of the law of evidence and procedure in a number of areas (particularly the exercise of the right to silence (**Chapter 10**) and the compellability of witnesses (**Chapter 4**)). The principle is also enshrined in Article 6(1) of the European Convention on Human Rights.

The privilege has a more general application. No person is obliged to reveal a fact if doing so renders it reasonably likely that proceedings will be commenced that expose him or her to the risk of any criminal charge or sanction (*Blunt v Park Lane Hotel Ltd* [1942] 2 KB 253). In explaining the above test in *R v Boyes* (1861) 1 B & S 311 Cockburn J said that the risk of prosecution and punishment must be 'real and appreciable with reference to the ordinary operation of the law in the ordinary course of things; not a danger of an imaginary and unsubstantial character'.

The rule does not apply where the risk posed is a civil liability (Witnesses Act 1806) or criminal liability under foreign law (*King of Two Sicilies v Willcox* (1851) 1 Sim NS 301; Civil Evidence Act 1968, s 14) but can extend to penalties under EC law (*Rio Tinto Zinc Corporation v Westinghouse Electric Company* [1978] AC 547).

The privilege extends not only to the evidence that the person might give but to documents, items or information that the person is requested to provide during proceedings.

#### 14.2.1.1    'Real and appreciable danger'

The evidence, document, etc must *create* the risk of incrimination. If there is already strong evidence against the witness on the matter to which the privilege is said to relate, the rule of exclusion will not apply (*Khan v Khan* [1982] 2 All ER 60).

Furthermore if the risk can be avoided, the privilege will not apply. So in *AT&T Istel v Tully* [1993] AC 45, HL, an offer by the CPS not to prosecute the defendant in respect of any frauds revealed was held to be sufficient protection for the defendant and therefore the privilege should not apply.

Where the sanction or punishment that is faced is trivial, the court may also conclude that there is no real and appreciable danger (*Rank Film Distributors Ltd v Video Information Centre* [1982] AC 380).

#### 14.2.1.2    To whom does the privilege apply?

In criminal cases the privilege only applies to the person asserting it. In other words, A could not exercise the privilege on the grounds that his answer would incriminate B (this is implicit from *R v Pitt* [1983] QB 25 where a witness was treated as compellable to give evidence against her spouse: this would not have been the case if she could have asserted a privilege against incriminating her spouse).

In civil cases the privilege does extend to spouses (Civil Evidence Act 1968, s 14(1)(b)) but no further.

Companies can be covered by the privilege (*Triplex Safety Glass Co Ltd v Lancegaye Safety Glass* [1939] 2 KB 395). However in such circumstances the privilege excuses an employee of the company from giving testimony (or disclosing evidence) that would incriminate the company; it does not excuse him or her from incriminating an employee of the company (*Rio Tinto Zinc v Westinghouse Electric*) other than himself.

#### 14.2.1.3    Privileged evidence that is revealed

If a witness answers questions without claiming the privilege (before or after but during the proceedings) the evidence can be used against the witness in subsequent proceedings

(*R v Coote* (1873) LR 4 PC 599). However if the witness does claim privilege and is wrongly refused (and therefore forced to answer), the evidence must be excluded in the subsequent proceedings (*R v Garbett* (1847) 1 Den CC 236).

### 14.2.1.4   Statutory exceptions

The privilege is subject to numerous statutory exceptions. First of all the privilege does not protect the accused in criminal proceedings from answering questions in respect of those proceedings (*Criminal Evidence Act 1898, s 1(2)*).

In the following situations evidence that reveals criminal conduct may be admitted in specific types of proceedings (the type of proceedings being illustrated in each situation below). However in each situation, there are restrictions on the extent to which the information revealed can be used in subsequent criminal proceedings:

(a) *Theft Act 1968, s 31(1)*: in proceedings concerning the recovery or administration of property, the execution of any trust or an account for property or dealings with property, a person is not excused from answering questions simply because doing so would reveal he or she may have committed an offence under the Theft Act 1968. However, any statement or testimony made as a result of this section is not admissible in a subsequent prosecution on the matter in question. This protection also extends to the spouse of the witness. If the evidence poses a real risk of both a Theft Act and a non-Theft Act prosecution the court will apply the privilege against self-incrimination (*Renworth Ltd v Stephansen* [1996] 3 All ER 244).

(b) The same provision exists in the *Criminal Damage Act 1971, s 9* relating to the same types of civil actions, but the criminal offences to which it relates are criminal damage offences.

(c) *Children Act 1989, s 98*: in proceedings concerning the care, supervision or protection of children, a person cannot refuse to answer questions on the grounds either that the person or his or her spouse would be incriminated. Again such evidence will not be admissible in subsequent proceedings except perjury proceedings (s 98(2)). It has been suggested that this protection extends to oral or written statements made before trial (*Oxfordshire County Council v P* [1995] 2 All ER 225, *Cleveland County Council v F* [1995] 2 All ER 236). However in *Re G (a minor)* [1996] 2 All ER 65, the Court of Appeal stated that the protection under s 98(2) should be restricted to evidence in the proceedings and not pre-trial statements. However the court recognised that the criminal courts were not bound by that view. In *A Chief Constable v A County Council* [2002] EWHC 2198 (Fam), the court took the view that statements made by parents to expert witnesses appointed by the court would be covered by s 98(2) privilege and therefore would not be admissible in subsequent criminal proceedings. Clearly such statements would be made before trial.

(d) *Criminal Justice Act 1987*, s 2: The Director of the Serious Fraud Office has broad powers to investigate persons in respect of offences of serious or complex fraud (ie those under Part 1 of that Act). Persons investigated can be required to answer questions or provide documentation. Such evidence can only be used at a later trial if the person is being prosecuted for the offence of providing false information under s 2 or subsequently makes a statement inconsistent with it (ie as a previous inconsistent statement: see **5.3.4**).

(e) *Insolvency Act 1986*: various statements that must be made under this Act could be incriminating. Section 433(1) of the Act provides that such statements may be used in evidence against the person who made them in subsequent proceedings. Section

433(2), however states that in subsequent criminal proceedings such statements may only be admitted (or questions asked about them) if the person who made the statement has already admitted evidence relating to that statement. This restriction does not apply in relation to perjury and related proceedings or criminal proceedings under the Insolvency Act.

(f) Similar restrictions to those under the Insolvency Act apply in relation to investigations under the *Companies Act 1985, ss 434 and 447* and various other statutes in Sch 3 to the Youth Justice and Criminal Evidence Act 1999.

Insofar as any other statute appears to have revoked the privilege against self-incrimination without any restriction upon the extent to which statements made can be used in subsequent criminal proceedings, there is a potential breach of Article 6(1) of the European Convention but this is not always so. In *Brown v Stott* [2001] 2 WLR 817, the Privy Council recognised that Article 6 allows limited qualification of the rights contained in it. Where there was a clear public interest in revoking the privilege, the statutory provision would not necessarily be held to be incompatible with Article 6. In *Office of Fair Trading v X* [2003] 2 All ER (Comm) 183, the High Court upheld powers to search premises and to question persons present about items found where the statutory framework for such searches included guarantees of a suspects' rights.

### 14.2.2    Legal professional privilege

Both civil and criminal litigation depends upon parties having access to effective legal advice. This in turn depends upon a party and his or her lawyer being able to communicate freely and without fear that the content of the discussion will be used by the other side. Furthermore legal professional privilege is a function of Article 6 of the European Convention on Human Rights.

There are two classes of legal professional privilege, which broadly are:

(a) Communications between a lawyer and his or her client (also known as 'lawyer-client privilege').

(b) Communications between the lawyer or client on the one hand and third parties on the other where such communication relates to pending or contemplated litigation: *Waugh v British Railways Board* [1980] AC 521 (also known as 'litigation privilege').

Under both classes the privilege applies to solicitors, barristers, foreign lawyers and in-house legal advisors (*Re Duncan* [1968] P 306; *Alfred Compton Amusement Machines Ltd v Customs & Excise Commissioners* [1974] AC 405).

#### 14.2.2.1    Lawyer-client privilege

Communications between a lawyer and his or her client for the purposes of obtaining or giving legal advice are privileged whether or not litigation is contemplated (*Greenough v Gaskell* (1833) 1 My & K 98).

The privilege clearly covers any requests for advice from a client to a lawyer and any advice given by the lawyer to the client. However, unlike litigation privilege (**14.2.2.2**) this privilege does not attach to communications between a lawyer or a client and a third party to the lawyer-client relationship. Therefore in *Wheeler v Le Marchant* (1881) 17 Ch D 675, no lawyer-client privilege could be attached to communications between a solicitor and a surveyor, the purpose of which communication was to provide advice concerning land included in a will. Therefore factual information communicated to a solicitor for the purpose of advice will not be protected when provided by a third party even if the third party was responding to a request for that information by the solicitor for the purpose of giving advice. In *Three Rivers District Council v Bank of England (No 5)* [2003] EWCA Civ 474, [2003] QB 1556, the Court of Appeal ruled that even internal communications between employees of the Bank of England would not be covered by lawyer-client privilege even though some of those communications were to and from employees responsible for seeking legal advice from the Bank's solicitors. It was only the communication between employees at the Bank and the Bank's solicitors that were covered by the privilege. However, if a communication to which privilege attaches is passed on to a third party or internally within an organisation, privilege will not be lost: *USP Strategies v London General Holdings Ltd and others* [2004] EWHC 373, Ch.

Lawyers do not restrict their advice and communication to explanation of the law. In *Belabel v Air India* [1988] Ch 317, Lord Taylor said at p 330:

> In most solicitor and client relationships, especially where a transaction involves protracted dealings, advice may be required [as] appropriate on matters great or small at various stages. There will be a continuum of communication and meetings between the solicitor and client...Where information is passed by the solicitor or client to the other as part of the continuum aimed at keeping both informed so that advice may be sought and given as required, privilege will attach...Moreover, legal advice is not confined to telling the client the law; it must include advice as to what should prudently and sensibly be done in the relevant legal context.

Even if between a solicitor and a client, only communications for the purposes of 'legal advice' are covered by this privilege. Therefore the purpose of any communication must be considered. In *Three Rivers District Council v Bank of England (No 10)* [2004] EWCA 373, Ch, the Court of Appeal concluded that 'legal advice' meant advice in relation to legal rights and obligations. Only such communications would be covered by this type of legal professional privilege. Therefore the provision of advice to the Bank of England concerning the presentation of evidence to an inquiry into the collapse of the private bank, BCCI, was held not to be 'legal advice' and therefore not covered by this sort of privilege.

However, lawyers do not restrict their advice to such matters. What if the purpose of the communication in question is mixed? In *Belabel v Air India* [1988] Ch 317, the Court of Appeal observed that whether communication was for the purposes of legal advice had to be interpreted broadly. In *Hellenic Mutual War Risks Association (Bermuda) Ltd v Harrison (The Sagheera)* [1997] 1 Lloyd's Rep 160, Rix J stated that documents would be privileged if the *dominant* purpose of the retainer (the employment of the lawyer) was the provision of legal advice. In both *Three Rivers District Council v Bank of England (No 5)* and *Three Rivers District Council v Bank of England (No 10)* (above), the Court of Appeal accepted without argument that 'purpose' in *Greenough v Gaskell* meant 'dominant purpose'. Therefore before lawyer-client privilege will attach to any communication, it must be established to have been predominantly about 'legal advice'.

The courts will not adopt a rigid or technical approach to determine whether one or more item is covered by lawyer-client privilege. As was noted above, in *Belabel* it was stated that the 'continuum' of communication rather than each individual communication is to be assessed when determining its purpose. However, in *United States of America v Philip Morris Inc* [2004] EWCA CIV 330, the Court of Appeal questioned the simple analysis of all communications under a solicitor's retainer and noted that *Belabel* had not created any rule that the 'continuum of communication' had to be entirely privileged or without privilege. In fact it was stated in *Belabel* that whether documents produced to note or record meetings would be covered by lawyer-client privilege would depend on whether they were 'part of that necessary exchange of information of which the object is the giving of legal advice as and when appropriate' (at p 332). The Court of Appeal in *USA v Morris* approved a decision of the judge at first instance not to award lawyer-client privilege to a series of communications but rather to order disclosure of all communications and to leave it to the respondent parties to claim privilege over any particular document when required. The effect of this judgment would appear to be to limit the extent of privilege to those documents which either requested or gave legal advice or (in the words used in *Belabel*) were 'necessary exchange of information of which the object is the giving of legal advice'. In *Belabel* the Court of Appeal held that whether communication was for the purposes of legal advice should be construed broadly but that did not necessarily mean that privilege only attached to communications asking for or receiving advice. There is extensive case law concerning what has or has not been considered to be covered by this head of privilege: see *Blackstone's Criminal Practice*, 2004, at F9.15.

Where the communication was intended to be passed on to other parties, such communications will not be privileged (*Conlon v Conlon's Ltd* [1952] 2 All ER 462). In *R (on the application of Hoare) v South Durham Justices* [2004] All ER (D) (Feb), the Divisional Court held that a solicitor could be called to prove the identity of his client and the fact of a previous conviction (at which the solicitor was present) without offending lawyer-client privilege.

It is not unusual for solicitors to provide advice on matters other than the law. When this happens the communication may or may not be privileged. In *Nederlandse Reassurantie Groep Holding v Bacon & Woodrow* [1995] 1 All ER 976 advice on the financial wisdom of a transaction was held to be privileged where it was provided along with advice about the legality of that transaction.

### 14.2.2.2    Third party or litigation privilege

The second class of legal professional privilege is aimed primarily at communications with potential experts of witnesses of fact although the rule is not restricted to persons in such classes.

Note that this class of privilege applies if either:

- the communication was between the party and a third party, or
- the communication was between the party's lawyer and a third party.

The key issue is whether the communication was for pending or contemplated litigation. Where the communication takes place before any dispute had arisen it is highly unlikely that it will be (*Wheeler v Le Marchant* (1881) 17 Ch D 675, CA). In *Re Highgrade Traders Ltd* [1984] BCLC 151, Oliver LJ at p 172 used the expression 'if litigation is reasonably in prospect' to define whether litigation was pending or contemplated and in *Mitsubishi Electric Australia Pty Ltd v Victorian Work Cover Authority* [2002] VSCA 59 an Australian court defined the test as 'a real prospect of litigation as distinct from a mere possibility'. This approach was approved in *United States of America v Philip Morris Inc* [2004] EWCA Civ 330, where it was noted that 'a mere possibility' of litigation being commenced would be inadequate.

In *Waugh v British Railways Board* [1980] AC 521, it was held that the dominant purpose had to be litigation. In that case the document in question was a report by an accident investigator that, it was alleged, had been prepared both so that the defendants could assess their liability in a crash and so that they could take steps to prevent any such accident from happening again. The House of Lords held that the two purposes had been of equal weight so the document was not privileged. Quite what the dominant purpose was will depend on the facts of each case.

In *Re L (A Minor) (Police Investigation: Privilege)* [1997] AC 16, the House of Lords decided that this type of privilege only applies in adversarial proceedings and therefore would not apply to advice concerning investigation and inquiries (see also *Three Rivers District Council v Bank of England (No 10)* (above), where it was accepted that communications in respect of a judicial enquiry formed by the government would not be privileged). Furthermore in *USA v Phillip Morris Inc* (above) it was stated that the prospect of a party being required to produce documents at the trial between two other parties did not amount to litigation for these purposes and therefore no privilege would attach to communication about such matters.

### 14.2.2.3   The effect of legal professional privilege

Communication falling under either class will not be admissible at trial unless the party who has the privilege waives it (see **14.2.2.4** below). The privilege renders the communications inadmissible and immune from discovery. However it does not prevent documents or items in the possession of the lawyer or third party from being admissible nor does it prevent the lawyer or third party from being called as a witness of fact on some matters (see **14.2.2.5** below). Furthermore there are two exceptions to the rule that communications are privileged (see **14.2.2.6** below).

The privilege is that of the client not of the lawyer or third party (*Schneider v Leigh* [1955] 2 QB 195).

The communication will remain privileged after the proceedings to which they relate has ended and will also pass to successors in title (*Minet v Morgan* (1873) 8 Ch App 361).

### 14.2.2.4   Waiver of privilege

As the privilege is that of the client, only he or she can waive it. Where the alleged waiver was made in excess of the powers of the person doing so, privilege will not have been waived: *GE Capital v Sutton* [2004] EWCA Civ 315. The court will look carefully at the circumstances of the waiver to determine whether and exactly how much of the privilege has been waived (*Great Atlantic Insurance Co v Home Insurance Co* [1981] 1 WLR 529).

Where a client has purported to waive privilege in respect of one matter or communication but not in respect of others, the court may infer that other communications have been waived (*General Accident Fire & Life Assurance Corporation Ltd v Tanter* [1984] 1 WLR 100). In large documents, the court will apply the waiver to the whole document unless parts of it are deemed to be distinct and severable in their nature (*British Coal Corporation v Dennis Rye Ltd (No 2)* [1988] 3 All ER 816).

Particular difficulties arise when a party is forced to give evidence as to the nature of discussions with his or her lawyer. This is most likely to be the case where the accused remains silent as a result of legal advice when questioned by the police and the prosecution in a criminal case seek to rely on s 34 of the Criminal Justice and Public Order Act 1994 (see **11.4.1.1**). To explain that such silence was not motivated by a consciousness of guilt, the lawyer may have to give evidence. In *R v Bowden* [1999] 2 Cr App R 176, the Court of Appeal concluded calling the lawyer in this way meant that he or she could be cross-examined as to the detail and reasons for the advice given and that it would be inappropriate for legal professional privilege to restrict this.

### 14.2.2.5   Limits on the scope of privilege

The privilege applies to the communications between lawyer and client not to facts that were perceived during the solicitor/client relationship such as the client's identity (*Studdy v Sanders* (1823) 2 Dow & Ry KB 347) or the fact of the client having attended the solicitor's office to receive advice (*R v Manchester Crown Court, ex p R* The Times, 15 February 1999).

Furthermore, documents or items do not become privileged simply because they are in the possession of a party's lawyer (*Dubai Bank v Galadari* [1989] 3 All ER 769). In *R v Peterborough Justice, ex p Hicks* [1977] 1 WLR 1371, the defendants were charged with forgery offences. The Court of Appeal refused to quash a warrant to search the party's solicitor's offices for allegedly forged documents stating that the solicitor had no better right to resist the warrant than the person upon whose behalf he or she held them. Therefore what determines whether or not such items can be obtained is whether the party has some right other than legal professional privilege to withhold them. This can be seen by contrasting the following two cases in which experts had received items of evidence for the purposes of advising a party and in which third party privilege was alleged:

(a) In *R v King* [1983] 1 WLR 411, CA, it was held that handwriting samples could be required from a handwriting expert who had previously been instructed by the defence.

(b) In *R v R* [1994] 4 All ER 260, CA, it was held that DNA samples that had been sent to an expert for his advice should not have been admitted (because the samples could not have been taken from the accused without his consent: see **11.4.3**).

In the two cases the items of evidence were admissible to prove facts in their own right. This principle also applies insofar as party A seeks to call party B's expert witness to prove *facts* as opposed to opinions he or she has perceived (*Harmony Shipping Co SA v Saudi Europe Line Ltd* [1979] 1 WLR 1380, CA).

What a lawyer receives by way of instructions will be privileged under the first class above. However, if the lawyer perceives facts that were not communicated to him whilst acting for the client, these will not be covered. In *Brown v Foster* (1857) 1 H & N 736, the plaintiff brought an action for malicious prosecution following an acquittal on a charge for embezzlement in which it was alleged he had not made an entry in a ledger. That charge had been dismissed when it was revealed that an entry in a ledger had in fact been made. The defendant in the malicious prosecution proceedings was allowed to call the plaintiff's barrister in the embezzlement proceedings to say that the day before the ledger was admitted as evidence, there was no such entry. This was a fact perceived by him rather than information received under privileged instructions.

### 14.2.2.6 Exceptions to legal professional privilege

The privilege applies absolutely. There is no general power to override the privilege because of public interest considerations (*R v Derby Magistrates' Court, ex p B* [1995] 3 WLR 681). However the privilege is subject to two qualifications set out below which reflect public interest concerns:

(a) *Legal professional privilege does not apply to communications made in pursuance of a crime or fraud* (*R v Cox and Railton* (1884) 14 QBD 153). In *Crescent Farm (Sidcup) Sport Ltd v Sterling Offices Ltd* [1972] Ch 553, it was stated that fraud went beyond the tort of deceit and included 'all forms of dishonesty such as fraudulent breaches of contract, fraudulent conspiracies, trickery and sham contrivances' (per Goff J). Clearly a lawyer will regularly be exposed to the criminal past of a client and will even have to advise them that future conduct might be unlawful in some way. However in *Barclays Bank plc v Eustice* [1995] 4 All ER 411, CA, a distinction was drawn between legal advice as to the legal affect of what had happened and advice as to how to carry out a fraudulent unlawful purpose in the future. However the timing of the criminal conduct does not fully determine the matter. Advice as to the potential illegality of future conduct will still be privileged (*Butler v Board of Trade* [1971] Ch 680). The test is whether the communication was made in pursuance of the fraud or crime (*R v Snaresbrook Crown Court, ex p DPP* [1988] QB 532).

The issue for the court to determine is whether it was the purpose of the lawyer *or* the client to pursue a fraud or crime. *R v Central Criminal Court, ex p Francis & Francis*, HL, concerned the powers of search and seizure under s 10 of the Police and Criminal Evidence Act 1984. The House stated that s 10 reflected the common law on legal professional privilege. The police, during a drugs investigation, had obtained orders requiring solicitors to produce documentation concerning the buying and selling of properties by a suspect and his family. The solicitors argued that the transactions and communications concerning them were privileged. However, the House concluded privilege would not apply if the intention of furthering a criminal purpose was that of the holder of the document or of any other party.

(b) *Third party legal professional privilege does not apply in cases concerning the welfare of children*. In any proceedings concerning the upbringing of children, the welfare of the child is the court's paramount consideration (s 1(1) of the Children Act 1989). In *Oxfordshire County Council v M* [1994] 2 All ER 269, the Court of Appeal held that the welfare of the child required that communications with third parties should not be subject to privilege. In children cases such communications will generally address various aspects of the welfare of the child such as his or her physical, educational or emotional needs or harm the child may or may not have suffered. The court was also influenced by the fact that such third parties were appointed by the court in any event. The position was confirmed by the House of Lords in *Re L (A Minor) (Police Investigation: Privilege)* [1996] 2 WLR 395. There the House noted the investigative nature of children proceedings and the requirement of leave for third parties to be instructed. It was therefore held to be inappropriate for third party privilege to apply in such cases.

Note that although most proceedings concerning the welfare of children will be those brought under the Children Act 1989, there are some proceedings in which this is not the case (such as wardship proceedings). Owing to the breadth of s 1(1) of the 1989 Act the welfare principle and its effect on third party privilege will be of equal application in such cases.

### 14.2.2.7 Proving evidence by other means

The privilege attaches only to the communications set out above. The facts contained in them are not covered by the privilege. Therefore if the fact can be proved by other means, other parties can attempt to do so. The extent to which the court must let them do so depends upon whether it is a criminal or civil case:

(a) *Criminal cases*: Once the information has been made available to the prosecution, the accused's privilege is lost. For example:

(i)    A note from the accused to his barrister that was found on the floor had been properly used in cross-examination (*R v Tompkins* (1977) 67 Cr App R 181, CA).

(ii)    The written account from the accused to his solicitor was accidentally sent to the prosecution. It had properly been used by them at trail (*R v Cottrill* [1997] Crim LR 56, CA).

However the court will consider whether the evidence has been obtained unfairly and should therefore be excluded under s 78 of the Police and Criminal Evidence Act 1984 (*R v Cottrill*).

(b) *Civil cases*: The position is now governed by CPR, r 31.20, which provides:

> Where a party inadvertently allows a privileged document to be inspected, the party who has inspected the document may use it or its contents only with the permission of the court.

In deciding whether or not to grant permission, the court will have regard to pre-CPR case law concerning the granting of injunctions to restrain the use of such evidence. Injunctions were generally granted where the documents had been obtained by fraud (*Ashburton v Pape* [1913] 2 Ch D 469) or obvious error (*Goddard v Nationwide Building Society* [1987] QB 670, CA) but what if the mistake is not obvious? In *International Business Machines Corporation v Phoenix International (Computers) Ltd* [1995] 1 All ER 413 numerous documents were made available by the defendant to the plaintiff. These documents included documents that were clearly privileged in principle. However the plaintiff's solicitors took the view that privilege had been waived in respect of the documents and told the defendant's solicitors this. The defendant therefore applied for an injunction restraining such use and seeking their return. The court held that test was whether a reasonable solicitor would have realised that privilege had not been waived. In doing so the court would take into account the extent to which privilege was claimed in respect of other documents, the nature of the case, of the documents and the way in which discovery (disclosure) had taken place thus far. On that basis the documents in question were clearly privileged.

However since the advent of the Civil Procedure Rules, the courts have adopted a stricter approach. In *USP Strategies v London General Holdings* [2004] EWHC 373, Ch, it was held that when a party obtains possession of communications to which an unwaived privilege attaches, the normal starting point is to order that the privileged material shall not be used and that any discretion to allow the use of such material should not be exercised merely to allow probative evidence to be admitted. However in extreme cases, the court could refuse to make an order restraining use of such evidence; in the public interest in the proper administration of justice: *ISTIL Group v Zahoor* [2003] 2 All ER 252.

Note also that paragraph 608(f) of the Code of Conduct for the Bar restricts the extent to which a barrister may use a document which has come into his or her possession by 'some means other than the normal and proper channels'. If the barrister accidentally reads such a document and then realises that he or she should not have done so, he or she may withdraw if he or she:

- would be embarrassed in the discharge of his or her duties by knowing what was revealed in the document; and

- he or she can do so without jeopardising the client's interests.

### 14.2.3  Activity

Now try **activity 14.1** in **Appendix 1**.

### 14.2.4  'Without prejudice' communications

It was noted above (**14.2.2.1**) that where the communication was intended to be passed on to other parties, such communications will not be privileged (*Conlon v Conlon's Ltd* [1952] 2 All ER 462 (see also *Paragon Finance plc v Freshfields* [1999] 1 WLR 1183)). Generally inter-parties communications are not privileged (after all the main purpose of the privilege is to prevent other parties from knowing the strength of the party's case). However this principle is subject to an exception where the parties are seeking to settle the case by negotiation so that parties need not fear that what they say when discussing whether or not to settle a case will be seen by the tribunal of fact, who might infer a weak case from a willingness to settle it, etc. This ground of excluding evidence resembles legal professional privilege but is different not least of all because the protection can only be waived by agreement between both parties.

Such communication is generally referred to as 'without prejudice' correspondence. As a matter of good practice those words should be clearly marked on any letters that are not intended to go before the judge however:

(a) the court is not bound to hold correspondence to be 'without prejudice' whenever the words are used (*Buckinghamshire County Council v Moran* [1990] Ch 623).

(b) the court is not bound to hold that correspondence without those words can never be 'without prejudice' (*Chocoladefabriken Lindt & Sprungli AG v Nestle Co Ltd* [1978] RPC 287).

(c) The real test is whether the correspondence is part of negotiations genuinely aimed at settlement (*South Shropshire District Council v Amos* [1986] 1 WLR 1271).

The rule prevents the correspondence from being admissible at trial (either on the matter or liability or on the issue of remedies). However there are limited circumstances in which such correspondence will be admissible:

(a) If the negotiations reach settlement, the correspondence can be used as evidence of what was agreed (*Walker v Wilshire* (1889) 23 QBD 335; *Tomlin v Standard Telephones & Cables Ltd* [1969] 1 WLR 1378). It is not evidence on any other matter nor is the agreement between the claimant and the first defendant in any way admissible in respect of the dispute between the claimant and the second defendant on exactly the same matter (*Rush & Tompkins Ltd v Greater London Council* [1989] AC 1280, HL). The reaching of an agreement is not necessarily recognition of the truth of the allegations to which it relates and should not therefore be allowed to prove anything other than the fact of agreement. However where one of the parties who reached a settlement brings proceedings against a third party for a contribution to the damages in the main claim and the without prejudice correspondence refers to the degrees of contribution, the correspondence can be referred to (*Gnitrow Ltd v Cape plc* [2000] 1 WLR 2327).

(b) Where subsequent proceedings relate to a wholly different subject matter and the correspondence reveals evidence in relation to that different subject matter then the correspondence will be admissible whether or not a settlement was reached (*Muller v Linsley & Mortimer* The Times, 8 December 1994).

(c) Where correspondence is marked 'without prejudice save as to costs' the court may, in limited circumstances, refer to the correspondence when determining costs issues. This detailed procedure is governed by CPR, Part 36 (see *Blackstone's Civil Practice*, 2003, Chapter 64) and in family proceedings by r 2.69 of the Family Proceedings Rules 1991, SI 1991/1247, and the case law deriving from *Calderbank v Calderbank* [1976] Fam 93. This will necessarily only apply where there was no settlement as the point of the analysis is to determine whether the party in question received a better order from the court than was offered by the other party.

(d) In proceedings relating to children, any admissions made by a parent concerning any harm that a child has suffered, whether made in an attempt to settle proceedings before trial of for other reasons will be admissible as evidence (*Re D (minor)* [1993] 2 All ER 693).

## 14.3  Public policy exclusion

The rules we have examined in this chapter so far have concerned the inadmissibility of evidence because one or both parties has asserted a privilege in respect of it. These privileges exist because of a concern to maintain the integrity of the litigation process and the interests of justice above and beyond the needs of the particular case. However there is also a rule of more general application that restricts the extent to which any otherwise admissible evidence can be revealed to parties and admitted as evidence. The concern for this rule is that there are other reasons for keeping evidence out of court than its impact upon the interests of justice.

You may at this point find it useful to carry out **activity 14.2** in **Appendix 1**. You will see from that activity that generally one party seeks to obtain evidence in the interests of justice and that another party resists such an attempt on the grounds of some other public interest.

This area of law is also commonly known as public interest immunity (or PII).

### 14.3.1  The general rule

The test of public policy exclusion is simply a matter of balancing the interest of justice in disclosing the evidence in question, on the one hand, against the public policy for excluding it, on the other hand (*Conway v Rimmer* [1968] AC 910). The claim of public policy exclusion should be decided by the courts.

The mere fact that a government agency or the prosecution alleges that it is not in the public interest for evidence in their possession to be revealed does not determine whether or not it should be (*R v Ward* [1993] 1 WLR 619 and the Criminal Procedure and Investigations Act 1996, Part I). Further, if no party requests that the evidence be excluded on public policy grounds the court may (and should) do so if necessary (*Duncan v Cammell Laird & Co Ltd* [1942] AC 624).

Determination of the public interest for these purposes is not determined by the class of document or source of information in question. Although such an approach used to be adopted in relation to documents such as high level government papers, the House of Lords stated in *Burmah Oil Company v Bank of England* [1980] AC 1090 that 'class' claims should be evaluated and decided on their merits just like any other type of document. Therefore public interest immunity from disclosure or use will not automatically be granted in respect of a document merely because it is diplomatic correspondence or a confidential economic report, for example. In 1996 the Lord Chancellor issued a statement (1997 147 NLJ 62) that government departments would no longer seek exclusion simply on the grounds that the document fell into a particular class. Instead ministers will:

... 'focus directly on the damage that disclosure of sensitive documents would cause ... Ministers will only claim immunity when they believe that disclosure ... will cause real damage or harm to the public interest. Damage will normally have to be in the form of a direct and immediate threat to the safety of an individual or to the nation's economic interest or relations with a foreign state, though in some cases the anticipated damage might be indirect or longer term, such as damage to a regulatory process.

Therefore a balancing exercise must be conducted in all cases. The fact that evidence from a particular class of source is more or less regularly excluded than that from other classes of source simply reflects the weight that is often attached to such sources when that balancing exercise is conducted rather than any absolute rule as to whether or not they should be excluded.

While in civil cases the interest of justice may vary from case to case, in criminal cases it has been said that where evidence may prove the accused's innocence or prevent a miscarriage of justice, the balance comes down heavily in favour of disclosing the evidence (*R v Keane* [1994] 1 WLR 746, CA). This does not prevent the court from having to consider the potential value of the evidence: where the evidence is not likely to do much to add to the issues in the case it is likely that the court will conclude that the evidence is unlikely to prove the innocence of the accused. The decision not to disclose material to the defence on the grounds of public interest immunity may undermine the right of the defendant to a fair trial in accordance with Article 6 of the European Convention. The European Court has recognised that the withholding of some information about prosecution investigative procedures is permissible without breaching the right of the accused to a fair trail (*Klass v Federal Republic of Germany* (1978) 2 EHRR 214, 232). However in *Rowe and Davis v United Kingdom* (2000) 30 EHRR 1, the European Court of Human Rights stated that only such withholding of evidence as was strictly necessary would be consistent with a fair trail. In *R v H, R v C* [2003] UKHL 2847, the House of Lords considered process for determining whether material in the possession of the prosecution could be withheld from the defence on the grounds of public interest immunity. As part of the identification of a seven-stage process for determining such disclosure issues (see **14.3.4.1** below), the House defined the test for public interest immunity in two stages:

3   Is there a real risk of serious prejudice to an important public interest (and, if so, what) if full disclosure of the material is ordered? If No, full disclosure should be ordered.

4   If the answer to...(3) is Yes, can the defendant's interest be protected without disclosure or disclosure be ordered to an extent or in a way which will give adequate protection to the public interest in question and also afford adequate protection to the interests of the defence?

### 14.3.2   The effect of public policy exclusion

Where evidence is excluded for reasons of public policy, no party can waive that right. Where no interested party has claimed that the evidence ought to be excluded on the grounds of public policy, that is simply a factor that the courts will consider in balancing the public policy against the interests of justice. In this sense the evidence is different to evidence excluded under one of the privileges set out in **14.2** above, as in privilege cases, the exclusion of the source of evidence depends upon a claim by someone that the evidence is privileged. Further, it is the fact or information contained in the document/ source that is excluded rather than the means of proving it (ie, the source or document itself) (*Rogers v Home Secretary* [1973] AC 388). Therefore, in contrast to evidence excluded on the grounds of a privilege, the information cannot be proved by some other route (for the contrast see **14.2.2.7**).

### 14.3.3   Examples

The following cases are all examples for the exercise of the principle of public policy exclusion. The list is not comprehensive. For further cases see *Blackstone's Criminal Practice*, 2004, at F9.1 to F9.8, *Archbold*, 2004, 12-34 to 12-44. While 'class' claims no longer determine whether or not evidence will be admitted, the type of document or type of information contained in the document tends to raise similar concerns and issues.

### 14.3.3.1   National security, affairs of state and foreign policy interests

It was this type of claim of public policy exclusion that previously led to automatic exclusion by class of document. However in Sir Richard Scott V-C's *'Report of the Inquiry into the Export of Defence Equipment and Dual-Use Goods to Iraq and Related Prosecutions'* (House of Commons Paper 115, 95/96, at G18.86) the use of class claims even in relation to national security interests was criticised leading to the Lord Chancellor's statement (at **14.3.1** above). Therefore any statement even that national security evidence should be excluded as a matter of course has to be looked at critically. However the trend has been for such evidence to be excluded. For example:

(a) In *Duncan v Cammell Laird & Co Ltd* [1942] AC 624 the court refused to order the disclosure of plans for a submarine that sank during trials.

(b) In *Burmah Oil Company v Bank of England* [1980] AC 1090, the bank's refusal to produce confidential records of dealings with bank and other businesses was upheld. The refusal was at the request of the government on the grounds of national economic interests.

(c) In *Buttes Gas & Oil Company v Hammer (No 3)* [1981] 1 QB 223, information relating to a company's dealings with a foreign State would not be revealed where that company was in a border dispute with its neighbour. The public interest served by refusing to disclose the evidence was international comity.

### 14.3.3.2   Police information

Information that has been used during investigations will often be of potential benefit to the accused in criminal proceedings or to parties taking action against the police in respect of their policing. Examples include:

(a) In *Evans v Chief Constable of Surrey* [1988] QB 588, a report sent to the DPP by the police was held not to be disclosable in a civil action to preserve the freedom of communication between the police and the DPP. Equally where the police have obtained evidence during a criminal investigation, the court must balance the confidentiality of such information obtained under the exercise of compulsory powers against the basic public interest in assuring a fair trial on full evidence in any subsequent civil proceedings: *Marcel v Commissioner of Police for the Metropolis* [1992] Ch 225, CA and *Taylor v Director of the Serious Fraud Office* [1999] 2 AC 177. In *Frankson v Home Office* [2003] EWCA Civ 655, the Court of Appeal rejected the argument that statements made to police officers under caution would necessarily be excluded in the public interest. There is therefore no general public interest in maintaining the confidentiality of statements made to prosecuting authorities that will outweigh the interest of a fair trial, although the court did leave open the possibility that an overriding public interest in non-disclosure could arise in specific cases.

(b) In *R v Horseferry Road Magistrates' Court, ex p Bennet (No 2)* [1994] 1 All ER 289, it was recognised that communications between prosecuting authorities in different countries could potentially be excluded although the evidence was admitted on that occasion as it showed that the accused had been unlawfully returned to the jurisdiction.

(c) In *R v Chief Constable of the West Midlands, ex p Wiley* [1995] 1 AC 274, it was held that whether or not statements made in the course of police complaints investigations should be excluded depended on the facts of each case.

(d) Where a criminal case appears to have been based upon informant evidence the courts have generally held that the identity of informants should not be disclosed although it may be ordered if it is necessary to establish the innocence of the accused (*Marks v Beyfus* (1890) 25 QBD 494). There is no general rule however that such evidence should not be disclosed, it is simply that generally the anonymity of the informant has been deemed to weigh heavily in the balance (*R v Keane* (above)). In *R v Agar* [1990] 2 All ER 442, the accused's case was that the informant and the police had cooperated in setting up the accused by inviting him to the informant's house and planting evidence there. The Court of Appeal held that the defence should have been entitled to cross-examine the police officers as to whether the informant had told them that the accused was due to visit his house.

(e) A similar approach has been adopted in relation to persons who have allowed their houses to be used as police surveillance posts (*R v Rankine* [1986] QB 861). In *R v Johnson (Kenneth)* (1989) 88 Cr App R 131, the Court of Appeal stated that before the court can admit evidence from a surveillance, two matters should be proved (as a minimum):

  (i)   A police officer in charge of the observations (no lower in rank than sergeant) testifies that *before the observation took place* he or she spoke to the occupiers of the premises to be used about their attitude to the observation, including the risk of disclosure of the use of the premises.

  (ii)  A police officer of the rank of at least chief inspector testifies that *immediately before trial* he or she visited the place of the observation and spoke to the occupiers at that time about their attitude to the disclosure of its use as an observation post at trial.

Where the court rules that the identity of informants or the details of information held by the police must be revealed, the prosecution may decide not to proceed on the charges in question. In this way they can preserve their sources.

### 14.3.3.3   Other confidential information

The approach of the courts in such cases rather depends on the issues being litigated (ie the interests of justice) on the one hand and the source of information and the importance of confidentiality (the public interest in exclusion) on the other. The results have therefore varied considerably, for example:

(a) *D v National Society for the Prevention of Cruelty to Children* [1978] AC 171, in which exclusion was granted in respect of anonymous reports made to the NSPCC concerning child abuse to children.

(b) *Science Research Council v Nasse* [1980] AC 1028, in which public policy exclusion was unsuccessfully sought in respect of documents used to determine promotion applications for employees.

(c) *Lonhro Ltd v Shell Petroleum Company Ltd* [1980] 1 WLR 627, in which information given in confidence to a government enquiry concerning a matter of foreign policy was held to have been properly excluded.

(d) *Re M (A Minor) (Disclosure of Material)* [1990] 2 FLR 36, in which social services reports and case notes concerning a child in care were not disclosable. (However such immunity does not operate against a guardian appointed for the child by the court in Children Act 1989 proceedings. Such a guardian can be ordered by the court to have access to all social service records under s 42 and no immunity would prevent such disclosure.)

(e) *R v Hampshire County Council, ex p K* [1990] 2 All ER 129, in which Social Services Department records were held not to be disclosed unless the judge ordered so.

(f) *Lonrho plc v Fayed (No 4)* [1994] QB 775, in which a taxpayer's tax returns held by the Inland Revenue were held potentially to be subject to public interest immunity as they had been obtained from the taxpayer by compulsion.

### 14.3.3.4    Journalistic sources

The provisions of the Contempt of Court Act 1981, s 10, make general provision as to the circumstances in which a journalist may be required by court order to reveal sources of information. Section 10 provides:

*No court may require a person to disclose, nor is any person guilty of contempt of court for refusing to disclose, the source of information contained in a publication for which he is responsible, unless it be established to the satisfaction of the court that disclosure is necessary in the interests of justice or national security or for the prevention of disorder or crime.*

Therefore a journalist is not generally under an obligation unless the evidence is necessary for one of four purposes: the interests of justice, national security, prevention of crime or prevention of disorder. The effect is that journalistic sources are covered by public policy exclusion and must be weighed against the other reason for revealing the source, of which one is the interests of justice, a phrase that has been interpreted narrowly (*Secretary of State for Defence v Guardian Newspapers* [1985] 1 AC 339). In *X Ltd v Morgan-Grampian (Publishers) Ltd* [1991] 1 AC 1, the interests of justice were defined as the protection of important legal rights or the protection against serious legal wrongs. Disclosure must be necessary for those purposes; therefore important factors will include the significance of the evidence and the difficulty of obtaining the information from other sources.

The 'prevention of disorder or crime' ground has been interpreted to relate to crime in general not specific crimes (*Re an Inquiry under the Companies Securities (Insider Dealing) Act 1985* [1988] AC 660). Therefore the section cannot be used in this way to force a journalist to disclose sources so that they can be called as witnesses in the case unless this is in the 'interests of justice'.

## 14.3.4    Determining whether to exclude evidence

As noted at the start of this chapter, whether or not evidence will be disclosed is a question of procedure rather than the rules of evidence. You should therefore refer to the ***Criminal Procedure*** and the ***Civil Procedure Manuals*** for detail. However in outline the procedures are as follows.

### 14.3.4.1    Criminal cases

Public policy exclusion will generally arise as part of the disclosure proceedings relating to unused material (ie evidence the prosecution will not rely upon). Under ss 3, 7 of the Criminal Procedure and Investigations Act 1996, the prosecution are under an obligation to reveal first any evidence that might undermine the prosecution case and at a later stage to reveal any information that assists the defence case. (When the Criminal Justice Act 2003 comes into force, s 32 will change the process to require the prosecution to disclose material at the primary disclosure stage which might reasonably be considered to undermine the prosecution case or assist the defence case.) The 1996 Act also provides the making of applications to the court to determine whether the evidence ought to be revealed. The extent to which the defence should be involved in such applications or should be informed depends on the degree of sensitivity of the material in question. There are three possibilities:

1. For the least sensitive class of material, the prosecution must inform the defence of the application (and the defence will be allowed to participate at the hearing) and of the class of material to which it relates at the very least.

2. For more sensitive material (where the prosecution allege that harm would be caused to a public interest by merely identifying the material in question), the prosecution must inform the defence of the application and the defence can make representations about the procedure to be adopted for determining the public interest immunity issue. However the prosecution do not have to reveal the nature of the material and the defendant and his or her representatives are not permitted to attend.

3. For the most sensitive cases (those in which the public interest to be protected would be threatened merely by revealing the fact of an application), the prosecution may apply to the court without notifying the defence of the application at all.

As the decision not to disclose evidence to the defence threatens the right to a fair trial, the process for determining what evidence should be revealed should itself safeguard the right to a fair trial protected by Article 6(1) of the European Convention of Human Rights. In *Rowe and Davis v United Kingdom* (2000) 30 EHRR 1, the European Court of Human Rights stated, at paragraph 61, 'any difficulties caused to the defence by a limitation on its rights must be sufficiently counterbalanced by the procedures followed by the judicial authorities'.

In *R v H, R v C* [2003] UKHL 2847, the House of Lords considered the procedures under the Criminal Procedure and Investigations Act 1996 in the light of developing practice in the UK courts and European Court of Human Rights jurisprudence. The result of this consideration was a seven stage process to be adopted when the prosecution opposed the disclosure of evidence on the grounds of public interest. The court must:

1. Identify and consider the material that the prosecution seek to withhold.

2. Determine whether the material is such as may weaken the prosecution case or strengthen that of the defence. (Disclosure does not have to be ordered for evidence that does not do one or the other.)

3. Determine whether there is a real risk of serious prejudice to an important public interest if full disclosure of the material is ordered. (If no serious prejudice, disclosure should be ordered.)

4. Determine whether the defendant's interest can be protected without disclosure or limited disclosure can be ordered that will both give adequate protection to the public interest and also to the interests of the defence. The court may have to consider what measures can be taken to offer adequate protection for the defence short of full disclosure.

5. Consider whether measures proposed in answer to (4) represent the minimum derogation necessary to protect the public interest in question. (The court is under a duty to get as close as possible to full disclosure while offering adequate protection for the interest in question.)

6. Consider whether any order for limited disclosure under (4) or (5) above may render the trial process unfair to the defendant. (If the trial process is rendered unfair fuller disclosure should be ordered even if this leads the prosecution to discontinue the proceedings so as to avoid having to make disclosure.)

7. Keep the fairness of the trial process under constant review during the trial in light of the order for limited disclosure. (The House noted that it was important that the answer to (6) should not be treated as final.)

The House therefore recognised that not only is there an issue of whether or not evidence ought to be disclosed but also that the court ought to consider ways in which evidence could be partially disclosed. The balance between disclosure and public interest immunity can therefore be achieved not simply by ordering or refusing disclosure of evidence but also by altering the way in which evidence is disclosed. The House noted in particular possibilities such as formal admissions of some or all of the facts the defence seek to prove with the evidence (see **1.5.1**), disclosure short of full disclosure by the preparation of summaries or extracts of evidence, or the provision of edited or anonymised documents.

The House also noted that occasionally a fair trial would require that the defendant was represented at disclosure hearings of the more sensitive types. In such cases, as noted above, the defendant and his or her representatives may not even be informed of the application. The House therefore approved the practice of appointing 'special counsel' to argue the defendant's case for disclosure at such hearings. However special counsel would only be appointed in exceptional circumstances. Special counsel would not be acting for the defendant and therefore would not be under any obligation to report to him or her about matters revealed during the disclosure hearing. However special counsel would be in a position to challenge the prosecution case from the a defence perspective so as to ensure that the adversarial nature of the trial process was safeguarded.

Where the person holding the information is not a party to the proceedings he or she may make an application to the court to rule the information should be excluded. Alternatively such matters fall to be resolved when the third party is the subject of a witness summons requiring him to attend court to produce the document or information.

### 14.3.4.2   Civil cases

CPR, r 31.19(1) makes detailed provision for determining whether evidence should be revealed. Such applications may be made without notice and will not generally be served on the other party unless the court orders otherwise. Where the information is sought from a non-party to the proceedings the application is made under CPR, r 31.17 (see also *Blackstone's Civil Practice*, 2004, Chapter 48).

# APPENDIX 1
# ACTIVITIES

This appendix contains the activities that are included in this Manual to assist you in understanding the subjects. These are not the questions that are to be used in the taught classes (they are contained in **Appendices 2** and **3**). Rather these activities are for you to complete on your own while reading the relevant chapter or immediately afterwards.

This appendix comes in two parts. Part 1 contains the activities and Part 2 the answers. Do not be tempted simply to look at the answers without attempting the activities as this will undermine their purpose. They are not simply tests of the law, but will often require you to use legal skills (such as legal research and fact analysis) and to think about how the rules work rather than just what the rules are.

Each activity is numbered according to the chapter in which it appears. For example the first activity from **Chapter 1** is numbered '**1.1**' while the second activity from **Chapter 3** is numbered '**3.2**'.

## Part 1: Activities

### Activity 1.1

Using *Blackstone's Criminal Practice* or *Archbold: Criminal Practice Pleading and Practice*, identify the facts in issue in a case of violent disorder contrary to s 3 of the Public Order Act 1986.

### Activity 1.2

Consider the following case:

Anil wishes to bring an action for breach of contract against Shedrite Ltd, a company that carried out building works in his offices. He entered into an oral contract with Brian, a sales representative for Shedrite. Anil alleges that it was agreed that Shedrite would build an extension to his office premises to accommodate three employees and their desks. He says that they promised to do this within four months but that they did not do so. As a result he had to delay the employment of three extra members of staff as a result of which he lost profit from a number of projects amounting to £25,000.

Now answer the following questions:

(a) What will the facts in issue be after Anil has drafted the particulars of claim in his statement of case?

(b) If Shedrite agree that a contract was agreed with Anil but that Brian had said to Anil that while they would aim to finish the work within four months, they could not guarantee they would do so in less than six months. They completed the contract within five months. They have no idea how much Anil might have lost in profit during that month. What would the facts in issue be?

(c) Alternatively, what if Shedrite stated that, while it was initially agreed that the work would be done in four months, the contract was in fact agreed when Anil signed Shedrite's standard-form written contract. This contract confirmed the four-month completion date but included an exclusion clause in the case of 'delays in completion due to scarcity or lack of materials'. They accept that there was a delay of one month but allege that this was because Anil had insisted on a particular South American wood and that labour shortages in the harvesting of this wood was the cause of the delay. Shedrite cannot comment on the loss alleged by Anil.

## Activity 2.1

You are instructed to act for Constantia Ltd who instruct you that they entered into a contract to transport three machines owned by Plumstead Manufacturing Ltd.

Clause 8(a) of the contract states:

> It is a condition of the contract that Constantia will deliver the machines in good working order and free of defects.

Clause 8(b) states:

> In the case of breach of clause 8(a), Plumstead shall be entitled to terminate the contract and shall not be liable for any payment thereunder save insofar as any breach of clause 8(a) is caused other than by the negligence or deliberate default of Plumstead, its servants or agents.

Plumstead agree to pay £5,000 for delivery within 30 days of delivery. Constantia have delivered the machines and have requested payment but no payment has been made. Plumstead have replied to requests for payment by saying that the machines were returned to them in a damaged state. Constantia state that the machines were fine when delivered to Plumstead but that an employee of Plumstead instructed the employees of Constantia to leave them in an uncovered area where they may have been subject to bad weather. When confronted with these allegations, Plumstead deny that their employee did any such thing but that the goods were left in the uncovered area due to the negligence of Constantia's employees.

(i) Bearing in mind that the party asserting a fact must generally prove it and the other rules of evidence, what facts should be alleged by Constantia in their Particulars of Claim to secure payment of the money they are owed?

(ii) Assuming Plumstead enter a defence to the action, invoking clause 8(b) what should they allege in their Defence?

(iii) How should Constantia reply to the Defence so as to preserve their action for the debt owing?

(iv) What facts are likely to be in issue at the close of the statement of case process and who is likely to bear the evidential and legal burdens of proof on those issues?

## Activity 2.2

Section 139 of the Criminal Justice Act 1988 states:

> (1) Subject to subsections (4) and (5) below, any person who has an article to which this section applies with him in a public place shall be guilty of an offence.

*(2) ... this section applies to any article which has a blade or is sharply pointed except a folding pocket knife.*

*...*

*(4) It shall be a defence for a person charged with an offence under this section to prove that he had good reason or lawful authority for having the article with him in a public place.*

*(5) Without prejudice to subsection (4) above, it shall be a defence for a person charged with an offence under this section to prove that he had the article with him—*

- *(a)    for use at work;*
- *(b)    for religious reasons; or*
- *(c)    as part of any national costume.*

You are instructed to prosecute the following cases:

(i) Alan is arrested in possession of a knife on the High Street at 6 am. When arrested, he says that he is a butcher and was taking the knife to his place of work, his other knives at work being blunt or broken. The police have obtained no other evidence.

(ii) Beatrice is arrested in possession of a knife on a lawn outside the University of Wessex. At trial she admits that she was in possession of the knife but that it was a folding pocket knife. She also alleges that the lawn upon which she was arrested was the private property of the University. She says that she had the knife because another student at the university, Carla, had made threats to her after Beatrice had reported Carla for selling drugs. She did not intend to use it, just to frighten Carla with it. The police have since lost the knife so it cannot be produced at court.

Who will bear the burden of proving the defences raised in each of those cases. Does either case present any difficulty in proving the offence (so far as it is possible to determine this on the limited facts provided above)? What impact will the European Convention of Human Rights have on the determination of the burden of proof?

## Activity 3.1

Consider the following example. Andrew and Beatrice are independently suing Edward, the trustee of a fund set up by Charlie. Charlie and Delia, his wife, died in a car crash. The terms of the trust are that all of the trust property (£125,000) should be held for the benefit of Charlie during his life. Upon Charlie's death the trust property would pass absolutely to Delia unless she predeceased him, in which case it would pass to Andrew or his successors. Beatrice, Delia's daughter, is sole beneficiary under Delia's will and had inherited all of her property. The evidence states that both Charlie and Delia would have died 'almost instantly'. Consider the following:

(a) What is the effect of this trust fund? In what circumstances will the trust property pass to Andrew? In what circumstances will it pass to Beatrice?

(b) What does Andrew have to prove to obtain the trust property?

(c) How will the court resolve this matter if it concludes that it is not possible to determine who died first and it is established that:

- (i)    Charlie was 72 and Delia 68, or
- (ii)   Charlie was 68 and Delia 72.

## Activity 3.2

Francis is prosecuted for theft of items from a clothing shop. The prosecution have proved that the items were taken by showing that the computer records that result from the scanning of the bar codes of items being lawfully sold do not show the items Francis had in his possession to have been sold. The items still have the labels of the shop in question upon them. Francis's advocate makes a submission of no case to answer on two bases: namely the prosecution have not shown that Francis appropriated the clothes from the shop nor that he did so dishonestly. Should the submission succeed or not? What presumptions will operate and what will have to have been established before they can do so? When you have considered these matters, refer back to this chapter and use either *Blackstone's Criminal Practice* or *Archbold*, if you feel them necessary.

### Activity 4.1

(a) Stephen is charged with assault occasioning actual bodily harm on his wife, Pattie. She would rather not give evidence. May the prosecution compel her to do so?

(b) Vince is charged with indecent assault on Andy, a 14-year-old boy. Wendy and Barbara (Vince's wife) are charged with the offence on the basis that they assisted Vince in committing this offence by luring Andy to Vince's house. Can Andy be compelled to give evidence for the prosecution? Can they call Barbara as a witness?

(c) Same facts as (b) above but Barbara has pleaded guilty. Vince wishes to call her to give evidence that he was not involved. Barbara does not wish to do so. Can Vince compel her? Can Wendy compel her to give evidence that Vince threatened both Barbara and her with serious violence if they did not get him a boy to assault.

### Activity 4.2

Consider the following case study.

You are instructed for the CPS to prosecute William Towers a 19 year old youth in the Crown Court for assault occasioning actual bodily harm. In your instructions to counsel you have, amongst other things, the following:

1. A witness statement of the victim, Jason Blue, a 13 year old boy who states that he was being bullied by William Towers and who was hit by Towers during a fight on the local recreation ground when Jason tried to stand up to him.

2. A witness statement from Mary Blue, Jason's mother in which she states that Jason has learning difficulties and a mental age of 9. He goes to a special school. This is why Towers has been picking on him. Mrs Blue also alleges that the whole Towers family has been trouble in the area for some time and have many previous convictions.

3. Subsequent statements from both Mary Blue and Jason Blue in which they state that they no longer wish to give evidence due to fear of Towers and his family.

4. Towers' previous convictions and findings of guilt, which include offences of violence and dishonesty from the age of 12.

5. Records of calls made to the police by Mrs Blue in which she alleged that various members of the Towers family have been threatening her and her son.

What procedural steps can be taken to ensure that both Mrs Blue and Jason Blue give effective testimony at trial?

### Activity 5.1

Consider the following case study:

Hazel Day is on trial for criminal damage to a car belonging to Geraldine Malory who had started going out with Hazel's ex-husband, Connor Greig. Answer the following questions:

(i)    The prosecution call Geraldine's elderly father, Terrance, who made a statement to the police just after the incident in which he says that he saw Hazel Day running a key along the bonnet of Geraldine's new car. He describes Hazel, whom he has never met. Terrance also identified her at an identification parade the day after the incident. At trial Terrance, who has difficulties with his memory, says that he cannot now remember anything about the incident. May he rely upon the statement he made to the police to refresh his memory?

(ii)   May the identification by Terrance at the police station be relied upon?

(iii)  The prosecution also call Connor. Hazel's barrister cross-examines Connor by suggesting that he has made up the allegation because of the acrimony of the divorce. Can the prosecution prove a statement made by Connor two days after the car had been damaged?

(iv)   Can the prosecution admit evidence of Hazel's statement when she was arrested by the police. The statemen was 'OK I admit I might have scratched the car but I didn't mean to. I was trying to put a letter to Geraldine under the windscreen wiper, telling her how useless Connor is and to keep clear of him. It was an accident'.

## Activity 5.2

Colin is prosecuted for dangerous driving having collided with Rajesh. At the trial, a witness for the prosecution, Mary, testifies that she clearly saw Colin's grey car, driving in excess of the speed limit, cross the white lines of the road and hit the side of the red car driven by Rajesh. You act for Colin and have a statement made by Thomas, in which he alleges that Mary sent him an e-mail at the time in which she said 'The driver of the red car was on his mobile phone and was veering into the middle of the road, sometimes straddling the white lines. His car had probably crossed the white line when it was hit. I cannot be sure because I was polishing my glasses at the time'. What use could you make of this statement? To what extent would the use of the statement differ if this evidence was adduced at a civil rather than a criminal trial? What questions would be asked of Mary so that the statement could become admissible evidence?

## Activity 6.1

Who should you call as a good character witness?

## Activity 6.2

Answer the following two questions:

(i)   What may amount to an assertion of good character?

(ii)  You are prosecuting a case where a defendant on a charge of indecent assault adduced evidence of sexual morality. Can you cross examine the witness about previous convictions for theft offences?

### Activity 6.3

On a trial concerning a plan to steal scrap metal, your client's defence is that he and the co-defendant did plan to steal the metal but the plan was not dishonest. The co-defendant's defence is that there was no plan at all. The co-defendant is allowed to cross-examine your client on your client's previous convictions.

Your instructing solicitor has asked you to advise whether your client can appeal on the ground that the material evidence was not 'against a co-defendant'. What would you advise?

### Activity 8.1

Have a look at the following proof of evidence for a witness in a criminal case concerning criminal damage and common assault. You act for the prosecution. There are two defendants, Patrick Bell and his father Charlie Bell, both charged with criminal damage. Patrick Bell is charged with common assault (to which, in police interview, he raised the defence of self-defence). The witness statement in question is that of Tony Ockford:

I was walking home from the pub, the Cricketers, with my friend Will. We were talking about Will's new car, which he had bought a couple of weeks back. He said that he had got it for a good price, considering it was brand new. I think he said it was about £11,000. When we crossed Marchmont Road and were approaching Will's house, I saw a couple of youths standing on the corner of Meadows Lane. That is where Will's house is. They had their bikes leaning against a low wall and were leaning over a car parked on the side of the road. Will said 'What are those youths doing to my new car?' He then started running forward. The car must have been about 150m away. One of the youths looked up and said 'Nice motor, mate. We thought we'd do it up for you' and laughed. The other shouted 'Come on Paddy. He looks pretty pissed off.' They then both jumped on their bikes and rode off. One of them, the one at the back, shouted back at Will, 'Come on Fatty Hendricks, you need to work out more'. Will caught up with one of them but the youth struck out behind him with his fist and Will fell over. They then got away. We looked at the car and saw that it had been scratched on the front with the word 'Scab'. Will said he thought he recognised one of the youths as Paddy Bell, the son of Charlie Bell, with whom Will works at a factory. The workers at the factory have recently gone on strike and Will refused to strike. He has told me that Charlie Bell had recently said to him 'You're getting a new car with strike money. Don't think you'll enjoy it for long.' Will's surname is Hendricks. He is quite large although I would not describe him as fat.

Now draw up a list of everything included in this witness statement that at trial will be an out of court statement. When you have done that try and identify how much of Tony Ockford's statement is based on things he has been told other than things he has personally experienced. This is slightly more tricky than simply identifying reported statements and it is not possible to be certain of the answers.

### Activity 8.2

Have another look at the statement of Tony Ockford (at **activity 8.1** above). For each of those statements work out (a) what the relevant purposes of those statements might be at trial and (b) whether to achieve that purpose the statement in question has to be true.

### Activity 8.3

Using either the table above or your own analysis, rewrite Tony Ockford's statement leaving out any hearsay evidence that Will would be better able to give authorative evidence. Also draw up a statement by Will that conveys the relevant information he is best able to comment upon. Remember that in reality Will's statement might also include details

Tony is unaware of. All we could draw up using Tony's statement is those parts of Tony's statement that we might expect to be in Will's statement (and testimony).

## Activity 8.4

Have a look at the following statement prepared by solicitors for Danny Kington, who is charged with assault occasioning actual bodily harm. Danny intends to plead not guilty and allege he acted in self-defence. The statement is signed by Angela Bairstow, who has since died.

I saw the whole incident. I heard a terrible shout and went to look out of my window. I saw Danny Kington and another boy shouting at one another on the other side of the road. There were two bikes lying in a tangle on the floor. I could not hear all of the words shouted but I did hear the other boy shout 'I will get you for that' just as he bent over to pick up a bit of wood that was lying on the floor. I think some bad language was used to. As the other boy straightened up and started waiving the wood, Danny tried to grab him by the arm holding the wood. The other boy struggled and fell over screaming. Danny then looked shocked and ran off. I later spoke to Danny's mother, Irene, who said that Danny and the other boy had run into each other on the road and that the other boy is a terrible bully.

How much of the statement could be proved using s 23?

## Activity 9.1

Answer the following questions:

   (i)   How, practically, could Y be protected where X makes adverse comments in her confession statement?

   (ii)  Where X has made a statement adverse to Y, can the prosecution cross-examine Y on the part of X's statement that implicates Y?

   (iii) What exception is there to the rule that a statement made by X and adverse to both X and Y is only admissible against Y? (This is something that has been considered earlier in this manual.)

## Activity 9.2

Research the following questions. You may find *Blackstone's Criminal Practice* 2004 or *Archbold* 2004 a useful place to start.

   (i)   Under what circumstances may a suspect's right to consult a solicitor be delayed?

   (ii)  What is meant by a 'serious arrestable offence'? Which offences are serious arrestable offences?

## Activity 9.3

Apply s 76(4) to (6) to the following scenario:

Tom is charged with burglary of Anne's house. Various items including an antique vase and a gold watch are taken from the property. Tom is arrested and questioned. The police officers breach Code C in a number of material ways. As a result of the breaches, Tom confesses to the burglary and tells the police that he has hidden the antique vase in his house and that he buried the watch at a particular place on Clapham Common (which is nowhere near his house). The police search for the items and find both of them. Anne is able to identify the watch but not the vase as her property. At the trial the confession is excluded under s 76(2).

Assuming no other evidence exists in the case, what evidence is there against Tom. If the defence were to make a submission of no case to answer, should it succeed?

## Activity 10.1

Consider the following case study:

Chris is charged with assault occasioning actual bodily harm and affray. The prosecution case is that the police were called to an incident that was taking place outside a chip shop. When the police arrived, the observed about five or six youths fighting. The youths ran away when they saw police officers and the police gave chase. One officer, PC Long, followed a youth into an adjoining street. There he saw Chris lying on the ground behind a car.

When found, Chris had a torn shirt and a bruised lip. PC Long cautioned Chris and told him that he had reason to suspect, due to his torn shirt, his injury and the fact that he was hiding where he was that he had been involved in the fight outside the chip shop. PC Long then requested Chris to explain these facts. Chris did not give any reply. The victim of the assault, Jack, identifies Chris and Chris is interviewed with his solicitor present. Chris declines to answer any questions put to him during the police interview under caution.

At trial Chris' barrister cross examines Jack and puts to him that Chris acted to stop the fight and in self defence, which Jack denies.

Answer the following questions:

(i)    Chris' barrister makes a submission of no case to answer. To what extent can sections 34, 36 or 37 be used in deciding whether there is a case to answer?

(ii)   Assume that the submission fails and Chris intends to give evidence. His instructions are that he had been standing outside of the chip shop when a fight started between people he did not know. He attempted to stop the fighting in the course of which he got hit and that he only struck out in self defence. He says that he ran away because he was frightened of the police, never having been in trouble before and that he hid and lied about his house keys because he was drunk and was frightened of the police. He says that he did not answer questions because his solicitor had advised him not to do so. The solicitor is also willing to testify that he advised Chris not to give evidence because he felt that Chris had drunk too much and the police should not have been questioning him when they did. What will be the effect to such testimony on any inferences that might be drawn by the jury?

(iii)  Should anything be done or have been done to exclude the no-comment interview?

## Activity 10.2

Gina is on trial in the Crown Court for theft from her employer, Bright Shoes. The prosecution call Ben, the owner of the shop, who testifies that, when asked if she knew anything about cash missing from the till, she said 'I think you should ask Henry. He is in need of money'. Henry is a fellow employee. Ben also states that he later saw Gina taking more money out of the till and called the police. The prosecution also adduce evidence to show that there was less money in the till than there should have been on a number of occasions and CCTV footage showing Gina acting suspiciously at the till. The police officer who arrested Gina, PC Armitage, also gives evidence that when Gina was questioned under caution at the shop before arrest, she did not say anything except, 'I want to see my lawyer'. However, at the police station, she produced a type-written statement in which she alleges that Ben had said to her that she could have £200 from the till in advance of her wages as she was short of money. It also states that at the time she and Ben were sleeping together but that she split up with Ben after she had found out that he was also sleeping with someone else and that the allegation of theft was made out of spite following that break-up. Gina then refused, on the advice of her solicitor, to answer any questions during the police interview.

Gina's barrister puts to Ben in cross-examination that he is lying due to their previous relationship. Gina does not to give evidence. She has four previous convictions, all for dishonesty offences.

What directions should the judge make to the jury in respect of Gina's silence at various stages of the process and also in respect of her statements about Henry?

## Activity 11.1

Write down, in no more than 200 words, a direction that you think a judge might give to a jury on the possible dangers of relying on visual identification evidence.

## Activity 11.2

Now consider the position in a case turning on aural (or voice) identification. Do you think that the same direction could be used again, suitably modified? Or would it need something different?

## Activity 11.3

### 11.3.1 First consider the following case:

A witness who was at or near a crime scene at or around the time when the offence occurred may be able to identify the offender again, later. How the witness might be asked to identify the offender will differ, according to whether or not the police have a suspect for the witness to make a comparison. Write down at least two methods which could be used when a witness makes a comparison, in a case where the identity of the suspect is known to the police.

### 11.3.2 Only attempt this part once you have looked at the answer to 11.3.1 in Part 2.

Take that list of methods and try to rank them in order of most probative method down to least probative.

Once you have considered the answer to **11.3.2** in Part 2, answer the following questions.

**11.3.3** Now write down some ways in which a witness might be asked to make a comparison where the identity of the suspect is not known to the police.

## Activity 11.4

The exercise allows you to practise your analysis of identification issues:

**11.4.1** Alan is walking along the High Road in Bigtown. Some way ahead, Alan sees an elderly woman come out of the Post Office. Alan recognises her as his Aunt Mabel. Alan looks at his aunt as he walks towards her. She is concentrating upon putting her purse into her shopping bag. Alan thinks to himself, 'Today is Thursday. I guess she has just collected her pension'. Just then, Alan sees a man suddenly appear on the pavement in the High Road, about 10 metres behind Mabel. The man runs up to Mabel and grabs her purse. Alan begins to run and shouts at the man, 'Hey you ...' The man looks in Alan's direction, puts the purse under one arm, turns and runs off in the direction from which he had come. Alan stops by Mabel and asks 'Are you OK?' Mabel says nothing; she is crying. Alan sees an alleyway which he thinks must be the way the man ran off. Alan runs into the alleyway but it is empty. There is no sign of the man. Alan returns to Mabel and calls the police on his mobile phone. Police officers attend the scene 10 minutes later. One police officer speaks to Mabel. She says she did not really see the person who took her purse.

Which of the following situations involves identification evidence?

(a) Alan is able to describe the man to police as 6 feet tall, slim build, dark hair cut short. Alan says the man was wearing dark shoes or trainers, blue jeans and a black shirt or jacket.

(b) Alan is unable to describe the man to police but says he was wearing a pair of lime green jogging pants and a red T-shirt with 'fcuk' on the chest.

(c) As in B. Additionally, some time later the police lawfully search a flat occupied by Barry Borrower. They find an empty purse, a pair of lime green jogging pants and an orange T-shirt with 'fcuk' on the front.

(d) As in B. Additionally, one police officer goes to the far end of the alleyway, turns the corner and sees a carrier bag on the pavement. She looks inside and finds a red T-shirt with 'fcuk' on the front, also a pair of lime green jogging pants. A man mending his car in the road says to the PC, 'I saw the man who dropped that bag. He went into the pub over there.' She enters the pub and sees a man dressed in singlet and shorts, drinking a glass of beer. She asks the barman how long the man has been in the pub and is told 'about ten minutes'. She asks the man his name and he says, 'Barry Borrower. Why?'

(e) Alan tells the police that he thinks he would recognise the man if he saw him again. Alan and the officer get into the police car and drive around the surrounding streets. After about five minutes, Alan points to a man standing by a minicab office and says, 'That's the man'. This man is dressed in black jeans and a blue jacket. The officer approaches the man who says he is Barry Borrower and is waiting for a cab. He says he has been waiting for about half an hour. The woman in the minicab office confirms that he ordered a cab about 30 minutes ago and then went to wait outside.

(f) Alan notices something on the floor in the alley. He picks it up and sees it is a library card. The name on it is 'Barry Borrower'.

(g) Alan tells the police officer, 'I know the man who did it. His name is Barry Borrower. We both work at Bigtown Laundry. I am sure it was him.'

Once you have checked your answers to these questions, complete the following:

**11.4.2** In each of these seven situations, Barry Borrower is eventually arrested on suspicion of robbery. When interviewed by police, he denies any involvement. In (a), (b), (c), (f) and (g), he says he was at home at the time of the robbery. Police confirm that he was not at work on the day of the robbery and that his home is 4 miles away from the Post Office. In (d), he says that he has been in the pub for at least half an hour. In (e), he says that he has been waiting just outside the minicab office since ordering the cab.

In which of these situations is identification a fact in issue? In which of these situations would it be appropriate for the police to hold an identification parade?

Having referred to Part 2 for the answers, consider the following:

**11.4.3** A police officer goes into the Post Office. He sees there is a CCTV camera on the wall above the counter. The Post Office manager says that the camera is positioned to show customers as they enter the Post Office and it also films a small area of the street directly outside. The manager gets the current tape and gives it to the police officer.

Now answer the following questions:

   (i)   In situation (a), is it permissible for the police to show Alan the CCTV tape?

  (ii)   How about in situation (b)? What could be done with the CCTV footage then?

 (iii)   Is it permissible for a police officer to watch the CCTV tape to see if the robbery was recorded?

 (iv)   If the robbery was recorded, is it permissible for the police officer to watch the CCTV tape to see if she can recognise the offender?

  (v)   If the police officer watches the CCTV tape and recognises the offender as Barry Borrower, can she be called as a witness at trial to say so?

## Activity 11.5

**Direction by a judge to a jury:**
For an illustration of the current position, we can consider the Privy Council decision in *R v Gilbert*, mentioned earlier. Read the summary of the case below.

The charge against Gilbert was attempted rape. The allegation was that he approached a woman (M) on a beach in St Lucia and told her that he was going to rape her. In the struggle that ensued, M scratched the man's back with her fingernails and she then ran off. M then went to a police station. She told them what had happened and that she knew her attacker. Even though the man's face had been partly obscured with a jumper, she had recognised him because they had both attended the same primary school (M was 21 years old at the time of the crime). The police officer who arrested G the next morning noticed scratch marks on his back, which appeared to be fingernail marks. G denied being the attacker, saying he was elsewhere at the time. He explained the marks as the result of falling into a bush.

What relevant directions do you think the trial judge should give when summing up the evidence to the jury?

## Activity 12.1

Think of two common issues in a trial where a witness' opinion would be unnecessary.

## Activity 12.2

**Example part 1**
D is on trial for murder. The allegation is that he stabbed a man some 26 times about the face and hands. At 11.30 pm, the man had gone to D's room, in a house where they both lived, to 'sort him out'. D does not deny that he stabbed the other man. His defence is that he must have done so whilst asleep, and thus acted as an automaton.

  (i)   Do you think that this is a matter of human behaviour, 'within the limits of normality'? Does the court need expert assistance?

 (ii)  Was a psychiatrist the correct type of expert to help the court with questions about sleep walking?

## Activity 12.3

**Example part 2**

Suppose the psychiatrist said in her evidence:

I just cannot accept that you are going to stay asleep for so long when a man is trying to strangle you and you are delivering a whole series of blows all over his body and face with a knife. I just cannot accept it, but if you are so deeply asleep that this is a conceivable state of affairs, then you are not going to come to very quickly so that you are awake for the end of the sequence and, indeed, awake with a knife in your hands. You can't have it both ways. You are either so extraordinarily deeply asleep it would take you up to half an hour to come round, or the more likely thing were if some drunken man comes barging into your small bedroom at night it wakes you up.

Would you consider that her evidence was actually of assistance to the court or not, in resolving the three points identified above?

## Activity 12.4

(i) Read the following phrases. Do you think any of them involves opinion evidence?

- 'Smith was really angry.'
- 'I could see Ethel was upset.'
- 'I saw the blue car being driven in a very dangerous manner along the High Street.'

(ii) Using the 'blue car' statement above, write down a question that you could ask the witness to bring out the facts that the witness originally perceived.

## Activity 12.5

Consider, in each of the following examples, what sort of an expert would be needed:

(a) Whether an accused (A) is suffering from a disease of the mind within the M'Naghten rules.

(b) Whether A is suffering from diminished responsibility; but note the distinction drawn between diminished responsibility and other forms of incapacity (for example, drunkenness).

(c) Whether A, who had put forward a defence of non-insane automatism, was sleepwalking.

(d) Whether a witness is suffering from a mental disability and, if so, that one of the effects is to render him incapable of giving reliable evidence. Expert evidence will *not* be permitted on the question whether a witness who has a normal capacity for reliability is actually giving reliable evidence — this is always a matter for the tribunal of fact.

(e) Whether two samples of handwriting were written by the same person.

(f) The effect of spiked drinks on the level of alcohol in A's blood, unless it would be obvious to a layman.

(g) The psychological effect *on children* of chewing gum cards depicting, in graphic detail, the horrors of war and, thus, whether the cards had a tendency to deprave or corrupt.

(h) The various ways of using cocaine and the adverse effects thereof and, thus, to help the jury decide whether a book describing these matters had a tendency to deprave or corrupt.

(i) The probable circumstances and causes of a fatal road accident.

(j) The possible effects of a *medical condition* on a person's mental processes and ability to form an intent.

(k) The reliability of a confession made by a person who was abnormally susceptible to suggestion.

(l) Evidence on whether the face appearing on a security video was that of the accused.

## Activity 13.1

Re-read CEA 1968, s 11 (see **13.3.1**). Write down your answers to the following questions:

(a) Which sub-section reverses the rule in *Hollington v Hewthorn*?

(b) Does s 11 apply only to convictions of the parties to the civil claim?

(c) Which sub-section creates the rebuttable presumption?

(d) Which sub-section explains how the conviction should be rebutted?

## Activity 13.2

Can you think of an example where it might be relevant and admissible to call evidence that an accused has previously committed an offence (other than that for which he is now on trial)? Write down your answer.

## Activity 13.3

Re-read the text on *R v Mahmood* at p 234. Did the trial judge in *Mahmood* fail to satisfy the first stage of the test or the second stage?

## Activity 13.4

Answer in no more than 250 words:

(a) Is the conviction of someone other than the accused admissible evidence and, if so, what is the effect of calling evidence of the conviction?

(b) Is the conviction of the accused admissible evidence and, if so, what is the effect of calling evidence of the conviction?

## Activity 14.1

Melkbos Foods Ltd, a company that imports fruit from South Africa is in dispute with Hornsey Refrigerators Ltd, a company that provides commercial refrigeration facilities. Melkbos allege Hornsey provided them with defective refrigerators for their storage depot in South London. Hornsey have an in-house lawyer who liaises with their solicitors, Farnham & Sons.

As part of the process of disclosure, Hornsey wish for advice as to whether they are obliged to disclose the following documents:

1. An internal memorandum in which an employee of Hornsey identified an error with the refrigeration system that was sold to Melkbos. The memorandum was sent to the in-house lawyer to be forwarded to Farnham & Sons.

2. A report by Dr Theodore Wick, which was commissioned by Hornsey following complaints from Melkbos about their refrigeration system. The report was

commissioned 'to identify errors in the system provided with a view to reaching a favourable settlement to any dispute between Melkbos and Hornsey'. The report identifies a number of key errors in installing the system that are attributable to employees of Hornsey.

3. A memorandum recommending that John Ripley, the engineer who installed Melkbos' system be disciplined for negligence in respect of another installation job he did a few months before the Melkbos job.

### Activity 14.2

Consider the following scenarios. Decide whether the evidence identified should, in principle, be admissible. Come up with arguments for and against admitting the evidence in each case and then decide which argument you think should prevail.

(a) A is tried for possession of drugs with intent to supply them. She admits that she is a drug user and that was in possession of the drugs which she received from her usual supplier. He asked her to look after the drugs and threatened to 'do her harm' if she didn't. Should A be entitled to know whether the police found about her possession of the drugs from an informant and, if so, who that informant was?

(b) B Ltd brings an action against C Ltd for non-payment of money's owing for machine parts provided by B to C. C Ltd says that parts were unsuitable for the machines, which were to be provided to the Ministry of Defence for military uses. The Ministry of Defence have refused to reveal details of the tests conducted on the machines for national security reasons.

(c) D is suing the police in respect of his arrest on burglary charges. He alleges that he was been arrested because he is black and that certain items of evidence that incriminated him were planted by the police officers investigating him. Can he obtain documentation from recent disciplinary hearings concerning those police officers?

(d) E is charged with indecent assault on a young boy in local authority care. He alleges that the boy made up the allegations against him to get attention and that there was no sexual activity between them. E is aware that the young boy was placed in local authority care following allegations of abuse on him by his uncle. Can E obtain the local authority records concerning the boy and his case history?

## Part 2: Answers to activities

### Activity 1.1

Having researched the offence of violent disorder, you should have come up with a list of facts in issue something like this:

(a) Identify of the defendant.

(b) *Actus reus*:

    (i)   three or more persons together;

    (ii)  either:

       • use unlawful violence; or

       • threaten unlawful violence; and

    (iii) the violence or threat of violence would cause a person of reasonable firmness to fear for his or her personal safety.

(c) *Mens rea*:

    (i)   Either:

- intention to use violence; or
- intention to threaten violence; or
- awareness that conduct may be violent or threatening.

Defences would only be facts in issue if raised at trial.

Your list may not look exactly the same as that set out above (breaking down a case like this is not an exact science but a matter of interpretation). The important thing is that the elements of the case have been sufficiently identified and separated that a practitioner has a clear idea of what must be proven and what any particular item of evidence is relevant to.

### Activity 1.2

(a) After Anil's statement of case the facts in issue will be:

    (i)   The existence of an oral contract between Anil and Shedrite to build an extension.

    (ii)  An express term of that contract that the extension would be completed within four months.

    (iii) Breach of that term (ie no completion within four months).

    (iv) The loss of £25,000 in profits.

    (v)  That loss having been caused by the breach of that term of the contract.

(b) As a result of the defence drafted on behalf of Shedrite, the facts in issue will be:

    (i)   An express term of that contract that the extension would be completed within four months.

    (ii)  Breach of that term (ie, no completion within four months).

    (iii) The loss of £25,000 in profits.

    (iv) That loss having been caused by the breach of that term of the contract.

Shedrite only admitted the existence of the contract. They did not add in a new issue by alleging that they completed the contract within five months. This is simply the detail of the challenge to Anil's allegations of breach. They have required Anil to prove the loss of profit (both the amount and that the loss was a result of their action).

(c) In the second scenario, Shedrite have raised more facts in issue (and closed off others):

    (i)   The formation of the contract, ie, whether it was made orally or in writing on Shedrite's standard form.

    (ii)  An express term excluding liability for delay due to scarcity or lack of materials.

    (iii) An express term as to which materials were to be used.

    (iv) The cause of delay.

    (v)  The loss of £25,000 in profits.

    (vi) That loss having been caused by the breach of that term of the contract.

Rather than having admitted the existence of the particular contract, Shedrite have denied the contract was formed orally and alleged that it was in fact a written contract. To succeed in their exclusion clause defence, not only will Shedrite have to prove the existence of the relevant term but they will also have to prove that the term applies in this case. Therefore, whether or not there was in fact scarcity will be a fact in issue. Loss and causation of loss remain facts in issue because Shedrite have not admitted them. Again they have required proof on each issue. Incidentally, Anil may wish to respond to these allegations by raising further issues by way of reply (for example, by relying an another term of the contract). If he goes beyond challenging Shedrite's allegations and opens up a new area of dispute, another fact in issue will exist in the case. It is only when the statement of case process has formally ended (ie, as a matter of procedural rules) that it will be possible to decide what in fact the facts in issue will be should the matter go to court. For these rules of procedure see the *Civil Litigation Manual*.

### Activity 2.1

It is important to remember that it is not possible to be certain about the facts in issue in a civil case until the close of the statement of case process at the very earliest. This is because it is not possible to determine which facts are in issue until all parties have entered all the pleadings they intend to during the statement of case process. However it is likely that the case will proceed as follows:

(i) The Particulars of Claim will allege that:

- There was a contract between Constantia and Plumstead.
- It was a term of the contract that Plumstead would pay Constantia £5,000 within 30 days of delivery of the machines.
- The machines were delivered.
- Plumstead have not paid the £5,000.

There is no need to allege any more than this at this point and doing so will potentially incur an obligation to prove anything alleged unnecessarily.

(ii) Plumstead's Defence is likely to:

- Admit all the facts alleged by Constantia (contract, term regarding payment, delivery and non-payment).
- Allege the existence of clauses 8(a) and (b).
- Allege that the goods were not in good working order or free from defects.
- Deny that Plumstead have any obligation to pay Constantia in the circumstances.

(iii) Constantia's Reply will:

- Admit the existence of clauses 8(a) and (b).
- Allege that under clause 8(b) Plumstead would not be excused from payment if damage occurred due to the negligence of Plumstead or its servants or agents.
- Not admit that the machines were damaged (assuming that Constantia do not know whether or not they are).
- Allege that any damage that has been caused was caused by the negligence of Plumstead or its employee.
- Allege that clause 8(b) therefore did not excuse Plumstead from making payment.

It is likely that Plumstead will in fact at this point enter further pleadings in which they will:

- Admit the detail of clause 8(b).
- Deny negligence of Plumstead or its employees.

(iv) Note that the following issues are not facts in issue as they have been admitted:

- The existence of a contract between Constantia and Plumstead.

- The term relating to payment.
- Delivery.
- Non-payment of £5,000.
- Existence of clauses 8(a) and (b).

The existing facts in issue and their burdens of proof will probably be as follows:

- Damage to the machines. Plumstead will bear the burden of proving these matters.
- The negligence of Plumstead's employee. This is difficult to resolve. It was first alleged by Constantia because Plumstead pleaded clause 8(b) and its effect selectively. However Constantia might argue that good pleading practice would require Plumstead to have pleaded their lack of negligence. They would rely upon *The Glendarroch* in support of an argument that regard to good pleading practice was an appropriate ground for resolving the burden of proof. However they would still have to prove what good pleading practice would require. This involves some use of broader policy considerataions such as the relative ease of each party to prove or disprove the allegation. Plumstead would argue that proving a negative is notoriously difficult (see for example *Joseph Constantine Steamship Line Ltd v Imperial Smelting Corp* [1942] AC 154) whereas Constantia might argue that Plumstead, as the party in possession of the goods, were in a better position to prove what did or did not happen to the goods (relying on bailment cases such as *Hurst v Evans* [1917] 1 KB 352). Ultimately there is no clear answer as to who would bear the burden of proving this issue and will therefore be a matter of legal argument (and possibly appeal).

## Activity 2.2

**Facts in Issue and Burdens of Proof (ignoring the impact of Article 6):** The facts in issue in Alan's case would be:

| Fact in issue | Evidential burden | Legal burden | Standard of proof |
|---|---|---|---|
| Identity of Alan | Prosecution | Prosecution | Beyond reasonable doubt |
| Possession | Prosecution | Prosecution | Beyond reasonable doubt |
| Bladed article | Prosecution | Prosecution | Beyond reasonable doubt |
| Public place | Prosecution | Prosecution | Beyond reasonable doubt |
| Use for work | Defence | Defence | Balance of probabilities |

Alan's explanation does not appear to have challenged the facts that the prosecution will have to prove. However, in contrast to civil cases, the fact that Alan may admit facts upon which the prosecution bear a burden will not prevent them from having to prove them. Alan would be entitled to make a submission of no case to answer if the prosecution failed to prove any of these facts. Note, however that the fact that Alan may have admitted aspects of the prosecution case when talking to the police may be evidence against him for the purposes of discharging burdens of proof (this will be discussed in **Chapter 9**).

Section 139(5) requires a party to prove the defence of possession of the knife for work purposes.

In Beatrice's case the facts in issue will be:

| Fact in issue | Evidential burden | Legal burden | Standard of proof |
| --- | --- | --- | --- |
| Identity of Beatrice | Prosecution | Prosecution | Beyond reasonable doubt |
| Possession | Prosecution | Prosecution | Beyond reasonable doubt |
| Bladed article | Prosecution | Prosecution | Beyond reasonable doubt |
| Public place | Prosecution | Prosecution | Beyond reasonable doubt |
| Not folding pen-knife | Defence | Defence | Balance of probabilities |
| Self defence | Defence | Prosecution | Beyond reasonable doubt |

As in Alan's case the prosecution must prove the elements of the offence and the identity of Beatrice. However, unlike Alan's case, Beatrice has challenged an element of the prosecution (public place). This does not affect who bears the burden or standard of proof: it simply makes it more likely that it is a live issue at trial.

The defence that the knife was a folding pen knife would appear to be an exception within the meaning of *R v Edwards* and s 101 of the Magistrates' Courts Act 1980. Therefore Beatrice will bear the burden of proving the nature of the knife. Given that knife has been lost, this may be more difficult than otherwise but not impossible; Beatrice can of course give evidence of the nature of the knife that could prove the issue and evidence in support might be obtained from the police officer. Self defence is a common law defence and therefore, following the normal rules for such defences, imposes only an evidential burden on Beatrice (*R v Lobell* [1957] 1 QB 547, CCA).

**The impact of Article 6:** Section 139(4) and (5) imposes reverse burdens which may be contrary to Article 6(2) of the European Convention. The matter has been considered in *DPP v Lynch* [2002] 2 All ER, HC and *R v Matthews* [2003] EWCA Crim 813. In *R v Matthews*, the Court of Appeal concluded that, on an ordinary interpretation, the sections imposed a legal burden on the defendant and that did contravene the presumption of innocence because the matters to which the sections related (good reason or other justification) were matters that went to the moral blameworthiness of the act in question (ie, the gravamen of the offence). However, the court concluded that s 139 was not a violation of Article 6(2) because the contravention was justified and proportionate. In reaching that conclusion the court had regard to a number of factors that meant that the imposition of a burden was not unfair. The defendant was in a better position to know the nature of the item in his possession than in drugs cases like *R v Lambert*. A defendant under s 139 would be in a better position to know whether he had a criminal item in his possession than under the Misuse of Drugs Act. Two further factors were that (a) the defendant would be proving something within his own knowledge and (b) that defences like 'good reason' were not really matters of burden of proof at all because a reason given was either good or bad without proof on the evidence. The court distinguished *Lambert* because the sentence for an offence under s 139 of the 1988 Act was less severe than one under the Misuse of Drugs Act and therefore the contravention of the presumption of innocence was less damaging. In the earlier case of *R v Lynch* the Divisional Court had also held that s 139(4) justifiably imposed a legal burden on the defendant.

## Activity 3.1

(a) The effect of the trust fund is that Andrew will inherit under it if Delia died before Charlie. If Charlie died before Delia, the property would pass to her absolutely and therefore would pass to Beatrice as her successor.

(b) Therefore Andrew must prove that Delia died first.

(c) Andrew would normally bear the burden of proving Delia died first as he will have alleged that he was entitled to the property (and why) in his particulars of claim. Without a presumption in his favour, he will not be able to succeed in doing so if the court decides that it cannot determine who died first. In that case he will have failed to discharge the burden of proof on the balance of probabilities because the court has decided that the probabilities are equal. However, there is a presumption that will determine this matter, that contained in s 184 of the Law of Property Act 1925 (see **3.4.3.3**). This will operate as follows:

    (i)    If Charlie was older than Delia, there is a rebuttable presumption that Charlie died first. Therefore the trust property will pass to Beatrice through Delia.

    (ii)    If, however, Delia is older than Charlie, then, according to s 184, Delia is taken to predecease Charlie and therefore Andrew will inherit the trust property.

Note that these presumptions can be rebutted.

## Activity 3.2

The prosecution will probably answer this submission relying on two presumptions:

(a) They could rely on the presumption of mechanical regularity (**3.4.4.2**) to establish that the scanning machinery of the court was operating properly whenever the goods were stolen. To do so they would have to establish the basic fact that the machinery was generally operating properly. This would probably be done by calling (or getting a written statement from) an employee of the shop. Note that the effect of this is that it would not be possible to prove that the goods were taken out of the shop at any precise time so long as it was established that they were ever in the shop (the labels would establish this).

(b) They could also rely on the presumption of guilty knowledge (see **3.5.2**) if Francis does not come up with a credible explanation for his possession when he was first found with them. Note that it will only operate if he is found in 'recent' possession, a notion that has not been precisely defined.

Again, these presumptions are both rebuttable. In fact the second presumption is only a presumption of fact: the magistrates or jury trying the case are not required to conclude at the end of the case that he had such guilty knowledge at all. However, both of these presumptions are being used to defeat a submission of no case to answer. In other words, they allow the prosecution to discharge the evidential burdens on various issues. In each case the fact that they *could* be disproved does not prevent them from discharging an evidential burden. By proof of relatively simple facts such as the fact that the machinery generally worked or that the defendant was found in possession of items and did not explain his possession, the prosecution have adduced sufficient evidence on other, more complicated facts, such as whether the machinery was working at some unknown time or that Francis came by the clothing dishonestly.

## Activity 4.1

(a) Yes they may. Pattie is a spouse of Stephen, the accused, and is not charged in the proceedings. Although not generally compellable for the prosecution, the offence is a specified offence under s 80(3)(a). Whether or not it is worth calling her as a witness given her unwillingness is another matter entirely.

(b) Andy may be compelled to give evidence for the prosecution. Section 80 does not apply in relation to him because he is not a spouse of the party. It would not make any difference whether he was the victim of an indecent assault or a theft. Barbara cannot be called as a witness because she is charged in the proceedings (s 80(4)). It is not suggested that she is no longer liable to conviction (s 80(5)) so she is not competent to give evidence on behalf of the prosecution. She is competent but not compellable on her own behalf and on behalf of Vince and Wendy, her co-accused parties.

(c) Once Barbara has pleaded guilty, she no longer stands to be convicted so can be dealt with like any other spouse of a party. That means that she is competent to give evidence for all parties. As Vince's spouse, she is compellable irrespective of the charge he faces. Wendy can compel her as well because Wendy has been charged with a specified offence (assault on a child under the age of 16).

## Activity 4.2

**Ensuring that Jason and Mary attend to give evidence:** Legally, both are compellable witnesses and therefore could be subject to compulsion to attend. (Technically, Jason is only really compellable if competent but it is likely that compulsion to attend will have to take place before any determination of competence.) Therefore it is possible that either could be made to attend by obtaining a witness summons under the Criminal Procedure (Attendance of Witnesses) Act 1965. However, it is worth bearing in mind that resort to such measures may not be that appropriate given the nature of witnesses and could be unproductive. The preferred method of ensuring attendance would be persuasion. It is also worth recognising that, whatever the rules of evidence and procedure might say, many prosecutions will fail due to a failure of prosecution witnesses to attend.

It will be seen at **8.6** of this Manual that the Criminal Justice Act 1988, ss 23, 24 may allow certain statements to be admitted as evidence of the matters stated in them if the witness is kept away from court through fear.

The rest of this answer assumes that the two witnesses can be persuaded to attend court.

**Determining Jason's competence to give evidence:** There is no need to determine the competence of a witness to give evidence unless the competence is challenged (whether by the court or by the defendant). However there is a strong likelihood that Jason's competence will be challenged. If so, the test is that set out in s 53(3) of the Youth Justice and Criminal Evidence Act 1999: whether he is able to understand questions put to him and give answers that can be understood. Competence will be determined by the judge asking questions of Jason to determine this. The papers referred to so far have not included any expert report. Such a report may be admissible and you should consider whether an expert report should be obtained in a case such as this and whether the expert should be at trial to give evidence to assist the court (see **Chapter 12** for more detail on this). When deciding whether Jason will be able to give meaningful testimony, the court can have regard to any special measures directions that might be made (see below).

**Note:** There will be no need to determine whether Jason can give sworn testimony because, being only 13, he is not eligible to do so (s 55(2)(a) of the 1999 Act).

**Determining whether any special measures directions are necessary:** Both Jason and Mary may wish for directions under s 16 and 17 of the 1999 Act to be made on their behalf.

Mary's entitlement to special measures would depend upon s 17, under which she will eligible for a direction if her evidence would be of less quality due to fear or distress related to testifying. This would require the concerns about Towers and his family to be addressed in front of the judge and decisions made about what, if any, measures are appropriate. The most important practical factor to bear in mind is that only measures that the court has available can be ordered. Not all courts have all of the facilities to make provision for all of the measures in ss 23 to 30 of the Act. However, subject to that, likely useful directions in favour of Mary might include the use of a screen round Mary while giving evidence (s 23) or even evidence by live link (s 24); the exclusion of members of the Towers family (but not the defendant) from court while Mary gives evidence (s 25) or even pre-recording of testimony (ss 27, 28). The court is likely to be aware of the need to limit such measures to those necessary and consistent with a fair trial of the defendant. In particular pre-recording of evidence might deprive the defendant of the opportunity properly to challenge the evidence of Mary in the light of other evidence adduced at trial.

Jason would be entitled to all of the measures listed above for Mary. However, he might also be entitled to further directions to facilitate a better understanding of his evidence if necessary such as the use of interpretation (s 29). Note also that as Jason is a child the court has less discretion as to whether to make a special measures direction (s 21). Having determined that he is a child the court *must* make a direction that any existing pre-recording will be admitted as evidence in chief and that evidence will be given by live link (s 21(3)) unless the court is satisfied that there is no need to do so (or the facilities for such measures are not available). The practical effect of this is that the court will have to persuaded not to make such a direction rather than the other way round.

## Activity 5.1

**(i) Memory refreshing document:** Terrance could have relied upon his statement to refresh his memory before giving evidence (*R v Richardson* [1971] 2 QB 484). However he can also use the statement while giving evidence as it was made at an earlier time and clearly shows a better recollection of the facts in issue (s 139 Criminal Justice Act 2003).

**(ii) Terrance's identification:** Evidence of a previous identification is generally admissible at trial as an exception to the rule against previous consistent statements. However in this case there is (unless the use of a memory refreshing document above achieves its desired result) not likely to be a statement of identification by Terrance with which it can be consistent. In *R v Christie* [1914] AC 545 it was held that identifications are admissible as evidence. However the law is less clear where the previous identification was used not to support an identification at court but in the absence of any such identification. Proof by a third person that Terrance identified Hazel will be contrary to the rule against hearsay (see **Chapter 8**). However in *R v McCay* [1990] 1 WLR 645 the Court of Appeal in effect ruled that such statements could be made. The law is in fact slightly unclear in this area and has been criticised (see for example *Andrews & Hirst on Criminal Evidence* (4th edition, Jordans) at 10.15). Any argument that out of court identification should not be admissible where not supporting an in-court identification by the witness will be assisted by the ruling in *Sealey v The State* [2002] UKPC 42 that identifications by persons not called as witnesses are not admissible. There cannot be much difference in principle between identifications by persons not called as witnesses and by persons called as witnesses who do not make identifications.

**(iii) Connor's previous statement:** This statement does not appear to be admissible. Although previous statements made to rebut a suggestion of fabrication are admissible (*R v Oyesiku* (1971) 56 Cr App R 240, CA), Connor's statement would not have this effect. There is a requirement that the statement precedes the time at which the motive to fabricate arose (*Fox v General Medical Council* [1960] 1 WLR 1017, PC). This does not appear to be the case here. The motive to fabricate (the divorce) precedes not only the statement in question but also the damage to the car to which it relates. Therefore the previous consistent statement would not *rebut* any allegation of recent fabrication because it was not made at a time when there was no motive to do so.

**(iv) Hazel's statement:** Statements made upon confrontation about the offence can be admissible if either wholly inculpatory (ie, if a confession to the offence) or 'mixed'. Hazel's statement would appear to be mixed in that she admits to the causing of the damage (which is part of the *actus reus* of a criminal damage charge) but denies intending to do so and in fact alleges that the damage was accidental. This could be a defence the charge (assuming it was not a reckless accident) and therefore part of the statement is exculpatory. Mixed statements are admissible as evidence of everything stated in it, not just the inculpatory parts (*R v Sharp* [1988] 1 All ER 65, HL). This is because the statement if only partly admissible would be rather confusing to a jury.

## Activity 5.2

It is first necessary to identify how the previous statement might be inconsistent. There would appear to be two inconsistencies:

- Who it was that crossed the white line. In her statement Mary says it might have been Rajesh. In her testimony she says it was Colin.
- Whether or not she could see what was happening clearly.

It is then necessary to identify the extent to which these two inconsistencies are covered by the 1865 Act. The first inconsistency is relevant to issue of whether or not Colin was driving dangerously. As that is a fact in issue, it is covered by the 1865 Act. The second matter, however, is an issue concerning the credibility of Mary as a witness (whether or not she should be believed on account of her potential short-sightedness and distraction). These matters are not facts in issue and therefore, following *R v Funderbark*, are not covered by the 1865 Act. This does not mean that no questions can be asked about the fact that Mary is short-sighted or may not have been looking; rather it means that if she were to deny that she was cleaning her glasses at the time of the accident, the previous statement that she was will not become evidence. Contrast the statement about the white line. If she persists in maintaining that Colin crossed the white line, the previous statement can be proved to have been made.

The main difference between a civil and criminal trial will be in what the previous statement can prove. In a civil case (presumably for damages for negligence) it will be evidence that what was said was true. In a criminal case it will only go to the credibility of Mary. In other words, the legitimate conclusion that could (not must) be reached by the tribunal of fact in each case would be as follows:

(a) In the civil case: Mary's previous statement alleges that Rajesh may have crossed the white line and therefore Rajesh may have crossed the line.

(b) In the criminal case: Mary's previous statement alleges that Rajesh may have crossed the white line and therefore I am less inclined to believe Mary's current testimony that Colin crossed the white line.

As for how questions would be put to the witness, assuming the statement was oral, the cross-examination might be conducted as follows:

Q: The red car drove across the white line didn't it?

A: No it was the grey car.

Q: You cannot be sure of that fact can you?

A: Yes I am sure.

Q: It is true is it not that you were cleaning your glasses at the time?

A: No I was not.

Q: Just after the incident you mentioned this event in an e-mail that you sent to an associate of yours called Thomas, didn't you?

A: Yes I did.

[The witness is then shown a copy of the e-mail.]

Q: Is that a copy of the e-mail that you sent?

A: It looks like it yes.

Q: And that was later on the same day as that on which the accident took place?

A: Yes.

Q: Could you please look at the third paragraph and read it to yourself?

[Mary reads the paragraph concerning the collision to herself.]

Q: Do you still say that it was the grey car that crossed the line?

A: Yes.

Q: Your honour, may the witness's statement be shown to the jury?

Notice the matter concerning the cleaning of glasses has not been pursued. The judge would have a discretion as to whether or not to allow the jury to see the whole of the e-mail including the part concerning the glasses. If the message just concerned the matter of the glasses or if Mary changed her testimony on the issue of which car straddled the white line, there would be no previous inconsistent statement to which the 1865 Act applied so the e-mail could not be proved.

## Activity 6.1

Practitioners differ in their approach to this question. Older practitioners would state that calling a vicar/priest or the defendant's mother would not carry as much weight as an employer or teacher. However, as society has become more secular, courts are more persuaded by a reference from a priest or a vicar. The usual witness counsel may call would be an employer, someone of standing in the community such as a community leader, a teacher or someone who has known the defendant for a long time.

## Activity 6.2

(i) Situations in which the courts have concluded that a witness had made an assertion of good character include:

- A defendant charged with larceny who gave evidence that on two occasions he had found property and had given it back to its owners: *R v Samuel* (1956) 40 Cr App R 8.
- An assertion of religious belief: *R v Ferguson* (1909) 2 Cr App R 250.
- An assertion by a defendant that he had been earning an honest living: *R v Baker* (1912) 7 Cr App R 217, CCA.
- The wearing of a regimental blazer while giving evidence: *R v Hamilton* [1969] Crim LR 486, CA.

It should be remembered that there are no rules of law as to what amounts to an assertion of good character sufficient to bring s 1(3)(ii) into operation. This is a matter for the judge to determine during trial. The cases above concern whether it was possible for the judge to determine that the above matters *could* be assertions of good character.

(ii) In *R v Winfield* (1939) 27 Cr App R 139 and in *R v Morris* (1959) 43 Cr App R 206, the Court of Appeal approved the admission of evidence of dishonesty offences in such circumstances. Humphreys J in *R v Winfield* said (at p 141), 'There is no such thing known to our procedure as putting half a prisoner's character in issue and leaving out the other half'. However there might still be an argument on behalf of the defence that the probative value of such evidence is outweighed by its prejudicial effect (see **1.7.2.1** and **6.3.5.7**).

## Activity 6.3

In *R v Hatton* [1976] 64 Cr App R 88, the Court of Appeal distinguished *R v Bruce* as the appellant's evidence had not provided a better defence for the co-defendant. Although the appellant's evidence had undermined the prosecution case on the issue of dishonesty it had, on balance undermined the co-defendant's case because it had both assisted the prosecution case by confirming a fact in issue (the existence of a plan) and had undermined the case presented by the co-defendant (that there was no plan).

## Activity 8.1

The trick to answering the first part of this question is simply to imagine that the text above is a transcript of the evidence Tony Ockford gave as testimony at trial and to then determine which parts of it were repetition of things said elsewhere ('out of court'). When you imagine the particular statement being produced as testimony the question is simple: is this thing something the witness is telling us in his own words now or is it something he is repeating (or summarising) that was said elsewhere?

As for statements Tony has repeated, you should come up with the following:

(a) Details of the conversation about the car. Although we cannot be certain from this witness statement, the suggestion is that the conversation was about the facts that:

   (i)   it was Will's car;

   (ii)  it was brand new;

   (iii) he had bought it a couple of weeks back;

   (iv) he got it for a good price (about £11,000).

(b) 'What are those youths doing to my new car?' (Will to Tony)

(c) 'Nice motor, mate. We thought we'd do it up for you.' (youth to Will)

(d) 'Come on, Paddy. He looks pretty pissed off.' (one youth to the other)

(e) 'Come on Fatty Hendricks, you need to work out more.'

(f) 'Scab' (scratched on the car). This is clearly a statement being made out of court (on the street). Remember that we are not yet identifying what the statement might be useful to prove or what exactly it means.

(g) Will said he thought he recognised one of the youths as Paddy Bell, the son of Charlie Bell, with whom Will works at the factory. Again this is a statement made out of court and repetition of a statement.

(h) 'He has told me that Charlie Bell had recently said to him "You're getting a new car with strike money. Don't think you'll enjoy it for long."' Here we have a statement within a statement. Tony is telling us what Will has said to him. Part of what Will said was the repetition of something Charlie had said to Will. Both what Will said and what Charlie said are out of court statements.

As for those parts of the witness statement that may be based on things Tony has been told rather than experienced, it is less possible to be certain. We shall have to speculate on this for the time being. If you were confronted with a witness statement with such statements in practice, you should ensure that you have determined, before trial, how much of what is related in a statement is the personal knowledge and experience of the witness in question and how much relates to matters they have been told but did not experience. As we shall see when we have completed this analysis, such information is probably inadmissible hearsay.

You should have come up with the following points:

(a) Some of the details of the new car such as that he had bought it a couple of weeks back could be the result of another, earlier conversation. One might need to ascertain whether Tony was with Will when he bought the car. If so, this information is not based on an out of court statement but on personal experience.

(b) The workers at the factory have recently gone on strike and Will refused to strike. Assuming that Will does not work at the same factory and therefore have personal experience of the strike, this is either part of the conversation on the night in question or something that Tony has been told previously.

## Activity 8.2

Look at the table (p 280). For the statements identified above, you might have reached conclusions along the lines suggested there. However the matters identified are not the only answers you might have come up with. If you had identified different purposes for the items of evidence, consider whether any of them were relevant to a fact in issue and whether the statement would have to be true to achieve the purpose you have identified.

## Activity 8.3

The statements might look like this:

Tony Ockford's statement:

I was walking home from the pub, the Cricketers, with my friend Will. When we crossed Marchmont Road and were approaching Will's house, I saw a couple of youths standing on the corner of Meadows Lane. That is where Will's house is. They had their bikes leaning against a low wall and were leaning over a car parked on the side of the road. Will started running forward. The car must have been about 150m away. One of the youths looked up and laughed. They then both jumped on their bikes and rode off. One of them, the one at the back, shouted back at Will, 'Come on Fatty Hendricks, you need to work out more'. Will caught up with one of them but the youth struck out behind him with

| The statement | Purpose | Does it have to be true? |
|---|---|---|
| The conversation about the car. | To prove that it was valuable as it was brand new and worth about £11,000 (this will be relevant to determine sentence at least). | Yes: to be a new car worth £11,000 Will's statement to Tony to that effect is being used to prove the truth of those facts. |
| 'What are those youths doing to my new car?' | To prove that it was Will's car the youths were attacking. | Yes: the implied statement in the question is 'those youths are doing something to my new car'. The statement is being relied on for its truth to prove ownership of the car. |
| 'Nice motor, mate. We thought we'd do it up for you.' | To prove that they had damaged the car. | Yes: that they had done something is implied from 'we thought we would do it up for you'. Again the statement is being relied upon for its truth. |
| 'Come on, Paddy.' | To prove that one of the two was called Paddy (and therefore Patrick?). | Yes: if the other youth was wrong or lying about the name, this statement would not prove that the youth was called Paddy. |
| 'He looks pretty pissed off.' | (For the defence) to prove that Will was threatening (and therefore Paddy was acting in self-defence). (For the prosecution) possibly to prove that there was not a denial when confronted. | Yes: self-defence will only be accepted in this way if the court decides Will did look that angry. No: all that would have to be proved is that these words were used as opposed to others like 'What are you upset about?' |
| 'Come on Fatty Hendricks, you need to work out more.' | To prove identity of the attacker by proving that the maker of the statement knew the person or the owner of the car to be Will Hendriks. If the youth knew the owner to be Hendriks it is more likely that he knew whose car he was damaging and therefore more likely that the car had been singled out. When it is also proved that Paddy and Charlie Bell had motives to damage the car there is circumstantial evidence that the attacker of the car was Paddy Bell. | No: the statement is not being used to prove that Hendriks needs to take exercise. Nor is it being used to prove that the person was Hendriks (we can prove that in other ways: not least of all by his testimony that he was there). Rather it is the fact that they correctly identified him that proves that the youth knew him. Having proved Will's name by other means the proof that this statement was made will lead to the inference that the maker knew him. |
| 'Scab.' | To prove that the motive related to strike action. Again, this is part of the circumstantial evidence that identifies the act as having been carried out by the Bells as they have a strike related motive. | No: the statement is not being used to prove that he is a strike-breaker but that the youths alleged that he was. The fact of this allegation having been made proves who might have damaged the car. Its probative value in no way depends on whether he is in fact a strike breaker but on the fact that the defendants think him to be one. |
| Will said he thought he recognised one of the youths as Paddy Bell, the son of Charlie Bell, with whom Will works at the factory. | To prove that the youth was Paddy Bell who is related to Charlie Bell who works at the factory. | Yes: the tribunal would rely on the truth of Will's statement to determine who committed the attack. |
| 'He has told me that Charlie Bell had recently said to him "You're getting a new car with strike money. Don't think you'll enjoy it for long."' | To prove that the offence was orchestrated or committed by Charlie Bell. | Yes: what Will said about these threats has to be true to show that Charlie had a motive to commit or organise the offence. Note, however, that what Charlie said does not have to be true. Rather Will's statement that Charlie said what he said has to be true. |
| The workers at the factory have recently gone on strike and Will refused to strike. | To prove that there was a real motive to carry out the threat. | Yes: if this is information that Tony has been told by Will, it is only of any value in the case if it is true. |

his fist and Will fell over. They then got away. We looked at the car and saw that it had been scratched on the front with the word 'Scab'. Will is quite large although I would not describe him as fat.

Will Hendrik's statement:

I was walking home from the pub, the Cricketers, with my friend Tony. When we crossed March-mont Road and were approaching my house, I saw a couple of youths standing on the corner of Meadows Lane. That is where I live. They had their bikes leaning against a low wall and were leaning over my car parked on the side of the road. I started running forward. The car must have been about 150m away. One of the youths looked up and laughed. They then both jumped on their bikes and rode off. One of them, the one at the back, shouted back at me, 'Come on Fatty Hendricks, you need to work out more'. I caught up with one of them but he struck out behind him with his fist and I fell over. They then got away. Tony and I looked at the car and saw that it had been scratched on the front with the word 'Scab'.

I recognised one of the youths as Paddy Bell, the son of Charlie Bell, who works in the same factory as me. The workers at the factory have recently gone on strike. I refused to strike.

A short while before this incident Charlie Bell said to me, 'You're getting a new car with strike money. Don't think you'll enjoy it for long.'

The car is brand new. I bought it a couple of weeks ago for £11,000.

One important point to note about the above two statements is that they have gone too far in removing hearsay evidence. Some of the statements will be admissible despite being hearsay. Just looking at the statements above, you might think that some of the sense of the incident and certainly some of the probative evidence has been lost. However, at this point we are simply identifying the hearsay evidence. Furthermore, by splitting up the statements in this way, we can see the way in which the hearsay rule encourages parties to call witnesses with first-hand experience.

Note also that the threats made by Charlie Bell to Will Hedricks have been included in his statement. As they are threats their purpose is to show Charlie's (and Paddy's) motive to commit the offence (to identify them as involved with the offence). To achieve this purpose, the statement (that he would not enjoy his new car for long) does not have to be true. It is relevant and probative because the statement was made (and then, in this case, acted upon).

## Activity 8.4

Nearly all of the statement would be admissible as there would not be any difficulty with most of it being admitted as the testimony of the witness. However it would not be possible to use it to prove the last sentence in which she explains the cause of the accident and the reputation of the other boy as these matters would be hearsay even if she had given evidence.

Note that there is no problem with the 'I will get you for that' statement as it would be relevant to prove that Danny was acting in self-defence. As such the statement is not admissible to prove a fact by reliance on what was said (that the other boy *would* get Danny) but that Danny believed he was about to be attacked. The relevance of that statement therefore stems from the fact of it having been made rather than from the truth of what was alleged.

## Activity 9.1

(i)    It would be possible to apply for separate trials of X and Y: *R v Gunewardene* [1951] 2 KB 600. However the courts will not agree to separate trials simply because of the existence of an adverse inadmissible statement. Separate trials will only occur in exceptional circumstances, such as where the jury are bound to be seriously prejudiced against one co-defendant by hearing the inadmissible confession: *R v Lake* (1977) 64 Cr App R 172.

(ii)   In *R v Gray* [1998] Crim LR 570, the Court of Appeal held that such cross-examination was not legitimate as the statement of X was not evidence against Y and should not be given weight as though it was.

(iii)  Where X makes a statement in furtherance of a common purpose between X and Y, X's statement is admissible against both X and Y. See **8.7.5.2**.

## Activity 9.2

(i)   The right of access to a solicitor is set out in s 58 of the Police and Criminal Evidence Act 1984. Section 58 provides that a delay of access to a solicitor of up to 36 hours is permitted if:

- The suspect is in police detention (s 58(6)(a)).

- The detention is for a "serious arrestable offence" (s 58(6)(a)).

- Delay has been authorised by an officer of the rank of at least superintendent (s 58(6)(b)).

- That officer has delayed access because there are reasonable grounds for believing one of the following:

  — Access will lead to the interference with or harm to evidence connected with the offence in question (s 58(8)(a)).

  — Access will lead to interference with or physical injury to other persons (s 58(8)(a)).

  — Access will lead to the alerting of other persons suspected of committing the serious arrestable offence who have not yet been arrested (s 58(8)(b)).

  — Access will hinder the recovery of property obtained as a result of the offence (s 58(8)(c)).

(ii)  A serious arrestable offence is defined in s 116 of the Police and Criminal Evidence Act 1984 and should be distinguished from arrestable offences, which simply give a police officer a power to arrest a suspect of such an offence. A serious arrestable offence determines various rights of suspects following arrest. A full list of such offences can be found in the *Criminal Litigation Manual*, **Chapter 1**.

## Activity 9.3

If the confession is excluded the only items that link Tom to the commission of the offence are the two items found by the police and the circumstances in which those items were found. Although revealed to the police as a result of a confession ruled inadmissible under s 76, the items and related evidence are not rendered inadmissible along with the confession (s 76(4)). However there are evidential difficulties with both items of evidence.

(a)  The antique vase does not prove Tom's commission of the offence on its own. Although found at his house, Anne's failure to identify it as hers means there is no evidence linking it to the burglary. The only other way in which it could be given relevance at Tom's trial is by showing how it came to be found at Tom's house. However s 76(5) states that evidence that a fact was discovered *as a result of* an inadmissible confession shall not be admissible. Therefore, assuming that the vase is not distinctive (which is likely given Anne's failure to recognise it), it will not support a conclusion that Tom burgled Anne's house.

(b) The watch also lacks a full evidential link to the offence. While it can be proven to have been stolen from Anne's house, there is no evidence linking it to Tom as the burglar. Having been found in a public place, there is nothing to link it to Anne's house. The prosecution cannot adduce evidence that Tom knew where it was (which would show some link to the burglary) because it will not be possible to show that the watch was found as result of the confession by virtue of s 76(5).

In both cases the items found are circumstantial evidence of the commission of the burglary but in each case it is the confession that links them to the offence. Given that such evidence is inadmissible by virtue of s 76(5), it is highly unlikely that the prosecution could succeed in defeating a submission of no case to answer.

Things would be different, of course, if there was scientific evidence (such as fingerprints) linking the watch to Tom. In such circumstances the watch would be admissible under s 76(4) and could be linked to Tom by the fingerprint evidence instead of by the confession. Equally if Anne's fingerprints were found on the vase, that would be strong evidence that it was hers and therefore again there would be a link between the burglary and Tom independent of the inadmissible confession.

## Activity 10.1

(i)   Submission of no case to answer:

- An inference under s 34 can be used to support a case to answer (s 34(2)(c)). Chris did not answer any questions when questioned under caution but a s 34 inference can only be drawn if he has since relied on a defence at trial. *R v Webber* [2004] 1 All ER 770 has established that this will be the case if questions are put in cross-examination that support a positive case. Chris has done so (through his barrister) by suggesting that he was preventing a fight and was acting in self defence, whether or not the witness accepts what is suggested. Section 34 will only operate if there was no good reason for failing to mention the facts relied upon at the earliest opportunity. However, as the defence has not given evidence at the submission of no case to answer stage and as, in any event, whether or not the reasons advanced are good reasons is a matter for the jury (*R v Argent* [1997] Crim LR 346) it will be the simple fact that no answers were given that supports a submission of no case to answer. The reasons for the failure to do so would only be relevant at the end of trial.

- Inferences under ss 36 and 37 can also support a case to answer (s 36(2)(c) and s 37(2)(c)). Section 36 would apply to the torn clothing (s 36(1)(a)(ii)) and to the bruised lip (s 36(1)(a)(i)). Section 37 would apply to the failure to explain being in the area of the incident 'at or about the time the offence...is alleged to have been committed (s 37(1)(a)). An inference could be drawn from a failure to explain these matters and neither s 36 nor s 37 require that the refusal be unreasonable. Therefore not only the state in which Chris was found and where he was found could amount to evidence for the court to consider at the submission of no case to answer stage but the *failure to explain* those matters would also be evidence in support of the prosecution case.

(ii)  The reasons given for not mentioning self defence under caution are matters for the jury. If they conclude that the only reason for not mentioning the defence at the first opportunity was Chris' consciousness of his own guilt then the jury may use the failure to explain when questioned under caution as further evidence of his guilt. The adequacy of any reasons given is a matter for the jury not an issue of law. If the police interviewed Chris while he was still drunk, this may be contrary to Code C. This will not necessarily mean that a refusal to answer questions will be justified. The question, so far as it relates to s 34, is whether the reason for not answering questions was a consciousness of guilt (*R v Argent* [1997] Crim LR 346).

(iii)   Defence counsel might have made an application under s 78 that the no-comment interview be excluded as unfair if the breaches of Code C were substantial. The no-comment interview will be evidence for the prosecution if used to support an adverse inference and therefore, if it has been obtained unfairly, the admission of interview could have an adverse effect on the fairness of proceedings. Of course, it will not be possible to rely on s 76 because there was no confession during the interview.

## Activity 10.2

**Summing up in relation to Henry:** What Gina said about Henry would appear to be a lie (note there is still the possibility that it is true). The statement is admissible to prove (on the prosecution's case) that Gina lied and is therefore not a hearsay statement (see **8.1** para (vi) and **8.3.2**). The judge should issue a *Lucas* direction (see **10.3**) which must direct the jury that they can only use the statement as further proof of Gina's guilt if they are satisfied so that they are sure that the statement was:

1. Deliberate.
2. Related to a material issue in the case.
3. Motivated by a realisation of guilt and fear of the truth as opposed to some other reason.
4. Untrue.

As Gina has not given any evidence or explanation for the lie, it is likely that the jury will not have much difficulty being convinced on the first three points. Gina's counsel would probably have sought in making his or her closing speech to stress the fourth point. The jury would have to be satisfied so that they are sure that Henry did not commit the theft before they can use Gina's statement in deciding whether they are sure that she did.

Note this is not a situation in which *R v Patrick* applies because rejecting Gina's allegation that Henry committed the offence does not necessarily mean that Gina did do so.

**Refusals to answer questions:** The refusal to give answers to questions at the shop might trigger s 34. She was questioned under caution and at that point failed to mention a fact that she subsequently relied upon in her defence in the proceedings, namely the suggestion put in cross-examination that the money was taken by Ben. Of course a s 34 inference can only be drawn by the jury if they are satisfied so that they are sure that the *only* reason for failing to mention the defence at an earlier point is a consciousness of guilt (*R v Argent*). It is a matter for the jury to decide whether this is the case. The fact that Gina has not called any evidence to explain why she did not do so will not assist her in raising a reasonable doubt on this matter. Remember that such reasons have to be adduced in evidence (*R v Cowan*). Defence counsel cannot raise them for the first time in her closing speech.

The refusal to answer questions at the police station is not quite the same. The statement made the same allegations as have been suggested in cross-examination. Therefore there is not the failure to mention a fact that is necessary for the application of s 34 (*R v*

*Ali*). If the defence advanced at trial departed in material ways from the prepared statement, s 34 could apply.

You should visit the Judicial Studies Board web site to see the specimen directions that will be issued in a case such as this: www.jsboard.co.uk.

**Failure to give evidence:** Assuming the formalities required before s 35 can apply have been met (ie, in effect Gina was properly warned by the judge of the potential effect of the failure to give evidence), the refusal to give evidence can give rise to an adverse inference of guilt as well.

It may well be that Gina did not wish to give evidence due to her previous convictions. Had she done so, having alleged that Ben a prosecution witness had stolen the money, she will be open to cross-examination about her previous convictions under s 1(3)(ii) of the Criminal Evidence Act 1898. Given that these are convictions for dishonesty offences, Gina may well fear that the jury will consider these to be proof of her dishonesty. Of course, in such a case, the judge could either have ruled the previous convictions inadmissible as being more prejudicial than probative or, if he did not do this, could have directed the jury that they were only relevant to Gina's credibility. However, it is easy to see why someone in Gina's position might not wish to take the risks that those protections do not work. In *R v Cowan* it was stated that the fact that a person does have previous convictions is not a ground for refusing to make a s 35 inference (although this may subsequently be dealt with by the House of Lords in *R v Becouarn*).

Overall one might think that Gina has not done herself many favours by refusing to give evidence. Not only will she face a s 35 inference for not having done so but she will also have failed to give any reason for the apparent lie about Henry or her failure to answer police questions at the shop. This is the sort of case in which her legal advisors would hopefully have given her clear advice at every stage about the consequences of her decisions.

As a final point, it is worth noting that her solicitor could have been called as a witness to give evidence as to the advice given to her concerning questioning at the police station and also at trial. This is a risky step to take because, by giving such evidence, the court might consider Gina to have waived her right for the discussions between her and her solicitor to remain inadmissible evidence under the rule of legal professional privilege. This area of law will be considered further in **Chapter 14**.

## Activity 11.1

The obvious need is to alert the jury to the risk of mistake on the part of the witness, which may be greater than the jury perceives it to be. See **11.4** for the specimen direction.

## Activity 11.2

The matter has not been considered by the Court of Appeal. The current view is that aural identification evidence is even more prone to error than visual identification. So, although a similar form of *Turnbull* direction can be given, it should warn the jury more forcefully of the risk that the witness is mistaken. See further **11.9.4** below.

## Activity 11.3

### 11.3.1

You might have written any of the following methods:

- video identification;

- identification parade;
- group identification;
- covert video identification or group identification;
- confrontation.

See Code D paras 2.16–2.20 and 2.3–2.10.

Before reading any further in this Part, go back to Part 1 and carry out **activity 11.3.2**.

### 11.3.2

The least probative is likely to be the confrontation, as the witness is presented with little choice and the circumstances are likely to signal to the witness that the person with whom they are confronted is already in trouble or under suspicion. See Code D, para 2.10.

Now look at **activity 11.3.3** from Part 1.

### 11.3.3

The police may put the witness in a police car and drive around the area; Code D, para 2.26. The witness may be shown photographs, a computerised likeness (e-fits), artists' sketches or similar; Code D, para 2.27, annex E.

## Activity 11.4

### 11.4.1

In all seven situations, there is evidence which may help to identify the offender. When the criminal courts express concern about 'identification evidence', however, the judges are concerned about the problems associated with visual identification by an eyewitness.

(a) This is a description, not an identification. It is left for the police to find someone, if they can, and charge that person with the robbery. Clearly, the police will look for a man who matches the physical characteristics and, in the short term, whose clothing matches. At trial, the fact finders would need to be persuaded that the accused is the offender. The fact that the accused is six feet tall is helpful as height is not easy to change. The build may be helpful, although people do put on and lose weight over time. Hair colouring is easy to change so perhaps not much weight should be put on that even if it matches what Alan said. Likewise, the hair length — hair grows and can be cut. What would help the fact finders most is to hear evidence of what the accused looked like on arrest, as that will be nearer in time to the offence, giving less opportunity to alter features such as weight, length of hair, etc.

(b) This is not identification evidence, according to the courts. A simple description of clothing is not thought to be very likely to be mistaken. Clearly, if this is all that we have to link Barry Borrower to the robbery, he should not be convicted.

(c) Again, none of this is identification evidence in the *Turnbull* sense. The purse would be helpful if it can be proved to belong to Mabel. She may be asked if she can identify it. If she cannot, it is irrelevant to the robbery. If she can, the fact of it being in Barry Borrower's possession is circumstantial evidence, suggesting a link to the robbery. The clothing is relevant to making a connection between Barry Borrower and the robbery, as it matches the clothing described by Alan. The weight to be attached to it will depend on the view of the fact finder(s) of how unusual it would be for anyone to possess either article or the combination.

(d) This is not *Turnbull* identification evidence. The police officer can put Barry Borrower in the area where the robbery occurred around the relevant time. The clothing *could* have been dropped by the robber. *If* the barman is correct on times, Barry Borrower could have done the robbery, dropped the bag and been drinking in the pub by the time the police officer entered. To make the necessary connection between Barry Borrower and the bag, it would be helpful if the man who was mending his car was able to say that Barry Borrower is the man he saw drop the bag. If he does so, *that* evidence will be identification evidence, in the *Turnbull* sense.

(e) Similar to D. Here, there is no clothing match that we know of. It would therefore have been sensible of the officer to have got a description of the robber from Alan *before* setting off on the drive. Of course, Alan could say in the police car, 'That's the man. I know because I recognise him and he is wearing the same clothes that the robber wore.' The weight of that evidence will be less than if Alan had described the physical features and clothing of the robber *before* seeing the man he now says is the robber.

(f) This is not identification evidence. It is circumstantial evidence which suggests that the library card was there because its possessor had previously been in the alleyway. It does not tell us when it was left there or by whom it was left. It may assist the police in their investigation as it suggests a possible line of enquiry. By itself, it cannot identify Barry Borrower as the robber.

(g) This is identification evidence. The fact that the alleged robber is already know to Alan does not mean that the fact-finder(s) should not be cautious before relying on Alan's evidence. It is clearly helpful that Alan says he recognised the robber but the courts have concluded that an eyewitness may be mistaken as to identification, wrongly thinking that they recognise someone.

Now consider **activity 11.4.2** in Part 1 before looking at the answer set out below.

**11.4.2** In each of the seven situations, Barry Borrower says he was not the perpetrator and, in effect, denies being present at the crime scene. Therefore, identification is in issue in all seven situations.

An identification parade (or other method permitted in Code D) should be used whenever identity is disputed and the police know of a witness who could confirm or deny that a particular suspect is the offender. However, it may be unnecessary where the witness claims to have recognised the offender.

Now see **activity 11.4.3** in Part 1.

**11.4.3**

(i) So far, no one knows if the tape shows either the robbery or the robber. If it shows the robbery, which anyone should be able to see, it would not advance the investigation to show Alan the tape. He will not be enabled to tell the police any more than he has already. If he is called as a witness at trial, the defence counsel may suggest that his description of the robber is based upon what he saw on the tape and not on his recollection of the incident. To forestall (or at least minimise) such cross-examination, it is good practice to take a statement from the witness, describing the offender, prior to showing the witness the CCTV footage. It was said in *R v Roberts* [1998] Crim LR 682 that it is permissible to show CCTV footage to a witness and then allow him to amend a statement he made earlier. This decision does not help to insulate the witness against damaging cross-examination at trial.

What if the tape does not show the robbery? It might help the investigation if Alan can identify the robber on the tape. The police would then have a better idea for themselves of the man they are looking for. However, this step does risk exposing

Alan to the criticism of defence counsel at trial. You should note that different purposes are served, depending upon whether the police are conducting the investigation or generating evidence for trial.

(ii)    As with (a), but the clothing is perhaps more distinctive. If the tape shows the robbery, there is no benefit to the investigation to show it to Alan and it may reduce the weight of his evidence at trial to do so. If the tape simply shows a man wearing these clothes, it is likely to be the robber. The police would not need Alan to tell them that, so there is no investigative need to show Alan the tape.

(iii)    Clearly it is, for the purposes of advancing the investigation.

(iv)    Again, this helps to advance the investigation and she can do so. It is clearly helpful if the officer recognises the offender as he commits the offence. If the video does not show the offence but the officer recognises Barry Borrower as someone in the vicinity at the approximate time of the offence, that is helpful to the investigation.

(v)    The case law says she can be called as an identification witness. Unlike a real eyewitness, who would probably have been surprised by the unfolding events and may have missed parts of it, the police officer can rewind and replay the tape many times. In this situation, the courts have suggested that the officer becomes something of an expert witness on the subject of identification (although only on the specific issue of the offender on the particular CCTV tape).

There is a danger of prejudicial information being put in front of the jury if the police witness says that she saw a man she knows as Barry Borrower on the video. It implies that Borrower may have a criminal past. Prosecuting counsel may need to conduct a careful examination-in-chief in order to minimise the risk of such inferences being made by the jury. See further **11.9.3**.

Further, the CCTV tape could be played at trial, for the fact finders to form their own views on identification. This may be rather a dangerous practice, though, and open to criticism by the defence at trial. A real eyewitness would usually be asked to participate in an identification parade. Such parades have certain safeguards to maximise their reliability, for example, having several people of similar appearance to the suspect participate in the parade. That cannot happen in the courtroom. The absence of such safeguards makes it dangerous for the fact finders to watch a CCTV tape and then look at the accused in the dock to see if she or he resembles the person on the tape.

## Activity 11.5

The trial judge actually directed the jury of the special need for caution before relying on M's evidence identifying G as her attacker (a *Turnbull* warning; see **11.7** above). The judge did not warn the jury of any possible danger if they relied on M's uncorroborated evidence to convict G. G was convicted and appealed.

The Privy Council said that G's plea of not guilty and his alibi defence put the issue of identification at the heart of the trial. Therefore the judge was correct to give a *Turnbull* warning. You might think that, if the jury were keen to find evidence to support M's identification of G, they could have used the evidence of the police officer about the scratch marks on G's back. At no stage of the trial did G assert that M was lying about the attack on her. As there was no suggestion that M had fabricated the allegation, there was no reason to warn the jury of any need for caution before acting upon M's evidence. See also *R v Chance* [1988] QB 932.

### Activity 12.1

One good example would be the reliability of a witness. This might be the witness who wants to offer an opinion of himself — 'You can trust me. I'm an honest man.' Or it might be an opinion about someone else — 'You can't believe a word he says. He has never liked me since I moved in next door to him.'

Another example is a person's state of mind. This often arises in criminal cases, where the *mens rea* of the accused is a fact in issue. So, a witness may feel able to offer the statement 'You could tell he meant to murder poor Daisy. You could see it in his eyes.' That is unhelpful opinion evidence. To say that 'Smith's face was flushed, his eyes were just staring at Daisy. They never left her face as he walked across the room towards her', offers factual information which the witness has perceived and from which the court can form its own opinion about Smith's state of mind and intention.

### Activity 12.2

(i) The court might need help on (a) whether D was sleepwalking at the time, (b) perhaps even whether such a condition exists, and (c) could a sleepwalker have behaved as D did? In the trial on which the example is based (*R v Smith* [1979] 1 WLR 1445), the prosecution needed to prove D's state of mind. They called a psychiatrist witness. The psychiatrist had examined D prior to the trial.

(ii) Perhaps an expert on sleep disorders might have been better qualified on the subject.

### Activity 12.3

Her initial opinion evidence is that someone in D's position could not be sleepwalking. She then seems to accept that D could possibly have been sleepwalking but that, if so, he would remain asleep for some time after the attack ended. If there was evidence from other witnesses (remember, the psychiatrist was not present) that D was awake and conscious by the end of the attack, the psychiatrist seems to say that this would contradict any suggestion of sleepwalking. An interesting question, which this expert does not seem to have dealt with, is whether a person, deeply asleep, who is being attacked by another could then sleepwalk his way across the room to the precise place where he keeps his butcher's knife, take it out and use it.

### Activity 12.4

(i) These statements are really just expressions of facts that the witness has perceived. If we asked the witness to do so, he or she could explain what led them to that conclusion. For example, 'Smith was really angry. He was red in the face. He was shouting at the top of his voice. His hands were clenched into fists.'

(ii) You may have written something like this: 'You say the blue car was being driven in a very dangerous manner, Mrs Hill-Start. What did you see to make you think that?' Or you might have asked a series of more closed questions: 'What was its speed? Which side of the road was it on? Were there any pedestrians in the High Street then? How were they affected by the blue car? Were there other vehicles in the High

Street? How did the way in which the blue car was driven affect them? Did the driver comply with the traffic signals?' etc Mrs Hill-Start may reply: 'The blue car swerved sharply around a parked car and went on to the 'wrong' side of the road. There were several cars coming towards the blue car then. They had to brake sharply to avoid colliding with it. The blue car was able to return to its own side of the road but it did so too fast. As a result, its nearside wheels mounted the pavement. It carried on like that for several yards, only getting all four wheels back on the road a few yards before it would have hit a phone box which had someone inside. The car then went over a crossroads, where the traffic lights were red against it. Several cars on the other road swerved and braked. Then I lost sight of the blue car.'

## Activity 12.5

The experts who were used in each example were:

(a) *R v Holmes* [1953] 1 WLR 686 — 'a medical man, Dr Woddis' — no suggestion of any particular psychiatric expertise in the law report.

(b) *R v Bailey* (1978) 66 Cr App R 31 — Dr Woddis (again), the other two were Dr Clegg (the Medical Superintendent of St Matthew's Hospital) and Dr Coates (the Senior Medical Officer of Birmingham Prison); again, no suggestion of any psychiatric qualification or expertise is made in the report of the case. *R v Tandy* [1989] 1 WLR 350 — doctors gave evidence on the level of alcohol in T's blood, forensic psychiatrists testified as to its effect on alcoholics generally and T in particular.

(c) *R v Smith* [1979] 1 WLR 1445 — a psychiatrist.

(d) *Toohey v Metropolitan Police Commissioner* [1965] AC 595, HL — a police surgeon who had examined the alleged victim shortly after the 'offence'. *R v MacKenney* (1983) 76 Cr App R 271 it was held that we do not need an expert to help diagnose whether a 'normal' witness is telling the truth.

(e) *R v Tilley* [1961] 1 WLR 1309 — no expert had been called and the Court of Appeal went no further than to observe that this was a matter calling for expert assistance. An experienced forensic document examiner would seem to be the obvious choice, not a graphologist. Remember, a non-expert witness could be called, if available, simply to say she saw the alleged author write the document.

(f) *Pugsley* v *Hunter* [1973] 1 WLR 578 — simply described in the report as 'medical evidence'. Possibly a qualification in biochemistry or pharmacology would be appropriate.

(g) *DPP v A and BC Chewing Gum Ltd* [1968] 1 QB 159 — experts on child psychiatry were said to be the relevant witnesses. But compare *R v Stamford* [1972] 2 QB 391 and *R v Anderson* [1972] 1 QB 304.

(h) *R v Skirving* [1985] QB 819 — a professor of addiction behaviour, whose evidence would be 'confined to the potentially deleterious effect of taking drugs, and not ... any other issue. The evidence was not aimed at establishing that the book had the necessary tendency [to deprave and corrupt] ... it was to give a scientific assessment of the characteristics of cocaine and their likely effect, both physical and mental, on the user ...; furthermore, to explain the different effects of the various methods of ingesting the substance.' Compare *R v Edwards* [2001] EWCA Crim 2185 — evidence about the practice of drug users given by a police officer and by someone who worked with addicts was valueless and so inadmissible. Both witnesses were relying upon accounts given by unidentified drug users, which were unsupported by any scientific material.

(i) *R v Oakley* (1979) 70 Cr App R 7 — the evidence was given by a police officer, trained in accident investigation.

(j) *R v Toner* (1991) 93 Cr App R 382 — the effect of hypoglycaemia on intent was not within the jury's knowledge; thus, the help of an expert, a consultant physician, was needed.

(k) *R v Silcott* The Times, 9 December 1991 — psychiatric or psychological evidence should have been allowed, to show that R was of lower than average intelligence and highly suggestible.

(l) *R v Stockwell* (1993) 97 Cr App R 260 — at this time, facial mapping was just developing. The proffered expert had 'no scientific qualifications, no specific training, no professional body and no database'. He was 'an artist working in the field of medicine and life science at the University of Manchester'. His work was to illustrate pictorially the essentials of anatomical features and surgical operations. He was also concerned in comparing photographs. The Court of Appeal felt that, on the basis of the witness's experience, and by the nature of the assistance he could give, the evidence was admissible.

## Activity 13.1

(a) See s 11(1).

(b) No, the section covers a conviction not just of a party but also of anyone else, so long as it is relevant to the facts in issue in the case. See s 11(1). This means that the section covers claims of vicarious liability, of which *Hollington v Hewthorn* was an example. Usually, though, the convicted person is a party to the subsequent civil claim.

(c) See s 11(2)(a).

(d) There is no such provision in the section. This was a matter which the CEA 1968 left to the courts to work out. How they did so is explained in **13.3.2**.

## Activity 13.2

You might have chosen an example where the commission of an earlier offence is itself an element of the current offence alleged against the defendant, D. So if D is on trial for murder, it could be relevant to show that D hit the victim, V, over the head, causing serious bodily harm. It is relevant because it shows the *actus reus* of the crime of murder and it also shows the identity of the alleged offender. Suppose the assault took place on 1 January 2003 but V did not die from his injuries until, say, 1 September 2003. By that date D may have been convicted of causing grievous bodily harm to V with intent (Offences against the Person Act 1861, s 18). The prosecution at D's murder trial could call the same witnesses that they used at the s 18 trial to prove the attack on V (there is no double jeopardy problem here). Or they could use PACE 1984, s 74(3) and just call evidence of the s 18 conviction. The advantage for the prosecution in using s 74(3) is that D must then be found to have attacked V unless he can prove otherwise. That is, D would need to prove, on a balance of probabilities, either that he did not attack V or that no one did.

Another example that you might have written down is where the commission of an earlier offence is admissible as similar fact evidence against the accused. In such cases, it is typically something about the way in which the earlier offence was committed that is important, *not* the mere fact of conviction. See further **Chapter 7**.

### Activity 13.3

The judge could not know whether L's plea was relevant to a fact in issue because he did not know what facts L was admitting in his plea. This failed to meet the first stage of the test.

### Activity 13.4

(a) Conviction of someone, X, other than the accused can be admissible as evidence to show that X committed that offence, where it is relevant to a fact in issue (PACE 1984, s 74(1)). Once evidence of that conviction is called, it will place a burden of proof on the party denying the commission of that offence to prove that it did not happen (PACE 1984, s 74(2)).

(b) Conviction of an accused is admissible in certain exceptional circumstances, unaffected by PACE 1984, s 4. If one of those exceptions occurs in a trial, calling evidence of the conviction will give rise to a rebuttable presumption that he committed that offence (PACE 1984, s 74(3)).

### Activity 14.1

**1. The memorandum identifying errors in the system:** This document is probably covered by lawyer-client privilege. It is a communication between a client and a lawyer. *Alfred Compton v Customs & Excise* [1974] AC 405 stated that in-house lawyers are covered by lawyer-client privilege. This memorandum is not the same as the types of memoranda that were considered in *Three Rivers v Bank of England (No 5)* [2003] EWCA Civ 474 because in that case the internal memoranda were between non-lawyers within the organisation.

**2. The report of Dr Wick:** This is clearly a communication between the 'client' (Hornsey) and a third party (Dr Wick). Therefore it can only be covered by privilege if its dominant purpose was pending or contemplated litigation. This is a question of fact that might have to be resolved by the court at an interlocutory hearing. The request for the report clearly envisages some future dispute but in *Waugh v British Railways Board* [1980] AC 521, it was stressed that the use for litigation had to be *dominant*. It is at least arguable that the request for the report recognises non-litigious disputes and possibly the fixing of the defects as other purposes for the report. There might therefore be some difficulty convincing a Master or District Judge that litigation was a dominant purpose.

**3. The memorandum concerning John Ripley:** There is no suggestion that this has been communicated to a lawyer (although dismissing employees is something on which there is a lot of law it is far from the case that most actions in dismissing employees involve resort to lawyers). Therefore it is an internal communication that is not for the dominant purpose of obtaining legal advice and therefore not covered by legal professional privilege: *Three Rivers v Bank of England (No 5)*. How relevant is this?

**Activity 14.2**

There is in fact no clear answer to the above questions although they all concern the types of public interest immunity. However you might have come up with the following answers:

(a) The argument in favour of revealing the informant is that A should know whether, for example, the dealer informed the police (he might do so to gain himself credit with the police or to deflect attention). However, set against that potential need is the public interest in police informants not being publicly known. Informants generally have to operate under cover both to be effective and for their own safety. If the identity of informants was publicly known there would be far fewer of them. A's argument was that revealing the informant was in the interests of justice. Set against that was the public interest in the detection and prevention of crime.

(b) B Ltd's claim for disclosure was that the details of the tests might assist them in proving that they were not in breach of the contract because the items were suitable for the purpose for which they were requested. The countervailing public interest is national security.

(c) D's claim for disclosure is based on the protection of D's rights not be arrested and prosecuted and his pursuit of remedies for damages for those rights having been breached. It would be in the interests of justice for any evidence that suggests that the police acted improperly to be admitted in his case. On the other hand there is a public interest in ensuring that internal policing matters are investigated fully and candidly without being concerned as to the risk that the products of that investigation are used against the police at a later date.

(d) E's claim for disclosure rests on his need to establish or support a defence that the allegations against him are unfounded. This defence would be strengthened by evidence that the boy had made previous allegations of a similar nature. The interests of justice served by ensuring that any evidence that raises a reasonable doubt as to E's commission of the offence must be set against the public interest in ensuring that the matters relating to the private lives of children in care should be kept as private as possible.

# APPENDIX 2
# SMALL GROUP QUESTIONS

This appendix sets out a series of 12 sessions that should help you in working through the subject matter of this Manual. For each session, any preparation that you must undertake will be identified. Usually this is simply the reading of the Manual. However occasionally you will be asked to look at other texts. There are numerous references in this appendix and in the Manual itself to *Blackstone's Criminal Practice*, *Blackstone's Civil Practice* and *Archbold*. Use of such practitioner works is an important aspect of practice as an advocate. While other works could have been referred to, references have been, where possible, limited to these for the sake of simplicity. You should use the 2003 editions of each (or the 2004 editions when available, although it is possible that specific references may change between versions).

As general guidance, you should remember that the focus of this Manual is on the practical application of the subject areas. This means that the questions below often require you to put yourself in the position of an advocate and to carry out particular activities that might be expected of a lawyer appearing at court. Furthermore these are *evidence* case studies. Any fact asserted, even in these problem questions, should be treated as something that a party will have to prove. Do not accept what is said uncritically.

## Session 1: fundamentals of evidence

This session is intended to lay the foundations for the rest of the evidence course by introducing fundamental concepts. By understanding these concepts you will be in a better position to understand the detailed rules of evidence and the principles behind them.

### Preparation

You should read **Chapter 1** of this Manual. While there are references to other Manuals and practitioner texts in this chapter, they are for deeper and further reference. You do not have to refer to them in preparing for this class.

### Objectives

This session is designed to ensure that you have a sound understanding of:

(a) the basic terminology of the law of evidence;

(b) the facts that are open to proof or disproof under English law;

(c) the distinction between the concepts of relevance, admissibility and weight;

(d) the division of functions between the judge and jury; and

(e) the discretion to exclude evidence (apart from evidence obtained by illegal or unfair means).

## Question 1: relevance

(a) Ian is charged with indecently assaulting John, a boy aged 13. The prosecution is able to prove that Ian is a homosexual.

  Is this evidence relevant? Why?

(b) Kevin is charged with the rape of Linda. The prosecution is able to prove that Kevin is a heterosexual.

  Is this evidence relevant? Why?

(c) Michael is charged with burglary. The prosecution is able to prove that he has ten previous convictions for burglary.

  Is this evidence relevant? Why?

## Question 2: evidential terms and concepts

Alan Smith has been charged with the theft of a bottle of claret from Walter's Wine Warehouse, Hackney. He intends to plead not guilty. The prosecution proposes to call, among others, Mrs Edwina Walter, the owner of the Warehouse, WPC Duncan, Mr Hughes and Inspector Jenkins.

The following are extracts from the witness statement made by Mrs Walter:

In late April 2002, I had an argument with a customer, Alan Smith, who claimed that I had short-changed him. I denied this. He became very angry and started swearing. He insisted that I was mistaken and said that I would live to regret it ... Mr Smith has been back in the Warehouse many times since then and I suspect that he has been up to no good ... My takings have been considerably lower than normal in the three months of May, June and July 2002. At about 1.20 pm on 7 August 2002, I saw Mr Smith enter the Warehouse. He was wearing a baggy brown coat. He went to the far end of the shop where we keep our best claret. He bent down behind some wine crates, out of my line of vision, then got up and hurriedly left the shop. Later that day, WPC Duncan showed me a bottle of claret priced £17.50 which I identified as having come from the Warehouse. She also asked me for a till roll to see if it showed the sale of any item priced £17.50. It did not.

WPC Duncan, in her witness statement, says:

I was passing the Warehouse at about 1.25 pm on 7 August when a man wearing a large brown trenchcoat emerged. He looked startled to see me and rushed off. I followed him. He kept looking over his shoulder and then ran off. I ran after him. He turned into Cambridge Passage but by the time I got to the Passage, he had disappeared. I inspected some dustbins there and inside one of them I found a bottle of claret bearing a small price sticker bearing the words 'Walter's Wine Warehouse', and a price, £17.50 ... At 4.15 pm I arrested and cautioned Alan Smith. He was still wearing the trenchcoat. I subsequently discovered inside the coat there was a false pocket, inexpertly stitched by hand, and measuring some 12 inches by 8 inches.

The statement of Mr Hughes, a suitably qualified expert, is to the effect that the bottle found by WPC Duncan bears fingerprints matching those taken from Alan Smith.

The statement of Inspector Jenkins relates to three interviews with Alan Smith at the police station. The third interview concludes as follows:

Q. Come on Al, don't waste any more of our time.
A. OK. OK. My hands are up. It was me. I took the bloody wine. That's what you thugs want to hear isn't it. Now lay off.

Alan Smith proposes to testify that he was, at the time of the alleged offence, with Mr Evans, whom he intends to call, at the Slug and Lettuce public house, Islington. He will say that Mrs Walter is lying because he once caught her out short-changing him, and proposes to cross-examine her about that and about the fact that she is blind in one eye and short-sighted in the other. He will also say that he confessed to the crime because Inspector Jenkins, exasperated by his constant denials in all three interviews, had threatened to punch him where it would hurt: a confession seemed the only way to prevent this from happening.

(a) Of the facts which the parties are proposing to prove, which will be:
  (i)   facts in issue; and
  (ii)  collateral facts; and
  (iii) preliminary facts?

(b) Which items of evidence are irrelevant (or not sufficiently relevant)?

(c) Which of the facts in issue
  (i)  can be proved by direct evidence; and
  (ii) must be proved by circumstantial evidence?

(d) For each such fact in issue to be proved by circumstantial evidence, identify
  (i)  the circumstantial evidence necessary to prove the fact in issue; and
  (ii) the generalisation or argument you would use to explain how those items of evidence combine to prove that fact in issue?

(e) Identify any items of real evidence that might be adduced in the case. What might they prove?

(f) Is it likely that there will be a need for a *voir dire* in this case? Why?

## Session 2: burdens and standards of proof; presumptions

How does the court decide who wins or loses a case? The rules of evidence place a burden on one side or another to prove the case at trial. This session considers how this risk of losing the case is apportioned. It also considers the concept of presumptions, which are rules of evidence that change the way in which burdens of proof work at trial.

### Preparation

Read **Chapters 2** and **3** of this Manual.

While reading the chapters you will have to conduct some research. It is suggested that you use either *Blackstone's Criminal Practice* or *Archbold* although you can conduct the research required in a law library or even online.

### Objectives

By the conclusion of this session, you should be able:

(a) to analyse the facts in issue in both civil and criminal cases and indicate who bears the legal burden of proof and who bears the evidential burden on each fact in issue;

(b) to decide who has the right to begin adducing evidence in a trial;

(c) to identify the standard of proof appropriate to a burden;

(d) to understand and to use properly the terminology applicable to both burdens and standards of proof;

(e) to classify presumptions;

(f)  to know when to apply a presumption to a given set of facts; and

(g)  to know the effect which a presumption has on the incidence of the legal and evidential burdens.

### Question 1: burden and standard

Have another look at the table at **2.1.3**. Using a similar table work out:

- the facts in issue;
- the incidence of the evidential burden;
- the incidence of the legal burden; and
- the standard of proof

for each case set out below.

### Case 1

Alan has been charged with possessing an offensive weapon, contrary to Prevention of Crime Act 1953, s 1. He is alleged to have had a chisel with him in a public street. He was found with the chisel at 2 am. He does not deny this but says he is a sculptor and while he was at a party, inspiration had struck him for a sculpture and he was on his way to his studio. He adds that he always carries a chisel in case he is attacked.

Prevention of Crime Act 1953, s 1(1), provides that:

*Any person who without lawful authority or reasonable excuse, the proof whereof shall lie on him, has with him in any public place any offensive weapon shall be guilty of an offence.*

Section 1(4) of the Act defines an offensive weapon as:

*any article made or adapted for use for causing injury to the person, or intended by the person having it with him for such use by him.*

### Case 2

Arabian Ltd, the charters of a ship, are suing Bulk Traffic Co, the owners of the ship, for breach of contract. The ship blew up and sank during its voyage. No one is able to determine the cause of the explosion.

Bulk Traffic alleges that the contract was frustrated by the explosion. Arabian Ltd says that any frustration was self-induced and does not afford a defence to its action.

### Case 3

Following a collision between his car and a lamp-post, Charles is accused of driving without due care and attention. He told the police officer who interviewed him at the hospital that he remembered nothing of the incident. Later, he told the police that his doctor told him that in all likelihood he simply blacked out (non-insane automatism).

### Question 2: determining burden of proof in civil cases

Explain the burdens and standard of proof in the following case.

In an action by A for breach of contract for the carriage of a consignment of television sets by lorry from London to Manchester, the contract provided that B, a lorry owner, was not liable for loss caused by fire provided that the lorry owner's servants were not negligent. The lorry and its load were destroyed by fire in a service area on the motorway. B claims that he is not liable for the loss. A asserts that B was facing bankruptcy and that the lorry was deliberately set on fire so that B could claim on his insurance from the insurers of the lorry. Alternatively A asserts that the fire was caused by the carelessness of the lorry driver.

(Think how each party might draft its statement of case.)

### Question 3: presumptions

On 1 January 1995 Mr and Mrs Bush (aged 22 and 24 respectively), set off from Folkestone, England in their yacht, *Mermaid,* to cruise to Australia. On 16 August 1997 the *Mermaid* was discovered adrift in open seas off the island of Bali in the Indian Ocean. Mr and Mrs Bush were not aboard.

Neither set of parents has heard from the couple since they left Folkestone, although Mrs Bush sent her parents a picture postcard of Cape Town which was postmarked '1 April 1996'. Title to Mr and Mrs Bush's house is registered at the Land Registry in Mrs Bush's name alone. Mr Bush's parents now claim:

(a) that as neither Mr Bush junior nor his wife have been heard from, save for the post-card, since they left Folkestone, they should be given up as dead; and

(b) that their son and daughter-in-law made mutual wills in which all property went to whichever outlived the other; that their son's will bequeathed the house to his parents should he survive his wife; and that since their son probably outlived his wife, they should inherit the house.

Mr and Mrs Bush bring an action under the will to secure the inheritance. Assuming that trial takes place on 1 October 2003, will Mr and Mrs Bush senior be able to rely on any presumptions to prove their case? Will any presumptions operate against them?

## Session 3: the calling and swearing of witnesses

This session concerns the rules that determine who is able to give evidence and who can be made to do so. Later chapters will address the rules concerning what a witness can say in evidence, this one simply addresses whether they will be in court at all.

### Preparation

Read **Chapter 4**. Again *Blackstone's Criminal Practice* or *Archbold* may prove useful in answering these questions as may *Blackstone's Civil Practice*. Not all of the answers to the questions below can be found in this Manual: you are expected to conduct some independent research.

### Objectives

By the conclusion of this session, you should be able:

(a) to identify when, during the course of a trial, the issue of competence is likely to arise;

(b) to know the procedure for determining the competence of a witness;

(c) to know whether any given witness is competent;

(d) to know whether any given witness is compellable;

(e) to know when a witness may give unsworn evidence; and

(f) to understand the procedural issues relating to witnesses.

### Question 1: vulnerable witnesses

John is 11 and Bob is 16. Bob is severely mentally handicapped and has difficulties in communicating with people. It is alleged that both John and Bob were sexually abused by

Graham. Both are very nervous about giving evidence and claim that Graham's brother, Joshua, has been rude and offensive to them each time he sees them.

What steps should be taken in respect of John and Bob before they give evidence at Graham's trial on indictment for indecent assault?

### Question 2: spouse and co-accused witnesses

Ellen leaves her husband, Edgar, and goes to live with George and Gary, his 12-year-old son. Edgar and his brother, Harry, are jointly charged with:

- assault occasioning actual bodily harm on Gary;
- inflicting grievous bodily harm on George;
- attempting to kidnap Ellen.

Consider the following issues:

(a) Are Ellen and Gary competent and compellable witnesses for the prosecution?

(b) If they are compellable, how can their attendance be secured if they prove unwilling?

(c) Edgar and Harry both wish to call Harry's wife, Hilda to give evidence in their favour. Hilda has left Harry and is reluctant to testify for either Edgar or Harry. Can she be compelled to do so?

(d) Advise whether Harry can be called as a defence witness either on his own behalf or for Edgar. To what extent can he be compelled to do so?

## Session 4: the examination of witnesses

Following on from the previous session, this session concerns various rules that regulate what questions may be asked of a witness and rules that regulate the extent to which the credibility of witnesses may be attacked.

### Preparation

Read **Chapter 5**. Using *Blackstone's Criminal Practice* or *Archbold* may be of use for answering questions on criminal matters while *Blackstone's Civil Practice* may prove a useful supplement for questions on civil evidence.

### Objectives

By the conclusion of this session, you should be able to understand and apply the rules (and exceptions) relating to leading questions, refreshing memory, previous consistent or self-serving statements, unfavourable and hostile witnesses, cross-examination on documents, cross-examination as to credit, previous inconsistent statements and the finality of answers to collateral matters.

### Question 1: cross-examination as to credit

Cecil is charged with the rape of Barbara at a party attended also by Dora, Edward and Francis. Cecil claims that Barbara consented to intercourse, being a prostitute of whom he is a regular client. Barbara, who has a conviction for soliciting, testifies that she was raped by Cecil. Among the prosecution witnesses to the circumstances immediately before and after the alleged rape are:

(a) Dora, who has a spent conviction for theft;

(b) Edward, who has a history of mental illness; and

(c) Francis, an importer of obscene films.

Advise Cecil whether the complainant and other prosecution witnesses may be cross-examined about the respective facts mentioned, and whether, if denied, those facts may be proved by the defence.

### Question 2: identifying errors at trial

Read the following witness statements. Then read the trial manuscript and as you do so, identify any procedural and evidential errors that occurred during the course of the hearing. Prepare skeleton arguments on any points of objection or other submissions that you would have made if appearing at this trial:

(a) for the prosecution; *and*

(b) for the defence.

### STATEMENT OF WITNESS

| | |
|---|---|
| Statement of: | Stephen WELHAM |
| Age of witness: | Over 18 |
| Occupation of witness: | Financial Services Manager |
| Address and telephone number: | 187 St John's Avenue, Friern Barnet |

This statement, consisting of two pages, each signed by me, is true to the best of my knowledge and belief and I make it knowing that, if it is tendered in evidence, I shall be liable to prosecution if I have wilfully stated in it anything which I know to be false or do not believe to be true.

Dated the 7th day of March 2003

Signed:   S. Welham

Signature witnessed by:   J. Osborn

On Wednesday 6 March 2003 I was returning from work at about 8 pm, and left the Underground at Highgate. It is a short walk round the corner to the bus stop for the bus home. I must have been thinking about work, because the next thing I knew a young fellow had stepped in front of me barring my path. He was in his early 20s, casually dressed with a waist-length dark cotton coat. He must have been about 5' 10" and well-built. He asked if I had a flyer. I started to say it was none of his business, when I noticed another youth standing against the railings a couple of yards away looking on casually. The man in front pulled me forward with one hand. I tried to push him away, but suddenly felt a sharp pain in my shin, followed by a blow to the side of my face. I lost my balance and fell to the ground. He then ran off in the direction of Muswell Hill. The other man simply disappeared — he must have gone in the other direction.

I picked myself up and went back to the main road. I saw a police car waiting at the lights. I flagged it down and explained to the driver that I had just been attacked by two muggers, and that one of them had run off towards Muswell Hill. I was told to get into the car and the other officer asked for a description. We went down a side road and stopped alongside some parked cars. The officers jumped out, and when I looked out of the side window I saw them with the man who had hit me.

I have a 2 inch long bruise on my left shin and am rather tender where I was hit in front of my right ear.

Signed:    S. Welham

Signature witnessed by:    J. Osborn

## STATEMENT OF WITNESS

| | |
|---|---|
| Statement of: | John WOOD |
| Age of witness: | Over 18 |
| Occupation of witness: | Joiner |
| Address and telephone number: | 157 Granville Avenue, London N22 |

This statement consisting of one page, each signed by me, is true to the best of my knowledge and belief and I make it knowing that, if it is tendered in evidence, I shall be liable to prosecution if I have wilfully stated in it anything which I know to be false or do not believe to be true.

Dated the 7th day of March 2003

Signed:    J. Wood

Signature witnessed by:    J. Osborn

Yesterday evening Alan LYNCH and myself went out for a drink. We are both unemployed at the moment. When we got to Highgate we both realised we didn't have any money. We stood talking outside the pub for a couple of minutes, a bit fed up. A City gent came round the corner, and Alan bumped into him. Alan asked for a flyer; it was all a piece of fun. I saw a police car coming up Archway Road, so decided to make myself scarce.

Signed:    J. Wood

Signature witnessed:    J. Osborn

## STATEMENT OF WITNESS

| | |
|---|---|
| Statement of: | D Sgt William CRANSTOUN |
| Age of witness: | Over 18 |
| Occupation of witness: | Detective Sergeant |
| Address and telephone number: | Muswell Hill Police Station |

This statement consisting of two pages, each signed by me, is true to the best of my knowledge and belief and I make it knowing that, if it is tendered in evidence, I shall be liable to prosecution if I have wilfully stated in it anything which I know to be false or do not believe to be true.

Dated the 7th day of March 2003

Signed:    W. Cranstoun

Signature witnessed by:    J. Osborn

On 6 March 2003 at 20.00 acting on information received I went with D.C. Henson and Stephen WELHAM towards Muswell Hill via Queen's Wood Road. I noticed a young man who I now know to be Alan LYNCH walking along the pavement. He looked over his shoulder and then ducked behind a parked car. I pulled up, and D.C. HENSON and I got out. I introduced myself. Stephen WELHAM called out 'He is the one'. I asked LYNCH where he was going. LYNCH replied, 'I am meeting some friends in Hornsey'. I asked him whereabouts, to which he replied, The Nightingale'. I asked, 'Where do you live?' Lynch said 'Lymington Avenue'. D.C. HENSON said Wood Green?' LYNCH said 'Yes'. I said, 'But that's in the opposite direction'. LYNCH replied, 'Yeah, but I've not come from home'. I said, 'Where have you come from?' LYNCH said, 'I don't have to answer these questions, do I?' D.C. HENSON said, 'Why did you try to hide from us?' LYNCH said, 'I was doing up my shoelace'. I said, 'Have you been near Highgate Underground station this evening?' LYNCH replied, 'What's it to you?' I said, 'I have reason to believe you assaulted this gentleman', indicating Stephen WELHAM, 'and I am arresting you on suspicion of assault'. I then cautioned him, to which he said, 'You've got the wrong man. You are making a big mistake'. LYNCH was then taken to the police station.

Later, I saw LYNCH at the police station with D.C. HENSON. I reminded LYNCH of the caution. D.C. HENSON said, The man in the car was punched and kicked this evening near Highgate tube a couple of minutes before we stopped you. He has positively identified you. You tried to hide from us when you saw our car. Do you want to tell us about it?' LYNCH looked into the corner of the room for a couple of minutes, then said, 'All right, I might have asked for money. It was a bit of a lark. It wasn't nothing serious. Give us a break'. I asked if he wanted to make a written statement, to which LYNCH replied, 'No. Nothing in writing'.

On 6 March 2003 at 22.15 LYNCH was charged, the charge was read over, arid he was cautioned. LYNCH made no reply.

Acting on local knowledge, on 7 September in company with D.C. HENSON, I attended at 157 Granville Avenue N22 where I saw John WOOD. As a result of our conversation John WOOD made a statement under caution at Muswell Hill Police Station.

Signed:   W. Cranstoun

Signature witnessed by:   J. Osborne

D.C. Henson made a statement in the same terms, with necessary changes.

Alan Lynch of 298 Lymington Avenue, Wood Green, N22 will say:

I am aged 22 and live at home with my parents, a brother and a sister. I am a car mechanic, but lost my job four months ago for bad timekeeping. I have several previous convictions for petty offences going back a long time. My most recent conviction was for fighting outside a pub when I was 20. I was fined £75.

On Wednesday 6 March I was arrested by the police. I was on my way to meet some friends at the Nightingale pub in Hornsey. We had nothing planned. We often meet for a drink and a game of pool. I had been to see a friend's car in Mill Hill, and decided to get off the tube at Highgate and walk through the woods and then across to the pub. I would say it was about a 1.5-mile walk.

The bloke in Mill Hill is really a friend of a friend. I had agreed with 'Trevor Jones, one of my friends, to look over a car one of 'Trevor's friends was going to buy. The car was in Oakhampton Road but I didn't go into the house so don't know the full address. I had been given a tenner for doing it, so didn't want to say anything to the police.

As I was coming up to the woods my shoelace came undone. I stopped to do it up. Then a car pulled up, and next thing I knew there were two policemen asking me a lot of questions about where I was going, where I had been and where I lived. They accused me of thumping a bloke they had in the car, arrested me and took me to Muswell Hill Police Station.

When I was seen by the police at the station I did not admit I had hit anybody. I did not do it and I never said that I did to the police. I might have said that I had asked for money to look over the car, and that I hadn't done anything seriously wrong, but those comments were not about hitting anybody.

'Trevor moved to Borehamwood a couple of years ago. I don't have his address, he just meets us every so often. I haven't seen him since I was arrested.

A. Lynch

## POLICE V ALAN LYNCH
'Trial 'Transcript

A    Clerk: The next case is Alan Lynch, sir, number 16 in the list. (*Lynch is brought* into *the court and enters the dock.*)

Clerk: Are you Alan Lynch?

Lynch: Yes.

Clerk: Alan Lynch, you are charged with assault occasioning actual bodily harm contrary to section 47 of the Offences Against the Person Act 1861 in that you, on the 6th day of March 2003, did assault one Stephen Welham thereby occasioning unto him actual bodily harm. Do you plead guilty or not guilty?

Lynch: Not guilty.

B    Clerk: You may sit down.

Prosecution Counsel: May it please you, sir, I appear on behalf of the prosecution and my learned friend Miss Lucy Davies appears for the defence. It is the prosecution's case that the defendant assaulted his victim outside the Three Thus public house in Highgate, which as I am sure you are aware is somewhat notorious. However, this case is not one in which alcohol is a factor. It is more in the nature of a mugging. The prosecution's first witness is the victim, Mr Stephen Welham, who will tell you about the circumstances of the assault on his way home from work and the extent of his injuries. The second witness will be Mr John Wood, an identification witness. He will be

C    followed by Detective Sergeant Cranstoun, the arresting officer. I should at this stage mention that the arrest occurred a matter of just a few minutes after the incident. The fourth witness will be Detective Constable Henson, who was also present at the time of the arrest. Without further ado, and with your permission, sir, I will call Stephen Welham.

Usher: Mr Welham, please hold the Testament in your right hand and read the words on the card.

Welham: I swear by Almighty God that the evidence I shall give shall be the truth, the whole truth and nothing but the truth.

D    Pros: Is your full name Stephen Welham and do you live at 187 St John's Avenue, Barnet?

Welham: Yes.

Pros: Are you a financial services manager?

Welham: That's right.

Pros: And who is your employer?

Welham: Barclays International, in the City.

A    Pros: How do you get to work?

Welham: I catch the bus on Colney Hatch Lane down to Highgate tube on Archway Road, then change from the Northern Line at Tottenham Court Road on to the Central Line to Bank.

Pros: And the reverse on the way home?

Welham: Yes.

Pros: Do you remember your journey home on Wednesday 6th March 2003?

Welham: I think so — I'm not sure of the date.

Pros: Was there an occasion when your usual routine was broken?

B    Welham: Yes, a couple of months ago I was threatened in the street by him (*points to defendant in the dock*).

Pros: Could you tell us where this happened?

Welham: I was leaving the Underground and walking round the corner to catch the bus. As I turned the corner I was confronted by the defendant.

Pros: What did he do?

Welham: He demanded money. Ten pounds, as I remember. Of course I refused. He had an accomplice with him. He grabbed me by the throat and started kicking me and punching — he was really wild. I managed to push him away and they ran off.

C    Pros: Could you tell us what your injuries were?

Welham: I had a large bruise on my shin and the side of my face became puffed up.

Pros: Were you cut at all?

Welham: No.

Pros: How clearly did you see your attacker?

Welham: He was facing me the whole time. He was a young man in his early 20s wearing a dark cotton jacket. It was still light and I remember the lights in the Three 'Tuns were on. I had a good look at him.

Pros: What did you do after the attack?

D    Welham: I went back to the main road, where there was a police car. We went off towards Muswell Hill. We caught up with him and he was arrested.

Pros: When the police car stopped, what did you do?

Welham: I remained in it until I was asked to move into the front passenger seat.

Pros: When the police officers left the car, did you see what they did?

Welham: They arrested the defendant.

Pros: Did anyone say anything at that stage?

Welham: Yes, the police asked the defendant a lot of questions.

Pros: Did anyone else say anything?

E    Welham: The defendant gave them his name, and ...

Pros: I had better stop you there. Did anyone apart from the police officers and the defendant say anything?

Welham: No.

Pros: Was anyone else present?

Welham: No. Only myself.

Pros: Did you say anything?

Welham: No. The policemen asked all the questions.

Pros: After the car stopped, did you identify anyone to the police officers?

F    Welham: Yes. When I looked out of the window I saw that they had caught my attacker, and I shouted something like That's him!'

Pros: Thank you Mr Welham. Please wait there in case there are any further questions.

*Cross-examination*

Def: Mr Welham, at what time do you finish work of an evening?

Welham: About 6 pm.

Def: Do you work overtime?

Welham: No. I am not in a grade that gets paid overtime.

Def: Do you ever work late?

G    Welham: Not normally. It depends on how much work we have on.

Def: How long does it take to get to Highgate from your office?

Welham: About 45 minutes.

Def: You seem unsure about the date of the alleged assault. How can you be sure it was the 6th of March?

A    Welham: I think I was working late that night.

Def: At what time did you arrive at Highgate?

Welham: About 8 p.m.

Def: That's after lighting-up time at that time of year?

Welham: I don't know.

Def: Do you remember if the street lights were on?

Welham: I didn't notice. It was quite light.

Def: Did you make a statement to the police after the incident?

Welham: Yes.

B    Def: Have you recently read that statement?

Welham: Why?

Def: I put it to you that you read your statement this morning before coming into court.

Welham: Well, I did, I wanted to get the facts straight.

Def: Do you drink, Mr Welham?

Welham: A little. Sometimes.

Def: Did you have a drink that evening?

Welham: No.

C    Def: I put it to you that the reason you were late that evening was that you had had a drink or two before leaving for home.

Welham: I have told you I was working late.

Def: You said you were confronted by your attacker, and after a brief exchange of words, he punched and kicked you, then ran off.

Welham: That's right.

Def: It would all have been over very quickly.

Welham: Yes, that must be right.

Def: He demanded ten pounds, Mr Welham?

D    Welham: Yes.

Def: But that is not right, is it?

Welham: Yes, I have already said he demanded money.

Def: You said ten pounds.

Welham: He demanded ten pounds.

Def: I put it to you, Mr Welham, that the man you saw did not demand ten pounds.

Welham: He demanded ten pounds.

Def: I put it to you, Mr Welham, that the man you saw did not demand ten pounds.

Welham: Yes, he did.

**E**  Def: I put it to you that when you described the attack to the police you did not mention a demand for ten pounds.

Welham: I did.

Def: It is true, is it not, that you told the police the day after the incident that the man who attacked you demanded five pounds not ten?

Welham: All right, it may have been five.

Def: May, or was, five pounds?

Welham: It was five pounds.

Def: After your attacker grabbed hold of you, would I be right in thinking you would

**F**  have been watching his hands?

Welham: I don't recall — but I did get a good look at his face.

Def: It's only a natural reaction to look at what his hands were doing, isn't it?

Welham: I'm not sure.

Def: You have already told this court that you were repeatedly kicked and punched.

Welham: That's right.

Def: The assault you mentioned to the police wasn't at all wild, was it?

Welham: I don't know what you mean.

Def: I am referring to the statement you made to the police after the attack. The ac-

**G**  count of the attack contained in your statement is rather different from what you have told the court today, isn't it?

Welham: Not so far as I remember.

Def: Sir, perhaps the witness could be shown his statement. Mr Welham do you recognise this statement?

Welham: Yes.

Def: And is it your signature at the bottom?

**A**  Welham: Yes.

Def: And have you signed a declaration to say that the statement is true to the best of your knowledge and belief?

Welham: I did.

Def: Would you look at the second half of the first paragraph of the statement. (*Witness reads statement to himself.*)

Def: Do you now wish to tell the justices again about the nature of the attack?

Welham: No.

Def: Very well. About half-way down the first page, the ninth sentence begins, 'I tried

**B**  to push him away'. Could you read that sentence?

Welham: I tried to push him away, but suddenly felt a sharp pain in my shin, followed by a ... This is rather underhand.

Def: Could you please continue.

Welham: Followed by a blow to the side of my face. It is rather immaterial how many times he hit me. The fact is he hit me, and nothing can take that away.

Def: Will you accept that at the time of the incident you said you were only kicked once and punched once?

Welham: Of course, I have to.

C     Def: Tell me, Mr Welham, have you yourself ever been in trouble?

Welham: What do you mean?

Def: Trouble with the police?

Welham: Er ... no.

Def: Is it not the case that you have a criminal record?

Welham: In a manner of speaking, but it was a long time ago.

Def: Is it true that you have a record for indecent exposure?

Welham: It was while I was a student. I was fined.

Chairman: Mr Welham, what was the date of that conviction?

D     Welham: It was when I was about 20. It must have been 1982, or thereabouts.

Def: Thank you, Mr Welham.

*Re-examination*

Pros: Mr Welham, I have one or two further questions to ask you. You were working late on the evening in question.

Welham: Yes.

Pros: At about what time did you leave the office?

Welham: Let me see. It must have been about 7.15 pm.

Pros: Did you stop off anywhere either before catching the Underground or *en route?*

E     Welham: No.

Pros: Can you remind the Court how long it took to get to Highgate?

Welham: 45 minutes.

Pros: And the time of the attack?

Welham: 8 pm.

Pros: You were asked a number of questions by the defence about the lighting conditions and the period over which you saw your attacker. How well did you see him?

Welham: Very well. We were face to face for some time, and I got a very good look at him.

F     Pros: Mr Welham, you have already described him as a man in his early twenties wearing a dark cotton jacket. How tall was he?

Welham: About 5' 10".

Pros: At the time of the attack, did you notice anyone else present?

Welham: There was an accomplice lounging against the railings.

Pros: Thank you, Mr Welham. Unless you have any questions, sir.

Chairman: Mr Welham, you go home via Highgate every day?

Welham: Yes

Chairman: Then you will appreciate that Muswell Hill Road slopes very steeply down

G     towards Muswell Hill?

Welham: It does.

Chairman: Which way were you facing when you were attacked?

A    Welham: Towards Muswell Hill.

Chairman: So you were uphill of your attacker?

Welham: Yes.

Chairman: When you described your attacker as 5' 10" did you take into account that you were uphill of him, and that he would therefore appear shorter than if you were at the same level as him?

Welham: I hadn't really thought about it. My impression was that he was about 5' 10". Bearing in mind what you say, it may be that he was a little taller than that.

Chairman: I have no further questions.

B    Pros: Sir, may the witness be released?

Def: I have no objection.

Chairman: Very well, thank you Mr Welham.

*(J. Wood is called and sworn).*

Pros: Are you John Wood of 157 Granville Avenue, London N22?

Wood: I am.

Pros: Are you an unemployed joiner?

Wood: No. I got a job.

Pros: Who are you employed by, Mr Wood?

C    Wood: I've been taken on by me uncle.

Pros: Do you remember the events of the evening of 6th of March 2003?

Wood: No.

Pros: Do you remember an arrangement to visit a public house in Highgate?

Wood: Nope.

Pros: Have you ever visited a public house called the Three Tuns in Highgate? It's located at the corner of Archway Road and Muswell Hill Road. Do you know the public house I am referring to?

Wood: I don't live in Highgate.

D    Pros: It's not very far from Wood Green. Have you ever been to Highgate?

Wood: I may have passed through.

Pros: Have you every stopped off at the Three Tuns?

Wood: I can't remember.

Pros: Do you recognise anyone in court today?

Wood: No.

Pros: Mr Wood, please look around the room, and think carefully before answering. Is there anyone here that you know?

Wood: No.

E    Pros: I have no further questions of this witness.

Def: No cross-examination, sir.

*(D. S. Cranstoun is called and sworn.)*

Pros: Are you Detective Sergeant William Cranstoun, attached to Muswell Hill Police Station?

Cranstoun: I am.

Pros: Were you on patrol with Detective Henson on the evening of 6th of March 2003?

Cranstoun: I was.

*(At this point D. S. Cranstoun produces a notebook from his top pocket and starts flicking*

**F** *through it.)*

Cranstoun: Do you mind if I refer to my notes, your worship?

Pros: If I may help, sir

Chairman: Please do.

Pros: Could you help us, Sergeant, by telling the court when the notes were written up?

Cranstoun: Contemporaneously, while the events were fresh in my memory.

Pros: In the circumstances I would ask that the witness be permitted to refresh his memory.

**G**   Chairman: Yes, please continue.

Pros: I think you were given a description of a person who was alleged to have committed an assault?

**A**   Cranstoun: Yes, I was driving towards Muswell Hill along Queen's Wood Road.

Pros: Why did you choose that route?

Cranstoun: The main road to Muswell Hill is very long with only one turning off for some distance that leads anywhere. I guessed that the suspect would leave Muswell Hill Road as soon as he could, so I did the same.

Pros: As you were driving, did you notice anything suspicious?

Cranstoun: I noticed a young man walking along the pavement. He looked over his shoulder and then ducked behind a parked car.

Pros: Why was he looking over his shoulder?

**B**   Cranstoun: He must have been looking to see if he was being followed.

Pros: Then what did you do?

Cranstoun: I stopped the car and got out. Detective Constable Henson did likewise.

Pros: Did you speak to the gentleman in the street?

Cranstoun: Yes, sir.

Pros: What did you say?

Cranstoun: I introduced myself. Mr Welham called out, 'He is the one'. At that time I ascertained that the man we had stopped was the defendant, Alan Lynch.

Pros: What did you say?

**C**   Cranstoun: I asked the defendant where he was going. He replied, 'I am meeting some friends in Hornsey'. I asked him whereabouts, to which he replied, The Nightingale'.

Pros: Where is that?

Cranstoun: It is about 2 miles from there, cutting through the side roads, on the corner of Nightingale Road and Hornsey High Street.

Pros: What did you say after that?

D    Cranstoun: I asked, Where do you live?' The defendant said, 'Lymington Avenue'. Detective Constable Henson asked if that was in Wood Green. The defendant said, 'Yes'. I said, 'But that's in the opposite direction'. The defendant said, 'Yeah, but I've not come from home'. I said, 'Where have you come from?' The defendant said, 'I don't have to answer these questions, do I?' Detective Constable Henson said, 'Why did you try to hide from us?' The defendant said, 'I was doing up my shoelace'. I said 'Have you been near Highgate Underground station this evening?' The defendant replied, 'What's it to you?'

Pros: I think you then told the defendant that you were arresting him for the assault on Mr Welham, and gave him the caution.

Cranstoun: That is right.

Pros: Did the defendant say anything in reply to the caution?

E    Cranstoun: Yes. He said, 'You've got the wrong man. You are making a big mistake'.

Pros: Was the accused then taken to Muswell Hill Police Station?

Cranstoun: Yes, sir.

Pros: Did you speak to the defendant at the station?

Cranstoun: Yes, together with Detective Constable Henson. I started by reminding Lynch of the caution.

Pros: Did Detective Constable Henson remind the accused of the facts of the incident?

Cranstoun: He did. The defendant looked into space for a while, then said, let me see,

F    'All right, I might have asked for money. It was a bit of a lark. It wasn't nothing serious. Give us a break'.

Pros: I think you then asked the defendant if he wanted to make a written statement.

Cranstoun: But he refused.

Pros: I understand the defendant was then charged.

Cranstoun: Yes, sir.

Pros: At what time was that?

Cranstoun: 10.15 pm, sir.

Pros: Did he make any reply?

G    Cranstoun: No. None.

Pros: Thank you Sergeant.

## Session 5: character evidence

This is the first of two sessions that concentrate on the issues of the character or parties in proceedings. The previous session considered the extent to which the character of other witnesses may be challenged but there are more restrictions when the character of a party is involved, especially in criminal cases.

### Preparation

Read **Chapter 6**. You should be able to access either *Blackstone's Criminal Practice* or *Archbold* while you do so. In answering the questions, you will also have to refer back to the subjects covered in session 3 and **Chapter 4**.

## Objectives

By the end of this session you should be able to:

(a) understand the reasons for the prohibition of cross-examination of the accused as to character;

(b) understand the nature of the exceptions contained in s 1(3)(i), (ii) and (iii) of the Criminal Evidence Act 1898;

(c) understand the distinction between character relevant to a fact in issue and character relevant to credit; and

(d) develop a sense of the tactical use of character evidence.

## Question 1: good character

Rajiv is tried for theft from his employer. What direction should be given in each of the following situations?

(a) He is of good character and gives evidence.

(b) He is of good character and does not give evidence.

(c) He is of good character and does not give evidence. However the prosecution have proved a written statement he gave to the police in which he admitted that he took the money from his employer but that he did so at the request of his employer, who said he wanted to test how effective his security procedures were.

(d) He gives evidence. Although he does not have any previous convictions, it was put to him in cross-examination that he had been dismissed from his previous employment under suspicion of having taken money from the company.

## Question 2: cross-examination under s 1(3) generally

Henry, James and Albert are jointly charged with burglary of a shop. They each have a number of previous convictions for the same offence. The only evidence which connects them with the crime is that of Sam, who claims to have driven their get-away car and has now turned Queen's evidence.

(a) Henry gives no evidence but his counsel puts to Sam in cross-examination that he has 14 previous convictions for offences involving dishonesty and Sam admits this to be true. Can the prosecution lead evidence of Henry's previous convictions?

(b) James says in evidence that Sam is a liar. Can the prosecution cross-examine James on his previous convictions?

(c) Albert says in evidence that Henry, James and Sam invited him to help with the break-in but he refused and did not take part. Can Henry's counsel cross-examine Albert on his previous convictions?

(d) Assuming Henry's counsel does not cross-examine Albert on his previous convictions, can the prosecution cross-examine Albert on them?

## Question 3: cross-examination of co-accused

Olive, Peter and Quentin are jointly charged with theft of computer equipment from their employer. Olive and Quentin plead not-guilty but Peter pleaded guilty at the plea and directions hearing. You represent Olive.

You see Olive in conference at which she says that she did not commit the offence. She has previous convictions for theft, drugs offences and some violence offences but was given this job and has not been in trouble for the last 11 years. She managed to work up to a position of trust. She says that only she and Quentin could have accessed the office in which the computer equipment was stored. She was approached by Peter who had asked her to help him to take some of the computer parts and that when she had refused he said that he would approach Quentin.

In your brief you have a copy of Peter's interview in which he alleges that both Olive and Quentin helped him to steal the computer parts. Quentin says nothing during his interview but his defence statement alleges that he took no part in the theft.

Advise Olive as to whether she should give evidence and what will happen to her if she does.

## Session 6: similar fact evidence

This is the second session in which character evidence is considered, this time concentrating on the concept of 'similar fact evidence'. This is often felt to be a difficult area but with some careful application of the principles and evaluation of the issues in a case, it is possible to get to grips with it.

### Preparation

Read **Chapter 7**. In addition to doing so you will have to read some of the case law in more detail. It does not matter whether you access them online or in hard copy but you should try to get hold of the full reports in one form or another rather than relying on an extract. In addition, you may also find it useful to re-read **Chapter 1**.

### Objectives

This session is designed to assist you:

    (a) to understand the rationale for the admission of evidence of disposition and behaviour on other occasions to prove commission of the offence by the accused despite the general rule to the contrary; and

    (b) to relate the rules discussed in this Chapter to the concepts of relevance, admissibility and weight discussed in **Chapter 2**.

### Question 1: on-indictment similar fact evidence

You represent Dorothy on four charges: counts 1 and 2 are charges of theft and counts 3 and 4 are charges of attempted theft. Your papers reveal the case to be that she is employed as a cleaner at various offices. Each count concerns handbags in offices. All four counts have the following similar details:

- The offices in which the bags were located are occupied by only one person (although in all four buildings most offices are open-plan there were some private offices for senior employees).
- The handbags were all brown.
- The offences all took place within three days of the end of the month.
- The offences all took place after 8 pm.
- The bags relating to counts 1 and 2 were found dumped in a bin outside Finsbury Park tube station.

The prosecution evidence is that Dorothy is a drug user and heavily in debt to her dealer. The dealer insists on payment of a large amount on the last day of each month. Dorothy lives in Finsbury Park. There are further details for the four counts:

- On counts 1 and 2 there is no evidence other than that set out above.
- On count 3 Dorothy was confronted when taking the handbag and said that it had fallen into her bucket by mistake while she was cleaning the office.
- On count 4 Dorothy said that she had mistaken the bag for her own.

Dorothy's solicitors have produced a defence statement that alleges that she did not commit the first offences at all and that repeats her assertions in respect of counts 3 and 4.

Advise Dorothy on the evidential value of the counts and of any applications that you might make before or during the trial. Be ready to play the role of counsel at the session.

### Question 2: off-indictment similar fact evidence

Jack is charged with one count of burglary. You act for the prosecution. The prosecution case is that Jack entered a building owned by Karen which had been damaged in flooding two weeks previously intending to steal property within it. The contents of the building had been moved into the upper floors to escape flood damage. Jack alleged during this police interview that he had been under the impression that the building was derelict. He also alleged that he was too drunk to intend to steal anything.

Advise the prosecution in each of the following (different) situations:

(a) The prosecution wish to prove that Jack has three previous convictions for burglary of domestic premises.

(b) The prosecution wish to prove that Jack has three previous convictions for burglary of abandoned houses in the same area spanning the previous four years.

(c) The prosecution wish to prove that Jack has been prosecuted on three previous occasions for burglary of abandoned houses or houses under construction and that on each occasion he has alleged that he believed the property to be derelict. On each occasion he was acquitted.

(d) The prosecution wish to prove that Jack entered three other properties on the same street on the same night. All of them had been damaged and deserted in the same flood.

## Session 7: hearsay

This session is the first of two that concern the challenging concept of hearsay evidence. As you will see from the reading for this session it is strongly recommended that you adopt a methodical approach to hearsay and its exceptions. In line with that approach the focus of this class is to determine whether or not the evidence might be classed as hearsay, original or real evidence. It is **not** about whether or not the evidence will be admissible at trial. That issue will be dealt with in session 8.

### Preparation

Read **Chapter 8**. You may find reference to *Blackstone's Criminal Practice, Archbold* and *Blackstone's Civil Practice* of use. This session addresses some revision points in addition to hearsay evidence. You will need to refresh your memory on previous consistent statements (**Chapter 5**) and character evidence (**Chapter 6**).

**Objectives**

By the end of this session, you should be able to:

(a) Distinguish between hearsay evidence and original evidence.

(b) Distinguish between hearsay evidence and real evidence.

(c) Apply the above distinctions in analysing a case study.

(d) Identify when evidence may be hearsay by implication.

(e) Identify when evidence may be original evidence under the doctrine of 'negative hearsay'.

### Question 1: identifying hearsay evidence

Peter is charged with indecently assaulting Ruth, a 14-year-old girl. The prosecution case is that Peter fondled her breast while standing at a bus stop. Peter instructs his solicitor as follows:

I was standing at a bus stop awaiting a number 17 bus at about 9 pm one evening. There were two other people there. One of them was an elderly lady. The other was a teenage girl. I heard the elderly lady shout out 'This child tried to pick my pocket. Catch the thief!' The girl looked as though she was about to escape so I caught hold of her from behind. She cried out 'Stop touching me up, you dirty old man'.

Unfortunately while all this was happening, a bus arrived and for some reason the old lady got onto it. She was probably frightened.

The police arrived soon afterwards and I told them what had happened. However Ruth said 'He grabbed me to fondle me. He is making this all up. There was no woman here'.

The police arrested me and charged me with indecent assault. I was released on bail. On my way home I noticed a wallet lying on the pavement at the bus stop. In it there was some cash and a photograph. The photograph had 'Dear Mum I thought you might like this photo of you and our Jack' written on the back and is dated '12/8/01'. It shows an old lady and a young boy at the seaside. The picture resembled the woman I had seen.

It is true that I have a previous conviction for indecent exposure arising out of some high spirited antics after a football match. Unfortunately I have also recently lost my job. Some female colleagues said that I had made indecent suggestions to them while working there.

(a) Discuss the evidential matters raised in these instructions (there are some revision points here).

(b) What are the likely consequences (if any) if Peter chooses to give evidence of his version of events?

(c) Of the matters raised in the statement above, which could be proved by Ruth if she gave evidence for the prosecution?

### Question 2: identifying hearsay evidence

The following is an extract from a prosecution witness statement concerning a fight between Tina and Carol, who have been charged with affray. The statement was made by a prosecution witness, Vicky.

I know both Tina and Carol and have done for some time. We work together in a shoe shop. A couple of years ago, Carol started going out with a bloke named Danny.

Last May I met Carol to do some shopping before we went to work. Carol said she had had a row with Danny and that he had stormed out. He had come back the following day and they had made up.

As we were having lunch someone who appeared to be a friend of Carol's came and spoke to us. She said that she had been in the local pub the previous evening and she had seen Danny who was with a girl with dark hair about 5' 5" tall. They had been chatting away in a very friendly manner. At one stage she had overheard the girl say, 'She won't find out if you don't tell her. We can go to my Dad's allotment'. Danny and the girl had then left. Danny had his arm around the girl.

I instantly knew that the girl was Tina. She is about 5' 5", has black hair and her dad owns an allotment. I was due to work the afternoon shift. Carol must have known too because she said 'That bitch, Tina. She is going to get it for this!'

When we got to work, Tina was there and Carol went straight over to her and said 'What do you think you are doing you dirty slag?' Tina replied 'What are you talking about?' Carol said 'You know. If you don't leave Danny alone, I will sort you out'. Carol and I then turned away to go and get changed for work. As we were leaving I heard Tina say 'Don't you think you can mess with me. Don't blame me if you can't keep your bloke.' I then heard a loud smacking sound and Carol fell over. Some of the other staff members and customers came over to hold Tina back. The manager and I took Carol upstairs. The manager gave her first aid while I went to call an ambulance.

Identify any hearsay statements or original evidence in the statement, and give reasons.

### Question 3: hearsay evidence of identifications

Robert Smith is being prosecuted for causing death by reckless driving and for failing to stop after an accident in Kensington, London. Robert says that on the night in question he was driving his car (registration number NFC 62P) in Bristol. Immediately after the accident, Mary saw a car disappearing and memorised the number, which she quickly wrote down with lipstick on the back of her hand. Later she showed her hand to a police officer, who wrote down the number in his notebook. Mary cannot remember the number any more but says she wrote the correct number on her hand, while the police officer says that he saw 'NFC 62P' written on her hand. May the *police officer* be called to give evidence to this effect?

## Session 8: hearsay exceptions

This session builds on the previous one by finishing the analysis that is necessary whenever evidence is alleged to be hearsay. The questions in the previous sessions concerned whether the evidence was hearsay whereas in this session, the concern is whether the evidence is *admissible* despite being hearsay.

### Preparation

Read **Chapter 9**.

### Objectives

This session is designed to ensure that you can:

    (a) demonstrate a sound understanding of the principles underlying the exceptions to the hearsay rule (other than the special provision relating to confessions which will be dealt with in **Chapter 10** of this Manual);

    (b) identify the circumstances in which the exceptions may apply;

    (c) identify which preliminary facts need to be proved and (when applicable) which procedural steps need to be taken; and

    (d) raise and/or counter an objection to hearsay evidence.

### Question 1: common law exceptions

Arthur is charged with murdering his ex-lover Edith in June 1996. He has pleaded not guilty and has given notice of an alibi defence.

(a) Advise the prosecution whether it will be possible to adduce the following items of evidence:

    (i)    Testimony by a police officer that as he was approaching the place where Edith was found dying from stab wounds he heard an unknown person shout, Hello Arthur, where are you rushing off to?'.

    (ii)   Testimony by a doctor that just before she died Edith said, 'I have a terrible pain in my back where Arthur stabbed me'.

    (iii)  Testimony by Oliver, a friend of Edith's, that several days before she was stabbed she told him that Arthur had threatened to kill her.

### Question 2: statutory and common law exceptions

Alvin is being prosecuted for causing death by dangerous driving. The prosecution case is that Alvin ran down Bert as he was crossing the road at a pelican crossing when the lights were on red to traffic. The prosecution alleges that Alvin was driving at excessive speed for the conditions (it was dark and raining), and that he failed to keep a proper look out.

Alvin's case is that he was driving at a reasonable speed and that Bert ran across the road in front of his car when the crossing lights were on green to traffic.

PC Trotter was on the scene soon after the accident and spoke to Charles who stated that the crossing lights were on red to traffic at the time of the accident and that another witness had told him (Charles) that Alvin was driving too fast. PC Trotter noted down Charles' statement. Unfortunately shortly after the accident Charles died of natural causes. It has not been possible to locate any other eye-witnesses.

Although he did not sustain any head injury Bert died in hospital several days after the accident. Whilst he was being taken to the hospital he told an ambulance-man that he had waited until the crossing lights changed in his favour before starting to walk across the road.

The prosecution proposes to call PC Trotter to prove the note and to call the ambulanceman to give evidence. Leaving aside any tactical considerations, prepare an objection to this evidence and, in each case, prepare an argument to support the overruling of the objection.

## Session 9: confessions and illegally obtained evidence

The last of the exceptions to the rule against hearsay that will be covered is confession evidence. However this exception is subject to so many rules and restrictions that it merits consideration in its own right. Furthermore confession evidence is also commonly rendered inadmissible under the broad discretion to exclude evidence on the grounds of fairness (s 78 of the Police and Criminal Evidence Act 1984) so this topic can usefully be considered at this point.

## Preparation

Read **Chapter 10**. You should have access to *Blackstone's Criminal Practice* or *Archbold* while preparing for this session. You should be prepared to use these sources to conduct further research on these subjects and on the questions.

## Objectives

By the end of this session, you should be able to:

(a) demonstrate a sound understanding of the principles governing the admissibility of confession evidence;

(b) apply those principles to specific factual situations;

(c) describe the procedural requirements when the admissibility of a confession is challenged;

(d) demonstrate a sound understanding of the basis upon which a judge might exclude evidence *other than* confessions on the ground that it is illegally or improperly obtained (including any procedural requirements); and

(e) raise and/or counter an objection to the admissibility of confessions and illegally or improperly obtained evidence.

### Question 1: s 78 and abuse of process

DI Alladice was investigating a gang believed to be involved in smuggling cannabis from Holland to the UK. Without obtaining proper authorisation, he planted a listening device in a flat rented by Ben, a suspected member of the gang. The listening device recorded a conversation between Ben and an unknown visitor, in which Ben said, 'There's a load of cannabis coming into Harwich tomorrow. Charlie is using the Volvo for the job. He'll drop the stuff off with Dave in Birmingham.' The following day Alladice kept watch at the ferry terminal at Harwich. He arrested Charlie as Charlie disembarked in a Volvo car from the ferry. The car was searched, and bags of cannabis were found concealed in the doors. There were no fingerprints on the bags.

At the police station Charlie was cautioned. He asked for his solicitor, Mr Grabbit, but was told that he could not see him, as any delay would lead to the alerting of Charlie's accomplices. He was then interviewed for several hours by Alladice. Charlie denied all knowledge of the cannabis or the gang. At one stage he said to Alladice, 'I've never had anything to do with drugs in my life.' At last Alladice said, 'Look son, do yourself some good. We've bugged your house and we've got cast iron evidence against you. You're going to go down, but just remember that the judge will make it easier for you if you co-operate.' Charlie then said, 'All right. I agreed to bring the cannabis in and take it to Dave, but only because Ben threatened to beat me up if I didn't.' Charlie's flat was later searched, and three ecstasy tablets were found in a bathroom cabinet.

Charlie agreed to deliver the Volvo to Dave under covert police surveillance. Alladice replaced the cannabis in the car and also hid a revolver under the back seat, instructing Charlie to tell Dave that Ben thought he would need it to protect the consignment of cannabis. Charlie followed these instructions. Alladice arrested Dave after Dave had taken possession of the cannabis and the revolver.

Ben, Charlie and Dave have been charged with conspiracy to evade the prohibition on the importation of a controlled drug, and Dave is also charged with unlawful possession of a firearm.

Advise the prosecution on the evidential matters arising.

### Question 2: ss 76 and 78

Steve and Dave were arrested on suspicion of committing a burglary. Steve and Dave were taken to the local police station where they were interviewed separately.

Steve claims that he asked to see his solicitor but that his request was refused on the ground that waiting for his solicitor would cause unreasonable delay to the investigation. He further claims that it was only when the police told him that Dave had confessed (and had implicated Steve) that he decided to confess. Steve then made a taped statement in which he admitted his part in the burglary but claimed that it had been master-minded by Dave. In fact Dave had not made any confession and he maintained his silence throughout his interrogation. Both men now stand jointly charged with burglary. During the trial a *voir dire* is held to determine the admissibility of Steve's confession.

On the assumption that the trial judge accepts in substance Steve's account of what took place during his interrogation, prepare an argument to support the exclusion of his confession (be prepared to make oral argument in class):

(a) under Police and Criminal Evidence Act 1984. s 76(2), and

(b) under Police and Criminal Evidence Act 1984, s 78.

## Session 10: lies and silence

This session concerns the evidential value of evasiveness by parties. Such behaviour can be circumstantial evidence of the guilt (or liability) of the party in question. Most of the rules are criminal although such evidence is admissible in civil cases at common law.

### Preparation

Read **Chapter 11**. You will also need to have access to either *Blackstone's Criminal Practice*, *JSB Guidelines or Archbold* to conduct further research during your reading.

### Objectives

By the conclusion of this session you should be able:

(a) to identify the general circumstances in which a party's evasive conduct can be put before the tribunal of fact as supporting an inference which is adverse to the party in question;

(b) as regards lies by the accused, to recognise which factors affect the probative value of the lies as circumstantial evidence against the accused and say how a judge should direct the jury on such evidence;

(c) as regards silence by the accused to recognise which factors affect:
   (i)   the probative value of such evidence, and
   (ii)  the public policy aspects of permitting such evidence to support any inference against the accused and state when silence can support an adverse inference against the accused;

(d) as regards a refusal to give body samples, to recognise that there are rules about the taking of such samples and state the evidential effect of a refusal without good cause to consent to the taking of such samples.

## Question

Alan, aged 30, is charged with having unlawful sexual intercourse with Martha, aged 15. The alleged offence came to light in the following circumstances. Martha's mother found Martha in bed with a naked man who promptly leapt out of the bedroom window and ran off. Martha's mother then telephoned the police. About two minutes after the phone call a police officer arrested Alan (who was naked) approximately a half mile away from Martha's house. The officer then asked Alan to explain his presence in that place in that condition (naked). Alan refused to do this. Meanwhile Martha told her mother that she had met Alan at a fun fair two weeks previously and that he had been the man in bed with her when her mother came into her bedroom. When interviewed by the police Alan claimed that, although he knew Martha, he had not met her at the fun fair. The police have now discovered that Martha's friend Louise can confirm that Martha met Alan at the fun fair.

Consider what, if any, inferences of guilt may be drawn from Alan's conduct.

## Session 11: identification

There are various ways in which it can be proved that the person committing an offence was the accused. This session concentrates on the rules and procedures relating to proof of identification by eye witnesses. It will be seen that in criminal cases there are various rules to ensure that identification evidence is used responsibly by tribunals of fact.

## Preparation

Read **Chapter 12**. There are a number of activities in this chapter (more than in others) and as usual you should attempt to do them before looking at the answers. You will also find that this session draws upon some of the other areas you have considered earlier in the course. You may also find it useful to have access to the Internet while reading through the chapter and while answering the questions.

## Objectives

This session is designed to ensure that, as regards corroboration, you are able to:

(a) identify when corroboration or a corroboration warning or a general warning to exercise caution is required/desirable;

(b) demonstrate an understanding of the legal definition of corroboration.

This session is designed to ensure that, as regards identification, you are able to:

(a) identify the circumstances in which a judge might withdraw from the jury a case based on identification evidence;

(b) identify the circumstances in which a *Turnbull* warning should be given and display knowledge of the usual terms and content of such a warning;

(c) display a sound understanding of the basis upon which a judge might exclude an item of identification evidence (including an understanding of the key points of the Code of Practice on Identification issued pursuant to PACE 1984, s 66); and

(d) raise and/or counter an objection to identification evidence (including knowledge of appropriate procedural matters).

### Question 1: identification evidence

Mark was tried and convicted on a charge of unlawfully wounding John (contrary to Offences against the Person Act 1861, s 20). The assault occurred when a fight broke out outside a public house at closing time. John was the only eye-witness called by the prosecution. He was a regular at the pub but his assailant was a stranger. Mark's defence throughout the trial was mistaken identity. John had identified Mark as his assailant shortly after the alleged assault when the police took him to the local bus station where Mark was waiting. He was suffering from a hand injury which was consistent with his being involved in a fight but he explained that he had fallen over when he was running to try to catch a bus. He claimed that he had spent the evening at the cinema but he could not remember the name of the film or the price he had paid to get in.

The police officers who took John to the bus station gave evidence at trial of his confident identification of Mark on that occasion. However, John (whose general confidence had deteriorated since the assault), when called as a witness, was unable to state whom he identified at the bus station. Mark had requested an identity parade but the police decided it was impracticable to hold one.

In summing up on the identification issue the trial judge said:

The defendant says that John has identified the wrong man. He says that he went to the cinema on that evening and that he had nothing to do with the events outside the pub. Of course, you should look with great care at the circumstances in which the identification was made. John did not know the defendant and he only had a short time to observe his attacker. Against this it is only fair to point out that only a short time had elapsed between the attack and John's clear identification of the defendant at the bus station. We have also heard how the defendant could remember nothing about the film he had just seen and there was the injury to his hand. Of course in the end, members of the jury, it is a matter for you to decide having heard the evidence of the prosecution witnesses and the defendant.

(a) Draft an argument in support of an appeal against conviction on behalf of Mark. You should also prepare a counter-argument on behalf of the prosecution.

(b) If Mark had admitted being present at the time of the assault but claimed that he had nonetheless been misidentified by John, would it have been unnecessary for the judge to give any *Turnbull* warning?

### Question 2: identification evidence, suspect witnesses and advocacy

Ed Hammond is charged with burglary and theft of a car. You represent him at trial. The prosecution case is that 10 Leaways Road was burgled at 9 pm on 5 June in which he stole various valuable items. The car was stolen for use in the robbery.

The prosecution intends to call a witness, Tina Thurlow, whose statement says she saw a man getting into a red Ford Escort with an M registration number plate at about 9.20 pm just outside the house. He was about 100 yards from her. She was standing across the street, which has good lighting. She saw the man emerge from the alley between 10 and 12 Leaways Road, quickly walk about 20 yards and get into a car and drive off (away from her). She did not subsequently identify Ed in an identification parade. The man she saw was wearing a black jacket, dark trousers and 'some sort of woolly hat', which she said she thought was odd because it was warm.

Tina has produced a plan of the street. The marked with an X indicates where she was standing.

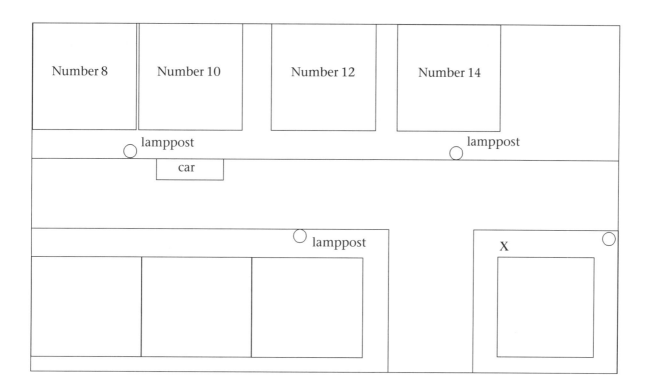

A police witness, PC Steel, says in his statement that he found the Ford Escort car stored in a garage belonging to a man named Alan Grayson. He searched the car and found a balaclava helmet in the footwell of the front passenger seat.

There is also a statement from Alan Grayson which states that he was phoned by Ed at about 10.30 on 5 June, who asked him to look after a car for him. He then arrived at about 11 pm and left the Ford Escort in Alan's garage. Before doing so he took a heavy bag out of the front passenger seat. Ed was wearing a black leather jacket and dark jeans at the time. Alan was not asked to identify Ed at a parade.

The car had been stolen a day previously. The unused material that the prosecution have revealed to the defence shows that Alan Grayson has numerous previous convictions including three for burglary (all of domestic premises) that all took place in the last eight years. It also reveals that the police attended Alan Grayson's property as a result of an anonymous phone call from a phone box, the message being 'If you're looking for the car what done a house in Leaways Road you should go to Grayson's place'.

Ed's instructions to you are that he was nowhere near 10 Leaways Road that night. He does know the road. It is generally well lit but there are lots of cars parked on it even late at night. There are also a lot of trees along the road. Your instructing solicitors instructs you that they have visited the street and think that the alleyway would have been in darkness and that there are two trees between the lamp posts on either side of number 10, one just outside number 10 and slightly to the right. Ed knows Alan. Alan does occasionally stores cars for Ed (who buys and sells cars). He also says that Alan does occasionally commit burglary.

(a) Prepare the cross-examination of Tina Thurlow concerning her identification evidence.

(b) What applications might you expect to make in respect of Tina and Alan's evidence at any point at trial?

## Session 12: opinion, privilege and public policy

This session covers a few areas. Unlike many of the subjects covered in this Manual, these subjects apply as much in civil cases as in criminal cases.

### Preparation

Read **Chapters 13** to **15**. You may find reference to *Blackstone's Civil Practice, Blackstone's Criminal Practice* and *Archbold* useful during your reading, especially where procedural issues are concerned. The ***Civil Litigation Manual*** may also prove useful.

### Objectives

By the end of this session you should be able to:

(a) demonstrate a sound understanding of the principles underlying the general exclusionary rule in relation to evidence of opinion;

(b) identify when opinion evidence will be admissible despite the rule of exclusion;

(c) apply the special rules concerning the evidence of expert witnesses;

(d) demonstrate a sound understanding of the rule restricting the admissibility of proof of judgments in previous cases and its exceptions;

(e) demonstrate a sound understanding of the privilege against self-incrimination and legal professional privilege;

(f) demonstrate a sound understanding of the principle of public policy exclusion.

### Question 1: expert evidence in civil cases

You are appearing for Susan, who is suing Thomas for negligence, alleging that a bad fall she had had on a slippery patch on the floor of Thomas's shop, when she was 18 weeks pregnant, had caused a miscarriage five days later.

(a) After Susan has given evidence, you call her mother, Una, an experienced midwife, who testifies that Susan was extremely shocked and that her symptoms started the next day. Thomas's counsel objects (i) when Una states that such a heavy fall as Susan's bruises suggest must have caused the miscarriage and (ii) when she offers in support of her view an article in a medical journal, which she produces. How would you try to meet these objections?

(b) A shop assistant, Vera, who saw Susan fall, says it was a bad fall as the floor was so slippery and the fall must have affected the course of the pregnancy. Counsel for the defendant objects. Do you consider that you can successfully counter the objection?

(c) The defence calls Dr White, an obstetrician, who testifies that Susan's miscarriage would probably have occurred spontaneously, and that his experience totally contradicts the views expressed in the article cited by Una. He adds that Susan's evidence is quite untrustworthy because her grief at the loss of her baby must have affected her veracity and the reliability of her memory. Do you consider that you can successfully object to the admission of any of Dr White's evidence?

### Question 2: proof of judgments in previous cases

Brian Laird and his brother Charles, together with three other men, have been jointly charged with conspiracy to obtain property by deception. It is alleged that all five men (who lived in the same block of flats) had obtained money from elderly house occupiers for whom they pretended to do substantial roofing work. Charles Laird will plead guilty but Brian and all the other co-accused will plead not guilty. Defence counsel are aware that at the trial, the prosecution, in reliance upon s 74(1) and (2) of the Police and Criminal Evidence Act 1984, will seek to admit in evidence Charles's conviction (of the offence charged).

(a) You are counsel for Brian Laird — what action will you take before the prosecution opens its case?

Make a note of the submissions you will make to the trial judge on the question whether this evidence should be excluded.

(b) You are counsel for the prosecution — make a note of the submissions you will make to the trial judge opposing the exclusion of this evidence.

### Question 3: without notice proceedings:

Consider the correspondence in the following cases:

(a) *Ackroyd v Smithson*: This correspondence concerns damages in respect of a motor car accident. The solicitors for the claimant are Adolphus & Ellis, those for the defendant are Carrington & Payne.

---

*From* Carrington & Payne
*To* Adolphus & Ellis

29 September 2003

Dear Sirs

*Ackroyd v Smithson*

Further to our telephone conversation of 28th September, we confirm that we have instructions to make an offer on behalf of our client of £17,500 by way of compensation for the physican injuries suffered by your client without prejudice as to liability. We also confirm that the special damages have been agreed at £377.25.

We look forward to hearing whether this offer is acceptable to your client.

Yours faithfully,

Carrington & Payne

---

```
                                                              Adolphus & Ellis

                                                              3 October 2003

    From Carrington & Payne

    Dear Sirs,

    Re Ackroyd v Smithson

    We thank you for your letter of 29th September.

    We regret that we do not have instructions to accept the offer of £17,500. However, an
    offer of £20,000 would be favourably considered by our client.

    Yours faithfully

    Adolphus v Ellis
```

```
    From Carrington & Payne
    To Adolphus & Ellis

    10 October 2003

    Dear Sirs

                        Ackroyd v Smithson

    We thank you for your letter of 3 October.

    Our client is not prepared to offer more than £17,500.

    Yours faithfully

    Carrington & Payne
```

No further correspondence is sent and the matter proceeds to trial.

    (i)   Is any part of this correspondence admissible in relation to the issue of liability?

    (ii)   Is any part of this correspondence admissible if the claimant seeks at trial to adduce evidence to show that the special damages to which he is entitled are in excess of £377.25?

(b) *Ball v Herbert.* This is a case which involves a claim by the claimant for damages for trespass to land and for an injunction restraining the defendant from parking motor cars on a field, the property of the claimant, known as Muddock's Square. The solicitors for the claimant are Carrington & Kirwan, those for the defendant are Ellis & Blackburn.

From Carrington & Kirwan
To Ellis & Blackburn

2nd October 2003

Dear Sirs,

**Re *Ball v Herbert*: Without Prejudice**

We have now taken our client's instructions. The terms upon which he would be prepared to discontinue proceedings against you are as follows:

1. Mr Herbert will forthwith remove any motor vehicles remaining parked on Muddock's Square and will thereafter refrain completely from parking motor vehicles of any description there.

2. Mr Herbert will pay to Mr Ball £25 by way of damages for trespass to land.

3. Mr Herbert will pay to Mr Ball £50 as a contribution towards Mr Ball's costs in this matter.

Are these terms acceptable to your client?

Yours faithfully,

*Carrington v Kirwan*

---

From Ellis & Blackburn
To Carrington & Kirwan

10 October 2003

Dear Sirs,

RE BALL: **WITHOUT PREJUDICE**

We have taken our client's instructions and confirm that the terms set out in your letter of 2nd October, for which we thank you, are acceptable to him.

We understand that no cars or other vehicles remain parked in Muddock's Square.

We enclose herewith our cheque for £75 in respect of damages and costs.

Yours faithfully,

Ellis & Blackburn

---

Some months have passed without incident but now Mr Herbert has started to park vehicles once more on Muddock's Square.

## Question 4: privilege and public policy exclusion

You are instructed for Country Farmers Ltd against Mammon Properties Ltd. Mammon Properties Ltd is the owner and occupier of land on which is constructed an irrigation work which, on 3 December 2001 flooded your lay client's farm. On 7 December 2001, your instructing solicitors intimated to Mammon Properties that their client would look to that company for compensation. Consider and advise whether the following documents can be obtained on discovery from the defendant:

(a) A report from surveyors, dated 1 January 2001, to Mammon Properties, advising that the irrigation work was prone to flooding and should be altered.

(b) A report from surveyors, dated 3 September 1989, to the Ministry of Defence tenants of the land before Mammon Properties. This report passed to Mammon Properties with the land.

(c) Advice from Mammon Properties Ltd's salaried solicitor as to the best method of evading liability for the nuisance by means of a tortious conspiracy with another of the company's servants.

# APPENDIX 3
# MULTIPLE CHOICE QUESTIONS

Multiple choice questions are a common way of assessing evidence on Bar Vocational Courses. As a means of assessment, they require a detailed knowledge of the subject area and an ability to apply that knowledge in relatively simple situations.

The appendix sets out the questions in a random order. This is mainly to help you resist the temptation to read ahead and pre-prepare the questions. This appendix is used on the Bar Vocational Course at the ICSL by presenting the questions for the first time in the class, which provides an opportunity to practice MCQ technique. It is intended that you will answer the questions without looking at the main chapters of the Manual (or any other textbooks or practitioner works). As such the questions will be an excellent test of the extent to which you have comprehended and remembered the subjects covered.

## Question 1

Noah and Max were en route to a party in a well-known gay bar. As they were walking to the entrance, a group of skinheads shouted abuse at them. The group then approached them in a menacing manner and Noah punched out at one of the skinheads, breaking his nose and cutting his face. Later Noah was charged with inflicting grievous bodily harm contrary to the Offences against the Person Act 1861, s 20. At his trial, Noah intends to raise the defence of self-defence. Who will bear the burden of proof on this particular issue?

[A] Noah bears both the legal and evidential burden.

[B] Noah bears the evidential burden only.

[C] Noah bears the tactical burden only.

[D] Noah bears the legal burden only.

## Question 2

After being arrested and detained for questioning in respect of the theft of a painting, Nick made a confession in which he informed the police that the painting was hidden in the garden shed at his allotment. The police found the painting hidden there. At Nick's trial the judge rules that Nick's confession was obtained by oppression. Subject to any discretion the judge may have to exclude it, which of the following items of evidence is admissible for the prosecution?

[A] The whole of the confession (because the successful search for the painting confirms its reliability).

[B] Evidence that the painting was recovered as a result of something said by Nick.

[C] Evidence that the painting was found in the garden shed at Nick's allotment.

[D] Evidence that the painting has been recovered, but not where it was found.

## Question 3

The following propositions relate to expert evidence in criminal trials. Only one of them is INCORRECT. Which one?

[A] Advance notice of expert evidence is generally required for both prosecution and defence.

[B] Where an expert does not give oral evidence, a written report by the expert will only be admissible with the leave of the court.

[C] Where an expert gives oral evidence, a written report by the expert will be inadmissible (except as a prior consistent or inconsistent statement).

[D] An expert may support his opinion by reference to authoritative works and research papers written by other persons.

## Question 4

One of the following statements about a defendant's good character is WRONG. Which one?

[A] If the defendant gives no evidence, the judge should not direct the jury that the defendant's good character is relevant to credibility unless the defendant, on being confronted with incriminating facts by the police, made a statement that was partly inculpatory and partly exculpatory.

[B] Where two defendants are tried together, only one of them being of good character, the judge should not make a good character direction in favour of either defendant.

[C] A defendant may be treated as not being of good character even if he or she has no previous convictions.

[D] A defendant may be treated as being of good character even if he or she has previous convictions.

## Question 5

Only one of the following propositions relating to the admissibility of similar fact evidence in criminal cases is CORRECT. Which one?

[A] Following the House of Lords decision in *R v P*, the test of admissibility is simply whether the evidence is relevant.

[B] Evidence of the accused's possession of incriminating articles should always be excluded as showing nothing more than the accused's criminal disposition.

[C] Where the defence seeks to exclude similar fact evidence on the basis of deliberate collusion on the part of two or more of the complainants, it is generally necessary to hold a *voir dire*.

[D] An accused may adduce similar fact evidence against a co-accused, ie evidence showing the misconduct of the co-accused on some other occasion, but only if it is relevant to the defence of the accused.

## Question 6

The following statements all refer to discharging the legal burden in civil cases. Which one is INCORRECT?

[A]  The more serious the allegation the more cogent is the evidence required to overcome the unlikelihood of what is alleged, and thus to prove it.

[B]  If the tribunal can say 'We think it more probable than not', or if the probabilities are equal, then the burden is discharged, but nothing short of that will suffice.

[C]  Facts in issue must be proved by a preponderance of probability.

[D]  If the tribunal can say 'We think it more probable than not', the burden is discharged but, if the probabilities are equal, it is not.

## Question 7

Adam is suspected of committing arson. He is arrested and detained for questioning. During this period there are several breaches of the Code of Practice — namely, failure to give adequate breaks for refreshment, failure to tape or otherwise record the interview and an unjustified refusal of access to legal advice. Adam eventually makes a full confession. At his trial his counsel represents to the court that the confession should be excluded. The judge rules that although there were breaches of the Code, they did not amount to oppression nor were they likely to render any confession made by Adam unreliable. He nevertheless decides to exclude the confession. On what legal basis could this ruling have been made?

[A]  Under PACE 1984, s 76(2)(a).

[B]  Because it is hearsay.

[C]  Under PACE 1984, s 76(2)(b).

[D]  Under PACE 1984, s 78.

## Question 8

Norman is charged with robbing Olivia. The facts alleged by the prosecution are that Olivia was walking down a road when Norman ran up behind, grabbed her handbag and ran off. Olivia continued her journey home. When her flatmate, Phillipa, arrived home about two hours later, Olivia told her what had happened. During examination-in-chief at Norman's trial, Olivia now wishes to refer to her conversation with Phillipa. Is Olivia's statement to Phillipa admissible?

[A]  No, because it is irrelevant.

[B]  Yes, as a previous consistent statement.

[C]  No, because it is a previous consistent statement.

[D]  Yes, as a recent complaint.

## Question 9

John is charged with indecently assaulting Kate, who is four years old, in a playground near her home. He has two previous convictions for indecent assaults on young girls and, when questioned by the police about the assault on Kate, and on being told that he had been identified leaving the playground shortly after the assault, he admitted that he had been in the locality. Some time after the alleged offence, Kate told her mother that the person who had attacked her had red hair and a curly ginger beard. John has black hair and no beard. The trial judge rules that Kate is not competent to be called as a witness in these proceedings. He also rules that her mother cannot give evidence of what Kate said as this is inadmissible hearsay. Is John entitled to rely on the statement made by Kate to her mother (in which she described her assailant)?

[A]  Yes, because it is relevant.

[B]  Yes, because the judge has a discretion to include such evidence.

[C]  No, because it has insufficient weight.

[D]  No, because the judge has no inclusionary discretion.

## Question 10

The following statements concern the circumstances in which a court may draw inferences from an accused's failure to mention, when being questioned or charged, any fact he subsequently relies on in his defence (Criminal Justice and Public Order Act 1994, s 34). If, in each case the fact was one which in the circumstances existing at the time the accused could reasonably have been expected to mention, which one is INCORRECT?

[A]  An inference may be drawn if the failure to mention the fact occurred when the accused was being questioned under caution by a constable (before he, the accused, was charged).

[B]  An inference may be drawn if the failure to mention the fact occurred when the accused was being questioned under caution by a customs officer (before he, the accused, was charged).

[C]  An inference cannot be drawn if the failure to mention the fact occurred on the accused being charged with the offence by a constable.

[D]  Section 34 does not prevent the admissibility of the silence of the accused in the face of questioning insofar as such evidence would be admissible at common law.

## Question 11

Ian is charged with the theft from a shop (ET Electrics) of a TV set which was found at Ian's house. Ian denies theft claiming that he has had the TV set for some time. In order to prove that the TV set is the one which was stolen from ET Electrics, the prosecution wish to adduce evidence of records obtained from the manufacturers of the TV set (Tosh Ltd) which show that the 'unit' number printed on the inside of the TV set found in Ian's house corresponds to the number on the TV set which was delivered to ET Electrics. The records were compiled by clerks at Tosh Ltd's factory on the basis of information given to them by employees on the production line. Are the records admissible or inadmissible?

[A]  Inadmissible hearsay.

[B]  Admissible in principle under the Criminal Justice Act 1988, s 23.

[C]  Admissible in principle under the Criminal Justice Act 1988, s 24.

[D]  Admissible at common law under the public records exception.

## Question 12

Mark was charged with assault and put forward an alibi defence. Norma, the alleged victim, and Oliver were called as identification witnesses and testified that they had observed

Mark for several minutes and that they were sure he was the assailant. In his summing up the trial judge told the jury (i) that the identification evidence given by Oliver (if believed) was capable of constituting support for that of Norma and vice versa but that it should be noted that a number of honest witnesses might all be mistaken and (ii) that he would have withdrawn the case from the jury if he had thought that the identification evidence was not supported by other evidence. Was the judge's direction proper or improper?

[A]  Improper because he was wrong to make the first point.

[B]  Improper because he was wrong to make both points.

[C]  Improper because he was wrong to make the second point.

[D]  Perfectly proper.

## Question 13

Adam and Ben are jointly charged with indecently assaulting Jane, aged 12 years. During examination-in-chief Adam gives evidence against Ben alleging that it was Ben who masterminded the plan and in fact carried out the assault single-handed. Adam has two previous convictions for similar offences. Can the *prosecution* cross-examine Adam in relation to his previous convictions?

[A]  Yes, if the judge grants leave.

[B]  Yes, irrespective of the judge's view of the matter.

[C]  No, because Adam has not cast imputations on a prosecution witness.

[D]  No, because the previous convictions are irrelevant.

## Question 14

Which of the following statements is CORRECT concerning which communications are covered by lawyer-client legal professional privilege?

[A]  All communications between lawyer and client.

[B]  Only those communications between lawyer and client which actually consist in giving or obtaining legal advice in respect of contemplated litigation.

[C]  All communications between lawyer and client which have as their main object the giving or obtaining of legal advice.

[D]  Only those communications between lawyer and client which are for the purpose of pending or anticipated litigation.

## Question 15

Arthur brings an action for breach of contract against Dan in respect of a contract for the sale of a car. Arthur, in order to prove the contract, wishes to call Stephen to testify that he heard Dan offer the car for sale to Arthur for £2,500. Is this evidence hearsay or not?

[A]  Not hearsay and Stephen can testify as to the details of what was said.

[B]  Hearsay, because what Stephen said has to be true to prove a relevant fact.

[C]  Hearsay, because what Dan said has to be true to prove a relevant fact.

[D]  Not hearsay but Stephen can only testify that something was said but not what it was.

## Question 16

Colin is charged with affray. His defence is that he was not present at the scene of the crime when the incident took place. The police accompany Anil, one of the victims, to the area of the crime, where he sees Colin and states that he was one of the attackers. Colin is arrested and requests an identification parade (pursuant to Code D of the Police and Criminal Evidence Act 1984). The police refuse on the grounds that Anil has already identified Colin.

Which of the following statements is CORRECT?

[A]  The court may take Code D into account when considering whether or not to exclude Anil's street identification but are not bound to do so.

[B]  The court must exclude Anil's street identification if there was any failure to observe Code D.

[C]  The court must take Code D into account when considering whether or not to exclude Anil's street identification but the court has a discretion as to whether or not to do so.

[D]  Code D does not apply where a witness has already identified the defendant in any way.

## Question 17

Only one of the following propositions is CORRECT. Which one?

[A]  If an atheist appears as a witness and takes an oath, it will be of no effect and therefore will not be binding on him or her.

[B]  All parties in all proceedings have a completely unfettered choice as to which competent and compellable witnesses they call in support of their case.

[C]  In a criminal trial the prosecution can call witnesses after the close of its case, but only (i) in order to make good a purely formal omission, or (ii) in order to rebut a matter which has arisen *ex improviso*.

[D]  In a trial on indictment a person (other than the accused) who is outside the United Kingdom may be permitted to give evidence through a live television link.

## Question 18

Which of the following propositions is INCORRECT?

[A]  In criminal proceedings, a formal admission, if made otherwise than in court, shall be in writing.

[B]  A judge may take judicial notice of a fact without enquiry if the fact is so notorious as to be beyond dispute.

[C]  In a Crown Court trial, questions relating to the weight of evidence are never decided by the judge.

[D]  In criminal proceedings, the discretion to exclude prosecution evidence because its prejudicial effect outweighs its probative value is of general application and is not confined to specific types of otherwise admissible evidence.

## Question 19

Len was convicted of stealing certain items of jewellery. The jewellery was returned to the alleged owner Oswald. Len then commenced a civil action for conversion against Oswald alleging that he (Len) was and always had been the owner of the jewellery. Oswald defends the action and proves Len's conviction.

Which of the following statements about Len's conviction is CORRECT?

[A]  It is inadmissible and should not have been proved.

[B]  It is admissible but only on the issue of credibility.

[C]  It is conclusive evidence that Len stole the jewellery.

[D]  It creates a rebuttable presumption that Len stole the jewellery.

## Question 20

Raymond is claiming damages for injuries sustained at work due to the negligence of his employers. When the matter comes to trial, some five years after the accident, Raymond has genuine difficulty in remembering the details of the accident and his evidence is confused and inconsistent. Counsel for the plaintiff applies to put in evidence, for the truth of its contents, a written statement made by Raymond to the defendant's insurance company two months after the accident.

Is the statement admissible for this purpose?

[A]  Yes, with the leave of the court.

[B]  Yes, without the leave of the court.

[C]  No, because Raymond is available as a witness.

[D]  No, because it would have been reasonable and practicable for Raymond's lawyers to have given notice of their intent to adduce the statement, but no such notice was given.

## Question 21

Which one of the following propositions is CORRECT?

[A]  A witness in civil proceedings, if asked to disclose the name of a police informer, has a free choice whether or not to answer.

[B]  A claim to public interest immunity will not necessarily succeed simply because it is a class claim relating to inter-departmental minutes concerning the formulation of government policy.

[C]  A civil court should generally uphold a claim to public interest immunity in respect of statements taken in the course of an inquiry undertaken by the Police Complaints Authority.

[D]  A civil court may require a person to disclose the source of information contained in a publication for which he is responsible, but *only* if it is established that disclosure is necessary in the interests of justice.

## Question 22

Amos is charged with robbing a bank. Just before the robbery, Ben, a traffic warden, noted in his note-book the registration number of a motorbike parked outside the bank. Other witnesses later confirmed that there was only one motorbike parked outside the bank at the time of the robbery. When the robber emerged from the bank, he made good his escape on this motorbike, knocking down Ben in the process. Ben has been in a coma ever since and is unfit to attend court as a witness. The police found Ben's note-book and traced the motorbike to Amos. Amos denies the robbery and claims that his motorbike was not parked outside the bank at any time on the day of the robbery. The prosecution seek to rebut this by proving the statement in Ben's note-book. Is the statement in the note-book admissible?

[A]  No, because it is hearsay.

[B]  Yes, as real evidence.

[C]  Yes, under the *res gestae* exception.

[D]  Yes, in principle, under Criminal Justice Act 1988, s 23.

## Question 23

Harry is charged with theft. PC Ings carried out most of the investigation, contemporaneously recording all his findings in his notebook. Two hours later, he used his notebook as the basis for his witness statement. PC Ings lost the notebook before the trial, and now has no independent recollection of the investigation. May he refresh his memory from the witness statement in the courtroom in the course of giving his evidence?

[A]  No, because the document used to refresh his memory must be the original.

[B]  No, because it would amount to relying on hearsay evidence.

[C]  Yes, if the court is satisfied that the witness statement contains substantially what was in his notes.

[D]  Yes, if the court exercised its discretion in favour of PC Ings.

## Question 24

Which one of the following is NOT a pre-condition to the drawing of an inference from the failure of an accused to testify (Criminal Justice and Public Order Act 1994, s 35)?

[A]  That the accused's physical condition is not such as to make it undesirable (in the court's view) for him to give evidence.

[B]  That the accused was present at the scene of the crime (and can therefore be expected to give evidence of what he saw).

[C]  That the accused's mental condition is not such as to make it undesirable (in the court's view) for him to give evidence.

[D]  That the accused's guilt is in issue.

## Question 25

Herbert, a bank manager, is charged with committing an act of bestiality with a sheep while on a walking tour of the Lake District. His defence is that he has been mistakenly identified as the culprit. The prosecution wishes to adduce evidence that when the police (lawfully) searched the lodgings where he was staying they discovered a quantity of farming magazines containing photographs of sheep. Is the evidence admissible?

[A]  Yes, because such evidence would rebut a defence of innocent association.

[B]  Yes, to establish Herbert's propensity towards bestiality.

[C]  No, because the law does not recognise a separate category of people who commit bestiality.

[D]  No, because it is irrelevant.

## Question 26

Only one of the following propositions concerning the rules about obtaining body samples (PACE 1984, ss 61–65) is CORRECT. Which one?

[A]  An intimate sample can be taken from a person without the appropriate consent if that person is suspected of committing a serious arrestable offence.

[B]  Saliva is an intimate sample.

[C]  Blood is a non-intimate sample.

[D]  A non-intimate sample may be taken from a person without the appropriate consent if he has been convicted of a recordable offence.

## Question 27

Brian is charged with indecently assaulting his neighbour's 15-year-old son, Charles. The prosecution wish to call as a witness, Daphne, Brian's wife; and Brian wishes to call as a witness, Edwina, Charles's mother. Both of these potential witnesses would prefer not to give evidence. Can they be compelled to do so?

[A]  Daphne can be compelled to testify, but not Edwina.

[B]  Edwina can be compelled to testify, but not Daphne.

[C]  Both Daphne and Edwina can be compelled to testify.

[D]  Neither Daphne nor Edwina can be compelled to testify.

## Question 28

Only one of the following statements about hearsay is WRONG. Which one?

[A]  The repetition of a question can never be caught by the rule against hearsay, because questions cannot be said to be either true or false.

[B]  Whether the rule against hearsay applies depends on the purpose for which the words uttered outside court are repeated in court.

[C]  An inference made from the absence of a record will not always be excluded by the rule against hearsay.

[D]  The hearsay rule does not exclude tapes or films that have directly recorded an incident under investigation.

## Question 29

Harold is suing Frank for fraudulent misrepresentation, alleging that Frank sold him a fake diamond ring after representing to him that the diamond was genuine. Frank defends the action, claiming that he mistakenly believed that the diamond was genuine. Harold wishes to prove that on several previous occasions over a period of years Frank has sold fake diamond rings having represented that they were genuine.

Is such evidence admissible?

[A] Yes, to show that Frank was not mistaken about the genuineness of the ring, provided such evidence is not oppressive or unfair to Frank.

[B] Yes, as there are no restrictions on the admissibility of similar fact evidence in civil trials except the judge's general discretion to exclude evidence under CPR, r 32.1(2).

[C] No, because the evidence is irrelevant.

[D] No, because Frank has no previous convictions for obtaining money by deception.

## Question 30

The following propositions relate to the inferences that may be drawn against the accused as a result of his silence at various stages of the prosecution process. Only one of them is CORRECT. Which one?

[A] At common law it is never permissible to draw inferences from the accused's silence in the face of the accusation.

[B] An inference which is properly drawn from the accused's failure to give a defence statement (when required to do so pursuant to the Criminal Procedure and Investigations Act 1996, s 5) may assist the prosecution to raise a prima facie case.

[C] An inference which is properly based on the accused's failure to testify may assist the prosecution to raise a prima facie case.

[D] An inference which is properly based on the accused's failure to explain the presence of blood stains on his clothing may assist the prosecution to raise a prima facie case.

## Question 31

Rupert, Sarah and Toby are charged with conspiracy between 1 April 2001 and 1 May 2001 fraudulently to evade the prohibition on the importation of cannabis. The prosecution relies on a confession made to the police by Sarah on 20 May 2001, in which she said, 'Toby and I were involved in importing cannabis. But it was Rupert who put us up to it. We'd never have got into it if it hadn't been for him.'

Which of the following propositions is CORRECT?

[A] The confession is evidence against Sarah but not against Toby or Rupert.

[B] The confession is evidence against Sarah and Rupert but not against Toby.

[C] If the confession was obtained by oppression it will not be admissible at trial for any party.

[D] If the confession was obtained unfairly no party will be able to rely upon it.

## Question 32

Concerning *non-expert* opinion evidence to be given by Odette, a witness in an action for damages for personal injuries arising out of a road traffic accident, which one of the following propositions is CORRECT?

[A] Such evidence is admissible provided that the party seeking to rely on it shall automatically disclose the substance of it to the other party or parties in the form of a written report which shall be agreed if possible.

[B]  Such evidence, if made as a way of conveying relevant facts personally perceived by Odette, is admissible as evidence of what she perceived.

[C]  Such evidence is inadmissible because Odette is not an expert witness.

[D]  Such evidence, although inadmissible in law, can be admitted by the judge under CPR, r 32.1(2).

## Question 33

Andrew and Bernard are charged with robbing Charlie of a gold watch in the lavatory of a restaurant. Charlie gives evidence and says that he was attacked by three men, two of whom he later identified as Andrew and Bernard, in the lavatory, and that one of the men stole his watch. The third man escaped. Andrew gives evidence and says that he and Bernard were both attacked in the lavatory by Charlie, who was drunk. He says that they fought to defend themselves, and that the watch must have been lost in the struggle. Bernard says that he went into the lavatory with Andrew, but that he at once entered one of the cubicles, where he heard and saw nothing. He says that when he came out, Andrew had left the lavatory. Bernard has a recent conviction for assault.

Can Andrew cross-examine Bernard about his conviction for assault?

[A]  No, because it is not a conviction for an offence of dishonesty.

[B]  Yes, because Bernard's evidence leaves Andrew as the only person who could have committed the robbery.

[C]  Possibly, because Bernard's evidence undermines the credibility of Andrew's testimony.

[D]  As in [C], but the judge has a discretion to exclude the cross-examination.

# INDEX

## A

**Absence of witness from court**  155
  Criminal Justice Act 2003  173-4
  death  156, 161
  kept away through fear  157-8, 161
  mentally incapable  161
  not found  157, 161
  outside UK  156-7, 161
  reasons  156-8
  unfit to attend  156, 161
**Accused**
  previous convictions  232-3
  witness
    for co-accused  61-2
    for defence  61-2
    for prosecution  61
    when to call  69
**Adducing evidence**  25-6
  documentary evidence  26
  real  26
  testimony  26
**Admissibility**  22-3
  confessions *see* **Confessions**
  preliminary facts  27-8
  *voir dire*  23, 27-8, 181
**Admissions, formal**  19-21
**Affirmations** *see* **Oaths and affirmations**
**Appeals**, identification evidence  208

## B

**Bankers' books**
  as evidence  65
  hearsay exception  165
**Body samples**
  destruction  217
  identification by  215, 216-19
  intimate  216, 217
  non-intimate  216, 217
  refusal to give  196
**Burden of proof**  3, 4, 297-8
  definitions  30
  evidential  30, 32, 33
    civil cases  37
    criminal cases  40-7
    defence  42-7
    directions to jury  47
    no case to answer submissions  47
    prosecution  40
    standard of proof  36
  facts in issue  31-2

  insanity  42
  legal  30, 32, 33
    civil cases  40
    contract  37-8
    criminal cases  40-7
    defence  42-7
    negative assertions  38-9
    policy considerations  40
    prosecution  40, 42
    statute law  40
  preliminary matters  47-8
  statutory exceptions
    express  42-5
    implied  46-7

## C

**CCTV identification**  213-14
**Character evidence**
  bad character  110-17
    previous convictions  112, 113, 117
  civil cases  107
  co-defendant  115-17
  credibility relevance  107
  criminal cases  107-18
  Criminal Evidence Act 1989  110-17
  Criminal Justice Act 2003  117, 118
  cross-examination on  110-17
    limits on  115
  defendant
    bad character  110-17
    good character  108-9
  defendant's shield  112
  disposition  114-15, 119
  fact in issue  107
    relevance to  108-17
  good character
    defendant  108-9
    non-defendant  109
  good character establishment  113
  imputations  113-14
  non-defendant's good character  109
  previous acquittals  113
  previous convictions  112, 113
    children  118
  questions  311-13
  similar fact *see* **Similar fact evidence**
**Children**
  actions involving
    legal professional privilege  245
    public policy exclusion  251
    self-incrimination privilege  239

age of responsibility   51
competence   58-61
    civil cases   60-1
    criminal cases   59-60
previous convictions   118
special measures directions   74-5
sworn evidence   59-61, 65
unsworn evidence   60, 65-6, 103
as witnesses   58-61, 74-5, 103
**Circumstantial evidence**   10-12
**Co-accused**
cross-examination by   115
evidence against   115-17
previous convictions   233-5
similar fact evidence   132
as witness   61-2
**Collateral evidence**   17-19
**Collusion**   131
**Common purpose**, furtherance of   171-2
**Competence and compellability**   57
accused
    for co-accused   61-2
    for defence   61-2
    for prosecution   61
bankers   65
children   58-61
co-accused   61-2
exceptions to rule   58
general rule   58
head of State   63
judges   65
persons of limited understanding   58-61
    civil cases   60-1
    mental illness   61
    sworn evidence   59-61, 65
    unsworn evidence   60, 65-6, 103
Sovereign   63
spouse of accused
    compellability   62-3
    competence   62
**Complainants in sexual cases**
cross-examination   91-5
examination-in-chief   84-5
as witnesses   103-4
**Confessions**
admissibility   177-80
    against defendant who made it   178
    anything said or done   178
    objections   178-9
Criminal Justice Act 2003   183
definition   177-8
deprivation of rights   181
discretion to exclude   180-1
exclusion   181-2
hearsay   171
legal advice   181
mentally handicapped persons   180
oppression
    anything said or done   178
    treatment   179
questions   317-19
reliability   179-80
statutory restrictions   178-80
*voir dire*   181
**Confidential information**   251-2
**Confrontation statements**   85-6

**Continuation of life presumption**   55
**Contract**, legal burden of proof   37-8
**Convictions** *see* **Previous convictions**
**Corroboration**, requirement for   106
**Credibility**
character evidence   107
cross-examination as to   96-7
hearsay evidence   164, 176
**Cross-examination**
bias or partiality   98-9
on character   110-17
    limits   115
co-accused
    by   115
    of   115-17
complainants in sexual cases   91-5
credibility of witness   96-7
disability affecting reliability   100
duty to cross-examine   91
finality rule   97-8
liability to   91
limits on   92-5
litigant in person   91-2
previous convictions   99
previous inconsistent statements   100-2
reputation for untruthfulness   100
restrictions   91-2

**D**

**Death**
of maker of statement *see* **Statements of persons now dead**
presumption of
    common law   52
    Law of Property Act 1925   53
    Matrimonial Causes Act 1973   53
of witness to hearsay   156, 161
**Defamation**, previous conviction use   231
**Detention**
deprivation of rights   181
legal advice   181
**Direct evidence**   10
**Directions to jury**
failure to testify   198-9
on lies   186-7
*Lucas* direction   186-7
silence of accused   192-3, 194
**Disclosure**
privilege and   237
public policy exclusion   237, 254
**DNA profiles**   215, 216-19
**Documentary evidence**   26
**Dying declarations**   169

**E**

**Evidence**
adducing   25-6
admissibility *see* **Admissibility**
character *see* **Character evidence**
circumstantial   10-12
collateral   17-19
direct   10
documentary   26
exclusion *see* **Exclusion of evidence**

facts *see* **Facts**
illegally or improperly obtained    182-3, 317-19
meaning    1-2
prejudicial effect    19, 24
probative value    19
proof *see* **Proof**
real    26
relevance *see* **Relevance**
sufficiency    28
sworn *see* **Oaths and affirmations**
testimony    26
unsworn *see* **Oaths and affirmations**
weight *see* **Weight**
**Examination-in-chief**
complainants in sexual cases    84-5
confrontation statements    85-6
general rules    80
hostile witnesses    89-90
previous consistent statements    83-8
complainants in sexual cases    84-5
Criminal Justice Act 2003    88-9
exculpatory statements    86-7
hearsay    84
identification    84
memory-refreshing documents    84
mixed statements    87
recent fabrication rebuttal    87-8
refreshing memory
before giving evidence    80-1
inspection of document    82-3
note made at time of event    81
original documents    82
previous consistent statements    84
verification of document    81
while giving evidence    81
unfavourable witnesses    89-90
**Exclusion of evidence**
civil cases    23-4
criminal cases    24-5
discretion    24-5
refusal to exercise    25
unfairly obtained    25
*see also* **Privilege**
**Expert evidence**    323
advance notice    225-6
basis of opinion    224-5
calling witness    68-9
civil cases    225, 226
criminal cases    225-6
experts    222-3
general principle    221-2
hearsay    226-7
issues requiring    221-2
notice    225-6
primary facts    224
privilege    68
secondary facts    224-5
status    223-4
ultimate issue    220

**F**

**Facial-mapping**    214
**Facts**
and arguments    3, 4
formal admissions    19-21

in issue    5
civil cases    7-8
criminal cases    6-7
significance    8-9
judicial notice    21-2
law and    2
meaning of words    28
personal knowledge    22
preliminary    27-8
presumptions of fact    54-5
proof    3-5
tribunal of fact    27-9
**Finality rule**    97-8
bias or partiality exception    98-9
disability affecting reliability    100
hearsay evidence    164
previous convictions    99
reputation for untruthfulness    100
**Fingerprints**    206, 215-16
**Foreign law**    29
**Formal admissions**
civil cases    20-1
criminal cases    20
**Fraud**
legal professional privilege    244-5
self-incrimination privilege    239

**G**

**Guilty knowledge**, presumption    54-5

**H**

**Head of State**, as witness    63
**Hearsay**    134-76
absence of witness    155-8
Criminal Justice Act 2003    173-4
death    156, 161
kept away through fear    157-8, 161
mentally incapable    161
not found    157, 161
outside UK    156-7, 161
reasons for    156-8
unfit to attend    156, 161
acting in course trade, business or profession    158-60, 169, 174
against interest of maker    170
assertion of fact    135, 138, 140-2
attacking credibility of statement    164, 176
bankers' books    165
business documents    158-60, 169, 174
challenging statement    153-4
common purpose, furtherance    171-2
competence of maker    176
confessions    171
criminal investigation documents    160-1
Criminal Justice Act 1988    154-64
Criminal Justice Act 2003    172-6
exclusion of statement    175-6
power to stop case    175
death
of witness to statement    156, 161
*see also* **Statements by persons now dead**
definition    136-7
dying declarations    169
exceptions    175, 316-17

civil cases   150-4, 172
  common law   154, 165-72
  criminal cases   154-65, 172
exclusion of document   161-3
expert opinion   226-7
finality rule   164
furtherance of common purpose   171-2
identification cases   147-9
identification of hearsay   136-42
implied
  from conduct   145-6
  from statements   145
knowledge of maker   155-60
leave requirement   151-2, 161-2
magistrates' courts   165
mechanical devices   149-50, 176
negative   146-7
notice requirement   151
original evidence   142-4
out of court statements   134-6, 139-40
pedigree   170
persons now dead
  witness to statement   156, 161
  see also **Statements of persons now dead**
police notebooks   160-1
previous consistent statements   84
proof of document   164
proof of false statement   144
proof of knowledge   144
proof of statement   152-3
  absence of witness   155-8
public documents   170-1
public rights   170
questions   314-17
*res gestae* statements   165-9
  admissibility   166-9
  contemporaneous   166-9
  mental state of maker   168
  performance of act   168-9
  physical state of maker   167-8
rule against   137-8
self-identification   148-9
statement other than testimony   139-40
statements by persons now dead   169-70
  against interest of maker   170
  in course of duty or business   169
  dying declarations   169
  pedigree   170
  public rights   170
statutory declarations   165
truth of statement irrelevant   135, 143
***Hollington* v *Hewthorn and Co Ltd* rule**   228-9, 233
**Hostile witnesses**   68, 89-90

**I**

**Identification**
admissibility   210
appeals   208
body samples   196, 215, 216-19
CCTV   213-14
confrontation   211
description   202, 203, 208
DNA profiles   215, 216-19
dock   211
exclusion of evidence   210

eyewitness
  confrontation   211
  in court   211
    group identification   211, 212
    out of court   147-8, 211-12
fingerprints   206, 215-16
fleeting glance   204
group identification   211, 212
hearsay and   147-9
identity known to police   211-12
identity not known to police   212
images   211
link between accused and crime   209-10
miscarriage of justice and   202-3
parades   210, 211, 212
photographs   213-14
poor quality
  no case to answer   205-6
  support for   206
previous consistent statements   84
questions   320-2
security film   213-14
self-identification   148-9
street   210
striking similarity   126-7
*Turnbull* warnings   203-6, 213, 214
  unnecessary   207-8
veracity of witness   207
video   211, 212
voice recognition   213
**Illegally or improperly obtained evidence**   182-3, 317-19
**Imputations**   113-14
**Informants**   251
**Insanity**, burden of proof   42
**Insolvency actions**, self-incrimination privilege   239-40
**Intention, presumption of**   54
**Internet**, fund transfers   150
**Intoximeters**   150
**Investigations**
body samples   196, 215, 216-19
fingerprints   206, 215-16
identification *see* **Identification**
silence *see* **Silence**

**J**

**Journalistic sources**   252
**Judges**
directions to jury
  failure to testify   198-9
  on lies   186-7
  *Lucas* direction   186-7
  silence of accused   192-3, 194
personal knowledge   22
summing up   27
as witnesses   65
**Judgments, as evidence of facts upon which based**
subsequent civil case   232
in subsequent criminal case   236
*see also* **Previous acquittals; Previous convictions**
**Judicial notice**
after enquiry   21-2
without enquiry   21
**Judicial warnings**, unreliable witnesses   104-6
**Juries**, directions *see* **Judges**, directions to jury

## K

**Knowledge**
personal, of judge    22
presumption of guilty knowledge    54-5

## L

**Law, tribunal of**    4-5, 27-9
**Legal advice**
confessions    181
to remain silent    191-2
**Legal professional privilege**
effect    243
exceptions    244-5
facts contained in communications    245-6
lawyer-client    240-2
limit on scope    243-4
pursuance of crime or fraud    244-5
third parties    242-3, 245
waiver    243
welfare of children    245
without prejudice communications    246-7, 324-6
**Legitimacy presumption**    52
**Libel**, questions of fact    28
**Lies**
civil cases    185
criminal cases    186-7
directions to jury    186
evidential value    184-5
identification witness    207
*Lucas* direction    186-7
questions    319-20
**Live television links**    75
*Lucas* direction    186-7

## M

**Magistrates' courts**    29
**Marriage presumption**    51, 56
**Mechanical devices**
internet transfers    150
intoximeters    150
presumption of regularity    54
statements produced by    149-50, 176
**Memory** *see* **Refreshing memory**
**Mentally handicapped persons**
confessions    180
*see also* **Persons of limited understanding**
**Miscarriage of justice**
identification    202-3
public policy exclusion    249

## N

**Newton hearings**    198
**No case to answer**
evidential burden    47
poor quality identification    205-6
sufficiency of evidence    28

## O

**Oaths and affirmations**    299-300
children    59-61
sworn evidence    59-61, 65
unsworn evidence    60, 103

civil cases    65-6
criminal cases    65
**Opinion evidence**    323
degree of precision    221
ultimate issue    220
witnesses of fact    220-1
*see also* **Expert evidence**
**Oppression**
anything said or done    178
treatment    179
**Out of court statements**    134-6
proof of facts contained in    135, 137, 140-2
proof that statement made    135, 143
*see also* **Hearsay**

## P

**Particulars of claim**    7
**Perjury**
corroboration    106
questions of fact    28
**Persons of limited understanding**
children *see* **Children**
civil cases    60-1
competence    58-61
criminal cases    59-60
mental illness    61
sworn evidence    59-60, 61, 65
unsworn evidence    60, 65-6, 103
*see also* **Mentally handicapped persons**
**Police complaints investigations**    250
**Prejudice**
prejudicial effect of evidence    19, 24
without prejudice communications    246-7, 324-6
**Preliminary matters**
burden of proof    47-8
standard of proof    47-8
*voir dire*    23
**Presumptions**    299-300
age of responsibility    51
conflicting    56
continuation of life    55
conviction as proof of crime    50
death
common law    52
Law of Property Act 1925    53
Matrimonial Causes Act 1973    53
definition    49
of fact    54-5
guilty knowledge    54-5
importance    50
intention    54
irrebuttable    50-1
legitimacy    52
marriage    51, 56
meaning    49
rebuttable    50, 51-4
regularity
mechanical    54
official    53
*res ipsa liquitur*    55
**Previous acquittals**
similar fact evidence    129
in subsequent civil case    232
in subsequent criminal case    236

**Previous consistent statements**   83-8
  complainants in sexual cases   84-5
  Criminal Justice Act 2003   88-9
  exculpatory statements   86-7
  hearsay   84
  identification   84
  memory-refreshing documents   84
  mixed statements   87
  recent fabrication rebuttal   87-8
**Previous convictions**
  accused   232-3
  challenging conviction   230-1
  children   118
  co-accused   233-5
  cross-examination on   99, 112, 113
  defamation cases   231
  as evidence of facts   228-36
  *Hollington* v *Hewthorn and Co Ltd* rule   228-9, 233
  inadmissible evidence of   113
  persons other than accused   233-5
  proving conviction   235
  relevant issues   235
  use in civil cases   229-32
  use in criminal cases   232-6
**Previous inconsistent statements**   100-2
**Privilege**   237
  expert witnesses   68
  journalistic sources   252
  legal professional   240-6
  public policy exclusion   248-54, 326-7
  self-incrimination   238-40
  *see also* **Individual types**
**Probative value**   19
**Proof**
  burden *see* **Burden of proof**
  of facts   3-5
    formal admissions   19-21
    judicial notice   21-2
    personal knowledge   22
    without evidence   19-22
  standard *see* **Standard of proof**
**Public documents,** hearsay   170-1
**Public policy exclusion**   248-54, 326-7
  affairs of state   250
  civil cases   297-8
  confidential information   251-2
  criminal cases   252-4
  effect   249
  foreign policy interests   250
  general rule   248-9
  informants   251
  miscarriage of justice   249
  national security   250
  police information   250-1
    complaints investigations   250
    informants   251
    surveillance posts   251

**R**

**Re-examination**   102, 106
**Real evidence**   26
**Recent fabrication,** rebuttal   87-8
**Refreshing memory**
  inside court   81
  inspection of document   82-3

  note made at time of event   81
  original documents   82
  outside court   80-1
  previous consistent statements   84
  verification of document   81
**Regularity presumption**
  mechanical   54
  official   53
**Relevance**   5
  circumstantial evidence   10-12
  conditional   14
  definition   9-10
  direct evidence   10
  importance of argument   15
  sufficiency   12-14
*Res gestae* **statements**   165-9
  admissibility   166-9
  contemporaneous statements   166-9
  mental state of maker   168
  performance of act   168-9
  physical state of maker   167-8
*Res ipsa liquitur*   55

**S**

**Security film identification**   213-14
**Self-incrimination privilege**
  child actions   239
  companies   238
  evidence revealed   238-9
  insolvency actions   239-40
  person asserting privilege   238
  real and appreciable danger   238
  serious fraud   239
  spouses   238
  statutory exceptions   239-40
**Sexual offences**
  complainants   84-5, 91-5, 103-4
  litigant in person cross-examination   91-2
**Silence**
  cannot alone justify conviction   106
  on charge   189
  civil cases   185
  common law position   193-4
  in court   197-9
    accused's guilt not in issue   198
    directions to jury   198-9
    failure to call evidence   199-200
    Newton hearings   198
    physical or mental condition   198
  criminal cases   187-96
  directions to jury   192-3, 194
    failure to testify   198-9
  duty to explain   189
  evidential value   184-5
  facts later relied upon in defence   189-90
  failure to account
    for objects, substances or marks   195-6
    for presence at scene   196
  failure to call evidence   199-200
  failure to disclose defence case   196-7
  legal advice   191-2
  on questioning   188-99
  questions   319-20
  refusal to give body samples   196
  unreasonable failure to mention   190-2

**Similar fact evidence**
background evidence   130-1
case law   121
civil law   121, 133
co-accused   132
collusion   131
criminal law   121, 122-33
discretion to exclude   132
exceptions to rule   120-1, 123
general rule   119-20
homosexuality   128
identification   126-7
incriminating articles   129-30
non-criminal behaviour   128-9
off-indictment   121
on-indictment   121
prejudice   120
previous acquittals   129
probative force   125, 126-8
propensity   119, 120, 122, 127-8
questions   313-14
separate trials   124
statutory   132-3
striking similarity   123-4, 125
identification   126-7
underlying link   124
**Sovereign, as witness**   63
**Speeding**, corroboration requirement   106
**Spouse of accused**
self-incrimination privilege   238
as witness   62-3
compellability   62-3
competence   62
**Standard of proof**   3, 4, 298
civil cases   34-5
crimes alleged   34-5
exceptions   34
criminal cases
defence   36
prosecution   35
definitions   31, 32
evidential burden   36
preliminary matters   47-8
**Statement of case**   7
**Statements by persons now dead**   169-70
against interest of maker   170
in course of duty or business   169
dying declarations   169
pedigree   170
public rights   170
**Street identification**   210
**Sufficiency of evidence**   28
**Summing up**   27
**Surveillance posts**   251
**Sworn evidence**   59-60, 61, 65-6

**T**

**Television links**
civil cases   75
criminal cases   75
**Testimony**, adducing   26
**Tribunal of fact**   27-9
meaning of words   28
**Tribunal of law**   4-5, 27-9
summing up   27

*Turnbull* **warnings**   213, 214
form   205
need for   203-6
unnecessary   207-8

**U**

**Unfavourable witnesses**   68, 89-90
**Unreliable witnesses**   102-6
complainants in sexual cases   103-4
corroboration   106
discretion of judge to warn   104-6
**Unsworn evidence**, children   60, 65-6, 103

**V**

**Victims**, collusion   131
**Video identification**   213-14
**Voice recognition**   213
*Voir dire*   23, 27-8
confessions   181

**W**

**Weight**   15
challenges   17
collateral evidence   17-19
importance at trial   16
**Witness statements**   66, 301-4
**Witnesses**
absent from court   155
Criminal Justice Act 2003   173-4
death   156, 161
kept away through fear   157-8, 161
mentally incapable   161
not found   157, 161
outside UK   156-7, 161
reasons   156-8
unfit to attend   156, 161
accused   61-2, 69
attendance at court   71-2
bankers   65, 165
calling
after close of case   69-71
civil cases   67, 69, 71
criminal cases   67-8, 71, 72-5
experts   68, 69
judges' powers   71
persons called   66-8
prevention   68-9
privileged information   68
when to call   69
character *see* **Character evidence**
children   58-61, 74-5, 103
co-accused   61-2
compellability *see* **Competence and compellability**
competence *see* **Competence and compellability**
complainants in sexual cases   84-5, 91-5, 103-4
credibility, cross-examination as to   96-7
dead
witness to hearsay   156, 161
*see also* **Statements by persons now dead**
examination   300-11
experts *see* **Expert evidence**
head of State   63
hostile   68, 89-90

judges   65
kept away through fear   157-8
live television links   75
opinions *see* **Expert evidence; Opinion evidence**
outside UK   156-7
persons of limited understanding   58-61
questions   299-300
securing attendance   71-2
Sovereign   63
special measures   72-5
   children   74-5
   directions   73-4
   eligibility   72-3

matters taken into account   77
spouse of accused   62-3
unfavourable   68, 89-90
unfit to attend court   156
unreliable   102-6
   children   103
   complainants in sexual cases   103-4
   corroboration   106
   discretion of judge to warn   104-6
vulnerable   72-5
**Words**, meaning of   28
**Without prejudice communications**   246-7, 324-6
   save as to costs   247